TEACHER'S RESOURCE BOOK

Mathematics
UNLIMITED

P9-CAN-673

Holt, Rinehart and Winston, Publishers
New York·Toronto·Mexico City·London·Sydney·Tokyo

AUTHORS

Francis "Skip" Fennell
Chairman, Education Department
Associate Professor of Education
Western Maryland College
Westminster, Maryland

Barbara J. Reys
Assistant Professor of Curriculum and Instruction
University of Missouri
Columbia, Missouri
Formerly Junior High Mathematics Teacher
Oakland Junior High, Columbia, Missouri

Robert E. Reys
Professor of Mathematics Education
University of Missouri
Columbia, Missouri

Arnold W. Webb
Senior Research Associate
Research for Better Schools
Philadelphia, Pennsylvania
Formerly Asst. Commissioner of Education
New Jersey State Education Department

Copyright © 1987 by Holt, Rinehart and Winston, Publishers
All rights reserved
Printed in the United States of America

ISBN: 0-03-006449-X

7890   066   987654

Table of Contents

III

GRADE 7

RETEACH

v

GRADE 7

ENRICH

GRADE 7

SKILLS INVENTORY

GRADE 7

PRETESTS

GRADE 7

POSTTESTS

GRADE 7

OTHER TESTS

GRADE 7

MANAGEMENT

MAKING MATH WORK

This section contains masters that are to be used for the situational problems presented on the chapter opener pages of the textbook. Detailed suggestions for their use can be found in the Teacher's Edition. These activities can be used for individual, small-group, or whole-class activities.

Name _____ Date _____

How much money will you need to buy publications to research your vacation spot? Use the chart to keep track of your costs. The first chart is for books, a one-time expense. The second chart is for magazines and newspapers, which you would buy regularly over a period of time.

	Book title	Cost
1.		
2.		
3.		
4.		
5.		
Total cost of books:		

	Newspaper or magazine	Newsstand cost	Yearly subscription cost
1.			
2.			
3.			
4.			
5.			
Totals:			

Besides publications, what other means of communication could you use to find out about your vacation spot? Make a list below.

1. _____

2. _____

3. _____

4. _____

5. _____

6. _____

MAKING MATH WORK

Now that you have gathered information for your trip, estimate the amount of money you will need in order to travel. How much money will you need for airfare? for hotel accommodations? What will you need to buy to take with you? How much money might you spend for meals? Find prices, and add them to the list below.

VACATION BUDGET

Expense	Cost
Airfare	
Hotel	
Total	

MAKING MATH WORK

Your arteries stretch after each heartbeat because blood is passing through them. That regular stretching of an artery is your pulse. How can you keep track of your heartbeat?

Find an artery near the surface of your skin where you can feel your pulse. Use a watch or clock that shows seconds, and count the number of pulses you feel in fifteen seconds.

How many times does your heart beat in one minute?

_____

How is your heartbeat affected by activity? Keep track of your heartbeats per minute for the activities listed below. Make a graph to show your results.

heartbeat while lying down   heartbeat after five minutes of running
heartbeat while walking   heartbeat after one minute of rest
heartbeat while running slowly   heartbeat after five minutes of rest

What do you think your heartbeat will be after you have viewed an exciting movie, read a magazine, or watched a football game? List three of your favorite activities below along with their corresponding heartbeat rates.

Activity	Heartbeats per minute

MAKING MATH WORK

How many times does your heart beat in a year? How fast does your hair grow? How much air do you breathe? To what length might your fingernails grow in a year? Use the information below to fill in the chart.

- My heart beats an average of _____ times per minute.

- The hair on an average person's head grows about $\frac{1}{2}$ inch each month.

- The average person consumes about 1 ton of food and drink every year.

- The average person's fingernails grow about 1 inch every 6 months.

	In 6 months	In 1 year	In 60 years
Heartbeats			
Hair growth			
Weight of food and drink			
Fingernail growth			

To work off 1 pound of fat, you need to walk 34 miles. About how many miles do you walk in a day? in a week? in a year? Make a chart below to find out how much fat you work off.

Name_____ Date_____

MAKING MATH WORK

This year, Griele Baggs won the annual Hullabaloo
Marathon. The drawing below shows the course he ran. The
length of each part of the course is given. Find the average
time in seconds per mile and in minutes per mile.

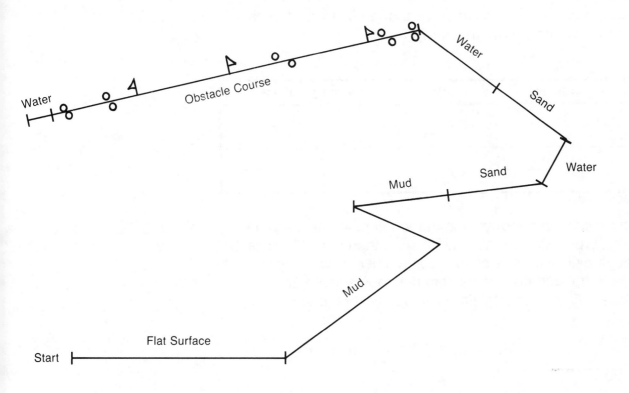

Miles traveled	Part of the course	Time per mile (in seconds)	Time per mile (in minutes)
3 miles in 1,260 seconds	Flat surface	**420 seconds**	**7 minutes**
3 miles in 1,620 seconds	Mud	**540 seconds**	**9 minutes**
2 miles in 1,800 seconds	Sand (running in bare feet)	**900 seconds**	**15 minutes**
4 miles in 5,040 seconds	Obstacle course	**1,260 seconds**	**21 minutes**
$1\frac{3}{4}$ miles in 1,050 seconds	Shallow water	**600 seconds**	**10 minutes**

MAKING MATH WORK

How far do you think you can run in 1 minute? in 5 minutes? in 10 minutes? Your average time per minute would depend on your endurance and the kind of terrain on which you are running.

Fill in the chart. How would you find the distance of each run? How would you measure it?

Distance	Time	Average per minute
	1 min	
	5 min	
	10 min	
	20 min	

In the space below, draw a marathon course similar to the one on Work Sheet 1. You might want the course to pass through different parts of your community, or you might want to make up your own course of crazy obstacles and surfaces. Find your total time and your average speed.

MAKING MATH WORK

How can you find the distance that an object falls without actually measuring the distance? There is a simple formula to find the distance that an object has fallen by the end of any second. Just multiply 16.08 times the square of the number of seconds the object takes to fall [$d = 16.08 \times (t^2)$]. Use a stopwatch to record an accurate time. Use the formula to measure different heights. You may want to use different objects. Record your results in the chart. One sample is shown.

Object/Location	Number of seconds it takes to fall	Height
Ball/Bridge over the river	2.5 seconds	100.5 feet

Are there any differences in the length of time it takes different objects to fall? Explain.

MAKING MATH WORK

To make a pendulum, you need three items: a small, heavy object such as a shoe or an unopened can; a length of rope or heavy cord; and a place from which to hang the rope, such as a hanging rod in a closet or an overhead beam. Tie one end of the rope to the rod or the beam. Attach the heavy object to the other end. Push the object, and it will swing back and forth.

What would happen to the speed of the swing if you tied the object halfway up the rope instead of at the rope's end? Suppose you tied it three fourths of the way up. How would the speed of the swing be affected?

You could experiment with lengths by moving the object up and down the rope. How could you use the graph below to record the number of swings you find at each length?

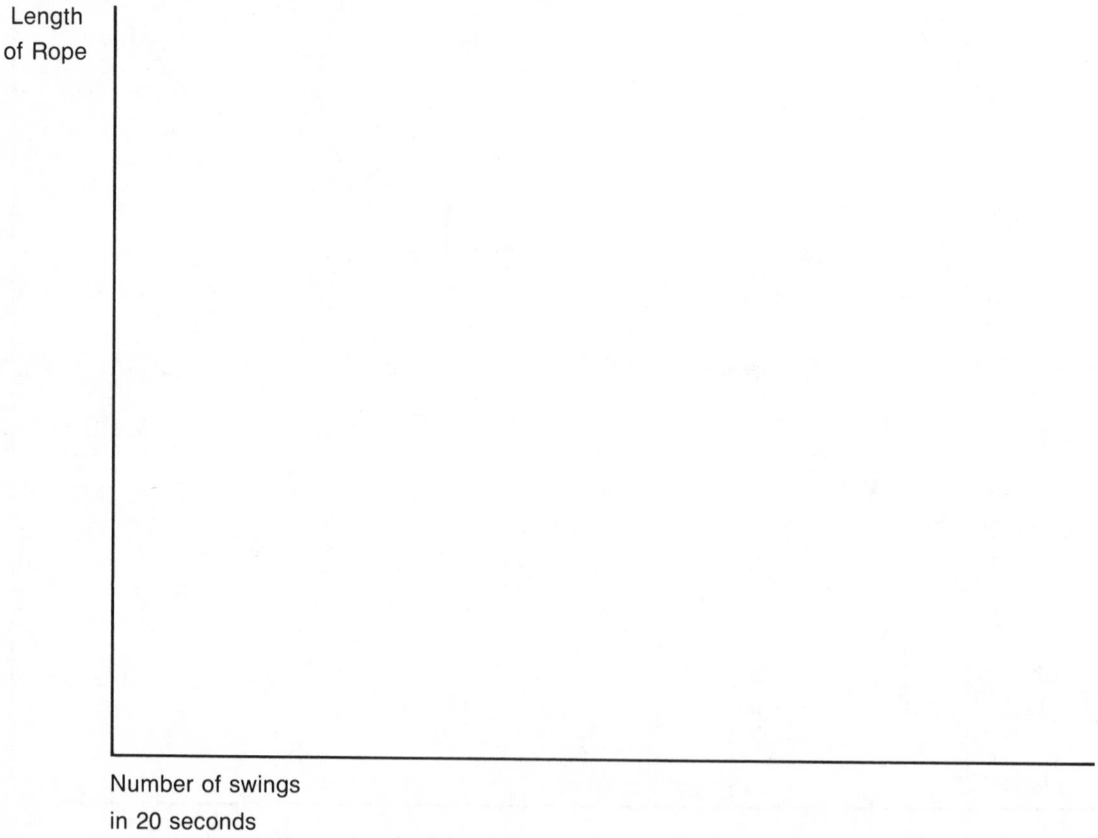

Length
of Rope

Number of swings
in 20 seconds

Name _____ Date _____

MAKING MATH WORK

Some people have unusual hobbies. There have been
reports of people who collect teeth, bottles, credit cards, salt
and pepper shakers, and even vegetables. Look at the list of
weights of some unusually large vegetables. Find each
weight in pounds by changing the fraction to a mixed
number.

Vegetable	Weight (fraction)	Weight (mixed number)
Mushroom	$\frac{88}{16}$ pounds	
Eggplant	$\frac{48}{16}$ pounds	
Cucumber	$\frac{69}{4}$ pounds	
Celery	$\frac{560}{16}$ pounds	
Beet	$\frac{89}{4}$ pounds	
Cabbage	$\frac{492}{4}$ pounds	
Carrot	$\frac{247}{16}$ pounds	
Radish	$\frac{100}{4}$ pounds	
Zucchini	$\frac{579}{16}$ pounds	

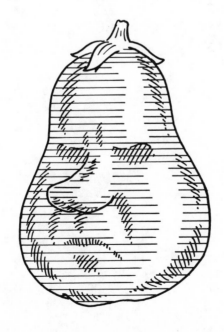

Name ______________________________ Date ______________

MAKING MATH WORK

Suppose your hobby was the creation of strange and fantastic costumes. You have to know how much fabric each costume requires. Suppose you were asked to make costumes for some friends. Use the chart below to figure out how much fabric you would need for different numbers of costumes.

Number of Costumes	Blue Fabric	Red Fabric	Ribbon	Total Fabric
1	$1\frac{2}{3}$ yd	$2\frac{1}{2}$ yd	$\frac{3}{4}$ yd	
2				
3				
4				
5				

Use with pupil page 161.

MAKING MATH WORK

The bicycle path in your community is planned to be $7\frac{1}{2}$ miles long. Where is the best place in your community to build the bicycle path? How could you plan the path? Use the grid below, and make a small scale drawing of the bicycle path. Before you begin, decide the distance that each square on the grid will stand for. Include distance markers every $\frac{1}{2}$ mile along the path and an entrance every $\frac{2}{5}$ mile.

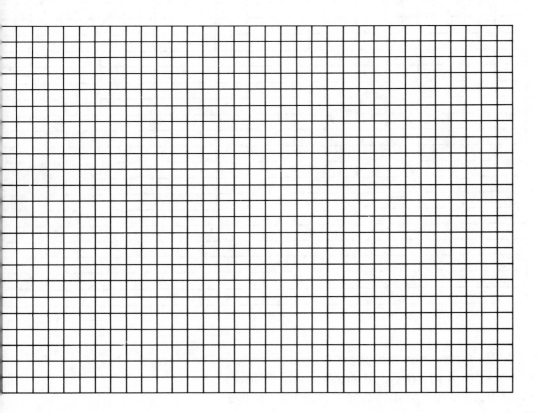

How far would you travel if you traveled the path $2\frac{1}{2}$ times?

_____

Suppose it took you $\frac{2}{3}$ hour (40 minutes) to travel the path. How many miles per hour would you have been traveling?

_____

Suppose it cost your community $89,025 to build the bicycle path. What was the cost of each mile? _____

Name_____ Date_____

Suppose you and your friends are hiking from Arlington to Prospect and back during one day. You have to be back in Arlington by 6:00 P.M. You think that the group can travel $2\frac{1}{2}$ miles during each hour of walking.

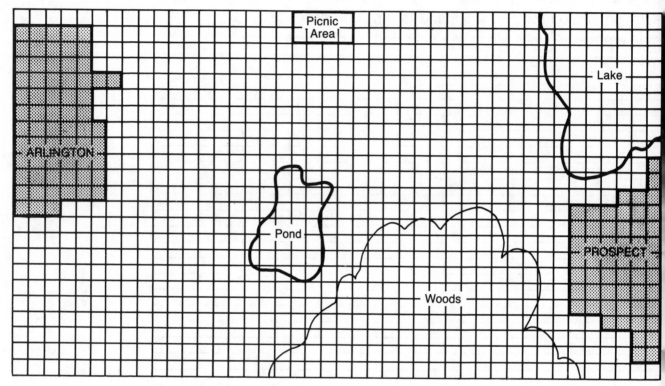

$\square = \frac{1}{4}$ mile

Plan a route for the hike. Complete the chart below to show the times of departure from and arrival at each point. Show how far you will travel from one point to another. Include the time spent at each stop.

Leave	Arrive	Distance traveled	Elapsed time	Arrival time
Arlington				
	Arlington			6:00 P.M.

Name _____ Date _____

In the space below, write a description of how you would use a stopwatch, a measuring cup, and a bucket to measure the amount of water it takes to fill a bathtub. How would you measure the amount of water your family drinks in one day? in one week? in one month?

Description: _____

_____

_____

_____

_____

_____

_____

_____

_____

_____

_____

_____

_____

_____

Now complete the chart by finding approximate water usage. List two more ways you use water, and try to measure each.

Use	Gallons per day	Gallons per week	Gallons per month
Drinking			
Bathing			

MAKING MATH WORK

How much of your body weight consists of fat? Men carry an average of about $\frac{1}{8}$ of their weight in fat; women carry about $\frac{1}{5}$ of their weight in fat. So, if a man weighs 145 pounds, about 18 pounds consist of fat. A woman of the same weight carries about 29 pounds of fat. Find the weights of ten people, and compute the approximate body fat for each. You may want to use the weights of different athletes or celebrities, members of your class, or your family. Use the chart below to list the results.

Person	Body weight	Fat	Person	Body weight	Fat
1.			6.		
2.			7.		
3.			8.		
4.			9.		
5.			10.		

Your body composition also reflects the weight of your muscles and the weight of the bones that make up your skeleton. If you weigh about 100 pounds, bones account for about 25 pounds and muscles account for about 63 pounds. Use these facts to find the weight of bones and muscles for each total body weight you used in the chart above.

Person	Weight of bone	Weight of muscle	Person	Weight of bone	Weight of muscle
1.			6.		
2.			7.		
3.			8.		
4.			9.		
5.			10.		

Name _____ Date _____

MAKING MATH WORK

How can you find out which recording artist is the most popular in your school? What method would you use to keep an accurate tally? Use the chart below to help you record your information. Write the tally for each artist as a fraction of the total tally. Then write each fraction as a percent.

Recording artist	Tally	Fraction	Percent

After you have completed your tally, find the top ten artists. Make a circle graph below to show this information.

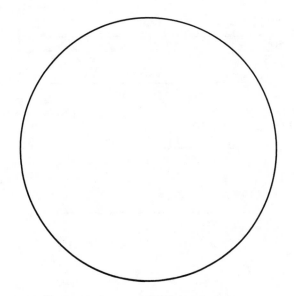

Use with pupil page 269.   **Making Math Work   15**

MAKING MATH WORK

How could you find out which songs were the top ten songs for this week? You might want to use magazines, newspapers, radio, or television. Make sure you can find out how many weeks each song has been on the chart and the position the song held last week. Fill in the information below, then answer each question.

Song	Position this week	Position last week	Number of weeks on the chart

What percent of the songs can you sing? _____

For what percent of the songs can you name the writer? _____

What percent of the songs have been on the chart for more than five weeks? _____

What percent of the songs have dropped from their positions last week? _____

What percent of the songs do you think will reach number one during the next three months? _____

Name _____ Date _____

MAKING MATH WORK

One way your class can earn money is to hold a bike-a-thon. Look at the chart below kept by one student from Grogan Hill School. The bike-a-thon course was 9.5 miles long. Complete the chart to find out how much money was earned.

Person	Donation	Total
Louis Shubert	$0.50 every half mile	
Amy Prage	$1.00 every mile	
Susan Sabot	$0.35 every quarter mile	
Harvey Mixx	$1.55 every mile	
Susanna Gold	$0.05 every half mile	
James Hype	$0.16 every quarter mile	
Dana Billa	$3.00 every mile	
Lisa Domingo	$16.00 every 5 miles	
David Bryan	$0.99 every quarter mile	

$150.58

How will your class organize a bike-a-thon? How long will the course be? How will you find people to donate the money? Will they pay you by the mile? by the half mile? by the quarter mile? Use the space below to keep track of the donations.

MAKING MATH WORK

Look at the numbers below. Complete the pattern that is begun in the first two rows. What figure does the pattern form? Then find the sum of each column. Do the sums have a pattern?

1	2	3	4	5	6	7	8	9	9	8	7	6	5	4	3	2	1
1	2	3	4	5	6	7	8			8	7	6	5	4	3	2	1
1																	1
1																	1
1																	1
1																	1
1																	1
1																	1
1																	1

MAKING MATH WORK

Do you know the boundaries of your community? Where might you find this information? How would you build a wall around your community so it has as great an area as possible within the wall? After finding your community's dimensions, choose a scale. Then make a scale drawing of your community that includes the protective wall you have designed.

MAKING MATH WORK

You have 200 feet of fencing to enclose a flower garden that you are planning. You want to enclose the largest possible area for your rectangular garden. What will the dimensions of your garden be? In the space below, draw the shape of your garden, and indicate its dimensions.

Look at the drawing of the property. Suppose you want to fence in a part of the property. The property lies along the river, so only three sides have to be fenced. You have 1,000 feet of fence. What is the largest number of square feet you can enclose within the fence? Draw the shape below, and indicate its dimensions.

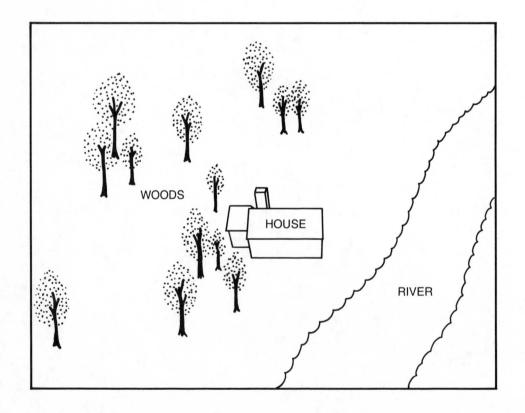

WOODS

HOUSE

RIVER

                                   Use with pupil page 351.

MAKING MATH WORK

On which day of the week were you born? Find out the days of the week on which three members of your family were born. Now interview four friends. On which days of the week were their family members born? Use the chart below to help organize the information.

You and your family (day of the week)		Friends' families	
1.			
2.			
3.			
4.			

How will you display the results of your survey? You might want to use a broken-line graph. Use the space below.

Name ______________________________ Date ______________

MAKING MATH WORK

In which month do you think most of the people in your class were born? First make a guess; then test your answer. Use the chart below to record the information. What do the results show?

Month	Tally
January	
February	
March	
April	
May	
June	
July	
August	
September	
October	
November	
December	

Were most of the students born in the first half of the year or in the second half? Explain your answer.

____

____

____

____

Use with pupil page 385.

ame _____ Date _____

ook at the coordinate map of a classroom. By looking at the
ey, you can find out where each student sits. Use the space
elow to draw a coordinate map of your classroom or town.
irst, use a scale to draw the map. Then make a grid to
iclude the coordinates. What will you include in your map?
emember to make a map key like the one shown.

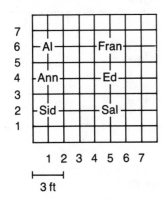

Al	(1,6)
Fran	(5,6)
Sid	(1,2)
Sal	(5,2)
Ann	(1,4)
Ed	(5,4)

MAKING MATH WORK

Look at the topographical map below. This map shows land elevations. The closer the lines are to one another, the steeper the land. Where the lines are far from one another, the land is flat. Use the map below to plot the locations of the archaeological findings listed in the chart. Use the labels to plot the points on the map.

Label	Finding	Location	Sector
A	Statues	⁻50 feet	(3,M)
B	Tombs	40 feet below statues	(8,P)
C	Jewelry	10 feet above tombs	(10,P)
D	Pots/tools	5 feet below statues	(11,R)
E	Ruins of homes	10 feet above statues	(6,L)
G	Fossils	20 feet below tombs	?

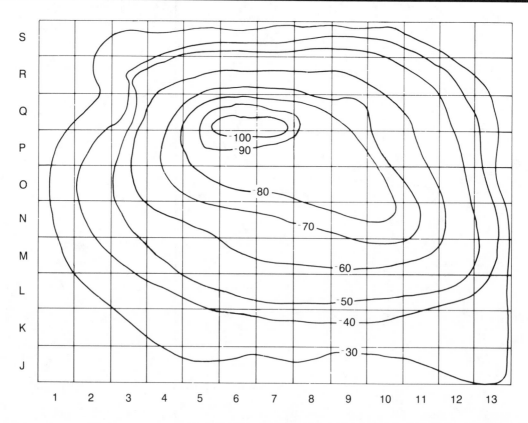

Use with pupil page 423.

Page 1

Chart for Books:
Answers will vary.
Chart for Newspapers or
Magazines:
Answers will vary.
List:
Answers will vary.

Page 2

Vacation Budget:
Answers will vary.

Page 3

Answers will vary.
Answers will vary.
Answers will vary.
Answers will vary.
Answers will vary.
Answers will vary.
Answers will vary.
Answers will vary.
Activity Chart:
Answers will vary.

Page 4

Answers will vary.
Chart:
Answers will vary. Answers will
vary. Answers will vary.
8 inches; 6 inches; 360 inches
½ ton; 1 ton; 60 tons;
1 inch; 2 inches; 120 inches

Page 5

420 seconds; 7 minutes
540 seconds; 9 minutes
900 seconds; 15 minutes
1,260 seconds; 21 minutes
600 seconds; 10 minutes

Page 6

Chart:
Answers will vary.
1. Answers will vary.

Page 7

Answers will vary.

Page 8

Answers will vary.

Page 9

$5\frac{1}{2}$ pounds

3 pounds

$7\frac{1}{4}$ pounds

35 pounds

$22\frac{1}{4}$ pounds

123 pounds

$15\frac{7}{16}$ pounds

25 pounds

$36\frac{3}{16}$ pounds

Page 10

1. $44\frac{11}{12}$ yd
2. Answers will vary.
3. Answers will vary.
4. Answers will vary.
5. Answers will vary.

Page 11

$18\frac{3}{4}$ miles

$11\frac{1}{4}$ mph

$11,870.00

Page 12

Answers will vary.

Page 13

Descriptions will vary.
Answers will vary.

Page 14

Answers will vary.
Answers will vary.

Page 15

Answers will vary.
Answers will vary.

Page 16

Answers will vary.

Page 17

$ 9.50
  9.50
 13.30
 14.73
  0.95
  6.08
 28.50
 30.40
 37.62
$150.58

Page 18

2, 3, 4, 5, 6, 7; 7, 6, 5, 4, 3, 2
2, 3, 4, 5, 6; 6, 5, 4, 3, 2
2, 3, 4, 5; 5, 4, 3, 2
2, 3, 4; 4, 3, 2
2, 3; 3, 2
2; 2
9; 16; 21; 24; 25; 24; 21; 16; 9; 9;
16; 21; 24; 25; 24; 21; 16; 9
Yes

Page 19

Answers will vary.

Page 20

Check students' drawings.

Page 21

Answers will vary.
Check students' graphs.

Page 22

Answers will vary.
Answers will vary.

Page 23

Check students' maps, scales,
and grids.

Page 24

(3, M)
(8, P)
(10, P)
(11, R)
(6, L)

PRACTICE

These masters provide additional practice for lessons found in the pupil's edition. Each master is keyed to the appropriate lesson, but could, of course, be used as extra practice or review at any time after the lesson.

PRACTICE   Whole-Number Place Value

Write in standard form.

1. fourteen thousand, twenty-five _____

2. 3 billion, 841 million, 2 hundred _____

3. 6 trillion, 34 million, 5 thousand _____

Write the word name for each number.

4. 92,957,000 _____

5. 4,005 _____

6. 1,352,729,000,321 _____

Give the value of each underlined digit.

7. 6̲64,125,428 _____

8. 33̲,000,500,891 _____

9. 2,67̲0,067 _____

10. 844,969,4̲20 _____

Write each number in standard form.

11. 800,000 + 50,000 + 5,000 + 3 _____

12. 9,000,000 + 300,000 + 80,000 + 1,000 + 60 _____

13. 70,000,000 + 40,000 + 200 + 30 + 7 _____

Write each number in expanded form.

14. 48,045 _____

15. 790,030 _____

16. 9,305,800 _____

PRACTICE   Comparing, Ordering Numbers

Write >, <, or = in the ◯.

1. 7,005,880 ◯ 7,050,008   **2.** 803 ◯ 823

3. 9,080 ◯ 990   **4.** 11,001 ◯ 10,111

5. 389,010,112 ◯ 3,980,999   **6.** 503,468,163 ◯ 503,648,165

7. 2,532,000 ◯ 2,523,000   **8.** 508,255,000,000 ◯ 508,255,000,000

9. 3,050,000,000 ◯ 3,008,000,000   **10.** 100,000,500,000 ◯ 100,000,050,000

11. 548 billion ◯ 548 trillion   **12.** 345 million ◯ 4 trillion

Write the numbers in order from the least to the greatest.

13. 234,386; 387,432; 645,200; 243,368

_____

14. 17,000,071; 7,107,000; 71,000,170; 17,017,000

_____

15. 17,345; 1,754; 173,543; 17,534; 1,745

_____

16. 8,954; 895; 89,452; 89,549; 8,945

_____

Write the numbers in order from the greatest to the least.

17. 521,615; 521,621; 8,501,400; 501,615   **18.** 18,250,000; 94,000; 18,000,250; 94,704,060

_____   _____

                                                       _____

19. 124,563; 12,456; 124,653; 1,246; 1,642   **20.** 749,345; 7,943; 794,345; 9,743; 794

_____   _____

Use with pages 4–5.

Name _____ Date _____

Write the missing number.

1. $171 + 89 = $ _____ $ + 171$

2. $3{,}793 - 0 = $ _____

3. $24 + (80 + 19) = 123$
$(24 + 80) + 19 = $ _____

4. $85 + 34 = 119$
$119 - 85 = $ _____

5. $391 + 0 = $ _____

6. $566 + 729 = $ _____ $ + 566$

7. $267 - 267 = $ _____

8. $55 + (8 + 4) = ($ _____ $ + 8) + 4$

9. $35 - 17 + 17 = $ _____

10. $14 + 3 + 22 = 3 + $ _____ $ + 14$

11. $733 - 0 = $ _____

12. $61 + (2 + 7) = (61 + 2) + $ _____

13. $844 - 233 = 611$
$611 + 233 = $ _____

14. $(67 + 5) + 48 = 120$
$67 + (5 + 48) = $ _____

15. $583 - 583 = $ _____

16. $707 + 0 = $ _____

17. $399 - $ _____ $ = 399$

18. $(1 + 15) + 49 = 1 + (15 + $ _____ $)$

19. $78 - $ _____ $ + 13 = 78 + 13$

20. $85 + 29 = $ _____ $ + 85$

21. $24 + 9 = 9 + $ _____

22. $14 - 0 = 14 + $ _____

23. $(6 + 4) + 3 = 6 + (4 + $ _____ $)$

24. $58 + 14 + 79 = 79 + $ _____ $ + 14$

25. $34 + 66 = $ _____ $ + 34$

26. $67 + (1 + 4) = ($ _____ $ + 1) + 4$

27. $245 + 92 - $ _____ $ = 245$

28. $362 - $ _____ $ = 0$

29. _____ $ - 5 + 5 = 50$

30. $183 - $ _____ $ = 183$

31. $119 + 11 = $ _____ $ + 119$

32. $22 - (8 + 10) = $ _____ $ - (10 + 8)$

33. $69 - $ _____ $ + 32 = 69$

34. $101 + 1 = $ _____ $ + 101$

35. $299 + (16 - 1) = (16 - 1) + $ _____

36. _____ $ - 3 + 3 = 71$

37. $99 - 0 = $ _____ $ + 99$

38. $3 + $ _____ $ = 472 + 3$

39. $500 + (1 + 4) = (1 + 4) + $ _____

40. $619 + 23 - $ _____ $ = 619$

PRACTICE   Estimation

Estimate to solve the problem. Ring the letter of the best answer.

1. Martha's father's birthday is a month away. Martha is saving to buy him a sweater. She needs $10 more. Martha earns from $3 to $9 each week baby-sitting. How many more weeks will it take her to earn enough money to buy the sweater?

   a. 1 week   b. at least 2 weeks   c. more than 3 weeks

2. After 2 weeks, Martha has earned only $6.00. She still needs $4.00. If she earns $1.50 per hour, how many more hours must she baby-sit?

   a. 2   b. 3   c. 4

3. Martha plans to take a bus into town and meet her friend Angela at the department store. Bus fare is $.85 each way. Lunch will cost Martha between $2 and $4. The sweater will cost between $20 and $23. To be safe, how much money should Martha bring with her?

   a. about $24   b. about $27   c. about $30

4. The next bus leaves in 10 minutes. The ride to the department store takes 15 minutes. It takes Martha 5 minutes to walk to the bus stop. When is the latest she can leave her house in order to take the next bus?

   a. in 5 minutes   b. in 10 minutes   c. in 15 minutes

5. Martha leaves her house at 1:00 P.M. Her mother has asked her to be home by 7:00 P.M. Suppose Martha allows about one hour for round-trip travel time, 2 to 3 hours for shopping, and 1 hour for lunch. How many hours can she spend taking a walk with Angela?

   a. less than 1 hour   b. from 1 to 2 hours   c. from 3 to 4 hours

6. At the department store, Angela browses through the book department. One of the paperback book racks is marked "All Books Here Priced Between $2 and $4!" Angela has $8. How many books can she buy?

   a. 2 or 3   b. 2, 3, or 4   c. 3, 4, or 5

Use with page 9.

Name _____ Date _____

PRACTICE   Estimating Sums of Whole Numbers

Estimate each sum.

1.	3,487	2.	6,384	3.	289,714	4.	2,598,214
	5,975		213		10,860		4,311,725
	2,219		4,425		147,233		2,685,340
	+ 4,290		+ 3,970		+ 2,108		+ 1,406,415

5.	3,487	6.	6,384	7.	289,714	8.	2,598,214
	5,975		213		10,860		4,311,725
	2,219		4,425		147,233		2,685,340
	+ 4,290		+ 3,970		+ 2,108		+ 1,406,415

9.	2,398	10.	9,248	11.	2,365,704	12.	4,025,713
	5,120		3,730		236,570		6,401
	3,015		6,329		3,398,443		238,972
	4,579		2,406		17,402		3,705,544
	+ 1,893		+ 3,275		+ 1,101,231		+ 28,376

13. 6,234 + 1,408 + 5,296 = _____

14. 8,192 + 650 + 3,275 = _____

Solve.

15. About how many people in all live in these cities?

_____

City	Population
Shanghai, China	10,820,000
Mexico City, Mexico	9,233,770
Tokyo, Japan	8,219,888
Moscow, Russia	7,831,000

16. Last week, Mr. Potter had gross sales from his butcher shop listed at right. About how much did he make for the week?

_____

Monday	$3,276
Tuesday	4,129
Wednesday	3,378
Thursday	5,892
Friday	5,315
TOTAL	

Use with pages 10–11.   5

PRACTICE Estimating Differences of Whole Numbers

Choose the letter of the best answer.

1. $6,398 - 2,842$ **a.** less than 4,000   **b.** more than 4,000

2. $8,569 - 3,125$ **a.** less than 5,000   **b.** more than 5,000

3. $9,720 - 6,643$ **a.** less than 3,000   **b.** more than 3,000

4. $4,620 - 4,415$ **a.** less than 200   **b.** more than 200

5. $18,175 - 11,580$ **a.** less than 7,000   **b.** more than 7,000

6. $27,315 - 6,502$ **a.** less than 21,000   **b.** more than 21,000

7. $75,238 - 49,600$ **a.** less than 25,000   **b.** more than 25,000

8. $369,240 - 171,920$ **a.** less than 200,000   **b.** more than 200,000

9. $825,376 - 439,725$ **a.** less than 400,000   **b.** more than 400,000

10. $782,175 - 763,200$ **a.** less than 20,000   **b.** more than 20,000

11. $8,375,216 - 5,142,960$ **a.** less than 3,000,000   **b.** more than 3,000,000

Estimate.

12. $\begin{array}{r} 8,765 \\ -\ 2,910 \\ \hline \end{array}$ 13. $\begin{array}{r} 9,326 \\ -\ 5,635 \\ \hline \end{array}$ 14. $\begin{array}{r} 62,392 \\ -\ 19,704 \\ \hline \end{array}$ 15. $\begin{array}{r} 78,632 \\ -\ 22,418 \\ \hline \end{array}$

16. $\begin{array}{r} 129,280 \\ -\ 63,716 \\ \hline \end{array}$ 17. $\begin{array}{r} 2,358,196 \\ -\ 2,146,720 \\ \hline \end{array}$ 18. $\begin{array}{r} 5,681,310 \\ -\ 3,726,189 \\ \hline \end{array}$ 19. $\begin{array}{r} 9,532,846 \\ -\ 2,486,355 \\ \hline \end{array}$

Solve.

20. In 1968, there were around 15,800 women in the U.S. Army. In 1980, the number had risen to 61,700. About how many more women were in the Army in 1980 than in 1968?

    _____

21. In 1983, the United States exported $7,767,000 of goods to the Netherlands. The United States imported $2,970,000 of goods from the Netherlands. About how much more did the United States export than import?

    _____

Use with pages 12–13.

PRACTICE | Adding Whole Numbers

Add. Check the answer by estimating.

1. 6,233
    + 714

2. 7,041
    + 775

3. 8,103
    + 464

4. 9,628
    + 130

5. 4,437
    + 2,657

6. $79.06
    + 55.18

7. 8,664
    + 3,137

8. 8,154
    + 1,047

9. 14,623
    + 71,371

10. 45,704
     + 53,707

11. 18,819
     + 37,406

12. $409.62
     + 211.76

13. 518,416
     + 878,673

14. 612,666
     + 778,498

15. 544,927
     + 393,299

16. 458,965
     + 595,638

17. $827
      345
    + 123

18. 2,708
     3,699
    + 5,265

19. 93,571
      2,781
    + 30,114

20. 18,810
     10,864
    + 17,269

21. 266,890
      20,092
           9
    +   33

22. 794,761
         360
       9,927
    + 19,732

23. 217,961
          66
          93
    + 66,330

24.   388
         2,447
        62,636
    + 119,496

Solve.

25. Greg shopped for new clothes. He bought a shirt for $15.25, a sweater for $17.00, and a pair of gym shorts for $6.83. How much did Greg spend?

_____

26. Maggie read about a sale at a department store. Dresses cost $36.45, jeans cost $12.88, and belts cost $2.39. If Maggie bought one of each item, how much did she spend?

_____

Name _____ Date _____

PRACTICE Subtracting Whole Numbers

Subtract.

| 1. | 31,289
–   58 | 2. | 96,363
–   973 | 3. | 9,485
–   895 | 4. | 95,826
–   99 | 5. | 9,426
–   73 |

| 6. | 8,892
– 1,476 | 7. | 5,838
– 1,222 | 8. | 6,974
– 3,138 | 9. | 9,585
– 3,115 | 10. | 5,909
– 4,253 |

| 11. | 60,024
–   3,739 | 12. | 52,994
–   8,104 | 13. | 86,430
–   6,313 | 14. | 95,055
–   5,732 | 15. | 98,869
–   4,816 |

| 16. | 70,166
– 63,036 | 17. | 76,998
– 58,306 | 18. | 72,176
– 52,424 | 19. | 54,786
– 25,969 | 20. | 29,628
– 10,170 |

| 21. | 951,972
–   52,142 | 22. | 987,338
–   9,376 | 23. | 799,824
–   7,151 | 24. | 464,924
–   72,448 | 25. | 35,104
– 16,927 |

26. 492 – 307 = _____

27. $291.05 – $152.73 = _____

28. $635.35 – $78.78 = _____

29. 9,971 – 3,808 = _____

Add or subtract.

30. 951,972 – 52,142 + 67 = _____

31. 3,843 – 41 + 36,671 = _____

32. 987,338 – 9,376 + 277 = _____

33. 1,745 + 49,756 – 7,639 = _____

Use with pages 16–17.

PRACTICE   Using the Help File

Kenny is a student who is trying to solve the problems below. For each problem, suggest which section of the Help File Kenny should consult for assistance: *Questions, Tools, Solutions,* or *Checks.* Then solve the problem.

1. Joanna received a camera for her birthday. The film that she loaded into the camera will allow her to take 36 pictures. So far she has taken 29. How many more pictures can she take?

   Kenny knows that he needs to subtract in order to solve the problem, but he is not sure how to check that his answer is correct. Which section of the Help File should he turn to?

   _____

2. Last week, Joanna shot 2 rolls of film. The first roll had 36 pictures. The second roll had 16 fewer pictures. How many pictures were there on the second roll?

   Kenny has read the problem several times, but he is not sure that he understands what he is being asked. Which section of the Help File should he turn to?

   _____

3. Joanna bought a telephoto lens for her camera. The lens normally costs $125, but the store was having a $10-off sale. How much did Joanna pay for her lens?

   Kenny understands the problem, but he is not sure what method to use to solve it. Which section of the Help File should he turn to? _____

4. In June, Joanna spent $38.73 for film developing, $16.95 on photography books, and $56.70 for a tripod. She has budgeted $100.00 for her hobby for the month. Did Joanna stay within her budget?

   Kenny thinks he knows how to approach the problem, but he does not know how to do the necessary math. Which section of the Help File should he turn to? _____

5. Joanna's rechargeable flash allows her to take 40 flash pictures without recharging. If she takes 10 flash pictures per day, after how many days will she have to recharge the flash?

   Kenny has read the problem several times, but he's not sure that he understands what he's being asked. Which section of the Help File should he turn to? _____

6. Joanna won first prize in her school's photography contest. She received a $50 gift certificate. She would like to buy a utility bag that costs $27. If she buys the bag, how much of her gift certificate will she have left to spend?

   Kenny knows how to solve the problem, but he's uncertain how to check his answer. Which section of the Help File should he turn to?

   _____

PRACTICE Extending Place Value

Write each missing word in the place-value chart. Then write
these numbers in the correct places: 10.419286; 4.0021; 0.19834.

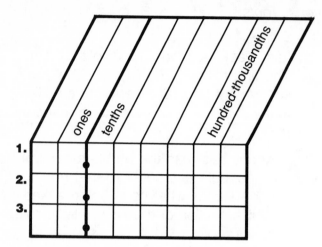

Write the value of each underlined digit.

4. 91.1<u>4</u>06 _____

5. 16.5984<u>1</u> _____

6. 20.49562<u>4</u> _____

7. 0.279<u>5</u>4 _____

Write in standard form.

8. 2 tenths _____

9. 45 hundredths _____

10. 352 thousandths _____

11. 5 ten-thousandths _____

12. 75 millionths _____

13. 1 hundred-thousandth _____

Write the word name for each number.

14. 6.8 _____

15. 0.033 _____

16. 0.0410 _____

Name _____ Date _____

PRACTICE Comparing and Ordering Decimals

Compare. Write >, <, or = in the ◯.

1. 0.07 ◯ 0.007   **2.** 1.015 ◯ 1.15   **3.** 0.004 ◯ 0.040

4. 6.15 ◯ 6.150   **5.** 0.0952 ◯ 0.9052   **6.** 0.0802 ◯ 0.08

7. 1.101 ◯ 1.0109   **8.** 8.201 ◯ 8.2   **9.** 0.03 ◯ 0.0300

10. 5.0050 ◯ 5.0500   **11.** 0.1098 ◯ 0.10980   **12.** 7.0032 ◯ 0.703

Write 14.5106; 14.051610; 14.511611; 14.005161 in order
from the greatest to the least.

13. _____

_____

Write the decimals in order from the least to the greatest.

14. 0.21; 0.201; 2.1; 0.021; 0.02   **15.** 6.431; 6.413; 0.6431; 6.4031

_____   _____

16. 0.07; 0.69001; 0.07103; 0.006913   **17.** 2.50038; 2.50308; 2.503008; 2.058003

_____   _____

The table lists the highest barometer reading in Woodstock
for each day of Michael's vacation.

Day	Monday	Tuesday	Wednesday	Thursday	Friday
Degrees	29.8	29.89	30.98	30.09	30.80

18. Write the days in order from the lowest to the highest
readings.

_____

19. On Saturday the barometer reached 30.08. Which days
had higher readings than Saturday?

_____

PRACTICE   Rounding Decimals

Round each number.

	To the nearest whole number	To the nearest tenth	To the nearest hundredth	To the nearest thousandth	To the nearest ten-thousandth
1.	4.89 _____	0.17 _____	0.024 _____	1.0036 _____	8.33041 _____
2.	31.256 _____	4.06 _____	2.5169 _____	0.4814 _____	1.09415 _____
3.	0.904 _____	15.108 _____	14.109 _____	3.6245 _____	2.68034 _____
4.	29.7 _____	11.98 _____	16.196 _____	0.42519 _____	0.80876 _____
5.	16.391 _____	0.3529 _____	10.2406 _____	25.5055 _____	15.98052 _____
6.	10.485 _____	3.534 _____	7.8949 _____	4.00062 _____	0.99995 _____

To which place is each number rounded? Write *W* for whole number, *TE* for tenth, *HU* for hundredth, *TH* for thousandth, and *TT* for ten-thousandth.

7. 4.0685 to 4.069 _____

8. 0.7531 to 0.75 _____

9. 6.01384 to 6.0138 _____

10. 161.49 to 161.5 _____

11. 0.6104 to 0.610 _____

12. 4.86 to 5 _____

13. 2.4076 to 2.41 _____

14. 3.7861 to 4.0 _____

Use with pages 24–25.

PRACTICE Using the Infobank

Solve each problem. Use the Infobanks on pages 469–474
to find the information you need.

1. A strong wind can make the air
temperature feel much colder than it is.
When the temperature is 25°F and the
wind is blowing at 10 miles per hour,
what is the equivalent temperature? ____

2. Schubert and Wagner were two great
composers of classical music. Both
lived in the nineteenth century. Which
of the two was born earlier in the
century? _____

3. Gauss, Pascal, and Cantor were
famous mathematicians. Which of them
lived in the 1600s?
_____

4. Which food has more calories: 1 cup
rice or 2 cups mashed potatoes?
_____

5. A phone bill for November–December
lists seven long-distance calls. Which of
the calls was the most expensive? ____

6. Which of the long-distance calls was
the least expensive? _____

7. The Sterns plan to move to Delbersville
Community Towers Senior Citizens
Community. They would like an
apartment with about 1,000 square feet
of space. Should they take an efficiency
apartment or a one-bedroom
apartment? _____

8. A significant year for classical music
was 1810. Two great composers were
born in that year. Who were they?
_____

9. As an after-school snack, Thomas had
a glass of milk and 2 carrots. How
many calories did he consume?
_____

10. Which baseball team won the most
games in the National League? Which
team won the fewest?
_____

11. Rene Descartes died fifteen years before
another great French mathematician.
Who was he? _____

12. A boiled egg has approximately the
same number of calories as which other
common food? _____

PRACTICE   Estimating Sums and Differences

Estimate. Write > or < in the space provided. Then, for each
problem with a >, cross out the corresponding numbered box
below. Answer the question: "Beijing is the capital of what
country?"

1. 2.3 + 0.95 + 1.6 ◯ 5

2. 0.56 + 0.329 + 0.421 ◯ 1

3. 3.32 + 4.39 + 2.15 ◯ 6

4. 7.21 + 0.368 + 0.67 ◯ 8

5. 12.15 + 15.72 + 11.29 ◯ 39

6. 3.763 − 0.9 ◯ 3

7. 58.47 − 9.36 ◯ 48

8. 32.18 + 10.63 + 0.112 ◯ 43

9. 68.34 + 2.52 + 3.61 ◯ 70

10. 19.47 − 5.691875 ◯ 13

11. 198.49 + 0.00217 + 0.014 ◯ 198

12. 59.23 + 0.562 + 19.1 ◯ 85

13. 38.666 − 14.58 ◯ 23

14. $19.95 − $9.29 ◯ $11

15. $19.59 + $18.36 + $17.50 ◯ $50

16. $109.20 + $115.99 ◯ $200

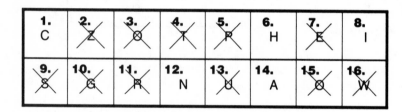

1. C	2. Z	3. O	4. X	5. P	6. H	7. E	8. I
9. S	10. G	11. R	12. N	13. U	14. A	15. O	16. W

_____

17. Lee made deposits of $145.32, $152.89, and $205.16 in
her checking account. About how much did she deposit
in all? _____

18. Rocio had $793.85 in her checking account. She wrote
checks for $35.49 and $178.99. About how much did she
have left in her account? _____

Name _____ Date _____

Add. Check by estimating.

1. 42.3322 + 47.4273	**2.** 24.243 + 42.612	**3.** 624.12 + 114.94	**4.** 6.3465 + 75.9854

5. 6.3465 8.0519 + 29.9911	**6.** 89.3780 14.0987 + 23.7846	**7.** 278.141 1,003.873 + 345.897	**8.** 98.9891 207.3879 + 3.4545

9. $9,820.45 6,851.94 + 639.82	**10.** $45,871.93 7,600.04 + 33,894.37	**11.** $83,609.51 76,475.28 + 23,368.41	**12.** $12,491.21 88,080.17 + 44,552.77

13. 12.6820 16.1083 + 47.8182	**14.** 15.4695 85.3964 + 15.2565	**15.** 33.1378 21.1191 + 96.4382	**16.** 123.8441 67.3394 + 36.7818

17. 42.3322 24.1437 51.5471 + 2.4237	**18.** 47.4273 42.6124 25.3426 + 91.8004	**19.** 16.3465 28.0513 33.5926 + 17.9901	**20.** 12.3311 73.4404 24.4273 + 23.5918

21. $0.013 + 1.3 + 22 =$ _____

22. $4.76 + 95.305 + 52.5 =$ _____

23. $6.01 + 0.4401 + 41.7593 =$ _____

24. $1.0001 + 2.032 + 0.9 =$ _____

25. $15.46 + 5.459 + 6.3701 =$ _____

26. $1.7961 + 0.8889 + 50 =$ _____

Name _____ Date _____

PRACTICE Subtracting Decimals

Subtract.

1. 3.4 − 3.3	**2.** 9.4 − 5.8	**3.** 9.3 − 6.1	**4.** 63.5 − 48.9
5. 80.8 − 50.2	**6.** 53.2 − 16.8	**7.** 44.9 − 32.2	**8.** 76.2 − 64.3
9. 90.33 − 66.94	**10.** 50.62 − 18.75	**11.** 3.82 − 1.19	**12.** 80.13 − 34.66
13. 51.536 − 5.70	**14.** 87.803 − 36.141	**15.** 95.108 − 3.3557	**16.** 3.82 − 1.676
17. 80.05 − 34.49	**18.** 68.93 − 60.62	**19.** 34.5 − 15.277	**20.** 7.86 − 3.05
21. 50.3963 − 8	**22.** 95.108 − 3.3557	**23.** 15.1 − 5.7137	**24.** 38.608፧ − 16
25. 9.2479 − 3.1227	**26.** 89.3797 − 78.1315	**27.** 4.6688 − 3.4264	**28.** 91.921፧ − 80.709፧

Solve.

29. Jessica wants to repair the old door on the barn. She goes to the lumberyard and buys one board for $8.59 and a sheet of plywood for $17.25. How much change does she receive if she gives the clerk two $20 bills? _____

30. Jessica gave the change from her purchase to her brother. He used the change to buy $3.50 worth of nails and a tape measure for $5.73. How much change was left? _____

Use with pages 32–33

Name _____ Date _____

Use the graph to solve.

1. In which year did the most children attend the Dawn County Annual Crafts Exhibition?

_____

2. What was the first year in which more than 400 adults attended the exhibition?

_____

3. How many adults came to the exhibition in 1982? _____

4. How many more adults than children attended the exhibition in 1984?

_____

5. What was the first year in which total attendance exceeded 700? _____

6. How many more adults and children came to the exhibition in 1985 than in 1981? _____

7. In which year did attendance figures for adults and for children differ the most?

_____

8. In which year did attendance figures for adults and for children differ the least?

_____

9. If 130 more people than previously had attended the exhibition in 1985, what would the total attendance have been?

_____

10. If 60 fewer adults and 30 fewer children had attended in 1983, what would the total attendance have been?

_____

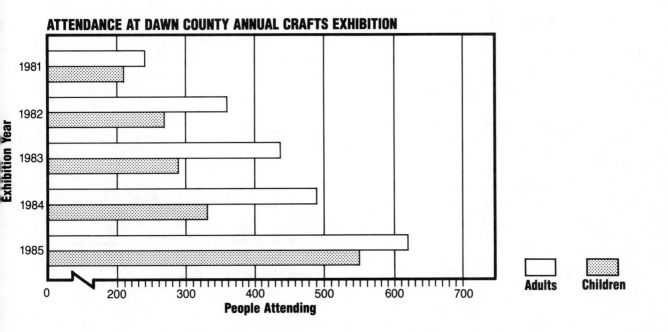

ATTENDANCE AT DAWN COUNTY ANNUAL CRAFTS EXHIBITION

Exhibition Year: 1981, 1982, 1983, 1984, 1985

People Attending: 0, 200, 300, 400, 500, 600, 700

Adults   Children

Name _____ Date _____

PRACTICE Multiplication

Write = or ≠ in the ◯

1. 14 × 7 ◯ 7 × 14

2. 8 × (3 × 9) ◯ (8 × 3) × 9

3. 43 × (8 + 2) ◯ (43 × 8) + (43 × 2)

4. 5 × (4 + 6) ◯ 54 + 56

5. 58 × 1 ◯ 1

6. 35 × 0 ◯ 0

7. (9 + 1) × 9 ◯ (9 × 9) + 9

8. 4 × 17 × 15 ◯ 17 × 15 × 4

9. 16 × 0 ◯ 16

10. (4 + 2) × 3 ◯ (4 × 2) + (2 × 4)

11. 1 × (5 + 29) ◯ 5 + 29

12. 24 × 1 ◯ 0

Which property does each equation demonstrate? Write *A* for Associative, *C* for Commutative, *D* for Distributive, *I* for Identity, and *Z* for Zero properties.

13. 450 × 12 × 81 = 81 × 450 × 12   _____

14. (21 + 42) × 7 = (21 × 7) + (42 × 7)   _____

15. 8 × (60 + 6) = (8 × 60) + (8 × 6)   _____

16. 4 × (31 × 2) = (4 × 31) × 2   _____

17. 4 × 2 × 0 = 0   _____

18. (31 + 6) × 1 = 31 + 6   _____

19. 21 × (3 × 8) = (21 × 3) × 8   _____

20. (47 × 19) × 55 = 47 × (19 × 55)   _____

Complete.

21. 16 × (5 + _____) = 16 × 5

22. _____ × 1 = 1,376

23. 146 × _____ = 0

24. 8 × 33 × 6 = 8 × 6 × _____

25. 23 × (1 + 27) = 23 + 23 × _____

26. 35 × 61 × 0 = _____

PRACTICE · Multiplying by Multiples of 10

Multiply.

1. 497 $\times$ 10	**2.** 4,252 $\times$ 600	**3.** 695 $\times$ 30	**4.** 8,166 $\times$ 3,000	**5.** 863 $\times$ 500
6. 2,968 $\times$ 1,000	**7.** 771 $\times$ 80	**8.** 240 $\times$ 70	**9.** 1,599 $\times$ 6,000	**10.** 645 $\times$ 50
11. 4,100 $\times$ 700	**12.** 189 $\times$ 90	**13.** 2,888 $\times$ 400	**14.** 315 $\times$ 20	**15.** 1,293 $\times$ 900
16. 5,001 $\times$ 300	**17.** 141 $\times$ 40	**18.** 1,710 $\times$ 5,000	**19.** 317 $\times$ 100	**20.** 1,285 $\times$ 8,000

21. $2,000,000 \times 1,000 =$ _____

22. $101,010 \times 10,000 =$ _____

23. $7,650 \times 10,000 =$ _____

24. $44,000 \times 2,000 =$ _____

25. $664 \times 100 =$ _____

26. $379 \times 1,000 =$ _____

27. $118 \times 10,000 =$ _____

28. $927 \times 100,000 =$ _____

Solve.

29. Ginger is watching her weight. She is trying not to eat more than 1,250 calories a day. If she keeps to her plan, how many calories will she eat in 10 days?

_____

30. A half-cup serving of low-fat cottage cheese contains about 100 calories. If Ginger eats 2 servings per day every day for the month of June, about how many calories is that?

_____

PRACTICE | Estimating Products of Whole Numbers

Find your way through the maze. Estimate each product by rounding. If the estimate adjusts up, go towards the number with a⁻. If the estimate adjusts down, go towards the number with a⁺.

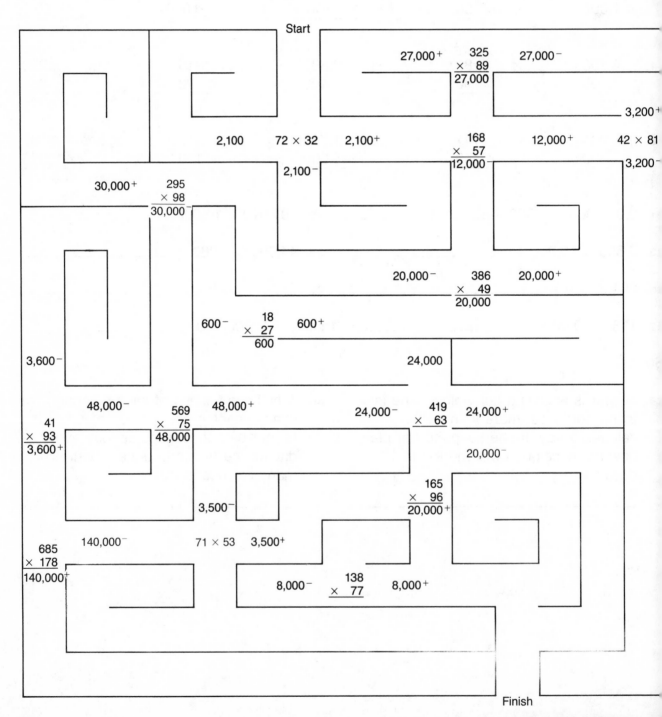

Use with pages 48–49

PRACTICE Multiplying by 1-Digit Numbers

Multiply.

1. 354 × 8	**2.** 496 × 2	**3.** 663 × 9	**4.** 175 × 5	**5.** 187 × 4
6. 1,221 × 3	**7.** $17.63 × 4	**8.** 7,161 × 7	**9.** 8,393 × 4	**10.** 4,572 × 9
11. 2,815 × 5	**12.** 9,564 × 8	**13.** 2,123 × 3	**14.** $68.41 × 7	**15.** 4,781 × 8
16. 54,270 × 5	**17.** 93,558 × 6	**18.** $129.47 × 9	**19.** 43,254 × 8	**20.** 34,170 × 9

21. $1,001.87 × 8	**22.** 187,169 × 4	**23.** 903,889 × 2	**24.** 177,531 × 5

25. $3 \times 784,213 =$ _____

26. $5 \times 328,754 =$ _____

27. $9 \times 681,992 =$ _____

Solve.

28. A new microscope costs $765.98. How much will the laboratory have to spend for 6 new microscopes?

_____

29. The lab technician can store 244 slides in one box. How many slides can be stored in 8 boxes?

_____

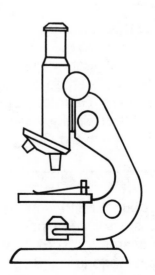

PRACTICE | Identifying Extra/Needed Information

Ring the letter of the sentence that describes the problem.

1. Gloria bought 200 shares of one stock at $8.00 per share and 100 shares of another stock at $20.25 per share. How many shares of stock did she buy?

   a. There is not enough information to solve the problem.

   b. There is more information than you need to solve the problem.

2. The price of Conway Corporation stock dropped $3 per share. Howard decided to buy 100 shares. How much did he pay for the stock?

   a. There is not enough information to solve the problem.

   b. There is more information than you need to solve the problem.

Solve.

3. Katherine invested $3,500 in American Industries stock. Later that year, she sold her stock for $4,325. How many shares of American Industries stock did Katherine own?

   _____

   _____

4. Cecilia bought 250 shares of GNE stock at $61 per share. If the company paid dividends of $2 per share, how much money in dividends did Cecilia receive? _____

5. Francis sold his shares of Riston Foods at $38.00 per share. He paid a broker's commission of $58.75. How much profit did he make?

   _____

   _____

6. Harriet invested $3,525 in Witchway stock when the shares sold for $47. Three months later, she sold her shares for $3,907. How much profit did Harriet make? _____

7. During the last year, Major Coal sold as high as $51.00 a share and as low as $39.75 a share. George bought 100 shares of Major Coal for $43.25 a share. How much did George's shares cost? _____

8. Fred purchased shares of Haward Tool for $10.00 per share. He later sold his shares at a small profit. He also received dividends of $1.07 per share. How much money did Fred earn in dividends?

   _____

   _____

9. Marjorie bought $840 worth of Century Furniture stock for $21 per share. She sold her shares for $775. How much money did Marjorie lose? _____

10. Marta bought 50 shares of Lion Oil stock each year for 3 years. She received dividends of $30 per share the first year, $60 per share the second year, and $90 per share the third year. How many shares of Lion Oil stock does Marta own? _____

PRACTICE | Multiplying by 2-Digit Numbers

Multiply.

1. 57,651
    ×   65

2.   59
    × 47

3. 1,473
    ×   55

4. 431
    × 15

5. 97
    × 24

6. 134
    × 36

7. 50,099
    ×   53

8. 9,747
    ×   68

9. 948
    × 85

10. 3,775
    ×   20

11. 82
    × 56

12. 745
    × 38

13. 18,247
    ×   98

14.   19
    × 92

15. 662
    × 72

16. 67
    × 56

17. $27.50 × 25 = _____

18. $39.45 × 92 = _____

19. $93.20 × 61 = _____

20. $530.03 × 86 = _____

21. $329.55 × 18 = _____

22. $801.21 × 77 = _____

23. $777.77 × 49 = _____

24. $101.01 × 34 = _____

Solve.

25. During strenuous exercise, the heart pumps about 12 gallons of blood per minute. How many gallons would the heart pump for a runner in a marathon that takes 2 hours 33 minutes?

_____

Name _____ Date _____

Multiply.

1. 914
    × 209

2. 5,260
    × 596

3. $1,873
    ×   400

4. 685
    × 655

5. 6,930
    ×   199

6. 169
    × 634

7. $555
    × 911

8. 170
    × 862

9. 712
    × 842

10. 4,609
     ×   260

11. 499
     × 864

12. $7,950
     ×   180

13. 1,160
     ×   774

14. 475
     × 704

15. $4,830
     ×   290

16. 376
     × 153

17. 535
     × 421

18. $708
     × 866

19. 1,723
     ×   550

20. 656
     × 490

Solve.

21. Maggie works in the mailing department
    of *Scientist Magazine*. She uses a
    computer to print 2,985 address labels
    per day. Last year she worked 247
    days. How many labels did she print?

    _____

22. *Scientist Magazine* sells 4,380 copies
    to newsstands each week. The
    newsstands pay the Scientist Magazine
    Company $1.35 per copy. What is the
    income from the sale of these
    magazines?

    _____

Use with pages 56–57

PRACTICE | Estimation

an the question be solved by estimation? Write *yes* or *no*.

1. Fernando spends $9.80 per week for a commuter booklet of bus tickets. If Fernando budgets $50.00 for the bus next month, will that be enough? _____

2. Jill takes a taxi to her grandmother's house. The taxi charges $0.90 for the first 0.1 mile and $0.20 for each additional 0.1 mile. Jill's grandmother lives 3 miles away. Jill pays the driver with a $10 bill. How much change does she receive? _____

olve. Estimate or figure exactly, as appropriate.

3. The Ghazanfar family is planning to drive 1,585 miles along the West Coast. If they travel an average of 185 miles per day, will they be able to complete their trip in less than 10 days? _____

4. Kim drives a truck. Last week, she drove from New York to Boston and back. The distance from New York to Boston is 206 miles. If Kim is paid 37 cents per mile, how much did she earn for the trip? _____

5. Vincent is taking a train to visit his aunt who lives 217 miles away. If he leaves at 9:00 A.M. and travels at an average speed of 50 miles per hour, will he arrive in time for lunch at noon? _____

6. Joseph and Dana Hauser and their two children plan to fly to Disney World. The plane fare is $79 each way for an adult and $35 for a child. If the Hausers plan to spend a maximum of $600 for the round-trip plane fare, did they budget enough money? _____

7. Betty travels to work by train. Each month, she buys a monthly commuter train ticket for $58.60. In a 6-month period, does Betty spend more or less than $350.00 for train tickets? _____

8. Mildred rented a car to take a trip through Rhode Island. She paid a $59.95 rental fee and a $41.20 mileage charge. She also spent $17.34 for gasoline. Was $110.00 enough to cover Mildred's car costs? _____

9. The round-trip distance from Ray's house to work is 48 miles. Ray's car has a 12-gallon gas tank. If his car gets 29 miles per gallon, will he be able to travel to and from work for 5 days on one tank of gas? _____

10. Before a recent vacation trip, Wendy's odometer read 21,317 miles. After the trip, it read 22,493 miles. Wendy's car averages 24 miles per gallon. How many miles did Wendy drive on her trip? _____

PRACTICE Estimating Products of Decimals

Choose the best answer.

1. Close to but greater than one   **a.** 0.95   **b.** 0.49   **c.** 1.1   **d.** 0.53

2. Close to but less than half   **a.** 1.4   **b.** 0.53   **c.** 0.92   **d.** 0.48

3. Close to but less than one   **a.** 0.96   **b.** 2.3   **c.** 1.2   **d.** 0.51

Use estimation to locate the decimal point.

4. $4.26 \times 0.98 = 4\ 1\ 7\ 4\ 8$ 5. $6.51 \times 0.49 = 3\ 1\ 8\ 9\ 9$

6. $1.1 \times 0.637 = 7\ 0\ 0\ 7$ 7. $0.53 \times 0.8218 = 4\ 3\ 5\ 5\ 5\ 4$

Estimate. Use numbers that are easy to mentally multiply.

8. $0.93 \times 6.01 = $ _____   9. $1.05 \times 2.9 = $ _____

10. $0.46 \times 0.82 = $ _____   11. $0.532 \times 4.817 = $ _____

12. $1.3 \times 3.9 = $ _____   13. $0.495 \times 10.2 = $ _____

Solve.

14. About how much would you pay for 3 pounds of chicken? for 5 pounds of hamburger? _____

AL'S BUTCHER SHOP	
Chicken	$0.49/lb
Hamburger	$1.19/lb

15. A survey showed that about 47% of Crown Point's economy can be attributed to tourism. If Crown Point's annual retail sales total $10.2 million, about how much is spent by tourists?

    _____

PRACTICE   Multiplying Decimals

Multiply. To check answers, estimate by rounding to the
highest place value in each number. Round dollar amounts to
the nearest cent.

1. 1.73 $\times$ 6.91	**2.** \$3.62 $\times$ 16.8	**3.** 81.051 $\times$ 0.08	**4.** 24.32 $\times$ 1.92	**5.** 18.6 $\times$ 2.81
6. 2.693 $\times$ 1.5	**7.** 35.42 $\times$ 7.9	**8.** 0.031 $\times$ 86.2	**9.** \$11.62 $\times$ 0.47	**10.** 19.83 $\times$ 1.21
11. 6.932 $\times$ 0.76	**12.** \$1.91 $\times$ 6.02	**13.** 8.394 $\times$ 0.97	**14.** 0.619 $\times$ 4.8	**15.** 88.635 $\times$ 0.19
16. 1.932 $\times$ 8.7	**17.** 21.65 $\times$ 0.61	**18.** \$19.77 $\times$ 0.42	**19.** 3.652 $\times$ 5.44	**20.** 8.413 $\times$ 0.91

21. $\$1.93 \times 2 =$ _____

22. $44.7 \times 4.86 =$ _____

23. $1.62 \times 4.9 \times 0.8 =$ _____

24. $11.6 \times 5.35 =$ _____

25. $0.9 \times 18.62 \times 2.3 =$ _____

26. $\$9.01 \times 5.8 =$ _____

27. $92.7 \times 0.08 =$ _____

28. $4.291 \times 8.4 \times 0.3 =$ _____

29. Chikako needs 12.8 yards of silk to make a kimono. It costs \$8.95 a yard. How much will she have to pay?

_____

30. Tender Leaf made a shawl. She used 9.6 yards of woven material that cost \$11.25 a yard. How much did she spend?

_____

PRACTICE   Choosing the Operation

Solve.

1. George and Lisa play one hour of racquetball every Tuesday and Thursday afternoon. When they play, they usually complete 2 or 3 games. What is the greatest number of games they can play in 4 weeks? _____

2. Last Tuesday, George won the first game 15 to 10. How many more points did George score than did Lisa?

_____

3. In the second game, Lisa beat George by 7 points. If Lisa needed 15 points to win, how many points did George score? _____

4. During the summer, George and Lisa played often. In July, they played 27 games. In August, they played 6 more games than that. How many games did they play in July and August? _____

5. George scored an average of 9.8 points per game in the club tournament. Lisa's average was 11.3 points. On the average, how many more points per game did Lisa score than did George?

_____

6. In team competition, George and Lisa played against Raphael and Inez. The competition lasted several days. On Monday, there were 35 spectators. Before the game was over, 6 spectators left. How many people stayed till the end? _____

7. On Tuesday, there were 46 spectators in the audience. On Wednesday, 58 people came to watch. On Thursday, 66 people watched. How much larger was the audience on Wednesday than on Tuesday? _____

8. The competition consisted of 7 games. George and Lisa won the first and second games and then lost the third. Raphael and Inez won the fourth and fifth games and then lost the sixth. George and Lisa won the seventh game. Who won the competition, and by how many games?

_____

9. George and Lisa each received a trophy and a $10 gift certificate. George used his certificate to help pay the next year's $35 club membership fee. How much money did he have to pay in addition to the certificate? _____

10. Lisa used her $10.00 gift certificate to buy a sweatshirt. The sweatshirt cost $16.75. Lisa paid with the gift certificate and two $5.00 bills. How much change did she receive? _____

PRACTICE Multiplying by Powers of 10

Multiply.

1.	4.00772	2.	5.6236	3.	3.02476	4.	30.241
	× 10		× 100		× 10,000		× 1,000

5.	0.69047	6.	0.00056	7.	0.21834	8.	0.1037
	× 100		× 1,000		× 10		× 10,000

9.	0.00078	10.	0.219	11.	0.000017	12.	9.58083
	× 100		× 10		× 10,000		× 1,000

13.	0.472671	14.	36.38	15.	1.3699	16.	0.0002
	× 10,000		× 1,000		× 10		× 100

17.	8.7196	18.	4.3315	19.	74.007	20.	0.76478
	× 10		× 1,000		× 100		× 100

21.	0.4441	22.	3.0648	23.	0.61978	24.	46.3
	× 100		× 10		× 1,000		× 100

25.	0.0519	26.	0.46257	27.	4.221	28.	0.82711
	× 1,000		× 10		× 1,000		× 10

29. $5.43 × 100 = _____

30. $0.16 × 10,000 = _____

31. $8.50 × 1,000 = _____

32. $2,931.88 × 10 = _____

Solve.

33. The diameter of a white blood cell is about 0.0015 cm. If 1,000 of these cells were lined up on a microscope slide, what would the total length be? _____

PRACTICE More Multiplying Decimals

Multiply.

1.	5.436 × 0.01	2.	0.97 × 0.05	3.	0.442 × 0.7	4.	4.925 × 0.002	5.	1.28 × 0.4

6.	72.8 × 0.03	7.	6.633 × 0.09	8.	18.175 × 0.006	9.	2.7262 × 0.3	10.	0.0141 × 0.3

11.	5.82 × 0.12	12.	11.2 × 0.086	13.	0.56 × 0.075	14.	0.21 × 0.0093	15.	17.8 × 0.011

16.	0.148 × 0.36	17.	0.053 × 0.27	18.	2.35 × 0.09	19.	1.26 × 0.048	20.	0.83 × 0.57

Multiply. Round the product to the nearest cent.

21. $8.66 × 9.5485 = _____

22. $25.43 × 0.0019 = _____

23. $504.00 × 6.1911 = _____

24. $1,986.99 × 0.008 = _____

25. $6,836.49 × 1.5762 = _____

26. $18,472.88 × 0.0002 = _____

Solve.

27. Carrie and Bob want to win the Super Science Award—a year's pass to their city museum. They clocked their dog Fred as he walked down the road. Fred walked at a rate of 3 miles per hour, or 4.4001 feet per second. It took Fred 954.52 seconds to walk down the road. To the nearest foot, how long is the road? _____

Use with pages 68–69

PRACTICE | Solving Two-Step Problems/Making a Plan

Write the step to complete the plan.

1. Evelyn Lyons decided to open her own clothing shop to be called The Clothing Palace. The store she rented has an area of 1,216 square feet. If her monthly rent is $1.05 per square foot, how much will Evelyn pay to rent the store for one year?

   Step 1: _____

   Step 2: Find Evelyn's rent for one year.

2. During the first month of operation, Evelyn's Clothing Palace used 1,827 kilowatt hours of electricity. If Evelyn paid a meter charge of $5 plus $.09 per kilowatt hour, find the amount she owed the electric company that month.

   Step 1: _____

   _____

   Step 2: Add the cost of 1,827 kilowatt hours of electricity to the meter charge.

Make a plan for each problem. Solve.

3. Evelyn's first telephone bill included a monthly charge of $11.35 plus 78 message units. Each message unit cost $0.23. Find the total amount of Evelyn's telephone bill. _____

4. Evelyn borrowed $10,000 from the bank in order to stock the Clothing Palace with merchandise. She agreed to repay the bank loan in 60 monthly installments of $233. How much interest is Evelyn paying on the loan? _____

5. Evelyn hired Orlando Ruiz to work in her shop. Orlando worked 5 hours per day Monday through Friday and 8 hours on Saturday. How many hours did Orlando work during the week? _____

6. The salesman for Zippy Designer Jeans sold Evelyn 122 pairs of jeans. 72 pairs of jeans were denim and cost $11.85 each. The rest of the jeans were corduroy and cost a total of $600. How much did Evelyn pay for the jeans? _____

7. Evelyn paid $12 apiece for corduroy jeans. She put them on sale for $19.95 each. How much profit will she make if she sells 50 pairs of corduroy jeans? _____

8. On Friday, Evelyn sold 9 dresses and 20 pairs of pants. On Saturday, she sold twice as many dresses and 10 more pairs of pants than on Friday. How many dresses did Evelyn sell on Friday and Saturday? _____

PRACTICE Division

Write the inverse problem.

1. 56 ÷ 8 _____   **2.** 5 × 5 _____

3. 17 × 6 _____   **4.** 156 ÷ 13 _____

5. 10 × 20 _____   **6.** 399 ÷ 19 _____

Write the problem three ways.

7. 22 divided by 11 _____, _____, _____   **8.** 140 divided by 7 _____, _____,

_____

9. 336 divided by 6 _____, _____, _____   **10.** 820 divided by 4 _____, _____,

_____

Write *true* or *false*.

11. 59 ÷ 0 = 0 ____   **12.** 46 ÷ 46 = 1 ____   **13.** 0 ÷ 15 undefined ____

14. 83 ÷ 1 = 1 ____   **15.** 87 ÷ 0 undefined ____   **16.** (48 ÷ 4) ÷ 2 = 48 ÷ (4 ÷ 2) ____

Write the missing number in the circle.

17. $\bigcirc$ ÷ 3 = 0   **18.** (7 × $\bigcirc$) × 8 = 56   **19.** 14 ÷ $\bigcirc$ = 1

20. 0 ÷ 87 = $\bigcirc$ **21.** 7 ÷ $\bigcirc$ = 7   **22.** $\bigcirc$ ÷ 1 = 5

23. (7 ÷ 7) × 4 = $\bigcirc$ **24.** (3 × 3) ÷ 4 = 9 ÷ $\bigcirc$ **25.** 41 ÷ 41 = $\bigcirc$

Cross out each pair of inverse operations.

26. How many balloons are left? _____

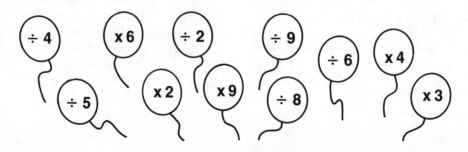

Use with pages 82–83

PRACTICE — Dividing by Multiples of 10

Divide.

1. 4)800

2. 9)2,700

3. 60)3,600

4. 90)4,500

5. 800)72,000

6. 200)2,800

7. 100,000 ÷ 1,000 = _____

8. 60,000,000 ÷ 60,000 = _____

9. 45,000,000 ÷ 300,000 = _____

10. 10,000,000 ÷ 1,000,000 = _____

11. 75,000 ÷ 25,000 = _____

12. 91,000,000 ÷ 13,000,000 = _____

13. 1,110,000 ÷ 10,000 = _____

14. 51,000,000 ÷ 17,000 = _____

15. 60)60,000

16. 400)83,600

17. 100)10,000

18. 30)84,900

19. 20)66,180

20. 80)98,800

21. 60)38,100

22. 120)480,000

23. 40)5,600

PRACTICE   Estimating Quotients of Whole Numbers

Estimate the quotient.

1. 224 ÷ 5 = _____

2. 735 ÷ 11 = _____

3. 6,289 ÷ 56 = _____

4. 426 ÷ 28 = _____

5. 8,952 ÷ 42 = _____

6. 65,120 ÷ 165 = _____

7. 57,943 ÷ 76 = _____

8. 3,531 ÷ 68 = _____

9. 30,492 ÷ 58 = _____

10. 22)$40.52

11. 58)$4.35

12. 39)$51.91

13. 78)$833.98

14. 66)7,253

15. 71)15,392

16. 16)83,496

17. 62)38,502

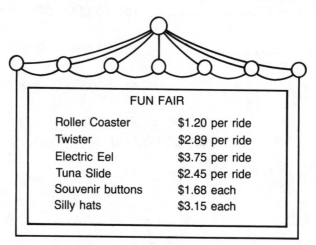

FUN FAIR	
Roller Coaster	$1.20 per ride
Twister	$2.89 per ride
Electric Eel	$3.75 per ride
Tuna Slide	$2.45 per ride
Souvenir buttons	$1.68 each
Silly hats	$3.15 each

Solve.

18. The members of the Ashura Swim Club decided to go to the Fun Fair. Everyone wants to ride the Tuna Slide. Estimate the number of rides they can buy for $235.00. _____

19. The members spend $62.40 on the roller-coaster ride, and no one rides more than once. Estimate the number of club members that rode the roller coaster. _____

20. Each club member decides to buy a silly hat and button. If $400.89 is spent on hats and buttons, estimate the number of club members.

_____

21. Karen wants to buy souvenirs for her brothers and sisters. Estimate the number of souvenir buttons she can buy if she spends $8.40.

_____

Use with pages 86–87

Name _____ Date _____

Divide.

1. 4)584   2. 2)290   3. 8)848   4. 7)756   5. 8)688

6. 6)486   7. 3)876   8. 2)595   9. 5)836   10. 6)461

11. 9)1,869   12. 8)2,437   13. 5)4,028   14. 7)4,232   15. 6)1,810

16. 3)1,227   17. 5)3,040   18. 6)48,341   19. 5)15,374   20. 7)42,731

21. 2)59,326   22. 9)98,111   23. 3)45,892   24. 4)30,166   25. 9)100,715

26. $99,073 \div 5 =$ _____

27. $92,002 \div 7 =$ _____

28. $790,073 \div 9 =$ _____

PRACTICE   Estimation

Estimate to solve each problem. Find the exact answer *only*
if you need to.

1. The Zabrowsky family is having a garage
   sale. On one table, Mark Zabrowsky has
   displayed 175 of his old comic books.
   He hopes to sell them all for 15 cents
   apiece. If he does, will Mark receive
   more or less than $30? _____

2. Mark's sister, Paula, is selling her
   collection of stuffed animals. There are
   27 animals in her collection: 13 bears, 6
   cats, 5 dogs, and 3 monkeys. The bears
   sell for $1.50 each. All the other animals
   sell for $1.00 each. If Paula sells all her
   animals, will she receive at least $40.00

   _____

3. Mr. Matthews wants to buy 3 old chairs.
   Each chair is priced at $4.75. Mr.
   Matthews has a $10.00 bill and a $5.00
   bill. Can he buy the chairs? _____

4. The Zabrowskys' numerous paperback
   books are popular sale items.
   Customers buy 38 books in the first 2
   hours. At that rate, will the Zabrowskys
   sell more or fewer than 150 books in 8
   hours? _____

5. One visitor to the garage sale wants to
   buy a lamp for $16.25, a bookcase for
   $24.50, and a mirror for $7.25. He sees
   a vase he wants that costs $1.95. If he
   has $50.00, can he afford to buy the
   vase, too? _____

6. The Zabrowskys have put a set of 9
   coffee mugs on sale for $8.00. Suppose
   they were able to sell each mug
   individually for $0.88. Would they make
   more or less money selling them that
   way than they would if they sold the
   mugs as a set? _____

7. A glass bowl contains 950 colored
   marbles. The red marbles are priced 3
   for a dime. Blue marbles sell 2 for a
   nickel. White marbles sell 5 for a
   quarter. If the Zabrowskys sell all the
   marbles in the bowl, will they receive
   more or less than $23? _____

8. The Zabrowsky family earns $387.62 at
   their garage sale. 46 customers made
   purchases. Was the average purchase
   made by a customer greater or less than
   $8.25? _____

Use with pages 90–91

PRACTICE   Dividing by 2-Digit Numbers

ivide.

1. 16)5,289

2. 23)23,989

3. 12)8,330

4. 51)143,162

5. 42)13,205

6. 75)405,465

7. 84)367,974

8. 38)76,821

9. 35)259,677

10. 68)274,184

11. 56)5,231,800

12. 47)425,915

3. 22)335,082

14. 93)93,468

15. 88)552,992

16. 71)995,562

What if we measured things in terms of other things?

7. How much does an Indian elephant weigh measured in terms of bald eagles?

_____

Indian elephant = 12,001 pounds
Bald eagle = 11 pounds

8. How much does a blue whale weigh in terms of trumpeter swans?

_____

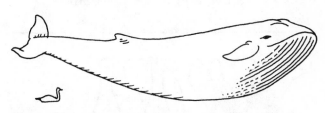

Blue whale = 230,014 pounds
Trumpeter swan = 38 pounds

Name _____ Date _____

Divide.

1. 828)‾301,392‾   2. 932)‾102,520‾   3. 167)‾119,572‾   4. 808)‾757,128‾

5. 329)‾284,317‾   6. 492)‾212,231‾   7. 584)‾154,760‾   8. 973)‾242,970‾

9. 355)‾646,100‾   10. 87)‾400,404‾   11. 332)‾830,334‾   12. 361)‾1,617,283‾

13. $\dfrac{480,318}{554}$ = _____   14. $\dfrac{300,202}{421}$ = _____   15. $\dfrac{18,383}{578}$ = ___

Complete.

16. 352,914 ÷ _____ = 393   17. 202,150 ÷ _____ = 650   18. 11,707 ÷ _____ = 23

19. 131,532 ÷ _____ = 291   20. 721,920 ÷ _____ = 3,840   21. 802,781 ÷ _____ = 1,57

Solve.

22. One year, a professional bowler scored 144,956 points in 668 games. What was his average score per game?

_____

23. Another bowler scored 137,783 points and had an average of 211 points per game. How many games did the bowle play?

_____

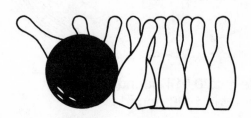

Name _____ Date _____

Read each problem. Without figuring the exact answer, ring
the letter of the most reasonable answer.

1. Memphis is 7.75 times farther away from El Paso than it is from Little Rock. Little Rock and Memphis are 140 miles apart. How far is Memphis from El Paso?

   a. fewer than 20 mi   b. about 1,100 mi

   c. about 11,000 mi

2. The distance from New York to Los Angeles is 2,875 miles. If a plane made 2 round-trips between these cities, how many miles would the plane fly?

   a. 5,750 miles   b. 8,625 miles

   c. 11,500 miles

3. Dallas, Texas, and Portland, Oregon, are 2,005 miles apart. If a car traveled from one city to the other in about 65 hours, what would be the car's average speed?

   a. about 15 miles per hour

   b. about 30 miles per hour

   c. about 50 miles per hour

4. Philadelphia is only 95 miles from Baltimore. Seattle, Washington, is 28.8 times farther away from Baltimore than Philadelphia is. How far is Seattle from Baltimore?

   a. fewer than 3,000 miles
   b. more than 3,000 miles
   c. can't tell

5. A bus traveled from Nashville, Tennessee, to Atlanta, Georgia, a distance of 235 miles. If the car's average speed was 47 miles per hour, how long did the trip take?

   a. 1 hour

   b. 5 hours

   c. 50 hours

6. Indianapolis is located halfway between Omaha and Washington, D.C. Traveling at a speed of 48 miles per hour, a car can go from Indianapolis to Washington, D.C., in 11 hours and 46 minutes. How far apart are Omaha and Washington, D.C.?

   a. about 600 miles

   b. about 1,100

   c. about 2,000 miles

7. A train traveling at an average speed of 65.3 miles per hour reaches Wilmington, Delaware, in 8 hours. A second train averaging 56.4 miles per hour reaches Wilmington in 7 hours. Both trains make the same number of stops. Which train traveled the greater distance?

   a. the first train

   b. the second train

   c. can't tell

8. A plane flies 1,665 miles from Birmingham, Alabama, to Phoenix, Arizona. After a one-hour stop, it takes off and flies 990 miles to Oklahoma City in 14 hours. What was the plane's average speed?

   a. about 75 miles per hour

   b. about 130 miles per hour

   c. about 200 miles per hour

Name _____ Date _____

Divide.

1. $6\overline{)13.02}$ **2.** $3\overline{)129.24}$ **3.** $9\overline{)495.549}$ **4.** $27\overline{)92.205}$

5. $45\overline{)288}$ **6.** $52\overline{)468.26}$ **7.** $16\overline{)1,076}$ **8.** $71\overline{)4.473}$

9. $33\overline{)\$167.31}$ **10.** $64\overline{)\$73.60}$ **11.** $26\overline{)\$25.48}$ **12.** $78\overline{)\$1,602.90}$

Divide. For each quotient, count the decimal places. Cross
out each domino that has that number of dots on one end.

13. $197.04 \div 8 =$ _____   **14.** $798 \div 38 =$ _____   **15.** $4,705.8 \div 93 =$ _____

16. $55.836 \div 54 =$ _____   **17.** $93.816 \div 15 =$ _____   **18.** $1,575 \div 63 =$ _____

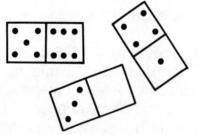

Add the dots on the dominoes you have *not* crossed out to
answer the question.

19. What is the shortest distance from England to
France? _____ miles

PRACTICE   Choosing the Operation

Decide whether you would add, subtract, multiply, or divide to solve each problem.

1. The Silverado Toy Company has factories located in 3 states. Each factory employs about 750 workers. About how many factory workers does Silverado employ?

   a. add   **b.** subtract

   c. multiply   **d.** divide

2. Silverado has sales offices in 7 foreign countries. The company has twice as many offices in the United States as it does abroad. How many sales offices does Silverado have in all?

   a. add   **b.** subtract

   c. multiply   **d.** divide

Solve.

3. Norman Kantor is a 38-year-old designer who works for the Silverado Toy Company. He's been with the company for 13 years. How old was Norman when he joined Silverado?

4. Norman's starting weekly salary at Silverado was $189.90, which was $94.23 less than his coworker, Jean. His salary has since quadrupled. How much is Norman earning now?

5. One of the most popular toys that Norman designed was the Binkiebonk Firefighter. Since Norman invented it 8 years ago, 688,000 of the toys have been sold. On the average, about how many Binkiebonk Firefighters have been sold per year?

6. The Binkiebonk Firefighter sells for $8.95. In November, Silverado sold 7,100 of the toys. How much money did the toy earn for the company in November?

7. Another popular Silverado toy is the Pepperpatch Bear. Since they were introduced 7 months ago, an average of 1,650 Pepperpatch Bears have been sold per month. The toy costs $12.50. How much money has the Pepperpatch Bear earned for the company since it was introduced?

8. Last year, Silverado earned $8,977,432 from toy sales. The company also earned $2,567,421 from its sales of games, and $57,007 from its sales of children's books. How much more did Silverado earn from toy sales than from sales of games and books last year?

PRACTICE Dividing Decimals by Powers of 10

Divide.

1. 45.38 ÷ 100 = _____

2. 1.12 ÷ 10 = _____

3. 948.6 ÷ 10 = _____

4. 21.09 ÷ 100 = _____

5. 0.53 ÷ 100 = _____

6. 5.2 ÷ 1,000 = _____

7. 17.4 ÷ 1,000 = _____

8. 0.01 ÷ 100 = _____

9. 90.01 ÷ 10,000 = _____

10. 83.38 ÷ 100 = _____

11. 1,000$\overline{)4,150}$

12. 10,000$\overline{)7.7}$

13. 100$\overline{)0.005}$

14. 1,000$\overline{)3.3}$

15. 10,000$\overline{)9,000}$

16. 10$\overline{)64.63}$

17. 100$\overline{)\$943.00}$

18. 1,000$\overline{)\$380.00}$

19. 10,000$\overline{)\$1,800.00}$

20. 10,000$\overline{)\$85,900.00}$

21. 1,000$\overline{)\$7,660.00}$

22. 10$\overline{)\$68.50}$

23. $40,000 ÷ 10,000 = _____

24. $3,200 ÷ 1,000 = _____

25. $57,600 ÷ 10,000 = _____

26. $462.50 ÷ 10 = _____

27. $200 ÷ 10,000 = _____

28. 3,590 ÷ 100 = _____

Use with pages 102–103.

Name _____ Date _____

PRACTICE Dividing Decimals by Decimals

Divide.

1. $0.4\overline{)1.464}$ **2.** $0.9\overline{)36.495}$ **3.** $3.7\overline{)1.406}$ **4.** $4.04\overline{)0.6060}$

5. $9.72\overline{)9.234}$ **6.** $7.8\overline{)7.41}$ **7.** $6.36\overline{)14.310}$ **8.** $0.005\overline{)0.410}$

9. $0.317\overline{)296.395}$ **10.** $1.5\overline{)14.96445}$ **11.** $0.348\overline{)4.350}$ **12.** $1.03\overline{)0.577933}$

13. $\$2,421.10 \div 3.1 =$ _____
14. $\$3,063.75 \div 0.75 =$ _____
15. $\$963.04 \div 1.3 =$ _____
16. $\$989.55 \div 4.5 =$ _____
17. $\$118.17 \div 0.101 =$ _____
18. $\$859.95 \div 2.457 =$ _____
19. $\frac{0.458}{9.16} =$ _____
20. $\frac{8.392}{0.01} =$ _____

Solve.

21. How many 0.33-liter servings are there in 7.92 liters of iuice?

_____

22. The refreshment stand sells a 0.4-liter serving of milk for 65¢. How much money is made if 9.2 liters are sold?

_____

Name _____ Date _____

PRACTICE Rounding Decimal Quotients

Divide. Round the quotient to the nearest tenth.

1. $5\overline{)7.63}$ **2.** $1.2\overline{)6.13}$ **3.** $4.6\overline{)50}$

Divide. Round the quotient to the nearest hundredth.

4. $1.8\overline{)1.492}$ **5.** $0.31\overline{)7}$ **6.** $1.01\overline{)4.839}$

Divide. Round the quotient to the nearest thousandth.

7. $0.6\overline{)1}$ **8.** $2.12\overline{)2.0843}$ **9.** $3\overline{)0.4508}$

Divide. Round the quotient to the nearest dollar.

10. $7\overline{)\$10.55}$ **11.** $4.2\overline{)\$2.65}$ **12.** $1.3\overline{)\$8}$

Divide. Round the quotient to the nearest cent.

13. $1.7\overline{)\$1.69}$ **14.** $3.7\overline{)\$0.72}$ **15.** $5\overline{)\$7.98}$

44

Name _____ Date _____

PRACTICE   Using a Map

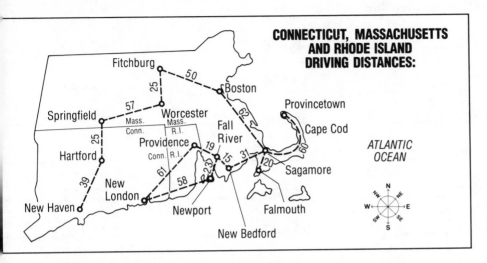

CONNECTICUT, MASSACHUSETTS AND RHODE ISLAND DRIVING DISTANCES:

The map above shows driving distances between some key cities and towns in New England. Use the map above to solve.

1. This summer, the Johnston family toured parts of New England by car. On the first day, they drove north from New Haven, Connecticut, to Hartford and then on to Springfield, Massachusetts. How many miles did the Johnstons travel on their first day? _____

2. From Springfield, the family drove east to Worcester. From Worcester, the Johnstons headed north for 25 miles and stopped at an art museum. In which city is the museum located? _____

3. After lunch, the Johnston family traveled southeast at an average speed of 42 miles per hour. How long did it take them to reach Boston? _____

_____

4. Two days later, the Johnstons left Boston and drove to scenic Cape Cod in easternmost Massachusetts. They drove all the way to Provincetown in about 4 hours. What was their average speed per hour? _____

5. From Provincetown, the Johnstons headed home. They stopped in Sagamore, took a side trip to a wildlife sanctuary in Falmouth, and then went to New Bedford, where they stopped for the night. How many miles had they driven that day? _____

6. After New Bedford, their next destination was New London on the southern coast of Connecticut. Mr. Johnston wanted to drive there via Fall River, Massachusetts, and Providence, Rhode Island. Mrs. Johnston wanted to go via Fall River and Newport, Rhode Island. Whose route to New London is shorter? by how many miles? _____

PRACTICE Divisibility

Write *yes* or *no* if the number is divisible.

1. by 5.	745 _____	6,458 _____	590,060 _____
2. by 3.	518 _____	13,456 _____	75,221 _____
3. by 8.	4,804 _____	35,000 _____	202,248 _____
4. by 2.	96 _____	5,720 _____	344,431 _____
5. by 10.	355 _____	4,000 _____	68,270 _____
6. by 4.	4,837 _____	85,347 _____	308,136 _____
7. by 9.	531 _____	1,352 _____	389,784 _____
8. by 6.	72 _____	9,536 _____	47,350 _____

Mr. Holmes has a piece of paper that has the following questions written on it. The answers provide a code for the combination lock on his safe. For each *no* answer, write the divisor on one of the lines on the safe.

9. Is 126,570 divisible by 6? _____   by 5? _____   by 10? _____

10. Is 35,451 divisible by 3? _____   by 9? _____   by 6? _____

11. Is 240,348 divisible by 9? _____   by 3? _____   by 2? _____

12. Is 600,000 divisible by 10? _____   by 5? _____   by 8? _____

13. Is 946,476 divisible by 4? _____   by 9? _____   by 10? _____

14. What is the combination of the safe?

Use with pages 118–119.

Name _____ Date _____

Write as a product of factors. Then multiply.

1. $3^4 =$ _____ = ____   **2.** $10^2 =$ _____ = ____

3. $5^3 =$ _____ = ____   **4.** $2^6 =$ _____ = ____

5. $1^7 =$ _____ = ____   **6.** $12^2 =$ _____ = ____

7. $9^3 =$ _____ = ____   **8.** $27^0 =$ _____

Use exponents to rewrite.

9. $7 \times 7 \times 7 =$ _____   **10.** $4 \times 4 \times 4 \times 4 \times 4 =$ _____

11. $13 \times 13 =$ _____   **12.** $20 \times 20 \times 20 =$ _____

13. $15 \times 15 \times 15 \times 15 =$ _____   **14.** $3 \times 3 \times 3 \times 3 \times 3 \times 3 =$ _____

Compare. Write $>$, $<$, or $=$ in the $\bigcirc$.

15. $2^4 \bigcirc 3^2$ **16.** $25^0 \bigcirc 5^2$ **17.** $7^2 \bigcirc 2^7$

18. $15^2 \bigcirc 6^3$ **19.** $60^5 \bigcirc 60^7$ **20.** $10^7 \bigcirc 7^1$

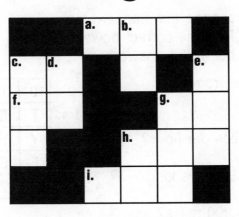

Across	**Down**
a. 11^2	**b.** the square root of 400
e. 13^0	**c.** the square of 15
f. the exponent in $28^{25} = x$	**d.** the greater of 75 and 4^3
g. the base in $10^2 = 100$	**e.** 100^1
h. 10×2^6	**h.** perfect square between 60 and 70
i. 12^2	**i.** 1^0

PRACTICE   Scientific Notation

Write in scientific notation.

1. 38 _____

2. 14.6 _____

3. 223 _____

4. 43.72 _____

5. 4,065 _____

6. 1.9 _____

7. 58 _____

8. 225,000 _____

9. 739 _____

10. 53,100 _____

Write in standard form.

11. 8.4×10^1 _____

12. 2.75×10^4 _____

13. 9.47×10^2 _____

14. 5.323×10^2 _____

15. 4.906×10^3 _____

16. 3.4×10^0 _____

17. 6.5×10^1 _____

18. 1.08×10^5 _____

19. 9.41×10^4 _____

20. 2.53×10^5 _____

To answer Exercises 21–24, change the standard-form
number to scientific notation. Find the correct power of 10 in
the grid for each. Write the letter in the answer box.

21. What is 141,000,000 miles from the
nearest star?

22. What travels at 54,000 miles per hour?

23. What has a year that is 687 days long?

24. What has a diameter of 4,200 miles?

	10^1	10^2	10^3	10^4	10^5	10^6	10^7	10^8
1.41 ×	T	D	R	E	O	S	P	M
5.4 ×	Y	H	G	A	I	L	D	X
6.87 ×	F	R	C	W	Q	H	T	N
4.2 ×	O	Z	S	J	U	B	V	K

The answer is

21.	22.	23.	24.
___	___	___	___

PRACTICE   Factors, Primes, and Composites

Write all the factors of each number.

1. 18 _____

2. 24 _____

3. 37 _____

4. 91 _____

5. 65 _____

6. 32 _____

7. 66 _____

8. 28 _____

Write *prime* or *composite*.

9. 64 _____   **10.** 13 _____   **11.** 17 _____

12. 2 _____   **13.** 23 _____   **14.** 36 _____

15. 15 _____   **16.** 33 _____   **17.** 90 _____

18. 37 _____   **19.** 27 _____   **20.** 73 _____

21. 12 _____   **22.** 49 _____   **23.** 55 _____

24. List all the prime numbers less than 30, from the least to the greatest.

_____

25. How many prime numbers are greater than 90 but less than 100?

_____

PRACTICE   Prime Factorization

Write the prime factorization of the number. Do not use exponents.

1. $315 =$ _____

2. $600 =$ _____

3. $99 =$ _____

4. $133 =$ _____

5. $1,470 =$ _____

6. $312 =$ _____

Write the prime factorization of the number. Use factor trees.
Use exponents to write the answer.

7. 400

8. 42

_____

_____

9. 175

10. 825

_____

_____

11. 280

12. 90

_____

_____

Write the number for the prime factorization.

13. $3^2 \times 5^2 =$ _____

14. $2^3 \times 3 =$ _____

15. $2^3 \times 3^2 \times 5 =$ _____

16. $7^2 \times 11 =$ _____

17. $5^3 \times 7^2 =$ _____

18. $11 \times 13^2 =$ _____

19. $2^5 \times 3^2 =$ _____

20. $2 \times 7^3 \times 13 =$ _____

21. $3^4 \times 5 \times 17 =$ _____

50

Name _____ Date _____

Use the graph below to answer the questions.

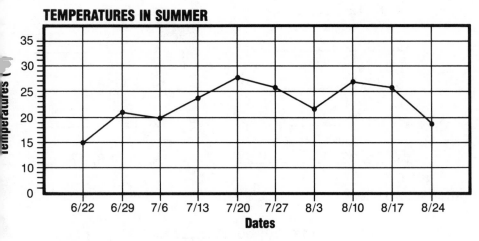

TEMPERATURES IN SUMMER

1. What was the average temperature during the week of July 6? _____

2. For how many weeks does this line graph extend? _____

3. Which week had the highest average temperature? _____

4. During which week was the average temperature 27°C? _____

5. During which two weeks was the average temperature the same?

_____

6. Was the temperature during the week of July 20 warmer or colder than during the week of June 22? by how many degrees? _____

7. For how many weeks was the average temperature above 25°C? _____

8. During which two weeks did the greatest decrease in average temperature occur?

_____

9. During the week of August 31, the average temperature was 4 degrees lower than it had been two weeks earlier. What was the average temperature during the week of August 31? _____

10. During which two weeks did the greatest increase in average temperature occur?

_____

PRACTICE   Greatest Common Factor (GCF)

Write the GCF by listing the factors.

1. 8, 16 _____

2. 6, 12 _____

3. 20, 5 _____

4. 12, 18 _____

5. 18, 24 _____

6. 40, 24 _____

7. 81, 27 _____

8. 52, 39 _____

9. 20, 35 _____

10. 12, 42 _____

11. 90, 7 _____

12. 19, 38 _____

13. 4, 16, 20 _____

14. 24, 32, 40 _____

15. 34, 68, 170 _____

Write the GCF by using prime factorization.

16. 15, 60 _____

17. 24, 60 _____

18. 69, 74 _____

19. 40, 32 _____

20. 34, 170 _____

21. 14, 35 _____

22. 11, 77 _____

23. 15, 45 _____

24. 34, 16 _____

25. 10, 125 _____

26. 27, 75 _____

27. 16, 52 _____

28. 16, 24, 80 _____

29. 27, 36, 45 _____

30. 31, 50, 75 _____

31. 45, 450 _____

32. 17, 181 _____

33. 304, 888 _____

Underline the two numbers that are relatively prime.

34. 4, 15, 20

35. 6, 21, 22

36. 6, 9, 40

37. 7, 14, 16

38. 22, 33, 39

39. 21, 70, 80

40. 21, 35, 48

41. 22, 45, 99

42. 7, 12, 21

43. 13, 52, 100

44. 65, 75, 91

45. 81, 90, 100

Name _____ Date _____

PRACTICE Least Common Multiple

Write the first five multiples of each number.

1. 4 _____

2. 17 _____

3. 5 _____

4. 8 _____

5. 12 _____

6. 25 _____

7. 221 _____

Write the LCM by listing multiples.

8. 8, 4 _____   **9.** 9, 9 _____   **10.** 6, 7 _____

11. 25, 15 _____   **12.** 10, 6 _____   **13.** 6, 8 _____

14. 22, 44 _____   **15.** 8, 9 _____   **16.** 5, 38 _____

17. 9, 8, 6 _____   **18.** 6, 13, 78 _____   **19.** 8, 4, 25 _____

Write the LCM by using prime factorization.

20. 11, 9 _____   **21.** 10, 6 _____   **22.** 6, 29 _____

23. 9, 26 _____   **24.** 6, 14 _____   **25.** 17, 36 _____

26. 4, 16, 72 _____   **27.** 15, 18, 36 _____   **28.** 9, 45, 12 _____

Solve.

? ?
How can you find the LCM of two prime numbers?

_____

? ?

PRACTICE Problem-Solving Practice

Solve. If a problem doesn't present all the facts you need,
write *There is not enough information.*

1. Lenny is planning a ski trip for February.
A 1-day lift ticket costs $21 at Mount
Campbell and $19 at Mount Hamilton.
How much will Lenny have to pay to ski
3 days at Mount Hamilton and 1 day at
Mount Campbell?
_____

2. Recent snowfall has made ski conditions
excellent. Mount Campbell received 8.5
inches of snow in the past week. Mount
Hamilton received 13 inches during the
same period. Nearby Freya Mountain
had 2.5 more inches of snow than did
Mount Campbell. How much more snow
did Mount Hamilton receive than Freya
Mountain?
_____

3. For his 4-day trip, Lenny budgets $300
for food and lodging. Lenny's friend Chet
budgets $35 less. How much money is
Chet planning to spend on food?
_____

4. The lodge where Lenny and Chet are
staying is surrounded by 3 tall
mountains. Their peaks have elevations
of 9,058 feet, 11,947 feet, and 12,526
feet. What is the average height of the
surrounding mountains?
_____

5. The current chair-lift capacity at Mount
Campbell is 13,800 skiers per hour. At
Mount Hamilton, the capacity is 4,800
skiers per hour. Newly proposed chair
lifts at Mount Hamilton will increase its
capacity by 2.6 times. If those lifts were
built, by how much would Mount
Campbell's lift capacity still exceed
Mount Hamilton's?
_____

6. On Sunday afternoon, Lenny makes 4
runs down an intermediate ski trail and 2
runs down an advanced trail. Chet
makes an equal number of runs down
the intermediate trail and 1 more than
Lenny on the advanced trail. How many
runs did Lenny make on Sunday
afternoon?
_____

Read each problem. Without figuring the exact answer, write
the letter of the most reasonable answer.

7. On Lenny and Chet's ride home, the bus
averaged 46 miles per hour. If the trip
took about $5\frac{1}{2}$ hours, how many miles
did the bus travel?

a. about 25

b. about 250

c. about 2,500

8. The total cost of Lenny's 4-day ski
weekend was $493.78. What was
Lenny's average cost per day?

a. about $100

b. about $125

c. about $180

PRACTICE Problem-Solving Practice

In swimming, a medley relay team consists of four members swimming backstroke, breaststroke, butterfly, and freestyle in succession. The chart below shows the recorded times for three teams competing in a 200-yard medley relay. Times are given in seconds.

	Backstroke (50 yards)	Breaststroke (50 yards)	Butterfly (50 yards)	Freestyle (50 yards)
Tanner High School	29.23	30.53	29.85	27.39
Riverside High School	31.73	32.35	30.41	24.47
Billings High School	28.75	33.01	29.26	24.70

Use the information in the chart above to solve.

9. How long did it take the Riverside High School swimmer to swim 50 yards of breaststroke? _____

10. In the 50-yard freestyle competition, how much faster was the Riverside swimmer than the Tanner swimmer? _____

11. The Alonzo High School swim team can swim the 200-yard relay in 2 minutes 17.91 seconds. If Alonzo had competed against Riverside, which team would have won? by how many seconds?

_____

12. If the four fastest swimmers had been members of the same all-star team, what would have been the team's time for the 200-yard medley relay?

_____

13. If the Billings High School's freestyle swimmer could have maintained her speed, how long would it have taken her to swim 400 yards?

_____

14. Which school had the greatest difference in time between breaststroke and freestyle? _____

15. Estimate to the nearest second the winner of the 200-yard medley relay competition. Then calculate the exact times. How close was your estimated time to the exact winning time?

_____

_____

_____

16. At Tanner High School, the second-best freestyle swimmer can swim 50 yards in 29.19 seconds. How many seconds per week would this swimmer have to improve in order to match the best Tanner swimmer's freestyle time in 6 weeks? _____

PRACTICE   Order of Operations

Simplify.

1. $3 \cdot 4 + 5 =$ _____

2. $4 + 2 \cdot 6 =$ _____

3. $8 \div 2 + 6 =$ _____

4. $3 + 5 - 1 \cdot 4 =$ _____

5. $2^3 + 8 \div 4 =$ _____

6. $(3 + 1)^2 - 8 \cdot 2 =$ _____

7. $8 \div 2 + 4 \div 2 =$ _____

8. $12 + 8 - 3 \div 3 =$ _____

9. $2^2 + 4 - 2^2 \div 4 =$ _____

10. $(16 - 4) \div 2 =$ _____

11. $9 \div 1 + 3 =$ _____

12. $(8 + 6) \div (7 - 5) =$ _____

13. $4^2 + 4 \div 2 =$ _____

14. $12 \div 3 - 4 + 2 =$ _____

15. $6 + 8 \cdot 4 =$ _____

16. $(3 - 1) \cdot (3^2 - 3) =$ _____

17. $16 \div 4 \div 2 =$ _____

18. $4 + 2^3 - 12 \div 3 =$ _____

Write parentheses to make each answer true.

19. $3 + 2 \cdot 4 = 20$

20. $14 - 6 \div 2 = 4$

21. $8 + 12 \div 4 \cdot 5 = 1$

22. $2 + 3 \cdot 2^2 = 38$

23. $2^2 \cdot 2 + 3^2 = 100$

24. $3 - 2 \cdot 7 - 7 = 0$

25. $16 - 4 \div 2 + 1 = 4$

26. $5^2 - 5 + 2 = 18$

27. $2^3 + 2 - 2 \div 2 = 9$

Write the expression, and simplify it.

28. Subtract the product of 2 and 9 from the sum of 40 and 10.

_____

29. Square the sum of 4 and 6; then divide by the difference between 50 and 30.

_____

PRACTICE Algebraic Expressions and Sentences (+ and −)

Complete the table. Write the value of the given expression if n has the value shown.

$n =$	2	0.4	11	7
1. $n + 7$				
2. $5 + n$				
3. $n - 0.24$				
4. $13 - n + 2$				

Write *true* or *false*.

5. $x - 5 = 0$, if $x = 10$ _____

6. $d + 11 = 18$, if $d = 7$ _____

7. $m - 1.5 = 0.8$, if $m = 2.3$ _____

8. $y + 6 = 20$, if $y = 12$ _____

9. $c + 5 = 8$, if $c = 2$ _____

Suppose z is any whole number from 0 through 15. Find the solution to each equation. Place the correct answer in the corresponding box in the magic square.

10. $z + 1 = 12$ **11.** $8 - z = 7$ **12.** $z - 2 = 10$

13. $13 - z = 4$ **14.** $2 + z = 10$ **15.** $15 - z = 8$

16. $9 - z = 5$ **17.** $z + 2 = 17$ **18.** $8 + z = 13$

The sum of each row, each column, and each diagonal should be the same.

19. What is the sum of each row, column, and diagonal?

_____

PRACTICE Solving Equations (+ and −)

Solve the equation.

1. $x + 4 = 14$ _____

2. $y - 13 = 5$ _____

3. $z - 10 = 4.7$ _____

4. $w + 38 = 75$ _____

5. $26 + q = 41$ _____

6. $z - 59 = 25$ _____

7. $90 + y = 151$ _____

8. $w - 100 = 169$ _____

9. $16.8 + y = 24.7$ _____

10. $x - 45 = 62$ _____

11. $r - 11 = 3$ _____

12. $n + 59 = 903$ _____

13. $q - 61 = 29$ _____

14. $85 + g = 178$ _____

15. $k + 79 = 126$ _____

16. $w - 4.2 = 3.4$ _____

17. $59 + b = 103$ _____

18. $s - 79 = 2$ _____

19. $x + 96 = 121$ _____

20. $p - 10 = 12$ _____

21. $f - 31 = 5$ _____

22. $29 + v = 120$ _____

23. $p - 7.2 = 8.9$ _____

24. $y + 12 = 55$ _____

25. $m + 869 = 1{,}764$ _____

26. $x - 1.5 = 6.5$ _____

27. $920 + d = 1{,}585$ _____

28. $m - 831 = 117$ _____

29. $q + 53.6 = 56.1$ _____

30. $x - 8 = 13$ _____

Write an equation for the problem, and solve.

31. A number decreased by 6.4 equals 3.8.
What is the number?

_____

Use with pages 140–141

PRACTICE | Using a Pictograph

he pictograph below shows the estimated number of people
vho listen to three radio stations.

HE RADIO STATIONS' AUDIENCE

Station	Listening Audience
WAAH-FM	🖩 🖩 🖩 🖩 🖩 🖩
WAGE-FM	🖩 🖩 🖩 🖩 🖩 🖩
KATE-FM	🖩 🖩

Each 🖩 stands for 10,000 listeners.

Jse the pictograph above to solve.

. How many people listen to KATE-FM?

_____

2. How many more listeners does WAGE-FM have than WAAH-FM?

_____

3. A sporting goods company pays WAAH-FM $2.35 per thousand listeners for each minute of advertising. How much does the company pay for 3 one-minute ads?

4. KATE-FM is changing from light rock to hard rock music. The station manager predicts that the number of listeners will double in 3 years. How many listeners would the station have then?

_____

. WAAH-FM decides to have a contest in order to draw more listeners. For one month, the station plays "Name That Song" five times each day. When the month is over, the station determines that its listening audience has grown by about 7,500. How many listeners do they have?

6. In an average hour, WAGE-FM has 18 minutes of advertising and 14 minutes of disc-jockey monologue. If songs average 3.5 minutes in length, how many records can they play in 1 hour? (HINT: There are 60 minutes in 1 hour.)

7. A one-minute prime-time ad on WAGE-FM costs $2.50 per 1,000 listeners. Next month, the price will go up by 15 cents. When that happens, how much will 10 minutes of prime-time advertising cost?

8. An automobile dealer believes he can sell 1 car for every 1,000 people who hear his ad on radio. If that's true, how many more cars would the dealer sell by advertising on WAAH-FM than on KATE-FM?

PRACTICE Algebraic Expressions and Sentences

Find the value of the given expression if $n = 9$.

1. $2.4n$ _____

2. $9n$ _____

3. $\dfrac{n}{3}$ _____

4. $\dfrac{27}{n}$ _____

5. $\dfrac{n}{1.5}$ _____

6. $5n$ _____

7. $3n - 10$ _____

8. $\dfrac{n}{9}$ _____

9. $4.3n$ _____

10. $n^2 + 1$ _____

11. $20 - n$ _____

12. $11n$ _____

Write *true* or *false*.

13. $6y = 6$, if $y = 1$ _____

14. $\dfrac{m}{2} = 7$, if $m = 3.5$ _____

15. $\dfrac{r}{5} = 2$, if $r = 10$ _____

16. $\dfrac{a}{3} = 8$, if $a = 24$ _____

17. $1.5t = 9$, if $t = 6$ _____

18. $10d = 10$, if $d = 0$ _____

19. $\dfrac{x}{3} = 5$, if $x = 15$ _____

20. $2.4k = 4.8$, if $k = 0.5$ _____

Suppose c is any whole number from 0 through 10. Find the solution for each equation, or write *no solution*.

21. $5c = 5$ _____

22. $3c = 90$ _____

23. $\dfrac{c}{2} = 4$ _____

24. $7c = 0$ _____

25. $8c = 100$ _____

26. $\dfrac{c}{3} = 2$ _____

Use with pages 144–145

PRACTICE Solving Equations (× and ÷)

Solve.

1. $67x = 536$ _____

2. $\frac{y}{13} = 2$ _____

3. $3n = 18$ _____

4. $42p = 42$ _____

5. $99r = 495$ _____

6. $\frac{m}{3} = 29$ _____

7. $\frac{q}{2} = 19$ _____

8. $42q = 252$ _____

9. $28x = 56$ _____

10. $71w = 142$ _____

11. $\frac{r}{2} = 203$ _____

12. $92y = 644$ _____

13. $\frac{y}{6} = 157$ _____

14. $25p = 75$ _____

15. $\frac{c}{14} = 38$ _____

16. $8.4x = 25.2$ _____

17. $0.16y = 1.28$ _____

18. $0.54x = 4.86$ _____

19. $\frac{x}{4} = 12$ _____

20. $58y = 232$ _____

21. $25x = 225$ _____

22. $23d = 207$ _____

23. $\frac{n}{7} = 11$ _____

24. $\frac{r}{16} = 9$ _____

25. $197x = 0$ _____

26. $45h = 405$ _____

27. $\frac{s}{9} = 45$ _____

28. $\frac{x}{9} = 85$ _____

29. $\frac{n}{17} = 28$ _____

30. $43m = 172$ _____

31. $\frac{v}{18} = 18$ _____

32. $\frac{q}{16} = 102$ _____

33. $\frac{x}{47} = 20$ _____

34. $\frac{q}{0.077} = 26$ _____

35. $\frac{x}{3} = 1.34$ _____

36. $\frac{n}{4.1} = 5.7$ _____

Write an equation, and solve.

37. If m divided by 5 is 1.4, what is m?

_____

38. The product of r and 15 is 90. What is r?

_____

PRACTICE   Solving Two-Step Equations

Solve.

1. $4n + 7 = 43$ _____

2. $\frac{n}{7} - 9 = 5$ _____

3. $8y - 6 = 58$ _____

4. $6q + 1 = 55$ _____

5. $4r - 9 = 35$ _____

6. $\frac{x}{7} - 7 = 5$ _____

7. $2p + 1 = 15$ _____

8. $\frac{f}{6} - 3 = 2$ _____

9. $5y + 4 = 49$ _____

10. $\frac{d}{7} - 1 = 8$ _____

11. $2h + 3 = 31$ _____

12. $\frac{b}{8} + 8 = 17$ _____

13. $3x - 3 = 54$ _____

14. $2v + 8 = 40$ _____

15. $7i - 6 = 50$ _____

16. $\frac{s}{6} - 7 = 7$ _____

17. $\frac{s}{7} + 7 = 19$ _____

18. $\frac{c}{3} - 5 = 4$ _____

Fill in the code message by solving each equation. Find your answer below one of the lines and write the variable for that answer above it.

$\overline{}$ $\overline{}$ $\overline{}$ $\overline{}$ $\quad$ $\overline{}$ $\overline{}$ $\overline{}$ $\overline{}$
56   5   45   28   20   4   11   9

$\overline{}$ $\overline{}$ $\quad$ $\overline{}$ $\overline{}$ $\overline{}$ $\overline{}$ $\overline{}$ $\overline{}$ $\overline{}$ $\overline{}$
36   7   1   5   14   20   27   9   6   9

19. $6e - 7 = 47$ _____

20. $\frac{y}{4} - 5 = 9$ _____

21. $5s - 1 = 34$ _____

22. $9o + 8 = 53$ _____

23. $6g - 9 = 57$ _____

24. $\frac{i}{3} - 6 = 6$ _____

25. $\frac{p}{2} + 1 = 11$ _____

26. $2m - 1 = 27$ _____

27. $7a + 2 = 30$ _____

28. $\frac{u}{5} + 4 = 13$ _____

29. $2l + 1 = 55$ _____

30. $\frac{r}{2} + 3 = 17$ _____

31. $6t - 2 = 34$ _____

32. $7c - 4 = 3$ _____

Use with pages 148–149.

PRACTICE   Writing an Equation

Write an equation, and then solve.

1. A *spelunker* is a person who explores caves. A group of spelunkers spent 2 hours exploring a large cave on Monday. On Tuesday, they spent twice as many hours exploring the same cave. How many hours did the group spend in the cave on Monday and Tuesday?

_____

2. Mammoth Cave in Kentucky was discovered in 1799. This limestone cavern has 150 miles of subterranean passageways. If a group of spelunkers walked an average of 6 miles per day, how many days would it take them to explore all the passageways?

_____

3. Exploring a cavern, a spelunker discovered a new passage. It was so narrow that the spelunker could only walk 50 feet in 20 minutes. At that rate, how far will the spelunker walk in 60 minutes?

_____

4. Fingal's Cave is located on an island off the coast of Scotland. This large cavern contains basalt, a kind of volcanic rock. Some of the columns are 40 feet high, which is 160 feet less than the depth of the cave. How deep is the cave?

_____

5. Aggtelek Cavern is located in Hungary. It is known for its *stalactites,* icicle-like formations that hang from the ceiling. About 0.33 of the length of this cavern is 1.67 miles. About how long is the cavern?

_____

6. Wyandotte Cave, located in southern Indiana, contains one of the largest caverns in North America. Inside the cavern is an underground mountain. If this mountain were 65 feet higher, it would be as tall as a 200-foot building. How high is the mountain?

_____

7. Carlsbad Caverns in New Mexico are the largest known caverns. They consist of three levels. The first is 754 feet below the surface. The second level is 146 feet below the first. The third level is 420 feet below the second. What is the depth of the third level?

_____

8. The temperature in Mammoth Cave remains fairly constant 24 hours a day. If half the cave's normal temperature plus 20 degrees equals 47, what is the normal temperature?

_____

Name _____ Date _____

Write the missing fractions.

1.

$\frac{0}{8}$ $\frac{1}{8}$ $\frac{2}{8}$ ___   ___ $\frac{5}{8}$ ___ $\frac{7}{8}$ ___

2.

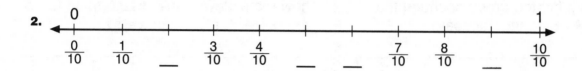

$\frac{0}{10}$ $\frac{1}{10}$ ___ $\frac{3}{10}$ $\frac{4}{10}$ ___   ___ $\frac{7}{10}$ $\frac{8}{10}$ ___ $\frac{10}{10}$

3.

$\frac{0}{5}$ ___   ___   ___ $\frac{4}{5}$ ___

Write each as a fraction. Then show the quotient as a whole number if possible.

4. $5 \div 9 =$ _____   **5.** $8 \div 4 =$ _____   **6.** $6 \div 7 =$ _____

7. $18 \div 6 =$ _____   **8.** $3 \div 5 =$ _____   **9.** $12 \div 3 =$ _____

10. $39 \div 1 =$ _____   **11.** $0 \div 9 =$ _____   **12.** $19 \div 21 =$ _____

13. $21 \div 7 =$ _____   **14.** $35 \div 5 =$ _____   **15.** $54 \div 9 =$ _____

16. $4 \div 7 =$ _____   **17.** $13 \div 16 =$ _____   **18.** $50 \div 25 =$ _____

Write each whole number as a fraction.

19. 12 _____   **20.** 5 _____   **21.** 11 _____   **22.** 8 _____   **23.** 33 _____

Ring the fraction that is the closest to 1.   Ring the fraction that is the closest to 0.

24. $\frac{1}{3}$ $\frac{88}{91}$ $\frac{5}{6}$ $\frac{12}{7}$ **25.** $\frac{1}{8}$ $\frac{12}{50}$ $\frac{2}{95}$ $\frac{3}{33}$

26. $\frac{1}{2}$ $\frac{50}{53}$ $\frac{4}{5}$ $\frac{55}{54}$ **27.** $\frac{3}{30}$ $\frac{2}{10}$ $\frac{3}{12}$ $\frac{1}{3}$

PRACTICE Equivalent and Simplifying Fractions

Write the missing number.

1. $\frac{12}{15} = \frac{4}{n}$ _____

2. $\frac{8}{24} = \frac{1}{n}$ _____

3. $\frac{8}{12} = \frac{n}{3}$ _____

4. $\frac{48}{60} = \frac{4}{n}$ _____

5. $\frac{6}{12} = \frac{1}{n}$ _____

6. $\frac{n}{5} = \frac{20}{25}$ _____

7. $\frac{3}{n} = \frac{9}{24}$ _____

8. $\frac{6}{n} = \frac{48}{56}$ _____

In around 2000 B.C., a famous Greek scholar did important work in the field of number theory. To find his name, write each fraction in simplest form on the line in row A. Find the code letter for each answer, and write it on the line in row B.

9. $\frac{7}{28}$

10. $\frac{37}{37}$

11. $\frac{6}{15}$

12. $\frac{70}{100}$

13. $\frac{4}{6}$

14. $\frac{20}{24}$

15. $\frac{28}{40}$

16. $\frac{24}{32}$

17. $\frac{2}{8}$

18. $\frac{45}{72}$

19. $\frac{12}{48}$

20. $\frac{15}{18}$

	9.	10.	11.	12.	13.	14.	15.	16.	17.	18.	19.	20.
A. Answer	___	___	___	___	___	___	___	___	___	___	___	___
B. Code letter	___	___	___	___	___	___	___	___	___	___	___	___

Answer Code

$\frac{2}{5}$	$\frac{1}{6}$	$\frac{1}{8}$	$\frac{1}{4}$	$\frac{3}{4}$	$\frac{3}{8}$	$\frac{7}{8}$	$\frac{1}{5}$	$\frac{3}{7}$
A	B	D	E	H	J	K	L	M

$\frac{5}{8}$	$\frac{2}{3}$	$\frac{1}{7}$	1	$\frac{5}{6}$	$\frac{7}{10}$	$\frac{1}{3}$	$\frac{4}{5}$	$\frac{5}{7}$
N	O	P	R	S	T	V	W	Y

PRACTICE   Mixed Numbers and Fractions

Write each fraction as a mixed number. The answer must be in simplest form.

1. $\frac{7}{3}$ _____

2. $\frac{17}{8}$ _____

3. $\frac{20}{9}$ _____

4. $\frac{12}{5}$ _____

5. $\frac{10}{7}$ _____

6. $\frac{16}{14}$ _____

7. $\frac{16}{7}$ _____

8. $\frac{11}{5}$ _____

Write each fraction as a whole number.

9. $\frac{9}{3}$ _____

10. $\frac{5}{1}$ _____

11. $\frac{17}{17}$ _____

12. $\frac{48}{12}$ _____

Write each mixed number as a fraction.

13. $3\frac{1}{5}$ _____

14. $3\frac{2}{3}$ _____

15. $2\frac{3}{7}$ _____

16. $6\frac{4}{5}$ _____

17. $8\frac{3}{8}$ _____

18. $10\frac{1}{4}$ _____

19. $1\frac{5}{7}$ _____

20. $2\frac{1}{2}$ _____

Write each as a mixed number in simplest form or as a whole number.

21. $2 + \frac{4}{5}$ _____

22. $5 + \frac{7}{7}$ _____

23. $7 + \frac{1}{3}$ _____

24. $5 + \frac{4}{6}$ _____

Become a math artist! There are five regular geometric shapes in the picture. Use your answers to the exercises above to connect the dots and to find the shapes. Follow the order of answers as shown in the table.

Shape 1: Answers for exercises 2, 9, 17, 23, 2	Shape 2: Answers for exercises 5, 12, 14, 22, 5	Shape 3: Answers for exercises 16, 19, 3, 16	Shape 4: Answers for exercises 20, 24, 7, 11, 30	Shape 5: Answers for exercises 10, 1, 13, 18, 10

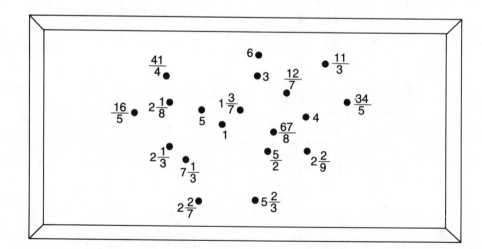

Name _____ Date _____

PRACTICE Comparing and Ordering Fractions

Write *true* or *false*. Use the LCD.

1. $\frac{3}{8} > \frac{5}{8}$ _____

2. $\frac{7}{11} < \frac{2}{3}$ _____

3. $\frac{13}{17} > \frac{9}{17}$ _____

4. $\frac{7}{12} < \frac{7}{15}$ _____

5. $7\frac{9}{10} > 7\frac{3}{4}$ _____

6. $3\frac{5}{6} < 3\frac{2}{3}$ _____

7. $2\frac{2}{5} > 2\frac{3}{8}$ _____

8. $9\frac{3}{5} > 9\frac{3}{7}$ _____

9. $\frac{13}{17} < \frac{9}{11}$ _____

10. $\frac{1}{4} < \frac{2}{3}$ _____

11. $\frac{4}{15} > \frac{5}{12}$ _____

12. $\frac{5}{14} < \frac{5}{13}$ _____

Write $<$, $>$, or $=$ in the circle. Use cross products.

13. $\frac{5}{8}$ ◯ $\frac{3}{4}$

14. $\frac{11}{12}$ ◯ $\frac{7}{9}$

15. $\frac{13}{15}$ ◯ $\frac{6}{7}$

16. $\frac{10}{18}$ ◯ $\frac{5}{9}$

17. $\frac{4}{12}$ ◯ $\frac{6}{18}$

18. $\frac{7}{9}$ ◯ $\frac{5}{6}$

19. $\frac{5}{6}$ ◯ $\frac{24}{30}$

20. $\frac{3}{8}$ ◯ $\frac{5}{12}$

21. $\frac{5}{8}$ ◯ $\frac{15}{24}$

Write the fractions from the least to the greatest.

22. $\frac{2}{3}, \frac{5}{6}, \frac{1}{2}$ _____

23. $\frac{5}{8}, \frac{7}{12}, \frac{13}{24}$ _____

24. $\frac{11}{12}, \frac{17}{24}, \frac{7}{8}$ _____

25. $\frac{9}{16}, \frac{3}{5}, \frac{7}{10}$ _____

26. $\frac{1}{3}, \frac{1}{5}, \frac{1}{4}, \frac{1}{2}$ _____

27. $\frac{3}{4}, \frac{2}{3}, \frac{5}{6}, \frac{7}{12}$ _____

Use with pages 168–169.

67

PRACTICE Check that the Solution Answers the Question

Which statement answers the question? Ring the correct answer.

1. Bill Bungle attempted a home-improvement project. He estimated that the job would take 30 days. He actually worked 28 days in September and 9 days in October. How close was his original estimate?

   a. He didn't work 30 days.

   b. He worked 37 days.

   c. He worked 7 more days than he'd estimated.

2. Bill began his home-improvement project with 250 nails. He bent 46 nails and successfully hammered 112 nails. How many nails did Bill have left?

   a. He successfully hammered 66 more nails than he bent.

   b. He had 92 nails left.

   c. He used 158 nails.

Solve.

3. Bill needed to cut 18 pieces of wood to a length of 21.75 inches each. If there are 12 inches to a foot, about how many feet of wood did Bill have to buy?

   _____

4. Bill's friend Jill tried to saw a board and ended up with a piece of wood 8.4 feet long. If she wants it to be 6.5 feet long, how much more must she trim?

   _____

5. Bill planned to install 2 identical windows that had panes of glass that measured 26 inches wide and 40 inches high. If the window frames enclosing the glass add 2 inches to each side of both windows, what are the dimensions of each window?

   _____

6. During one 8-hour work-day, Bill began work one hour late, took 2 breaks of a half hour each, and went to lunch for an hour. How many hours did Bill spend not working that day? _____

7. Bill and Jill bought 3 cans of purple paint at the hardware store. Each can covers 450 square feet. Bill will be painting 660 square feet of walls, and Jill will be painting 745 square feet. Did they buy enough paint? _____

8. To celebrate the completion of the project, Bill invited 16 friends to a pizza party. Bill ordered 4 pizzas, and each guest at the party ate 2 slices. If there were 8 slices per box, how many slices were left for Bill to eat? _____

Use with pages 170–171.

Name _____ Date _____

Circle the better estimate.

1. $2\frac{1}{3} + 5\frac{1}{4}$ over 8   under 8   **2.** $4\frac{2}{7} + 5\frac{3}{8}$ over 10   under 10

3. $7\frac{4}{5} + 6\frac{2}{3}$ over 14   under 14   **4.** $8\frac{1}{2} - 2\frac{1}{3}$ over 6   under 6

5. $10\frac{3}{11} - 6\frac{8}{15}$ over 4   under 4   **6.** $12\frac{17}{25} - 6\frac{2}{15}$ over 6   under 6

Write > or < for ◯.

7. $4\frac{1}{10} + 3\frac{2}{9}$ ◯ 8   **8.** $2\frac{3}{4} + 7\frac{2}{3}$ ◯ 10

9. $6\frac{7}{10} + 5\frac{8}{11}$ ◯ 12   **10.** $8\frac{17}{30} + 5\frac{8}{15}$ ◯ 14

11. $10\frac{18}{25} + 9\frac{11}{14}$ ◯ 20   **12.** $15\frac{11}{45} + 11\frac{8}{30}$ ◯ 27

13. $8\frac{2}{3} + 6\frac{3}{8} + 4\frac{5}{7}$ ◯ 19   **14.** $23\frac{5}{6} + 12\frac{2}{11} + 8\frac{4}{15}$ ◯ 45

15. $5\frac{1}{7} - 3\frac{3}{5}$ ◯ 2   **16.** $11\frac{3}{10} - 5\frac{3}{11}$ ◯ 6

Estimate; then adjust your estimate.

17. $5\frac{2}{3} + 7\frac{1}{4} =$ _____   **18.** $8\frac{3}{10} + 6\frac{2}{15} =$ _____

19. $12\frac{4}{7} + 5\frac{2}{3} =$ _____   **20.** $9\frac{1}{2} + 4\frac{11}{20} =$ _____

21. $8\frac{2}{3} - 5\frac{3}{4} =$ _____   **22.** $6\frac{1}{9} - 4\frac{1}{5} =$ _____

Solve.

23. Terry and Leon collected newspapers for the school's paper drive. Terry collected $135\frac{13}{16}$ pounds of paper while Leon collected $129\frac{2}{3}$ pounds. About how many more pounds of paper did Terry collect than Leon? _____

PRACTICE   Adding Fractions

Add. The answer must be in simplest form.

1. $\frac{4}{10} + \frac{1}{10} =$ _____

2. $\frac{2}{5} + \frac{1}{5} =$ _____

3. $\frac{1}{6} + \frac{3}{6} =$ _____

4. $\frac{2}{7} + \frac{3}{7} =$ _____

5. $\frac{1}{10} + \frac{3}{5} =$ _____

6. $\frac{1}{2} + \frac{1}{10} =$ _____

7. $\frac{1}{2} + \frac{1}{4} =$ _____

8. $\frac{3}{10} + \frac{1}{5} =$ _____

9. $\frac{3}{4} + \frac{3}{4} + \frac{3}{4} =$ _____

10. $\frac{7}{10} + \frac{7}{10} + \frac{5}{10} =$ _____

11. $\frac{1}{4} + \frac{2}{4} + \frac{3}{4} =$ _____

12. $\frac{1}{3} + \frac{2}{3} + \frac{2}{3} =$ _____

13. $\frac{8}{9} + \frac{7}{9} + \frac{2}{9} =$ _____

14. $\frac{5}{6} + \frac{1}{6} + \frac{4}{6} =$ _____

15. $\frac{4}{9} + \frac{7}{9} + \frac{4}{9} =$ _____

16. $\begin{array}{r} \frac{1}{3} \\ + \frac{1}{9} \\ \hline \end{array}$

17. $\begin{array}{r} \frac{1}{3} \\ + \frac{1}{6} \\ \hline \end{array}$

18. $\begin{array}{r} \frac{1}{4} \\ + \frac{1}{8} \\ \hline \end{array}$

19. $\begin{array}{r} \frac{1}{2} \\ + \frac{1}{6} \\ \hline \end{array}$

20. $\begin{array}{r} \frac{3}{8} \\ + \frac{1}{2} \\ \hline \end{array}$

21. $\begin{array}{r} \frac{1}{2} \\ + \frac{5}{6} \\ \hline \end{array}$

22. $\begin{array}{r} \frac{3}{5} \\ + \frac{7}{10} \\ \hline \end{array}$

23. $\begin{array}{r} \frac{5}{8} \\ + \frac{3}{4} \\ \hline \end{array}$

24. $\begin{array}{r} \frac{3}{4} \\ \frac{3}{5} \\ + \frac{2}{5} \\ \hline \end{array}$

25. $\begin{array}{r} \frac{7}{8} \\ \frac{3}{4} \\ + \frac{1}{2} \\ \hline \end{array}$

26. $\begin{array}{r} \frac{4}{9} \\ \frac{5}{9} \\ + \frac{2}{3} \\ \hline \end{array}$

27. $\begin{array}{r} \frac{5}{6} \\ \frac{1}{3} \\ + \frac{3}{4} \\ \hline \end{array}$

PRACTICE   Subtracting Fractions

Subtract. The answer must be in simplest form.

1. $\frac{2}{5} - \frac{1}{5} =$ _____   **2.** $\frac{7}{8} - \frac{6}{8} =$ _____   **3.** $\frac{8}{9} - \frac{2}{9} =$ _____   **4.** $\frac{3}{4} - \frac{1}{4} =$ _____

5. $\frac{9}{10} - \frac{4}{5} =$ _____   **6.** $\frac{1}{3} - \frac{2}{9} =$ _____   **7.** $\frac{2}{3} - \frac{1}{6} =$ _____   **8.** $\frac{5}{8} - \frac{1}{2} =$ _____

9. $\frac{5}{8} - \frac{1}{4} =$ _____   **10.** $\frac{1}{3} - \frac{1}{6} =$ _____   **11.** $\frac{7}{9} - \frac{2}{3} =$ _____   **12.** $\frac{9}{10} - \frac{4}{5} =$ _____

13. $\begin{array}{r} \frac{4}{5} \\ -\ \frac{2}{3} \\ \hline \end{array}$ **14.** $\begin{array}{r} \frac{1}{4} \\ -\ \frac{1}{6} \\ \hline \end{array}$ **15.** $\begin{array}{r} \frac{7}{10} \\ -\ \frac{1}{4} \\ \hline \end{array}$ **16.** $\begin{array}{r} \frac{5}{6} \\ -\ \frac{4}{9} \\ \hline \end{array}$

17. $\begin{array}{r} \frac{1}{3} \\ -\ \frac{1}{5} \\ \hline \end{array}$ **18.** $\begin{array}{r} \frac{3}{4} \\ -\ \frac{1}{6} \\ \hline \end{array}$ **19.** $\begin{array}{r} \frac{1}{4} \\ -\ \frac{1}{32} \\ \hline \end{array}$ **20.** $\begin{array}{r} \frac{6}{7} \\ -\ \frac{1}{2} \\ \hline \end{array}$

21. $\begin{array}{r} \frac{3}{5} \\ -\ \frac{1}{3} \\ \hline \end{array}$ **22.** $\begin{array}{r} \frac{55}{81} \\ -\ \frac{28}{81} \\ \hline \end{array}$ **23.** $\begin{array}{r} \frac{19}{27} \\ -\ \frac{7}{30} \\ \hline \end{array}$ **24.** $\begin{array}{r} \frac{12}{25} \\ -\ \frac{4}{15} \\ \hline \end{array}$

Solve.

25. Mr. Rosewald is setting up his company's new warehouse. He wants $\frac{3}{4}$ of the room to hold all the supplies and equipment. The forklift will occupy $\frac{3}{10}$ of the entire room. What fraction of the room is left for the supplies? _____

PRACTICE | Problem-Solving Practice

Write the letter of the equation you would use to solve the problem.

1. Unicorn Airlines flew 63 scheduled flights last month, and carried a total of 3,024 passengers. On the average, how many passengers were there on each flight?

   a. $n = 63 \times 3{,}024$ b. $n = 3{,}024 \div 63$

   c. $n = 63 \div 3{,}024$ d. $n = 3{,}024 \div 31$

2. Unicorn Airlines flies into Hollow Rock 6 more times each week than it flies into Orange Grove. Unicorn flies into Orange Grove 13 times per week. How many times weekly does the airline fly into Hollow Rock?

   a. $n + 63 = 13$ b. $6n = 13$

   c. $n = 13 + 6$ d. $6 = n + 13$

Write an equation and solve.

3. Unicorn is a "no-frills" airline. The typical passenger spends $2.75 for food and beverages. At that rate, how much money would Unicorn earn from 8 flights averaging 45 passengers per flight?

_____

4. Last year, Unicorn Airlines charged $149 for a one-way ticket to Miami. This year, the cost of a one-way ticket increased by $15. How much would 2 people pay to fly to Miami this year on Unicorn Airlines?

_____

Without computing the exact answer, write the letter of the most reasonable answer.

5. The passengers of Flight 315 to Chicago brought aboard 51 suitcases weighing an average of 23 lb each. About how many pounds of luggage is the airline carrying?

   a. 70 lb   b. 100 lb
   c. 1,000 lb   d. 10,000 lb

6. It took a flight attendant about 14 minutes to serve dinner to the 47 passengers of Flight 315. On the average, how long did it take the attendant to serve each passenger?

   a. $\frac{1}{2}$ minute   b. 3 minutes
   c. 12 minutes   d. 11 hours

Solve.

7. Captain Chance, Unicorn's best pilot, rated his landings as follows: 15 smooth, 3 rough; and 2 very rough. What fraction of his landings were not smooth?

_____

8. Unicorn Airlines conducted a survey of 100 of its passengers. Of the passengers, $\frac{1}{3}$ surveyed rated Unicorn's service "excellent." $\frac{1}{2}$ rated the service "good." The rest felt that service "needs improvement." What fraction of the passengers surveyed were less than satisfied?

_____

Use with pages 178–179.

Name _____ Date _____

PRACTICE Problem-Solving Practice

Use the broken-line graph to solve.

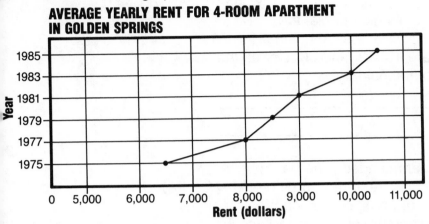

AVERAGE YEARLY RENT FOR 4-ROOM APARTMENT IN GOLDEN SPRINGS

9. What was the average rent for a 4-room apartment in Golden Springs in 1979? _____

10. How much higher was the yearly rent for an apartment in 1985 than in 1977? _____

11. What was the average rent per month for a 4-room apartment in 1983? _____

12. The Hilzen family rented an apartment in Golden Springs for all of 1975. During that time, the Hilzens had a family income of $19,500. What fraction of their income went for rent? _____

Solve. Make a plan if necessary.

13. An apartment-building owner has 16 units, 6 of which are 4-room units. What fraction of the units are not 4-room units? _____

14. A high-rise building is being converted from rented apartments to condominiums. At present, $\frac{2}{3}$ of the apartments are rented, and $\frac{1}{4}$ have been sold as condominiums. The remaining apartments are vacant. What fraction of the apartments are vacant? _____

15. The landlord at 1812 Orchard Street paid fuel bills of $870 for November, $1,370 for December, and $2,430 for January. He had budgeted $5,000 for this 3-month period. Was the landlord's estimated amount higher or lower than the actual cost? how much? _____

16. The Zubermans pay a monthly rent of $760. The Oshers pay $55 more than the Zubermans. The Freys pay $925 per month. How much more do the Freys pay in rent per month than the Oshers? _____

PRACTICE   Making an Organized List

Solve. Use a list if needed.

1. Tom can't remember the order in which to dial the numbers of his combination lock. He does know that the 3 numbers in the combination are 10, 19, and 30. List all the possible combinations that Tom should try.

   _____

   _____

2. Lisa wants to order an ice cream sundae. She has a choice of 9 different flavors of ice cream and 5 different toppings. If a sundae consists of one flavor of ice cream and one topping, how many different sundaes can Lisa choose from? _____

3. Frieda, Morris, Jesse, Donna, and Lee are all members of the same racquetball club. Each of them plays each of the others 3 times. How many games are played? _____

4. A camp director is planning tomorrow morning's program. At 9:00, campers may choose either canoeing or sailing. At 10:00, they can select crafts or drama. At 11:00, they can choose swimming, archery, or softball. How many possible program combinations does each camper have to choose from? _____

5. The programming director of Station KRVX is designing the format for a news show. The program is to include feature stories, weather, sports, and a movie review. The feature stories will always lead off the program. List all the different formats he can use.

   _____

   _____

   _____

   _____

   _____

     Use with pages 180–181.

Name _____ Date _____

Complete the list at the right to solve the problem.

6. Rodney is getting dressed to go to the beach. He plans to wear shorts, a shirt, and a hat. He has white shorts and blue shorts. His shirts are red, gray, and black, and he has a gold hat and a green one. How many different clothing combinations can he choose? _____

Shorts	Shirt	Hat	Shorts	Shirt	Hat
white	red	gold	blue	red	gold
white	red	green	blue	red	_____
white	gray	gold	blue	_____	_____
white	gray	green	_____	_____	_____
white	black	gold	_____	_____	_____
white	black	green	_____	_____	_____

Solve. Use a list if needed.

7. Rodney and his friend Lauren meet for breakfast at a diner. For $0.75, the diner offers coffee, tea, or juice with a hard roll, danish, or doughnut. How many different combinations can they choose from? _____

8. Lauren brings along her metal detector to the beach. Immediately, she finds $0.10. How many different coin combinations could she have found? __

9. Lauren and Rodney find 11 rings with the help of the metal detector. Some are women's rings and some are men's rings. How many different combinations of rings could they have found? _____

10. For lunch, Rodney and Lauren stop at a sandwich wagon. Rodney wants to order a sandwich, juice, and a snack. He would like either a cheese sandwich, a ham sandwich, or a salami sandwich. He can select orange, tomato, or apple juice. For a snack, he can choose an apple, banana chips, or carrot cake. How many different lunch combinations can Rodney choose from? _____

11. In the afternoon, Lauren finds $0.75 in nickels and dimes. How many different coin combinations could she have found if there were at least 2 nickels and 2 dimes? _____

12. While walking along the beach, Rodney and Lauren fill a pail with various objects they find. There are 5 objects in the pail, including at least one shell, one rock, and one crab claw. How many different combinations of objects can there be in the pail? _____

PRACTICE   Adding Mixed Numbers

Add. The answer must be in simplest form.

1. $8\frac{1}{4}$
    $+ 6\frac{1}{2}$

2. $16\frac{1}{4}$
    $+ 5\frac{5}{8}$

3. $37\frac{1}{5}$
    $+ 16\frac{1}{2}$

4. $10\frac{3}{4}$
    $+ 10\frac{1}{10}$

5. $8\frac{1}{4}$
    $+ 7\frac{2}{3}$

6. $37\frac{1}{6}$
    $+ 5\frac{1}{6}$

7. $78\frac{2}{3}$
    $+ 84\frac{2}{3}$

8. $42\frac{5}{8}$
    $+ 93\frac{7}{8}$

9. $61\frac{2}{9}$
    $+ 42\frac{1}{9}$

10. $88\frac{4}{7}$
    $+ 6\frac{6}{7}$

11. $49\frac{4}{5}$
    $+ 67\frac{1}{10}$

12. $37\frac{1}{4}$
    $+ 26\frac{5}{8}$

13. $42\frac{3}{5}$
    $+ 14\frac{1}{2}$

14. $94\frac{1}{2}$
    $+ 65\frac{2}{3}$

15. $62\frac{5}{6}$
    $+ 51\frac{5}{9}$

16. $17\frac{2}{8} + 12\frac{3}{8} + 8\frac{2}{8} =$ _____

17. $19\frac{4}{5} + 6\frac{3}{5} + 14\frac{1}{5} =$ _____

18. $13\frac{9}{10} + 7\frac{3}{10} + 11\frac{1}{10} =$ _____

19. $1\frac{3}{8} + 10\frac{5}{8} + 15\frac{5}{8} =$ _____

20. $9\frac{5}{7} + 2\frac{1}{2} + 16\frac{6}{7} =$ _____

21. $8\frac{1}{9} + 14\frac{5}{6} + 7\frac{1}{3} =$ _____

22. $65\frac{3}{4} + 28\frac{1}{6} + 4\frac{1}{3} =$ _____

23. $12\frac{5}{6} + 87\frac{3}{5} + 34\frac{3}{10} =$ _____

Solve.

24. Tamiko's grandmother told her she could have the family rolltop desk. There is only one wall against which Tamiko can put the desk, which is $3\frac{3}{4}$ feet wide. Her bookcase and dresser stand against the same wall. The bookcase is $2\frac{7}{8}$ feet wide and the dresser is $3\frac{1}{3}$ feet wide. If the wall is $9\frac{11}{12}$ feet wide, will the family rolltop desk fit? _____

Use with pages 182–183.

PRACTICE Subtracting Mixed Numbers without Renaming

Subtract. The answer must be in simplest form.

1. $20\frac{4}{5}$
$-13\frac{1}{5}$

2. $17\frac{7}{10}$
$-11\frac{3}{5}$

3. $34\frac{3}{4}$
$-13\frac{7}{10}$

4. $179\frac{25}{36}$
$-\ \ 65$

5. $12\frac{1}{2}$
$-10\frac{1}{4}$

6. $80\frac{2}{3}$
$-44\frac{1}{3}$

7. $26\frac{3}{5}$
$-\ \ 7\frac{1}{3}$

8. $20\frac{3}{4}$
$-\ \ 7\frac{1}{6}$

9. $16\frac{3}{9}$
$-\ \ 9\frac{2}{9}$

10. $60\frac{74}{83}$
$-\ \ 21$

11. $15\frac{7}{9}$
$-14\frac{1}{3}$

12. $20\frac{5}{7}$
$-14\frac{1}{2}$

13. $29\frac{5}{7}$
$-\ \ 14$

14. $5\frac{8}{9}$
$-3\frac{4}{9}$

15. $65\frac{5}{9}$
$-\ \ 1\frac{1}{3}$

16. $16\frac{9}{10}$
$-\ \ 3\frac{1}{6}$

17. $13\frac{5}{6}$
$-12\frac{1}{4}$

18. $14\frac{5}{10}$
$-\ \ 9\frac{4}{10}$

19. $12\frac{5}{6}$
$-11\frac{1}{2}$

20. $71\frac{6}{7}$
$-35\frac{2}{3}$

21. $15\frac{8}{9} - 4\frac{3}{9} =$ _____

22. $17\frac{3}{8} - 8\frac{1}{4} =$ _____

23. $9\frac{6}{7} - 6 =$ _____

24. $8\frac{2}{3} - 2\frac{1}{6} =$ _____

25. $7\frac{5}{7} - 2\frac{1}{7} =$ _____

26. $15\frac{2}{5} - 10\frac{1}{4} =$ _____

Use with pages 184–185.

PRACTICE Subtracting Mixed Numbers with Renaming

Subtract. The answer must be in simplest form.

1. $13\frac{1}{4}$
   $- \ 2\frac{5}{6}$

2. $14\frac{1}{2}$
   $- \ 2\frac{2}{3}$

3. $11\frac{1}{3}$
   $- \ 7\frac{1}{2}$

4. $8\frac{2}{3}$
   $- \ 2\frac{3}{4}$

5. $6\frac{1}{2}$
   $- \ 4\frac{8}{9}$

6. $18\frac{1}{2}$
   $- \ 13\frac{5}{7}$

7. $10\frac{1}{5}$
   $- \ 5\frac{1}{4}$

8. $15\frac{1}{2}$
   $- \ 11\frac{5}{9}$

9. $18\frac{1}{4}$
   $- \ 10\frac{5}{6}$

10. $16\frac{1}{6}$
    $- \ 6\frac{1}{4}$

11. $14\frac{1}{3}$
    $- \ 6\frac{3}{5}$

12. $18\frac{1}{6}$
    $- \ 9\frac{8}{9}$

13. $10\frac{1}{2}$
    $- \ 4\frac{4}{5}$

14. $15\frac{3}{5}$
    $- \ 13\frac{2}{3}$

15. $13\frac{1}{4}$
    $- \ 4\frac{7}{10}$

16. $20\frac{3}{20}$
    $- \ 17\frac{3}{4}$

17. $27\frac{5}{18}$
    $- \ 26\frac{5}{6}$

18. $40\frac{48}{51}$
    $- \ 39\frac{49}{51}$

19. $59\frac{2}{7}$
    $- \ 37\frac{4}{9}$

20. $89\frac{1}{4}$
    $- \ 77\frac{3}{5}$

21. $86\frac{3}{7} - 59\frac{2}{3} = $ _____

22. $90\frac{2}{9} - 88\frac{1}{2} = $ _____

23. $52\frac{1}{2} - 34\frac{5}{7} = $ _____

24. $75\frac{2}{5} - 62\frac{3}{4} = $ _____

25. $43\frac{1}{4} - 38\frac{9}{10} = $ _____

26. $244\frac{7}{12} - 231\frac{11}{15} = $ _____

  Use with pages 186–187

Name _____ Date _____

Solve.

1. $a + 10\frac{1}{8} = 19\frac{3}{8}$ _____

2. $12\frac{9}{10} - y = 9\frac{1}{10}$ _____

3. $6\frac{1}{2} + q = 7\frac{11}{14}$ _____

4. $10\frac{1}{6} + c = 16\frac{2}{3}$ _____

5. $6\frac{1}{2} - b = 2\frac{5}{18}$ _____

6. $j + 7\frac{1}{4} = 17\frac{13}{20}$ _____

7. $9\frac{5}{12} = r - 5\frac{1}{3}$ _____

8. $12\frac{13}{18} = 2\frac{5}{9} + z$ _____

9. $12\frac{1}{2} - c = 9\frac{5}{18}$ _____

10. $10\frac{1}{2} + r = 15\frac{3}{4}$ _____

11. $9\frac{1}{6} - f = \frac{11}{12}$ _____

12. $20\frac{14}{15} = 10\frac{5}{6} + t$ _____

13. $10\frac{1}{2} = 13\frac{2}{3} - a$ _____

14. $2\frac{2}{3} = 1\frac{1}{6} + m$ _____

15. $\frac{13}{20} = z - 12\frac{3}{4}$ _____

Where did the first movie theater in the United States open?
To answer the question, write the answer to each equation in
simplest form on the line in row A. Find the code letter for
each answer, and write it on the line in row B.

16. $d + 8\frac{1}{6} = 16\frac{7}{18}$

17. $8\frac{1}{4} - z = 6\frac{5}{12}$

18. $15\frac{3}{5} = n + 7\frac{11}{10}$

19. $3\frac{3}{8} + 1\frac{1}{2} = s$

20. $17\frac{2}{3} - r = 11\frac{1}{6}$

21. $4\frac{1}{6} = u + \frac{1}{6}$

22. $9\frac{19}{20} = 4\frac{1}{5} + t$

23. $1\frac{1}{4} = 3\frac{1}{12} - s$

24. $1\frac{1}{4} + c = 10\frac{3}{4}$

25. $w + 5\frac{1}{6} = 13\frac{7}{18}$

26. $6\frac{5}{6} = 12\frac{1}{2} - d$

27. $2\frac{1}{4} + x = 7\frac{1}{8}$

	16.	17.	18.	19.	20.	21.	22.	23.	24.	25.	26.	27.
A. Answer												
B. Code letter												

Answer Code

$1\frac{5}{6}$	$5\frac{3}{4}$	$8\frac{2}{9}$	$7\frac{1}{8}$	$6\frac{1}{2}$	$13\frac{7}{10}$	$9\frac{1}{2}$	$7\frac{1}{2}$	$3\frac{1}{2}$	$5\frac{2}{3}$	4	$15\frac{1}{2}$	$4\frac{7}{8}$
E	L	N	X	O	P	A	W	Q	S	R	C	

PRACTICE   Writing a Simpler Problem

Ring the letter of the better plan for simplifying each problem.

1. Justine works at Barker Kennels. She feeds and tends the dogs. Every day she feeds each large dog $6\frac{3}{4}$ ounces of food. A bag of food contains 30 ounces. If there are 13 large dogs in the kennel, how many bags of food does Justine use per day?

a. Step 1: $7 \times 13 = 91$
Step 2: $91 \div 30 = 3$

b. Step 1: $30 + 7 = 37$
Step 2: $37 - 13 = 24$

2. Small puppies are fed $1\frac{1}{4}$ ounces of food each day, while medium-sized puppies are fed $2\frac{2}{3}$ ounces. How much more food does a medium-sized puppy eat in one week than a small puppy?

a. Step 1: $1 \times 7 = 7$
Step 2: $7 - 3 = 4$

b. Step 1: $3 - 1 = 2$
Step 2: $2 \times 7 = 14$

Solve. Solve a simpler problem first if you need to. Then solve the original problem.

3. Justine is paid $3.90 per hour for working at the kennel. If she works $2\frac{1}{2}$ hours on Monday, Wednesday, and Friday, and 7 hours on Saturday, how much does she earn in one week?

4. Many of the dogs at the kennel eat canned dog food. The cost of 4 cans is $1.89. If Justine has $40 to spend for dog food, does she have enough money to buy 90 cans? _____

5. Ralph exercises the dogs at the kennel. Each dog gets $\frac{3}{4}$ of an hour of exercise each day. Ralph works from 9:00 to 4:00. He has a 1-hour lunch break. How many dogs can he exercise? _____

6. Ralph clocked the distance from the kennel to the veterinarian's office at 4.2 miles and from the kennel to the pet supply store at 6.7 miles. Ralph made 5 round-trips to the veterinarian and 3 round-trips to the supply store. Did he drive more than 75 miles? _____

7. This week, 48 dogs are being boarded at the Barker Kennels. It costs an owner $7.85 per day to board one dog. How much will the kennel earn this week in boarding fees? _____

8. Every dog cage has a 16.8-square-foot exercise yard. If there are cages for 38 dogs, are there more than 500 square feet of exercise yard? _____

Use with pages 190–191.

Name _____ Date _____

Multiplying Fractions

Each code box contains one part of a message. Solve each
problem below. Look for your answer above a code box.
Copy what you see into the correct message box. The
answer must be in simplest form.

1. $\frac{1}{3} \times \frac{2}{5} =$ _____ 2. $\frac{5}{4} \times \frac{7}{6} =$ _____   3. $\frac{1}{4} \times \frac{3}{8} =$ _____   4. $\frac{1}{8} \times \frac{2}{5} =$ _____

5. $\frac{3}{4} \times \frac{1}{6} =$ _____ 6. $\frac{3}{7} \times \frac{5}{8} \times \frac{2}{3} =$ _____ 7. $\frac{5}{7} \times \frac{3}{10} =$ _____ 8. $\frac{2}{3} \times \frac{3}{2} =$ _____

9. $\frac{4}{9} \times \frac{2}{9} =$ _____ 10. $\frac{6}{7} \times 14 =$ _____ 11. $\frac{5}{7} \times \frac{5}{6} =$ _____ 12. $8 \times \frac{3}{7} =$ _____

13. $\frac{3}{5} \times \frac{5}{6} =$ _____ 14. $\frac{3}{4} \times \frac{5}{12} \times \frac{2}{3} =$ _____ 15. $\frac{2}{9} \times \frac{4}{5} \times \frac{6}{16} =$ _____ 16. $\frac{1}{9} \times \frac{1}{10} \times \frac{1}{2} =$ _____

17. $3 \times \frac{1}{4} =$ _____ 18. $\frac{1}{2} \times \frac{2}{3} \times \frac{3}{4} =$ _____ 19. $5 \times \frac{2}{5} =$ _____ 20. $\frac{2}{11} \times \frac{5}{3} =$ _____

Code Boxes

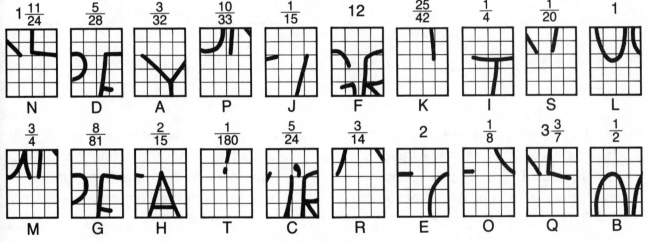

$1\frac{11}{24}$	$\frac{5}{28}$	$\frac{3}{32}$	$\frac{10}{33}$	$\frac{1}{15}$	12	$\frac{25}{42}$	$\frac{1}{4}$	$\frac{1}{20}$	1
N	D	A	P	J	F	K	I	S	L

$\frac{3}{4}$	$\frac{8}{81}$	$\frac{2}{15}$	$\frac{1}{180}$	$\frac{5}{24}$	$\frac{3}{14}$	2	$\frac{1}{8}$	$3\frac{3}{7}$	$\frac{1}{2}$
M	G	H	T	C	R	E	O	Q	B

Message Boxes

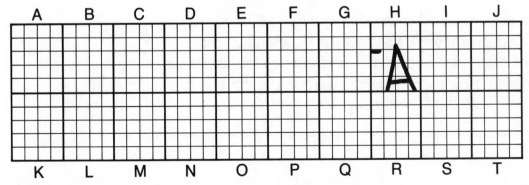

PRACTICE   Simplifying Before Multiplying

Multiply. The answer must be in simplest form.

1. $\frac{4}{5} \times \frac{5}{16} =$ _____

2. $\frac{4}{7} \times \frac{21}{28} =$ _____

3. $\frac{1}{3} \times \frac{3}{2} \times \frac{3}{7} =$ _____

4. $\frac{3}{8} \times \frac{4}{9} \times \frac{3}{4} =$ _____

5. $\frac{8}{3} \times \frac{5}{6} \times \frac{1}{5} =$ _____

6. $\frac{5}{12}$ of $\frac{24}{25} =$ _____

7. $\frac{2}{15} \times \frac{5}{6} =$ _____

8. $\frac{7}{9}$ of 3 = _____

9. $\frac{1}{5} \times 10 \times \frac{7}{2} =$ _____

10. $\frac{18}{25} \times \frac{5}{9} =$ _____

11. $\frac{10}{3} \times \frac{9}{20} =$ _____

12. $\frac{2}{9} \times 27 =$ _____

13. $\frac{11}{14} \times \frac{7}{22} \times 3 =$ _____

14. $7 \times \frac{5}{6} \times \frac{3}{14} =$ _____

15. $\frac{4}{7} \times \frac{5}{12} =$ _____

16. $\frac{1}{4} \times \frac{8}{13} =$ _____

17. $\frac{3}{11}$ of 11 = _____

18. $\frac{7}{25}$ of $\frac{3}{14} =$ _____

19. $\frac{5}{7} \times \frac{3}{5} =$ _____

20. $\frac{1}{10} \times 100 \times \frac{2}{5} =$ _____

21. $\frac{2}{9} \times \frac{27}{32} =$ _____

22. $4 \times \frac{9}{22} =$ _____

23. $\frac{4}{5} \times \frac{7}{16} \times \frac{10}{7} =$ _____

24. 6 of $\frac{5}{18} =$ _____

25. $3 \times \frac{11}{12} \times \frac{5}{22} =$ _____

26. $\frac{3}{8}$ of $\frac{2}{3} =$ _____

27. $\frac{1}{4} \times \frac{8}{3} \times \frac{6}{7} =$ _____

Solve.

28. Mr. Rodriquez sells trees at a nursery. He sold $\frac{1}{8}$ of all the nursery trees. Of the trees sold, $\frac{3}{4}$ were pines, and he sold every pine tree. What fraction of the nursery trees were pines?

_____

29. Grover tends flowers in the nursery. It takes him $\frac{4}{5}$ hour to prune the roses, $\frac{1}{4}$ hour to weed the geraniums, and $\frac{2}{3}$ hour to water the flowers. How much time does he work?

_____

30. Maria sells roses. This morning she had 25 bunches. She sold $\frac{1}{5}$ of them for $12.00 per bunch, and then reduced the price and sold $\frac{7}{10}$ of the ones left for $9.00 per bunch. How many bunches were left at the end of the day? How much money did Maria earn?

_____

                                    Use with pages 202–203

PRACTICE   Choosing or Writing a Sensible Question

Read each statement below. Then write two questions for each that should be answered before making a decision.

The Service Club of Lockhart Junction is planning its calendar of activities for the coming year.

1. The Service Club plans to award scholarships to two college-bound seniors at graduation time. The club must decide how much to give and how to earn the money.

_____

_____

2. The club is planning a fund-raising auction for the fall. The club must decide whether to sell a large quantity of low-priced items or a smaller quantity of high-priced items.

_____

_____

3. A barbecue is planned for Independence Day. The club needs to decide how much to charge per person.

_____

_____

4. The club must determine how many ribs to order for the barbecue.

_____

_____

5. One of the club's planned service projects is for its members to spend a week working at a community center for underprivileged children. The center is 20 miles away, and the club must make transportation arrangements for its members.

_____

_____

6. The Service Club wants to sponsor an arts and crafts showcase for local craftspersons. The club must select a date and place.

_____

_____

PRACTICE   Estimating Products of Mixed Numbers

Write > or < for ○.

1. $2\frac{1}{9} \times 5\frac{1}{3}$ ○ 10

2. $6\frac{3}{4} \times 4\frac{5}{6}$ ○ 35

3. $8\frac{9}{10} \times 3\frac{1}{3}$ ○ 27

4. $12\frac{1}{7} \times 5$ ○ 60

5. $9\frac{15}{16} \times 8\frac{11}{14}$ ○ 90

6. $15\frac{9}{11} \times 3$ ○ 48

7. $4\frac{1}{3} \times 11\frac{3}{4}$ ○ 47

8. $3\frac{7}{10} \times 9\frac{7}{8}$ ○ 30

9. $7 \times 8\frac{2}{11}$ ○ 56

10. $5\frac{17}{20} \times 6\frac{8}{9}$ ○ 42

11. $14\frac{13}{15} \times 5\frac{7}{9}$ ○ 90

12. $9\frac{1}{8} \times 6\frac{2}{3}$ ○ 60

13. $8\frac{1}{10} \times 9\frac{5}{6}$ ○ 81

14. $6\frac{1}{3} \times 12\frac{3}{8}$ ○ 72

15. $15\frac{5}{6} \times 8\frac{4}{5}$ ○ 144

16. $8 \times 19\frac{6}{7}$ ○ 160

17. $12\frac{1}{5} \times 10\frac{1}{8}$ ○ 120

18. $5\frac{2}{3} \times 8\frac{1}{6}$ ○ 49

19. $2\frac{1}{8} \times 5\frac{2}{11} \times 10\frac{1}{4}$ ○ 100

20. $7\frac{2}{3} \times 4\frac{9}{10} \times 9\frac{8}{11}$ ○ 400

Estimate.

21. $3\frac{1}{7} \times 6\frac{1}{3} =$ _____

22. $4\frac{5}{6} \times 8\frac{5}{7} =$ _____

23. $9\frac{4}{5} \times 8\frac{1}{10} =$ _____

24. $7 \times 6\frac{8}{11} =$ _____

25. $14\frac{3}{4} \times 6\frac{1}{8} =$ _____

26. $19\frac{5}{8} \times 5\frac{1}{5} =$ _____

27. $9\frac{3}{4} \times 12\frac{2}{3} =$ _____

28. $8\frac{4}{7} \times 10\frac{2}{9} =$ _____

Name _____ Date _____

Multiply. The answer must be in simplest form.

1. $1\frac{3}{4} \times 1\frac{1}{2} =$ _____

2. $3\frac{1}{6} \times 2 \times \frac{3}{8} =$ _____

3. $\frac{1}{5} \times 2\frac{3}{7} \times \frac{5}{14} =$ _____

4. $3\frac{2}{5} \times 4\frac{3}{8} \times \frac{1}{14} =$ _____

5. $2\frac{1}{9} \times 6\frac{3}{4} =$ _____

6. $4\frac{5}{8} \times 9 \times \frac{3}{74} =$ _____

7. $1\frac{1}{2} \times 4 \times 3\frac{2}{5} =$ _____

8. $7\frac{1}{7} \times 1\frac{2}{5} \times 3 =$ _____

9. $3\frac{4}{5} \times \frac{3}{38} \times 11 =$ _____

10. $4\frac{2}{5} \times 1\frac{1}{11} \times \frac{5}{7} =$ _____

11. $7\frac{2}{9} \times 0 \times 3\frac{1}{6} =$ _____

12. $1\frac{15}{16} \times 1\frac{2}{5} \times \frac{5}{21} =$ _____

13. $3\frac{7}{8} \times 1\frac{3}{5} =$ _____

14. $2\frac{9}{11} \times 3\frac{7}{8} \times \frac{8}{31} =$ _____

15. $1\frac{1}{2} \times 2\frac{4}{9} \times 2\frac{1}{4} =$ _____

16. $8\frac{3}{4} \times 2\frac{2}{9} =$ _____

17. $4\frac{2}{9} \times 3 \times \frac{2}{7} =$ _____

18. $1\frac{1}{15} \times 1\frac{7}{9} \times \frac{3}{16} =$ _____

19. $2\frac{4}{13} \times 7\frac{2}{3} =$ _____

20. $1\frac{6}{7} \times 3\frac{4}{5} \times \frac{15}{19} =$ _____

21. $3\frac{1}{14} \times \frac{14}{43} =$ _____

22. $9\frac{1}{3} \times \frac{2}{9} =$ _____

23. $1\frac{1}{4} \times \frac{1}{5} \times 6\frac{2}{3} =$ _____

24. $7\frac{1}{2} \times \frac{1}{16} \times 1\frac{3}{5} =$ _____

25. Augustus Stanley, captain of the *North Moth,* lands on a small deserted island. He decides to stay and explore the island for 4 days. He plans to explore for $3\frac{1}{2}$ hours after breakfast and for $4\frac{1}{4}$ hours after lunch each day. How much time does Augustus wish to spend exploring?

_____

26. Augustus has just been appointed admiral of the navy. His first assignment is to assist his fellow officers and sailors in repainting the fleet. If they can paint $5\frac{3}{5}$ ships every hour, how many ships can they paint in $12\frac{1}{2}$ hours? _____

PRACTICE Dividing Fractions

Write the reciprocal.

1. $\frac{4}{13}$ _____

2. $\frac{8}{9}$ _____

3. $\frac{1}{4}$ _____

4. $\frac{3}{11}$ _____

5. $\frac{7}{6}$ _____

6. 5 _____

7. $3\frac{3}{5}$ _____

8. $\frac{10}{7}$ _____

Divide. The answer must be in simplest form.

9. $\frac{3}{5} \div \frac{1}{3} =$ _____

10. $6 \div \frac{4}{5} =$ _____

11. $\frac{2}{9} \div \frac{1}{6} =$ _____

12. $\frac{6}{13} \div \frac{3}{26} =$ _____

13. $\frac{4}{7} \div \frac{2}{5} =$ _____

14. $\frac{21}{32} \div \frac{7}{8} =$ _____

15. $\frac{11}{14} \div \frac{3}{7} =$ _____

16. $\frac{8}{15} \div \frac{32}{35} =$ _____

17. $3 \div \frac{1}{10} =$ _____

18. $\frac{3}{8} \div 6 =$ _____

19. $\frac{3}{5} \div \frac{14}{15} =$ _____

20. $\frac{7}{10} \div 8 =$ _____

21. $\frac{2}{7} \div \frac{6}{7} =$ _____

22. $\frac{8}{9} \div \frac{1}{3} =$ _____

23. $\frac{5}{6} \div \frac{7}{12} =$ _____

24. $1 \div \frac{2}{7} =$ _____

25. $\frac{11}{15} \div \frac{4}{5} =$ _____

26. $\frac{4}{9} \div \frac{5}{12} =$ _____

Solve.

27. Keith is making salad dressing for his family picnic. He makes $\frac{3}{4}$ pint of dressing. If 12 people use all the dressing, how large a serving does each person receive?

_____

28. Keith's sister Maria and her cousins tell stories for $\frac{3}{4}$ hour at the picnic. If each of the 15 cousins tells a story for the same amount of time, how many minutes long is each story?

_____

Use with pages 210–211

PRACTICE   Dining Mixed Numbers

Ring the letter of the correct answer.

1. $3\frac{4}{7} \div \frac{5}{14}$ **a.** $\frac{5}{2}$ **b.** 10 **c.** $\frac{1}{10}$ **d.** $\frac{2}{5}$

2. $6\frac{2}{7} \div 11$ **a.** $69\frac{1}{7}$ **b.** $\frac{7}{4}$ **c.** $\frac{8}{7}$ **d.** $\frac{4}{7}$

3. $2\frac{1}{5} \div 1\frac{3}{10}$ **a.** $2\frac{43}{50}$ **b.** $\frac{21}{13}$ **c.** $1\frac{9}{13}$ **d.** $\frac{13}{22}$

Divide. The answer must be in simplest form.

4. $2\frac{1}{7} \div 2\frac{8}{11} =$ _____   **5.** $2\frac{4}{9} \div 2\frac{3}{4} =$ _____   **6.** $3\frac{3}{8} \div 1\frac{2}{7} =$ _____

7. $3\frac{4}{15} \div 1\frac{1}{20} =$ _____   **8.** $1\frac{1}{8} \div 3\frac{3}{5} =$ _____   **9.** $1\frac{1}{8} \div 5\frac{2}{5} =$ _____

10. $1\frac{7}{8} \div 1\frac{1}{4} =$ _____   **11.** $\left(\frac{1}{4} \times 2\frac{1}{2}\right) \div \frac{7}{10} =$ _____   **12.** $3\frac{1}{2} \div 2\frac{1}{3} =$ _____

13. $4 \div 5\frac{1}{7} =$ _____   **14.** $\frac{3}{4} \div 2\frac{2}{5} =$ _____   **15.** $4\frac{1}{5} \div \frac{14}{25} =$ _____

16. $4\frac{1}{6} \div 1\frac{1}{4} =$ _____   **17.** $3\frac{1}{3} \div 4\frac{1}{6} =$ _____   **18.** $3\frac{1}{6} \div 5\frac{3}{7} =$ _____

Solve.

19. The cook at Trucker's Heaven Diner bakes all her blueberry muffins before the early-morning crowd arrives. This morning she has $2\frac{3}{4}$ hours before they arrive. If each batch of muffins takes $\frac{1}{2}$ hour to bake, how many complete batches can she bake in that time? Will she have any time left? If so, how much time?

_____

20. Trucker's Heaven Diner uses hundreds of plates, glasses, and cups each day. The dishwashers start a new load of dishes every $1\frac{1}{4}$ hours. If the dishwashers work for 10 hours, how many loads of dishes do they wash in that time?

_____

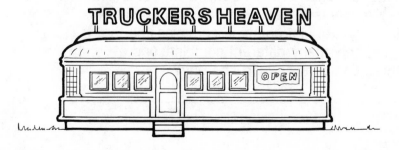

TRUCKERS HEAVEN

PRACTICE   Selecting Notation

Solve. Use notation where appropriate.

1. The Arrows and the Dragons are playing for the basketball championship. The Arrows trail 50–45 with time running out. List the different combinations of baskets (2 points) and/or free throws (1 point) that the Arrows could score in order to win the game by one point.

_____

_____

2. Each of 5 teams in a basketball league plays each of the other teams once. Two league officials are present at each game. If the league pays an official $21 per game, how much money will the league pay its officials for this first round of play? _____

3. The telephone company in Paddington charges $0.31 for the first minute and $0.16 for each additional minute for a weekday call. How many quarters would a Paddington resident need to make a 10-minute call on a weekday from a pay phone? _____

4. The leader of the Explorer's Club camping trip needs to measure 4 pints of water for the meal he is preparing. However, he brought along only a 6-pint kettle, a 5-pint kettle, and a 3-pint kettle. Show how the leader can measure 4 pints using the kettles he has.

_____

_____

5. Mrs. Ridero has $240 that she wants to invest in three companies traded on the stock market. She wants to buy at least 6 shares of Dynamo, which sells for $24 per share, and at least 3 shares of Plurotron, which costs $12 per share. She also wants to buy no more than 10 shares of Acme, at $6 per share. Not counting commissions that she'd have to pay, how many different combinations of shares in the three companies could she buy?

_____

_____

Use with pages 214–21

PRACTICE   Selecting Notation

Select an appropriate model and solve. Write the letter of the correct answer.

6. Carol manages Dryden Junior High School's field-hockey teams. Before today's practice session, she wants to divide a 4-gallon container of water equally between the varsity team and the junior varsity team. If she has empty 3-gallon and 1-gallon containers, how can she evenly divide the water? The first number in the ordered pairs represent gallons of water in the 3-gallon container. The second number represents gallons of water in the 1-gallon container.

a. (3, 0)   (0, 1)   (2, 0)   c. (0, 1)   (1, 0)   (2, 0)
b. (0, 1)   (1, 1)   (2, 0)   d. (3, 0)   (2, 1)   (2, 0)

_____

7. There are 5 field-hockey teams in the league. If each team plays every other team once, how many games will be played? Each dot represents a team in the league and each line represents a game played.

A.    B.    C. 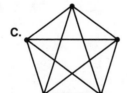   D.

8. One day at practice, Carol found $0.47 on the field. If she found only dimes and pennies, list the possible different combinations she could have found.

_____

9. Six field-hockey teams went to a tournament. If the coach of each team shook hands with every other coach, how many handshakes were there? Use a drawing to represent your answer.

_____

10. Nancy and Erica are players on one of the teams. Nancy has an 8-oz box of juice. She offers half to Erica. If they locate an empty 5-oz and 3-oz cup, how can they divide the juice equally?

_____

PRACTICE Decimals and Fractions

Write as a decimal.

1. $\frac{7}{25}$ = _____

2. $\frac{87}{1,000}$ = _____

3. $\frac{2}{50}$ = _____

4. $\frac{3}{4}$ = _____

5. $\frac{99}{100}$ = _____

6. $\frac{23}{100}$ = _____

7. $\frac{14}{25}$ = _____

8. $\frac{13}{40}$ = _____

9. $\frac{11}{20}$ = _____

10. $2\frac{1}{4}$ = _____

11. $\frac{9}{10}$ = _____

12. $\frac{904}{1,000}$ = _____

13. $\frac{7}{10}$ = _____

14. $\frac{3}{20}$ = _____

15. $\frac{17}{50}$ = _____

16. $\frac{2}{100}$ = _____

Write as a fraction or a mixed number. The answer must be in simplest form.

17. 0.125 = _____

18. 0.66 = _____

19. 0.2 = _____

20. 0.7000 = _____

21. 0.95 = _____

22. 0.65 = _____

23. 27.24 = _____

24. 0.008 = _____

25. 0.05 = _____

26. 2.375 = _____

27. 0.77 = _____

28. 28.04 = _____

29. 0.6000 = _____

30. 15.6 = _____

31. 0.225 = _____

32. 4.75 = _____

Solve.

33. Mrs. Lincoln owns the Hot Stuff food company. She sends out catalogs every month to interest people in her spices and canned chili. Of the 600 people she sent catalogs to last month, 0.35 sent back order forms for various goods. What fraction of the people who were sent catalogs placed orders? How many people did not place orders?

_____

34. Mrs. Lincoln spends three quarters of a dollar to mail each catalog. How much did it cost her to mail 600 catalogs last month?

PRACTICE   Using a Recipe

Use information from the recipe to answer the questions that follow.

ROGER'S HEAVENLY HAMBURGER SOUP	$\frac{1}{2}$ hour preparation time 1 hour cooking time

2 tbsp butter	1 c diced potatoes
$\frac{2}{3}$ c chopped onions	$1\frac{1}{4}$ tsp salt
$\frac{3}{4}$ c sliced carrots	$\frac{1}{8}$ tsp pepper
$\frac{1}{2}$ c chopped green peppers	$\frac{1}{3}$ c flour
1 lb ground beef	4 c milk
2 c tomato juice	$\frac{3}{4}$ tsp seasoned salt

Sauté butter, onions, carrots, and green peppers. Add beef and cook until crumbly. Stir in tomato juice, potatoes, and seasonings. Cover and cook for about $\frac{1}{2}$ hour. Combine flour and milk and stir in gradually. Makes 12 servings.

1. Mrs. Dudek's home-economics class is making Roger's Heavenly Hamburger Soup. If the class wanted to prepare 18 servings instead of 12, how much ground beef would they need? _____

2. Mrs. Dudek divides the class into 3 groups. Each group will follow the recipe as shown. If ground beef costs $1.89 per pound, how much will Mrs. Dudek spend on ground beef for the class? _____

3. One chopped green pepper equals about $\frac{3}{4}$ of a cup. How many green peppers will Mrs. Dudek need to buy for the 3 cooking groups? _____

4. Hugh is measuring the butter for his group. If one stick of butter equals 8 tablespoons, what part of a stick should Hugh add to the recipe? _____

PRACTICE Terminating and Repeating Decimals

Write each fraction as a decimal. Write a bar to show a repeating decimal.

1. $\frac{17}{18} =$ _____

2. $\frac{11}{6} =$ _____

3. $\frac{23}{10} =$ _____

4. $\frac{1}{80} =$ _____

5. $8\frac{1}{8} =$ _____

6. $4\frac{1}{6} =$ _____

7. $\frac{1}{9} =$ _____

8. $\frac{17}{5} =$ _____

9. $\frac{3}{16} =$ _____

10. $\frac{4}{37} =$ _____

11. $\frac{17}{24} =$ _____

12. $\frac{3}{25} =$ _____

13. $\frac{8}{9} =$ _____

14. $\frac{17}{27} =$ _____

15. $\frac{5}{22} =$ _____

16. $\frac{5}{12} =$ _____

Write the greater decimal.

17. 0.60 or $0.\overline{6}$ _____

18. 0.177 or $0.\overline{17}$ _____

19. 15.09 or $15.\overline{09}$ _____

Solve.

20. Mr. Schlomo wants to prepare a budget to help him save money for a trip to the Grand Canyon. He begins by listing his expenses. He spends $\frac{2}{9}$ of his salary on groceries. How would Mr. Schlomo write this fraction as a decimal?

_____

21. Mrs. Chan spends $\frac{1}{2}$ of her salary on rent, $\frac{1}{3}$ on groceries, and $\frac{1}{12}$ on entertainment. She wants to save the rest. What fraction of her salary will she try to save? If her salary is $300 a week, how much will she spend on groceries?

_____

Use with pages 220–221

PRACTICE Solving Equations with Fractions

Ring the letter of the correct answer.

1. $\frac{7}{8}a + 14 = 28$ a. $\frac{49}{4}$ b. $\frac{1}{16}$ c. 16 d. $12\frac{1}{4}$

2. $\frac{1}{4}c - \frac{3}{8} = 3\frac{1}{8}$ a. 11 b. $12\frac{1}{2}$ c. 14 d. $\frac{1}{11}$

3. $\frac{5}{6}b = 1$ a. $\frac{1}{6}$ b. $\frac{6}{5}$ c. 1 d. $\frac{4}{5}$

Solve. The answer must be in simplest form.

4. $\frac{5}{6}a = 10$ _____

5. $\frac{3}{4}e - 4 = 8$ _____

6. $\frac{1}{3}y = \frac{7}{27}$ _____

7. $\frac{2}{7}c + 5\frac{1}{2} = 9\frac{1}{2}$ _____

8. $\frac{1}{7}r - \frac{1}{5} = 4\frac{4}{5}$ _____

9. $\frac{5}{8}z + 4 = 5.25$ _____

10. $\frac{1}{2}w - 4 = 3\frac{1}{10}$ _____

11. $\frac{2}{5}b = \frac{6}{7}$ _____

12. $\frac{1}{4}y - 0.6 = 1\frac{1}{5}$ _____

13. $\frac{1}{8}z + \frac{1}{10} = \frac{11}{20}$ _____

14. $2\frac{1}{2} + \frac{7}{9}x = 2\frac{5}{6}$ _____

15. $\frac{1}{6}c + 1\frac{1}{12} = 3\frac{1}{4}$ _____

Solve.

16. A number minus $\frac{2}{5}$ is $\frac{1}{10}$. _____

17. What number times $1\frac{3}{4}$ is 1? _____

18. A number times $\frac{1}{4}$ increased by $\frac{3}{8}$ is $1\frac{1}{8}$. _____

19. A number plus $\frac{1}{6}$ is $\frac{5}{12}$. _____

Amazin' Equations! There is something very interesting about the variables in each pair of equations. Solve each pair of equations and see how the two relate to one another.

20. a. $5 + x = 6\frac{1}{4}$ b. $5x = 6\frac{1}{4}$ $x =$ _____

21. a. $9 + y = 10\frac{1}{8}$ b. $9y = 10\frac{1}{8}$ $y =$ _____

22. a. $3 + t = 4\frac{1}{2}$ b. $3t = 4\frac{1}{2}$ $t =$ _____

23. a. $13 + c = 14\frac{1}{12}$ b. $13c = 14\frac{1}{12}$ $c =$ _____

24. a. $100 + r = 101\frac{1}{99}$ b. $100r = 101\frac{1}{99}$ $r =$ _____

Name _____   Date _____

Write the letter of the correct answer.

1. Ricardo Martinez owns an automobile rental and repair business. If he buys 74 new tires, how many cars can he equip with new tires?

   a. 18 cars

   b. $18\frac{1}{4}$ cars

   c. 19 cars

2. Ricardo paid $2,701.00 for the 74 new tires he purchased. How much did each tire cost?

   a. $36.00

   b. $36.50

   c. $37.00

Solve.

3. The mechanics in Ricardo's repair shop used 317 spark plugs last year. If Ricardo buys the plugs in boxes of 24, how many boxes did he purchase last year? _____

4. The towns of Deauville and Carney Heights are 180 miles apart. If a map in Ricardo's office has a scale of 1 in. equals 50 miles, how many inches apart are the towns on the map? _____

5. Ricardo estimates that it will cost about $590 next year to insure each of his rental cars. If Ricardo has $8,000 budgeted to pay for insurance, how many cars will he be able to insure? _____

6. Ricardo advertises in the newspaper every week. His ad is 189 characters long. If the newspaper sells space by the line, and if each line is 22 characters long, how many lines of space must he buy? _____

7. Mrs. Chan rented a new compact car. She drove the car 285 miles. If the car averaged 25 miles per gallon, how much gas did Mrs. Chan need? _____

8. On Monday mornings, Ricardo provides coffee and bagels for his workers. He buys the bagels in half-dozen bags. If Ricardo has 5 workers and they eat an average of 2 bagels each, how many bags of bagels does Ricardo buy? _____

9. In December, many customers drop off their cars at Ricardo's to have their snow tires put on. It takes a mechanic's assistant about $\frac{1}{3}$ hour to mount the snow tires on one car. At that rate, how many cars could the assistant finish in $1\frac{1}{2}$ hours? _____

10. Ricardo charges $29.50 per hour for repair services. One customer's bill had a service charge of $44.25. How many hours of service were included on the bill? _____

Name _____ Date _____

PRACTICE Metric Units of Length

Write the most likely unit of measurement (km, m, cm, mm).

1. width of a hand   _____

2. distance across an ocean   _____

3. height of a flagpole   _____

4. thickness of a glass window   _____

5. length of a finger   _____

6. length of a table   _____

7. length of a sheet of paper   _____

8. thickness of a mattress   _____

9. distance between towns   _____

10. thickness of a saw blade   _____

Ring the letter of the best estimate.

11. height of a house   a. 1 m   b. 30 cm   c. 10 m

12. thickness of a spoon   a. 0.2 mm   b. 2 mm   c. 200 mm

13. length of a shoe   a. 2 cm   b. 20.3 cm   c. 203 cm

14. length of a river   a. 18 km   b. 18 cm   c. 18 m

Estimate the length of each string to the nearest centimeter.
Then measure each to the nearest centimeter and to the
nearest millimeter.

15. _____

16. _____

Solve.

17. Erin cuts lengths of cloth to line flower
baskets. If she had 6 m of cloth, how
many 63-cm pieces of cloth was she
able to cut? _____

18. Each day, Erin walks 560 meters to
the flower show and from the flower
show. How much more than a
kilometer does she walk each day?

_____

PRACTICE Renaming Metric Units of Length

Complete each table.

m	mm
1. 45	
4. 0.06	
7. 170	
10. 8	

m	cm
2. 13	
5. 87,000	
8. 2,400	
11.	900

km	m
3.	4
6.	36
9.	4,725
12.	290

Write the missing number.

13. 20 cm = _____ km

14. 0.07 hm = _____ km

15. 0.69 dam = _____ mm

16. 67,300 cm = _____ km

17. 0.1 km = _____ hm

18. 120 dam = _____ m

19. 6,472 m = _____ km

20. 2,640 mm = _____ cm

21. 8.92 m = _____ cm

22. 5,000 cm = _____ m

23. 12 mm = _____ m

24. 27.62 km = _____ m

25. 1.94 km = _____ cm

26. 0.6 cm = _____ mm

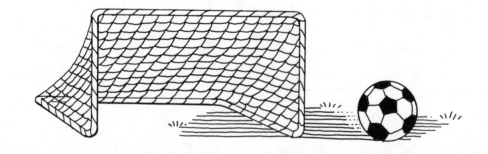

Solve.

27. Marni and Sally live on opposite sides of town. They always ride their bicycles to meet at the soccer field. Marni rides 2.3 km and Sally rides 2,030 m. Who has a longer ride?

_____

28. Each of the girls scored a goal in the last soccer game. Marni kicked hers from 9 m away, and Sally kicked hers from 1,240 cm away. Whose goal was longer? by how much?

_____

Use with pages 238–239.

Name _____ Date _____

PRACTICE   Metric Units of Capacity and Mass

Compare. Write >, <, or =.

1. 480 g $\bigcirc$ 5 kg

2. 241 mL $\bigcirc$ 0.2 L

3. 0.35 kg $\bigcirc$ 350 g

4. 6.24 L $\bigcirc$ 625 mL

5. 255 mg $\bigcirc$ 0.28 g

6. 2.85 L $\bigcirc$ 2,800 mL

7. 0.282 L $\bigcirc$ 282 mL

8. 0.01 g $\bigcirc$ 9 mg

9. 165 mL $\bigcirc$ 1.62 L

10. 8.08 kg $\bigcirc$ 8,100 g

11. 188 mL $\bigcirc$ 0.2 L

12. 21.45 g $\bigcirc$ 0.0215 kg

Write the missing number.

13. 5,000 mL = _____ L

14. 5,000 g = _____ kg

15. 25 kg = _____ g

16. 2.5 L = _____ mL

17. 10 L = _____ mL

18. 1,000 mg = _____ g

19. 10.5 g = _____ mg

20. 45 g = _____ kg

21. 300 g = _____ kg

22. 1,500 mL = _____ L

23. 59 L = _____ mL

24. 2,980 g = _____ kg

Panic in the Lab

Dr. M. I. Stake discovered a leak in a 5-liter drum of distilled water in his lab. Before he could catch any of the liquid, 250 mL leaked onto the floor. He then used all the beakers in the lab to catch the leaking liquid. He used four 1-liter bottles, seven 100-milliliter jars, and three 10-milliliter vials.

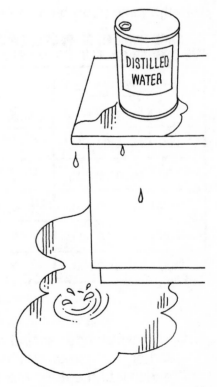

25. Could Dr. M. I. Stake catch all the leaking liquid in his beakers? _____

26. Did he need more 10-milliliter vials, or did he have extras? _____

27. How many more did he need? _____

PRACTICE   Problem-Solving Practice

Write an equation and solve.

1. Seventh graders at the Kennedy School held a mock election. $\frac{2}{3}$ of the students voted for the Republican-party candidate for governor. If 411 students voted in the election, how many voted Republican?

   _____

2. A guest speaker for the Democratic party told students that the Democratic party had spent $1,298,700 campaigning in the state. If there are 4,329,000 registered voters in the state, how much did the Democratic party spend per vote?

   _____

Ring the letter of the best answer.

3. One candidate for governor campaigned throughout the state by train. The train traveled a total of 17,600 kilometers. If the train covered an average of 320 kilometers per day, for approximately how many weeks did the candidate travel?

   a. 8   b. 21   c. 60

4. Another candidate drove throughout the state. One week, he drove 220 km. The next week, he drove 311 km, and the week after that he drove 190 km. If his average speed was 51 km per hour, about how many hours did he drive during the 3-week period?

   a. 14   b. 230   c. 700

Use the pictograph below to solve.

**AVERAGE NUMBER OF PEOPLE PASSING
THE CORNER OF MAIN STREET AND BROADWAY PER HOUR**

Time	Number of people
7:00 A.M.–8:00 A.M.	♀ ♀ ♀ ♀ ⸹
8:00 A.M.–9:00 A.M.	♀ ♀ ♀ ♀ ♀ ⸹
12:00 P.M.–1:00 P.M.	♀ ♀ ♀ ♀ ♀
3:00 P.M.–4:00 P.M.	♀ ♀ ♀
4:00 P.M.–5:00 P.M.	♀ ♀ ♀ ♀ ⸹
5:00 P.M.–6:00 P.M.	♀ ♀ ♀ ♀ ♀

Each ♀ stands for 100 people.

5. During which hour should a candidate stand on the corner of Main Street and Broadway to meet the most people?

   _____

6. About how many more people pass the corner from 8:00 A.M. to 9:00 A.M. than from 5:00 P.M. to 6:00 P.M.?

   _____

Use with pages 242–243.

PRACTICE Problem-Solving Practice

Solve.

7. Harrison Middle School is holding Student Council elections. The budget for campaign spending is $65.70, $7.00 less than last year. What was last year's campaign budget? _____

8. For this year's election, the students spent $18.48 on decorations, $14.81 on materials for signs, and $31.19 on campaign literature. How much of their $65.70 budget remains? _____

9. 410 of the school's 438 students voted for Student Council president. Irene received $\frac{3}{5}$ of the votes. How many students voted for Irene?

_____

10. Three students ran for Student Council treasurer. Of the 406 votes cast, Howard received 141 votes and Beth received 14 votes fewer than Howard. How many votes did Vincent receive? Who won the election?

_____

Use the double-bar graph to solve.

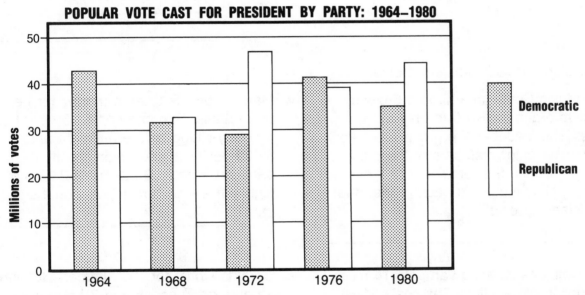

POPULAR VOTE CAST FOR PRESIDENT BY PARTY: 1964–1980

11. In which years did the Democratic-party candidate receive more votes than the Republican-party candidate?

_____

12. In which year was the margin of victory the greatest? _____

13. How many more people voted for the Republican candidate than for the Democratic candidate in 1968?

_____

14. How many more votes did the Republican-party candidate receive in 1980 than the Republican candidate received in 1976?

_____

PRACTICE Solving Multistep Problems/Making a Plan

Write the steps to complete each plan.

1. Plans are underway for the Jefferson High School senior prom. 75 couples will attend. The total cost will be $3,625. If the senior class has $850 in its treasury to help pay for the prom, how much will each couple have to pay?

Step 1: _____

_____

_____

Step 1: Find the cost per couple.

2. Mr. Kimmer, the caterer for the prom, purchased 60 pounds of roast beef, 52 pounds of potatoes, and 27 pounds of green beans for the main course. If he paid $2.46 per pound for roast beef, $0.21 per pound for potatoes, and $0.47 per pound for green beans, how much did he spend in all?

Step 1: Find the cost of the roast beef.

Step 2: _____

_____

Step 3: _____

_____

Step 4: _____

_____

Make a plan for each problem. Solve.

3. The Music Committee hired a 5-piece musical group for $780 to play at the prom. The leader of the group received $210. The other members of the group equally divided the remainder of the money. How much did each of the other musicians receive?

_____

4. Maria baby-sits to earn money for her prom dress. She charges $1.50 per hour for baby-sitting before midnight and $2.00 per hour after midnight. If she baby-sat from 7:00 P.M. until 2:00 A.M. 2 nights in a row, how much would she earn?

_____

5. Mr. Kimmer's catering van gets 14 miles per gallon of gasoline. Gas costs $1.38 per gallon. What does it cost Mr. Kimmer for gas if his van travels 266 miles one week and twice as many miles the next?

_____

6. Geraldo works for Mr. Kimmer. He works 5 hours on Tuesday and 7 hours a day Friday through Sunday. If he is paid $5.20 per hour, how much does he earn in a week?

_____

Use with pages 244–245.

Name _____ Date _____

PRACTICE   Customary Units of Length

Write the missing number.

1. 4 ft = _____ in.

2. 9 yd = _____ ft

3. 36 in. = _____ ft

4. 2 yd = _____ in.

5. 180 in. = _____ yd

6. $3\frac{1}{4}$ ft = _____ in.

7. 5,280 ft = _____ mi

8. $6\frac{1}{3}$ yd = _____ ft

9. 66 ft = _____ yd

10. 5 yd = _____ in.

11. 108 in. = _____ ft

12. 21,120 ft = _____ mi

13. 72 in. = _____ yd

14. 8 ft = _____ yd

15. $14\frac{1}{3}$ ft = _____ in.

Ring the most likely measure.

16. the length of a baseball bat   **a.** 12 in.   **b.** 1 yd   **c.** 108 in.

17. the height of a door   **a.** 1 yd   **b.** 40 in.   **c.** 7 ft

18. the width of a file cabinet   **a.** 1 yd   **b.** 5 ft   **c.** 16 in.

19. the length of a shoe   **a.** 10 in.   **b.** 0.25 in.   **c.** 2 ft

20. the length of a pencil   **a.** 2 in.   **b.** 20 in.   **c.** $\frac{1}{6}$ yd

Complete.

21.   6 ft 8 in.
      + 3 ft 9 in.

22.   4 yd 3 ft
      + 7 yd 8 ft

23.   5 yd 2 ft 9 in.
      − 4 yd 3 ft 6 in.

Solve.

24. Michelle had her yellow canary kite flying the full length of a 100-yd string. Andy gave her 400 ft more string. How high could she fly her kite with the additional string? _____

25. Paul is making orange fish kites. He bought rolls of crepe paper that are each 12 yd long to make the tails. If each tail is 28 in. long, how many tails can he make from one roll? _____

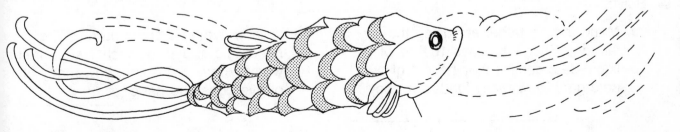

Use with pages 246–247.

PRACTICE Customary Units of Capacity and Weight

Ring the letter of the most likely measure.

1. a carton of milk   **a.** 32 pt   **b.** 32 fl oz   **c.** 32 qt

2. a can of peas   **a.** 3 lb   **b.** 12 oz   **c.** 2 oz

3. a bag of flour   **a.** 5 fl oz   **b.** 5 oz   **c.** 5 lb

Write the missing number.

4. 8 gal = _____ qt

5. 16 c = _____ gal

6. 4 qt = _____ gal

7. 20 fl oz = _____ c

8. 3 T = _____ lb

9. 7 lb = _____ oz

10. 4 pt = _____ fl oz

11. 3 qt = _____ pt

12. 21 pt = _____ gal

13. $1\frac{1}{4}$ T = _____ lb

14. 112 oz = _____ lb

15. 40 fl oz = _____ pt

16. 2 lb 3 oz = _____ oz

17. $1\frac{1}{2}$ gal = _____ fl oz

18. 120 c = _____ qt

19. $\frac{3}{4}$ qt = _____ c

20. 56 oz = _____ lb

21. 3,000 lb = _____ T

22. 5 gal = _____ pt

23. 9 pt = _____ qt

24. 36 c = _____ gal

25. 35 c = _____ pt

26. 68 oz = _____ lb

27. 14 c = _____ fl oz

28. 118 oz = _____ lb

Solve.

29. Mark and his father are doing the laundry. Each load uses 10 fl oz of liquid detergent. If they have 1 qt of detergent, how many loads can they do? _____

30. Julia is dyeing T-shirts purple. She needs 6 c of dye for each T-shirt. If she wants to dye 3 T-shirts, how many pints of dye does she need? _____

PRACTICE Time

Write the missing number.

1. 2 d = _____ h

2. 6 min = _____ s

3. 2 y = _____ d

4. 8 h = _____ d

5. 21 d = _____ wk

6. 90 s = _____ min

7. 480 min = _____ h

8. 5 wk = _____ d

9. 30 min = _____ h

10. 1 wk = _____ h

11. 60 mo = _____ y

12. 3 d = _____ h

13. $2\frac{1}{3}$ h = _____ min

14. 96 h = _____ d

15. $2\frac{1}{4}$ centuries = _____ y

16. 400 min = _____ h

17. 6 h = _____ d

18. 180 s = _____ min

Add or subtract.

19. 3 wk 5 d
    + 2 wk 4 d

20. 6 y 10 mo
    + 4 y 5 mo

21. 4 h 12 min
    − 1 h 30 min

22. 5 h 48 min
    + 2 h 22 min

23. 12 wk 4 d
    − 8 wk 5 d

24. 3 centuries 42 y
    − 1 century   18 y

25. 1 h 16 min 49 s
    + 3 h 50 min 20 s

26. 2 wk 3 d 12 h
    − 1 wk 5 d 9 h

27. 2 h 38 min 45 s
    + 6 h 29 min 45 s

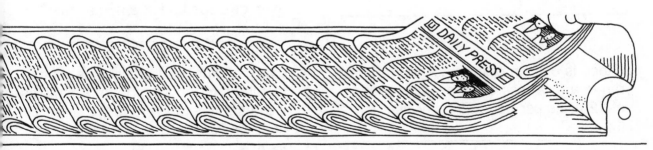

Solve.

28. Tom spends 40 minutes delivering the morning newspapers. He does this every day except Saturday. How many hours does he spend on his paper route each week? _____

29. It takes 40 minutes for Tom's distributor to get the papers from the publisher, and 50 minutes for the distributor to get them to Tom. How many hours does it take for the papers to get from the publisher to Tom? _____

Name _____ Date _____

PRACTICE Using a Formula (*d = rt*)

Which part of the formula *d = rt* will you solve for? Ring the letter of the correct answer.

1. The Stanton University football team traveled to its first game by bus. The bus averaged 50 miles per hour, and the trip took 4 hours. How far did the bus travel?

a. rate

b. time

c. distance

2. For a tournament in Chicago, the university basketball team traveled by plane. The plane flew 1,505 miles and averaged 430 miles per hour. How long did the flight take?

a. rate

b. time

c. distance

Solve for the unknown factor.

3. The gold team took a train to a match in a neighboring state. If the trip took 3 hours and the train averaged 43 miles per hour, find the distance the train traveled. _____

4. Neil Chessa is a member of the track team. He entered a 26-mile marathon and finished the race in 2.67 hours. What was his average speed for the race? _____

5. The soccer team traveled by ship to England for a summer tour. The ship left port at 7:00 A.M. on August 6 and arrived in England 22 hours later. Find the average speed of the ship. _____

6. Fay Welker plans to drive from her home to Newport College in Midville. She wants to leave at 9:45 A.M. and arrive in Midville $2\frac{1}{4}$ hours later. If Midville is 108 miles away, what average speed must she maintain? _____

7. Eileen is captain of the track team. She ran in a mile race at an average speed of 12 miles per hour. Find her time for the race. _____

8. Every afternoon at practice sessions, members of the swim team swim laps. If the swimmers average 3.5 miles per hour for 30 minutes, how far do they swim? _____

9. Carlos ran a mile in $7\frac{1}{2}$ minutes. Juan ran the same distance $\frac{3}{4}$ of a minute faster. How long did it take Juan to run the mile? _____

10. Brenda walked an average of 11.23 miles per day for $4\frac{1}{2}$ days. About how far did she walk in $3\frac{1}{2}$ days? _____

104

Use with pages 252–253.

PRACTICE Time Zones

Write the time zone for each city. Refer to the map on page 256 of your text.

1. Los Angeles _____   **2.** St. Louis _____   **3.** Santa Fe _____

4. Washington, D.C. _____   **5.** San Francisco _____   **6.** New York _____

7. Dallas _____   **8.** Boston _____   **9.** New Orleans _____

It is 9:00 A.M. in Denver. Write the time in each city.
Refer to the map on page 254 of your text.

10. New York _____   **11.** Atlanta _____   **12.** Los Angeles _____

13. Miami _____   **14.** Boston _____   **15.** Dallas _____

Pilot's Convention

Three pilots, Mary, Mark, and Tom, have to arrive in Chicago at 2:00 P.M. for a pilot's convention. Their flight plans are listed below.

Pilot	City of origin	First stop	Duration (first flight)	Layover	Duration (second flight)
Mary	Phoenix	Seattle	$2\frac{1}{2}$ h	1 h	3 h
Mark	Atlanta	Los Angeles	4 h	2 h	$3\frac{1}{2}$ h
Tom	New Orleans	Boston	3 h	$\frac{1}{2}$ h	2 h

16. What time should Mark leave Los Angeles to arrive in Chicago by 2:00 P.M.? _____

17. Tom leaves New Orleans at 9:00 A.M. Will he arrive on time? _____

18. When must Mary leave Phoenix to arrive in Chicago on time? _____

19. Mark leaves Atlanta at 6:00 A.M. He is delayed an extra hour in Los Angeles, making his layover 3 hours. Will he arrive on time? If not, when will he arrive? _____

PRACTICE Temperature

Ring the letter of the most likely temperature for each.

1. skiing   **a.** 40°F   **b.** 18°F   **c.** 75°F

2. playing volleyball   **a.** 75°F   **b.** 20°F   **c.** 124°F

3. ice cream   **a.** 40°F   **b.** ⁻10°F   **c.** 30°F

4. water in a bathtub   **a.** 212°F   **b.** 32°F   **c.** 100°F

5. hot cup of soup   **a.** 100°F   **b.** 200°F   **c.** 32°F

6. person with a fever   **a.** 98.6°F   **b.** 101°F   **c.** 200°F

Ring the letter of the best estimate.

7. day at the beach   **a.** 33°C   **b.** 80°C   **c.** 90°C

8. sledding   **a.** 30°C   **b.** 50°C   **c.** ⁻5°C

9. warm radiator   **a.** 9°C   **b.** 70°C   **c.** 19°C

10. playing softball   **a.** 6°C   **b.** 75°C   **c.** 22°C

11. ice cube   **a.** ⁻1°C   **b.** 5°C   **c.** 30°C

12. cup of hot tea   **a.** 85°C   **b.** 185°C   **c.** 45°C

Solve.

13. Water boils at 212°F. Methyl alcohol boils at 148°F. How much higher is water's boiling point? _____

14. Gold melts at 1,064.43°C. Iron melts at 1,535°C. How much lower is gold's melting point? _____

Use with pages 256–257.

Name _____ Date _____

Ring the more precise measurement.

1. 600 cm or 6 m

2. 95 cm or 950 mm

3. 6 ft or 2 yd

4. 380.0 g or 380 g

5. 2 ft or 24 in.

6. 180 min or 3 h

7. 3 lb or 48 oz

8. 16 km or 16.0 km

9. 5 m or 5.0 m

10. 1 cm or 10 mm

1. 4 pt or 2 qt

12. 1 wk or 168 h

3. 63.0°F or 63°F

14. 0.5 kg or 500 g

5. the temperature of an ice cube   a. 30.00°F   b. 30°F   c. 30.0°F

6. the length of a kitchen   a. 4.0 m   b. 4 m   c. 400 cm

7. the mass of an elephant   a. 1,202 kg   b. 1.2 T   c. 1.20 T

8. the capacity of a soup bowl   a. 0.3 L   b. 0.32 L   c. 320 mL

9. the weight of a watermelon   a. 20 lb   b. 320 oz   c. $20\frac{1}{2}$ lb

0. the length of a carpet   a. 5 yd   b. 180 in.   c. 15 ft

Solve.

1. Kathy measured the length of a piece of fabric. She said it was 1.4 m long. Her friend Jessica measured the fabric and said it was 142 cm long. Which measurement was more precise?

_____

22. Kathy measured the width of the fabric to be 1.1 m. The actual width may be between which two numbers?

_____

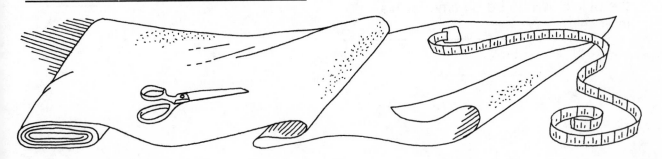

PRACTICE   Using a Schedule

Use the bus schedule to solve each problem. Write either *true* or *false*.

1. Ceva is a nurse at Valley Hospital in Ridgewood. If she takes the 6:34 A.M. bus from West Broadway and Katz Avenue in Paterson, she will arrive at Valley Hospital in Ridgewood at 7:11 A.M.

_____

2. Donald is a lab technician at the same hospital. It takes Donald 12 minutes to walk from the Ridgewood Bus Terminal to the hospital. If he boards the bus at Ratzer Road and Route 23 in Wayne at 2:29 P.M., he will arrive at the hospital at 3:45 P.M.

_____

POMPTON LAKES Bus Station	WAYNE Ratzer Rd. and Rt. 23	WAYNE Alps and Ratzer Rd.	WAYNE Valley Rd. and Hamburg Tpk.	PATERSON West Broadway and Katz Av.	PATERSON City Hall	PATERSON Madison and Third Aves.	GLEN ROCK Maple Av. and Rock Rd.	RIDGEWOOD Bus Terminal	RIDGEWOOD Valley Hospital
A.M.	A.M.	A.M.	A.M.	A.M.	A.M.	A.M.	A.M.	A.M.	A.M
W —	—	—	—	—	5:50	6:03	6:09	6:16	—
W —	—	—	—	—	6:15	6:28	6:34	6:41	—
W 6:10	—	—	6:21	6:34	6:45	6:58	7:04	7:11	7:1(
W 7:25	7:34	7:37	—	7:49	8:00	8:13	8:20	8:28	—
W 7:50	—	—	8:01	8:14	8:25	8:38	8:45	8:53	—
W 8:30	8:39	8:42	—	8:54	9:05	9:18	9:25	9:33	—
W —	—	—	—	9:24	9:35	9:48	9:55	10:03	—
W 9:20	9:29	9:35	9:42	9:54	10:05	10:18	10:25	10:33	—
P.M.	P.M.	P.M.	P.M.	P.M.	P.M.	P.M.	P.M.	P.M.	P.M.
W 1:20	1:29	1:35	1:42	1:54	2:05	2:18	2:25	2:33	—
W 2:20	2:29	2:35	2:42	2:54	3:05	3:18	3:25	3:33	—

Solve.

3. Leonard travels daily from Pompton Lakes to City Hall in Paterson. If he boards the bus at 7:25 A.M., how long does the trip take?

_____

4. Teresa lives in Pompton Lakes and works at the Manhattan Hospital Supply Company in Glen Rock. She wants to arrive in Glen Rock no later than 9:00 A.M. but no earlier than 8:30 A.M. What bus should she catch?

_____

5. At 9:24 A.M., Emil boards a bus at West Broadway and Katz Avenue in Paterson. He has a job interview at an office in Glen Rock at 10:15 A.M. It will take Emil 18 minutes to walk from the bus stop to the office. Will he be on time for his interview?

_____

6. Dorothy is going from Alps and Ratzer roads in Wayne to Madison and 3rd avenues in Paterson. How much longer would it take if she leaves at 9:35 A.M. rather than at 7:37 A.M.?

_____

Use with pages 260-261.

PRACTICE Ratio and Rate

Write each ratio as a fraction in simplest form.

1. 12 to 18 _____   **2.** 8:64 _____   **3.** $\frac{27}{54}$ _____

4. $\frac{24}{9}$ _____   **5.** 39 to 72 _____   **6.** 8:2 _____

7. 6 m to 10 m _____   **8.** 21 to 2 dozen _____   **9.** 45 s to 1 min _____

0. 40 cm to 2 m _____   **11.** 10 min to 1 h _____   **12.** 3 dimes:16 nickels _____

3. 5,200 copies in 13 minutes. _____   **14.** 420 km in 5 hours _____

Write each ratio as a fraction in simplest form. In a class of
9 students, there are 17 boys and 12 girls.

5. What is the ratio of boys to girls? _____

6. What is the ratio of boys to students? _____

7. What is the ratio of girls to boys? _____

8. What is the ratio of girls to students? _____

For each box, write the answer to the
corresponding problem above. Then check
each row across and down.

9. Do all the rows across and down have
the correct answer?

_____

0. Which box is wrong? What number
should appear in the box to make
it right?

_____

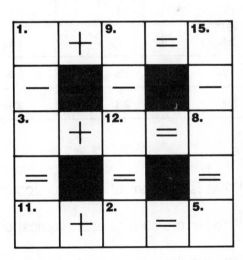

PRACTICE   Proportion

Are the ratios equal? Write *yes* or *no.* Use cross products to find the answer.

1. $\frac{3}{7}, \frac{12}{28}$ _____

2. $\frac{5}{2}, \frac{2}{5}$ _____

3. $\frac{13}{13}, \frac{17}{13}$ _____

4. $\frac{14}{10}, \frac{42}{30}$ _____

5. $\frac{7}{42}, \frac{1}{6}$ _____

6. $\frac{5}{9}, \frac{18}{10}$ _____

7. $\frac{8}{12}, \frac{2}{3}$ _____

8. $\frac{7}{6}, \frac{35}{30}$ _____

9. $\frac{15}{12}, \frac{24}{30}$ _____

Solve each proportion. Write the answer in the corresponding box below.

10. $\frac{x}{7} = \frac{9}{21}$

11. $\frac{142}{2} = \frac{x}{1}$

12. $\frac{4}{x} = \frac{16}{20}$

13. $\frac{19}{19} = \frac{2}{x}$

14. $\frac{x}{106} = \frac{1}{2}$

15. $\frac{33}{x} = \frac{6}{2}$

16. $\frac{5}{10} = \frac{x}{74}$

17. $\frac{60}{5} = \frac{1}{x}$

18. $\frac{x}{19} = \frac{34}{38}$

19. $\frac{39}{15} = \frac{x}{5}$

20. $\frac{40}{x} = \frac{120}{123}$

21. $\frac{2}{2} = \frac{31}{x}$

22. $\frac{3}{9} = \frac{x}{87}$

23. $\frac{5}{35} = \frac{1}{x}$

24. $\frac{6}{x} = \frac{24}{76}$

25. $\frac{x}{5} = \frac{94}{10}$

10.	11.	12.	13.
14.	15.	16.	17.
18.	19.	20.	21.
22.	23.	24.	25.

Solve.

26. What is the sum of each horizontal row? _____

27. What is the sum of each vertical column? _____

28. What is the sum of each diagonal? _____

29. Are the sums all the same? _____

Use with pages 272–273

Name _____ Date _____

Ring the letter of the correct proportion.

1. The architect who designed a large office complex used a blueprint scale of 1 in. = 20 ft. If a steel beam is 90 feet long, what length is shown on the blueprint?

   a. $\frac{1}{20} = \frac{90}{X}$ b. $\frac{1}{20} = \frac{X}{90}$ c. $\frac{20}{X} = \frac{1}{90}$

2. The general contractor for the construction work hired 2 supervisors for every 17 laborers. If the contractor hired 6 supervisors, how many laborers were hired?

   a. $\frac{2}{17} = \frac{X}{6}$ b. $\frac{2}{X} = \frac{17}{6}$ c. $\frac{2}{17} = \frac{6}{X}$

Use a proportion where appropriate to solve.

3. An electrician on the project was paid $56 for 4 hours of work. How much would the electrician receive for working a 36-hour week? _____

4. The ratio of men to women in the local chapter of the mason's union is 7 to 5. If there are 35 men in the union, how many women are there?

   _____

5. It takes 618 bricks to build 100 square feet of wall. A crew of masons on the project laid 2,163 bricks on Monday. How many square feet of wall did they build?

   _____

6. A gasoline generator provides the power to light the project at night. The generator uses 5 gallons of gasoline for every 3 hours of operation. How much gasoline is used in 10 hours?

   _____

7. Ruthann, a supervisor on the project, saves $2 of every $25 she earns. If Ruthann earns $1,750 per month, how much does she save? _____

8. A cement truck mixes 1 part cement with 4 parts sand. If 2.5 cubic yards of cement are used, how much sand is needed for the mixture?

   _____

9. A large crane used at the construction site has a 200-foot reel of cable. A 3-foot section of cable weighs 2 pounds. What is the weight of the cable on the reel?

   _____

10. Four bricks weigh 18 pounds. Stanley, a mason's helper, can push 243 pounds of brick in his wheelbarrow. How many bricks can he push in the wheelbarrow?

    _____

PRACTICE   Scale Drawings

Use the scale and drawing to answer each question.

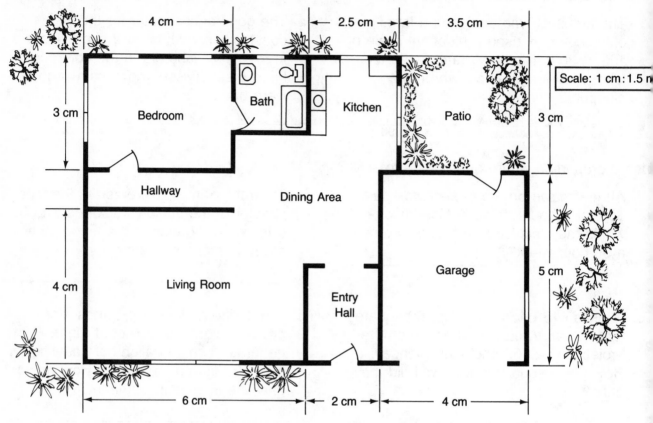

1. What is the actual length of the living room? _____

2. What is the actual width of the living room? _____

3. What is the actual width of the entry hall? _____

4. How long is the front of the house? _____

5. How wide is the kitchen? _____

6. How long is the side of the house? _____

7. How long is the hallway? _____

8. How long is the patio? _____

9. How wide is the patio? _____

10. How wide is the hallway? _____

11. How wide is the bath? _____

PRACTICE Percent

Write each fraction as a percent.

1. $\frac{55}{100}$ = _____

2. $\frac{42}{100}$ = _____

3. $\frac{33}{100}$ = _____

4. $\frac{5}{100}$ = _____

5. $\frac{64}{100}$ = _____

6. $\frac{12}{100}$ = _____

7. $\frac{26}{100}$ = _____

8. $\frac{18}{100}$ = _____

9. $\frac{79}{100}$ = _____

10. $\frac{88}{100}$ = _____

11. $\frac{10}{100}$ = _____

12. $\frac{20}{100}$ = _____

13. $\frac{6}{10}$ = _____

14. $\frac{8}{10}$ = _____

15. $\frac{2}{10}$ = _____

16. $\frac{3}{10}$ = _____

17. $\frac{25}{100}$ = _____

18. $\frac{17}{100}$ = _____

19. $\frac{9}{10}$ = _____

20. $\frac{5}{10}$ = _____

21. $\frac{8}{100}$ = _____

22. $\frac{7}{10}$ = _____

23. $\frac{75}{100}$ = _____

24. $\frac{82}{100}$ = _____

25. 40 poets of 100 writers _____

26. 38 guppies of 100 fish _____

27. 6 girls of 10 classmates _____

28. 4 comic books of 10 magazines _____

29. 55 cats of 100 pets _____

30. 2 sandals of 10 shoes _____

31. 67 oaks of 100 trees _____

32. 9 sculptors of 10 artists _____

Solve.

33. A company published 100 books last year, of which 9 were best-sellers. What percent were best-sellers? _____

34. Of the 100 books published last year, 100 were romance novels. What percent were romance novels? _____

35. Of the 10 mystery books published, 2 were best-sellers. What percent were best-sellers? _____

36. The publisher considered 10 manuscripts for publication and accepted 3. What percent were rejected? _____

PRACTICE Decimals and Percents

Write each as a decimal.

1. 82% = _____

2. 3% = _____

3. 35% = _____

4. 19.5% = _____

5. 33.3% = _____

6. 18.7% = _____

7. 10.14% = _____

8. 120% = _____

9. 17.25% = _____

10. 241% = _____

11. 355% = _____

12. 0.65% = _____

13. 21% = _____

14. 8.25% = _____

15. 9.5% = _____

16. 0.06% = _____

17. 7.3% = _____

18. 47.84% = _____

Write as a percent.

19. 0.55 = _____

20. 0.27 = _____

21. 0.99 = _____

22. 0.484 = _____

23. 0.466 = _____

24. 0.078 = _____

25. 3.47 = _____

26. 7.06 = _____

27. 0.0672 = _____

28. 1.8 = _____

29. 0.37 = _____

30. 0.0762 = _____

31. 0.76 = _____

32. 0.089 = _____

33. 1.065 = _____

34. 0.0501 = _____

35. 5.2 = _____

36. 0.73 = _____

37. 6.89 = _____

38. 43.3 = _____

39. 0.865 = _____

Use with pages 280–281

PRACTICE   Fractions and Percents

Write each percent as a fraction or as a mixed number. The
answer must be in simplest form.

1. 85% = _____

2. $12\frac{1}{2}\%$ = _____

3. 150% = _____

4. 4% = _____

5. 13% = _____

6. 34% = _____

7. 90% = _____

8. 40% = _____

9. $83\frac{1}{3}\%$ = _____

10. $266\frac{2}{3}\%$ = _____

11. 12% = _____

12. 128% = _____

3. $6\frac{1}{4}\%$ = _____

14. 35% = _____

15. 79% = _____

16. 48% = _____

Write each fraction as a percent.

7. $\frac{1}{4}$ = _____

18. $\frac{5}{12}$ = _____

19. $\frac{9}{50}$ = _____

20. $\frac{7}{8}$ = _____

1. $1\frac{1}{3}$ = _____

22. $\frac{17}{2}$ = _____

23. $\frac{7}{16}$ = _____

24. $\frac{19}{10}$ = _____

5. $\frac{15}{16}$ = _____

26. $\frac{4}{25}$ = _____

27. $\frac{25}{25}$ = _____

28. $\frac{48}{50}$ = _____

Write each percent in the corresponding triangle as a fraction
in simplest form. Then begin at the top, and trace a path
through the fractions whose sum, when they are added
together, is 1.

a. 50%

b. $33\frac{1}{3}\%$

c. 20%

d. 10%

e. $41\frac{2}{3}\%$

f. $12\frac{1}{2}\%$

g. $11\frac{1}{9}\%$

h. $13\frac{1}{3}\%$

i. $6\frac{2}{3}\%$

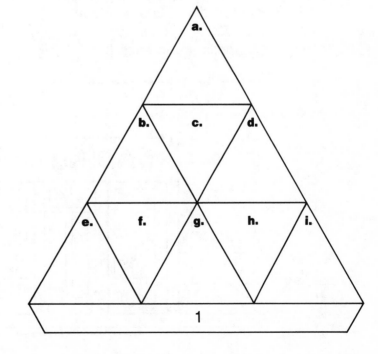

Name _____ Date _____

Write the percent of the number.

1. 45% of 60 _____

2. 50% of 38 _____

3. 4% of 50 _____

4. 5.5% of 600 _____

5. 20% of 115 _____

6. 7.4% of 6 _____

7. 23% of 50 _____

8. 30% of 100 _____

9. 80% of 525 _____

10. 150% of 71 _____

11. 98% of 80 _____

12. 2% of 43 _____

13. $33\frac{1}{3}$% of 600 _____

14. $37\frac{1}{2}$% of 64 _____

15. 90% of $300 _____

16. 11% of $116 _____

17. 56% of 90 _____

18. 2% of 65 _____

19. 42.2% of 3,000 _____

20. 45% of $45 _____

21. 28% of $160 _____

Solve.

22. On a certain day, the sales in Kadir's Health Food Store amounted to 185 items. Of those items, 20% were health-food drinks. How many health-food drinks were sold? _____

23. Gabriel sells 50 pounds of fruit to Kadir's each day. Of that, 30% is bananas. How many pounds of bananas does Gabriel sell to the store each day? _____

24. Kadir's carries small boxes of sunflower seeds. There are about 200 seeds in each box, but 7% are just shells. How many empty shells are in each box? _____

25. Kadir's stocks 42 large bags of raisins. Only $16\frac{2}{3}$% of this inventory is sold in a month. How many bags of the raisins are sold? _____

PRACTICE | Computing with Commission Using Percent

olve.

1. Mr. Hamilton's career education class is doing research on the different ways in which people earn income. Dominic, Olga, Patrick, and Juana are on the committee researching commission income. They will interview salespersons who earn some or all their money by commission. Dominic's brother, for example, works in an appliance store. He receives a 13% commission on all his sales. One week his sales totaled $2,435. What was his commission that week? _____

2. Olga's neighbor, Ruth, is the sales manager at Auto World. Ruth receives a salary of $150 per week plus a 5% commission on each sale. Last week she sold a car for $9,180 and a minivan for $13,495. How much did Ruth earn for the week? _____

3. Juana's Aunt Monica sells encyclopedias part-time. Each 26-volume set costs $419. Monica receives a 14% commission on each set she sells. Last year she sold 28 sets. What were her earnings for the year? _____

4. Patrick's father sells new cars. He is paid a 5% commission on each sale. During the first week of August, he sold one car for $8,273 and another car for $11,570. Find his earnings for the week. _____

5. Olga's father sells medical supplies. He is paid a salary of $65 per week, and also earns a 10% commission on sales. Last week, Olga's father sold $2,731 worth of medical supplies. How much more did he earn in commissions than in salary for the week? _____

6. Juana's neighbor, George Hascup, sells copying machines and supplies. George's commission is 16% of sales. His sales for this week were: Monday, $825.95; Tuesday, $430.25; Wednesday, $58.70; Thursday, $1,475.60; Friday, $208.35. What were his earnings for the week? _____

7. Patrick's neighbor, Jacob Cohen, works at the Center Furniture Mart. He receives an 11% commission on all the furniture he sells. Recently, Jacob sold a dining room set for $1,990, a sofa for $650, a bedroom set for $1,495, and a coffee table for $251. How much commission did he earn on the dining room set? _____

8. Dominic's older brother, Ernest, is selling magazine subscriptions in the neighborhood to earn money for a new bicycle. The magazine company pays Ernest a 25% commission. Ernest sold 3 $6 subscriptions, 5 $8 subscriptions, and 2 $11 subscriptions. How much money did he earn in commissions? _____

PRACTICE Computing with Commission Using Percent

Read the paragraph, and answer the questions below. Make a plan when you need to.

Agencies that sell real estate receive a commission on each property they sell. When an agency represents or "lists" a house, that agency is called the *listing agency.* The agency that sells the house is the *selling agent.* When one agency acts as both listing and selling agent, that agency receives the entire sales commission. Where there are two agencies involved, the listing agent receives 40% of the commission and the selling agent receives 60%. In all transactions, the salesperson who makes the actual sale receives half the commissions, and the agency he or she works for gets the other half. The commission on all sales is 6% of the selling price.

9. You are a salesperson for the Marshall Real Estate Agency. You've just sold a house for which Marshall was the listing agent. The selling price was $87,000. What will your commission be? _____

10. Your friend Donna is a salesperson who works for Crossroads Realty. Last week she sold a house that was listed by the Marshall Real Estate Agency. What was Donna's commission if the house sold for $71,500?

_____

11. You received a commission of $3,000 for selling a house listed by your agency. Find the selling price of the house.

_____

12. Crossroads Realty is the listing agent for a new complex of town houses. If you sell one of these town houses for $104,600, how much commission will Crossroads Realty receive? _____

13. Your agency listed a house, but Donna sold it. If the selling price was $41,300, find Donna's commission.

_____

14. You sold a house that Donna's agency had listed. What percentage of the commission did you receive?

_____

PRACTICE   Finding the Percent

ing the letter of the correct answer.

1. What percent of 20 is 18?

   a. 111% **b.** 9% **c.** 0.9% **d.** 90%

2. 90 is what percent of 360?

   a. 400% **b.** 4% **c.** 25% **d.** 2.5%

3. What percent of 35 is 70?

   a. 200% **b.** 50% **c.** 20% **d.** 5%

4. 8 is what percent of 80?

   a. 1,000% **b.** 10% **c.** 1% **d.** 0.1%

Write the percent.

5. What percent of 300 is 60? _____

6. 45 is what percent of 90? _____

7. 16 is what percent of 4? _____

8. What percent of 240 is 90? _____

9. 25 is what percent of 75? _____

10. 3 is what percent of 600? _____

11. What percent of 144 is 18? _____

12. What percent of 5 is 15? _____

13. 26 is what percent of 208? _____

14. 6 is what percent of 72? _____

15. What percent of 8 is 10? _____

16. What percent of 320 is 80? _____

17. What percent of 500 is 3? _____

18. 20 is what percent of 150? _____

19. 38 is what percent of 19? _____

20. What percent of 100 is 19? _____

21. What percent of 18 is 60? _____

22. 9 is what percent of 630? _____

23. 11 is what percent of 25? _____

24. What percent of 27 is 36? _____

Solve.

25. Heather counts the fruit on one orange tree to give herself an idea of how much fruit is ready to be picked from the orchard. The tree she counts has 208 oranges on it, of which 52 are ripe. What percent of the oranges are ripe? About how many oranges are ripe on Heather's 1,000 trees?

_____

26. Heather's shipping boxes contain 64 pieces of fruit each. Usually, 8 pieces of fruit in each box are bruised during transport. What percent of the fruit in each box is bruised?

_____

PRACTICE   Finding the Total Number

Ring the letter of the correct answer.

1. 45 is 20% of what number?

    a. 450   b. 225   c. 900   d. 90

2. 150 is 50% of what number?

    a. 300   b. 250   c. 450   d. 75

3. $66\frac{2}{3}$% of what number is 42?

    a. 66   b. 63   c. 84   d. 126

4. 75% of what number is 84?

    a. 140   b. 168   c. 42   d. 112

Write the number.

5. 10% of what number is 66? _____

6. 60 is 60% of what number? _____

7. 90% of what number is 54? _____

8. 25% of what number is 13? _____

9. $12\frac{1}{2}$% of what number is 35? _____

10. $33\frac{1}{3}$% of what number is 35? _____

11. $87\frac{1}{2}$% of what number is 49? _____

12. 110 is 55% of what number? _____

13. 3% of what number is 9? _____

14. 20% of what number is 0.1? _____

15. 1.7 is 50% of what number? _____

16. 5% of what number is 12? _____

17. 20 is $62\frac{1}{2}$% of what number? _____

18. 40% of what number is 24? _____

19. 45 is 150% of what number? _____

20. $33\frac{1}{3}$% of what number is 7.82? _____

21. 900% of what number is 3.24? _____

22. 1 is 2% of what number? _____

23. $20\frac{1}{4}$ is 15% of what number? _____

24. 75% of what number is 42? _____

Solve.

25. Bill "Irontoe" Nelson, the placekicker, was the school football team's star player. Last season, he kicked 32 field goals in 10 games and led his team to second place in their division. If his rate of success at scoring field goals was 80%, how many field goals did he attempt last season?

    _____

26. Unfortunately, the school's quarterback Tommy "Wobbly-Arm" Jones, wasn't as skillful as "Irontoe" Nelson. In the 10 games last year, he only completed 6 passes. His 8% rate of pass completion was the worst in the state. How many passes did Jones attempt last season?

    _____

PRACTICE Using a Formula ($i = prt$)

Write the letter of the correct interest formula.

1. Hector wants to borrow $2,000 to buy a motorcycle. The bank will lend him the money at 14% interest for 2 years. How much will he pay in interest?

   a. $p = i \div rt$ b. $r = i \div pt$

   c. $i = prt$ d. $t = i \div pr$

2. Linda borrowed $5,500 to purchase a bright red convertible. She paid $2,475 in interest during the 3 years it took to repay the loan. What rate of interest did Linda pay?

   a. $p = i \div rt$ b. $r = i \div pt$

   c. $i = prt$ d. $t = i \div pr$

Use the correct form of the interest formula to solve.

3. Aaron borrowed $425 from a finance company to buy a moped. The interest rate was 13%, and the loan was for one year. How much interest did he pay?

   _____

4. Margo borrowed $14,000 to buy a sports car. She repaid $21,840. If she paid 14% interest, for how long had she borrowed the money?

   _____

5. Mr. Macones paid $3,219 in interest over 3 years on a loan he took out to buy a new van. The loan rate was 14.5%. How much money did he borrow?

   _____

6. Walter made a down payment of $3,500 on a station wagon that cost $11,480. He borrowed the rest at an annual interest rate of 14% for 4 years. How much interest will he have to pay?

   _____

7. Russell borrowed $4,400 to restore a 1932 Model T Ford. He repaid $6,160 in $2\frac{1}{2}$ years. What rate of interest did he pay?

   _____

8. In order to repair the transmission on his car, Calvin borrowed $440 at $17\frac{1}{4}$% interest for 18 months. How much interest will he have to pay?

   _____

9. Virginia plans to buy a used pickup truck for $3,785. She will pay 20% down and borrow the rest at a rate of 15.5%. She will owe $1,642.69 in interest. How long does Virginia have to repay the loan?

   _____

10. A car dealer is offering loans at a special low interest rate of 7.7% for any new car purchase. Jean borrows $7,400 at this special rate for 4 years. If she had borrowed the same amount from a local bank, the interest rate would have been 14.5%. How much money did Jean save by borrowing from the dealer?

   _____

PRACTICE Percent Using Proportions

Use a proportion to solve each problem.

1. What is 45% of 150? _____

2. 12 is what percent of 240? _____

3. 14 is 35% of what number? _____

4. 60% of what number is 27? _____

5. What percent of 88 is 22? _____

6. 40% of 115 is what number? _____

7. 13 is 20% of what number? _____

8. 4% of what number is 22? _____

9. What percent of 30 is 9? _____

10. Find 15% of 60. _____

11. 22 is what percent of 55? _____

12. 21 is 7% of what number? _____

13. 12% of 50 is what number? _____

14. 3% of what number is 15? _____

Solve.

15. Larry, Harry, Barry, and Beatrice are members of the
Westville All-Star baseball team. Larry has a total of 8
hits after 32 times at bat. Harry has 9 hits after 36 times
at bat. Barry has 13 hits after 26 times at bat. Beatrice
has 13 hits after 25 times at bat. What is the batting
average in percent of each player?

Larry _____

Harry _____

Barry _____

Beatrice _____

16. Which player has the best batting percent? _____

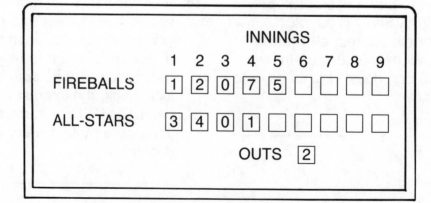

PRACTICE   Percent Increase and Decrease

ing the correct percent of increase or decrease.

1. Original value: 40
Increase: 5

   a. 80%   **b.** 8%

   c. 12.5%   **d.** 25%

2. Original value: 536
Decrease: 96

   a. 20%   **b.** 17.9%

   c. 36%   **d.** 8%

3. Original price: $76
New price: $114

   a. 25%   **b.** 15%

   c. 32%   **d.** 50%

4. Original price: $25
New price: $20

   a. 25%   **b.** 20%

   c. 80%   **d.** 10%

Write the percent of increase or decrease.

5. _____
Original value: 45
Increase: 4.5

6. _____
Original value: 72
Decrease: 8

7. _____
Original value: 300
Increase: 50

8. _____
Original value: 25
New value: 45

9. _____
Original price: $2.50
New price: $3.00

10. _____
Original value: 68
Increase: 17

1. _____
Original price: $85.00
Increase: $15.00

12. _____
Original price: $120
New price: $80

13. _____
Original price: $80
New price: $120

14. _____
Original value: 1,000
New value: 1,325

15. _____
Original value: 400
Decrease: 80

16. _____
Original value: 250
New value: 300

17. _____
Original value: 6,000
Decrease: 250

18. _____
Original price: $19.00
New price: $25.00

19. _____
Original value: 200
New value: 175

20. _____
Original price: $20
New price: $35

21. _____
Original value: 1,600
New value: 1,000

22. _____
Original value: 9,000
New value: 10,000

Name_____ Date_____

Use the circle graph to answer the questions. Ring the letter of the correct answer.

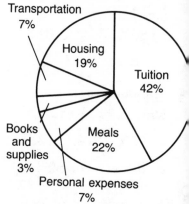

VALERIE CHEN'S YEARLY COLLEGE COSTS

Transportation 7%

Housing 19%

Tuition 42%

Books and supplies 3%

Meals 22%

Personal expenses 7%

Total costs: $9,730 per year

1. On which category of items did Valerie spend the least amount of money?

a. Personal expenses

b. Tuition

c. Transportation

d. Books and supplies

2. The combined costs of Housing and Meals is about equal to the cost of which other item?

a. Tuition

b. Transportation

c. Personal expenses

d. Books and supplies

Solve.

4. How much did Valerie spend on meals for the year?

_____

5. Did Valerie spend more on books or on supplies?

_____

_____

6. How much did Valerie spend on transportation for the year? _____

7. Did Valerie pay more for books, supplies, and meals combined than she paid for housing and personal expenses combined? _____

8. If college costs remain the same, how much can Valerie expect to spend on housing for 4 years? _____

9. How much more money did Valerie pay for Tuition than for Housing and Meals combined? _____

ame _____ Date _____

Name the figure.

1.

2.

3.

4.

_____   _____   _____   _____

Write the notation for the figure.

5.

•Z

6.

S

T

7. D•

C•

8.

M

L   N

_____   _____   _____   _____

Draw the figure and write its name.

9. $\overrightarrow{UV}$

10. point R

11. $\overleftrightarrow{GH}$

_____   _____   _____

Point J is on line segment PQ.

12. Name all the line segments in the figure.

_____

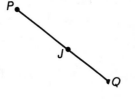

P•

J

•Q

13. How many line segments have J as an endpoint? _____

Refer to the figure at the right.

14. Name a point not on $\overleftrightarrow{MP}$. _____

15. Name two angles. _____

16. Name a ray with endpoint N. _____

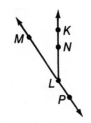

M   K
     N

L
P

Refer to the figure at the right. Write *true* or *false*.

17. $\overleftrightarrow{CD}$ and $\overleftrightarrow{XZ}$ are skew lines. _____

18. $\overleftrightarrow{PR}$ and $\overleftrightarrow{WY}$ are skew lines. _____

19. $\overleftrightarrow{PR}$ and $\overleftrightarrow{SU}$ are skew lines. _____

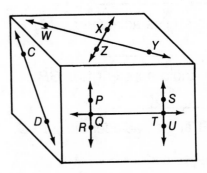

W   X

C   Z   Y

P   S

D   Q   T U
  R

Name _____ Date _____

Find the measure of each angle. Write *acute, right, obtuse,*
or *straight* for each angle.

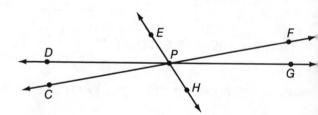

1. ∠RYS _____ ; _____

2. ∠QYR _____ ; _____

3. ∠PYT _____ ; _____

4. ∠RYT _____ ; _____

5. ∠QYT _____ ; _____

6. ∠QYS _____ ; _____

Draw an angle for each measure. Identify each angle as
acute, right, obtuse, or *straight.*

7. 142° _____

8. 180° _____

9. 38° _____

Write the measure of the angle that is complementary to the
angle whose measure is given.

10. 80° _____

11. 11° _____

12. 39° _____

13. 65° _____

14. 23° _____

15. 43° _____

16. 17° _____

17. 86° _____

Write the measure of the angle that is supplementary to the
angle whose measure is given.

18. 165° _____

19. 32° _____

20. 101° _____

21. 94° _____

22. 7° _____

23. 156° _____

24. 170° _____

25. 51° _____

Refer to the figure at the right. Name

26. two angles adjacent to ∠GPH.

_____

27. two angles adjacent to ∠EPF.

_____

28. an angle adjacent to ∠GPE.

_____

29. two angles adjacent to ∠CPH.

_____

30. two angles adjacent to ∠EPD.

_____

31. two angles adjacent to ∠GPF.

_____

Use with pages 312–313

ame _____ Date _____

PRACTICE Constructing Segments and Angles

Determine which pairs of line segments or angles are
congruent. Write *congruent* or *not congruent* for each.

1.

2.

3.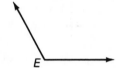

_____ _____ _____

Construct a figure congruent to each figure.

4.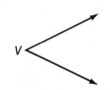

5.

6.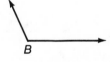

7.

8. Construct an angle congruent to the supplement of ∠*B*.

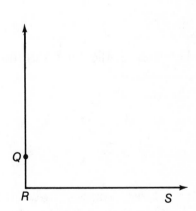

9. Angle *QRS* is a right angle. Follow these steps to
construct a square in which each of its four sides has the
same length as $\overline{RS}$.

a. Construct a line segment, $\overline{RT}$, on $\overrightarrow{RQ}$ that is congruent to
$\overline{RS}$.

b. Find point *U* so that $\overline{TU}$ and $\overline{SU}$ are congruent to $\overline{RS}$.

PRACTICE   Bisecting Segments and Angles

Complete.

1.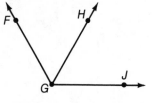

$\overrightarrow{GH}$ bisects $\angle FGJ$

$\angle FGH \cong$ _____

2.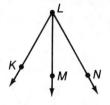

$\overrightarrow{LM}$ bisects $\angle KLN$.

$\angle MLN \cong$ _____

3.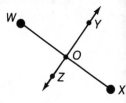

$\overleftrightarrow{YZ}$ bisects $\overline{WX}$.

$\overline{WO} \cong$ _____

Construct the bisector of each figure.

4.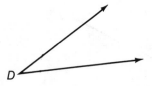

5.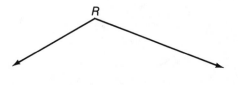

6.

7.

Draw a line segment for each length. Construct its bisector.

8. 5 cm

9. 6 cm

Draw an angle for each measure. Construct its bisector.

10. 90°

11. 64°

12. Carl Compass drew an angle with measure 60° and bisected it. Then he bisected one of the two angles in his construction. He said, "Now I have three angles. Each must have measure 20° because 3 × 20 = 60." Is Carl correct?

Use with pages 316–317.

PRACTICE Making a Table to Find a Pattern

Solve. Make a table if needed.

1. A parcel delivery service charges $2.50 to deliver packages that weigh up to 2 lb. The delivery charge for packages weighing over 2 lb, but less than $3\frac{1}{2}$ lb, is $2.95. For packages weighing over $3\frac{1}{2}$ lb, but less than 5 lb, the fee is $3.40, and so on. Rosanna uses the service to send a package and is charged $4.75. What is the range of the weight of her package?

_____

2. If Rosanna had sent a package that weighed $11\frac{1}{2}$ lb, what would she have been charged?

_____

3. Suppose Rosanna had sent 2 packages separately, each weighing $3\frac{3}{4}$ lb. What would the delivery fee have been?

_____

4. Tim has an after-school delivery service that he provides for several small retailers in town. He uses his bicycle and charges $1.25 for a delivery made within $1\frac{1}{2}$ mi, $1.70 for a delivery of at least $1\frac{1}{2}$ mi but less than $1\frac{3}{4}$ mi, $2.15 for a delivery of at least $1\frac{3}{4}$ mi but less than 2 miles, and so on. How much would Tim charge to make a delivery $2\frac{5}{8}$ mi away?

_____

5. A store owner had Tim deliver 3 packages. The first went to a customer $3\frac{7}{8}$ mi away. The second went to a customer $2\frac{1}{4}$ mi away. The third package was delivered just around the corner. How much money did Tim receive?

_____

6. If Tim raised his rates by 10%, what would he be paid to deliver a package $3\frac{1}{8}$ miles?

_____

PRACTICE   Making a Table to Find a Pattern

Complete the table in order to solve.

7. Mrs. Hawks and Mr. Green teach 6 cooking classes of
   12 students each. They have decided to hold a holiday
   open house before winter vacation. In order to advertise
   the open house, they ask the students in each cooking
   class to tell 2 classmates apiece next period. Each
   student told is then to pass the word to 2 more students
   in the next class period, and so on. How many students
   will know about the open house by the end of the sixth
   period? _____

PERIOD	1	2	3	4	5	6
Students in cooking class	12	12	12			
Students told	—	24	48			
Total number of students who know	12	48	108			

8. How many more students will know about the open
   house at the end of sixth period than at the end of fourth
   period? _____

9. If there were 14 students in each cooking class, instead
   of 12, by the end of what period would 200 students
   know about the open house? _____

10. Mrs. Hawks receives a recipe chain letter in the mail.
    The letter lists the names and addresses of 5 people.
    Mrs. Hawks is to send her favorite recipe to the person
    at the top of the list, cross out that person's name, and
    add her name to the bottom of the list. Then she is to
    send one copy of the chain letter to 5 of her friends in a
    week. If everyone who receives a copy of the chain letter
    follows these instructions, how many lists will Mrs.
    Hawks's name appear on at the end of the third week?

    _____

11. If no one breaks the chain, at the end of which week will
    Mrs. Hawks's name appear on over 600 lists?

    _____

Use with pages 318–319.

PRACTICE Perpendicular and Parallel Lines

Identify each pair of lines as *perpendicular, parallel,* or *neither.*

1.

2.

3.
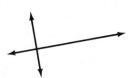

4.

_____   _____   _____   _____

Draw each figure.

5. $\overleftrightarrow{RS} \perp \overline{GH}$

6. $\overline{JK} \perp \overleftrightarrow{KL}$

7. $\overline{ST} \parallel \overrightarrow{AB}$

8. $\overleftrightarrow{DE} \parallel \overleftrightarrow{GH}$ with transversal *m*

9. $\overleftrightarrow{XY}$ intersecting $\overleftrightarrow{PQ}$ at *Z*

Identify each pair of angles as *vertical angles, corresponding angles,* or *supplementary angles.*

10. ∠3 and ∠5 _____

11. ∠7 and ∠ 6 _____

12. ∠8 and ∠5 _____

13. ∠6 and ∠1 _____

14. ∠5 and ∠2 _____

15. ∠1 and ∠8 _____

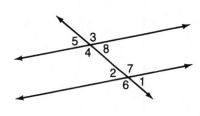

Name _____ Date _____

1. Construct a line that is parallel to line *p* and passes through point *M*.

    • *M*

2. Construct a line perpendicular to $\overline{DE}$.

D •————————————————• *E*

3. Construct a line perpendicular to line *n* at point *G*.

n ←———————•———————→
          G

4. Construct a line parallel to line *r*.

                  r

5. Construct a line that is parallel to line *b* and passes through point *G*.

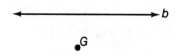
←————————————→ *b*
      •*G*

6. Construct a line parallel to $\overline{MN}$.

M •
       •
    N •

7. Construct $\overrightarrow{MK}$ perpendicular to $\overleftrightarrow{MN}$. Then construct $\overrightarrow{KL}$ perpendicular to $\overrightarrow{MK}$. Make $\overrightarrow{KL}$ congruent to $\overleftrightarrow{MN}$. Draw the transversal $\overleftrightarrow{LN}$. When you have completed the construction, use a protractor to measure ∠*MNL*. It should be a right angle.

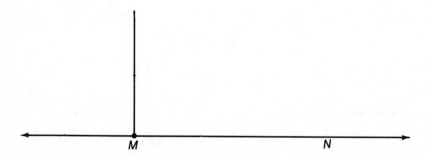

PRACTICE   Problem-Solving Practice

Use the circle graph to solve.

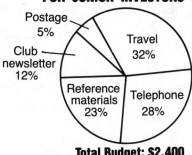

**ANNUAL EXPENSE BUDGET
FOR JUNIOR INVESTORS CLUB**

Postage 5%
Club newsletter 12%
Travel 32%
Reference materials 23%
Telephone 28%

Total Budget: $2,400

1. Which category of expenses represents the greatest percentage of the Junior Investors Club's budget?

   _____

2. How many dollars are budgeted to cover the cost of reference materials? _____

3. How much more money is budgeted for telephone expenses than for the club newsletter? _____

4. On the average, how much does the club budget for postage per month? ____

Use the formula $d = rt$ to solve.

5. Alice, the president of the Junior Investors Club, has to drive 80 miles per month on club business. If she travels at an average speed of 35 miles per hour, about how many hours does Alice spend driving?

   _____

6. On Sunday, Alice left home at 10:15 A.M. and arrived at the library at 11:00 A.M. If the distance she traveled was 29 miles, what was Alice's average speed? _____

Use the formula $i = prt$ to solve.

7. The Junior Investors Club lends money to its members at an interest rate of 1% per month. Tom borrowed $200 to be repaid in 3 months. How much interest will he pay? _____

8. Judy, another club member, plans to borrow a sum of money for 1 year. The treasurer has told Judy that she will owe $21 in interest. How much does Judy plan to borrow? _____

PRACTICE Problem-Solving Practice

Write a proportion, and then solve.

9. A manufacturing company owns two factories. Its Houston factory employs 1,320 workers and 40 supervisors. Its Denver factory operates with a worker-to-supervisor ratio in proportion to that of the Houston factory. If the Denver factory has 17 supervisors, how many workers does it employ? _____

10. Company supervisors negotiated a salary increase. Supervisor making $33,000 this year will earn $36,500 next year. Suppose the workers were to receive an increase in proportion to that of the supervisors. If a worker currently earns $5.26 per hour, how much would the worker make next year? _____

Cross out the facts that won't help you answer the question. Then solve.

11. John D. Rockefeller, who was born in 1839, was once the world's richest man. He made his fortune in the oil business, which he entered at the age of 23. He died in 1937. In what year did Rockefeller enter the oil business?

_____

12. Born in Scotland in 1835, Andrew Carnegie made his fortune in the steel business. In 1900, he founded part of what is today known as Carnegie-Mellon University. He sold his steel firm to the United States Steel Corporation in 1901. How old was he at the time of the sale? _____

Solve.

13. Mr. and Mrs. Olson own a hardware store. In 1983, their business grossed $228,000. In 1985, the Olsons grossed $241,000. By what percent did their business increase from 1983 to 1985?

_____

14. The Olsons have built a two-room addition to their house and want to wallpaper both rooms. The first room has 384 feet of wall to paper. The second room has $\frac{2}{5}$ more wall to cover than the first. About how many feet of wallpaper will the Olsons need?

_____

15. This year, the Olsons plan to raise the price of a pint of wood stain by 5% over last year's price of $2.80. If the price were to increase by 5% next year, what would next year's price be? _____

16. At the Olson's store, three 12-in. spikes sell for $1.35. If a customer had exactly $20, could he buy 45 spikes? _____

Name _____ Date _____

PRACTICE Triangles

Name each triangle according to the measures of its angles.

1.

_____

2.

_____

3.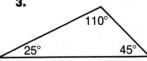

_____

4. 50°, 70°, 60°

_____

5. 100°, 70°, 10°

_____

6. 20°, 20°, 140°

_____

7. 15°, 90°, 75°

_____

8. 79°, 60°, 41°

_____

9. 16°, 82°, 82°

_____

Name each triangle according to the lengths of its sides.

10.

_____

11.

_____

12.

_____

13. 3 km, 7 km, 5 km

_____

14. 18 m, 20 m, 14 m

_____

15. 10 cm, 10 cm, 10 cm

_____

16. 11 cm, 15 cm, 11 cm

_____

17. 82 mm, 21 mm, 82 mm

_____

18. 5 m, 8 m, 10 m

_____

Find the measure of the missing angle in each triangle.

19.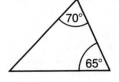

_____

20.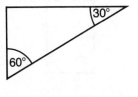

_____

21.

_____

22. 46°, 19°, _____

23. 103°, 20°, _____

24. 25°, 25°, _____

25. 32°, 100°, _____

26. 80°, 70°, _____

27. 41°, 57°, _____

PRACTICE   Polygons

Name each polygon.

1.

_____

2.

_____

3.

_____

4.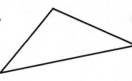

_____

5.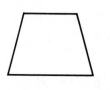

_____

6.

_____

7.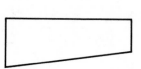

_____

8.

_____

9. Which figure in Exercises 1–8 is a regular polygon? _____

Write the letter or letters of the figures described.

10. trapezoid   _____

11. regular polygon _____

12. parallelogram   _____

13. rectangle   _____

14. quadrilateral   _____

15. rhombus   _____

Find the measure of the missing angle in each quadrilateral.

16.

71°
109° 71°

_____

17.

_____

18.

95°   116°
89°

_____

Name _____ Date _____

List each pair of polygons that appear to be congruent.

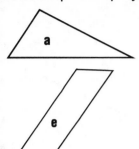
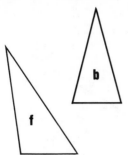
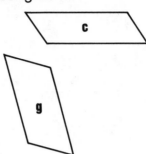
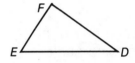

1. _____

△ABC ≅ △DEF. Complete the following.

2. $\overline{BC}$ ≅ _____   **3.** ∠BAC ≅ _____

4. $\overline{DE}$ ≅ _____   **5.** ∠FDE ≅ _____

6. $\overline{AB}$ ≅ _____   **7.** ∠DFE ≅ _____

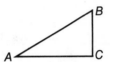

Quadrilateral MNOP ≅ Quadrilateral WXYZ.

8. List four pairs of congruent sides.

_____

9. List four pairs of congruent angles.

_____

△RST ≅ △FGH. Find the measure of each.

10. $\overline{RT}$ _____   **11.** $\overline{FG}$ _____

12. ∠RST _____   **13.** ∠HFG _____

14. $\overline{GH}$ _____   **15.** ∠GHF _____

△ABC has angles with measures of 72°, 54°, and 54°.

16. How many triangles congruent to △ABC are needed to form a regular polygon? _____

17. What polygon is formed? _____

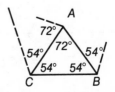

PRACTICE   Similar Polygons

Is each pair of polygons similar? Write *yes* or *no*.

1. _____

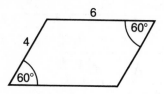

2. _____

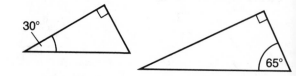

3. _____

4. _____

Each pair of polygons is similar. Find each missing length or missing angle.

5. *a* = _____

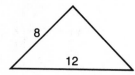

6. *a* = _____

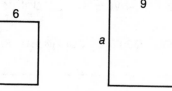

7. *a* = _____

 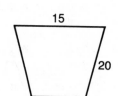

8. *a* = _____

9.

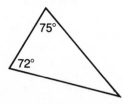

∠*p* = _____; ∠*q* = _____; ∠*r* = _____

10.

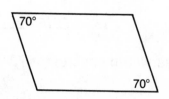

∠*m* = _____; ∠*n* = _____

Use with pages 332–333.

Name _____ Date _____

Work backward. Then choose the correct solution.

1. Yukiko, Mario, Tom, and Lisa have organized a computer club in their community. Yukiko recruited $\frac{1}{2}$ of the members, Mario recruited $\frac{1}{3}$ of the rest of the members, Tom brought in 4 members, and Lisa brought in 2 members. How many members besides the four organizers are there in the computer club?

a. 36   b. 18   c. 24

2. Warren, a member of the club, earned money to buy some new hardware for his home-computer system. He spent $\frac{3}{5}$ of his earnings on disk drives, $\frac{2}{3}$ of the rest of the money on a modem, and the remaining $80 on a "mouse." How much did Warren earn?

a. $300   b. $600   c. $400

Solve.

3. The first month's dues will be used to rent a film about computer-related careers, to purchase a reference book, and to buy refreshments for the next meeting. If $\frac{1}{2}$ of the money is spent on the film rental, $\frac{1}{4}$ of the remainder is used for refreshments, and $7.50 is spent on the book, how much money will be spent? _____

4. Club members wrote a program together, with several people working on each of 4 parts. If the first part of the program required $\frac{1}{3}$ of the total time, the second part needed $\frac{1}{2}$ of the remaining time, the third part took 30 minutes, and the fourth part took 60 minutes, how many hours did the program take to write?

_____

5. Four students at a computer fair competed against each other in a space-travel game. Chris scored $\frac{2}{3}$ as many points as the winner, Pat. Rich scored $\frac{1}{2}$ as many points as Chris. Tom scored 100 points, which was 90 points less than Rich's score. How many points did Pat score? _____

6. While cataloging the software library, students found that $\frac{3}{8}$ of the available programs were in books or magazines. Of the remainder, $\frac{2}{3}$ were on disk, and the rest were on cassette tape. If there were 50 programs on cassette tape, how many programs were there on the software library? _____

7. In the adult-school classes held several nights per week, $\frac{1}{2}$ of the adults enrolled fall into the 41–60 age group, $\frac{1}{3}$ of the remainder are over 60, 14 are in the 30–40 age group, and 12 are under 30. How many adults are enrolled in the school? _____

8. A prize for a computer contest includes a computer worth $\frac{1}{2}$ of the value of the prize, a monitor worth $\frac{1}{2}$ of the remaining value, a modem worth $200, and software worth $150. What is the total value of the prize? _____

Name _____ Date _____

PRACTICE Working Backward

Solve.

9. Ozzie went to the Cover-To-Cover Bookstore to buy school supplies. He spent $\frac{1}{3}$ of the money he had on a looseleaf notebook, $\frac{1}{2}$ of the rest for paper, and whatever was left for pens and pencils. If Ozzie spent $3 on pens and pencils, what was his total bill?

10. A table at the front of the bookstore is used for the display of calendars. Of the different types, $\frac{1}{3}$ have famous paintings as their theme, $\frac{1}{4}$ use movies, 12 use animal themes, and 6 are humorous. How many calendars are displayed on the table?

11. One shelf at Cover-to-Cover Bookstore contains copies of several books on the best-seller list. Half of the books on the shelf are copies of the Number 1 best-seller. Of the remainder, $\frac{1}{4}$ are copies of the Number 4 book and $\frac{1}{3}$ are copies of the Number 3 book. The rest are copies of the Number 2 book. If there are 5 copies of the Number 2 book, how many best-sellers are on the shelf?

12. Ozzie's mother bought an assortment of greeting cards while she was at the bookstore. She bought twice as many birthday cards as anniversary cards. She bought 2 fewer anniversary cards than general greetings cards, but 2 more anniversary cards than get-well cards. If she bought 2 get-well cards, how many cards did she buy in all?

13. Allyson came to Cover-to-Cover Bookstore to pick up new magazines for the doctor's waiting room. One-fourth of her choices were children's magazines. Of the rest, $\frac{1}{3}$ were news magazines, 3 were sports magazines, and 5 were health-oriented publications. How many magazines did Allyson buy at the bookstore?

14. Of the bundles delivered daily to the store, $\frac{1}{3}$ consist of the morning edition of *The Daily Sun*. Another 2 bundles are made up of the afternoon edition of the same paper. Of the remaining bundles, $\frac{1}{2}$ are regional, one is a local newspaper, and one is from another state. How many bundles of papers are delivered daily to the bookstore?

15. Of the books in a library, $\frac{1}{3}$ came from Robbie's collection and 15 came from Marta's. Of the rest, 15 were Elena's, $\frac{1}{5}$ were Winfield's, and 5 were purchased from the bookstore. How many books are there in the library?

16. Of the money spent at the bookstore, Winfield contributed twice as much as Robbie. Robbie gave $150 less than Marta, but $1.50 more than Elena. Marta gave $3.50. How much did each person contribute to the money spent at the bookstore?

140

Use with pages 334–335.

PRACTICE Circles

Refer to the circle at the right for Questions 1–5.

1. Name four radii. _____

2. Name a diameter. _____

3. Name two chords. _____

4. Name the smallest central angle. _____

5. Name two arcs that are smaller than $\overset{\frown}{BC}$. _____

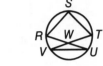

Use the circle at the right to identify each as either a *center,*
a *radius,* a *chord,* a *diameter,* an *arc,* or a *central angle.*

6. ∠TWU _____   7. $\overline{VU}$ _____

8. W _____   9. $\overset{\frown}{ST}$ _____

10. ∠VWR _____   11. $\overline{RU}$ _____

12. $\overline{RS}$ _____   13. $\overset{\frown}{RS}$ _____

14. $\overline{VW}$ _____   15. ∠VWU _____

16. $\overline{VT}$ _____   17. $\overline{WR}$ _____

In the circle at the right, the measure of $\overline{MQ}$ is 10 cm,
m∠MTN is 46°, and m∠NTP is 85°. Find the measure of
each.

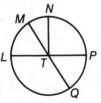

18. $\overline{LP}$ _____   19. $\overline{TQ}$ _____

20. ∠MTL _____   21. ∠PTQ _____

22. $\overline{NT}$ _____   23. ∠LTQ _____

Solve.

24. On another sheet of paper construct a circle with center
Z. Draw diameters $\overline{VW}$ and $\overline{XY}$. Name an angle that is
supplementary to ∠VZX. Name an angle that is
congruent to ∠VZX.

_____

_____

Name ______________________ Date ______________

PRACTICE Symmetry and Reflections

Draw the line or lines of symmetry for each figure.

1.

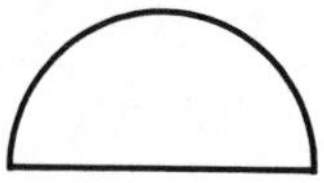

2.

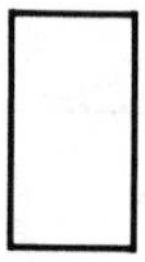

3.

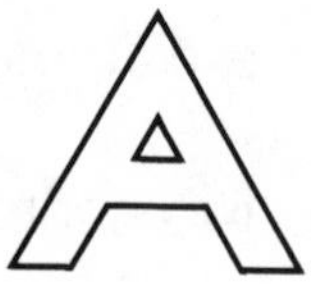

4.

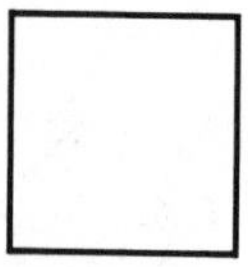

5.

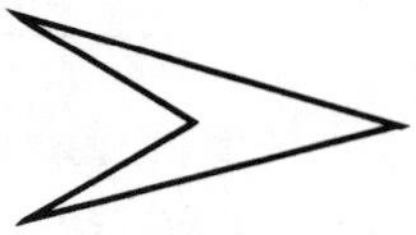

6.

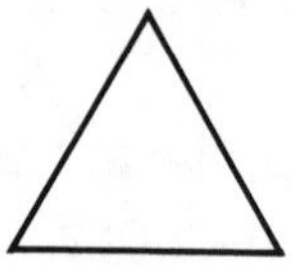

How many lines of symmetry does each figure have?

7.

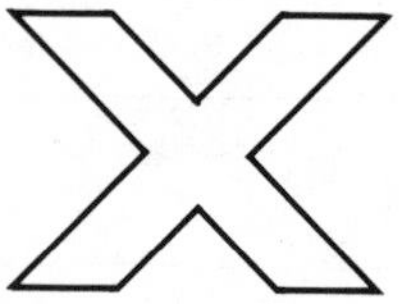

______

8.

______

9.

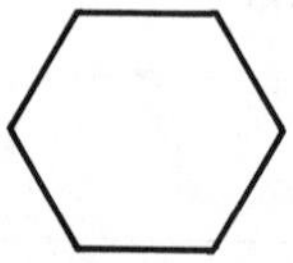

______

Draw a line of symmetry between the two figures in each pair.

10.

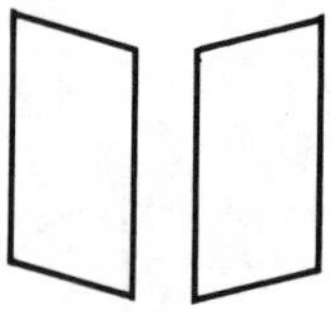

11.

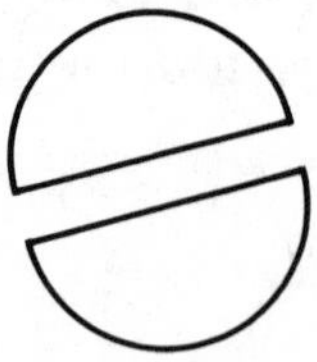

12.

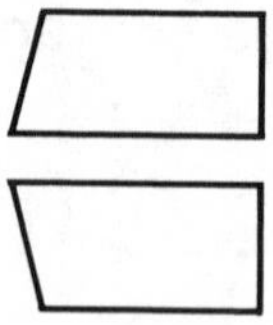

Draw the reflection of each figure. Use the line of symmetry given.

13.

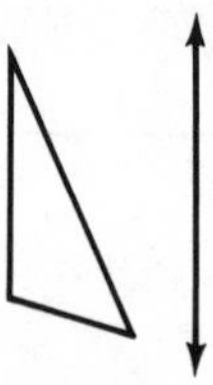

14.

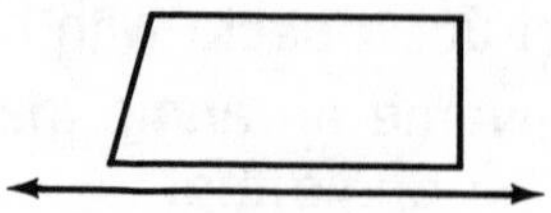

15.

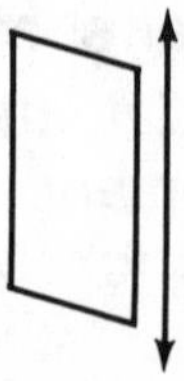

Use with pages 338–339.

PRACTICE   Translations and Rotations

Translate each figure as specified.

1. six units to the right   **2.** four units   **3.** five units to the left

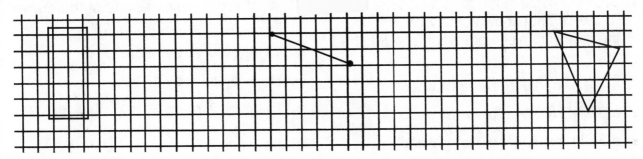

4. three units up   **5.** two units to the right   **6.** four units up

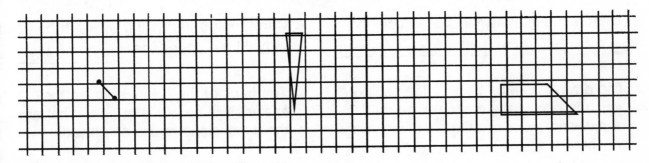

Choose the figure in each problem that is the rotation of
Figure *F* around point *Z*.

7.

8.

9.

10.

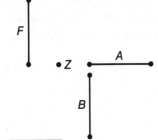

11.

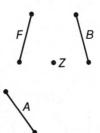

PRACTICE   Using a Picture or Model

Use the picture below to solve each problem. Ring the letter
of the correct answer.

1. Blair is buying wood to make the doors
   of the cabinet shown below. Which of
   the following pieces of wood should she
   buy?

   a. a 14-in. by 29-in. piece of wood

   b. a 32-in. by 20-in. piece of wood

   c. a 34-in. by 30-in. piece of wood

Solve.

2. What are the dimensions of the drawer
   in the cabinet shown below?

   a. 15 in. by 6 in. by 15 in.

   b. 30 in. by 6 in. by 15 in.

   c. 15 in. by 9 in. by 30 in.

3. What is the total height of the cabinet?

   _____

4. Can a board that is 3 ft by $1\frac{1}{2}$ ft be used
   to build the upper shelf?

   _____

5. The drawer and the back of the cabinet
   which is behind the doors will be made
   of plywood. What are the dimensions of
   this plywood back?

   _____

6. The back of the cabinet behind the
   shelves will be made of oak. What are
   the dimensions of this oak back?

   _____

7. How many $1\frac{1}{4}$-in. books will fit across
   the lower shelf?

   _____

8. Blair builds 2 shelves inside the doors.
   The shelves are spaced evenly inside.
   How many inches apart are these two
   shelves?

   _____

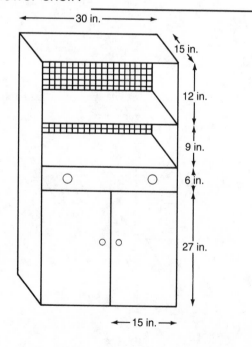

PRACTICE Perimeter

Write the perimeter of each polygon.

1.
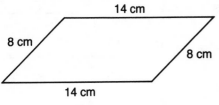
14 cm
8 cm
8 cm
14 cm

_____

2.
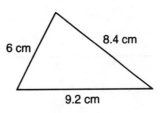
6 cm
8.4 cm
9.2 cm

_____

3.
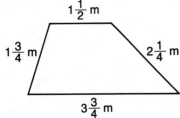
$1\frac{1}{2}$ m
$1\frac{3}{4}$ m
$2\frac{1}{4}$ m
$3\frac{3}{4}$ m

_____

4.
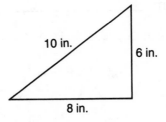
10 in.
6 in.
8 in.

_____

5.
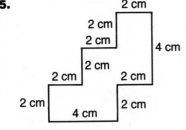
2 cm
2 cm
2 cm
2 cm
4 cm
2 cm
2 cm
2 cm
2 cm
2 cm
4 cm

_____

6.
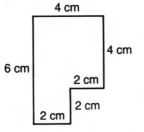
4 cm
4 cm
6 cm
2 cm
2 cm
2 cm

_____

7.
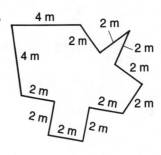
4 m
2 m
2 m
4 m
2 m
2 m
2 m
2 m
2 m
2 m
2 m
2 m

_____

Write the perimeter of each square. One side is given.

8. _____
$s = 56$ cm

9. _____
$s = 22.7$ m

10. _____
$s = 5\frac{3}{8}$ in.

11. _____
$s = 1$ m

Write the perimeter of each rectangle. Two sides are given.

12. _____
$l = 6.4$ cm
$w = 3.8$ cm

13. _____
$l = 56$ mm
$w = 14$ mm

14. _____
$l = 13\frac{2}{3}$ in.
$w = 8\frac{3}{4}$ in.

15. _____
$l = 43$ m
$w = 17$ m

Name _____ Date _____

PRACTICE | Circumference

Write the circumference. Use 3.14 for π.

1. radius = 22 m _____ **2.** radius = 12.3 cm _____

3. radius = 13 in. _____ **4.** radius = $5\frac{1}{2}$ in. _____

Write the circumference. Use $3\frac{1}{7}$ for π.

5. diameter = 25 cm _____ **6.** diameter = 84 cm _____

7. diameter = 9 m _____ **8.** diameter = 28 m _____

Write the circumference. Use 3.14 for π.

9.

10 cm

10.
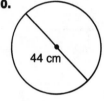
44 cm

11.
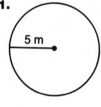
5 m

12.
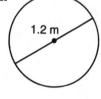
1.2 m

_____ _____ _____ _____

Write the circumference. Use $3\frac{1}{7}$ for π.

13.
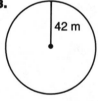
42 m

14.

35 cm

15.
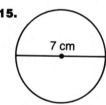
7 cm

16.
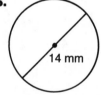
14 mm

_____ _____ _____ _____

A computer has calculated π to over one million decimal places. Use the decoder circle to write the value of π to the first fifteen places. Find the answer to each problem above in the outer circle. Write the code number for the answer in the space marked with the number of the problem.

$= \dfrac{3}{\underset{\textbf{1.}}{}} . \underset{\textbf{2.}}{} \ \underset{\textbf{3.}}{} \ \underset{\textbf{4.}}{} \ \underset{\textbf{5.}}{} \ \underset{\textbf{6.}}{} \ \underset{\textbf{7.}}{} \ \underset{\textbf{8.}}{}$

$\underset{\textbf{9.}}{} \ \underset{\textbf{10.}}{} \ \underset{\textbf{11.}}{} \ \underset{\textbf{12.}}{} \ \underset{\textbf{13.}}{} \ \underset{\textbf{14.}}{} \ \underset{\textbf{15.}}{} \ \underset{\textbf{16.}}{}$

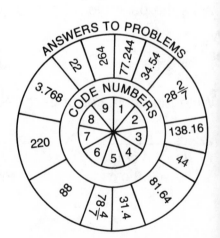

ANSWERS TO PROBLEMS

CODE NUMBERS

22 264 77.244 34.54 28$\frac{2}{7}$ 138.16 44 81.64 31.4 78$\frac{4}{7}$ 88 220 3.768

ame _____ Date _____

PRACTICE Area of Parallelograms

Write the area of each square.

1.

4 m

_____

2.

6.2 m

_____

3.

14.2 m

_____

4.

25 cm

_____

Write the area of each rectangle.

5.

12 mm

18.3 mm

_____

6.

0.85 cm

7.4 cm

_____

7.

42 in.

27 in.

_____

8.

146 m

8 m

_____

Write the area of each parallelogram.

9.

12 cm

15 cm

_____

10.

14.2 ft

8.4 ft

_____

11.

16 m   22 m

28 m

_____

12.

18.2 in.

15 in.

16.8 in.

_____

Write the formula you would use to determine the area of each figure.

13.

square

_____

14.

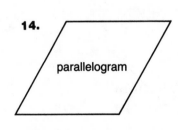

parallelogram

_____

15.

rectangle

_____

PRACTICE Areas of Triangles and Trapezoids

Place the numbers 10, 20, 30, 40, 50, 60, 70, and 80 in the circles in such a way that the numbers in any two connecting circles differ by more than 10. Use each number exactly once. Need help? One possible solution can be found by finding the answer to each problem below and placing it in the corresponding circle. If the answer to problem 1 were 50, the number 50 would go in circle 1.

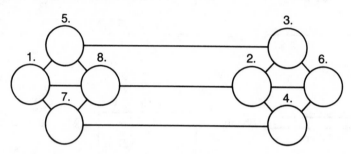

Find the area.

1.

10 m
14 m

_____

2.

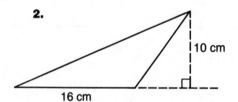

10 cm
16 cm

_____

3.

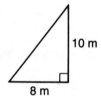

10 m
8 m

_____

4.

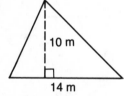

10 cm
12 cm

_____

5.

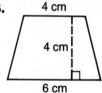

4 cm
4 cm
6 cm

_____

6.

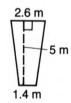

2.6 m
5 m
1.4 m

_____

7.

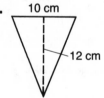

9 m
6 m
4 m

_____

8.

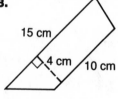

15 cm
4 cm
10 cm

_____

9.

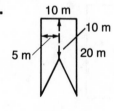

10 m
10 m
5 m
20 m

_____

PRACTICE | Multistep Problems/Making a Plan

Fill in the missing steps of the plan.

1. Elena does black-and-white or pastel-chalk drawings of tourists. She charges $7 for a black-and-white profile and $11 for a black-and-white front view. She charges $3 more for each pastel drawing. A customer asked Elena to draw black-and-white profiles of his 3 children and a pastel front view of his wife. He paid her with a $50 bill. How much change did he receive?

a. _____

_____

b. _____

c. _____

2. Elena's husband, Louis, sells umbrellas and other items at his store in North Shore Seaport. On Monday morning, his first customer bought 2 umbrellas for $11.95 each. The sales tax was 6 percent. The customer handed Luis $25.00. How much more money did the customer owe Luis?

a. _____

b. _____

c. _____

_____

d. _____

_____

Make a plan for each problem. Solve.

3. After moving to a new house, the McGraths budgeted $250 for landscaping. On their visit to a local nursery, they chose 8 yews priced at $14.95 each, 6 rhododendruns priced at $10.95 apiece, and 12 azaleas priced at $11.95 each. By how much did the McGraths exceed their budget? _____

4. The McGraths' new property is 200 ft long and 75 ft wide. Their previous property was 160 ft long and 80 ft wide. Is the area of the McGraths' new property greater or less than that of their old property? By how much?

_____

5. The recycler pays a penny per pound for newspaper and a nickel per pound for aluminum. Rob wants to earn $20 for his club. He has collected 1,100 lb of newspaper. How many cans must Rob collect if each can weighs approximately 1 oz? _____

6. A large sculpture in North Shore Seaport's town square is triangular in shape. Its area is 6,405 ft^2. Its base is 61 ft wide. A similar sculpture in South Shore has an area of 11,505 ft^2 and a base that is 59 ft wide. How much taller is the sculpture in North Shore than the one in South Shore? _____

PRACTICE Area of Circles

Write the area. Use $3\frac{1}{7}$ for π.

1.
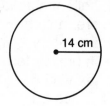
14 cm

_____

2.

7 in.

_____

3.
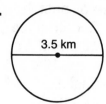
3.5 km

_____

4.
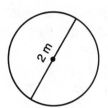
2 m

_____

Write the area. Use 3.14 for π. Round to the nearest tenth.

5.
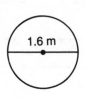
1.6 m

_____

6.

11 m

_____

7.
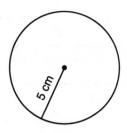
5 cm

_____

8.

8 mm

_____

9.

6 cm

_____

10.
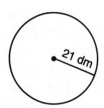
21 dm

_____

11.

3 m

_____

12.
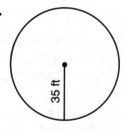
35 ft

_____

Write *true* or *false*.

13.
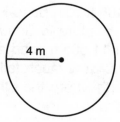
4 m

$A = 50.2$ m^2

_____

14.
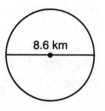
8.6 km

$A = 51.8$ km^2

_____

15.

4.4 in.

$A = 15.2$ in.^{2}

_____

16.

10 cm

$A = 31.4$ cm^2

_____

Use with pages 362–363.

PRACTICE   Guessing and Checking

Use the guess-and-check method to solve.

1. The Fremont Public Library has 3,124 members. For every 3 adult members, there is 1 child member. How many members are adults? How many are children? _____

2. The MacRae family checked out 11 library books. Each of the 2 children checked out the same number of books, which was 3 more than their father checked out. Mrs. MacRae took out twice as many books as her husband. How many books did each family member check out?

_____

_____

3. A librarian noted that during the summer, volume 1 of a popular 3-volume series of mystery books had been borrowed 2 more times than volume 3. Volume 3 had been borrowed one time less than volume 2. The 3 books had been checked out 39 times. How many times was each volume checked out?

_____

_____

4. Barbara, Steve, and Lisa are avid readers. In the last year, they read 121 books among them. Barbara read 3 more books than Steve. Steve read 2 more books than Lisa. How many books did each read?

_____

_____

5. During the past 3 years, the library acquired 1,584 new books. If the librarian purchased 30 books more each year than she purchased the year before, how many books did the librarian buy last year? _____

6. One morning, the library held a book sale. All books were priced at $0.10, $0.25, and $1. The number of $0.25 books sold was twice the number of $1 books sold. The number of $0.10 books sold was four times the number of $1 books sold. If the library received $15.20, how many books did it sell at each price? _____

7. In addition to books, the Fremont Library has a collection of 108 "book cassettes." If there are 20 more fiction than nonfiction cassettes, how many of each kind does the library have?

_____

8. Four people are in line waiting to check out books. They have selected 15 books. Each person has half as many books as the person standing in front of him or her. The last person in line is borrowing 3 fewer books than the second person in line. How many books is each person checking out?

_____

_____

PRACTICE   Guessing and Checking

Use the guess-and-check method to solve.

9. At Woodston Junior High School, 3 candidates were running for seventh grade president. Before the election, a reporter for the school newspaper polled 13 students. The number of students who said they intended to vote for Alicia was twice the number who said they intended to vote for Jason. The number who intended to vote for Eileen was 2 less than the number who intended to vote for Alicia. According to the poll, how many students intended to vote for each candidate?

_____

10. Doreen was elected treasurer. She estimated that the seventh grade would need $600 to pay for next year's activities. About $\frac{1}{3}$ of the amount needed would be covered by student dues. The rest would come from the sale of candy and holiday decorations. Candy sales generally produce 3 times as much money as sales of holiday decorations. How much of the $600 will come from candy sales? How much will come from the sale of decorations?

_____

11. T. J. and Emily were candidates for vice president. T. J. spent $1.65 more than Emily on posters and balloons. If their campaign costs came to $11.85, how much did each candidate spend?

_____

12. A postelection dance was held in the school gym. Of the 178 students in the seventh grade, 24 did not attend the dance. The ratio of boys to girls at the dance was 3 to 4. How many boys and how many girls attended the dance?

_____

13. The cost of refreshments for the dance was $82. A committee of 4 students paid for the necessary food, drinks, and paper goods. Dave spent 3 times as much money as Cindy, Sharon spent $8 less than Dave, and Tim spent $2 more than Cindy. How much did each committee member spend for refreshments?

_____

14. There were 8 elected positions to fill. After the election, the number of female officeholders exceeded the number of male officeholders by 2. How many girls were elected?

_____

Use with pages 364–365.

PRACTICE   Solid Figures

Write the letter of the correct name under each solid figure.

a. cone
c. cylinder
e. rectangular pyramid
g. triangular prism

b. cube
d. rectangular prism
f. sphere
h. triangular pyramid

1.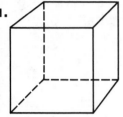
_____

2.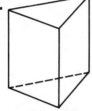
_____

3.
_____

4.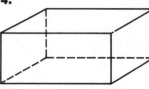
_____

5.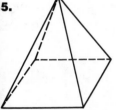
_____

6.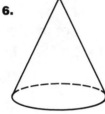
_____

7.
_____

8.
_____

Write the answer in the chart below.

Figure	Number of Vertices (V) +	Number of Faces (F)	Number of Edges (E)	
1.	+	−	=	2
2.	+	−	=	2
3.	+	−	=	2
4.	+	−	=	2
5.	+	−	=	2

The number of vertices, faces, and edges of prisms and pyramids have a special relationship. This relationship is called *Euler's formula.* Using the chart above, what is the formula?

_____

PRACTICE Making a Picture, a Drawing, a Model

Draw a picture or diagram to help you solve each problem.

1. Mrs. Smollet made a table that has 4 folding leaves. The center of the table is square, and each leaf is a semicircle whose diameter is equal to one side of the square. The square is 3 feet per side. What is the area of the table?

_____

2. Lee is a designer. The sketch that he is working on is a 13-in.-by-15-in. rectangle. One of the 13-in. sides is also the base of the triangle that has a height of 10 in. One of the 15-in. sides is also the base of a triangle that has a height of 12 in. What is the total area of the sketch?

_____

3. Kyle is watering a row of plants at Wayside Garden Center. He waters the first plant, skips 2 plants, and waters the next. He then skips 2 more plants, goes back 1, and moves ahead 6. There are 2 more plants left in the row. How many plants make up the row?

_____

4. Milo has a round vegetable garden enclosed by a low square wall. The wall is 25 feet to a side. What is the area of the vegetable garden?

_____

5. In front of an office building there is a round pound that has a flower garden around it. The diameter of the entire garden is 37 feet. The diameter of the pond is 5 feet. What is the area of the garden around the pond?

_____

6. Emilio is building a miniature staircase for a dollhouse. The first step is $1\frac{1}{2}$ in. high. Each of the other steps is 2 in. higher than the step before it. How high is the fifth step?

_____

PRACTICE   Making a Picture, a Drawing, or a Model

Draw a picture or diagram to help you solve each problem.

7. For a game of musical chairs, Rhoda arranges some chairs in a circle. She sits in one chair, then moves 2 chairs to the right. She then moves 1 chair to the left, and 4 to the right. Next, she moves 3 chairs to the right and finds herself back in the chair where she started. How many chairs are in the circle?

_____

8. Outside the Kelly Museum, there are 2 gardens: one circular and the other square. The distance between the centers of the gardens is 78 feet. The circular garden has a diameter of 20 feet. Each side of the square garden is 54.6 feet. How many feet apart are the two gardens?

_____

9. Lars is walking in a park. He walks 50 feet north, 40 feet east, 20 feet south, 60 feet west, 50 feet north, and 20 feet east. How far is he from his starting point?

_____

10. Portia is enlarging a triangular garden. The original garden has a base of 15 feet and a height of 12 feet. Portia increases the height by 4 feet and the base by 8 feet. How much larger is the new garden?

_____

11. The centers of 3 circles lie along the same straight line. The circles have radii of 12 in., 16 in., and 25 in., in that order. How far is the center of the first circle from the center of the last?

_____

12. Teddy is painting a mural of an ice cream cone. The cone is a triangle that has a height of 25 feet and a base of 12.5 feet. The ice cream is a semicircle that sits on the base of the triangle. What is the total height of the mural?

_____

Name _____ Date _____

PRACTICE Surface Area

Write the area of each figure. Use 3.14 for π.

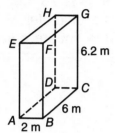

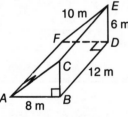

1. Area of *ABFE* _____

2. Area of *EFGH* _____

3. Area of *ABCD* _____

4. Area of *BCGF* _____

5. Area of *CDHG* _____

6. Area of *DAEH* _____

7. total of surface area _____

8. Area of top circle _____

9. Area of rectangle _____

10. Area of bottom circle _____

11. total of surface area _____

12.

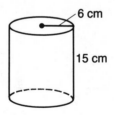

_____

13.

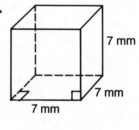

_____

14.

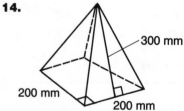

_____

15.

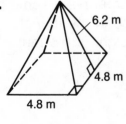

_____

16.

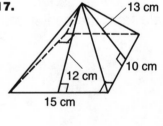

_____

17.

_____

156

Use with pages 370–37

PRACTICE Volume

Write the answer to each question.

1. What shape is the base? _____

2. What is the height of the base? _____

3. What is the area of the base? _____

4. What is the height of the solid? _____

5. What is the volume of the solid? _____

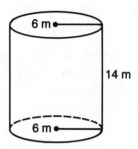

6. What shape is the base? _____

7. What is the radius of the base? _____

8. What is the area of the base? _____

9. What is the height of the solid? _____

10. What is the volume of the solid? _____

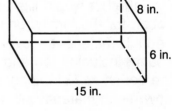

Write the volume. Round your answer to the nearest tenth.

11.

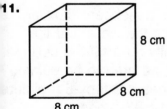

_____

12.

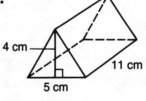

_____

13.

_____

14.

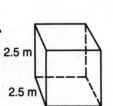

_____

15.

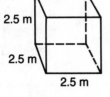

_____

16.

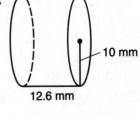

_____

PRACTICE Choosing the Formula

Ring the letter of the correct formula.

1. The Sanchez family built a new room 21 ft long, 11 ft wide, and 8 ft high. They plan to cover the floor with wall-to-wall carpeting. How many feet of carpeting will they need?

   a. $P = 2(l + w)$

   b. $A = l \times w$

   c. $A = \frac{1}{2}bh$

2. In one corner of the room, Ray's father has built a rectangular planter. It is 2 ft long, 8 in. wide, and 8 in. high. About how many cubic feet of potting soil will be needed to fill the planter?

   a. $V = r^2h$

   b. $A = \frac{1}{2}bh$

   c. $V = bh$

Use the correct formula to solve each problem. Use the room's dimensions given in the first problem when needed.

3. Ray wants to add baseboard molding. If the lumberyard sells molding in 10-ft lengths, about how many lengths will Ray need to buy? _____

4. Ray's mother bought an unfinished round end table at a furniture store. After sanding, staining, and sealing the table, she ordered a piece of glass for the table top. If the diameter of the circular top is 26 in., what is the area of the piece of glass she ordered?

   _____

5. Ray's father would like to recover an old couch for the family room. He needs enough material to cover the entire couch, including top and all four sides. If the couch is 23 in. long and 18 in. wide, how much material will he need?

   _____

6. After installing the baseboard molding, Ray wants to paint the walls and the ceiling of the family room. If the ceiling is 8 ft high, what is the area to be painted? NOTE: The room has a 3-ft-by-5-ft picture window and a 2-ft-by-7-ft doorway.

   _____

7. Ray found a 3-ft tall cylindrical fish tank at a garage sale. He plans to buy colored sand to make an unusual sand sculpture as a decoration for the new family room. If the fish tank has a circular base $1\frac{1}{2}$ ft in diameter, how many cubic feet of sand will Ray need to make the sand sculpture?

   _____

8. Because of the distance of the new room from the furnace, Ray's mother thinks that a space heater may be needed to keep the room warm in winter. In order to determine what size heater to buy, she must know the number of cubic feet of space enclosed by the room. Calculate the number.

   _____

Use with pages 374–375.

PRACTICE Arranging Data

ems in a warehouse are coded with letters that indicate
here they should be sent. There are six different codes—
, J, K, L, M, and N. These items are waiting for shipment.

	N,	L,	L,	M,	H,	K,	H
	K,	K,	J,	H,	K,	N,	J
	N,	J,	M,	H,	K,	N,	K
	K,	M,	L,	M,	H,	H,	L
	N,	K,	K,	H,	J,	K,	L
	L,	L,	K,	M,	L,	N,	L
	J,	K,	M,	J,	J,	L,	M

Code	Tally	Frequency	Relative frequency
H			
J			
K			
L			
M			
N			

Complete the frequency table for the codes. Express relative
requency as a fraction and a percent. Use the table to
answer Questions 1–3.

1. What is the total number of items? _____

2. What percent of the items are coded N? _____

3. What is the relative frequency of items coded M?

_____

PRACTICE Range, Median, and Mode

Write the range of each set of numbers.

1. 44, 16, 32, 27, 35 _____

2. 58, 106, 731, 22, 59 _____

3. 6.4, 3.3, 2.6, 5.5, 2.1 _____

4. 10.2, 12.4, 8.3, 11.1, 7.9 _____

5. 234, 666, 23, 572, 14 _____

6. 216, 212, 214, 211, 213 _____

7. $5.63, $1.98, $2.20, $3.82, $1.02 _____

8. $4.22, $2.22, $1.39, $4.52, $3.99 _____

Write the median of each set of numbers.

9. 15, 22, 18, 14, 25 _____

10. 120, 98, 33, 112 _____

11. 12, 21, 25, 12 _____

12. $3.50, $5.60, $6.30, $3.50 _____

13. $37.00, $12.00, $4.26, $55.00 _____

14. 7.3, 9.3, 3.7, 3.1 _____

15. 2.4, 5.9, 6.7, 5.6, 6.3 _____

16. 10.2, 6.8, 12.5, 3.4, 5.1 _____

Write the mode(s) of each set of numbers.

17. 15, 18, 22, 15, 20 _____

18. 34, 42, 22, 6, 10, 22, 43 _____

19. 21, 612, 5, 45, 21, 5 _____

20. 2, 4, 2, 4, 4, 4, 2, 4, 2, 2 _____

21. $2.46, $5.42, $2.46, $3.46 _____

22. 8.1, 8.4, 8.0, 8.1, 8.2, 8.3 _____

Dr. Myra Marvelous is conducting an experiment to determine how much the temperature of bowls of chicken noodle soup changes as ice cubes of different sizes are added to them. These were her results:
2.5°, 2.6°, 1.8°, 2.6°, 1.6°, 2.2°, 2.4°, and 2.3°.

23. What was the range of the temperature changes?

_____

24. What was the median of the temperature changes? _____

25. What was the mode of the temperature changes?

_____

26. If the scientist added one more measurement of 2.5° to her data, how many modes would there be? _____

Use with pages 388–389.

PRACTICE   Mean

Write the mean for each set of data. Round to the nearest
whole number.

1. 40, 50, 35, 35, 60 _____

2. 6.5, 3.2, 5.3, 6.5, 3.5 _____

3. 82, 80, 74, 73, 66 _____

4. 151, 121, 111, 131, 141 _____

5. 5.3, 5.5, 2.2, 4.8, 3.2 _____

6. 2, 10, 6, 3, 5, 20, 3 _____

7. 22 km, 31 km, 17 km, 26 km _____

8. 7.2, 11.1, 4.2, 2.7, 3.2, 1.6 _____

9. 33, 10, 2, 14 _____

10. 49, 12, 78, 108 _____

11. 147, 45, 89, 42, 30 _____

12. $3.26, $7.00, $1.78, $2.63 _____

13. $23.60, $7.89, $21.01, $55.49 _____

14. 9.2, 5.6, 1.1, 3.3 _____

Write the mean for each set of data. Round to the nearest tenth.

15. 2.6, 7.2, 3.5, 9.8, 2.5 _____

16. 5.1, 2.4, 7.8, 2.3, 4.4, 1.1 _____

17. 23.5, 32.3, 98.6, 21.9 _____

18. 429, 407, 410, 235 _____

19. 152, 344, 233, 667, 321 _____

20. 9.7, 3.8, 4.5, 1.2, 6.2 _____

Solve.

21. The Kaufman family drove through five
states during their summer vacation.
The price per gallon of gasoline in each
of the states was $1.09, $1.16, $1.19,
$1.14, and $1.17. What is the mean
price per gallon in these states? _____

22. The Kaufmans have to drive an
average of 250 miles each day to
complete their vacation on time. On the
first four days, they travel 220 miles,
300 miles, 210 miles, and 275 miles.
What is the mean distance traveled? If
they maintain this average, will the
Kaufmans finish on time?

PRACTICE Pictographs and Bar Graphs

This pictograph represents the number of people who went on tours with different offices of the Travel Association.

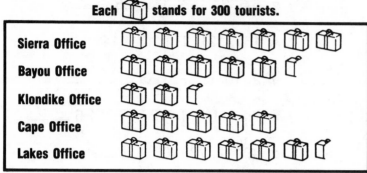

TRAVEL ASSOCIATION TOURISTS

1. How many tourists did the Bayou Office serve? _____

2. How many more tourists did Sierra serve than Lakes? _____

3. What percent of all the tourists are represented by a single 🧳 ? (Round to the nearest tenth.) _____

4. The tourists from the Klondike office were housed in different places. There were 350 in motels, 200 in hostels, 150 in campgrounds; 50 others found different housing. Use the information to make a vertical bar graph, then answer Questions 7–11.

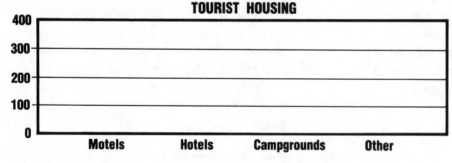

5. How many tourists were housed in motels? _____

6. How many camped? _____

7. What percent of all the Klondike tourists stayed in hostels? (Round to the nearest tenth.) _____

Name _____ Date _____

The directors of the Science Exhibit at the Orangeburg City Center took a survey of visitors one Saturday morning. They noted each person's age and how long the person remained at the exhibit. Here is the information they obtained.

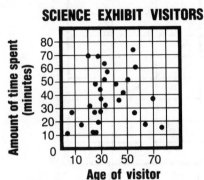

SCIENCE EXHIBIT VISITORS

Use the scattergram above to solve.

1. What was the longest anyone stayed at the exhibit? _____

2. How old was the youngest person who visited the exhibit? _____

3. How old was the oldest person who visited the exhibit? _____

4. How many people stayed less than 20 minutes? _____

Write the letter of the correct answer.

5. Most of the people who entered the exhibit were

  a. between 10 and 30 years old.

  b. between 30 and 50 years old.

  c. between 50 and 70 years old.

6. Of the 30 visitors surveyed, the greatest number stayed

  a. between 20 and 30 minutes.

  b. between 30 and 40 minutes.

  c. between 40 and 50 minutes.

7. The age range of the visitors surveyed was

  a. 63 years.

  b. 72 years.

  c. 76 years.

8. The visitor who stayed the longest was

  a. 70 years old.

  b. 74 years old.

  c. 53 years old.

9. The average age of visitors to the exhibit was about

  a. 25 years.

  b. 35 years.

  c. 45 years.

10. The average amount of time spent at the exhibit was about

  a. 27 minutes.

  b. 38 minutes.

  c. 49 minutes.

Name _____ Date _____

An ornithologist made this broken-line graph to show how much time a pair of birds—Pair A—spent building a nest.

Fig. 11-4

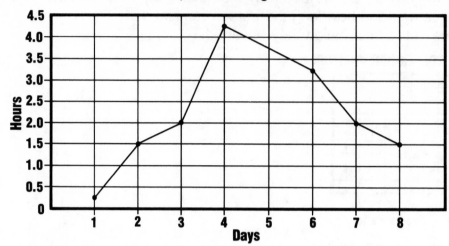

1. On what day did Pair A spend the most time nest-building? _____

2. How much more time did Pair A spend nest-building on day 7 than on day 2? _____

3. On what day did Pair A spend only 15 minutes building their nest? _____

4. What was the total amount of time spent nest-building?

   _____

5. Make a double broken-line graph by adding these data for a second pair of birds—Pair B—to the graph above.

Day	1	2	3	4	5	6	7	8
Hours	1.0	2.75	2.75	2.75	3.0	2.0	2.5	0.5

6. On what day did the difference between Pair A's time and Pair B's time equal a half hour? _____

7. Which of the pairs showed the greatest increase of nest-building between two consecutive days? _____

8. Which of the pairs showed a steady decrease in time each day from day 4 to day 8? _____

                                                                 Use with pages 396–397

Name _____ Date _____

PRACTICE | Circle Graphs

There are six companies competing for the state's fruit-juice market. Use the information below to complete the chart and draw a circle graph. Calculate the measure of each central angle and use a protractor to draw the angles. Label the graph.

DAILY SALES IN GALLONS

Consolidated Juices	4,000	Natural Juices	1,000
General Juice, Inc.	1,000	Juice-Tek	2,000
Juicy Works	1,000	Smile Juice Co.	3,000

Company	Daily sales in gallons	Fraction of market	Central angles
Consolidated			
Natural			
General			
Juice-Tek			
Juicy Works			
Smile			

To help increase its sales, Juice-Tek needs to know how much it sells in each part of the state. Its sales in five parts of the state are given. Use the information to complete the chart and draw a circle graph. Calculate the measure of each central angle and use the protractor to draw the angles. Label the graph.

JUICE-TEK DAILY SALES IN GALLONS BY REGION

North	600
East	200
Central	200
South	400
West	600

Region	Daily sales in gallons	Percent sold	Central angles
North			
East			
Central			
South			
West			

Name _____ Date _____

PRACTICE Estimation

Decide whether you can estimate or whether you must find
the exact answer, Write *estimate* or *exact answer*.

1. The Bensons are driving from their home
to Gifford State Park, a distance of 97
miles. Their car's gas tank contains 12.1
gallons of gasoline. If their car gets 22.9
miles per gallon, do they have enough
gas to get there and back? _____

2. On their way to the park, the Bensons
drive along a toll road. The average cost
per mile for tolls is $0.03. If the Bensons
drive 83 miles each way on the toll road,
would $5 be enough money to cover the
cost of tolls? _____

3. When they arrive at the park, Mr.
Benson gives the attendant a $10 bill. Is
that enough money to pay for 4
admissions plus parking? _____

4. The Bensons arrive at the park at
11:00 A.M.. If they hike along Valley
Trail, take an hour for lunch, and then
hike along Snake Trail, will they have
finished hiking by 3:30 P.M.? _____

Estimate the answer to each problem. Find the exact answer
only if you need to.

5. During the past year, the Bensons went
hiking at Gifford State Park three times.
They hiked along the Ridge Trail three
times, along the Valley Trail once, and
along the Snake Trail twice. Did they
hike more than 20 miles in all?

_____

6. Mrs. Fromm and Mr. Jacobs took 41
students on a trip to the state park. The
cost of the charter bus was $159.90. If
the students paid for their admission and
paid half of the cost of the bus, was a
charge of $6 per student enough to
cover the total cost? _____

7. A park ranger told the students that in
the first week of June, 291 people hiked
along Valley Trail and 432 people hiked
along Snake Trail. At that rate, should
the park ranger expect more than 3,500
people to hike along those trails during
the entire month of June? _____

8. On Saturday, the parking lot at Gifford
State Park contained 112 cars and 5
buses. Each car had carried an average
of 3 passengers, and each bus had
carried an average of 30 passengers.
Did the state park take in more than
$1,500 in admissions and parking that
day? _____

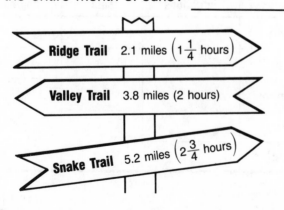

> **Ridge Trail** 2.1 miles $\left(1\frac{1}{4} \text{ hours}\right)$

> **Valley Trail** 3.8 miles (2 hours)

> **Snake Trail** 5.2 miles $\left(2\frac{3}{4} \text{ hours}\right)$

Gifford State Park
Admission: $1.95 per person
Parking: Cars—$2.25 Buses—$4.75
Park Closes at Dusk

Use with pages 400–401.

Name _____ Date _____

Refer to the spinner to answer the questions.

1. How many possible outcomes are there? _____

2. Are all the possible outcomes equally likely? _____

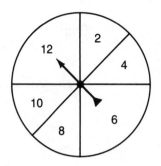

3. Are spinning a 2 and spinning an 8 equally likely? _____

4. Are spinning a 2 and spinning a 6 equally likely? _____

5. Luisa wants to spin a 10. If she spins a 4, is that a favorable outcome? _____

6. Jon does *not* want to spin a 2. How many favorable outcomes are possible when he spins? _____

7. Cyndi wants to spin a 4 and Mark wants to spin a 12. Do they both have an equally likely chance of obtaining a favorable outcome? _____

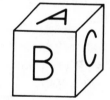

8. Is the number of possible outcomes different for Cyndi and Mark? _____

You are going to toss the letter cube once. The letters on the 6 faces are *A, B, C, D, E, F.* Write each probability.

9. P(*A*) _____   10. P(*D*) _____

11. P(not *E*) _____   12. P(not *B*) _____

13. P(*B* or *D*) _____   14. P(*C* or *F*) _____

Solve.

15. Sam keeps all his socks in a drawer. He picked a brown sock just before a power blackout. He knows there are 5 brown socks, 8 black socks, and 2 blue socks left in the drawer. If Sam picks a sock, what is the probability he will have a pair?

_____

16. What is the probability Sam will end up wearing two different socks?

_____

PRACTICE   Tree Diagrams and Sample Space

Janette will have two tries spinning the spinner pictured here. Below is a tree diagram and a sample space showing the possible outcomes.

Spin 1	Spin 2	Sample space
A	A B C	AA AB AC
B	A B C	BA BB BC
C	A B C	CA CB CC

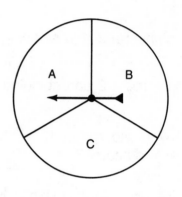

1. How many possible outcomes are there for Janette's first spin? _____

2. How many possible outcomes are there for Janette's second spin? _____

3. How many possible combined outcomes are there for both spins together? _____

4. A blue card and a red card are dropped into a hat. In the space below, draw a tree diagram and make a sample space for three draws from the hat—the card drawn will be put back in the hat after each draw.

Use with pages 404–405.

PRACTICE Probability and Sample Space

The letters of the word *serendipity* are written on a set of cards:

S	E	R	E	N	D	I	P	I	T	Y

The cards are shuffled and placed facedown on a table. After a card is drawn, it is returned to the deck, the cards are shuffled, and they are placed facedown again. Write each probability.

1. P(S) _____

2. P(E) _____

3. P(I) _____

4. P(not D) _____

5. P(Y or N) _____

6. P(a letter before J in the alphabet) _____

7. P(I or E) _____

8. P(W) _____

9. P(not W) _____

10. P(R or M) _____

You are going to toss a penny, a nickel, and a dime.

1. Write the sample space as ordered triples.

_____

_____

2. How many possible outcomes are there in the sample space? _____

3. How many outcomes have at least two heads?

_____

4. What is the probability of tossing exactly one tail?

_____

5. What is the probability of an outcome with at least one head or at least one tail? _____

6. What is the probability of an outcome with all three tosses the same? _____

Name _____ Date _____

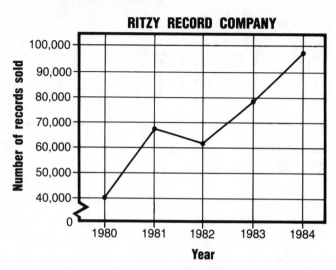

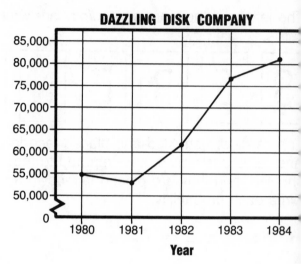

The two graphs above show the record sales of two companies from 1980 through 1984. Use the graphs to answer these questions.

1. Which company sold more records in 1981? how many more? _____

2. Both companies were formed in 1980. Which company sold more records during its first three years?

_____

3. In which year did the two companies sell the same number of records? _____

4. In which year was the difference in the number of records sold by the two companies the greatest? _____

5. Which company had higher average yearly sales for the five-year period shown in the graph? how much higher?

_____

_____

6. From 1980 to 1981, by what percent did the Ritzy Record Company's sales increase? _____

7. Which company had a greater increase in sales from 1982 to 1983? How much greater was the percent of increase?

_____

Use with pages 408–409.

Name _____ Date _____

The spinner below is spun and a coin is tossed.
Write each probability.

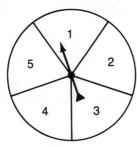

1. P(3, heads) _____

2. P(5, tails) _____

3. P(odd number, tails) _____

4. P(not 1, heads) _____

5. P(6, tails) _____

6. P(4, heads) _____

The spinner is spun twice in a row. Write each probability.

7. P(1, 3) _____

8. P(odd number, even number) _____

9. P(5, 5) _____

10. P(4, not 2) _____

11. P(even number, not 6) _____

12. P(3, not 3) _____

The coin is tossed twice and the spinner is spun once.
Write each probability.

13. P(tails, tails, 3) _____

14. P(heads, tails, odd number) _____

15. P(heads, tails, not 5) _____

16. P(tails, heads, 8) _____

17. P(tails, heads, not 8) _____

18. P(heads, heads, even number) _____

A box holds 4 pearl buttons, 3 ivory buttons, 2 plastic
buttons, and 1 wooden button. You pick a button, put it back
into the box, and then pick again.
Write the probability.

19. P(plastic, pearl) _____

20. P(wooden, wooden) _____

21. P(wooden, not plastic) _____

22. P(pearl, pearl) _____

23. P(ivory, not pearl) _____

24. P(plastic, ivory) _____

Name _____ Date _____

PRACTICE Dependent Events

There are 10 marbles in a jar: 4 red, 3 blue, 2 yellow, and 1 white. You pick a marble from the jar and then pick another, without replacing the first. Write each probability.

1. P(red; then white) _____
2. P(blue; then blue) _____
3. P(yellow; then not red) _____
4. P(blue; then red) _____
5. P(white; then not blue) _____
6. P(white; then not white) _____
7. P(yellow; then yellow) _____
8. P(red; then black) _____

Students at lunch are being asked at random to participate in a taste test of a new spinach-flavored yogurt. There are 6 ninth graders, 5 eighth graders, 4 seventh graders, and 3 sixth graders in the lunchroom. Write each probability.

9. P(eighth grader; then sixth grader) _____
10. P(ninth grader; then ninth grader) _____
11. P(seventh grader; then not eighth grader) _____
12. P(sixth grader; then any student) _____

A box contains 15 snapshots: 1 of Jeanne, 2 of Vicki, 3 of Phil, 4 of Elliot, and 5 of Donald. You pick out a photo, and then pick another, without putting the first one back. Write each probability.

13. P(Vicki; then Donald) _____
14. P(Donald; then Donald) _____
15. P(Elliot; then Jeanne) _____
16. P(Jeanne; then Vicki) _____
17. P(Phil; then Elliot) _____
18. P(Donald; then Phil) _____

Use with pages 412–413.

PRACTICE Using Outside Sources Including an Infobank

HE WORLD'S LARGEST ISLANDS

Island	Location	Area (square miles)
Baffin	Arctic	183,000
Borneo	Asia	288,243
Great Britain	Europe	88,787
Greenland	Arctic	840,000
Honshu (Japan)	Asia	88,930
Madagascar	Indian Ocean	226,658
New Guinea	Oceania	316,856
Sumatra	Asia	182,860

Solve each problem. Use the information contained in the chart above. When you need more information, consult an outside source, such as an almanac or other reference book.

1. How much larger is the world's largest island than the next larger island?

_____

2. Baffin Island has a small population. About how many people per square mile live on the island?

_____

3. Sicily and Sardinia are the two largest islands in the Mediterranean Sea. Is their combined area greater or less than the area of Honshu?

_____

4. How much greater is the area of Greenland than the combined area of the next three larger islands?

_____

5. Cuba is the largest island in the West Indies. About how many times larger than Cuba is the largest island in Asia?

_____

6. Only 131,930 square miles of Greenland are free of ice. Approximately what percentage is that of the island's total land area?

_____

Name_____ Date_____

Write the integer for each point on the number line.

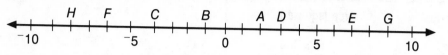

1. A _____

2. B _____

3. C _____

4. D _____

5. E _____

6. F _____

7. G _____

8. H _____

9. Solve. Write each integer in the correct circle.

⁻4	7	⁻3	3	⁻15
85	⁻51	⁻25	42	10
19	⁻85	66	⁻70	94

Less than 0   Greater than 0

Write the integers in order from the least to the greatest.

10. 9, 6, ⁻4, ⁻27 _____

11. ⁻4, 4, 5, ⁻5 _____

12. ⁻1, ⁻2, ⁻3, ⁻10 _____

Write the integers in order from the greatest to the least.

13. ⁻27, ⁻14, 39, ⁻39 _____

14. 124, 22, ⁻17, ⁻150, 96 _____

Compare. Write > or <.

15. 9 ◯ 6

16. ⁻6 ◯ ⁻10

17. 55 ◯ ⁻55

18. ⁻70 ◯ ⁻58

19. 0 ◯ ⁻1

20. 35 ◯ ⁻9

21. 12 ◯ ⁻12

22. ⁻81 ◯ ⁻18

23. 12 ◯ 48

PRACTICE   Properties of Integers

Use the properties to find the missing number.

1. $22 + (1 + {}^-12) = (22 + $ _____ $) + {}^-12$

2. $13 \cdot 0 = $ _____

3. ${}^-9 \cdot $ _____ $= 3 \cdot {}^-9$

4. _____ $\cdot (14 + 11) = (3 \cdot 14) + (3 \cdot 11)$

5. $16 + 31 = 31 + $ _____

6. ${}^-8 + $ _____ $= {}^-8$

7. $($ _____ $+ 13) + 19 = 23 + (13 + 19)$

8. $19 \cdot $ _____ $= 19$

9. $12 \cdot ({}^-3 \cdot 1) = (12 \cdot {}^-3) \cdot $ _____

10. $52 \cdot ({}^-12 + {}^-2) = (52 \cdot $ _____ $) + (52 \cdot {}^-2)$

11. $29 + $ _____ $= {}^-3 + 29$

12. _____ $\cdot 13 = 13 \cdot {}^-14$

13. $16 \cdot ($ _____ $\cdot 6) = (16 \cdot 36) \cdot 6$

14. ${}^-23 \cdot 1 = $ _____

Use the Commutative Property to reorder the integers.

15. $2{,}673 + {}^-12$

16. ${}^-32 \cdot {}^-14$

17. ${}^-1{,}236 + 29$

18. $367 \cdot {}^-50$

_____   _____   _____   _____

19. ${}^-36 + {}^-62$

20. ${}^-319 \cdot 93$

21. $7{,}211 \cdot {}^-3$

22. $99 + {}^-457$

_____   _____   _____   _____

Use the Associative Property to reorder the integers.

23. $(3{,}061 \cdot {}^-14) \cdot 601$

24. ${}^-333 + ({}^-24 + 89)$

25. ${}^-96 + (3 + {}^-419)$

_____   _____   _____

26. ${}^-601 \cdot ({}^-13 \cdot 1)$

27. $(1{,}300 + {}^-69) + 14$

28. $(319 \cdot {}^-2{,}001) \cdot {}^-197$

_____   _____   _____

Use the Distributive Property to reorder the integers.

29. ${}^-390 \cdot ({}^-3 + 62)$

30. $10 \cdot (69 + {}^-99)$

31. ${}^-607 \cdot (32 + {}^-6)$

_____   _____   _____

32. ${}^-315 \cdot ({}^-3 + 69)$

33. $277 \cdot (34 + {}^-1{,}268)$

34. ${}^-3 \cdot (18 + {}^-925)$

_____   _____   _____

Name _____ Date _____

PRACTICE Adding Integers

Add.

1. $^-25 + {}^-75 =$ _____

2. $60 + {}^-98 =$ _____

3. $86 + {}^-64 =$ _____

4. $^-36 + {}^-87 =$ _____

5. $^-12 + {}^-48 =$ _____

6. $^-75 + 96 =$ _____

7. $88 + {}^-69 =$ _____

8. $96 + {}^-9 =$ _____

9. $^-83 + {}^-32 =$ _____

10. $^-44 + {}^-41 =$ _____

11. $^-73 + {}^-61 =$ _____

12. $98 + {}^-37 =$ _____

13. $88 + {}^-35 + 53 =$ _____

14. $^-23 + 66 + {}^-100 =$ _____

15. $12 + {}^-89 + {}^-37 =$ _____

16. $^-93 + {}^-8 + {}^-82 =$ _____

Write = or ≠ in the blank space.

17. $^-41 + 9$ _____ $^-41 + {}^-9$

18. $^-40 + {}^-72$ _____ $^-40 - {}^-72$

19. $^-19 + {}^-11$ _____ $^-19 + 11$

20. $46 + {}^-89$ _____ $46 - 89$

Add. Use the properties.

21. $^-99 + ({}^-12 + 99) =$ _____

22. $^-74 + (74 + {}^-90) =$ _____

23. $67 + ({}^-89 + {}^-37) =$ _____

24. $55 + ({}^-55 + 39) =$ _____

25. $^-21 + (21 + {}^-34) =$ _____

26. $^-59 + ({}^-94 + {}^-59) =$ _____

Solve.

27. Pure water boils at 212°F. If a certain chemical compound is added to the water, the boiling point changes by $^-24$°F. Write an addition problem to express this change, and solve to find the new boiling point.

28. Pure water freezes at 32°F. When another chemical compound is added, the freezing point changes by $^-45$°F. Write an addition problem to express this change, and solve to find the new freezing point.

Name _____ Date _____

PRACTICE Subtracting Integers

Subtract.

1. $^-65 - {}^-21 =$ _____

2. $^-72 - 52 =$ _____

3. $97 - {}^-79 =$ _____

4. $^-71 - {}^-4 =$ _____

5. $^-4 - {}^-79 =$ _____

6. $^-55 - {}^-32 =$ _____

7. $53 - 85 =$ _____

8. $^-35 - 52 =$ _____

9. $^-91 - {}^-51 =$ _____

10. $55 - 83 =$ _____

11. $^-11 - {}^-19 =$ _____

12. $^-95 - {}^-24 =$ _____

13. $^-44 - 54 =$ _____

14. $^-42 - 99 =$ _____

15. $23 - 58 =$ _____

16. $84 - 19 =$ _____

17. $66 - {}^-24 =$ _____

18. $30 - 56 =$ _____

19. $^-75 - {}^-10 =$ _____

20. $67 - 59 =$ _____

21. $^-43 - 75 =$ _____

22. $^-81 - 25 =$ _____

23. $^-25 - {}^-48 =$ _____

24. $^-33 - {}^-2 =$ _____

25. $^-58 - {}^-52 =$ _____

26. $^-17 - 72 =$ _____

27. $59 - {}^-38 =$ _____

28. $^-83 - {}^-71 =$ _____

29. $^-64 - 44 =$ _____

30. $^-59 - {}^-38 =$ _____

31. $^-23 - 40 =$ _____

32. $^-72 - {}^-11 =$ _____

33. $^-38 - 55$ _____

34. $4 - {}^-82 =$ _____

35. $^-46 - {}^-24 =$ _____

36. $79 - 10 =$ _____

37. $^-72 - {}^-20 =$ _____

38. $^-4 - {}^-94 =$ _____

39. $^-24 - {}^-18 =$ _____

40. The greatest recorded change in temperature in a 24-hour period was 100°F and took place in Browning, Montana, January 23–24, 1916. The high temperature was 44°F. How low did the temperature drop that night?

_____

41. The highest temperature ever recorded in North America was 134°F. The lowest was $^-81$°F. What is the difference between the highest and the lowest temperatures?

_____

PRACTICE Problem-Solving Practice

Use the guess-and-check strategy to solve.

1. The Crestview Athletic League is holding its annual track-and-field day on Saturday, May 17, from 10:30 A.M. to _____ P.M. The time is a three-digit number. The first digit is a prime number. The sum of all 3 digits is 9. The last digit is 2 more than the first.

_____

Make a picture, model, or diagram to solve.

2. There are 4 entrants in the boys' 200-meter dash. At the finish, Rick is 4 meters ahead of Carl. Kevin is 2 meters behind Austin, and Carl is 6 meters ahead of Kevin. How many meters separate the winner from the runner in last place?

_____

Make a list on the right to solve.

3. The snack bar at the athletic field sells hamburgers and hot dogs for $1 apiece. Irene has $3, which she can spend all or part of. How many different orders can she place?

_____

Make a table on the right to solve.

4. Once the stadium gates open, the number of spectators sitting in the bleachers doubles every 15 minutes. If 4 spectators were sitting in the bleachers at 9:30 A.M., at what time did the bleachers contain 256 spectators?

_____

Use appropriate notation to solve.

5. At the conclusion of the 1,500-meter run, Dana and Yvonne want to share the contents of an 8-oz container of orange juice. They have an empty 5-oz cup and an empty 3-oz cup. How can they evenly divide the juice between them?

_____

_____

Use with pages 432–433.

PRACTICE   Problem-Solving Practice

Solve.

6. At the Crestview Athletic League's annual track-and-field day, 5 runners competed in the girls' 800-meter race. At the conclusion of the race, each runner shook the hand of every other runner. How many handshakes were there in all? _____

7. At the snack bar a milk shake and an apple cost $1.70. What is the cost of each if the milk shake costs $1 more than the apple? _____

8. Ann is getting dressed to attend the track-and-field events. She has 3 skirts and 4 sweaters in her drawer. If she decides to wear a skirt and sweater, how many different possible outfits can she choose from? _____

9. During the lunchtime break, Sal and Brenda take a walk around the neighborhood. Starting at the entrance to the field, they walk 5 blocks east. Then they turn north and walk 2 blocks. They turn west for 1 block, south for 2 blocks, west again for 3 blocks, and then north for 4 blocks. They then turn left, walk for 3 blocks, turn south and walk 4 blocks, and stop. How far are they from the entrance to the field? _____

10. David asked a worker at the snack bar for change for a quarter. How many different combinations of nickels, dimes, and pennies could David receive?

_____

11. At the conclusion of the girls' discus competition, Rona is $\frac{1}{2}$ meter behind Janice. Marie is $9\frac{3}{4}$ meters ahead of Angie. If Rona is $3\frac{1}{2}$ meters behind Marie, how far is Janice ahead of Angie?

_____

Name _____ Date _____

PRACTICE **Multiplying Integers**

Write + or − in the space to indicate whether each product
will be positive or negative.

1. 17 · 2 _____

2. ⁻2 · 21 _____

3. ⁻11 · ⁻3 _____

4. ⁻333 · ⁻1 _____

5. 403 · ⁻18 _____

6. ⁻606 · ⁻1,008 _____

Find the product.

7. ⁻84 · ⁻14 = _____

8. 90 · ⁻59 = _____

9. 93 · 26 = _____

10. ⁻84 · 48 = _____

11. 483 · ⁻42 = _____

12. ⁻836 · ⁻26 = _____

13. 147 · 31 = _____

14. ⁻722 · 60 = _____

15. ⁻267 · 14 = _____

The chart lists the names and locations of several of Earth's
high and low places. Find the product for each of the
problems below, and enter it on the corresponding line in
the chart. The completed chart will tell you the elevation in
feet above or below sea level for each location.

16. 1,130 · 25

17. ⁻635 · ⁻32

18. 967 · 20

19. 652 · 19

20. ⁻110 · ⁻87

21. 838 · 5

22. 3 · ⁻94

23. ⁻2,011 · 18

	Name	Location	Elevation (in feet)
16.	Mount Goodwin Austen	Kashmir	
17.	Mount McKinley	Alaska (U.S.)	
18.	Mount Kilimanjaro	Tanzania	
19.	Mount Fuji	Japan	
20.	Mount Olympus	Greece	
21.	Mount Vesuvius	Italy	
22.	Death Valley	California (U.S.)	
23.	Mariana Trench	Pacific Ocean	

PRACTICE   Dividing Integers

Divide.

1. $6\overline{)^-48}$

2. $^-3\overline{)12}$

3. $8\overline{)^-56}$

4. $^-9\overline{)18}$

5. $^-7\overline{)28}$

6. $^-5\overline{)10}$

7. $^-4\overline{)20}$

8. $^-9\overline{)81}$

9. $61\overline{)^-244}$

10. $31\overline{)^-279}$

11. $16\overline{)^-128}$

12. $^-39\overline{)^-273}$

13. $^-56\overline{)168}$

14. $^-2\overline{)^-188}$

15. $53\overline{)^-106}$

16. $^-6\overline{)252}$

17. $^-4,576 \div 52 =$ _____

18. $^-5,395 \div 83 =$ _____

19. $^-1,428 \div 84 =$ _____

20. $^-3,040 \div 80 =$ _____

21. $^-5,307 \div ^-61 =$ _____

22. $3,478 \div ^-74 =$ _____

23. $1,936 \div ^-88 =$ _____

24. $^-2,277 \div 33 =$ _____

25. $^-3,360 \div 56 =$ _____

26. $^-1,164 \div ^-4 =$ _____

27. $7,636 \div ^-83 =$ _____

28. $^-3,600 \div 80 =$ _____

Solve.

29. Excavation Industries' stock lost 16 points over a 4-day period. What was the stock's average change per day?

_____

30. On Tuesday, Salvage Systems' stock lost 5 points, on Wednesday it gained 3 points, and on Thursday it lost 7 points. What was the average daily change?

_____

PRACTICE   Problem-Solving Practice

Solve.

1. In 1984, a 612-pound pumpkin won the International Pumpkin Association's competition. Second place was awarded to a pumpkin that weighed about 8 percent less than the winner. How much did the second-place pumpkin weigh?

_____

2. The squash, which is related to the pumpkin, can also grow to a surprising size. Three of the largest squashes ever grown weighed 365, 402, and 466 pounds. What was their average weight?

_____

3. A good thing about pumpkins is that they can be used to make pies. If an 8-pound pumpkin is needed to make a single pumpkin pie, about how many pies could you make from three 11-pound pumpkins?

_____

4. On Saturday of the annual Pumpkin Festival weekend, the Souvenir Committee sold 66 Great Pumpkin T-shirts and 45 copies of *The Pumpkin Cookbook*. On Sunday, $\frac{1}{3}$ more T-shirts and $\frac{2}{5}$ more books are sold than were sold on Saturday. How many souvenirs were sold in all?

_____

Think about the remainder. Then ring the letter of the correct answer.

5. Glenda Mayer grew 3,363 pumpkins on her farm this summer. Her truck can hold about 354 pumpkins. How many trips will it take her to transport all the pumpkins to the market?

   a. 9   **b.** 9.5   **c.** 10

6. A farmer picks 8 pumpkins. If he can carry 3 pumpkins at a time, how many trips to the truck will he have to make?

   a. 2   **b.** 2.7   **c.** 3

Write a proportion and solve.

7. The average customer at the Meadowland Farmers Market buys about 6 apples, 7 plums, and 4 peaches. One morning, customers buy 234 apples and 156 peaches. About how many plums were sold?

_____

8. Ricardo is sketching a picture of the scarecrow in the pumpkin patch. He estimates that it is about 7.5 feet tall and that the horizontal stick that forms the scarecrow's arms is 4 feet long. If the figure he draws is 6 inches high, how wide should it be?

_____

PRACTICE Problem-Solving Practice

Solve.

9. The Austrian composer Wolfgang Amadeus Mozart was born in 1756 and died in 1791. The Italian composer Antonio Salieri was born 6 years earlier and died in 1825. About how many years longer did Salieri live than Mozart? _____

10. Last season, the Cosmopolitan Opera performed *Tosca* 12 times, *Aida* 17 times, *Lulu* 4 times, *Salome* 5 times, and *Carmen* 19 times. The first two operas are Italian; the next two are Austrian; and the last one is French. How many more performances were there of Italian operas than of non-Italian operas?

_____

Write an equation and solve.

11. A new production of *The Threepenny Opera* requires 36 costumes. The costume designer decides that he can adapt $\frac{2}{3}$ of the costumes that he created for last year's production of *Porgy and Bess.* How many new costumes must he make?

_____

12. Last year, 1,356 people in Australia attended a performance of Prokofiev's *The Love for Three Oranges.* When the same company performed the opera in Japan, 1,728 people attended. How much larger was the Japanese audience?

_____

13. Concert organizers predict that for every 2 children who come to this afternoon's performance, 5 adults will attend. If the organizers are correct, how many children will come to the concert if 315 adults attend?

_____

14. At the concert, albums and T-shirts are sold as souvenirs. About 7 T-shirts are sold for every 3 albums. At that rate, if 133 T-shirts are purchased, about how many albums will be sold?

_____

Ring the letter of the formula that would help you solve the problem.

15. For a production of *A Midsummer Night's Dream,* the designer plans to fill the stage with dozens of cubes painted in different colors. Each cube is 34 inches high. What is its volume?

a. $V = Bh$ **b.** $V = c^3$ **c.** $V = lwh$

16. The stage of a planned music hall will be rectangular in shape. To accommodate the huge productions to be presented there, the stage will be 33 meters wide and 21 meters deep. What will be its area?

a. $A = lw$ **b.** $A = \frac{1}{2}bh$ **c.** $P = 2l + 2w$

PRACTICE Solving Equations with Integers

Solve the equation.

1. $45 + x = 39$ _____

2. $^-82 - y = 15$ _____

3. $22m = {}^-374$ _____

4. $q \div 34 = {}^-1$ _____

5. $85 + r = 139$ _____

6. $y + 14 = {}^-2$ _____

7. $^-187q = 8{,}041$ _____

8. $n \div {}^-7 = 49$ _____

9. $x + {}^-18 = {}^-65$ _____

10. $u - 93 = 193$ _____

11. $^-629t = {}^-23{,}273$ _____

12. $p \div 3 = {}^-40$ _____

13. $138 + s = 276$ _____

14. $g - {}^-20 = 15$ _____

15. $^-63x = 4{,}914$ _____

16. $y \div 58 = {}^-21$ _____

17. $^-67 + b = 60$ _____

18. $^-76 - r = 59$ _____

19. $^-784t = {}^-24{,}304$ _____

20. $h \div 56 = {}^-25$ _____

21. $\frac{x}{^-4} - 4 = 9$ _____

22. $^-6y - 3 = 27$ _____

23. $3r + 2 = {}^-58$ _____

24. $\frac{t}{2} - 5 = 8$ _____

25. $\frac{m}{3} - 8 = {}^-20$ _____

26. $^-9g - 1 = 53$ _____

27. $\frac{n}{^-4} + 4 = 17$ _____

28. $^-2x - 5 = 33$ _____

Write the equation and solve.

29. If $^-6$ is subtracted from a certain number, the result is $^-24$. What is the number?

_____

30. If an integer is multiplied by $^-12$, the product is 252. What is the integer?

_____

31. If a number is multiplied by 7 and $^-42$ is added to the product, the result is $^-133$. What is the number?

_____

32. If a certain number is divided by $^-6$ and 14 is subtracted from the quotient, the result is $^-89$. What is the number?

_____

Use with pages 440–441

PRACTICE Solving Inequalities

Write *equality* or *inequality*.

1. $^-4 \geq 6 + n$ _____

2. $x + 2 \leq 5$ _____

3. $^-1 + y \neq 4$ _____

4. $7 + m = 3$ _____

5. $^-19 - x \neq 4$ _____

6. $15p \leq 125$ _____

Solve the inequality.

7. $p - 5 \leq 6$ _____

8. $k + 5 \geq 4$ _____

9. $3m \geq 21$ _____

10. $x + 41 \geq 19$ _____

11. $4h \leq ^-24$ _____

12. $73 + j \leq 1$ _____

13. $q - 1 \geq 4$ _____

14. $347 \geq x + 167$ _____

15. $x - 2 \leq 7$ _____

16. $25 \geq 5a$ _____

17. $7y \leq 35$ _____

18. $7x \leq 28$ _____

19. $4m \geq 36$ _____

20. $13 + p \leq ^-28$ _____

21. $x - 300 \leq 10$ _____

22. $y - ^-72 \leq 71$ _____

Write the inequality and solve.

23. The Hartville Volunteer Fire Department throws a picnic every summer to raise money. The fire fighters need 100 pounds or more of hamburger to feed everyone. If there are already 35 pounds in their freezer, how much more hamburger do they need to buy?

24. Mr. Ng, Mrs. Burn, and Mr. Gold volunteer to bring lemonade for the picnic. They calculate that they need at least 50 gallons of lemonade altogether. If each brings the same amount, how many gallons of lemonade must each bring?

_____

PRACTICE Writing an Equation

Ring the letter of the correct equation.

1. An anchor is lowered from the deck of a fishing boat until it touches the bottom of the bay. The boat's deck is 8 feet above the water, and the bottom of the bay is 27 feet below the surface of the water. How much anchor rope was let out?

   a. $27 - 8 = n$

   b. $^-27 + 8 = n$

   c. $27 + 8 = n$

2. In the late eighteenth century, there were 264 French fishing boats and 10,000 registered crew members. The English fishing fleet had 400 boats and 20,000 crew members. How many crew members were there for every boat in the French fleet?

   a. $10,000 \div 264 = n$

   b. $10,000 \times 264 = n$

   c. $20,000 \div 400 = n$

Write an equation and solve.

3. In 1980, the population of the world was approximately 4,000,000,000, which was about 12 times as much as the estimated population of the world in 1300. About how many people were there in 1300?

   _____

   _____

4. Spanish explorers discovered the potato when they reached Peru in 1539. It was brought to England by Sir Walter Raleigh 49 years later and was first grown in France about 70 years after that. In what year did the potato reach France?

   _____

   _____

5. Pepper was the most valuable import of the Dutch East Indies Company in 1648. It accounted for 33% of the total value of products and materials brought from India to Europe. By 1780, it had fallen to fourth place. By what percent did its value drop per year?

   _____

   _____

6. Dried fish was once used as a form of money in Iceland. According to a regulation issued in 1426, a pair of women's shoes were worth 3 fish, and a cask of butter was worth 120 fish. How many pairs of women's shoes could you buy with a cask of butter?

   _____

   _____

7. In the mountains of Switzerland, the spring sunshine often raises daytime temperatures to a very comfortable level. On one sunny day, the temperature rose to 17°C by noon. Twelve hours later, however, the temperature dropped 29°. What was the temperature at midnight?

   _____

   _____

8. In the year 1086, tax collectors counted 287,045 tenants and landowners living in the 34 counties of England. If each tenant and landowner had 5 other people living in his or her household, what was the average number of people living in each county?

   _____

   _____

Use with pages 444–445

PRACTICE Graphing Sentences

Solve. Graph each solution on the number line.

1. $x + {}^-6 \le {}^-3$ _____

$\xleftarrow{\hspace{0.3cm}}$ | $\overset{{}^-8}{}$ | $\overset{{}^-7}{}$ | $\overset{{}^-6}{}$ | $\overset{{}^-5}{}$ | $\overset{{}^-4}{}$ | $\overset{{}^-3}{}$ | $\overset{{}^-2}{}$ | $\overset{{}^-1}{}$ | $\overset{0}{}$ | $\overset{1}{}$ | $\overset{2}{}$ | $\overset{3}{}$ | $\overset{4}{}$ | $\overset{5}{}$ | $\overset{6}{}$ | $\overset{7}{}$ | $\overset{8}{}$ $\xrightarrow{\hspace{0.3cm}}$

2. $t + {}^-9 = {}^-15$ _____

$-8\ -7\ -6\ -5\ -4\ -3\ -2\ -1\ 0\ 1\ 2\ 3\ 4\ 5\ 6\ 7\ 8$

3. $z + 4 \ge 3$ _____

$-8\ -7\ -6\ -5\ -4\ -3\ -2\ -1\ 0\ 1\ 2\ 3\ 4\ 5\ 6\ 7\ 8$

4. $\frac{1}{2} + p \ge 4\frac{1}{2}$ _____

$-8\ -7\ -6\ -5\ -4\ -3\ -2\ -1\ 0\ 1\ 2\ 3\ 4\ 5\ 6\ 7\ 8$

5. $n - 4 = 3$ _____

$-8\ -7\ -6\ -5\ -4\ -3\ -2\ -1\ 0\ 1\ 2\ 3\ 4\ 5\ 6\ 7\ 8$

6. ${}^-6 + y = {}^-8$ _____

$-8\ -7\ -6\ -5\ -4\ -3\ -2\ -1\ 0\ 1\ 2\ 3\ 4\ 5\ 6\ 7\ 8$

7. $\frac{1}{5}s \le 1$ _____

$-8\ -7\ -6\ -5\ -4\ -3\ -2\ -1\ 0\ 1\ 2\ 3\ 4\ 5\ 6\ 7\ 8$

8. ${}^-3.8 + t \ge {}^-1.8$ _____

$-8\ -7\ -6\ -5\ -4\ -3\ -2\ -1\ 0\ 1\ 2\ 3\ 4\ 5\ 6\ 7\ 8$

9. $2r = {}^-4$ _____

$-8\ -7\ -6\ -5\ -4\ -3\ -2\ -1\ 0\ 1\ 2\ 3\ 4\ 5\ 6\ 7\ 8$

10. $m - 6 \le 2$ _____

$-8\ -7\ -6\ -5\ -4\ -3\ -2\ -1\ 0\ 1\ 2\ 3\ 4\ 5\ 6\ 7\ 8$

11. $3y > {}^-15$ _____

$-8\ -7\ -6\ -5\ -4\ -3\ -2\ -1\ 0\ 1\ 2\ 3\ 4\ 5\ 6\ 7\ 8$

PRACTICE Graphing Ordered Pairs

Write the ordered pair for each point on the coordinate plane.

1. A _____   2. B _____

3. C _____   4. D _____

5. E _____   6. F _____

7. G _____   8. H _____

9. I _____   10. J _____

11. K _____   12. L _____

13. M _____   14. N _____

15. O _____   16. P _____

17. Q _____   18. R _____

Write the coordinate points on each axis.

19. x-axis _____   20. y-axis _____

Write the coordinate points that define each figure.

21. A rectangle with point E as a vertex. _____

22. A right triangle with side 3 and point R as a vertex.

_____

23. A parallelogram with side 4 and point P as a vertex.

_____

24. Suppose R, H, and Q are vertices of a square. Mark the fourth vertex, S, on the coordinate plane and write the coordinates. _____

Use with pages 448–449.

Name _____ Date _____

PRACTICE Using a Broken-Line Graph

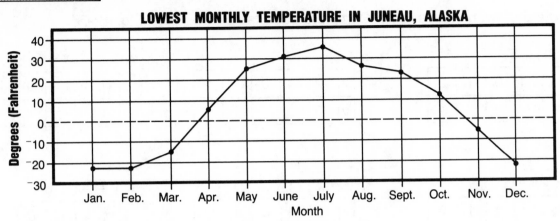

LOWEST MONTHLY TEMPERATURE IN JUNEAU, ALASKA

Use the broken-line graph above to answer questions 1–6.

1. What was the lowest temperature recorded in Juneau in November? _____

2. During which month was the lowest recorded temperature 6°F? _____

3. In which two months was the same low temperature recorded?

_____

4. In how many months shown was the temperature below 0°F? _____

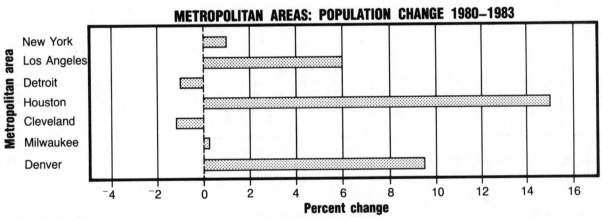

METROPOLITAN AREAS: POPULATION CHANGE 1980–1983

Use the broken-line bar graph above to answer questions 1–10.

5. Which metropolitan area had the greatest percent of increase? _____

6. Which metropolitan area had a greater change in population—Detroit or Cleveland? how much greater?

_____

7. Which metropolitan area had the least change in population between 1980 and 1983?

_____

8. If the Houston area had a population of 3,100,000 in 1980, what was its population in 1983? _____

Use with pages 450–451.

189

PRACTICE   Solving Equations in Two Variables

Substitute the given values for x. Complete each table.   Fig. 12-7

1. $y = 2x + 5$

x	$^-2$	$^-1$	0	1	2
y	1				

2. $y = x - 3$

x	$^-2$	$^-1$	0	1	2
y	$^-5$				

3. $y = {}^-3x + 2$

x	$^-2$	$^-1$	0	1	2
y					

4. $y = {}^-2x + 1$

x	$^-2$	$^-1$	0	1	2
y	5				

5. $y = x - 1$

x	$^-2$	$^-1$	0	1	2
y					

6. $y = 4x + 3$

x	$^-2$	$^-1$	0	1	2
y					

Substitute values for x. Complete each table.

7. $y = x - 5$

x	$^-2$	$^-1$	0	1	2
y					

8. $y = {}^-2x - 2$

x	$^-2$	$^-1$	0	1	2
y					

9. $y = 3x + 3$

x	$^-2$	$^-1$	0	1	2
y					

10. $y = x + 7$

x	$^-2$	$^-1$	0	1	2
y					

11. $y = {}^-4x - 5$

x	$^-2$	$^-1$	0	1	2
y					

12. $y = 6x + 2$

x	$^-2$	$^-1$	0	1	2
y					

Set up a table to find three ordered-pair solutions to each equation.

13. $y = x + 9$

14. $y = {}^-3x - 2$

15. $y = 7x + 4$

16. $y = x - 12$

17. $y = 5x - 2$

18. $y = {}^-3x - 5$

Use with pages 452–453.

ame _____ Date _____

PRACTICE   Graphing Equations in Two Variables

Complete each table. Use it to graph each equation.

1. $y = 2x + 6$

x	−5	−3	−2	0
y				

2. $y = {}^-2x + 6$

x	0	1	3	5
y				

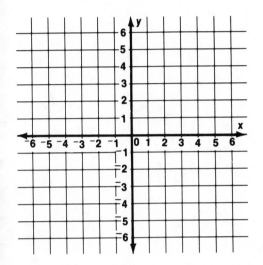

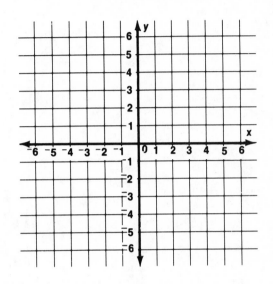

3. $y = {}^-x + 4$

x	−2	0	1	4
y				

4. $y = 3x − 1$

x	−1	0	1	2
y				

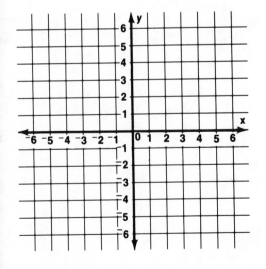

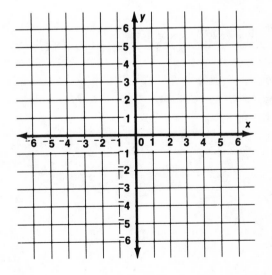

PRACTICE ANSWER KEY

Page 1

1. 14,025
2. 3,841,000,200
3. 6,000,034,005,000
4. 92 million, 957 thousand
5. 4 thousand, 5
6. 1 trillion, 352 billion, 729 million, 321
7. 600 million
8. 3 billion
9. 70 thousand
10. 4 hundred
11. 855,003
12. 9,381,060
13. 70,040,237
14. 40,000 + 8,000 + 40 + 5
15. 700,000 + 90,000 + 30
16. 9,000,000 + 300,000 + 5,000 + 800

Page 2

1. < 2. < 3. > 4. > 5. >
6. < 7. > 8. = 9. > 10. >
11. < 12. >
13. 234,386; 243,368; 387,432; 645,200
14. 7,107,000; 17,000,071; 17,017,000; 71,000,170
15. 1,745; 1,754; 17,345; 17,534; 17,543
16. 895; 8,945; 8,954; 89,452; 89,549
17. 8,501,400; 521,621; 521,615; 501,615
18. 94,704,060; 18,250,000; 18,000,250; 94,000
19. 124,653; 124,563; 12,456; 1,642; 1,246
20. 794,345; 749,345; 9,743; 7,943; 794

Page 3

1. 89 2. 3,793 3. 123 4. 34
5. 391 6. 729 7. 0 8. 55
9. 35 10. 22 11. 733 12. 7
13. 844 14. 120 15. 0 16. 707
17. 0 18. 49 19. 0 20. 29
21. 24 22. 0 23. 3 24. 58
25. 66 26. 67 27. 92 28. 362
29. 50 30. 0 31. 11 32. 22
33. 32 34. 1 35. 299 36. 71
37. 0 38. 472 39. 500 40. 23

Page 4

1. b 2. b 3. c 4. a 5. b 6. b

Page 5*

1. 15,000–17,000
2. 14,000–15,000
3. 400,000–500,000
4. 10,000,000–11,000,000
5. 15,000–17,000
6. 14,000–16,000
7. 400,000–500,000
8. 11,000,000–12,000,000
9. 16,000–18,000
10. 24,000–26,000
11. 6,000,000–8,000,000
12. 7,000,000–9,000,000
13. 12,000–14,000
14. 11,000–13,000
15. 35,000,000–40,000,000
16. $20,000–$23,000

Page 6*

1. a 2. b 3. b 4. b 5. a
6. a 7. b 8. a 9. a 10. a
11. b
12. $6,000^-$
13. $4,000^-$
14. $40,000^+$
15. $50,000^+$
16. $60,000^+$
17. $200,000^+$
18. $2,000,000^-$
19. $7,000,000^+$
20. $50,000^-$ women
21. $\$5,000,000^-$

Page 7

1. 6,947 2. 7,816 3. 8,567
4. 9,758 5. 7,094 6. $134.24
7. 11,801 8. 9,201 9. 85,994
10. 99,411 11. 56,225
12. $621.38 13. 1,397,089
14. 1,391,164 15. 938,226
16. 1,054,603 17. $1,295
18. 11,672 19. 126,466
20. 46,943 21. 287,024
22. 824,780 23. 284,450
24. 184,967 25. $39.08
26. $51.72

Page 8

1. 31,231 2. 95,390 3. 8,950
4. 95,727 5. 9,353 6. 7,416
7. 4,616 8. 3,836 9. 6,470
10. 1,656 11. 56,285 12. 44,890

*Answers may vary. Accept any reasonable estimate.

Page 8 (cont'd.)

13. 80,117 14. 89,323
15. 94,053 16. 7,130 17. 18,692
18. 19,752 19. 28,817
20. 19,458 21. 899,830
22. 977,962 23. 792,673
24. 392,476 25. 18,177 26. 185
27. $138.32 28. $556.57
29. 6,163 30. 899,897
31. 40,473 32. 978,239
33. 43,862

Page 9

1. Checks; 7 more pictures
2. Questions; 20 pictures
3. Tools; $115
4. Solutions; no
5. Questions; 4 days
6. Checks; $23

Page 10

Check students' charts.
1. 10.419286
2. 4.0021
3. 0.19834
4. 4 hundredths
5. 1 hundred-thousandth
6. 4 millionths
7. 5 ten-thousandths
8. 0.2
9. 0.45
10. 0.352
11. 0.0005
12. 0.000075
13. 0.00001
14. six and eight tenths
15. thirty-three thousandths
16. four hundred ten ten-thousandths

Page 11

1. > 2. < 3. < 4. = 5. <
6. > 7. > 8. > 9. = 10. <
11. = 12. >
13. 14.511611; 14.5106; 14.051610; 14.005161
14. 0.02; 0.021; 0.201; 0.21; 2.1
15. 0.6431; 6.4031; 6.413; 6.431
16. 0.006913; 0.07; 0.07103; 0.69001
17. 2.058003; 2.50038; 2.503008; 2.50308
18. Monday, Tuesday, Thursday, Friday, Wednesday
19. Wednesday, Thursday, Friday

PRACTICE ANSWER KEY

Page 12

1. 5, 0.2, 0.02, 1.004, 8.3304
2. 31, 4.1, 2.52; 0.481, 1.0942
3. 1, 15.1, 14.11, 3.625, 2.6803
4. 30, 12, 16.2, 0.425, 0.8088
5. 16, 0.4, 10.24, 25.506, 15.9805
6. 10, 3.5, 7.89, 4.001, 1
7. TH 8. HU 9. TT 10. TE
11. TH 12. W 13. HU 14. W

Page 13

1. 9°F
2. Schubert
3. Pascal
4. 2 cups mashed potatoes
5. no. 4
6. no. 1
7. one-bedroom apartment
8. Schumann and Chopin
9. 225 calories
10. Montreal; Pittsburgh
11. Pierre de Fermat
12. an apple

Page 14

1. < 2. > 3. > 4. > 5. >
6. < 7. > 8. < 9. > 10. >
11. > 12. < 13. > 14. <
15. >
16. >; **Code:** CHINA
17. $400–$600
18. $500–$600
17.–18. Answers will vary. Accept any reasonable estimate.

Page 15

1. 89.7595 2. 66.855
3. 739.06 4. 82.3319
5. 44.3895 6. 127.2613
7. 1,627.911 8. 309.8315
9. $17,312.21 10. $87,366.34
11. $183,453.20 12. $145,124.15
13. 76.6085 14. 116.1224
15. 150.6951 16. 227.9653
17. 120.4467 18. 207.1827
19. 95.9805 20. 133.7906
21. 23.313 22. 152.565
23. 48.2094 24. 3.9321
25. 27.2891 26. 52.685

Page 16

1. 0.1 2. 3.6 3. 3.2 4. 14.6
5. 30.6 6. 36.4 7. 12.7
8. 11.9 9. 23.39 10. 31.87
11. 2.63 12. 45.47 13. 45.836

Page 16 (cont'd.)

14. 51.662 15. 91.7523
16. 2.144 17. 45.56 18. 8.31
19. 19.223 20. 4.81 21. 42.3963
22. 91.7523 23. 9.3863
24. 22.6082 25. 6.1252
26. 11.2482 27. 1.2424
28. 11.2123 29. $14.16
30. $4.93

Page 17

1. 1985 2. 1983 3. 360 adults
4. 160 more adults 5. 1983
6. 720 more adults and children
7. 1984 8. 1981
9. 1,300 people 10. 640 people

Page 18

1. = 2. = 3. = 4. ≠ 5. ≠
6. = 7. = 8. = 9. ≠
10. ≠ 11. = 12. ≠ 13. C
14. D 15. D 16. A 17. Z 18. I
19. A 20. A 21. 0 22. 1,376
23. 0 24. 33 25. 27 26. 0

Page 19

1. 4,970 2. 2,551,200
3. 20,850
4. 24,498,000 5. 431,500
6. 2,968,000 7. 61,680
8. 16,800
9. 9,594,000 10. 32,250
11. 2,870,000 12. 17,010
13. 1,155,200 14. 6,300
15. 1,163,700 16. 1,500,300
17. 5,640 18. 8,550,000
19. 31,700 20. 10,280,000
21. 2,000,000,000
22. 1,010,100,000
23. 76,500,000 24. 88,000,000
25. 66,400 26. 379,000
27. 1,180,000 28. 92,700,000
29. 12,500 calories
30. 6,000 calories

Page 20

Check students' mazes.

Page 21

1. 2,832 2. 992 3. 5,967
4. 875 5. 748 6. 3,663
7. $70.52 8. 50,127 9. 33,572
10. 41,148 11. 14,075
12. 76,512 13. 6,369
14. $478.87 15. 38,248
16. 271,350 17. 561,348

Page 21 (cont'd.)

18. $1,165.23 19. 346,032
20. 307,530 21. $8,014.96
22. 748,676 23. 1,807,778
24. 887,655 25. 2,352,639
26. 1,643,770 27. 6,137,928
28. $4,595.88 29. 1,952

Page 22

1. b 2. a
3. There is not enough information to solve this problem.
4. $500
5. There is not enough information to solve this problem.
6. $382
7. $4,325
8. There is not enough information to solve this problem.
9. $65
10. 150 shares

Page 23

1. 3,747,315 2. 2,773
3. 81,015 4. 6,465 5. 2,328
6. 4,824 7. 2,655,247
8. 662, 796 9. 80,580
10. 75,500 11. 4,592
12. 28,310
13. 1,788,206
14. 1,748
15. 47,664
16. 3,752
17. $687.50
18. $3,629.40
19. $5,685.20
20. $45,582.58
21. $5,931.90
22. $61,693.17
23. $38,110.73
24. $3,434.34
25. 1,836 gallons

Page 24

1. 191,026
2. 3,134,960
3. $749,200
4. 448,675
5. 1,379,070
6. 107,146
7. $505,605
8. 146,540
9. 599,504
10. 1,198,340
11. 431,136
12. $1,431,000
13. 897,840

PRACTICE ANSWER KEY

Page 24 (cont'd.)

14. 334,400
15. $1,400,700
16. 57,528
17. 225,235
18. $613,128
19. 947,650
20. 321,440
21. 737,295 labels
22. $5,913.00 per week

Page 25

1. yes
2. no
3. yes
4. $152.44
5. no
6. yes
7. more
8. no
9. yes
10. 1,176 miles

Page 26*

1. c 2. d 3. a 4. 4.1748
5. 3.1899 6. 0.7007
7. 0.435554
8. 6^+ 9. 3^+ 10. 0.4^-
11. 2.5^+ 12. 5^+ 13. 6^-
14. $1.00–$1.50; $5.00–$6.00
15. $4 million–$5.5 million

Page 27

1. 11.9543 2. $60.82
3. 6.48408 4. 46.6944
5. 52.266 6. 4.0395
7. 279.818 8. 2.6722 9. $5.46
10. 23.9943 11. 5.26832
12. $11.50 13. 8.14218
14. 2.9712 15. 16.84065
16. 16.8084 17. 13.2065
18. $8.30 19. 19.86688
20. 7.65583 21. $3.86
22. 217.242 23. 6.3504
24. 62.06 25. 38.5434
26. $52.26 27. 7.416
28. 10.81332 29. $114.56
30. $108.00

Page 28

1. 24 games
2. 5 more points
3. 8 points
4. 60 games
5. 1.5 points
6. 29 people

Page 28 (cont'd.)

7. 12 people more
8. George and Lisa won by one game.
9. $25
10. $3.25

Page 29

1. 40.0772 2. 562.36
3. 30,247.6 4. 30,241
5. 69.047 6. 0.56 7. 2.1834
8. 1,037 9. 0.078 10. 2.19
11. 0.17 12. 9,580.83
13. 4,726.71 14. 36,380
15. 13.699 16. 0.02 17. 87.196
18. 4,331.5 19. 7,400.7
20. 76.478 21. 44.41 22. 30.648
23. 619.78 24. 4,630 25. 51.9
26. 4.6257 27. 4,221 28. 8.2711
29. $543.00 30. $1,600.00
31. $8,500.00 32. $29,318.80
33. 1.5 cm

Page 30

1. 0.05436 2. 0.0485
3. 0.3094 4. 0.00985 5. 0.512
6. 2.184 7. 0.59697
8. 0.10905 9. 0.81786
10. 0.00441 11. 0.6984
12. 0.9632 13. 0.042
14. 0.001953 15. 0.1958
16. 0.05328 17. 0.01431
18. 0.2115 19. 0.06048
20. 0.4731 21. $82.69 22. $0.05
23. $3,120.31 24. $15.90
25. $10,775.68 26. $3.69
27. 4,200 feet

Page 31

1. Find Evelyn's rent for one month.
2. Find the cost of 1,827 kilowatt-hours of electricity.
3. $29.29
4. $3,980
5. 33 hours
6. $1,453.20
7. $397.50
8. 27 dresses

Page 32

1. 7×8
2. $25 \div 5$
3. $102 \div 6$
4. 12×13
5. $200 \div 20$

Page 32 (cont'd.)

6. 21×19
7. 22/11; $22 \div 11$; $11\overline{)22}$
8. 140/7; $140 \div 7$; $7\overline{)140}$
9. 336/6; $336 \div 6$; $6\overline{)336}$
10. 820/4; $820 \div 4$; $4\overline{)820}$
11. false
12. true
13. false
14. false
15. true
16. false
17. 0 18. 1 19. 14 20. 0 21. 1
22. 5 23. 4 24. 4 25. 1
26. 3 balloons

Page 33

1. 200 2. 300 3. 60 4. 50
5. 90 6. 14 7. 100 8. 1,000
9. 150 10. 10 11. 3 12. 7
13. 111 14. 3,000 15. 1,000
16. 209 17. 100 18. 2,830
19. 3,309 20. 1,235 21. 635
22. 4,000 23. 140

Page 34*

1. 40^+ 2. 70^+ 3. 120^+
4. 20^+ 5. 200^+ 6. 400^+
7. 800^+ 8. 500^+
9. 600^+ 10. 2.00^+
11. 0.08^+ 12. 2.00^+
13. 10.00^+
14. 100^+ 15. 200^+
16. $8,000^+$
17. 600^+
18. 100^+ rides
19. 60^+ members
20. 100^+ members
21. 8^+ souvenir buttons

Page 35

1. 146 2. 145 3. 106 4. 108
5. 86 6. 81 7. 292 8. 297 R1
9. 167 R1 10. 76 R5
11. 207 R6 12. 304 R5
13. 805 R3 14. 604 R4
15. 301 R4 16. 409 17. 608
18. 8,056 R5 19. 3,074 R4
20. 6,104 R3 21. 29,663
22. 10,901 R2 23. 15,297 R1
24. 7,541 R2 25. 11,190 R5
26. 19,814 R3 27. 13,143 R1
28. 87,785 R8

*Answers may vary. Accept any reasonable estimate.

PRACTICE ANSWER KEY

Page 36

1. less
2. no
3. yes
4. more
5. yes
6. less
7. more
8. greater

Page 37

1. 330 R9   2. 1,043   3. 694 R2
4. 2,807 R5   5. 314 R17
6. 5,406 R15   7. 4,380 R54
8. 2,021 R23   9. 7,419 R12
10. 4,032 R8   11. 93,425
12. 9,062 R1   13. 15,231
14. 1,005 R3   15. 6,284
16. 14,022
17. 1,091 bald eagles
18. 6,053 trumpeter swans

Page 38

1. 364   2. 110   3. 716
4. 937 R32   5. 864 R61
6. 431 R179   7. 265
8. 249 R693   9. 1,820
10. 4,602 R30   11. 2,501 R2
12. 4,480 R3   13. 867
14. 713 R29   15. 31 R465
16. 898   17. 311   18. 509
19. 452   20. 188   21. 511
22. 217 points
23. 653 games

Page 39

1. Ring b.
2. Ring c.
3. Ring b.
4. Ring a.
5. Ring b.
6. Ring b.
7. Ring a.
8. Ring c.

Page 40

1. 2.17   2. 43.08   3. 55.061
4. 3.415   5. 6.4   6. 9.005
7. 67.25   8. 0.063   9. $5.07
10. $1.15   11. $0.98
12. $20.55
13. 24.63
14. 21
15. 50.6
16. 1.034

Page 40 (cont'd.)

17. 6.2544
18. 25
19. 21

Page 41

1. c
2. c
3. 25 years old
4. $759.60 per week
5. 86,000
6. $63,545
7. $144,375
8. $6,353,004

Page 42

1. 0.4538   2. 0.112   3. 94.86
4. 0.2109   5. 0.0053   6. 0.0052
7. 0.0174   8. 0.0001
9. 0.009001   10. 0.8338
11. 4.15   12. 0.00077
13. 0.00005   14. 0.0033   15. 0.9
16. 6.463   17. $9.43   18. $0.38
19. $0.18   20. $8.59   21. $7.66
22. $6.85   23. $4.00   24. $3.20
25. $5.76   26. $46.25   27. $0.02
28. 35.9

Page 43

1. 3.66   2. 40.55   3. 0.38
4. 0.15   5. 0.95   6. 0.95
7. 2.25   8. 82   9. 935
10. 9.9763   11. 12.5   12. 0.5611
13. $781.00   14. $4,085.00
15. $740.80   16. $219.90
17. $1,170   18. $350.00   19. 0.05
20. 839.2
21. 24 servings
22. $14.95

Page 44

1. 1.5   2. 5.1   3. 10.9   4. 0.83
5. 22.58   6. 4.79   7. 1.667
8. 0.983   9. 0.150   10. $2
11. $1   12. $6   13. $0.99
14. $0.19   15. $1.60

Page 45

1. 64 miles
2. Fitchburg
3. 1.19 hours (or about 1 hour 11 minutes)
4. 30.5 miles per hour
5. 131 miles

Page 45 (cont'd.)

6. Mr. Johnston's route is one mile shorter.

Page 46

1. yes, no, yes
2. no, no, no
3. no, yes, yes
4. yes, yes, no
5. no, yes, yes
6. no, no, yes
7. yes, no, no
8. yes, no, no
9. yes, yes, yes
10. yes, yes, no
11. no, yes, yes
12. yes, yes, yes
13. yes, yes, no
14. 6, 9, 10

Page 47

1. $3 \times 3 \times 3 \times 3 = 81$
2. $10 \times 10 = 100$
3. $5 \times 5 \times 5 = 125$
4. $2 \times 2 \times 2 \times 2 \times 2 \times 2 = 64$
5. $1 \times 1 \times 1 \times 1 \times 1 \times 1 \times 1 = 1$
6. $12 \times 12 = 144$
7. $9 \times 9 \times 9 = 729$
8. 1   9. 7^3 10. 4^5 11. 13^2
12. 20^3 13. 15^4 14. 3^6 15. >
16. <   17. <   18. >
19. <   20. >

Across:
A. 121
E. 1
F. 25
G. 10
H. 640
I. 144
Down:
B. 20
C. 225
D. 75
E. 100
H. 64
I. 1

Page 48

1. 3.8×10^1
2. 1.46×10^1
3. 2.23×10^2
4. 4.372×10^1
5. 4.065×10^3

Page 48 (cont'd.)

6. 1.9×10^0
7. 5.8×10^1
8. 2.25×10^5
9. 7.39×10^2
10. 5.31×10^4
11. 84 **12.** 27,500 **13.** 947
14. 532.3 **15.** 4,906 **16.** 3.4
17. 65 **18.** 108,000 **19.** 94,100
20. 253,000 **21.** M **22.** A **23.** R
24. S

Page 49

1. 1, 2, 3, 6, 9, 18
2. 1, 2, 3, 4, 6, 8, 12, 24
3. 1, 37
4. 1, 7, 13, 91
5. 1, 5, 13, 65
6. 1, 2, 4, 8, 16, 32
7. 1, 2, 3, 6, 11, 22, 33, 66
8. 1, 2, 4, 7, 14, 28
9. composite
10. prime
11. prime
12. prime
13. prime
14. composite
15. composite
16. composite
17. composite
18. prime
19. composite
20. prime
21. composite
22. composite
23. composite
24. 2, 3, 5, 7, 11, 13, 17, 19, 23, 29
25. one

Page 50

1. $3 \times 3 \times 5 \times 7$
2. $2 \times 2 \times 2 \times 3 \times 5 \times 5$
3. $3 \times 3 \times 11$
4. 7×19
5. $2 \times 3 \times 5 \times 7 \times 7$
6. $2 \times 2 \times 2 \times 3 \times 13$
7.–12. Check factor trees.
7. $2^4 \times 5^2$
8. $2 \times 3 \times 7$
9. $5^2 \times 7$
10. $3 \times 5^2 \times 11$
11. $2^3 \times 5 \times 7$
12. $2 \times 3^2 \times 5$
13. 225 **14.** 24 **15.** 360 **16.** 539

Page 50 (cont'd.)

17. 6,125 **18.** 1,859 **19.** 288
20. 8,918 **21.** 6,885

Page 51

1. 20°
2. 10 weeks
3. July 20
4. August 10
5. July 27 and August 17
6. 13 degrees warmer
7. 4 weeks
8. August 17 to August 24
9. 22°C
10. June 22 to June 29

Page 52

1. 8 **2.** 6 **3.** 5 **4.** 6 **5.** 6
6. 8 **7.** 27 **8.** 13 **9.** 5 **10.** 6
11. 1 **12.** 19 **13.** 4 **14.** 8
15. 34 **16.** 15 **17.** 12 **18.** 1
19. 8 **20.** 34 **21.** 7 **22.** 11
23. 15 **24.** 2 **25.** 5 **26.** 3 **27.** 4
28. 8 **29.** 9 **30.** 1 **31.** 45 **32.** 1
33. 8 **34.** 4,15 **35.** 21,22
36. 9,40 **37.** 7,16 **38.** 22,39
39. 21,80 **40.** 35,48 **41.** 22,45
42. 7,12 **43.** 13,100 **44.** 75,91
45. 81,100

Page 53

1. 0, 4, 8, 12, 16
2. 0, 17, 34, 51, 68
3. 0, 5, 10, 15, 20
4. 0, 8, 16, 24, 32
5. 0, 12, 24, 36, 48
6. 0, 25, 50, 75, 100
7. 0; 221; 442; 663; 884
8. 8 **9.** 9 **10.** 42 **11.** 75
12. 30 **13.** 24 **14.** 44 **15.** 72
16. 190 **17.** 72 **18.** 78 **19.** 200
20. 99 **21.** 30 **22.** 174 **23.** 234
24. 42 **25.** 612 **26.** 144 **27.** 180
28. 180
Solution for the boxed question:
Multiply them.

Page 54

1. $78
2. 2 inches more
3. There is not enough information.
4. 11,177 feet
5. 1,320 skiers per hour
6. 6 runs

Page 54 (cont'd.)

7. Ring b.
8. Ring b.

Page 55

9. 32.35 seconds
10. 2.92 seconds more
11. Riverside, by 18.95 seconds
12. 1 minute 53.01 seconds
13. 3 minutes 17.6 seconds
14. Billings High School
15. Estimated winner is Billings — 1 minute 56 seconds; exact time was 1 minute 55.72 seconds, which is within 0.28 seconds of the estimated time.
16. 0.3 seconds

Page 56

1. 17 **2.** 16 **3.** 10 **4.** 4 **5.** 10
6. 0 **7.** 6 **8.** 19 **9.** 7 **10.** 6
11. 12 **12.** 7 **13.** 18 **14.** 2
15. 38 **16.** 12 **17.** 2 **18.** 8
19. $(3 + 2)$
20. $(14 - 6)$
21. $(8 + 12)$, $(4 \cdot 5)$
22. $(3 \cdot 2)^2$
23. $(2 + 3)^2$
24. $(3 - 2)$
25. $(16 - 4)$, $(2 + 1)$
26. $(5 + 2)$
27. $(2 \div 2)$
28. $(40 + 10) - (2 \cdot 9) = 32$
29. $(4 + 6)^2 \div (50 - 30) = 5$

Page 57

1. 9, 7.4, 18, 14
2. 7, 5.4, 16, 12
3. 1.76, 0.16, 10.76, 6.76
4. 13, 14.76, 4, 8
5. false
6. true
7. true
8. false
9. false
10. 11 **11.** 1 **12.** 12 **13.** 9
14. 8 **15.** 7 **16.** 4 **17.** 15 **18.** 5
19. 24

Page 58

1. $x = 10$
2. $y = 18$
3. $z = 14.7$
4. $w = 37$

Page 58 (cont'd.)

5. $q = 15$
6. $z = 84$
7. $y = 61$
8. $w = 269$
9. $y = 7.9$
10. $x = 107$
11. $r = 14$
12. $n = 844$
13. $q = 90$
14. $g = 93$
15. $k = 47$
16. $w = 7.6$
17. $b = 44$
18. $s = 81$
19. $x = 25$
20. $p = 22$
21. $f = 36$
22. $v = 91$
23. $p = 16.1$
24. $y = 43$
25. $m = 895$
26. $x = 8$
27. $d = 665$
28. $m = 948$
29. $q = 2.5$
30. $x = 21$
31. $n - 6.4 = 3.8; n = 10.2$

Page 59

1. 15,000 people
2. 5,000 more listeners
3. $387.75
4. 30,000 listeners
5. 62,500 listeners
6. 8 records
7. $1,590.00
8. 45 more cars

Page 60

1. 21.6 2. 81 3. 3 4. 3 5. 6
6. 45 7. 17 8. 1 9. 38.7
10. 82 11. 11 12. 99
13. true
14. false
15. true
16. true
17. true
18. false
19. true
20. false
21. $c = 1$
22. no solution
23. $c = 8$
24. $c = 0$

Page 60 (cont'd.)

25. no solution
26. $c = 6$

Page 61

1. $x = 8$
2. $y = 26$
3. $n = 6$
4. $p = 1$
5. $r = 5$
6. $m = 87$
7. $q = 38$
8. $q = 6$
9. $x = 2$
10. $w = 2$
11. $r = 406$
12. $y = 7$
13. $y = 942$
14. $p = 3$
15. $c = 532$
16. $x = 3$
17. $y = 8$
18. $x = 9$
19. $x = 48$
20. $y = 4$
21. $x = 9$
22. $d = 9$
23. $n = 77$
24. $r = 144$
25. $x = 0$
26. $h = 9$
27. $s = 405$
28. $x = 765$
29. $n = 476$
30. $m = 4$
31. $v = 324$
32. $q = 1,632$
33. $x = 940$
34. $q = 2.002$
35. $x = 4.02$
36. $n = 23.37$
37. $m/5 = 1.4; m = 7$
38. $15r = 90; r = 6$

Page 62

1. $n = 9$
2. $n = 98$
3. $y = 8$
4. $q = 9$
5. $r = 11$
6. $x = 84$
7. $p = 7$
8. $f = 30$
9. $y = 9$
10. $d = 63$
11. $h = 14$

Page 62 (cont'd.)

12. $b = 72$
13. $x = 19$
14. $v = 16$
15. $i = 8$
16. $s = 84$
17. $s = 84$
18. $c = 27$
19. $e = 9$
20. $y = 56$
21. $s = 7$
22. $o = 5$
23. $g = 11$
24. $i = 36$
25. $p = 20$
26. $m = 14$
27. $a = 4$
28. $u = 45$
29. $l = 27$
30. $r = 28$
31. $t = 6$
32. $c = 1$
Code: YOUR PAGE IS COMPLETE.

Page 63

1. $n = 2 + 4; 6$
2. $n = 150 \div 6$, 25 days
3. $n = 50 \times 3$; 150 feet
4. $40 = n - 160$; 200 feet
5. $0.33n = 1.67$; about 5 miles
6. $n = 200 - 65$; 135 feet
7. $n = 754 + 146 + 420$; 1,320 feet
8. $n/2 + 20 = 47$; 54

Page 64

1. $\frac{3}{8}, \frac{4}{8}, \frac{6}{8}, \frac{8}{8}$
2. $\frac{2}{10}, \frac{5}{10}, \frac{6}{10}, \frac{9}{10}$
3. $\frac{1}{5}, \frac{2}{5}, \frac{3}{5}, \frac{5}{5}$
4. $\frac{5}{9}$
5. $\frac{8}{4}$, or 2
6. $\frac{6}{7}$
7. $\frac{18}{6}$, or 3
8. $\frac{3}{5}$
9. $\frac{12}{3}$, or 4
10. $\frac{39}{1}$, or 39
11. $\frac{0}{9}$, or 0
12. $\frac{19}{21}$

Page 64 (cont'd.)

13. $\frac{21}{7}$, or 3

14. $\frac{35}{5}$, or 7

15. $\frac{54}{9}$, or 6

16. $\frac{4}{7}$

17. $\frac{13}{16}$

18. $\frac{50}{25}$, or 2

19. $\frac{12}{1}$

20. $\frac{5}{1}$ **21.** $\frac{11}{1}$ **22.** $\frac{8}{1}$ **23.** $\frac{33}{1}$

24. $\frac{88}{91}$ **25.** $\frac{2}{95}$ **26.** $\frac{55}{54}$ **27.** $\frac{3}{30}$

Page 65

1. 5 **2.** 3 **3.** 2 **4.** 5 **5.** 2
6. 4 **7.** 8 **8.** 7

9. A. $\frac{1}{4}$ B. E

10. A. 1 B. R

11. A. $\frac{2}{5}$ B. A

12. A. $\frac{7}{10}$ B. T

13. A. $\frac{2}{3}$ B. 0

14. A. $\frac{5}{6}$ B. S

15. A. $\frac{7}{10}$ B. T

16. A. $\frac{3}{4}$ B. H

17. A. $\frac{1}{4}$ B. E

18. A. $\frac{5}{8}$ B. N

19. A. $\frac{1}{4}$ B. E

20. A. $\frac{5}{6}$ B. S

Page 66

1. $2\frac{1}{3}$ **2.** $2\frac{1}{8}$ **3.** $2\frac{2}{9}$ **4.** $2\frac{2}{5}$

5. $1\frac{3}{7}$ **6.** $1\frac{1}{7}$ **7.** $2\frac{2}{7}$ **8.** $2\frac{1}{5}$

9. 3 **10.** 5 **11.** 1 **12.** 4

13. $\frac{16}{5}$ **14.** $\frac{11}{3}$ **15.** $\frac{17}{7}$ **16.** $\frac{34}{5}$

17. $\frac{67}{8}$ **18.** $\frac{41}{4}$ **19.** $\frac{12}{7}$ **20.** $\frac{5}{2}$

21. $2\frac{4}{5}$ **22.** 6 **23.** $7\frac{1}{3}$ **24.** $5\frac{2}{5}$

Students will connect the dots to find the five geometric shapes.

Page 67

1. false
2. true

Page 67 (cont'd.)

3. true
4. false
5. true
6. false
7. true
8. true
9. true
10. true
11. false
12. true
13. < **14.** > **15.** > **16.** =
17. = **18.** < **19.** >
20. < **21.** =

22. $\frac{1}{2}$, $\frac{2}{3}$, $\frac{5}{6}$

23. $\frac{13}{24}$, $\frac{7}{12}$, $\frac{5}{8}$

24. $\frac{17}{24}$, $\frac{7}{8}$, $\frac{11}{12}$

25. $\frac{9}{16}$, $\frac{3}{5}$, $\frac{7}{10}$

26. $\frac{1}{5}$, $\frac{1}{4}$, $\frac{1}{3}$, $\frac{1}{2}$

27. $\frac{7}{12}$, $\frac{2}{3}$, $\frac{3}{4}$, $\frac{5}{6}$

Page 68

1. c
2. b
3. about 33 feet
4. 1.9 feet
5. 30 inches wide, 44 inches high
6. 3 hours
7. no
8. none

Page 69

1. under 8
2. under 10
3. over 14
4. over 6
5. under 4
6. over 6
7. < **8.** > **9.** > **10.** > **11.** >
12. < **13.** > **14.** < **15.** <
16. >
17.–22. Answers will vary. Accept any reasonable estimate.
17. 13$^-$
18. 14$^+$
19. 19$^-$
20. 14$^+$
21. 2$^+$
22. 2$^-$
23. 6$^+$ lb

Page 70

1. $\frac{1}{2}$ **2.** $\frac{3}{5}$ **3.** $\frac{2}{3}$ **4.** $\frac{5}{7}$

5. $\frac{7}{10}$ **6.** $\frac{3}{5}$ **7.** $\frac{3}{4}$ **8.** $\frac{1}{2}$

9. $2\frac{1}{4}$ **10.** $1\frac{9}{10}$ **11.** $1\frac{1}{2}$ **12.** $1\frac{2}{3}$

13. $1\frac{8}{9}$ **14.** $1\frac{2}{3}$ **15.** $1\frac{2}{3}$ **16.** $\frac{4}{9}$

17. $\frac{1}{2}$ **18.** $\frac{3}{8}$ **19.** $\frac{2}{3}$ **20.** $\frac{7}{8}$

21. $1\frac{1}{3}$ **22.** $1\frac{1}{3}$ **23.** $1\frac{3}{8}$ **24.** $1\frac{3}{4}$

25. $2\frac{1}{8}$ **26.** $1\frac{2}{3}$ **27.** $1\frac{11}{12}$

Page 71

1. $\frac{1}{5}$ **2.** $\frac{1}{8}$ **3.** $\frac{2}{3}$ **4.** $\frac{1}{2}$

5. $\frac{1}{10}$ **6.** $\frac{1}{9}$ **7.** $\frac{1}{2}$ **8.** $\frac{1}{8}$

9. $\frac{3}{8}$ **10.** $\frac{1}{6}$ **11.** $\frac{1}{9}$ **12.** $\frac{1}{10}$

13. $\frac{2}{15}$ **14.** $\frac{1}{12}$ **15.** $\frac{9}{20}$ **16.** $\frac{7}{18}$

17. $\frac{2}{15}$ **18.** $\frac{7}{12}$ **19.** $\frac{7}{32}$ **20.** $\frac{5}{14}$

21. $\frac{4}{15}$ **22.** $\frac{1}{3}$ **23.** $\frac{127}{270}$

24. $\frac{16}{75}$ **25.** $\frac{9}{20}$

Page 72

1. b
2. c
3. $n = 8 \times 45 \times 2.75$; $n =$ $990
4. $n = 2 \times (149 + 15)$; $n =$ $328
5. c
6. a

7. $\frac{1}{3}$

8. $\frac{1}{6}$

Page 73

9. $8,500
10. $2,500
11. $833.33

12. $\frac{1}{3}$

13. $\frac{5}{8}$

14. $\frac{1}{12}$

15. $330 higher
16. $110

Page 74

1. 10, 19, 30; 19, 10, 30; 30, 10, 19; 10, 30, 19; 19, 30, 10; 30, 19, 10

PRACTICE ANSWER KEY

Page 74 (cont'd.)

2. 45 different sundaes
3. 30 games
4. 12 combinations
5. feature stories, weather, sports, movie; feature stories, weather, movie, sports; feature stories, sports, weather, movie; feature stories, sports, movie, weather; feature stories, movie, sports, weather; feature stories, movie, weather, sports

Page 75

6. 12 17. 9 8. 4 9. 10 10. 27
11. 5 12. 6

Page 76

1. $14\frac{3}{4}$ 2. $21\frac{7}{8}$ 3. $53\frac{7}{10}$ 4. $20\frac{17}{20}$

5. $15\frac{11}{12}$ 6. $42\frac{1}{3}$ 7. $163\frac{1}{3}$ 8. $136\frac{1}{2}$

9. $103\frac{1}{3}$ 10. $95\frac{3}{7}$ 11. $116\frac{9}{10}$

12. $63\frac{7}{8}$ 13. $57\frac{1}{10}$ 14. $160\frac{1}{6}$

15. $114\frac{7}{18}$ 16. $37\frac{7}{8}$ 17. $40\frac{3}{5}$

18. $32\frac{3}{10}$ 19. $27\frac{5}{8}$ 20. $29\frac{1}{14}$

21. $30\frac{5}{18}$ 22. $98\frac{1}{4}$ 23. $134\frac{11}{15}$

24. no

Page 77

1. $7\frac{3}{5}$ 2. $6\frac{1}{10}$ 3. $21\frac{1}{20}$ 4. $114\frac{25}{36}$

5. $2\frac{1}{4}$ 6. $36\frac{1}{3}$ 7. $19\frac{4}{15}$ 8. $13\frac{7}{12}$

9. $7\frac{1}{9}$ 10. $39\frac{74}{83}$ 11. $1\frac{4}{9}$ 12. $6\frac{3}{14}$

13. $15\frac{5}{7}$ 14. $2\frac{4}{9}$ 15. $64\frac{2}{9}$ 16. $13\frac{11}{15}$

17. $1\frac{7}{12}$ 18. $5\frac{1}{10}$ 19. $1\frac{1}{3}$ 20. $36\frac{4}{21}$

21. $11\frac{5}{9}$ 22. $9\frac{1}{8}$ 23. $3\frac{6}{7}$ 24. $6\frac{1}{2}$

25. $5\frac{4}{7}$ 26. $5\frac{3}{20}$

Page 78

1. $10\frac{5}{12}$ 2. $11\frac{5}{6}$ 3. $3\frac{5}{6}$ 4. $5\frac{11}{12}$

5. $1\frac{11}{18}$ 6. $4\frac{11}{14}$ 7. $4\frac{19}{18}$ 8. $3\frac{17}{18}$

9. $7\frac{5}{12}$ 10. $9\frac{11}{12}$ 11. $7\frac{11}{15}$ 12. $8\frac{5}{18}$

13. $5\frac{7}{10}$ 14. $1\frac{14}{15}$ 15. $8\frac{11}{20}$ 16. $2\frac{2}{5}$

17. $\frac{4}{9}$ 18. $\frac{50}{51}$ 19. $21\frac{53}{63}$ 20. $11\frac{13}{20}$

Page 78 (cont'd.)

21. $26\frac{16}{21}$ 22. $1\frac{13}{18}$ 23. $17\frac{11}{14}$

24. $12\frac{13}{20}$ 25. $4\frac{7}{20}$ 26. $12\frac{51}{60}$

Page 79

1. $9\frac{1}{4}$ 2. $3\frac{4}{5}$ 3. $1\frac{2}{7}$ 4. $6\frac{1}{2}$

5. $4\frac{2}{9}$ 6. $10\frac{2}{5}$ 7. $14\frac{3}{4}$ 8. $10\frac{1}{6}$

9. $3\frac{2}{9}$ 10. $5\frac{1}{4}$ 11. $8\frac{1}{4}$ 12. $10\frac{1}{10}$

13. $3\frac{1}{6}$ 14. $1\frac{1}{2}$ 15. $13\frac{2}{5}$

16. A. $8\frac{2}{9}$ B. N

17. A. $1\frac{5}{6}$ B. E

18. A. $7\frac{1}{2}$ B. W

19. A. $4\frac{7}{8}$

20. A. $6\frac{1}{2}$ B. O

21. A. 4 B. R

22. A. $5\frac{3}{4}$ B. L

23. A. $1\frac{5}{6}$ B. E

24. A. $9\frac{1}{2}$ B. A

25. A. $8\frac{2}{9}$ B. N

26. A. $5\frac{2}{3}$ B. S

27. A. $4\frac{7}{8}$

Page 80

1. a
2. b
3. $56.55
4. no
5. 8 dogs
6. yes
7. $2,637.60
8. yes

Page 81

1. $\frac{2}{15}$ 2. $1\frac{11}{24}$ 3. $\frac{3}{32}$ 4. $\frac{1}{20}$ 5. $\frac{1}{8}$

6. $\frac{5}{28}$ 7. $\frac{3}{14}$ 8. 1 9. $\frac{8}{81}$ 10. 12

11. $\frac{25}{42}$ 12. $3\frac{3}{7}$ 13. $\frac{1}{2}$ 14. $\frac{5}{24}$ 15. $\frac{1}{15}$

16. $\frac{1}{180}$ 17. $\frac{3}{4}$ 18. $\frac{1}{4}$ 19. 2 20. $\frac{10}{33}$

Check art.
"You're Great!"

Page 82

1. $\frac{1}{4}$ 2. $\frac{3}{7}$ 3. $\frac{3}{14}$ 4. $\frac{1}{8}$ 5. $\frac{4}{9}$ 6. $\frac{2}{5}$

Page 82 (cont'd.)

7. $\frac{1}{9}$ 8. $2\frac{1}{3}$ 9. 7 10. $\frac{2}{5}$ 11. $1\frac{1}{2}$

12. 6 13. $\frac{3}{4}$ 14. $1\frac{1}{4}$ 15. $\frac{5}{21}$ 16. $\frac{2}{13}$

17. 3 18. $\frac{3}{50}$ 19. $\frac{3}{7}$ 20. 4 21. $\frac{3}{16}$

22. $1\frac{7}{11}$ 23. $\frac{1}{2}$ 24. $1\frac{2}{3}$ 25. $\frac{5}{8}$ 26. $\frac{1}{4}$

27. $\frac{4}{7}$ 28. $\frac{3}{32}$ 29. 1 h 43 min

30. 6 bunches; $186.00

Page 83

1. How much money will be helpful to the seniors? What fund-raising activities are usually successful?
2. What kind of items can they obtain? How much are people willing to spend?
3. How much will the barbecue cost? How much are people willing to spend?
4. How many people will come? How many ribs will each person eat?
5. How many people will be going? Which form of transportation is the cheapest?
6. What time of year is the best? What location would be accessible to most people?

Page 84

1. > 2. < 3. > 4. > 5. <
6. < 7. > 8. > 9. > 10. <
11. < 12. > 13. < 14. >
15. < 16. < 17. > 18. <
19. > 20. <
21.–28. Answers will vary. Accept any reasonable estimate.
21. 18+ 22. 45− 23. 80−
24. 49− 25. 90− 26. 100+
27. 130− 28. 90−

Page 85

1. $2\frac{5}{8}$ 2. $2\frac{3}{8}$ 3. $\frac{17}{98}$ 4. $1\frac{1}{16}$

5. $14\frac{1}{4}$ 6. $1\frac{11}{16}$ 7. $20\frac{2}{5}$ 8. 30

9. $3\frac{3}{10}$ 10. $3\frac{3}{7}$ 11. 0 12. $\frac{31}{48}$

13. $6\frac{1}{5}$ 14. $2\frac{9}{11}$ 15. $8\frac{1}{4}$ 16. $19\frac{4}{9}$

17. $3\frac{13}{21}$ 18. $\frac{16}{45}$ 19. $17\frac{9}{13}$ 20. $5\frac{4}{7}$

21. 1 22. $2\frac{2}{27}$ 23. $1\frac{2}{3}$ 24. $\frac{3}{4}$

25. 31 hours
26. 70 ships

PRACTICE ANSWER KEY

Page 86

1. $\frac{13}{4}$ 2. $\frac{9}{8}$ 3. 4 4. $\frac{11}{3}$ 5. $\frac{6}{7}$ 6. $\frac{1}{5}$

7. $\frac{5}{18}$ 8. $\frac{7}{10}$ 9. $1\frac{4}{5}$ 10. $7\frac{1}{2}$ 11. $1\frac{1}{3}$

12. 4 13. $1\frac{3}{7}$ 14. $\frac{3}{4}$ 15. $1\frac{5}{6}$ 16. $\frac{7}{12}$

17. 30 18. $\frac{1}{16}$ 19. $\frac{9}{14}$ 20. $\frac{7}{80}$ 21. $\frac{1}{3}$

22. $2\frac{2}{3}$ 23. $1\frac{3}{7}$ 24. $3\frac{1}{2}$ 25. $\frac{11}{12}$

26. $1\frac{1}{15}$

27. $\frac{1}{16}$ pint

28. 3 minutes

Page 87

1. B 2. D 3. C 4. $\frac{11}{14}$ 5. $\frac{8}{9}$

6. $2\frac{5}{8}$ 7. $3\frac{1}{9}$ 8. $\frac{5}{16}$ 9. $\frac{5}{24}$ 10. $1\frac{1}{2}$

11. $\frac{25}{28}$ 12. $1\frac{1}{2}$ 13. $\frac{7}{9}$ 14. $\frac{5}{16}$ 15. $7\frac{1}{2}$

16. $3\frac{1}{3}$ 17. $\frac{4}{5}$ 18. $\frac{7}{12}$

19. 5; yes; $\frac{1}{4}$ h

20. 8 loads

Page 88

1. 3 baskets, 0 free throws, 2 baskets; 2 free throws, 1 basket, 4 free throws; 0 baskets, 6 free throws

2. $420

3. 7 quarters

4. $(6,0,0) \rightarrow (3,0,3) \rightarrow (0,3,3) \rightarrow$ $(0,5,1) \rightarrow (1,5,0) \rightarrow (1,2,3) \rightarrow$ $(4,2,0)$

5. 9(D8, P3, A2; D7, P4, A4; D7, P5, A2; D6, P7, A2; D6, P6, A4; D6, P5, A6; D6, P4, A8; D7, P3, A6; D6, P3, A10

Page 89

6. d

7. C

8. (0,47), (1,37), (2,27), (3,17), (4,7)

9. 15 handshakes

10. $(5,0) \rightarrow (2,3) \rightarrow (2,0) \rightarrow$ $(0,2) \rightarrow (5,2) \rightarrow (4,3) \rightarrow (4,0)$

Page 90

1. 0.28 2. 0.087 3. 0.04
4. 0.75 5. 0.99 6. 0.23
7. 0.56 8. 0.325 9. 0.55

Page 90 (cont'd.)

10. 2.25 11. 0.9 12. 0.904
13. 0.7 14. 0.15 15. 0.34

16. 0.02 17. $\frac{1}{8}$ 18. $\frac{33}{50}$ 19. $\frac{1}{5}$

20. $\frac{7}{10}$ 21. $\frac{19}{20}$ 22. $\frac{13}{20}$ 23. $27\frac{6}{25}$

24. $\frac{1}{125}$ 25. $\frac{1}{20}$ 26. $2\frac{3}{8}$ 27. $\frac{77}{100}$

28. $28\frac{1}{25}$ 29. $\frac{3}{5}$ 30. $15\frac{3}{5}$ 31. $\frac{9}{40}$

32. $4\frac{3}{4}$

33. $\frac{7}{20}$; 390 people

34. $450.00

Page 91

1. $1\frac{1}{2}$ lb

2. $5.67

3. 2 green peppers

4. $\frac{1}{4}$ stick

Page 92

1. $0.9\overline{4}$ 2. $1.8\overline{3}$ 3. 2.3
4. 0.0125 5. 8.125 6. $4.1\overline{6}$
7. $0.\overline{1}$ 8. 3.4 9. 0.1875
10. $0.\overline{108}$ 11. $0.708\overline{3}$ 12. 0.12
13. $0.\overline{8}$ 14. $0.6\overline{29}$ 15. $0.2\overline{27}$
16. $0.41\overline{6}$ 17. $0.\overline{6}$ 18. 0.177
19. $15.\overline{09}$ 20. $0.\overline{2}$ 21. $\frac{1}{12}$; $100

Page 93

1. c
2. c
3. B
4. $A = 12$
5. $E = 16$
6. $Y = \frac{7}{9}$
7. $C = 14$
8. $R = 35$
9. $Z = 2$
10. $W = 14\frac{1}{5}$
11. $B = 2\frac{1}{7}$
12. $Y = 7\frac{1}{5}$
13. $Z = 3\frac{3}{5}$
14. $X = \frac{3}{7}$
15. $C = 13$
16. $\frac{1}{2}$ 17. $\frac{4}{7}$ 18. 3 19. $\frac{1}{4}$ 20. $1\frac{1}{4}$
21. $1\frac{1}{8}$ 22. $1\frac{1}{2}$ 23. $1\frac{1}{12}$ 24. $1\frac{1}{99}$

Page 94

1. a
2. b
3. 14 boxes
4. $3\frac{3}{5}$ in.
5. 13 cars
6. 9 lines
7. $11\frac{2}{5}$ gallons
8. 2 bags
9. 4
10. $1\frac{1}{2}$ hours

Page 95

1. cm
2. km
3. m
4. mm
5. cm
6. m
7. cm
8. cm
9. km
10. mm
11. c
12. b
13. b
14. a
15.–16. Estimates will vary.
15. 5 cm; 50 mm
16. 13 cm; 127 mm
17. 9 pieces
18. 120 meters

Page 96

1. 45,000 2. 0.13 3. 0.004
4. 60 5. 870 6. 0.036
7. 170,000 8. 24 9. 4.725
10. 8,000 11. 9 12. 0.290
13. 0.0002 14. 0.007 15. 6,900
16. 0.673 17. 1 18. 12
19. 6.472 20. 264 21. 892
22. 50 23. 0.012 24. 27,620
25. 194,000 26. 6
27. Marni
28. Sally's; 340 cm

Page 97

1. < 2. > 3. = 4. > 5. <
6. > 7. = 8. > 9. < 10. <
11. < 12. < 13. 5 14. 5
15. 25,000 16. 2,500 17. 10,000
18. 1 19. 10,500 20. 0.045

PRACTICE ANSWER KEY

Page 97 (cont'd.)

21. 0.3 **22.** 1.5 **23.** 59,000
24. 2.98
25. no
26. He needed more.
27. 2 more

Page 98

1. $\frac{2}{3} \times 411 = n$; 274 students
2. $1,298,700 ÷ 4,329,000 = n$;
$0.30
3. Ring a.
4. Ring a.
5. 8:00 A.M.–9:00 A.M.
6. about 50 more people

Page 99

7. $72.70
8. $1.22
9. 246 students
10. 138; Howard
11. 1964 and 1976
12. 1972
13. 1 million
14. 5 million

Page 100

1. Find the cost to be divided by the 75 couples.
2. Find the cost of the potatoes. Find the cost of the green beans. Find the amount Mr. Kinner spent in all.
3. $142.50 **4.** $23 **5.** $78.66
6. $135.20

Page 101

1. 48 **2.** 27 **3.** 3 **4.** 72 **5.** 5
6. 39 **7.** 1 **8.** 19 **9.** 22
10. 180 **11.** 9 **12.** 4 **13.** 2
14. $2\frac{2}{3}$ **15.** 172 **16.** b **17.** c
18. c **19.** a **20.** c
21. 10 ft 5 in.
22. 14 yd 2 ft
23. 2 ft 3 in.
24. 700 ft
25. 15 tails

Page 102

1. b **2.** b **3.** c **4.** 32 **5.** 1
6. 1 **7.** $2\frac{1}{2}$ **8.** 6,000 **9.** 112
10. 64 **11.** 6 **12.** $2\frac{5}{8}$ **13.** 2,500

Page 102 (cont'd.)

14. 7 **15.** $2\frac{1}{2}$ **16.** 35 **17.** 192
18. 30 **19.** 3 **20.** $3\frac{1}{2}$ **21.** $1\frac{1}{2}$
22. 40 **23.** $4\frac{1}{2}$ **24.** $2\frac{1}{4}$ **25.** $17\frac{1}{2}$
26. $4\frac{1}{4}$ **27.** 112 **28.** $7\frac{3}{8}$
29. 3 loads
30. 9 pints

Page 103

1. 48 **2.** 360 **3.** 14 **4.** $\frac{1}{3}$
5. 3 **6.** $1\frac{1}{2}$ **7.** 8 **8.** 35 **9.** $\frac{1}{2}$
10. 168 **11.** 5 **12.** 72 **13.** 140
14. 4 **15.** 225 **16.** $6\frac{2}{3}$ **17.** $\frac{1}{4}$
18. 3
19. 6 wk 2 d
20. 11 y 3 mo
21. 2 h 42 min
22. 8 h 10 min
23. 3 wk 6 d
24. 2 centuries 24 y
25. 5 h 7 min 9 s
26. 5 d 3 h
27. 9 h 8 min 30 s
28. 4 hours
29. $1\frac{1}{2}$

Page 104

1. c
2. b
3. 129 miles
4. 9.74 mph
5. cannot answer
6. 48 mph
7. 5 minutes
8. 1.75 miles
9. $6\frac{3}{4}$ minutes
10. 39.3 miles

Page 105

1. Pacific
2. Central
3. Mountain
4. Eastern
5. Pacific
6. Eastern
7. Central
8. Eastern
9. Central
10. 11:00 A.M.
11. 11:00 A.M.

Page 105 (cont'd.)

12. 8:00 A.M.
13. 11:00 A.M.
14. 11:00 A.M.
15. 10:00 A.M.
16. 8:30 A.M.
17. no
18. 6:30 A.M.
19. no; 3:30 P.M.

Page 106

1. b **2.** a **3.** c **4.** c **5.** b
6. b **7.** a **8.** c **9.** b **10.** c
11. a **12.** a **13.** 64°F
14. 470.57°C

Page 107

1.–20. Students will ring the more precise measurement.
21. Jessica's 142 cm
22. 1.05 m and 1.15 m

Page 108

1. false
2. true
3. 35 minutes
4. the 7:50 A.M. bus
5. yes
6. 7 minutes

Page 109

1. $\frac{2}{3}$ **2.** $\frac{1}{8}$ **3.** $\frac{1}{2}$ **4.** $\frac{8}{3}$ **5.** $\frac{13}{24}$
6. 4 **7.** $\frac{3}{5}$ **8.** $\frac{7}{8}$ **9.** $\frac{3}{4}$ **10.** $\frac{1}{5}$
11. $\frac{1}{6}$ **12.** $\frac{3}{8}$ **13.** $\frac{400}{1}$ **14.** $\frac{84}{1}$
15. $\frac{17}{12}$ **16.** $\frac{17}{29}$ **17.** $\frac{12}{17}$ **18.** $\frac{12}{29}$
19. no **20.** 2; $\frac{3}{8}$

Page 110

1. yes
2. no
3. no
4. yes
5. yes
6. no
7. yes
8. yes
9. no
10. 3 **11.** 71 **12.** 5 **13.** 23
14. 53 **15.** 11 **16.** 37 **17.** 1
18. 17 **19.** 13 **20.** 41 **21.** 31
22. 29 **23.** 7 **24.** 19 **25.** 47

Page 110 (cont'd.)

6. 102 **27.** 102 **28.** 102
29. yes

Page 111

1. b
2. c
3. $504
4. 25 women
5. 350 square feet
6. 16.7 gallons
7. $140
8. 10 cubic yards
9. $133\frac{1}{3}$ (or 133.3) lb
10. 54 bricks

Page 112

1. 9 m
2. 6 m
3. 3 m
4. 18 m
5. 3.75 m
6. 12 m
7. 6 m
8. 5.25 m
9. 4.5 m
10. 1.5 m
11. 3.75 m

Page 113

1. 55% **2.** 42% **3.** 33%
4. 5% **5.** 64% **6.** 12% **7.** 26%
8. 18% **9.** 79% **10.** 88%
11. 10% **12.** 20% **13.** 60%
14. 80% **15.** 20% **16.** 30%
17. 25% **18.** 17% **19.** 90%
20. 50% **21.** 8% **22.** 70%
23. 75% **24.** 82% **25.** 40%
26. 38% **27.** 60% **28.** 40%
29. 55% **30.** 20% **31.** 67%
32. 90% **33.** 9% **34.** 100%
35. 20% **36.** 70%

Page 114

1. 0.82 **2.** 0.03 **3.** 0.35
4. 0.195 **5.** 0.333 **6.** 0.187
7. 0.1014 **8.** 1.2 **9.** 0.1725
10. 2.41 **11.** 3.55 **12.** 0.0065
13. 0.21 **14.** 0.0825 **15.** 0.095
16. 0.0006 **17.** 0.073 **18.** 0.4784
19. 55% **20.** 27% **21.** 99%
22. 48.4% **23.** 46.6% **24.** 7.8%
25. 347% **26.** 706% **27.** 6.72%

Page 114 (cont'd.)

28. 180% **29.** 37% **30.** 7.62%
31. 76% **32.** 8.9% **33.** 106.5%
34. 5.01% **35.** 520% **36.** 73%
37. 689% **38.** 4,330%
39. 86.5%

Page 115

1. $\frac{17}{20}$ **2.** $\frac{1}{8}$ **3.** $1\frac{1}{2}$ **4.** $\frac{1}{25}$ **5.** $\frac{13}{100}$
6. $\frac{17}{50}$ **7.** $\frac{9}{10}$ **8.** $\frac{2}{5}$ **9.** $\frac{5}{6}$ **10.** $2\frac{2}{3}$
11. $\frac{3}{25}$ **12.** $1\frac{7}{25}$ **13.** $\frac{1}{16}$ **14.** $\frac{7}{20}$
15. $\frac{79}{100}$ **16.** $\frac{12}{25}$ **17.** 25% **18.** $41\frac{2}{3}\%$
19. 18% **20.** $87\frac{1}{2}\%$ **21.** $133\frac{1}{3}\%$
22. 850% **23.** $43\frac{3}{4}\%$ **24.** 190%
25. $93\frac{3}{4}\%$ **26.** 16% **27.** 100%
28. 96%
A. $\frac{1}{2}$
B. $\frac{1}{3}$
C. $\frac{1}{5}$
D. $\frac{1}{10}$
E. $\frac{5}{12}$
F. $\frac{1}{8}$
G. $\frac{1}{9}$
H. $\frac{2}{15}$
I. $\frac{1}{15}$

Page 116

1. 27 **2.** 19 **3.** 2 **4.** 33 **5.** 23
6. 0.44 **7.** 11.5 **8.** 30 **9.** 420
10. 106.5 **11.** 78.4 **12.** 0.86
13. 200 **14.** 24 **15.** $270
16. $12.76 **17.** 50.4 **18.** 1.3
19. 1,266 **20.** $20.25 **21.** $44.80
22. 37 **23.** 15 lb **24.** 14 **25.** 7

Page 117

1. $316.55 **2.** $1,283.75
3. $1,642.48 **4.** $992.15
5. $208.10 **6.** $479.82
7. $218.90 **8.** $20

Page 118

9. $2,610 **10.** $1,287
11. $100,000 **12.** $2,510.40
13. $743.40 **14.** 30%

Page 119

1. d **2.** c **3.** a **4.** b **5.** 20%
6. 50% **7.** 400% **8.** $37\frac{1}{2}\%$
9. $33\frac{1}{3}\%$ **10.** 0.5%
11. $12\frac{1}{2}\%$ **12.** 300% **13.** $12\frac{1}{2}\%$
14. $8\frac{1}{3}\%$ **15.** 125% **16.** 25%
17. 0.6% **18.** $13\frac{1}{3}\%$ **19.** 200%
20. 19% **21.** $333\frac{1}{3}\%$ **22.** $1\frac{3}{7}\%$
23. 44% **24.** $133\frac{1}{3}\%$
25. 25%, 5,200 **26.** $12\frac{1}{2}\%$

Page 120

1. b **2.** a **3.** b **4.** d **5.** 660
6. 100 **7.** 60 **8.** 52 **9.** 280
10. 105 **11.** 56 **12.** 200 **13.** 300
14. 0.5 **15.** 3.4 **16.** 240 **17.** 32
18. 60 **19.** 30 **20.** 23.46
21. 0.36 **22.** 50 **23.** 135 **24.** 56
25. 40 **26.** 75

Page 121

1. c
2. b
3. $55.25
4. 4 years
5. $7,400
6. $4,468.80
7. 16%
8. $113.85
9. $3\frac{1}{2}$ years
10. $2,012.80

Page 122

1. $67\frac{1}{2}$ **2.** 5% **3.** 40 **4.** 45
5. 25% **6.** 46 **7.** 65 **8.** 550
9. 30% **10.** 9 **11.** 40%
12. 300 **13.** 6 **14.** 500
15. Larry = 25%
    Harry = 25%
    Barry = 50%
    Beatrice = 52%
16. Beatrice

Page 123

1. c **2.** b **3.** d **4.** b **5.** 10%
6. $11\frac{1}{9}\%$ **7.** $16\frac{2}{3}\%$ **8.** 80%

Page 123 (cont'd.)

9. 20% 10. 25% 11. $17\frac{11}{17}$%

12. $33\frac{1}{3}$% 13. 50% 14. $32\frac{1}{2}$%

15. 20% 16. 20% 17. $4\frac{1}{6}$%

18. $31\frac{11}{19}$% 19. $12\frac{1}{2}$% 20. 75%

21. $37\frac{1}{2}$% 22. $11\frac{1}{9}$%

Page 124

1. d 2. a 4. $2,140.60
5. There is not enough information to answer the question.
6. $681.10 7. no 8. $7,394.80
9. $97.30

Page 125

1. ray 2. line segment
3. angle 4. plane 5. point
6. $\overleftrightarrow{ST}$ or $\overleftrightarrow{TS}$
7. $\overline{DC}$ or $\overline{CD}$ 8. ∠LMN or
∠NML
9. ray 10. point 11. line
12. $\overline{PJ}$ ($\overline{JP}$), $\overline{JQ}$ ($\overline{QJ}$), $\overline{PQ}$ ($\overline{QP}$)
13. two 14. N or K 15. ∠MLN,
∠KLP 16. $\overrightarrow{NK}$ 17. true
18. true 19. false

Page 126

1. 59°; acute
2. 17°; acute
3. 148°; obtuse
4. 74°; acute
5. 90°; right
6. 75°; acute
7. obtuse/Check student's
drawing.
8. straight/Check student's
drawing.
9. acute/Check student's
drawing.
10. 10° 11. 79° 12. 51° 13. 25°
14. 67° 15. 47° 16. 73° 17. 4°
18. 15° 19. 148° 20. 79°
21. 86° 22. 173° 23. 24°
24. 10° 25. 129°
26. ∠FPG, ∠HPC
27. ∠FPG, ∠EPD
28. ∠DPE or ∠HPG
29. ∠CPD, ∠HPG
30. ∠EPF, ∠DPC
31. ∠EPF, ∠GPH

Page 127

1. not congruent
2. congruent 3. congruent
4.–7. Check students' drawings.
8.–9. Check students'
constructions.

Page 128

1. ∠HGJ
2. ∠KLM
3. $\overline{OX}$
4.–11. Check students'
constructions.
12. No; he had one 30° angle and
two 15° angles.

Page 129

1. over 8 lb, but less than $9\frac{1}{2}$ lb
2. $5.65
3. $6.80
4. $3.50
5. $10.05
6. $4.84

Page 130

7. 816 students
8. 600
9. fourth period
10. 125
11. the fourth week

Page 131

1. perpendicular
2. neither
3. perpendicular
4. parallel
5.–9. Check students' drawings.
10. supplementary
11. vertical
12. vertical
13. supplementary
14. corresponding
15. corresponding

Page 132

1.–7. Check students'
constructions.

Page 133

1. travel 2. $552 3. $384
4. $10 5. 2.29 h (2 h 17 min)
6. 3.87 mi/h 7. $6 8. $175

Page 134

9. 561 workers
10. $5.82
11. 1862
12. 66 years old
13. 6%
14. about 922 feet
15. $3.09
16. no

Page 135

1. right
2. acute
3. obtuse
4. acute
5. obtuse
6. obtuse
7. right
8. acute
9. acute
10. isosceles
11. equilateral
12. isosceles
13. scalene
14. scalene
15. equilateral
16. isosceles
17. isosceles
18. scalene
19. 45° 20. 90° 21. 101°
22. 115° 23. 57° 24. 130°
25. 48° 26. 30° 27. 82°

Page 136

1. hexagon
2. pentagon
3. decagon
4. triangle
5. quadrilateral
6. hexagon
7. quadrilateral
8. octagon
9. the hexagon in Ex. 6

PRACTICE ANSWER KEY

Page 136 (cont'd.)

0. d
1. a, c
2. a, b, f
3. a, b
4. a, b, d, f
5. f **16.** 109° **17.** 90° **18.** 60°

Page 137

1. a and f, c and e, d and g
2. $\overline{EF}$
3. $\angle EDF$
4. $\overline{AB}$
5. $\angle CAB$
6. $\overline{DE}$
7. $\angle ACB$
8. $\overline{NO} \cong \overline{XY}$; $\overline{NM} \cong \overline{XW}$; $\overline{OP} \cong \overline{YZ}$; $\overline{MP} \cong \overline{WZ}$
9. $\angle N \cong \angle X$; $\angle O \cong Y$; $\angle M \cong \angle W$; $\angle P \cong \angle Z$
10. 7 m
11. 16 m
12. 40°
13. 55°
14. 12 m
15. 85°
16. 5
17. regular pentagon

Page 138

1. yes
2. no
3. no
4. yes
5. 3 **6.** 12 **7.** 9 **8.** 4
9. 75°; 33°; 72° **10.** 110°; 70°

Page 139

1. b
2. b
3. $20
4. $4\frac{1}{2}$ hours
5. 570
6. 240
7. 78
8. $1,400

Page 140

9. $9.00 **10.** 36 **11.** 42 **12.** 20
13. 16 **14.** 9 **15.** 60
16. Winfield, $4.00; Marta, $3.50; Robbie, $2.00; Elena, $0.50

Page 141

1. $\overline{XA}$, $\overline{XB}$, $\overline{XC}$, $\overline{XD}$
2. $\overline{AD}$
3. $\overline{AD}$ and $\overline{BC}$
4. $\angle CXD$
5. $\overline{AB}$ and $\overparen{CD}$
6. central angle
7. chord
8. center
9. arc
10. central angle
11. diameter
12. chord
13. arc
14. radius
15. central angle
16. diameter
17. radius
18. 10 cm
19. 5 cm
20. 49°
21. 49°
22. 5 cm
23. 131°
24. $\angle XZW$ or $\angle VZY$; $\angle YZW$

Page 142

1.–15. *Check diagrams.*
7. 2 **8.** 4 **9.** 6

Page 143

1.–6. Check students' drawings.
7. B **8.** B **9.** A **10.** B **11.** A

Page 144

1. c
2. b
3. 54 in.
4. yes
5. 30 in. by 33 in.
6. 30 in. by 21 in.
7. 24 books
8. 9 inches apart

Page 145

1. 44 cm
2. 23.6 cm
3. $9\frac{1}{4}$ m
4. 24 in.
5. 24 cm
6. 20 cm
7. 28 m
8. 224 cm
9. 90.8 m

Page 145 (cont'd.)

10. $21\frac{1}{2}$ in.
11. 4 m
12. 20.4 cm
13. 140 mm
14. $44\frac{5}{6}$ in.
15. 120 m

Page 146

1. 138.16 m
2. 77.244 cm
3. 81.64 in.
4. 34.54 in.
5. $78\frac{4}{7}$ cm
6. 264 cm
7. $28\frac{2}{7}$ m
8. 88 m
9. 31.4 cm
10. 138.16 cm
11. 31.4 m
12. 3.768 m
13. 264 m
14. 220 cm
15. 22 cm
16. 44 mm
3.141592653589793

Page 147

1. 16 m^2
2. 38.44 m^2
3. 201.64 m^2
4. 625 cm^2
5. 219.6 mm^2
6. 6.29 cm^2
7. 1,134 in.^{2}
8. 1,168 m^2
9. 180 cm^2
10. 119.28 ft^2
11. 352 m^2
12. 252 in.^{2}
13. $A = S^2$
14. $A = b \cdot H$
15. $A = l \cdot w$

Page 148

1.–8. Students will complete the puzzle. *Solution:* **1.** 70; **2.** 80; **3.** 40; **4.** 60; **5.** 20; **6.** 10; **7.** 30; **8.** 50.
1. 70 m^2
2. 80 cm^2
3. 40 m^2
4. 60 cm^2

Page 148 (cont'd.)

5. 20 cm^2
6. 10 m^2
7. 30 m^2
8. 50 cm^2
9. 150 m^2

Page 149

1. Find the price of three black-and-white profiles. Add the price of one pastel front view. Subtract the total price from $50.
2. Find the price of the umbrellas. Find the sales tax. Find the total amount of the customer's bill. Subtract $25 from the total amount of the bill.
3. $78.70
4. greater; 2,200 ft^2
5. 2,880 cans
6. 15 ft

Page 150

1. 616 cm^2
2. 154 in.^{2}
3. $9\frac{5}{8}$ km^2
4. $3\frac{1}{7}$ m^2
5. 2.0 m^2
6. 379.9 m^2
7. 78.5 cm^2
8. 50.2 mm^2
9. 28.3 cm^2
10. 1,384.7 dm^2
11. 7.1 m^2
12. 3,846.5 ft^2
13. true
14. false
15. true
16. false

Page 151

1. 2,343 adults; 781 children
2. Mrs. MacRae–2; Mr. MacRae–1; each child–4
3. volume 1–14; volume 2–13; volume 3–12
4. Barbara–43; Steve–40; Lisa–38
5. 528 books
6. 8 @ $1; 16 @ 25¢; 32 @ 10¢
7. 44 nonfiction and 64 fiction cassettes
8. first person, 8; second, 4; third, 2; last, 1

Page 152

9. Alicia: 6; Jason: 3; Eileen: 4
10. $300 from candy sales; $100 from the sale of decorations
11. T.J.: $6.75; Emily: $5.10
12. 66 boys and 88 girls
13. Cindy: $11; Sharon: $25; Dave: $33; Tim: $13
14. 5 girls

Page 153

1. b 2. g 3. h 4. d 5. e 6. a
7. f 8. c
Chart:
Figure 1. 8 + 6 − 12
Figure 2. 6 + 5 − 9
Figure 3. 4 + 4 − 6
Figure 4. 8 + 6 − 12
Figure 5. 5 + 5 − 8
The formula: $V + F − E = 2$.

Page 154

1. Check students' diagrams. 23.1 ft^2
2. Check students' diagrams. 350 in.^{2}
3. Check students' diagrams. 14 plants
4. Check students' diagrams. 490.6 ft^2
5. Check students' diagrams. 1,055 ft^2
6. Check students' diagrams. $9\frac{1}{2}$ in.

Page 155

7–12. Check students' diagrams.
7. 8 chairs
8. 40.7 feet
9. 80 feet
10. 94 ft^2
11. 69 in.
12. 31.25 ft

Page 156

1. 12.4 m^2
2. 12 m^2
3. 12 m^2
4. 37.2 m^2
5. 12.4 m^2
6. 37.2 m^2
7. 123.2 m^2
8. 28.26 m^2
9. 169.56 m^2
10. 28.26 m^2

Page 156 (cont'd.)

11. 226.08 m^2
12. 336 m^2
13. 791.28 cm^2
14. 160,000 mm^2
15. 82.56 m^2
16. 294 mm^2
17. 460 cm^2

Page 157

1. triangle
2. 4 m
3. 36 m^2
4. 12 m
5. 432 m^3
6. circle
7. 6 m
8. 113.04 m^2
9. 14 m
10. 1,582.56 m^3
11. 512 cm^3
12. 110 cm^3
13. 720 in.^{3}
14. 168.5 m^3
15. 15.6 m^3
16. 3,956.4 mm^3

Page 158

1. b
2. c
3. about 7; $P = 2 (l + w)$
4. $531\frac{1}{7}$ in.^{2}; $A = \pi r^2$
5. not enough information to answer
6. 714 ft^2; $A = lw$
7. $5\frac{17}{56}$ ft^3; $V = \pi r^2 h$
8. 1,848 ft^3; $V = lwh$

Page 159

Check students' tables.
1. 56
2. 12.5%
3. $\frac{9}{56}$ or 16.1%

Page 160

1. 28 2. 709 3. 4.3 4. 4.5
5. 652 6. 5 7. $4.61
8. $3.13 9. 18 10. 105 11. 16
12. $4.55 13. $24.50 14. 5.5 15.
16. 6.8 17. 15 18. 22 19. 5; 21
20. 2 · 4 21. $2.46 22. 8.1
23. 1.0° 24. 2.35° 25. 2.6°
26. two

PRACTICE ANSWER KEY

Page 161

1. 44 **2.** 5 **3.** 75 **4.** 131
5. 4 **6.** 7 **7.** 24 km **8.** 5
9. 15 **10.** 62 **11.** 71 **12.** $4.00
13. $27.00 **14.** 5 **15.** 5.1
16. 3.9 **17.** 44.1 **18.** 370.3
19. 343.4 **20.** 5.1 **21.** $1.15
22. 251.25 miles; yes

Page 162

1. 1,650
2. 150
3. 3.8%
4. Check students' graphs.
5. 350
6. 150
7. 26.7%

Page 163

1. 74 minutes
2. 4 years old
3. 76 years old
4. 6 **5.** a **6.** a **7.** b **8.** c
9. b **10.** b

Page 164

1. day 4 **2.** a half hour
3. day 1 **4.** 14.75 hours
5. Check student's graphs.
6. day 7 **7.** Pair A **8.** Pair A

Page 165

Top chart:
4,000; $\frac{1}{3}$; 120°

1,000; $\frac{1}{12}$; 30°

1,000; $\frac{1}{12}$; 30°

2,000; $\frac{1}{6}$; 60°

1,000; $\frac{1}{12}$; 30°

3,000; $\frac{1}{4}$; 90°

Bottom chart:
600; 30; 108°
200; 10; 36°
200; 10; 36°
400; 20; 72°
600; 30; 108°

Page 166

1. estimate
2. exact answer
3. exact answer
4. estimate
5. yes; 20.5 miles
6. yes
7. no
8. no

Page 167

1. 6 **2.** no **3.** yes **4.** no

5. no **6.** 5 **7.** no **8.** no **9.** $\frac{1}{6}$

10. $\frac{1}{6}$ **11.** $\frac{5}{6}$ **12.** $\frac{5}{6}$ **13.** $\frac{1}{3}$ **14.** $\frac{1}{3}$

15. $\frac{1}{3}$ **16.** $\frac{2}{3}$

Page 168

1. 3 **2.** 3 **3.** 9
4. Check students' diagrams.

Page 169

1. $\frac{1}{11}$ **2.** $\frac{2}{11}$ **3.** $\frac{2}{11}$ **4.** $\frac{10}{11}$

5. $\frac{2}{11}$ **6.** $\frac{5}{11}$ **7.** $\frac{4}{11}$ **8.** 0

9. 1 **10.** $\frac{1}{11}$ **11.** (H, H, H)

(H, H, T) (H, T, H) (H, T, T)
(T, H, H) (T, H, T) (T, T, H)
(T, T, T)

12. 8 **13.** 4 **14.** $\frac{3}{8}$ **15.** 1

16. $\frac{1}{4}$

Page 170

1. Ritzy; 15,000 more records
2. Ritzy Record Company
3. 1982
4. 1984
5. Ritzy Record Company averaged 4,000 more records per year.
6. about 70%
7. Ritzy Record Company; about 4%

Page 171

1. $\frac{1}{10}$ **2.** $\frac{1}{10}$ **3.** $\frac{3}{10}$ **4.** $\frac{2}{5}$ **5.** 0

6. $\frac{1}{10}$ **7.** $\frac{1}{25}$ **8.** $\frac{6}{25}$ **9.** $\frac{1}{25}$ **10.** $\frac{4}{25}$

11. $\frac{2}{5}$ **12.** $\frac{4}{25}$ **13.** $\frac{1}{20}$ **14.** $\frac{3}{20}$ **15.** $\frac{1}{5}$

16. 0 **17.** $\frac{1}{4}$ **18.** $\frac{1}{10}$ **19.** $\frac{2}{25}$ **20.** $\frac{1}{100}$

21. $\frac{2}{25}$ **22.** $\frac{4}{25}$ **23.** $\frac{9}{50}$ **24.** $\frac{3}{50}$

Page 172

1. $\frac{2}{45}$ **2.** $\frac{1}{15}$ **3.** $\frac{1}{9}$ **4.** $\frac{2}{15}$ **5.** $\frac{1}{15}$

6. $\frac{1}{10}$ **7.** $\frac{1}{45}$ **8.** 0 **9.** $\frac{5}{102}$ **10.** $\frac{5}{51}$

11. $\frac{8}{51}$ **12.** $\frac{1}{6}$ **13.** $\frac{1}{21}$ **14.** $\frac{2}{21}$ **15.** $\frac{2}{105}$

16. $\frac{1}{105}$ **17.** $\frac{2}{35}$ **18.** $\frac{1}{14}$

Page 173

1. 523,144 square miles
2. about 92 people per square mile
3. Their combined area is less than the area of Honshu.
4. 8,243 square miles greater
5. about 6.5 times larger
6. about 16% (15.7%)

Page 174

1. 2 **2.** ⁻1 **3.** ⁻4 **4.** 3 **5.** 7
6. ⁻6 **7.** 9 **8.** ⁻8
9. ⁻4, ⁻3, ⁻15, ⁻51, ⁻25, ⁻85, ⁻70; 7, 3, 85, 42, 10, 19, 66, 94
10. ⁻27, ⁻4, 6, 9
11. ⁻5, ⁻4, 4, 5
12. ⁻10, ⁻3, ⁻2, ⁻1
13. 39, ⁻14, ⁻27, ⁻39
14. 124, 96, 22, ⁻17, ⁻150
15. > **16.** > **17.** > **18.** <
19. > **20.** > **21.** > **22.** <
23. <

Page 175

1. 1 **2.** 0 **3.** 3 **4.** 3 **5.** 16
6. 0 **7.** 23 **8.** 1 **9.** 1 **10.** ⁻12

Page 175 (cont'd.)

11. ⁻3 12. ⁻14 13. 36
14. ⁻23
15. ⁻12 + 2,673
16. ⁻14 · ⁻32
17. 29 + ⁻1,236
18. ⁻50 · 367
19. ⁻62 + ⁻36
20. 93 · ⁻319
21. ⁻3 · 7,211
22. ⁻457 + 99
23. 3,061 · (⁻14 · 601)
24. (⁻333 + ⁻24) + 89
25. (⁻96 + 3) − 419
26. (⁻601 · ⁻13) · 1
27. 1,300 + (⁻69 + 14)
28. 319 · (⁻2,001 · ⁻197)
29. (⁻390 · ⁻3) + (⁻390 · 62)
30. (10 · 69) + (10 · ⁻99)
31. (⁻607 · 32) + (⁻607 · ⁻6)
32. (⁻315 · ⁻3) + (⁻315 · 69)
33. (277 · 34) + (277 · ⁻1,268)
34. (⁻3 · 18) + (⁻3 · ⁻925)

Page 176

1. ⁻100 2. ⁻38 3. 22
4. ⁻123 5. ⁻60 6. 21 7. 19
8. 87 9. ⁻115 10. ⁻85
11. ⁻134 12. 61 13. 106
14. ⁻57 15. ⁻114 16. ⁻183
17. ≠ 18. ≠ 19. ≠ 20. =
21. ⁻12 22. ⁻90 23. ⁻59
24. 39 25. ⁻34 26. ⁻212
27. 212°F + ⁻24°F = 188°F
28. 32°F + ⁻45°F = ⁻13°F

Page 177

1. ⁻44 2. ⁻124 3. 176
4. ⁻67 5. 75 6. ⁻23 7. ⁻32
8. ⁻87 9. ⁻40 10. ⁻28 11. 8
12. ⁻71 13. ⁻98 14. ⁻141
15. ⁻35 16. 65 17. 90 18. ⁻26
19. ⁻65 20. 8 21. ⁻118
22. ⁻106 23. 23 24. ⁻31
25. ⁻6 26. ⁻89 27. 97 28. ⁻12
29. ⁻108 30. ⁻21 31. ⁻63
32. ⁻61 33. ⁻93 34. 86
35. ⁻22 36. 69 37. ⁻52 38. 90
39. ⁻6
40. 44°F − 100°F = ⁻56°F
41. 134°F − ⁻81°F = 215°F

Page 178

1. 3:15
2. Check students' diagrams.
   10 meters

Page 178 (cont'd.)

3. Check students' lists. She can make 9 different orders.
4. Check students' tables.
   11:00 A.M.
5. (5,0) → (2,3) → (2,0) → (0,2) → (5,2) → (4,3) → (4,0)
   Teacher's note: The first coordinate represents the 5-oz cup and the second coordinate represents the 3-oz cup.

Page 179

6. 10 handshakes
7. milk shake: $1.35; apple: $0.35
8. 12 outfits
9. 2 blocks
10. 12 combinations
11. $6\frac{3}{4}$ meters

Page 180

1. + 2. − 3. + 4. + 5. −
6. + 7. 1,176 8. ⁻5,310
9. 2,418 10. ⁻4,032
11. ⁻20,286 12. 21,736
13. 4,557 14. ⁻43,320
15. ⁻3,378 16. 28,250
17. 20,320 18. 19,340
19. 12,388 20. 9,570 21. 4,190
22. ⁻282 23. ⁻36,198

Page 181

1. ⁻8 2. ⁻4 3. ⁻7 4. ⁻2
5. ⁻4 6. ⁻2 7. ⁻5 8. ⁻9
9. ⁻4 10. ⁻9 11. ⁻8 12. 7
13. ⁻3 14. 94 15. ⁻2 16. ⁻42
17. ⁻88 18. ⁻65 19. ⁻17
20. ⁻38 21. 87 22. ⁻47
23. ⁻22 24. ⁻69 25. ⁻60
26. 291 27. ⁻92 28. ⁻45
29. ⁻4 points
30. ⁻3 points

Page 182

1. about 563 pounds
2. 411 pounds
3. about 4
4. 262
5. Ring c.
6. Ring c.
7. 273 plums
8. 3.2 inches

Page 183

9. about 40 years
10. one more performance
11. $n = \frac{1}{3} \times 36$; 12 new costumes
12. $n = 1,728 - 1,356$; 372 more people
13. 126 children
14. about 57 albums
15. b
16. a

Page 184

1. $x = ⁻6$
2. $y = ⁻97$
3. $m = ⁻17$
4. $q = ⁻34$
5. $r = 54$
6. $y = ⁻16$
7. $q = ⁻43$
8. $n = ⁻343$
9. $x = ⁻47$
10. $u = 286$
11. $t = 37$
12. $p = ⁻120$
13. $s = 138$
14. $g = ⁻5$
15. $x = ⁻78$
16. $y = ⁻1,218$
17. $b = 127$
18. $r = ⁻135$
19. $t = 31$
20. $h = ⁻1,400$
21. $x = ⁻52$
22. $y = ⁻5$
23. $r = ⁻20$
24. $t = 26$
25. $m = ⁻36$
26. $g = ⁻6$
27. $n = ⁻52$
28. $x = ⁻19$
29. $n - ⁻6 = ⁻24$; $n = ⁻30$
30. $⁻12n = 252$; $n = ⁻21$
31. $7n + ⁻42 = ⁻133$; $n = ⁻13$
32. $(n \div ⁻6) - 14 = ⁻89$; $n = 450$

Page 185

1. inequality
2. inequality

Page 185 (cont'd.)

3. inequality
4. equality
5. inequality
6. inequality
7. $p \leq 11$
8. $k \geq {}^-1$
9. $m \geq 7$
10. $x \geq {}^-22$
11. $h \leq {}^-6$
12. $j \leq {}^-72$
13. $q \geq 5$
14. $x \leq 180$
15. $x \leq 9$
16. $5 \geq a$ or $a \leq 5$
17. $y \leq 5$
18. $x \leq 4$
19. $m \geq 9$
20. $p \leq {}^-41$
21. $x \leq 310$
22. $y \leq {}^-1$
23. $x + 35 \geq 100$; $x \geq 65$ pounds
24. $3x \geq 50$; $x \geq 16\frac{2}{3}$ gallons

Page 186

1. c
2. a
3. $4,000,000,000 \div 12 = n$; about 333,333,333 people
4. $1,539 + 49 + 70 = n$; 1,658
5. There is not enough information.

Page 186 (cont'd.)

6. $120 \div 3 = n$; 40 pairs
7. $17 - 29 = n$; $^-12°C$
8. $287,045 \times 6 = n$ (1,722,270); $1,722,270 \div 34 = n$; 50,655 people

Page 187

Check students' graphs.
1. $x \leq 3$
2. $t = {}^-6$
3. $z \geq {}^-1$
4. $p \geq 4$
5. $n = 7$
6. $y = {}^-2$
7. $s \leq 5$
8. $t \geq 2$
9. $r = {}^-2$
10. $m \leq 8$
11. $y \geq {}^-5$

Page 188

1. 3, 5 2. 4, $^-2$ 3. 3, 2
4. 3, 0 5. $^-4$, $^-2$ 6. $^-1$, 0
7. $^-1$, 2 8. 0, 4 9. 4, 4
10. 5, $^-4$ 11. 0, $^-6$ 12. $^-3$, $^-5$
13. $^-4$, 1 14. $^-6$, 5 15. 6, 4
16. 1, $^-4$ 17. $^-4$, 4 18. 0, 0
19. F, D, R
20. H, R, K
21. E, B, I, Q
22. R, D, H

Page 188 (cont'd.)

23. P, J, D, F; F, H, I, D; Answers will vary.
24. ($^-4$, 0)

Page 189

1. $^-5°F$
2. April
3. January and February
4. 5 months
5. Houston
6. Cleveland; 0.2% greater
7. Milwaukee
8. 3,565,000

Page 190

1. 3, 5, 7, 9
2. $^-4$, $^-3$, $^-2$, $^-1$
3. 8, 5, 2, $^-1$, $^-4$
4. 3, 1, $^-1$, $^-3$
5. $^-3$, $^-2$, $^-1$, 0, 1
6. $^-5$, $^-1$, 3, 7, 11
4.–6. Check students' graphs.

Page 191

1. $^-4$, 0, 2, 6
2. 6, 4, 0, $^-4$
3. 6, 4, 3, 0
4. $^-4$, $^-1$, 2, 5
1.–4. Check students' graphs.

RETEACH

These masters reteach material covered in the
lessons in the pupil's edition. Where appropriate,
the emphasis of these masters is directed at
remediation of common errors.

RETEACH Whole-Number Place Value

In one year, light travels 9,460,563,614,000 kilometers. Give the place value name of the 5.

Remember

Be sure to use the correct position of the digit in a number to find its place value.

PERIODS	Trillions			Billions			Millions			Thousands			Ones		
	hundred trillions	ten trillions	trillions	hundred billions	ten billions	billions	hundred millions	ten millions	millions	hundred thousands	ten thousands	thousands	hundreds	tens	ones
			9	4	6	0	5	6	3	6	1	4	0	0	0

The place value of 5 is hundred millions.

Jupiter has twelve moons. The distances of nine of these moons from Jupiter are shown in the table. Complete the table by writing the place value of the underlined digit.

Satellite	Distance from Jupiter	Place Name
1.	1<u>8</u>1,500	
2.	<u>4</u>22,000	
3.	<u>6</u>71,400	
4.	<u>1</u>,071,000	
5.	1,<u>8</u>84,000	
6.	<u>1</u>1,500,000	
7.	11,750,0<u>0</u>0	
8.	11,7<u>5</u>0,000	
9.	<u>2</u>1,000,000	

RETEACH | Comparing and Ordering Whole Numbers

The table lists the heights, in feet, of several famous mountains of the world. Order these heights from the least to the greatest.

Mountain	Height (feet)
Everest	29,028
Manaslu	26,658
St. Helens	9,677
Nanga Parbat	26,650

Remember

When ordering whole numbers, line up the digits in a vertical column. Then compare the digits, beginning at the left.

Compare to find the least.

9,677
29,028
26,658
26,650

9,677 has no ten thousands.
So, 9,677 is the least.

Continue comparing to order the remaining numbers.

$26,65\textcircled{0} < 26,65\textcircled{8}$
$2\textcircled{6},650 < 2\textcircled{9},028$
$2\textcircled{6},658 < 2\textcircled{9},028$

So, $2\textcircled{6},65\textcircled{0} < 2\textcircled{6},65\textcircled{8} < 2\textcircled{9},028$.

The order from the least to the greatest is 9,677; 26,650; 26,658; 29,028.

Compare. Write >, <, or =.

1. 6,453 _____ 6,385

2. 4,475 _____ 795

3. 5,377,337 _____ 5,389,373

4. 21,001 _____ 21,010

5. 382,000 _____ 382 thousand

6. 483,860,267 _____ 483,869,267

7. 475 trillion _____ 479 billion

8. 396 billion _____ 369 billion

Order the numbers from the least to the greatest.

9. 8,846; 8,836; 37,733; 896

10. 283,389; 263,398; 28,837; 29,375

_____

_____

11. 476,743,648; 498,498,374; 54,475,279; 582,298; 832,382,221

_____

RETEACH　Addition and Subtraction

ubtract.

$5 - (16 - 8) = \blacksquare$

Remember

Subtraction is not associative. In subtraction, the grouping of the numbers may change the answer. Do the operation within parentheses first.

$$25 - (16 - 8) = \blacksquare$$
$$25 - \quad 8 \quad = 17$$

If you subtract 16 from 25 and then subtract 8, you reach a wrong answer. $25 - (16 - 8) \neq 1$

$5 - (16 - 8) = 17$

Use the properties to complete.

1. $50 - (21 - 6)$
$50 - $ _____ = _____

2. $35 + (9 + 8)$
$35 + $ _____ = _____

3. $89 - (63 - 7)$
$89 - $ _____ = _____

4. $74 + (42 + 11)$
$74 + $ _____ = _____

5. $752 + (90 + 30)$
$752 + $ _____ = _____

6. $105 - (78 - 26)$
$105 - $ _____ = _____

7. $1,892 - (599 - 66)$
$1,892 - $ _____ = _____

8. $916 + (36 + 72)$
$916 + $ _____ = _____

9. $623 + (56 + 45)$
$623 + $ _____ = _____

10. $876 - (89 - 23)$
$876 - $ _____ = _____

Solve.

11. The Noh family drove 100 miles to the beach. The next day, they drove 14 miles to a restaurant and 7 miles to a shopping mall. How many miles did they travel in all? _____

12. Mrs. Noh began the trip with $1,575. She gave $84 to her son James. He spent $30 to rent a sailboat. How much was left of the original $1,575? _____

RETEACH Estimating Sums—Front-End and Rounding

According to the 1980 census, the census figures for the four largest states in the United States are as shown in the table at the right. About how many people live in these states?

State	Population
Calif.	23,699,000
N.Y.	17,557,000
Tex.	14,228,000
Pa.	11,867,000

Remember

Adjust by grouping to ten millions.

$$\begin{matrix} 23{,}669{,}000 \\ 17{,}557{,}000 \end{matrix} \Big\rangle \rightarrow \text{about } 10{,}000{,}000$$

$$\begin{matrix} 14{,}228{,}000 \\ +\ 11{,}867{,}000 \end{matrix} \Big\rangle \rightarrow \text{about } 10{,}000{,}000$$

$$50{,}000{,}000 + 20{,}000{,}000 = 70{,}000{,}000$$

About 70 million people live in these states.

Estimate each sum.

1. 7,235
    5,956
    6,010
    + 4,782

2. 3,520
    6,231
    4,489
    + 2,690

3. 4,289,425
    6,302,761
    + 2,410,986

4. 28,39.
    9,41'
    12,02!
    + 10,57!

5. 7,235
    5,956
    6,010
    + 4,782

6. 3,520
    6,231
    4,489
    + 2,690

7. 4,289,425
    6,302,761
    + 2,410,986

8. 28,39;
    9,41'
    12,02!
    + 10,57!

Estimate. Write > or <.

9. $228{,}475 + 63{,}920 + 119{,}680 \bigcirc 450{,}000$

10. $12{,}965{,}287 + 20{,}689{,}305 + 17{,}652{,}381 \bigcirc 50{,}000{,}000$

11. $6{,}408{,}215 + 596{,}380 + 4{,}926{,}846 \bigcirc 15{,}000{,}000$

Use with pages 10–11

RETEACH   Estimating Differences

About how many more people were there living in the United States in 1980 than in 1970?

United States Population	
1970	203,235,298
1980	226,504,825

Remember

Round numbers so that it is easy to compute.

230	or	227 million
− 200		− 203 million
30		24 million

About 24 million people more lived in the United States in 1980 than in 1970.

Estimate. Choose the best answer.

1. 5,319 − 2,675   a. less than 3,000   b. more than 3,000

2. 8,237 − 3,910   a. less than 5,000   b. more than 5,000

3. 7,840 − 5,753   a. less than 2,000   b. more than 2,000

4. 12,365 − 9,429   a. less than 3,000   b. more than 3,000

5. 19,726 − 15,308   a. less than 4,000   b. more than 4,000

6. 48,275 − 26,419   a. less than 20,000   b. more than 20,000

7. 48,275 − 26,419   a. less than 22,000   b. more than 22,000

8. 125,238 − 110,407   a. less than 15,000   b. more than 15,000

Estimate.

9.	7,248	10.	28,723	11.	85,239
	− 3,650		− 20,566		− 36,404

12.	6,789,435	13.	8,235,910	14.	4,635,129
	− 2,901,753		− 943,686		− 4,614,350

Name _____ Date _____

A class is collecting aluminum cans for recycling. On Monday, they collected 965; Tuesday, 1,462; Wednesday, 843; Thursday, 761; and Friday, 2,462. How many cans did the class collect this week?

Remember	
Line up whole numbers in the ones place and the others will fall in the right place. Regroup when necessary.	965 1,462 843 761 + 2,462 6,493

The class collected 6,493 cans this week.

The number of cans collected each day for the past four weeks is shown in the chart. Find the total for each week.

Week	Monday	Tuesday	Wednesday	Thursday	Friday	Total for the week
1.	1,250	872	1,114	901	1,015	
2.	2,714	915	517	872	1,673	
3.	1,141	646	622	962	2,589	
4.	979	899	419	1,005	1,243	

Add.

5. $453 + 29 + 8 =$ _____

6. $267 + 152 + 27 =$ _____

7. $385 + 468 + 1,412 =$ _____

8. $9,841 + 983 + 17 =$ _____

9. $8,467 + 29 + 986 =$ _____

10. $10,842 + 8,743 + 12,403 =$ _____

11. $8,422 + 12,675 + 819 =$ _____

12. $152,643 + 28,444 + 88,972 =$ _____

13. $26,453 + 8,752 + 181,499 =$ _____

14. $1,899,743 + 6,970,463 + 152,600 =$ _____

6

RETEACH Subtracting Whole Numbers

The circulation of *Science Today* magazine increased from 85,921 subscriptions last year to 102,732 subscriptions this year. How many more subscriptions are there this year?

Remember

Regroup when necessary.

Subtract the ones and then the tens.		Subtract the hundreds.	Subtract the thousands.	Subtract the ten thousands.
102,732 − 85,921 1	102,732 − 85,921 11	102,732 − 85,921 811	102,732 − 85,921 6,811	102,732 − 85,921 16,811

There are 16,811 more subscriptions this year.

Solve.

Last year *Science Today* magazine sold 85,921 copies. The year before that, it sold 83,785 copies. Three years ago, it sold 82,972 copies; four years ago, 79,546.

1. How many more copies were sold last year than two years ago? _____

2. How many more were sold two years ago than three years ago? _____

3. How many more were sold three years ago than four years ago? _____

4. How many more were sold last year than four years ago? _____

Subtract.

5. 91
 − 79

6. 304
 − 146

7. 672
 − 98

8. 64,000
 − 4,961

9. 61,004 − 22,114 = _____

10. 64,671 − 14,986 = _____

11. 661,563 − 62,843 = _____

12. 1,907,843 − 1,384,642 = _____

RETEACH Extending Place Value

It takes a radio wave 0.005368 seconds to travel one mile. What is the name for 0.005368?

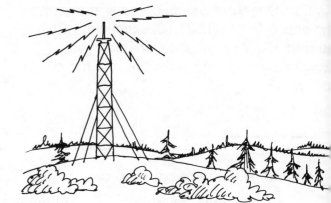

Remember

Use the position of the 8 (the millionths place) in the number to name the decimal.

The name is five thousand, three hundred sixty-eight millionths.

Write the letter of the correct number.

1. Forty-three ten-thousandths _____

  a. 0.043   **b.** 0.00043   **c.** 43,000   **d.** 0.0043

2. One thousand, three hundred ninety-nine hundred-thousandths _____

  a. 1,399   **b.** 0.01399   **c.** 0.1399   **d.** 0.001399

3. One thousand, eight hundred seventy-nine hundred-thousandths _____

  a. 1,879   **b.** 1879   **c.** 0.01879   **d.** 0.001879

4. Four thousand, one hundred fifty-five ten-thousandths _____

  a. 4,155,000   **b.** 0.4155   **c.** 0.04155   **d.** 0.041550

5. One and two thousand, seven hundred seventy-seven hundred-thousandths _____

  a. 1.002777   **b.** 0.12777   **c.** 1.02777   **d.** 1.2777

Name the number.

6. 0.05 _____   **7.** 0.004 _____

8. 0.0006 _____   **9.** 0.00009 _____

10. 0.45 _____   **11.** 0.045 _____

RETEACH | Comparing and Ordering Decimals

Sally's mother works with a micrometer, an instrument that makes very precise measurements. Two measurements she makes of gears are 3.276 inches and 3.2758 inches. Use one of the symbols >, <, or = to compare these decimals.

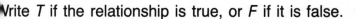

Remember

To compare decimals, line up the decimal points. Write extra zeros if necessary, and then compare the digits from left to right. The symbol < means less than. The symbol > means greater than.

$$3.2760$$
$$3.2758$$

3.2760 > 3.2758 (or 3.2758 < 3.2760)

Write *T* if the relationship is true, or *F* if it is false.

1. 6.234 < 6.240 _____

2. 0.00730 < 0.00729 _____

3. 27.973 > 27.980 _____

4. 0.0008470 > 0.0008467 _____

5. 5.04320 = 5.43200 _____

Write >, <, or =.

6. 2.37 _____ 2.372   **7.** 2.814 _____ 2.82   **8.** 0.0057 _____ 0.00563

9. 0.972 _____ 0.9665   **10.** 1.843 _____ 0.962   **11.** 3.675 _____ 2.676

12. 1.005 _____ 1.0006   **13.** 3.4617 _____ 3.462   **14.** 0.00561 _____ 0.000562

Order the decimals from the least to the greatest.

15. 0.005; 0.0005; 0.05   **16.** 1.35; 1.349; 1.3492

_____   _____

RETEACH | Rounding Decimals

The area of Czechoslovakia is 0.011951 of the area of
Europe. Round this number to the nearest ten-thousandth.

Remember

Examine the digit to the right of the place to which you
are rounding. When the digit is 5 or greater, round up.
When the digit is less than 5, round down. When
rounding 9 up, regroup.

0.011951 is between 0.0119 and 0.0120.

0 . 0 1 1 ⑨ 5 1   The number to the right is 5; so, round
up to 0.0120.

The number 0.011951 rounded to the nearest ten-thousandth
is 0.0120.

This chart shows the decimal part of the area of South
America that several countries occupy. Complete the chart.

Country	Decimal part of area of South America	Round to	Rounded number
1. Columbia	0.063799	hundredths	
2. Bolivia	0.059875	thousandths	
3. Venezuela	0.0510796	tenths	

This chart shows the decimal part of the area of the United
States occupied by several states. Complete the chart.

State	Decimal part of area of United States	Round to	Rounded number
4. Vermont	0.002493	ten-thousandths	
5. Kansas	0.022695	thousandths	
6. Missouri	0.019124	hundredths	
7. Oklahoma	0.0191643	thousandths	
8. Virginia	0.0110195	ten-thousandths	

Use with pages 24–25

RETEACH Estimating Decimal Sums

Kim has $10 to spend. Does she have enough to pay the bill?

BILL
$2.75
3.29
2.49
2.59
$

Remember

Round or adjust by grouping cents to dollars.

Rounding	Adjusting
$2.75 → $3	$2.75 ⎤
3.29 → 3	3.29 ⎦ around $1
2.49 → 2	2.49 ⎤
+ 2.59 → 3	+ 2.59 ⎦ around $1
$11	$9 + $2 = $11

No, $10 is probably not enough.   No, $10 is not enough.

Estimate. Write > or <.

1. $3.59 + $2.75 + $1.45 ◯ $8

2. $2.40 + $0.95 + $6.75 ◯ $10

3. $8.99 + $12.25 + $6.10 ◯ $27

4. $28.49 + $53.10 ◯ $81

5. $25.25 + $32.19 + $18.79 ◯ $80

6. 3.2 + 4.68 + 0.03 ◯ 8

Estimate.

7. 12.35
     6.091
   + 0.003

8. 25.41
     6.98
   + 12.65

9. 58.2
    14.71
   + 16.05

10. $129.39
    + 249.89

11. 43.026
      0.91
    + 38.5

12. 75.21
     24.9
    + 0.018

13. 215.2
     29.81
    + 12.37

14. 387.46
      0.0097
    + 12.82

RETEACH   Adding Decimals

The four members of a 400 meter relay team finished their legs of the race with times of 10.33 seconds, 10.7 seconds, 11.2 seconds, and 10.12 seconds. Find the total time that the relay team took to complete the race.

┌─ **Remember** ─────────────────────────────────────┐

Be sure to line up the decimal points when adding decimals. Add zeros if needed. Place the decimal in the sum correctly.

$$\begin{array}{r} 10.33 \\ 10.7\textcircled{0} \\ 11.2\textcircled{0} \\ +\ 10.12 \\ \hline 42.35 \end{array}$$

└──┘

The total time was 42.35 seconds.

Three teams compete in a 400-meter relay. The times for each leg of the race are shown in the table. Complete the table.

Team	First leg	Second leg	Third leg	Fourth leg	Total time
1.	10.43	10.7	11.1	10.3	$\begin{array}{r} 10.43 \\ 10.7\textcircled{0} \\ 11.1\textcircled{0} \\ +\ 10.3\textcircled{0} \end{array}$
2.	10.51	10.31	10.96	10.41	$\begin{array}{r} 10.51 \\ 10.31 \\ 10.96 \\ +\ 10.41 \end{array}$
3.	10.6	10.43	10.85	10.6	$\begin{array}{r} 10.6\textcircled{0} \\ 10.43 \\ 10.85 \\ +\ 10.6\textcircled{0} \end{array}$

RETEACH — Subtracting Decimals

In a hurdles race, the first-place runner finished with a time of 15.7 seconds. The second-place runner finished in 16.12 seconds. What was the difference in time between the runners?

Remember

Be sure to line up the decimal points when subtracting decimals. Add zeros if needed. Place the decimal point in the difference correctly.

$$\begin{array}{r} 16.12 \\ -\ 15.70 \\ \hline 0.42 \end{array}$$

The difference in time between the two runners was 0.42 seconds.

Subtract.

1. $3.62 - 1.07 = $ _____

2. $1.87 - 0.89 = $ _____

3. $\$14 - \$8.75 = $ _____

4. $\$35 - \$26.94 = $ _____

5. $0.65 - 0.5 = $ _____

6. $1.875 - 0.025 = $ _____

7. $6.03 - 0.962 = $ _____

8. $7.13 - 1.875 = $ _____

9. $87 - 0.003 = $ _____

10. $962.3 - 15.677 = $ _____

11. $0.56172 - 0.421843 = $ _____

12. $0.004375 - 0.000673 = $ _____

Solve.

13. The highest speed in the time trials for a 500-mile Indianapolis race was 209.872 miles per hour. The second-best time was 209.87 miles per hour. Find the difference.

_____

14. The average speed for the winner in a 500-mile race in Indianapolis was 165.173 miles per hour. The second-place car averaged 165.069 miles per hour. Find the difference in speeds.

_____

RETEACH Multiplication

1. Name the property that is illustrated by this expression.

$$6 \times (8 \times 4) = 6 \times (4 \times 8)$$

Remember

The numbers have not been regrouped, but have only changed position.

The property is the Commutative Property of Multiplication.

2. Name the property that is illustrated by this expression.

$$3 \times (5 + 8) = (5 + 8) \times 3$$

Remember

Again, the numbers have changed position but have not been regrouped.

The property is the Commutative Property of Multiplication.

Name the property that is illustrated by the expression.

1. $(4 \times 3) \times 5 = (3 \times 4) \times 5$

_____

2. $(4 \times 3) \times 5 = 4 \times (3 \times 5)$

_____

3. $8 \times (6 + 4) = (6 + 4) \times 8$

_____

4. $8 \times (6 + 4) = 8 \times 6 + 8 \times 4$

_____

Find n.

5. $(6 \times 8) = n \times 6; \ n =$ _____

6. $(6 \times 8) \times 9 = 6 \times (n \times 9); \ n =$ _____

7. $(3 + 4) \times n = 3 \times 9 + 4 \times 9; \ n =$ _____

8. $(18 + 20) \times n = 31 \times (18 + 20); \ n =$ _____

9. $n \times (31 + 40) = 9 \times 31 + 9 \times 40; \ n =$ _____

10. $16 \times (18 + n) = 16 \times 18 + 16 \times 20; \ n =$ _____

Use with pages 44–45.

Name _____ Date _____

RETEACH **Multiplying by Multiples of 10**

In a recent year, the federal government spent about $2,000 for each person in the United States. How much did the government spend for the residents of a town with a population of 3,000?

Remember

The number of zeros in the product is the sum of the numbers of zeros in the factors.

$$2,000 \times 3,000 = 6,000,000$$
$$(3 + 3) \text{ zeros} = 6 \text{ zeros}$$

The government spent $6,000,000 for the residents of the town.

Complete the table.

	Number	Multiply by			
		10	100	1,000	10,000
1.	5				
2.	8				
3.	10				
4.	28				
5.	150				

Solve.

6. In a recent year, the state of Hawaii collected about $1,000 in taxes for each person in the state. In a city of 2,000 people, about how much state tax was collected?

_____

7. In a recent year, the federal government spent about $400 on projects for each resident of Hawaii. If there are 300,000 people in a city, about how much money was spent on federal projects?

_____

Use with pages 46–47.   15

RETEACH Estimating Products

Clearview School is planning to take 6 buses to the state tournament. If each bus will hold 78 passengers, about how many people can ride the bus to the game?

┌─────────────────────┐
│ STATE │
│ TOURNAMENT │
│ │
│ Final: │
│ Clearview │
│ vs. │
│ Jamestown │
└─────────────────────┘

Remember

Round to numbers that are easy to compute mentally, yet close to the given number.

Underestimate		Overestimate	
$78 \rightarrow$ 70		$78 \rightarrow$ 80	
$\times\ 6$ $\times\ 6$		$\times\ 6$ $\times\ 6$	
420		480	

Between 420 and 480 people can ride the bus.

Pick the best estimate of each product.

1. 8×380 **a.** 8×300 **b.** 8×400 **c.** 10×300 **d.** 10×400

2. 17×49 **a.** 10×40 **b.** 10×50 **c.** 20×40 **d.** 20×50

3. 63×72 **a.** 60×70 **b.** 60×80 **c.** 70×70 **d.** 70×80

Use mental computation to find these products.

4. 300×4 _____   5. 20×70 _____   6. 80×30 _____

7. 200×50 _____   8. 400×100 _____   9. $6,000 \times 300$ _____

10. $5,000 \times 500$ _____   11. $8,000 \times 2,000$ _____

Estimate each product.

12. 28×5 _____   13. 42×81 _____   14. 36×59 _____

15. 188×31 _____   16. 531×52 _____   17. 608×320 _____

Use with pages 48–49

RETEACH Multiplying by 1-Digit Numbers

The Williams family traveled an average of 340 miles per day
on their vacation. If they spent 7 days on vacation, how
many miles did they travel?

Multiply 340 × 7.

Remember

Be sure to regroup when multiplying.

Multiply by the ones.	Multiply by the tens. Regroup the 2 hundreds.	Multiply by the hundreds. Add the 2 hundreds.
$\begin{array}{r} 340 \\ \times\ \ 7 \\ \hline 0 \end{array}$	$\begin{array}{r} ②\\ 3④0 \\ \times\ \ \ 7 \\ \hline ⑧0 \end{array}$	$\begin{array}{r} ②\\ ③40 \\ \times\ \ \ 7 \\ \hline 2,③80 \end{array}$

The Williams family traveled 2,380 miles on their vacation.

Multiply.

1. 360 × 8 = _____

2. 142 × 9 = _____

3. 28 × 7 = _____

4. 46 × 9 = _____

5. 143 × 6 = _____

6. 280 × 9 = _____

7. 238 × 5 = _____

8. 462 × 7 = _____

9. 1,004 × 8 = _____

10. 1,307 × 9 = _____

11. 3,265 × 6 = _____

12. 12,861 × 4 = _____

13. $146.98 × 3 = _____

14. $1,467.88 × 8 = _____

Solve.

15. The Williams spent an average of $78 per day for meals on their 7-day vacation. How much did they spend for meals?

_____

16. The average cost per day for lodging for 6 nights was $63.85. How much did they spend for lodging?

_____

Name _____ Date _____

RETEACH Multiplying by 2-Digit Numbers

A machine at a bottling plant places caps on 3,272 bottles per hour. If the machine operates for 18 hours per day, how many bottles are capped per day by the machine?

Remember

Multiply 3,272 by 18.

Multiply by the ones.	Place a zero in the units place.	Multiply by the tens.	Add.
3,272 × 18 26176	3,272 × 18 26176 0	3,272 × 18 26176 32720	3,272 × 18 26176 32720 58,896

The machine caps 58,896 bottles per day.

Multiply.

1. 189 → 189
       × 32   × 32
              378
                0

2. $28.95 → $28.95
        × 46   × 46
               17370
                   0

3. 84 × 48 = _____

4. 62 × 18 = _____

5. 89 × 26 = _____

6. 106 × 12 = _____

7. 263 × 19 = _____

8. 486 × 72 = _____

9. 1,007 × 23 = _____

10. 1,841 × 40 = _____

11. 6,214 × 84 = _____

Solve.

12. A packing machine at the bottling plant can package 84 six-packs per hour. How many six-packs can the machine package in an 18-hour day?

13. Bottled juices sell for $6.35 a case. The refreshment committee for the class picnic ordered 14 cases. How much did they spend?

18

Use with pages 54–55.

Name _____ Date _____

RETEACH — Multiplying by Larger Numbers

Delaware has a land area of about 1,982 square miles. The population density is 306 people per square mile. What is the approximate population of the state?

Remember

Multiply 1,982 × 306.

Multiply by the ones.	Place a zero in the tens place.	Multiply by the hundreds.	Add.
1,982 × 306 11892	1,982 × 306 11892 0	1,982 × 306 11892 59460	1,982 × 306 11892 59460 606,492

Be sure to use the zero in the tens place as a multiplier.

The population of the state is about 606,492.

Multiply. Show all work for numbers 1 and 2.

1. 355 × 207

2. 678 × 306

_____   _____

3. 38 × 105 = _____

4. 103 × 107 = _____

5. 462 × 106 = _____

6. 458 × 307 = _____

7. 981 × 609 = _____

8. 4,641 × 205 = _____

9. 481 × 1,004 = _____

10. 3,681 × 3,007 = _____

RETEACH   Estimating Decimal Products

Juan needs 3.75 pounds of apples. They are $0.44 per pound. About how much will they cost?

Estimate 3.75 × $0.44.

Remember

It is not necessary to round both factors to the same place value. Round factors to their front digit, or take advantage of closeness to 1 or $\frac{1}{2}$.

3.75 → 4	
0.44 → 0.4	4 × $0.40 = $1.60
OR	
3.75 → 4	
0.44 → 0.5	4 × $0.50 = $2.00

The apples cost $1.60 to $2.00.

Choose the best answer.

1. Close to but greater than half   a. 0.46   b. 0.53   c. 0.96   d. 1.05

2. Close to but less than one   a. 0.45   b. 0.55   c. 0.97   d. 1.1

3. Close to but greater than one   a. 0.47   b. 0.58   c. 0.957   d. 1.26

Use estimation to locate the decimal point.

4. 5.07 × 1.2 = ___6 0 8 4___   5. 0.975 × 4.26 = ___4 1 5 3 5___

6. 0.866 × 0.53 = ___4 5 8 9 8___   7. 0.459 × 0.28 = ___1 2 8 5 2___

Estimate. Use numbers that are easy to multiply mentally.

8. 0.963 × 0.708 = _____   9. 1.1 × 3.26 = _____

10. 1.05 × 0.2369 = _____   11. 2.42 × 0.52 = _____

12. 0.482 × 6.12 = _____   13. 1.3 × 8.1 = _____

Use with pages 60–61.

Name _____ Date _____

A gram of water contains about 0.11 g of hydrogen. To the nearest 0.01 g, how much hydrogen is there in 12.35 g of water?

┌─ **Remember** ──────────────────────────────────────┐

Multiply 12.35 × 0.11.

```
   12.35  ←    2 places          The number of decimal
 ×  0.11  ←  + 2 places          places in the product
   1235                          is the sum of the
   1235                          numbers of decimal places
  1.3585  ←    4 places          in the factors.
```
└──┘

There are about 1.36 g of hydrogen in 12.35 g of water.

Place the decimal point in the product.

1. 6.8 × 3.75 = ___**25 500**___

2. 5.98 × 8.3 = ___**49 634**___

Multiply.

3. 18 × 5.9 = _____

4. 322 × 0.6 = _____

5. 14.3 × 8.6 = _____

6. 13.2 × 1.71 = _____

7. 85.3 × 0.12 = _____

8. 14.5 × 0.35 = _____

9. 18.9 × 0.3 = _____

10. 10.45 × 1.72 = _____

11. $18.45 × 1.5 = _____

12. $187.50 × 0.05 = _____

13. 36.8 × 1.09 = _____

14. 4,641.85 × 2.36 = _____

Solve.

15. There is about 0.375 g of carbon in 1 g of carbon dioxide. How much carbon is there in 17.5 g of carbon dioxide?

_____

16. A gram of salt contains about 0.39 g of sodium. How much sodium is there in 28.5 g of salt? _____

RETEACH Multiplying by Powers of 10

Of each pound of body weight, about 0.65 lb is water. If the "front-four" linemen on a defensive football team have a total weight of 1,000 lb, about how much of that weight is water?

Remember

To multiply a decimal by a power of 10, move the decimal point to the right the same number of places as there are zeros in the power of 10. Write as many zeros as necessary.

$$0.65 \times 1,000 = 0.\underline{650}$$
$$= \quad 650$$

About 650 lb of that weight is water.

Multiply.

1. $0.05 \times 1,000 = 0.\underline{050} =$ _____

2. $0.36 \times 10,000 = 0.\underline{3600} =$ _____

Complete the table.

	Number	Multiply by			
		10	100	1,000	10,000
3.	1.9				
4.	0.04				
5.	0.872				
6.	19.6				
7.	0.0032				

Solve.

8. A 50-person football team has a total weight of about 10,000 lb. If there is 0.65 lb of water in each pound of body weight, how many pounds of water do the 10,000 lb contain?

_____

Use with pages 66–67.

Name _____ Date _____

Each kilogram of brass alloy contains 0.015 kg of lead. A brass part for a motorcycle weighs 0.25 kg. How much lead is in the motorcycle part?

Remember

Multiply 0.25 by 0.015.
The number of decimal places in the product is the sum of the numbers of places in the factors. Add additional zeros if necessary.

$$0.015 \leftarrow 3 \text{ places}$$
$$\times \quad 0.25 \leftarrow 2 \text{ places}$$
$$0.00375 \leftarrow 5 \text{ places}$$

There is 0.00375 kg of lead in the brass part.

Place the decimal point in the product.

1. $0.43 \times 0.21 = \underline{\quad 903 \quad}$

2. $0.052 \times 0.17 = \underline{\quad 884 \quad}$

3. $0.75 \times 1.26 = \underline{\quad 945 \quad}$

4. $0.375 \times 0.064 = \underline{\quad 240 \quad}$

Multiply.

5. $0.085 \times 0.3 = \underline{\hspace{2cm}}$

6. $0.267 \times 0.3 = \underline{\hspace{2cm}}$

7. $1.36 \times 0.37 = \underline{\hspace{2cm}}$

8. $1.4 \times 0.036 = \underline{\hspace{2cm}}$

9. $1.72 \times 0.103 = \underline{\hspace{2cm}}$

10. $.234 \times 1.7 = \underline{\hspace{2cm}}$

11. $0.637 \times 0.4 = \underline{\hspace{2cm}}$

12. $0.046 \times 0.372 = \underline{\hspace{2cm}}$

13. $0.709 \times 15.3 = \underline{\hspace{2cm}}$

Solve.

14. The brass alloy in the example contains 0.58 kg of copper for each kilogram of brass. How much copper is there in a 0.25 kg piece of brass?

_____

15. Each kilogram of the brass alloy contains 0.405 kg of zinc. How much zinc is there in a 0.25 kg piece of brass?

_____

RETEACH Division

An I-beam is 12 meters long. If it is divided into 3 equal parts, how long is each piece? Check your answer by multiplication.

> **Remember**
>
> $12 \div 3 = 4$
> Check: $4 \times 3 = 12$.

Each piece is 4 meters long.

Write the multiplication statement that checks each answer.

1. $18 \div 2$ _____ × _____ = _____

2. $34 \div 2$ _____ × _____ = _____

3. $0 \div 32$ _____ × _____ = _____

4. $365 \div 5$ _____ × _____ = _____

5. $32 \div 32$ _____ × _____ = _____

6. $100 \div 4$ _____ × _____ = _____

7. $0 \div 16$ _____ × _____ = _____

8. $81 \div 3$ _____ × _____ = _____

9. $38 \div 2$ _____ × _____ = _____

10. $188 \div 47$ _____ × _____ = _____

11. $90 \div 15$ _____ × _____ = _____

12. $18 \div 1$ _____ × _____ = _____

13. $6 \div 1$ _____ × _____ = _____

14. $6 \div 2$ _____ × _____ = _____

15. $27 \div 9$ _____ × _____ = _____

16. $45 \div 15$ _____ × _____ = _____

17. $87 \div 87$ _____ × _____ = _____

18. $36 \div 6$ _____ × _____ = _____

Write *true* if the pair of statements is equivalent. Write *false* if they are not.

19. $56 \div 4 = n$; $4 \times n = 56$ _____

20. $85 = 5 \times n$; $n \times 85 = 5$ _____

Solve.

21. A box contains 144 books. The books are to be shared equally by 16 people. Write the division statement to solve for how many books each person receives, and the multiplication statement that checks the answer.

_____   _____

Use with pages 82–83.

Name _____ Date _____

An airplane used 760,000 liters of jet fuel in 200 hours of operation. How many liters of fuel were used per hour of operation?

┌─ **Remember** ──────────────────────────────────────┐

To divide by a multiple of 10, rewrite the division as an easier problem.

$$x = 760,0\boxed{0}\boxed{0} \div 2\boxed{0}\boxed{0}$$
$$= 7,600 \div 2$$
$$= 3,800$$

└──┘

The plane used 3,800 liters of fuel per hour.

Solve.

1. 300 ÷ 10 = _____

2. 400 ÷ 20 = _____

3. 600 ÷ 30 = _____

4. 3,000 ÷ 10 = _____

5. 4,000 ÷ 20 = _____

6. 6,000 ÷ 300 = _____

7. 5,000 ÷ 200 = _____

8. 6,000 ÷ 3,000 = _____

9. 7,000 ÷ 200 = _____

10. 3,800 ÷ 190 = _____

11. 4,200 ÷ 70 = _____

12. 48,000 ÷ 60 = _____

13. 48,000 ÷ 600 = _____

14. 48,000 ÷ 6,000 = _____

Solve.

15. An automobile used 3,000 gallons of gasoline in 1,200 hours of operation. Calculate the number of gallons per hour used by the car.

16. An airplane traveled 150,000 miles in 300 hours of operation. What was the average number of miles traveled per hour?

Use with pages 84–85.

RETEACH | Estimating Quotients of Whole Numbers

Mr. Davis is budgeting $2,500 for expenses during his 12-day trip to the mountains. About how much can he spend per day?

Remember

• Find out where the first digit in the quotient belongs.

$$12\overline{)2,500}$$ 12 divides 25.

• Count remaining digits in dividend.

$$12\overline{)2,500}^{\,\text{---}}$$ 3 digits in quotient

$$\begin{array}{r} 200\ + \\ 12\overline{)2,500} \end{array}$$

He can spend around $200 per day.

How many digits will the quotient contain?

1. $4\overline{)5,275}$ _____

2. $7\overline{)2,928}$ _____

3. $5\overline{)4,806}$ _____

4. $6\overline{)16,734}$ _____

5. $12\overline{)3,948}$ _____

6. $23\overline{)16,923}$ _____

Choose the best estimate.

7. $6\overline{)7,385}$ **a.** 10   **b.** 100   **c** 1,000   **d.** 10,000

8. $8\overline{)3,520}$ **a.** 40   **b.** 400   **c.** 4,000   **d.** 40,000

9. $15\overline{)4,936}$ **a.** 3   **b.** 30   **c.** 300   **d.** 3,000

Estimate.

10. $7\overline{)8,025}$

11. $9\overline{)4,631}$

12. $16\overline{)3,509}$

13. $22\overline{)17,940}$

14. $31\overline{)16,780}$

15. $58\overline{)180,311}$

16. $41\overline{)216,528}$

17. $61\overline{)623,155}$

18. $38\overline{)203,747}$

Use with pages 86–87.

Name _____ Date _____

Matt has 2,927 new records. He sends the same number to each of his 4 stores. He gives the rest to a school. How many does each store receive? How many does the school receive?

Remember

Be sure to bring digits down in the correct place.

$$
\begin{array}{r}
731 \text{ R3} \\
4\overline{)2{,}927} \\
28 \\
\hline
1\,2 \\
1\,2 \\
\hline
7 \\
4 \\
\hline
3
\end{array}
$$

Each store receives 731 records. The school will receive 3 records.

Solve.

1. $1{,}070 \div 5 =$ _____

2. $896 \div 7 =$ _____

3. $2{,}877 \div 9 =$ _____

4. $973 \div 7 =$ _____

5. $288 \div 8 =$ _____

6. $105 \div 7 =$ _____

7. $4{,}041 \div 9 =$ _____

8. $3{,}148 \div 7 =$ _____

9. $1{,}796 \div 4 =$ _____

10. $7{,}014 \div 7 =$ _____

11. $498{,}666 \div 7 =$ _____

12. $20{,}065 \div 5 =$ _____

13. $7{,}744 \div 7 =$ _____

14. $9{,}261 \div 9 =$ _____

Solve.

15. Karim bought 7 albums for $46.13. What was the average cost per album? _____

16. Jane bought 6 single records for $12.72. What was the average cost per record? _____

RETEACH   Dividing by 2-Digit Numbers

Luke's father raised 9,588 bushels of corn on a 47-acre field.
How many bushels per acre did he raise?

Remember

Write zeros in the quotient
when necessary.

$$\begin{array}{r} 20 \\ 47\overline{)9{,}588} \\ 9\ 4 \\ \hline 18 \end{array} \qquad \begin{array}{r} 204 \\ 47\overline{)9{,}588} \\ 9\ 4 \\ \hline 188 \\ 188 \\ \hline 0 \end{array}$$

Luke's father raised 204 bushels per acre.

Solve.

1. 8,925 ÷ 85 = _____

2. 12,454 ÷ 61 = _____

3. 12,627 ÷ 61 = _____

4. 1,717 ÷ 17 = _____

5. 3,259 ÷ 31 = _____

6. 21,843 ÷ 27 = _____

7. 5,833 ÷ 19 = _____

8. 4,284 ÷ 14 = _____

9. 10,818 ÷ 18 = _____

10. 11,055 ÷ 11 = _____

11. 17,017 ÷ 17 = _____

12. 68,085 ÷ 17 = _____

13. 28,054 ÷ 14 = _____

14. 110,077 ÷ 11 = _____

15. Luke's father also raised soybeans. He
calculated that he raised 46 bushels per
acre. The total number of bushels was
4,922. How many acres did he plant?

_____

16. A neighbor of Luke's raised 5,040
bushels of soybeans. He raised 48
bushels per acre. How many acres did
he plant?

_____

Name _____ Date _____

The charity fund drive netted $6,162.84 from 323 contributors. What was the average contribution?

┌─ **Remember** ──┐
│ Write zero in the quotient when necessary. │
│   19.0   19.08 │
│   323)6,162.84 $\frac{258}{323}$ < 1   323)6,162.84 │
│   3 23↓│   3 23↓││ │
│   ─────   ───── │
│   2 932   2 932 ││ │
│   2 907↓   2 907 ↓↓│ │
│   ─────   ───── │
│   25 8   25 84 │
│   25 84 │
│   ───── │
│   0 │
└───┘

The average donation was $19.08.

Divide.

1. 11,025 ÷ 105 = _____

2. 11,881 ÷ 109 = _____

3. 92,416 ÷ 304 = _____

4. 21,628 ÷ 104 = _____

5. 38,257 ÷ 125 = _____

6. 95,130 ÷ 315 = _____

7. $6,187.72 ÷ 343 = _____

8. $2,727.45 ÷ 261 = _____

9. $4,566.24 ÷ 453 = _____

10. 343,200 ÷ 165 = _____

11. 21,528 ÷ 207 = _____

12. 271,416 ÷ 263 = _____

13. 331,350 ÷ 165 = _____

14. 185,555 ÷ 185 = _____

Solve.

15. A heart-fund solicitor received $27.25 from 25 contributors in the neighborhood. What was the average donation?

_____

Name _____ Date _____

A 68-oz can of apple juice is listed with a sale price of $1.36. Find the cost per oz of the juice by dividing $1.36 by 68.

Remember

Write zeros to place the decimal point correctly.

$$
\begin{array}{r}
0.02 \\
68\overline{)1.36} \\
1.36 \\
\hline
0
\end{array}
$$

The juice costs $0.02 per ounce.

In comparing prices of items, the idea of a **unit cost** is important. The unit cost of an item is the cost of one unit of the item.

Complete the table by calculating the unit cost for each item.

Item	Size	Cost	Unit	Unit cost
1. Green beans	9 oz	$0.63	oz	
2. Mixed fruit	12 oz	$0.72	oz	
3. Potatoes	10 lb	$1.90	lb	
4. Milk	3 qt	$1.92	qt	
5. Peanuts	15 oz	$1.65	oz	
6. Flour	5 lb	$1.20	lb	
7. Orange juice	4 pt	$1.92	pt	
8. Peas	12 oz	$0.48	oz	
9. Broccoli spears	10 oz	$1.20	oz	

Name _____ Date _____

A stack of 1,000 sheets of notebook paper
is 3.82 inches high. Calculate the
approximate thickness of a single sheet of
paper by dividing 3.82 inches by 1,000.

Remember

To divide by a power of 10, move the decimal point one
place to the left for each zero in the divisor.

$$3.82 \div 1,000$$
$$0.0382 \div 10 = 0.00382$$

A sheet of notebook paper is about 0.00382 in. thick.

Write the letter of the correct quotient.

1. $316.7 \div 1,000 =$ _____   **a.** 31.67   **b.** 3.167   **c.** 0.3167   **d.** 0.03167

2. $38.62 \div 100 =$ _____   **a.** 3.862   **b.** 0.3862   **c.** 0.03862   **d.** 0.003862

3. $5,168 \div 10 =$ _____   **a.** 516.8   **b.** 51.68   **c.** 5.168   **d.** 0.5168

4. $386.52 \div 10,000 =$ _____   **a.** 38.652   **b.** 3.8652   **c.** 0.38652   **d.** 0.038652

5. $6.26 \div 1,000 =$ _____   **a.** 6.26   **b.** 0.626   **c.** 0.0626   **d.** 0.00626

6. $0.56 \div 100 =$ _____   **a.** 0.056   **b.** 0.0056   **c.** 0.00056   **d.** 0.000056

Solve.

7. A book that contains 100 pages is 0.27 in. thick, excluding
   the covers. Find the approximate thickness of each
   sheet. _____

8. A 2,000-page telephone book is 3.84 in. thick. What is the
   approximate thickness of each sheet? _____

9. A bag containing 5,000 small steel balls weighs 10.75
   pounds. The weight of the bag itself is too small to
   register on the scale. How many pounds does each steel
   ball weigh? _____

Use with pages 102–103.

RETEACH Dividing Decimals by Decimals

Frank's father traveled 488.4 miles and used 26.4 gallons of gasoline. How many miles per gallon did he get for the trip?

Remember

1. Multiply the divisor and the dividend by 10.

$$26.4\overline{)488.4}$$

2. Place the decimal point in the quotient.

$$264\overline{)4{,}884.0}$$

3. Divide.

$$\begin{array}{r} 18.5 \\ 264\overline{)4{,}884.0} \\ 2\ 64 \\ \hline 2\ 244 \\ 2\ 112 \\ \hline 132\ 0 \\ 132\ 0 \\ \hline 0 \end{array}$$

Write zero when necessary.

Frank's father got 18.5 miles per gallon for the trip.

Write the quotient.

1. $8.5\overline{)27.20}$ _____

2. $0.32\overline{)1.696}$ _____

3. $0.16\overline{)1.312}$ _____

4. $6.72\overline{)0.3360}$ _____

5. $7.1\overline{)45.156}$ _____

6. $6.8\overline{)0.204}$ _____

Solve.

7. $24.42 \div 6.6 =$ _____

8. $2.43 \div 8.1 =$ _____

9. $3.36 \div 0.35 =$ _____

10. $0.6084 \div 0.78 =$ _____

11. $0.185 \div 0.5 =$ _____

12. $0.1443 \div 0.185 =$ _____

13. On a trip, the Peduk family traveled 396 miles on 14.4 gallons of gasoline. How many miles per gallon did they get on the trip?

_____

14. Along the highway, the guard-rail posts are 11.5 feet apart. How many posts are needed for a rail which is 977.5 feet long? (HINT: The number of posts is $977.5 \div 11.5 + 1$).

_____

Use with pages 104–105.

RETEACH — Rounding Decimal Quotients

The Johnson family traveled 2,170 miles on their vacation. The gasoline for the trip cost $122.83. To the nearest cent, what was the cost per mile for gasoline?

Remember

When rounding decimal quotients, divide to one place more than the one to which you are rounding. Then round the quotient.

$$
\begin{array}{r}
0.056 \\
2{,}170\overline{)122.830} \\
108.50 \\
\hline
14.330 \\
13.020 \\
\hline
1.310
\end{array}
$$

The gasoline cost $0.06 per mile, to the nearest cent.

Divide, rounding the answer to tenths.

1. $1.87 \div 0.35 =$ _____

2. $6.283 \div 1.7 =$ _____

3. $43 \div 8.2 =$ _____

4. $0.372 \div 0.05 =$ _____

5. $18.3 \div 1.7 =$ _____

6. $69.75 \div 3.4 =$ _____

Round the answer to hundredths.

7. $1.732 \div 1.03 =$ _____

8. $69.94 \div 3.85 =$ _____

9. $0.075 \div 0.13 =$ _____

10. $0.003 \div 0.0028 =$ _____

Round the answer to thousandths.

11. $17.2 \div 3.5 =$ _____

12. $89.975 \div 0.3 =$ _____

13. $0.013 \div 0.03 =$ _____

14. $17.29 \div 1.2 =$ _____

Round the answer to ten-thousandths.

15. $12 \div 11 =$ _____

16. $4.55 \div 0.27 =$ _____

17. $3.33 \div 8 =$ _____

18. $67.7 \div 43 =$ _____

RETEACH   Divisibility

Lucius and two of his friends are planting a large garden as part of a 4-H project. They have started 117 tomato plants in a seed bed. Can they plant them in 3 even rows?

Remember

To check for divisibility by 3, find out whether the *sum of the digits* is evenly divisible by 3. Since 1 + 1 + 7 = 9 and 9 is evenly divisible by 3, the number *117* is evenly divisible by 3.

They can plant the tomato plants in 3 even rows.

Write *yes* if the number is evenly divisible by 3, *no* if it is not.

1. 79 _____   2. 129 _____   3. 369 _____

4. 879 _____   5. 1,469 _____   6. 8,749 _____

7. 12,659 _____   8. 189,159 _____   9. 92,466 _____

Test for divisibility by 9. (A number is evenly divisible by 9 if the sum of its digits is evenly divisible by 9.)

10. 169 _____   11. 189 _____   12. 579 _____

13. 819 _____   14. 1,689 _____   15. 8,379 _____

16. 13,869 _____   17. 199,999 _____   18. 33,966 _____

Solve.

19. Can Lucius and his friends put the 119 plants in 9 even rows? _____

20. The group has started 126 pepper plants. Can these plants be placed in 9 even rows? _____

Name _____ Date _____

RETEACH Powers and Roots

In the expression 5^4, 5 is called the base and 4 is called the exponent. Write 5^4 as a product of factors. Then multiply to find the product.

Remember

The exponent 4 tells you how many times to multiply the number.

$$5^4 = 5 \underbrace{\times 5 \times 5 \times 5}_{4 \text{ factors}}$$

$5^4 = 625$

Write the product of the factors and solve.

1. $6^2 = 6 \times 6 =$ _____

2. $1.3^4 = 1.3 \times 1.3 \times 1.3 \times 1.3 =$ _____

3. $7^2 =$ _____ $=$ _____

4. $4^3 =$ _____ $=$ _____

5. $2^6 =$ _____

6. $8^3 =$ _____

7. $15^2 =$ _____

8. $1.5^2 =$ _____

9. $3.1^3 =$ _____

10. $4^5 =$ _____

Use exponents to rewrite.

11. $2 \times 2 \times 2$

12. $4 \times 4 \times 4 \times 4 \times 4$

13. 9×9

14. $7 \times 7 \times 7$

15. $3 \times 3 \times 3 \times 3$

16. $5 \times 5 \times 5 \times 5$

17. 12×12

18. $11 \times 11 \times 11$

19. $10 \times 10 \times 10 \times 10 \times 10$

RETEACH   Scientific Notation

The population of the North American continent is about 395,000,000 people. Write this number in scientific notation.

Remember

Move the decimal point to the left enough places so that the number formed is between 1 and 10.

395,000,000.

8 places

$395,000,000 = 3.95 \times 10^8$

The number in scientific notation is 3.95×10^8.

Write in scientific notation.

1. 62,500 = _____   2. 8,420 = _____

3. 1,620 = _____   4. 1,500 = _____

5. 10,000 = _____   6. 15,000 = _____

7. 150 = _____   8. 20 = _____

9. 85,600 = _____   10. 653.7 = _____

11. 5,621.2 = _____   12. 8,907,000 = _____

Solve.

13. The population of Europe was recently estimated to be 696,400,000. Write the number in scientific notation.

_____

14. The population of Australia was recently estimated to be 15,500,000. Write the number in scientific notation.

_____

Write the number represented by the scientific notation.

15. 1.85×10^4 = _____   16. 2×10^3 = _____

17. 3.741×10^2 = _____   18. 1.8932×10^5 = _____

RETEACH   Factors, Primes, and Composites

Tanya has 48 petunias to plant in her flower garden. She wants to place them in rows so that each row has the same number of plants. What different numbers of rows of plants are possible?
What are the different factors of 48?

> **Remember**
>
> The number *48* can be written as a product in these ways: 1×48, 2×24, 3×16, 4×12, 6×8. The factors of 48 are 1, 2, 3, 4, 6, 8, 12, 16, 24, 48.

Tanya can plant the flowers in 1, 2, 3, 4, 6, 8, 12, 16, 24, or 48 rows.

Find all the factors of each number.

1. 36: 1×36, 2×18, 3×12, 4×9, 6×6; _____

2. 30: 1×30, 2×15, 3×10, 5×6; _____

3. 6: _____ **4.** 7: _____

5. 14: _____ **6.** 21: _____

7. 31: _____ **8.** 56: _____

9. 25: _____ **10.** 49: _____

11. 98: _____ **12.** 100: _____

Solve.

13. Tanya has 32 marigolds. She wants to plant them in rows, each having the same number of plants. What different numbers of rows are possible?

_____

14. She also has 13 geraniums. Can she plant them evenly using more than one row and more than one plant per row?

_____

15. What are the possible combinations of the numbers of even columns and rows for 40 geraniums if there are to be planted more geraniums in a column than in a row?

_____

Name _____ Date _____

Find the prime factorization of 250.

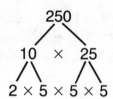

Use the factor tree at the right.

┌─ **Remember** ──────────────────────────────────┐
│ Write each factor as the product of two factors until all of │
│ the factors are prime. │
│ $250 = 2 \times 5 \times 5 \times 5 = 2 \times 5^3$ │
└──┘

The factors of 250 are 2×5^3.

Complete the factor trees.

1.   **2.**   **3.**

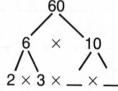   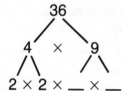   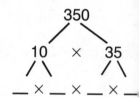

Write the prime factorization. Use exponents where possible.

4. 30 = _____   **5.** 22 = _____   **6.** 56 = _____

7. 190 = _____   **8.** 350 = _____   **9.** 400 = _____

10. 512 = _____   **11.** 2,500 = _____   **12.** 90 = _____

Write the number for the prime factorization.

13. $2 \times 3^2 \times 7$ **14.** $2^2 \times 3 \times 5$ **15.** $2^3 \times 3$

_____   _____   _____

16. $2 \times 3^3 \times 5$ **17.** $2^4 \times 5$ **18.** $2 \times 3 \times 5^2$

_____   _____   _____

Solve.

19. Find the prime factors of 36 and 20. Which factor(s) are the same for the two numbers? _____

20. Find the prime factors of 15 and 48. Which factors are the same for the two numbers? _____

RETEACH Greatest Common Factor

A landscape architect is planning to plant trees along two sides of a rectangular lot. She wants the trees equally spaced a whole number of feet apart. If the rectangle is 140 ft long and 120 ft wide, how far apart can she plant the trees?

Find the greatest common factor of 120 and 140.

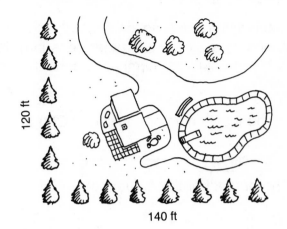

140 ft

Remember

The greatest common factor (GCF) is the product of the common prime factors of the numbers.

$$120 = 2 \times 2 \times 2 \times 3 \times 5$$
$$140 = 2 \times 2 \times 5 \times 7$$
$$GCF = 2 \times 2 \times 5 = 20$$

The landscape architect can plant the trees 20 ft apart.

Find the greatest common factor.

1. 65, 95: $\begin{cases}(65 = 5 \times 13)\\(95 = 5 \times 19)\end{cases}$ _____

2. 60, 150: $\begin{cases}(60 = 2 \times 2 \times 3 \times 5)\\(150 = 2 \times 3 \times 5 \times 5)\end{cases}$ _____

3. 16, 28: _____

4. 22, 33: _____

5. 18, 24: _____

6. 49, 56: _____

7. 20, 50: _____

8. 45, 105: _____

9. 250, 300: _____

10. 60, 72: _____

11. 180, 240: _____

12. 93, 99: _____

13. 71, 73: _____

14. 30, 75, 90: _____

Solve.

15. A triangular region is being fenced in. The sides of the triangle are 56 ft, 64 ft, and 72 ft long. What is the greatest whole number of feet apart the fence posts can be placed and still be equally spaced? _____

16. Susan is planting flowers around the edges of a rectangular flower bed that is 72 in. by 80 in. What is the greatest whole number of inches apart she can plant the flowers so that they are equally spaced? _____

RETEACH   Least Common Multiple (LCM)

A manufacturer packages pens in boxes of 12 each. The
school supply store must order pens in multiples of 200.
What is the smallest number of pens that the store can
order?

Find the least common multiple (LCM) of 12 and 200.

Remember

The product of the *highest* power of each of the prime factors yields the LCM.

$$12 = 2 \times 2 \times 3 = 2^2 \times 3$$
$$200 = 2 \times 2 \times 2 \times 5 \times 5 = 2^3 \times 5^2$$
$$LCM = 2^3 \times 3 \times 5^2 = 600$$

The smallest number of pens that the store can order is 600.

Complete the table.

Numbers	Prime factorization	LCM
1. 80, 120	$80 = 2^4 \times 5$ $120 = 2^3 \times 3 \times 5$	_____
2. 40, 60	$40 = 2^3 \times 5$ $60 = 2^2 \times 3 \times 5$	_____
3. 18, 24	$18 =$ _____ $24 =$ _____	_____
4. 30, 45	$30 =$ _____ $45 =$ _____	_____
5. 95, 190	$95 =$ _____ $190 =$ _____	_____
6. 13, 16	$13 =$ _____ $16 =$ _____	_____
7. 25, 60	$25 =$ _____ $60 =$ _____	_____
8. 36, 48	$36 =$ _____ $48 =$ _____	_____

RETEACH Order of Operations

Evaluate the expression $5 \cdot 3 + 7(6 - 4) \div 2$.

Remember

Simplify within parentheses first. Multiply as indicated by exponents. Multiply and divide before adding and subtracting. Then, add and subtract in the order they are given.

$$5 \cdot 3 + 7(6 - 4) \div 2$$
$$= 5 \cdot 3 + 7 \cdot 2 \div 2$$
$$= 15 + 14 \div 2$$
$$= 15 + 7$$
$$= 22$$

So, $5 \cdot 3 + 7(6 - 4) \div 2 = 22$.

Solve.

1. $6 \cdot 4 + 5 \cdot 3 - 2 \cdot 7 = 24 + 15 - 14 =$ _____

2. $3 + 6 \cdot 5 + 8 \div 4 = 3 + 30 + 2 =$ _____

3. $2 \cdot 6 + 3 \cdot 2 =$ _____

4. $5 \cdot 7 + 8 \div 2 =$ _____

5. $4 \cdot 7 - 8 \cdot 2 =$ _____

6. $6 \cdot 3 + 8 \cdot 7 - 2 \cdot 7 =$ _____

7. $8 \cdot 9 + 6 \cdot 3 - 14 \cdot 2 =$ _____

8. $8 \cdot 10 - 7 \cdot 8 + 16 \cdot 3 =$ _____

9. $84 \div 4 + 7 =$ _____

10. $95 \div 5 - 11 =$ _____

11. $87 \div 3 + 48 - 36 =$ _____

12. $86 \div 43 - 36 \div 18 =$ _____

13. $3 \cdot (6 + 7) - 4 =$ _____

14. $(12 + 7) \cdot (10 - 5) =$ _____

Solve.

15. George bought 6 coins for $2 each, 5 coins for $3 each, and 1 coin for $8 at a meeting of the Coin Collectors Club. How much did he spend? _____

RETEACH Algebraic Expressions and Sentences (+, −)

Suppose x is any whole number from 12 through 15. Find the solution to the equation $x - 7 = 6$. If there is no solution, write *no solution*.

Remember

Substitute all the numbers from 12 through 15 for x.

12 is not a solution since $12 - 7 \neq 12$
13 is a solution since $13 - 7 = 6$
14 is not a solution since $14 - 7 \neq 12$
15 is not a solution since $15 - 7 \neq 12$

The equation $x - 7 = 6$ has the solution $x = 13$.

Complete the table by finding whether the equation has a solution given the range of values indicated for x. Write *yes* or *no*.

Equation	Values for x	Solution in set?
1. $x - 5 = 14$	2, 4, 6, 8, 10, 12, 14	
2. $x - 4 = 7$	3, 6, 9, 11, 15, 18	
3. $x + 6 = 15$	2, 4, 6, 9, 10, 12	
4. $x - 3.1 = 5.1$	1, 2, 3, 4, 5, 6	

Suppose x is any even whole number from 2 through 20. Find the solution to each question, or write *no solution*.

5. $x + 4 = 10$ _____   **6.** $x - 5 = 7$ _____   **7.** $x + 3 = 12$ _____

8. $x - 15 = 10$ _____   **9.** $x + 1 = 21$ _____   **10.** $x + 10 = 30$ _____

11. $x - 15 = 3$ _____   **12.** $18 - x = 8$ _____   **13.** $31 - x = 15$ _____

14. $x + 5.1 = 9.1$ _____   **15.** $x - 6.7 = 11.3$ _____   **16.** $x - 9.7 = 3.7$ _____

Use with pages 138–139

RETEACH | Solving Equations (+ and −)

Gina purchased a game cassette for her home computer for
$18. The price of the cassette was advertised as a reduction
of $13. What was the original cost of the cassette?

Remember

Be sure to perform the same operation on both sides of
the equation.
Let x represent the original price.

$$x - 13 = 18$$
$$x - 13 + 13 = 18 + 13$$
$$x = 31$$

The cassette originally cost $31.

Solve the equation.

1.
$$x + 12 = 37$$
$$x + 12 - 12 = 37 - 12$$
$$x = \rule{2cm}{0.4pt}$$

2.
$$x - 6.7 = 8.3$$
$$x - 6.7 + 6.7 = 8.3 + 6.7$$
$$x = \rule{2cm}{0.4pt}$$

3. $x + 9 = 18$ _____

4. $x + 3 = 21$ _____

5. $x + 4 = 25$ _____

6. $x - 7 = 9$ _____

7. $x - 2 = 14$ _____

8. $x - 46 = 46$ _____

9. $x + 14 = 23$ _____

10. $x - 14 = 23$ _____

11. $x + 15 = 125$ _____

12. $x + 14.3 = 16$ _____

13. $x - 3.2 = 7.8$ _____

14. $x - 15.65 = 21.35$ _____

Solve.

15. Gina also bought a voice synthesizer
for her home computer for $37.95. It
was advertised as having been "marked
down $20." What was the original
price? _____

16. The store also advertised the price of a
printer as "$150 off." The reduced price
of the printer was $299.95. Find the
original price of the printer.
_____

RETEACH | Algebraic Expressions and Sentences (×, ÷)

Suppose x is any even whole number from 2 through 8. Find the solution of $\frac{x}{1.25} = 6.4$

Remember

If the solution is not clear by inspection, substitute to find the solution.

2 is not a solution since $\frac{2}{1.25} \neq 6.4$.

4 is not a solution since $\frac{4}{1.25} \neq 6.4$.

6 is not a solution since $\frac{6}{1.25} \neq 6.4$.

8 is the solution since $\frac{8}{1.25} = 6.4$.

Find the value of the given expression if $t = 14$.

1. $5t = $ _____

2. $8t = $ _____

3. $\frac{t}{14} = $ _____

4. $\frac{t}{7} = $ _____

5. $6t = $ _____

6. $\frac{2t}{4} = $ _____

7. $t^2 = $ _____

8. $\frac{t^2}{2} = $ _____

Write *true* or *false*.

9. $5z = 14$ if $z = 3$ _____

10. $\frac{y}{9} = 3$ if $y = 54$ _____

11. $4.8r = 38.4$ if $r = 8$ _____

12. $9.3u = 18.2$ if $u = 2$ _____

13. $\frac{12}{t} = 3$ if $t = 4$ _____

14. $\frac{38.4}{a} = 3$ if $a = 5.4$ _____

Suppose x is any of these numbers: 3, 6, 9, 12, 15, 18, 21, 24. Find the solution for each equation, or write *no solution*.

15. $\frac{x}{4} = 6$ _____

16. $\frac{x}{3} = 5$ _____

17. $\frac{x}{4} = 7$ _____

18. $3x = 27$ _____

19. $5x = 20$ _____

20. $16x = 96$ _____

21. $\frac{x}{4} = 1$ _____

22. $\frac{x}{18} = 1$ _____

23. $14x = 98$ _____

24. $\frac{x}{3.2} = 5$ _____

25. $\frac{x}{1.5} = 12$ _____

26. $\frac{x}{2} = 7.5$ _____

Use with pages 144–145.

RETEACH   Solving Equations (× and ÷)

A discount store received a large shipment of records that it decided to sell for $4 each. Shelly spent $28 for records. How many records did she buy?

Remember

Be sure to perform the same operation on both sides of the equation.

Let n represent the number of records purchased.

$$4n = 28$$
$$\frac{4n}{4} = \frac{28}{4}$$
$$n = 7$$

Shelly bought 7 records.

Solve the equation for n.

1. $6n = 1.5$
$\frac{6n}{6} = \frac{1.5}{6}$ (Divide by 6.)
$n = $ _____

2. $\frac{n}{3} = 7.2$

$3 \cdot \frac{n}{3} = 3 \cdot 7.2$ (Multiply by 3.)
$n = $ _____

3. $5n = 60$ _____

4. $6n = 72$ _____

5. $9n = 81$ _____

6. $\frac{n}{4} = 1$ _____

7. $\frac{n}{3} = 5$ _____

8. $\frac{n}{6} = 12$ _____

9. $\frac{n}{2} = 1.6$ _____

10. $\frac{n}{1.6} = 2$ _____

11. $3n = 3.6$ _____

12. $5n = 9.5$ _____

13. $\frac{n}{3.5} = 8$ _____

14. $\frac{n}{1.5} = 7.5$ _____

Solve.

15. Shelly also purchased 12 pencils for 96¢. What was the cost per pencil?

_____

16. At the shop near the discount store, Shelly paid $1.56 for small boxes of raisins. If the raisins cost $0.39 per box, how many boxes did she buy?

_____

RETEACH — Solving Two-Step Equations

A two-step equation contains two operations. For example, the equation $50x + 25 = 275$ uses multiplication and addition. Solve the equation $50x + 25 = 275$.

Remember

In order to solve a two-step equation, you must undo both operations.

$$50x + 25 = 275$$

Subtract 25 from both sides.

$$50x + 25 - 25 = 275 - 25$$

$$50x = 250$$

Divide both sides by 50.

$$\frac{50x}{50} = \frac{250}{50}$$

$x = 5.$

Solve for x.

1.
$$2x - 6 = 18$$
$$2x - 6 + 6 = 18 + 6$$
$$2x = 24$$
$$x = \underline{\qquad}$$

2.
$$\frac{x}{5} + 4 = 7$$
$$\frac{x}{5} + 4 - 4 = 7 - 4$$
$$\frac{x}{5} = 3$$
$$x = \underline{\qquad}$$

3.
$$\frac{x}{4} - 5 = 2.5$$
$$\frac{x}{4} - 5 + 5 = 2.5 + 5$$
$$\frac{x}{4} = \underline{\qquad}$$
$$x = \underline{\qquad}$$

4. $3x - 7 = 14$ _____

5. $5x - 6 = 19$ _____

6. $6x + 7 = 25$ _____

7. $\frac{x}{3} - 5 = 1$ _____

8. $\frac{x}{4} - 3 = 6$ _____

9. $\frac{x}{7} + 3 = 8$ _____

10. $14x - 7 = 91$ _____

11. $16x - 3 = 77$ _____

12. $19x + 14 = 109$ _____

13. $\frac{x}{14} - 3 = 1$ _____

14. $\frac{x}{6} - 17 = 13$ _____

15. $\frac{x}{8} + 7 = 27$ _____

16. $2x - 19 = 15$ _____

17. $9x + 18 = 63$ _____

18. $11x - 9 = 68$ _____

19. $\frac{x}{5} - 7 = 7$ _____

20. $\frac{x}{9} + 18 = 23$ _____

21. $\frac{x}{12} + 9 = 16$ _____

22. $4x + 15 = 31$ _____

23. $7x - 4 = 87$ _____

24. $9x + 7 = 61$ _____

25. $\frac{x}{9} - 9 = 10$ _____

26. $\frac{x}{8} + 12 = 17$ _____

27. $\frac{x}{4} - 3 = 17$ _____

Use with pages 148–149.

Name _____ Date _____

A jogging path in Lewis Park is divided into 8 equal parts. Mario ran along the shaded part. What fraction names the part of the track around which he ran?

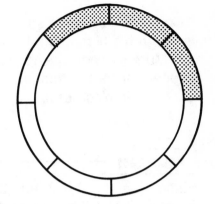

Remember

Use the total number of parts in the whole, 8, as the denominator.

$$\frac{3}{8} = \frac{\text{parts run by Mario}}{\text{total number of parts in the park}}$$

He ran around $\frac{3}{8}$ of the park.

The shaded area represents the part of the track covered by each jogger. Write the fraction which names that part.

Jogger   Fractional part

1. Mike

_____

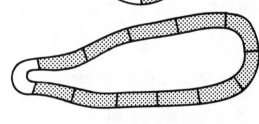

2. Maria

_____

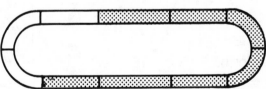

3. April

_____

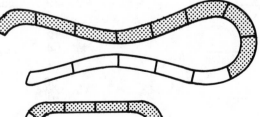

4. Joe

_____

5. Anita

_____

RETEACH | Equivalent Fractions and Simplifying Fractions

Mr. Cohen is taking his son, Abe, fishing at a stream 24 miles from his home. On the way, they will pick up Abe's friend Murray, who lives 18 miles from the stream. What fractional part of the total trip will Murray take? Write the fraction in simplest form.

Remember

Since $18 = 2 \times 3 \times 3$, and $24 = 2 \times 2 \times 2 \times 3$, 18 and 24 have 2 and 3 as common factors. $2 \times 3 = 6$, so, 6 is the greatest common factor.

$$\frac{18 \div 6}{24 \div 6} = \frac{3}{4}$$

Murray will travel $\frac{3}{4}$ of the total trip.

Use the map to solve each question. Write the fraction in simplest form.

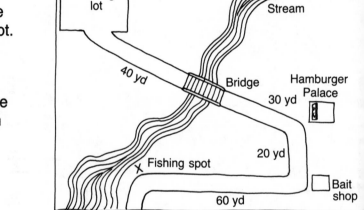

1. Compare the distance between the parking lot and bridge to the distance from the parking lot to the fishing spot.

   _____

2. Compare the distance from the bridge to the Bait Shop to the distance from the parking lot to the fishing spot.

   _____

Write in simplest form.

3. $\frac{14}{34} =$ _____

4. $\frac{18}{39} =$ _____

5. $\frac{36}{48} =$ _____

6. $\frac{39}{117} =$ _____

7. $\frac{12}{54} =$ _____

8. $\frac{24}{32} =$ _____

9. $\frac{30}{75} =$ _____

10. $\frac{90}{135} =$ _____

11. $\frac{34}{85} =$ _____

Use with pages 164–165.

Name _____ Date _____

Sam is camping, and it is his turn to prepare the meal. He has $2\frac{3}{4}$ cups of wild raspberries. If each portion will be $\frac{1}{4}$ cup, how many portions can Sam make? Write the fraction that shows this.

Remember

Be sure to multiply the whole number part by the denominator before you add the fractional part.

$$2\frac{3}{4} = \frac{(2 \times 4) + 3}{4} = \frac{11}{4}$$

Sam can make 11 portions.

Write as a fraction.

1. $5\frac{1}{4}$ _____

2. $3\frac{7}{8}$ _____

3. $3\frac{3}{5}$ _____

4. $6\frac{7}{10}$ _____

5. $4\frac{7}{12}$ _____

6. $1\frac{1}{16}$ _____

7. $3\frac{3}{20}$ _____

8. $9\frac{3}{8}$ _____

9. $7\frac{7}{10}$ _____

Write the letter of the equivalent fraction.

10. $\frac{8}{24}$ _____ **a.** $\frac{4}{6}$ **b.** $\frac{2}{12}$ **c.** $\frac{1}{3}$ **d.** $\frac{1}{6}$

11. $\frac{5}{9}$ _____ **a.** $\frac{10}{90}$ **b.** $\frac{25}{18}$ **c.** $\frac{15}{27}$ **d.** $\frac{15}{18}$

12. $\frac{2}{3}$ _____ **a.** $\frac{4}{12}$ **b.** $\frac{8}{24}$ **c.** $\frac{6}{18}$ **d.** $\frac{10}{15}$

13. $\frac{4}{7}$ _____ **a.** $\frac{20}{35}$ **b.** $\frac{8}{56}$ **c.** $\frac{20}{45}$ **d.** $\frac{12}{28}$

RETEACH | Comparing and Ordering Fractions

One recipe calls for $\frac{2}{3}$ cup milk and a second recipe calls for $\frac{5}{8}$ cup milk. Use cross products to determine which recipe requires the greater amount of milk.

Remember

Use the cross product that has the numerator as one factor to represent that fraction.

$$\frac{2}{3} \times \frac{5}{8}$$
$$2 \times 8 > 3 \times 5$$
$$\frac{2}{3} > \frac{5}{8}$$

The first recipe requires more milk.

Compare the fractions. Write >, <, or =.

1. $\frac{5}{6}$ _____ $\frac{7}{8}$

2. $\frac{3}{7}$ _____ $\frac{1}{3}$

3. $\frac{5}{8}$ _____ $\frac{2}{3}$

4. $\frac{15}{16}$ _____ $\frac{16}{19}$

5. $\frac{5}{12}$ _____ $\frac{6}{13}$

6. $\frac{11}{9}$ _____ $\frac{10}{7}$

7. $3\frac{4}{7}$ _____ $3\frac{5}{8}$

8. $13\frac{1}{3}$ _____ $\frac{40}{3}$

9. $7\frac{3}{7}$ _____ $7\frac{1}{2}$

Write the numbers from the least to the greatest.

10. $\frac{5}{6}, \frac{7}{8}, \frac{8}{9}$

11. $\frac{8}{3}, \frac{9}{4}, \frac{3}{2}$

12. $\frac{10}{3}, \frac{13}{4}, \frac{7}{2}$

_____

_____

_____

Solve.

13. Which holds the greater amount, 13 fourth-cup containers or 7 half-cup containers?

_____

14. Three containers of oregano contain $2\frac{2}{3}$ ounces, $2\frac{5}{8}$ ounces, and $2\frac{3}{4}$ ounces. Order the numbers from the least to the greatest.

_____

Name _____ Date _____

RETEACH **Estimating Sums and Differences**

Would a 5-gallon pitcher hold this fruit punch?

┌─────────────────────────────────┐
│   FRUIT PUNCH   │
│ $1\frac{3}{8}$ gal orange juice │
│ $\frac{1}{6}$ gal cranberry juice │
│ $2\frac{4}{5}$ gal lemon-lime soda │
└─────────────────────────────────┘

┌─ **Remember** ──────────────────────────────┐
│ $\frac{3}{8} \approx \frac{1}{2}$; $\frac{1}{6} \approx 0$; $\frac{4}{5} \approx 1$ │
│ Whole numbers: $1 + 2 = 3$ │
│ Estimate: $3 + \frac{1}{2} + 0 + 1 = 4\frac{1}{2}$. │
└──┘

A 5-gallon pitcher will hold the fruit punch.

Estimate. Write $>$ or $<$.

1. $2\frac{3}{7} + 4\frac{2}{3} \bigcirc 6$

2. $1\frac{1}{7} + 1\frac{3}{10} \bigcirc 3$

3. $6\frac{4}{11} + 3\frac{2}{9} \bigcirc 10$

4. $3\frac{3}{4} + 4\frac{7}{8} \bigcirc 9$

5. $2\frac{1}{6} + 3\frac{1}{9} \bigcirc 5$

6. $5\frac{8}{15} + 8\frac{3}{4} \bigcirc 14$

7. $6\frac{1}{2} - 3\frac{1}{4} \bigcirc 3$

8. $9\frac{7}{11} - 4\frac{2}{3} \bigcirc 5$

9. $3\frac{11}{12} - 1\frac{2}{7} \bigcirc 2$

10. $8\frac{1}{10} - 7\frac{12}{19} \bigcirc 1$

Estimate. Use numbers that are easy to work with.

11. $3\frac{5}{8} + 2\frac{6}{11} =$ _____

12. $8\frac{2}{3} + 4\frac{15}{19} =$ _____

13. $4\frac{1}{7} + 5\frac{3}{22} =$ _____

14. $6\frac{1}{10} + 1\frac{7}{12} =$ _____

15. $7\frac{13}{30} + 9\frac{9}{20} =$ _____

16. $4\frac{9}{22} - 2\frac{17}{19} =$ _____

17. $6\frac{8}{15} - 5\frac{1}{9} =$ _____

18. $7\frac{1}{3} - 4\frac{10}{11} =$ _____

19. $38\frac{22}{25} - 26\frac{17}{19} =$ _____

20. $15\frac{3}{7} + 18\frac{1}{2} + 6\frac{17}{20} =$ _____

RETEACH Adding Fractions

Anna and Pancho are collecting money at the shopping center for the Muscular Dystrophy Fund. At the end of the first day, their container was $\frac{2}{3}$ full, and at the end of the second day their container was $\frac{3}{5}$ full. How many containers did they collect in all?

Remember

Find the least common multiple of 3 and 5.

Write $\frac{2}{3}$ as $\frac{10}{15}$, and $\frac{3}{5}$ as $\frac{9}{15}$.

Add the numerators, and use the common denominator.

$$\frac{2}{3} + \frac{3}{5} = \frac{10}{15} + \frac{9}{15} = \frac{10+9}{15} = \frac{19}{15} = 1\frac{4}{15}$$

They collected $1\frac{4}{15}$ containers.

Write the answer in simplest form.

1. $\frac{4}{5} + \frac{9}{10} =$ _____

2. $\frac{1}{3} + \frac{1}{4} =$ _____

3. $\frac{1}{8} + \frac{1}{4} + \frac{1}{3} =$ _____

4. $\frac{1}{5} + \frac{1}{2} =$ _____

5. $\frac{5}{9} + \frac{1}{6} =$ _____

6. $\frac{4}{5} + \frac{1}{3} + \frac{3}{10} =$ _____

Write the answer in simplest form.

7. Jim's container was $\frac{3}{4}$ full after the first day and $\frac{3}{5}$ full at the end of the second day. What was the total number of containers for Jim's collection?

_____

8. Matt had a container $\frac{7}{8}$ full the first day and $\frac{9}{16}$ full the second day. What was Matt's total?

_____

9. The container Karen had the first day was $\frac{9}{10}$ full. The second day it was $\frac{4}{5}$ full. Write Karen's total.

_____

Use with pages 174–175.

RETEACH | Subtracting Fractions

Joyce invited Gina to Joyce's house for a pizza. Before Gina arrived, Joyce's brother ate all but $\frac{5}{8}$ of the pizza. If Joyce and Gina ate $\frac{1}{2}$ of the pizza, what part was left?

Remember

Use the least common multiple to find the least common denominator. Write the equivalent fractions and then subtract the numerators.

$$\frac{5}{8} - \frac{1}{2} = \frac{5}{8} - \frac{4}{8} = \frac{5-4}{8} = \frac{1}{8}$$

The remaining part was $\frac{1}{8}$.

Write the answer in simplest form.

1. $\frac{7}{8} - \frac{1}{2} =$ _____

2. $\frac{3}{2} - \frac{3}{4} =$ _____

3. $\frac{7}{8} - \frac{9}{16} =$ _____

4. $\frac{9}{10} - \frac{1}{2} =$ _____

5. $\frac{9}{10} - \frac{4}{5} =$ _____

6. $\frac{15}{16} - \frac{7}{8} =$ _____

Solve.

7. $\left(\frac{7}{10} - \frac{3}{8}\right) - \frac{3}{20} =$ _____

8. $\frac{1}{3} - \left(\frac{7}{9} - \frac{1}{2}\right) =$ _____

Solve for n.

9. $n - \frac{5}{12} = \frac{11}{24}$; $n =$ _____

10. $n - \frac{5}{8} = \frac{2}{5}$; $n =$ _____

RETEACH   Adding Mixed Numbers

Craig is buying material to make a costume for a Halloween party. He needs $2\frac{5}{8}$ yards of red material and $1\frac{1}{2}$ yards of black material. How much material does he need?

Remember

Rename $3\frac{9}{8}$ as $4\frac{1}{8}$. Remember to simplify.

$$
\begin{array}{ccc}
 & 2\frac{5}{8} & \rightarrow & 2\frac{5}{8} \\
+ & 1\frac{1}{2} & \rightarrow & +\ 1\frac{4}{8} \\
\hline
 & & & 3\frac{9}{8} = 3 + 1\frac{1}{8} = 4\frac{1}{8}
\end{array}
$$

He needs $4\frac{1}{8}$ yards of material.

Write the answer in simplest form.

1. $\begin{array}{r} 1\frac{7}{8} \\ +\ 2\frac{1}{4} \\ \hline \end{array}$

2. $\begin{array}{r} 1\frac{9}{16} \\ +\ \ \ \frac{1}{2} \\ \hline \end{array}$

3. $\begin{array}{r} 3\frac{3}{5} \\ +\ 1\frac{1}{4} \\ \hline \end{array}$

4. $\begin{array}{r} 2\frac{9}{10} \\ +\ 1\frac{1}{5} \\ \hline \end{array}$

5. $\begin{array}{r} 1\frac{4}{5} \\ +\ 1\frac{1}{2} \\ \hline \end{array}$

6. $\begin{array}{r} 2\frac{3}{7} \\ +\ 1\frac{5}{7} \\ \hline \end{array}$

7. $\begin{array}{r} 1\frac{2}{3} \\ +\ 2\frac{7}{9} \\ \hline \end{array}$

8. $\begin{array}{r} 3\frac{4}{5} \\ +\ 2\frac{2}{3} \\ \hline \end{array}$

9. $2\frac{7}{16} + 1\frac{3}{4} = $ _____

10. $6\frac{7}{8} + 1\frac{1}{5} = $ _____

Solve.

11. Amy needs three kinds of material for her costume. The amounts needed are $1\frac{1}{4}$ yd, $1\frac{3}{5}$ yd, and $2\frac{3}{10}$ yd. How much material must she buy?

_____

12. Ralph needs three kinds of material. He needs $2\frac{5}{8}$ yd, $\frac{7}{8}$ yd, and $\frac{3}{4}$ yd of each kind respectively. How much material should he buy?

_____

13. Raajiv needs three kinds of material. The amounts needed are $2\frac{2}{3}$ yd, $\frac{3}{4}$ yd, and $1\frac{1}{12}$ yd. How much material must he buy?

_____

Use with pages 182–183.

RETEACH Subtracting Mixed Numbers Without Renaming

A bolt used in shop class is $1\frac{7}{16}$ in. long. All except $1\frac{1}{4}$ in. of the bolt is threaded. What is the length of the threaded part of the bolt?

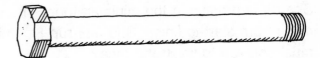

Remember

Find a common denominator for the fractions. Subtract the fractions, and subtract the whole numbers.

$$
\begin{array}{r}
1\frac{7}{16} \rightarrow \quad 1\frac{7}{16} \\
- 1\frac{1}{4} \rightarrow -1\frac{4}{16} \\
\hline
\frac{3}{16}
\end{array}
$$

The threaded part of the bolt is $\frac{3}{16}$ in. long.

Write the answer in simplest form.

1. $\begin{array}{r} 7\frac{3}{4} \\ -4\frac{1}{4} \\ \hline \end{array}$ **2.** $\begin{array}{r} 7\frac{3}{4} \\ -6\frac{9}{16} \\ \hline \end{array}$ **3.** $\begin{array}{r} 7\frac{3}{4} \\ -7\frac{3}{8} \\ \hline \end{array}$ **4.** $\begin{array}{r} 11\frac{5}{12} \\ -9\frac{1}{4} \\ \hline \end{array}$

5. $11\frac{7}{12} - 7\frac{1}{6} =$ _____   **6.** $14\frac{7}{8} - 10\frac{1}{16} =$ _____

7. $18\frac{3}{4} - 16\frac{3}{16} =$ _____   **8.** $6\frac{11}{16} - 4\frac{1}{2} =$ _____

9. $3\frac{9}{64} - 1\frac{1}{8} =$ _____   **10.** $17\frac{17}{32} - 15\frac{3}{64} =$ _____

Solve.

11. Jamie's term paper will be $6\frac{3}{4}$ typewritten pages. She has typed the first $2\frac{2}{3}$ pages. How much more must she type?

_____

Name _____ Date _____

Sharon is running in the minimarathon. The race is $13\frac{1}{8}$ miles from start to finish. She has run $8\frac{1}{2}$ miles. How far must she run to finish the race?

Remember

$13\frac{1}{8}$ must be regrouped as $12 + 1\frac{1}{8} = 12\frac{9}{8}$.

$$
\begin{array}{cccc}
13\frac{1}{8} \rightarrow & 13\frac{1}{8} \rightarrow & 12 + 1\frac{1}{8} \rightarrow & 12\frac{9}{8} \\
- 8\frac{1}{2} \rightarrow & - 8\frac{4}{8} \rightarrow & - \quad 8\frac{4}{8} \rightarrow & - 8\frac{4}{8} \\
\hline
& & & 4\frac{5}{8}
\end{array}
$$

Sharon must run $4\frac{5}{8}$ miles to complete the race.

Write the answer in simplest form.

1. $26\frac{1}{4}$
    $- 13\frac{1}{2}$

2. $26\frac{1}{4}$
    $- 10\frac{3}{4}$

3. $26\frac{1}{4}$
    $- 8\frac{5}{8}$

4. $26\frac{1}{4}$
    $- 7\frac{9}{16}$

5. $13\frac{1}{8}$
    $- 10\frac{1}{4}$

6. $13\frac{1}{8}$
    $- 8\frac{3}{16}$

7. $13\frac{1}{8}$
    $- 10\frac{3}{5}$

8. $13\frac{1}{8}$
    $- 11\frac{3}{10}$

9. $8\frac{3}{10} - 2\frac{3}{4} =$ _____

10. $42\frac{1}{3} - 19\frac{3}{8} =$ _____

11. $9\frac{1}{10} - 2\frac{23}{100} =$ _____

12. $9\frac{1}{8} - 8\frac{5}{6} =$ _____

Solve.

13. Tony has run $6\frac{3}{16}$ miles of a $13\frac{1}{8}$-mile marathon. How much more must he run?

_____

14. Ardiff has run $4\frac{3}{6}$ miles of a $13\frac{1}{8}$-mile marathon. How much more must he run?

_____

Use with pages 186–187.

RETEACH Solving Equations with Fractions (+ and −)

At the Stevens Junior High track meet, the winner threw the discus $202\frac{7}{8}$ ft. The second-place throw was $6\frac{1}{8}$ ft less. How long was the second-place throw? Use the equation $S + 6\frac{1}{8} = 202\frac{7}{8}$.

Remember

Perform the same operation, using the identical value, on both sides of the equation.

$$S + 6\frac{1}{8} = 202\frac{7}{8}$$
$$S + 6\frac{1}{8} - 6\frac{1}{8} = 202\frac{7}{8} - 6\frac{1}{8}$$
$$S = 196\frac{3}{4}$$

The second-place throw was $196\frac{3}{4}$ ft.

Fill in the blanks with an operation sign or a number.

1. $S + 7\frac{8}{15} = 16\frac{2}{5}$; $S + 7\frac{8}{15} -$ _____ $= 16\frac{2}{5} -$ _____

2. $N - 6\frac{2}{3} = 18\frac{3}{4}$; $N - 6\frac{2}{3}$ _____ $6\frac{2}{3} = 18\frac{3}{4}$ _____ $6\frac{2}{3}$

3. $F - 8\frac{1}{4} = 6\frac{1}{2}$; $F - 8\frac{1}{4}$ _____ _____ $= 6\frac{1}{2} +$ _____

Solve.

4. $X + 2\frac{1}{3} = 7$; $X =$ _____

5. $3\frac{1}{4} + X = 7\frac{3}{5}$; $X =$ _____

6. $Y - 4\frac{1}{3} = 5\frac{2}{3}$; $Y =$ _____

7. $Y - 1\frac{7}{16} = 3\frac{9}{64}$; $Y =$ _____

8. $Y - 1\frac{3}{32} = \frac{3}{4}$; $Y =$ _____

9. $Y - 7\frac{4}{7} = 3\frac{1}{5}$; $Y =$ _____

Solve.

10. The second-place high jump was $5\frac{3}{4}$ ft. The first place was $\frac{2}{3}$ ft higher. Use the equation $F - \frac{2}{3} = 5\frac{3}{4}$ to find the height of the first-place jump.

_____

RETEACH | **Multiplying Fractions**

The March of Dimes is sponsoring a bicycle "riding-for-health" fund-raising activity. Riders are encouraged to get pledges for each lap that they ride around a $\frac{3}{8}$ mile track. Julio completed 17 laps. How many miles did he ride?

Remember

Write the whole number as a fraction. Then multiply the numerators and multiply the denominators.

$$\frac{3}{8} \times 17$$

$$\frac{3}{8} \times \frac{17}{1} = \frac{3 \times 17}{8 \times 1} = \frac{51}{8} = 6\frac{3}{8}$$

Julio rode $6\frac{3}{8}$ miles.

Find the missing fact.

Distance around the track	Number of laps	Distance covered
1. $\frac{3}{8}$ mile	16	
2. $\frac{3}{8}$ mile	21	
3. $\frac{1}{2}$ mile	17	
4. $\frac{3}{4}$ mile	15	
5. $\frac{5}{8}$ mile	10	
6. $\frac{6}{8}$ mile	12	
7. $\frac{11}{20}$ mile	17	
8. $\frac{15}{16}$ mile	8	
9. $\frac{19}{24}$ mile	15	

Use with pages 200–201.

RETEACH — Simplifying Before Multiplying

The class conducted a taste test for Brand X and Brand Y juices. The results showed that $\frac{9}{20}$ of the people preferred Brand X juice. Of these students, $\frac{2}{3}$ were girls. What part of the sample were girls who preferred Brand X?

Remember

Simplify the fractions. Then multiply the numerators and multiply the denominators.

$$\frac{2}{3} \text{ of } \frac{9}{20} = \frac{\overset{1}{\cancel{2}}}{\underset{1}{\cancel{3}}} \times \frac{\overset{3}{\cancel{9}}}{\underset{10}{\cancel{20}}} = \frac{1 \times 3}{1 \times 10} = \frac{3}{10}$$

Three tenths of those who preferred Brand X were girls.

Complete the table.

1. $\frac{9}{20}$ of students preferred Brand X. $\frac{1}{3}$ of these were boys.	proportion that chose Brand X and were boys $\frac{1}{3} \times \frac{9}{20} = \underline{\dfrac{\times}{\times}} = \underline{\qquad}$
2. $\frac{2}{5}$ of students preferred Brand Y. $\frac{5}{12}$ of these were girls.	proportion that chose Brand Y and were girls $\frac{2}{5} \times \frac{5}{12} = \underline{\qquad}$
3. $\frac{2}{5}$ of students preferred Brand Y. $\frac{7}{12}$ of these were boys.	proportion that chose Brand Y and were boys $\frac{2}{5} \times \frac{7}{12} = \underline{\qquad}$
4. $\frac{3}{8}$ of students preferred Brand W. $\frac{4}{7}$ of these were girls.	proportion that chose Brand W and were girls $\frac{3}{8} \times \frac{4}{7} = \underline{\qquad}$
5. $\frac{4}{19}$ of students preferred Brand Z. $\frac{11}{13}$ of these were boys.	proportion that chose Brand Z and were boys $\frac{4}{19} \times \frac{11}{13} = \underline{\qquad}$

RETEACH — Estimating Fraction and Mixed-Number Products

What is the area of Bernard's bedroom? Will a can of paint that covers 85 square feet be enough to paint its ceiling?

Remember

Whenever possible, round just one of the factors. Your estimate will be closer to the exact value.

$$7\frac{5}{8} \rightarrow 8$$

$$10 \times 8 = 80; \frac{1}{4} \times 8 = 2$$

$$80 + 2 = 82 \text{ ft}^2$$

Since we rounded up, 82 is an overestimate. Therefore, there is enough paint to cover the ceiling.

Estimate by rounding only one factor. Adjust by writing + or − if possible.

1. $4\frac{1}{2} \times 5\frac{7}{8} =$ _____

2. $2\frac{1}{3} \times 8\frac{4}{5} =$ _____

3. $1\frac{3}{5} \times 3\frac{1}{2} =$ _____

4. $2\frac{2}{5} \times 10\frac{1}{3} =$ _____

5. $4\frac{2}{7} \times 13\frac{7}{9} =$ _____

6. $6\frac{1}{4} \times 10\frac{2}{3} =$ _____

Estimate. Write > or <.

7. $5\frac{1}{3} \times 4\frac{1}{6}$ ◯ 20

8. $9\frac{2}{3} \times 5$ ◯ 54

9. $6\frac{9}{10} \times 2\frac{1}{7}$ ◯ 18

10. $8\frac{4}{5} \times 10$ ◯ 90

11. $7\frac{1}{4} \times 12\frac{3}{20}$ ◯ 84

12. $6\frac{7}{8} \times 7\frac{1}{5}$ ◯ 42

13. $9\frac{11}{12} \times 14\frac{2}{3}$ ◯ 150

14. $5\frac{1}{9} \times 15\frac{2}{5}$ ◯ 76

15. $11\frac{5}{7} \times 8\frac{5}{6}$ ◯ 108

16. $9\frac{3}{4} \times 19\frac{7}{10}$ ◯ 200

17. $2\frac{1}{8} \times 3\frac{2}{15} \times 6\frac{1}{6}$ ◯ 36

18. $4\frac{5}{6} \times 3\frac{8}{11} \times 5\frac{2}{3}$ ◯ 120

Estimate.

19. $4\frac{3}{4} \times 8\frac{1}{7} =$ _____

20. $10\frac{2}{9} \times 8 =$ _____

21. $8\frac{1}{6} \times 9\frac{7}{8} =$ _____

22. $19\frac{11}{15} \times 4\frac{6}{7} =$ _____

23. $12\frac{1}{5} \times 4\frac{2}{15} =$ _____

24. $4\frac{1}{5} \times 25\frac{1}{10} =$ _____

Use with pages 206–207.

RETEACH Multiplying Mixed Numbers

George and Mike have been selected to provide pizza for the class picnic. They decided to make biscuit pizza crust, which requires $\frac{3}{4}$ cup water, $\frac{1}{4}$ ounce yeast, and $2\frac{1}{2}$ cups biscuit mix. They need to make $6\frac{2}{5}$ times as much as the recipe produces. How much water should they use?

Remember

Write the product as a mixed number.

$$6\frac{2}{5} \times \frac{3}{4} = \frac{\overset{8}{\cancel{32}}}{5} \times \frac{3}{\underset{1}{\cancel{4}}} = \frac{24}{5} = 4\frac{4}{5}$$

They should use $4\frac{4}{5}$ cups water.

Multiply. Write your answer in simplest form.

1. $6\frac{2}{5} \times 2 = $ _____

2. $2\frac{1}{2} \times 2 = $ _____

3. $\frac{1}{4} \times 2 = $ _____

4. $3\frac{1}{3} \times \frac{1}{2} = $ _____

5. $4\frac{3}{8} \times 2\frac{1}{2} = $ _____

6. $1\frac{1}{2} \times 3\frac{1}{4} = $ _____

7. $11\frac{1}{2} \times 1\frac{1}{2} = $ _____

8. $1\frac{3}{4} \times 6\frac{1}{3} = $ _____

9. $12\frac{1}{2} \times \frac{2}{5} = $ _____

10. $12\frac{1}{2} \times 1\frac{3}{5} = $ _____

11. $7\frac{1}{2} \times \frac{1}{3} = $ _____

12. $3\frac{2}{3} \times 2\frac{1}{2} = $ _____

13. $6\frac{7}{9} \times \frac{3}{4} = $ _____

14. $5\frac{1}{7} \times 3\frac{1}{7} = $ _____

15. $8\frac{8}{9} \times 2\frac{1}{4} = $ _____

16. $3\frac{3}{8} \times 4\frac{2}{9} = $ _____

17. $6\frac{3}{5} \times 3\frac{1}{8} = $ _____

18. $6\frac{5}{7} \times 4\frac{3}{8} = $ _____

19. $3\frac{3}{5} \times 2\frac{7}{9} = $ _____

20. $7\frac{1}{3} \times 1\frac{8}{11} = $ _____

RETEACH Dividing Fractions

The Hernandez family is camping at Rocky Ledge State Park. The campsite is located at the top of a sheer cliff overlooking a lake. The trail to the lake is more than a mile long. So, Juan decided to cut strips from a piece of heavy cloth to make a rope to lower a bucket for lake water. The cloth is $\frac{3}{4}$ yard wide and the strips are $\frac{1}{12}$ yard wide. How many strips of this size can Juan cut from the cloth?

Remember

To divide fractions, multiply the first fraction by the reciprocal of the divisor.

$$\frac{3}{4} \div \frac{1}{12} = \frac{3}{\underset{1}{4}} \times \frac{\overset{3}{\cancel{12}}}{1} = \frac{3 \times 3}{1 \times 1} = \frac{9}{1} = 9$$

Juan can cut 9 strips from the cloth.

Divide. Write your answer in simplest form.

1. $\frac{3}{4} \div \frac{1}{8} =$ _____

2. $\frac{3}{4} \div \frac{1}{6} =$ _____

3. $\frac{5}{6} \div \frac{1}{8} =$ _____

4. $\frac{1}{2} \div \frac{1}{16} =$ _____

5. $\frac{1}{2} \div \frac{3}{32} =$ _____

6. $\frac{35}{36} \div \frac{1}{16} =$ _____

7. $\frac{2}{3} \div \frac{3}{4} =$ _____

8. $\frac{2}{3} \div \frac{5}{8} =$ _____

9. $\frac{3}{4} \div \frac{2}{5} =$ _____

10. $\frac{1}{5} \div \frac{2}{7} =$ _____

Use with pages 210–211.

RETEACH Dividing Mixed Numbers

Divide $2\frac{1}{2}$ by $1\frac{1}{3}$.

Remember

Rename the mixed numbers as fractions. Then write as a multiplication problem, using the reciprocal of the divisor.

reciprocals

$$2\frac{1}{2} \div 1\frac{1}{3} = \frac{5}{2} \div \frac{4}{3} = \frac{5}{2} \times \frac{3}{4} = \frac{15}{8} = 1\frac{7}{8}$$

So, $2\frac{1}{2}$ divided by $1\frac{1}{3}$ is $1\frac{7}{8}$.

Divide. Write the answer in simplest form.

1. $1\frac{1}{2} \div 3 =$ _____

2. $1\frac{1}{2} \div 6 =$ _____

3. $5\frac{1}{2} \div 12 =$ _____

4. $3\frac{3}{8} \div 12 =$ _____

5. $1\frac{7}{8} \div 7 =$ _____

6. $2\frac{1}{2} \div 6 =$ _____

7. $1\frac{1}{2} \div \frac{1}{2} =$ _____

8. $3\frac{3}{8} \div \frac{9}{32} =$ _____

9. $1\frac{7}{8} \div \frac{15}{16} =$ _____

10. $2\frac{1}{2} \div \frac{5}{12} =$ _____

Solve.

11. Joey has 7 dogs. He has $5\frac{1}{2}$ pounds of dog food. If he divides the dog food evenly, how much food will each dog get?

_____

Name _____ Date _____

RETEACH Decimals and Fractions

Many instruments are used to take linear measurements.
Rulers are used to divide inches into 8, 16, 32, and 64 parts.
Fractions such as $\frac{3}{8}$, $\frac{5}{16}$, and $\frac{19}{64}$ describe fraction parts.
Micrometers use decimals to measure inches.

The thickness of a metal plate is $\frac{1}{16}$ in. If the plate is
measured with a micrometer, what decimal thickness would it
have?

Remember

Place the decimal point correctly, adding zeros if
necessary.

$$\begin{array}{r} 0.0625 \\ 16\overline{)1.0000} \\ \underline{96} \\ 40 \\ \underline{32} \\ 80 \\ \underline{80} \\ 0 \end{array}$$ $\frac{1}{16} = 0.0625$

The thickness of the plate would be 0.0625 inches.

Rewrite each fraction as a decimal.

1. $\frac{1}{10} =$ _____

2. $\frac{1}{20} =$ _____

3. $\frac{1}{40} =$ _____

4. $\frac{1}{50} =$ _____

5. $\frac{3}{32} =$ _____

6. $\frac{1}{80} =$ _____

7. $\frac{3}{50} =$ _____

8. $\frac{3}{25} =$ _____

9. $\frac{1}{25} =$ _____

Solve.

10. An automobile's odometer measures distance by tenths
of a mile. If you travel two and a half miles, how would
that register on an odometer? _____

11. How would a micrometer show the measurement of a
sheaf of papers $\frac{13}{16}$ inch thick? _____

12. How would a micrometer show the measurement of a
glass slide $\frac{5}{64}$ inch thick? _____

64   **Use with pages 216–217.**

| RETEACH | Terminating and Repeating Decimals |

Ship canals save time and energy. The Chesapeake–
Delaware Canal is 19 miles long. The Amsterdam–Rhine
Canal is 45 miles long. Compare the lengths in terms of a
repeating decimal.

Remember

Place the line *only* over the digits that repeat.

$$\frac{19}{45} = 0.42222 \ldots = 0.4\overline{2}$$

The Chesapeake–Delaware Canal is $0.4\overline{2}$ times the length of
the Amsterdam–Rhine Canal.

The table compares the lengths of other canals with the
length of the Amsterdam–Rhine Canal. Write each fraction as
a repeating decimal.

Canal	Length	Fraction	Decimal
1. Cape	13	$\frac{13}{45}$	
2. Chicago	30	$\frac{30}{45}$	
3. Beaumont– Port Arthur	40	$\frac{40}{45}$	
4. Corinth	4	$\frac{4}{45}$	

5. $\frac{11}{12} = $ _____

6. $\frac{14}{15} = $ _____

7. $\frac{7}{12} = $ _____

8. $\frac{21}{27} = $ _____

9. $\frac{31}{33} = $ _____

10. $\frac{4}{9} = $ _____

11. $\frac{13}{15} = $ _____

12. $\frac{11}{15} = $ _____

RETEACH | Solving Equations That Have Fractions

Louis, a stonemason, can lay $10\frac{1}{2}$ rows of bricks in 1 hour.
How long will it take him to lay 91 rows of bricks?
Use the formula $10\frac{1}{2}h = 91$, where h = number of hours.

Remember

Multiply both sides of the equation by the reciprocal of $10\frac{1}{2}$, which is $\frac{2}{21}$.

$$10\frac{1}{2}h = 91$$
$$10\frac{1}{2} = \frac{21}{2}$$
$$\frac{2}{21} \times \frac{21}{2}h = 91 \times \frac{2}{21}$$
$$h = 8\frac{2}{3}$$

It will take him 8 hours 40 minutes to lay 91 rows.

Solve.

1. $\frac{2}{3}h = 30$ $\frac{3}{2} \times \frac{2}{3}h = 30 \times \frac{3}{2}$ $h =$ _____

2. $4\frac{4}{5}h = 96$ $\frac{5}{24} \times \frac{24}{5}h = 96 \times \frac{5}{24}$ $h =$ _____

3. $1\frac{1}{2}h = 18$ $h =$ _____   4. $4\frac{1}{2}h = 90$ $h =$ _____

5. $\frac{13}{15}h = 39$ $h =$ _____   6. $2\frac{7}{8}h = 138$ $h =$ _____

7. $1\frac{3}{4}h = 12\frac{1}{4}$ $h =$ _____   8. $3\frac{2}{3}h = 14\frac{1}{2}$ $h =$ _____

9. If Louis can lay $14\frac{2}{3}$ rows of bricks in 1 hour, how many hours would it take him to lay 66 rows?

_____

Use with pages 222–223.

RETEACH   Metric Units of Length

Olympic events, such as running races, are measured in metric units. An Olympic-sized track is 400 meters long. The basic unit of length in the metric system is the *meter*, or *m*. Other metric units of length are the *kilometer*, or *km*, which is 1,000 meters; the *centimeter*, or *cm*, which is 0.01 meter; and the *millimeter*, or *mm*, which is 0.001 meter.

Which unit would be used to measure a runner's stride?

Remember

Since runners' strides vary greatly, from about 1 meter, it would be a good idea to measure them in units smaller than a meter.

Centimeters would be used to measure a runner's stride.

Write the most likely unit (*m, cm, mm,* or *km*) used to measure each item.

1. the height of a door _____

2. the width of this sheet of paper _____

3. the height of a dog _____

4. the thickness of a coin _____

5. the length of a piece of chalk _____

6. the distance you walk in one hour _____

7. your height _____

8. the diameter of a quarter _____

Write the letter of the best estimate.

9. the length of a car _____   **a.** 4.6 m   **b.** 46 m   **c.** 4.6 km

10. the length of your shoe _____   **a.** 24 mm   **b.** 24 cm   **c.** 24 m

11. the height of your room _____   **a.** 3 m   **b.** 3 cm   **c.** 3 km

12. the length of a baseball bat _____   **a.** 100 m   **b.** 100 cm   **c.** 100 mm

13. José kicks a soccer ball a fair distance. Which unit *(km, m, cm)* would be best for describing the distance of such a kick? _____

14. Which unit *(m, cm, mm)* would be best for measuring the length of a flea's jump? _____

RETEACH | Renaming Metric Units of Length

In the 1936 Olympics, United States track star Jesse Owens
set a record in the long jump. His record jump measured
806 cm. How many meters is this?

Remember

To rename centimeters (small units) with meters (larger
units), divide by 100.

$$806 \div 100 = 8.06$$

Jesse Owens jumped 8.06 meters.

Write the missing number.

1. 0.53 mm = _____ cm

2. 1.5 mm = _____ cm

3. 5,000 m = _____ km

4. 0.315 km = _____ m

5. 53 dm = _____ m

6. 390 m = _____ cm

7. 3,000 m = _____ km

8. 274 cm = _____ m

9. 96.74 km = _____ m

10. 19 m = _____ dm

11. 9.5 km = _____ m

12. 0.315 km = _____ m

13. 0.9042 m = _____ km

14. 36,106 cm = _____ m

15. 152 cm = _____ dm

Solve.

16. How many kilometers long is a 32,000-meter race?

_____

17. One race is referred to as the "800" because it is 800 m
long. How many kilometers long is the race? _____

RETEACH   Metric Units of Capacity and Mass

In Mexico, Luis Sanchez buys cat food for his pet cat. The container indicates that it contains 1.81 kg of cat food. Luis also feeds his cat some milk. The milk container contains one liter of milk. Liters are measures of capacity, and kilograms are measures of mass. Other measures of capacity and mass are listed in these tables.

1,000 milliliters (mL) = 1 liter (L)
1,000 liters (L)   = 1 kiloliter (kL)

1,000 milligrams (mg) = 1 gram (g)
1,000 grams (g)   = 1 kilogram (kg)

How many grams of cat food does Luis buy? (Rename 1.81 kg with grams.)

Remember

To rename larger units with smaller units, multiply. To rename small units with larger units, divide. To rename kilograms (larger units) with grams (smaller units),

multiply the number of kilograms by 1,000.

$$1.18 \times 1,000 = 1,810$$

Luis buys 1,810 grams of cat food.

Write which unit (*mg, g,* or *kg*) you would use to measure the mass of each item.

1. a cat _____

2. an apple _____

3. a motorbike _____

4. a toy truck _____

5. your shoes _____

6. a drop of rain _____

7. a dictionary _____

8. a loaf of bread _____

9. a bug _____

Write the missing number.

10. 35 mg = _____ g

11. 2,500 kg = _____ g

12. 400 g = _____ kg

13. 2.5 L = _____ kL

14. 45,000 kL = _____ L

15. 99 g = _____ mg

16. 5 kL = _____ L

17. 45 mL = _____ L

RETEACH | Customary Units of Length

In the United States, length is measured in inches, feet (12 inches) and yards (3 feet). A football field is 100 yards long. How many feet long is a football field?

Remember

To rename yards (a larger unit) with feet (a smaller unit), multiply the number of yards by 3.

$$100 \times 3 = 300$$

A football field is 300 feet long.

Write the missing number.

1. 4 ft = _____ in.   **2.** 6 ft = _____ yd   **3.** 3,520 yd = _____ mi

4. 3 yd = _____ ft   **5.** 72 in. = _____ ft   **6.** 108 in. = _____ ft

7. 4 yd = _____ ft   **8.** 2 mi = _____ yd   **9.** 6 ft = _____ in.

Solve.

10. On a baseball diamond, the distance from home plate to first base is 90 feet. How many yards is that?

_____

11. A baseball hit 300 yards travels how many feet?

_____

12. A football player who carries the ball 60 feet travels how many yards? _____

13. If a football team needs 1.5 feet to reach a first down, how many inches is that? _____

14. Each end zone is 10 yards long. How many feet are there in an end zone? _____

15. How long is a football field if you include the playing field and the end zones? _____ feet _____ yards

Use with pages 246–247.

RETEACH   Customary Units of Capacity and Weight

These are some units of measure.

8 fluid ounces (fl oz) = 1 cup (c)
2 cups (c)   = 1 pint (pt)
2 pints (pt)   = 1 quart (qt)
4 quarts (qt)   = 1 gallon (gal)

These are some units of weight.

16 ounces (oz) = 1 pound (lb)
2,000 pounds (lb) = 1 ton (T)

The zookeeper at the Oakwood Zoo told
the seventh-grade class that Jumbo, the
elephant, has a weight of 5 tons. What is
Jumbo's weight in pounds?

Remember

To rename a larger unit (tons) with a smaller unit
(pounds), multiply the number of tons by 2,000.

$$5 \times 2000 = 10,000$$

Jumbo weighs 10,000 pounds.

Write the missing number.

1. 6 gal = _____ qt

2. 10 pt = _____ c

3. 368 oz = _____ lb

4. 3 qt = _____ pt

5. 48 c = _____ pt

6. 6,000 lb = _____ T

7. 23 gal = _____ qt

8. 27 lb = _____ oz

9. 22 pt = _____ qt

10. 24 fl oz = _____ c

11. 48 oz = _____ lb

12. 36 c = _____ pt

Solve.

13. Jumbo eats 36,000 pounds of hay each year. How many
tons of hay does he eat each year? _____

RETEACH   Time

These are units used to measure time.

60 seconds (s)	= 1 minute (min)	365 days (d)	= 1 year (y)*
60 minutes (min)	= 1 hour (h)	52 weeks (wk)	= 1 year (y)
24 hours (h)	= 1 day (d)	12 months (mo)	= 1 year (y)
7 days (d)	= 1 week (wk)	100 years (y)	= 1 century

*366 days in a leap year

If you traveled around the world in 80 days, how many hours would such a trip take you?

Remember

To rename a larger unit (days) with a smaller unit (hours), multiply the number of days by 24.

$$80 \times 24 = 1{,}920$$

The trip would take 1,920 hours.

Write the missing number.

1. 15 min = _____ s

2. 3 h = _____ min

3. 10 h = _____ min

4. 6 d = _____ h

5. 8 min = _____ s

6. 2 d = _____ h

7. 36 h = _____ d

8. 1 h = _____ s

9. 400 min = _____ h

Solve.

10.
```
  6 min 16 s
+ 3 min 28 s
_____
```

11.
```
  10 h  2 min
+  2 h 35 min
_____
```

12.
```
  6 h 34 min
+ 2 h 28 min
_____
```

13.
```
  35 h 30 min
- 12 h 16 min
_____
```

14.
```
  27 h 35 min
- 15 h 20 min
_____
```

15.
```
  14 h 15 min
-  8 h 44 min
_____
```

Solve.

16. The longest intentional single-handed voyage on a raft was made by William Willis of the United States. In 1963 he made a 130-day voyage across the Pacific Ocean. How many hours did the trip take? _____

Use with pages 250–251.

RETEACH   Time Zones

Going west, time is one hour earlier per time zone.

Going east, time is one hour later per time zone.

UNITED STATES TIMES ZONES

Alaska Hawaii Time
9:00 A.M.

Pacific Time
11:00 A.M.

Mountain Time
12:00 NOON

Central Time
1:00 P.M.

Eastern Time
2:00 P.M.

It takes 24 hours for Earth to make one complete rotation on its axis. For this reason we have created 24 time zones around the world. There are 7 time zones between the Atlantic coast and Hawaii, as the time zone map above indicates.

When it is 2:00 P.M. in Boston, what time is it in Seattle?

┌─ **Remember** ──────────────────────────────────┐
The map indicates that it is 11 o'clock in Seattle, but it is *earlier* in the West than it is in the East.
└──┘

It is 11:00 A.M. in Seattle.

It is 7:00 A.M. in St. Louis. Find the time in each city.

1. Anchorage _____

2. Atlanta _____

3. Santa Fe _____

4. New Orleans _____

5. Chicago _____

6. Denver _____

7. Boston _____

8. Cheyenne _____

RETEACH Temperature

Most temperatures in the United States are measured in degrees Fahrenheit. Temperatures in many other parts of the world are measured in degrees Celsius.

Choose the most likely temperature for a cold glass of orange juice. Write the letter of the correct answer.

a. 37°C
b. 0°C
c. 10°C

Remember

Water boils at 100°C.
A hot cup of tea is 85°C.
A warm bath is 50°C.
A swimming pool is 25°C.
Water freezes at 0°C.

The best estimate of the temperature of a cold glass of orange juice is **c.** 10°C.

Choose the most likely temperature for each. Write the letter of the correct answer.

1. ice skating _____   a. 15°C   b. ‾1°C   c. 32°C

2. nice summer day _____   a. 30°C   b. 20°C   c. 10°C

3. boiling water _____   a. 75°C   b. 90°C   c. 100°C

4. a cold day _____   a. 25°C   b. 5°C   c. 30°C

5. ice cube _____   a. 30°F   b. 40°F   c. 50°F

6. warm summer day _____   a. 60°F   b. 80°F   c. 45°F

7. boiling water _____   a. 212°F   b. 100°F   c. 32°F

Solve.

8. The body temperature of a dog can be as high as 102°F. Mary's dog, Mr. Chips, has a fever of 103.2°F. What is the difference between these two temperatures? _____

Use with pages 256–257.

RETEACH   Measurement and Precision

Jenny and Arthur are guitarists in the rock band The
Centimeters. Jenny's guitar pick is 0.15 mm thick. Arthur's
guitar pick is 0.3 mm thick. Which measurement is more
precise?

Remember

The precision of a measurement depends on both the
unit and number used when the measurement is
recorded.

Although both guitar picks use the same unit of
measurement, the thickness of Jenny's guitar pick is
measured more precisely. Since the number 0.15 is to
the nearest hundredth, whereas the number 0.3 is only
to the nearest tenth, the number 0.15 is more precise.

The more precise measurement is 0.15 mm thick.

Write the more precise measurement.

1. 8 qt or 2 gal _____   **2.** 2 m or 2,000 mm _____

3. 74 cm or 730 mm _____   **4.** 17 oz or 17.0 oz _____

5. 3 m or 300 cm _____   **6.** 1 y or 360 d _____

7. 48.0°C or 48°C _____   **8.** 6 c or 3 pt _____

9. 1.5 mi or 7,920 ft _____   **10.** 9 g or 9,000 mg _____

11. 51 ft or 17 yd _____   **12.** 6.09 m or 6.0 m _____

Ring the more precise measure.

13. the length of a drumstick	0.5 m	0.50 m	50 cm
14. the mass of a guitar pick	1.2 g	0.0012 kg	1,200 mg
15. the temperature of an oven	168.50°C	168°C	168.5°C
16. the capacity of a bowl	2.0 L	205 mL	2.05 L

RETEACH   Ratio and Rate

In 3 hours, an airplane travels 756 miles. Write the ratio of the distance traveled to the travel time as a fraction in simplest form.

Remember

A rate is a ratio that compares different kinds of quantities. Select the correct value for the *terms* (distance and time).

$$756 : 3$$
Distance : Time

$$\frac{756}{3} = \frac{756 \div 3}{3 \div 3} = \frac{252}{1}$$

The rate is $\frac{252}{1}$.

Write and compare the rate of the distance traveled to the amount of time required as a fraction in simplest form.

		Rate	Fraction
1.	A bicycle traveled 34 miles in 4 hours.	_____ : _____	_____
2.	A train traveled 290 miles in 3 hours.	_____ : _____	_____
3.	In 2 hours, Mike walked 8 miles.	_____ : _____	_____
4.	In 6 hours, a boat traveled 92 miles.	_____ : _____	_____
5.	A distance of 500 miles covered in 4 hours.	_____ : _____	_____
6.	A distance of 125 miles covered in 10 hours.	_____ : _____	_____
7.	It takes 6 hours to travel 150 miles.	_____ : _____	_____
8.	It takes 2 seconds to travel 162 feet.	_____ : _____	_____
9.	It takes 5 hours to travel 250 miles.	_____ : _____	_____
10.	It takes 40 minutes to travel 5 miles.	_____ : _____	_____

RETEACH Proportion

The Chang family is traveling on a summer vacation. On Monday, they traveled 300 miles in 6 hours. On Tuesday, they plan to travel for 4.5 hours. At about the same rate of speed, how far can they expect to travel the second day? Solve as a proportion and write the answer.

Remember

Solve the proportion by using the cross products.

$$\frac{x}{4.5} = \frac{300}{6}$$
$$6x = 4.5 \cdot 300 \qquad \text{Cross multiply.}$$
$$\frac{6x}{6} = \frac{1,350}{6} \qquad \text{Solve.}$$
$$x = 225$$

The Changs can expect to travel 225 miles on Tuesday.

Solve.

The Banz family traveled 480 miles in 8 hours on Sunday when they started their vacation. At the same rate of speed, they traveled 420 miles on Monday and 240 miles on Tuesday. Write how long they traveled on each day and solve as a proportion. Show all work.

1. Monday: $\frac{420}{x} = \frac{480}{8}$

_____ = _____

$x =$ _____

2. Tuesday: $\frac{240}{x} = \frac{480}{8}$

_____ = _____

$x =$ _____

3. An airplane traveled 1,125 miles in $4\frac{1}{2}$ hours. Write how many miles it would travel in 8 hours at that speed. Show all work.

_____ = _____

_____ = _____

$x =$ _____

RETEACH Scale Drawing

A map is a scale drawing. Linda uses a ruler to approximate the air distance between Missoula and Great Falls, which she finds is 6 cm. The scale of the map is 1 cm:22 mi. Use a proportion to find the distance.

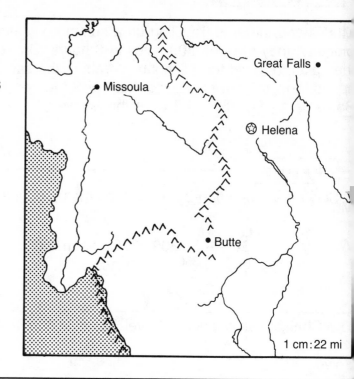

1 cm:22 mi

Remember

Set up the proportion with the units corresponding to the map scale.

$$\frac{\text{Length in drawing (cm)}}{\text{Actual length (mi)}} \rightarrow \frac{1}{22} = \frac{6}{x} \leftarrow \frac{\text{Length in drawing (cm)}}{\text{Actual length (mi)}}$$
$$1x = 6 \cdot 22 \quad \text{Cross multiply.}$$
$$x = 132$$

The distance is 132 mi.

Complete the table.

Cities	Scale	Map Distance	Proportion	Actual distance
1. Missoula to Butte	1 cm = 22 mi	5 cm		_____ mi
2. Butte to Great Falls	1 cm = 22 mi	5.5 cm		_____ mi
3. Helena to Butte	1 cm = 22 mi	3.2 cm		_____ mi
4. Missoula to Helena	1 cm = 22 mi	4.3 cm		_____ mi

RETEACH Percent

Moussa got 8 out of 10 correct on an arithmetic test. What percent did he get correct?

Remember

Write the fraction with a denominator of 100.

$$\frac{8}{10} = \frac{8 \cdot 10}{10 \cdot 10} = \frac{80}{100} = 80\%$$

Moussa got 80% on his test.

Write as a percent.

1. $\frac{7}{10} = \frac{70}{100} =$ _____

2. $\frac{15}{20} = \frac{75}{100} =$ _____

3. $\frac{19}{20} = \frac{95}{100} =$ _____

4. $\frac{16}{25} = \frac{64}{100} =$ _____

5. $\frac{3}{10}$ _____

6. $\frac{6}{10}$ _____

7. $\frac{10}{10}$ _____

8. $\frac{5}{10}$ _____

9. $\frac{38}{100}$ _____

10. $\frac{94}{100}$ _____

11. $\frac{91}{100}$ _____

12. $\frac{18}{20}$

13. $\frac{16}{20}$ _____

14. $\frac{20}{20}$ _____

15. $\frac{22}{25}$ _____

16. $\frac{18}{25}$ _____

Solve.

17. On a test containing 25 problems, Wanda got 20 items correct. What percent did she get correct? _____

18. On a 20-item test, Frank had 3 errors. What percent did he get correct? _____

19. A true/false test had 200 questions. Laurel got 190 of the items correct. What percent did she get correct? _____

20. On the 200-item true/false test, Roosevelt had 20 errors. What percent did he get correct? _____

Use with pages 278–279.

RETEACH   Decimals and Percents

The department store had a sidewalk sale to close out the
winter merchandise. The store advertised gloves at 5% off.
Write the percent as a decimal.

Remember

Percent means "hundreds." Move the decimal point two
places to the left, and omit the percent sign. Add zeros if
necessary.

$$5\% = \underset{\smile}{05}\% = 0.05$$

5% as a decimal is 0.05.

Write as a decimal.

1. $50\% = \underset{\smile}{50}. =$ _____

2. $12.5\% = \underset{\smile}{12.5} =$ _____

3. $7.5\% = \underset{\smile}{07}.5 =$ _____

4. $4\% = \underset{\smile}{04}. =$ _____

5. $2.5\% =$ _____

6. $1.5\% =$ _____

7. $1.2\% =$ _____

8. $1.75\% =$ _____

9. $43\% =$ _____

10. $16\% =$ _____

11. $0.5\% =$ _____

12. $0.05\% =$ _____

Write as a percent.

13. $0.05 =$ _____

14. $0.075 =$ _____

15. $0.112 =$ _____

16. $0.003 =$ _____

17. $0.142 =$ _____

18. $1.05 =$ _____

Solve.

19. A credit-card company charges 1.8% per month on the
unpaid balance. Write the percent as a decimal. _____

20. A suit is advertised at a 12.5% discount. Write the
percent as a decimal. _____

Use with pages 280–281.

RETEACH Fractions and Percents

n a poll of voter preferences for class president, $\frac{3}{8}$ of the
oters said that they would vote for Vito. What percent does
he fraction $\frac{3}{8}$ represent?

Remember

Divide the numerator by the denominator to obtain a
decimal. Move the decimal point two places to the right
and write the percent sign.

$$\frac{3}{8} = 8\overline{)3.000} \qquad \frac{3}{8} = 0.375 = 37.5\%$$

$$\begin{array}{r} 0.375 \\ 8\overline{)3.000} \\ \underline{2\,4} \\ 60 \\ \underline{56} \\ 40 \\ \underline{40} \\ 0 \end{array}$$

Vito would get 37.5% of the vote.

Write each fraction as a percent.

1. $\frac{5}{8}\left[\begin{array}{c} 0.625 \\ 8\overline{)5.000} \end{array}\right]$ _____

2. $\frac{1}{4}\left[\begin{array}{c} 0.25 \\ 4\overline{)1.00} \end{array}\right]$ _____

3. $\frac{5}{16}\left[\begin{array}{c} 0.3125 \\ 16\overline{)5.0000} \end{array}\right]$ _____

4. $\frac{1}{16}\left[\begin{array}{c} 0.0625 \\ 16\overline{)1.0000} \end{array}\right]$ _____

5. $\frac{1}{2}$ _____ 6. $\frac{1}{3}$ _____ 7. $\frac{1}{6}$ _____ 8. $\frac{9}{24}$ _____

9. $\frac{1}{60}$ _____ 10. $\frac{5}{24}$ _____ 11. $\frac{7}{16}$ _____ 12. $\frac{19}{64}$ _____

A preference poll for class secretary shows Joe with 20
votes, Mike with 6 votes, and "no preference" with 4 votes.

Solve.

13. What percent of the votes did Joe receive?

14. What percent of the votes did Mike receive? _____

15. What percent of the students had no preference?

_____

RETEACH   Finding the Percent of a Number

Yousop's father is buying the materials to build a storage shed in the yard. The lumberyard offers a $7\frac{1}{2}$% discount for cash. Two-by-fours for the framework cost $1.90 each. How much can be saved by paying cash?

Remember

Change the percent to a decimal before multiplying.
Think: What is $7\frac{1}{2}$% of $1.90?

$$7\frac{1}{2}\% = 7.5\% = 0.075$$
$$\$1.90 \cdot 0.075 = \$0.1425$$

He will save about $0.14 per board.

Find the percent of the number.

1. $5\frac{1}{2}$% of 21.5 = 0.055 × 21.5 = _____

2. $2\frac{1}{2}$% of 0.75 = 0.025 × 0.75 = _____

3. 9.25% of $12.95 = _____ × $12.95 = _____

4. 10% of 0.62 = _____ × 0.62 = _____

5. 5% of 0.85 = _____   6. 5.3% of 11.5 = _____

7. 10% of $3.85 = _____   8. $9\frac{1}{4}$% of $21.50 = _____

9. 15% of 4.9 = _____   10. 11.4% of 5.1 = _____

11. 5.75% of 3.85 = _____   12. $4\frac{1}{2}$% of 2.73 = _____

Solve.

13. Yousop's father bought an outdoor light for his shed. The light was listed at $28.95. If he received a 15% discount, how much did he save?
_____

14. His father needs 42 two-by-fours for his shed at $1.90 each. If he receives a $7\frac{1}{2}$% discount, how much will he save?
_____

     Use with pages 284–285.

Name _____ Date _____

Susan is the official statistician for the seventh-grade basketball team. One of her jobs is to keep track of the shooting percentage of the players. In a game today, Linda made 6 shots out of 15 attempts. What is her shooting percentage?

Remember

Write an equation that matches the statement of the question.

6 is what percent of 15?

$$6 = n \qquad 15$$

$$6 = 15n$$

$$\frac{6}{15} = \frac{15n}{15} \qquad 15\overline{)6.0}^{\,0.4}$$

$$0.4 = n$$

Since 0.4 = 40%, then 6 is 40% of 15.

Linda made 40% of her shots.

Calculate each team member's season percentages.

1. Martha: Tried 94   shots, made 47   _____

2. Noor: Tried 168   shots, made 56   _____

3. Amy: Tried 50   shots, made 13   _____

4. Jenny: Tried   7   shots, made   0   _____

5. Juanita: Tried   6   shots, made   1   _____

6. Karen: Tried 75   shots, made 38   _____

7. Debbie: Tried 10   shots, made   8   _____

8. Team: Tried _____ shots, made _____ _____

Solve.

9. Sean has 137 stamps in his collection, and all but 26 are stamps from foreign countries. What percent of his stamps are stamps from foreign countries? _____

RETEACH   Finding the Total Number

At Janine's Bicycle Store, Janine has been told by her
supplier that she has received 85% of her total shipment of
bicycles. If she has received 255 bicycles, how many will she
receive altogether?

> **Remember**
>
> Change the decimal to a percent before solving the
> equation.
>
> $$85\% \text{ of } n = 255$$
> $$0.85n = 255$$
> $$\frac{0.85n}{0.85} = \frac{255}{0.85}$$
> $$n = 300$$

Janine will receive 300 bicycles altogether.

Find the number. Fill in the blanks.

1. 406 is 70% of what number? 70% of $n = 0.70n = 406$

   $n =$ _____

2. 286 is 65% of what number? 65% of $n =$ _____ $n = 286$

   $n =$ _____

3. 74% of $n = 185$ $n =$ _____

4. 20% of $n = 97$ $n =$ _____

5. 40% of $n = 70$ $n =$ _____

6. 82% of $n = 328$ $n =$ _____

7. 30% of $n = 48$ $n =$ _____

8. 45% of $n = 162$ $n =$ _____

Solve.

9. Last year by this time, Janine had received 80% of her
   total shipment of bicycles. If she had received 176
   bicycles, what was the total for the year?

   _____

10. Janine hopes that this year's shipment of bicycles (300)
    will only be 80% the size of next year's. What does she
    hope the size of next year's shipment will be?

_____

Use with pages 290–291.

RETEACH Percent Using Proportions

A survey of schools in a region showed that 25.2% of the schools had personal computers. The number of schools having personal computers was 63. Use a proportion to find out how many schools were surveyed. 25.2% of what number is 63?

Remember

Compare like parts in both ratios.

$$\text{Part} \rightarrow \frac{25.2}{100} = \frac{63}{n} \leftarrow \text{Part}$$
$$\text{Whole} \rightarrow \qquad\quad\ \ \leftarrow \text{Whole}$$

$$25.2n = 63 \cdot 100$$
$$25.2n = 6{,}300$$
$$\frac{25.2n}{25.2} = \frac{6{,}300}{25.2}$$
$$n = 250$$

The number of schools surveyed was 250.

Use a proportion to solve each problem.

1. 62 is 24.8% of what number?

$$\frac{24.8}{100} = \frac{62}{n} \qquad n = \text{_____}$$

2. 24% of 60 = n

$$\frac{24}{100} = \frac{n}{60} \qquad n = \text{_____}$$

3. What percent of 30 is 12?

$$\frac{n}{100} = \frac{12}{30} \qquad n = \text{_____}$$

4. 5.5% of what number is 11? _____

5. 94 is 23.5% of what number? _____

6. 2.5% of what number is 13? _____

7. 7.4% of what number is 333? _____

8. What number is 13.6% of 1,250? _____

9. What number is 0.5% of 200? _____

10. What number is 74% of 111? _____

11. What percent of 180 is 9? _____

12. What percent of 500 is 22? _____

13. 124 is what percent of 800? _____

RETEACH — Percent of Increase and Decrease

Jody keeps a record of attendance at the meetings of the mathematics club. The attendance at the first meeting was 25. At the second meeting, the attendance dropped to 18. What was the percent of decrease?

Remember

Compare the amount of decrease with the number *before* the decrease. Think: What percent of 25 is 7?

$$25n = 7$$
$$n = \frac{7}{25} \longrightarrow \frac{\text{Amount of decrease}}{\text{Amount } before \text{ the decrease}}$$
$$n = \frac{7}{25} = \frac{28}{100} = 0.28 = 28\%$$

There was a 28% decrease in attendance.

Find the percent of increase or decrease between meetings of high-school clubs. Label *increase* or *decrease*.

1. Science Club
15 attended 1st meeting; 12 attended 2nd meeting

_____

2. Student Council
30 attended 1st meeting; 27 attended 2nd meeting

_____

3. Tennis Club
32 attended 1st meeting; 36 attended 2nd meeting

_____

4. Soccer Club
75 attended 1st meeting; 90 attended 2nd meeting

_____

Solve.

5. What was the percentage of increase if the total number of students who attended the first meetings of all high-school clubs was 300 and the total number who attended the second meetings was 336? _____

Name _____ Date _____

Basic Ideas of Geometry

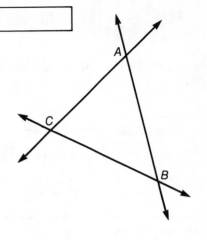

What is another symbol that represents the same set of points as ∠ACB?

┌─ **Remember** ─────────────────────────────────────┐
│ Look at the vertex when renaming angles. The vertex of │
│ an angle is the middle letter in the symbol for an angle. │
│ Both ∠BCA and ∠ACB have C as the vertex and │
│ consist of $\overrightarrow{CB}$ and $\overrightarrow{CA}$. │
└───┘

∠BCA represents the same set of points as ∠ACB.

Refer to the figure at the right. Write *true* or *false*.

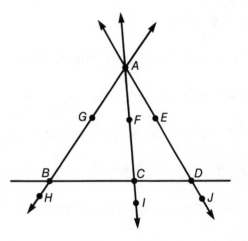

1. $\overleftrightarrow{AG}$ is a ray. _____

2. $\overrightarrow{AH}$ is a ray. _____

3. $\overleftrightarrow{JA}$ is a ray. _____

4. $\overrightarrow{DJ}$ is a ray. _____

5. ∠ABD = ∠DBA _____

6. ∠ADB = ∠ADC _____

7. ∠BDE = ∠BDA _____

8. ∠BDE = ∠BDJ _____

9. ∠JAI = ∠JAH _____

10. ∠JAH = ∠JAG _____

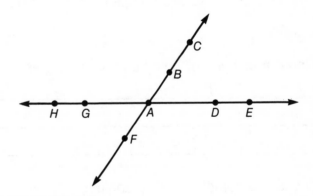

Refer to the figure at the right. Write another symbol for the given symbol.

11. $\overrightarrow{AE}$ _____

12. $\overrightarrow{AC}$ _____

13. $\overleftrightarrow{GE}$ _____

14. ∠CAG _____

15. ∠DAF _____

16. ∠CAE _____

17. What angle has $\overrightarrow{AE}$ and $\overrightarrow{AF}$ as sides? _____

Use with pages 310–311.

RETEACH   Angles

Are ∠JFH and ∠IFG complementary angles?

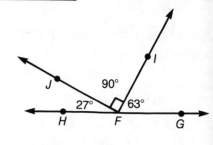

> **Remember**
>
> Complementary angles do not have to be adjacent angles. The sum of the measures of ∠JFH and ∠IFG = 27° + 63° = 90°.

The angles are complementary.

Write *true* or *false*.

1. ∠CAF and ∠FAB are complementary angles. _____

2. ∠CAF and ∠DAE are complementary angles. _____

3. ∠CAD and ∠CAB are complementary angles. _____

4. ∠FAB and ∠BAE are complementary angles. _____

5. ∠FAB and ∠DAE are complementary angles. _____

6. ∠CAD and ∠DAE are complementary angles. _____

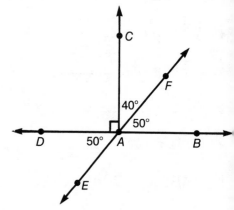

Solve.

7. Name four pairs of complementary angles.

_____

_____

_____

8. Name the complementary angles.

_____

_____

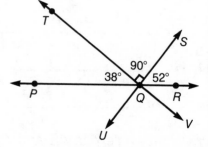

Use with pages 312–313.

Name _____ Date _____

Use a compass and a straightedge to construct an angle congruent to ∠A.

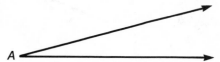
A

Remember

Congruent angles have the same measure.

E   F

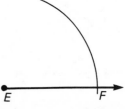
B
A   C

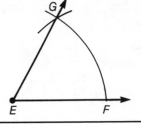
E   F

Draw a ray $\overrightarrow{EH}$.
Label the endpoint E.

Place the compass point at A. Draw an arc to intersect both sides of ∠A. Label the points B and C.

Use the same compass opening to draw an arc from E. Label the point F on $\overrightarrow{EH}$.

Using a compass opening equal to $\overline{BC}$, place the compass point at F and draw an arc that intersects the first arc. Label the intersection G.

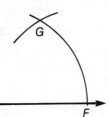
G
E   F

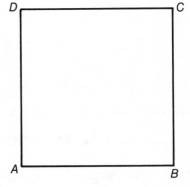
G
E   F

∠E ≅ ∠A

---

1. Use line $\overline{EF}$ to construct a figure congruent to ABCD.

2. Use A′ as an endpoint to construct $\overline{A'B'} = \overline{AB}$.

3. At A′ construct an angle congruent to ∠DAB.

4. At B′ construct an angle congruent to ∠ABC.

5. On the ray constructed at A′, construct $\overline{A'D'} = \overline{AD}$.

6. On the ray constructed at B′, construct $\overline{B'C'} = \overline{BC}$. Draw $\overline{D'C'}$.

7. Name four pairs of line segments that are congruent.

_____

8. Name four pairs of angles that are congruent.

_____

D _____ C

A _____ B

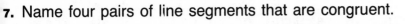

A

Bisecting Segments and Angles

Bisect ∠A.

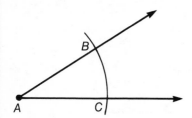

Remember

Keep the same compass opening to draw the intersecting arcs.

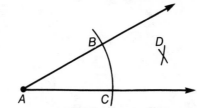 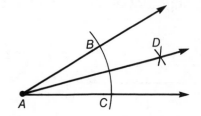

Place the compass point at A and draw an arc that bisects both sides of ∠A. Label the intersections B and C.

Use the same compass opening to draw intersecting arcs from B and C. Label the intersection D.

Draw $\overrightarrow{AD}$.

$\overrightarrow{AD}$ bisects ∠A

Trace each figure.

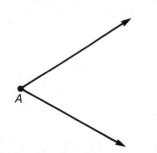 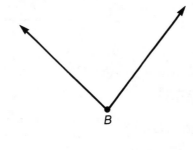 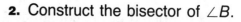

1. Construct the bisector of ∠A.

2. Construct the bisector of ∠B.

3. Construct the bisector of $\overline{CD}$.

4. Construct the bisector of $\overline{EF}$.

Draw a line segment for each length. Construct its bisector.

5. 3 in.   **6.** 8 in.   **7.** 6 cm.   **8.** 9 cm.

Draw an angle for each measure. Construct its bisector.

9. 40°   **10.** 64°   **11.** 70°   **12.** 142°

Use with pages 316–317.

RETEACH Perpendicular and Parallel Lines

Given that $\overleftrightarrow{AB}$ and $\overleftrightarrow{CD}$ are parallel lines, identify ∠1 and ∠5 as vertical angles, corresponding angles, or neither.

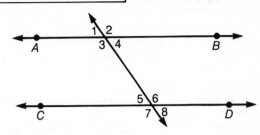

Remember

Vertical angles have equal measures. Corresponding angles have equal measures. ∠1 and ∠4, ∠2 and ∠3, ∠5 and ∠8, and ∠6 and ∠7 are the vertical angles formed by these lines. ∠2 and ∠6, ∠4 and ∠8, ∠1 and ∠5, and ∠3 and ∠7 are the corresponding angles formed by these lines.

∠1 and ∠5 are corresponding angles.

Identify pairs of angles as *vertical* angles, *corresponding* angles, or *supplementary* angles.

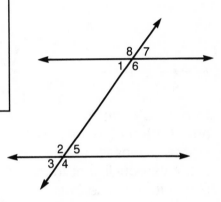

1. ∠8 and ∠6 _____

2. ∠2 and ∠4 _____

3. ∠8 and ∠7 _____

4. ∠6 and ∠1 _____

5. ∠8 and ∠2 _____

6. ∠5 and ∠3 _____

7. ∠4 and ∠6 _____

8. ∠6 and ∠7 _____

9. ∠1 and ∠7 _____

10. ∠1 and ∠3 _____

11. ∠5 and ∠7 _____

12. ∠2 and ∠5 _____

$\overleftrightarrow{AB}$, $\overleftrightarrow{EF}$, and $\overleftrightarrow{DC}$ are parallel.

13. Name four pairs of vertical angles.

_____

_____

_____

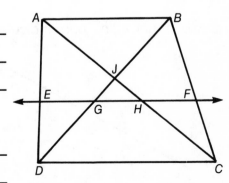

14. Name two pairs of corresponding angles.

_____

_____

RETEACH | **Constructing Perpendicular and Parallel Lines**

Construct a line perpendicular to line *l*.

_____ *l*

Remember

Change to a wider compass width for the second set of arcs.

 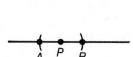 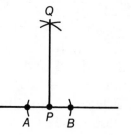

Choose a point *P* anywhere on the line. With a compass, draw two arcs equidistant from *P* to intersect line *l* at points which you label *A* and *B*.

Open the compass wider than $\overline{AP}$. Draw intersecting arcs above *P* with *A* as a base point, and then with *B* as a base point. Label the intersection *Q*.

Draw $\overline{PQ}$.

$ADP \quad \overline{QP}$
$\perp \overline{AB}$

$\overline{PQ} \perp l$.

Trace each line.

1. Construct a line perpendicular to $\overline{AB}$.

2. Construct a line parallel to $\overline{CD}$.

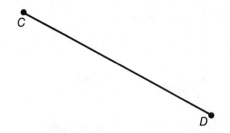

3. Construct a line perpendicular to $\overline{EF}$.

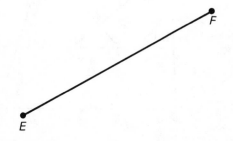

4. Construct a line parallel to $\overline{GH}$.

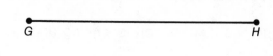

RETEACH   Triangles

Triangles are classified by the measures of the angles they contain and by the lengths of the sides of the triangles.

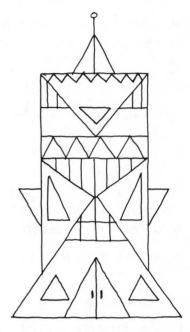

Remember

These are the major kinds of triangles.

Angle Classifications
An *acute* triangle has three acute angles.
An *obtuse* triangle has an obtuse angle.
A *right* triangle has a right angle.

Classifications by Lengths of Sides
A *scalene* triangle has no congruent sides.
An *isosceles* triangle has two congruent sides.
An *equilateral* triangle has three congruent sides.

In figure *ABCD*, $\overline{AD}$, $\overline{AE}$, $\overline{BE}$, and $\overline{BC}$ are congruent, and $\overline{DE} \cong \overline{CE}$.

1. Name three isosceles triangles.

_____

2. Name three right triangles.

_____

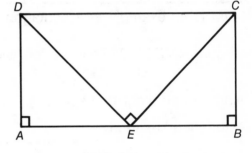

In *FGHI*, $\overline{IH}$ and $\overline{FG}$ are parallel and congruent, $\overline{IF} \perp \overline{IH}$ and $\overline{FG}$, and $\overline{HG} \perp \overline{IH}$ and $\overline{FG}$.

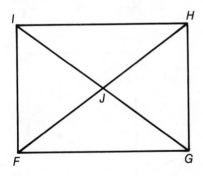

3. Name four right triangles.

_____

4. Name two acute triangles.

_____

5. Name two obtuse triangles.

_____

6. Name four isosceles triangles.

_____

Name _____ Date _____

RETEACH Polygons

A polygon is a closed figure that consists of three or more line segments. Some of the common polygons are shown here.

triangle

square

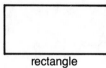
rectangle

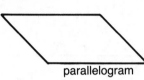
parallelogram

pentagon

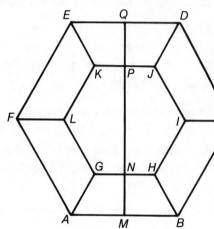

Polygons are named using the vertices in order. For example, the pentagon above is named as *GHIJK*.

Name a pentagon in Figure *ABCDEF*.

Remember

A pentagon does not have to be a regular pentagon.

BCDQM is an example of a pentagon.

Use Figure *AMBCDQEF* for the following problems.

1. Name three other pentagons. _____

2. Name two hexagons. _____

3. Name seven trapezoids. _____

Use Figure *RSTUVW* for the following problems.

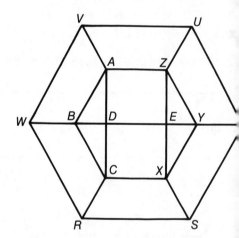

4. Name two squares. _____

5. Name a rectangle. _____

6. Name four quadrilaterals that are not squares, rectangles, or trapezoids; for example, *WDAV*. _____

7. Name five trapezoids. _____

8. Name two pentagons. _____

Use Figure *FGHIJK* for the following problems.

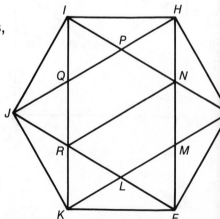

9. Name three parallelograms that are not a rectangle; for example, *JRNP*. _____

10. Name two pentagons. _____

94

Use with pages 328–329.

RETEACH   **Congruent Polygons**

△ACB and △FDE are congruent.
List three pairs of congruent sides.
List three pairs of congruent angles.

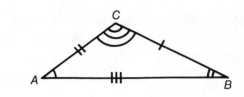

> **Remember**
>
> Slash marks on each polygon indicate
> the sides and angles that are
> congruent.

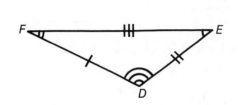

Corresponding angles	Corresponding sides
∠F ≅ ∠B	$\overline{FE}$ ≅ $\overline{AB}$
∠E ≅ ∠A	$\overline{FD}$ ≅ $\overline{CB}$
∠D ≅ ∠C	$\overline{DE}$ ≅ $\overline{AC}$

Write the congruent sides and angles.

1.

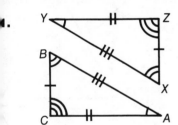

2.

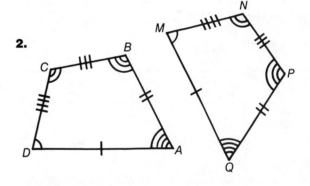

_____

_____

_____

_____

_____

Find the corresponding sides and angles for the
congruences.

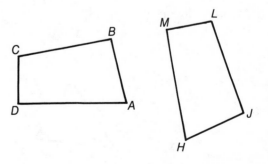

3. ABCD ≅ HJLM

$\overline{AB}$ ≅ _____   ∠A ≅ _____

$\overline{BC}$ ≅ _____   ∠B ≅ _____

$\overline{CD}$ ≅ _____   ∠C ≅ _____

$\overline{DA}$ ≅ _____   ∠D ≅ _____

RETEACH   Similar Polygons

Sara and Maria want to find the distance across the pond (the length of $\overline{DE}$ on the diagram). They stake off $\triangle ABC$, which is similar to $\triangle DEC$. Then they make the measurements shown on the diagram. What is the length of $\overline{DE}$?

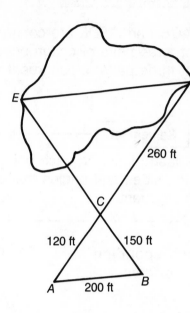

Remember

The lengths of the corresponding sides of similar polygons are proportional.

$\overline{AB} \sim \overline{DE}$
$\overline{AC} \sim \overline{CD}$
$\overline{BC} \sim \overline{CE}$

Let $x =$ length of $\overline{DE}$.

$$\dfrac{x}{\text{length of } \overline{AB}} = \dfrac{\text{length of } \overline{CD}}{\text{length of } \overline{AC}}$$

$\dfrac{x}{200} = \dfrac{260}{120}$

$120x = 200 \cdot 260$

$120x = \dfrac{52{,}000}{120}$

$x = 433\tfrac{1}{3}$

The distance is $433\tfrac{1}{3}$ ft.

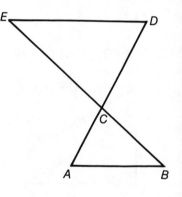

Complete the table.

	$\overline{AC}$	$\overline{AB}$	$\overline{BC}$	$\overline{CD}$	$\overline{DE}$	$\overline{CE}$
1.	60	100	75	130		
2.	12	16	15	24		
3.	9	13	12	18		
4.	4.1	6.7	7.2	8.3		

Find the missing dimensions.

5.

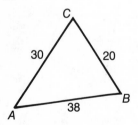

6.

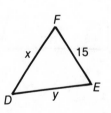
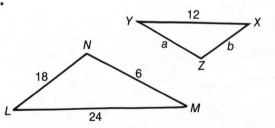

    Use with pages 332–333.

RETEACH   Circles

There are five basic terms associated with circles.

Radius: a line segment that extends from the center of a circle to any point on a circle.

Chord: a line segment whose endpoints are on a circle.

Diameter: a chord that passes through the center of a circle.

Arc: part of a circle.

Central angle: an angle whose vertex is the center of a circle.

Use the figure on the right to solve the problems.

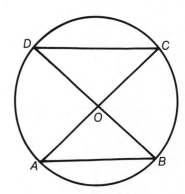

1. Name two diameters of the circle. _____

2. Name four radii of the circle. _____

3. Name four chords of the circle. _____

4. Name four central angles of the circle.

_____

Use the figure on the right to complete the statements.

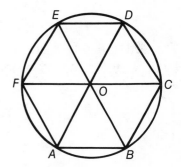

5. $\overline{DO}$ is a _____ of the circle.

6. $\overline{AB}$ is a _____ of the circle.

7. $\angle AOB$ is a _____ of the circle.

8. $\overline{BE}$ is both a _____ and a _____ of the circle.

Identify each segment of the figure below as a *radius, diameter, chord,* or *none of these.*

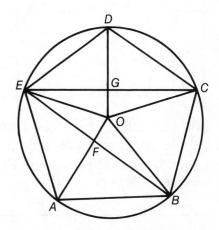

9. $\overline{AB}$ _____

10. $\overline{CE}$ _____

11. $\overline{OC}$ _____

12. $\overline{OG}$ _____

RETEACH   Symmetry and Reflections

Many objects have natural symmetry. The butterfly is one example of such symmetry. Many geometric figures also have lines of symmetry. Is line *EF* a line of symmetry for parallelogram *ABCD*?

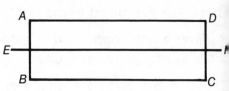

Points *A* and *D* and points *B* and *C* are images of one another, using *EF* as a reflection line. Therefore, *EF* is a line of symmetry.

For each figure decide whether or not the line is a line of symmetry. Write *yes* or *no*.

1.

_____

2.

_____

3.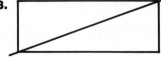

_____

4.

_____

5.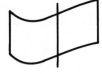

_____

6.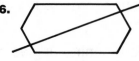

_____

The letter *A* has a line of symmetry. Draw all lines of symmetry for the other letters. If there are none, write *none*.

$\cancel{A}$

B ___   C ___   D ___   E ___

H ___   I ___   K ___   L ___

N ___   T ___   X ___   Y ___

The name *DEBBIE* has a line of symmetry. Hold the page upside down and look at it in a mirror. What do you observe? Draw the line of symmetry. Print another name which has a horizontal line of symmetry.

DEBBIE

_____

Use with pages 338–339.

RETEACH | Translations and Rotations

Describe the translation that makes △DEF become △ABC.

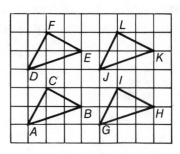

Remember
A **translation (slide)** is the movement of a figure from one position to another along a line.

The translation that makes △DEF become △ABC is 3 units down.

Describe the following translations.

1. △ABC becomes △DEF. _____

2. △ABC becomes △GHI. _____

3. △ABC becomes △JKL. _____

4. △JKL becomes △GHI. _____

5. △JKL becomes △DEF. _____

6. △DEF becomes △GHI. _____

Draw a grid system, and place △ABC at the positions A(2,2), B(0,3),and C(2,4). Show these translations of △ABC.

7. three units to the right

8. six units up

9. four units to the right and three units up

0. five units up and six units to the right

Choose the figure that is the rotation of Figure X around point P.

1.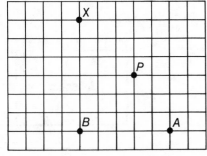

12.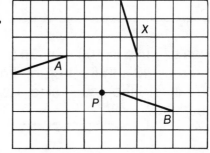

RETEACH   Perimeter

Yoshika is helping her father install a fence around the backyard. The yard is a rectangle that has a length of 42 ft and a width of $35\frac{1}{2}$ ft. How much fencing do they need?

> **Remember**
>
> To find the perimeter of a rectangle, add two lengths and two widths.
>
> $$P = 2l + 2w$$
> $$P = 2 \cdot 35\frac{1}{2} + 2 \cdot 42$$
> $$P = 71 + 84$$
> $$P = 155$$

They need 155 ft of fencing.

Find the perimeter of each rectangle.

1. $l = 46$ ft, $w = 30\frac{1}{4}$ ft $P = 2(46) + 2\left(30\frac{1}{4}\right) =$ _____

2. $l = 45\frac{1}{2}$ in., $w = 27\frac{1}{4}$ in. $P = 2\left(45\frac{1}{2}\right) + 2\left(27\frac{1}{4}\right) =$ _____

3. $l = 58$ cm, $w = 30$ cm $P = 2(58) + 2(30) =$ _____

4. $l = 35$ ft, $W = 33\frac{1}{-}$ ft, $P =$ _____

5. $l = 10\frac{1}{-}$ in., $w = 7\frac{1}{-}$ in., $P =$ _____

6. $l = 10\frac{3}{4}$ in., $w = 8\frac{1}{2}$ in., $P =$ _____

7. $l = 16.2$ cm, $w = 8$ cm, $P =$ _____

8. $l = 14$ cm, $w = 6.8$ cm, $P =$ _____

9. $l = 11.3$ m, $w = 7.5$ m, $P =$ _____

Solve.

10. How many feet of fencing is needed to enclose an area 40 ft wide and 55 ft long? _____

11. What is the perimeter of a square lot 80 ft on a side? _____

12. The Jobson's house is 100 ft by 70 ft. A fence is to be built which runs 40 ft in front of the house, 30 ft behind the house, and 10 ft on each side. How many feet of fence is needed? _____

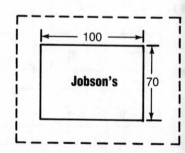

Use with pages 352–353.

Name _____ Date _____

Swen's bicycle wheels each have a radius of 13 inches. How far does he ride as the wheels make one revolution?

Remember

To find the circumference of a circle when the radius is known, use the formula $C = 2\pi r$.

$$C \approx 2 \cdot 3.14 \cdot 13$$
$$C \approx 81.64$$

The bicycle travels approximately 81.64 inches.

Find the circumference of each circle. Use 3.14 for π.

1. $r = 13.5$ in. $C = 2 \cdot \pi \cdot 13.5 = 2 \cdot 3.14 \cdot 13.5$

$C =$ _____ in.

2. $r = 10$ in. $C = 2 \cdot \pi \cdot 10 = 2 \cdot 3.14 \cdot 10$

$C =$ _____ in.

3. $r = 8$ in. $C = 2 \cdot \pi \cdot 8 = 2 \cdot$ _____ $\cdot$ _____

$C =$ _____ in.

4. $r = 6.5$ cm $C = 2 \cdot \pi \cdot 6.5 = 2 \cdot$ _____ $\cdot$ _____

$C =$ _____ cm

5. $r = 5$ in. $C =$ _____ in.   **6.** $r = 12$ ft $C =$ _____ ft

7. $r = 13.5$ cm $C =$ _____ cm   **8.** $r = 15.3$ cm $C =$ _____ cm

Find the circumference of each circle. Use $\frac{22}{7}$ for π.

9. $r = 98\frac{1}{3}$ cm $C =$ _____ cm   **10.** $r = 16\frac{1}{4}$ in. $C =$ _____ in.

11. $r = 15\frac{4}{5}$ ft $C =$ _____ ft   **12.** $r = 9\frac{1}{7}$ ft $C =$ _____ ft

Solve.

13. Swen's brother has a tricycle. The radius of each back wheel is 3.5 inches. About how many inches does the tricycle travel for each revolution of the back wheels?

_____

Name _____ Date _____

RETEACH Area of Squares, Rectangles, Parallelograms

Amy is making a trivet in crafts class. It is a square 9 inches on a side. She is making the top with 1-inch tiles. How many tiles does she need?

Remember

Use the formula for the area of a square.

$$A = s^2 = 9 \cdot 9 = 81$$

Amy needs 81 tiles.

Find the area of each square. Fill in the blanks.

1. $s = 20$ in. $A = s^2 = 20^2 = 20 \times 20 =$ _____ in.^{2}

2. $s = 38$ in. $A = s^2 = 38^2 =$ _____ $\times$ _____ $=$ _____ in.^{2}

3. $s = 7.5$ cm $A = s^2 =$ _____ $=$ _____ $\times$ _____ $=$ _____ cm^2

4. $s = 14.5$ cm $A =$ _____ $\times$ _____ $=$ _____ cm^2

5. $s = 3\frac{1}{2}$ in.
 $A =$ _____

6. $s = 7\frac{1}{4}$ in.
 $A =$ _____

7. $s = 16\frac{7}{8}$ in.
 $A =$ _____

8. $s = 4.3$ cm
 $A =$ _____

9. $s = 6.8$ cm
 $A =$ _____

10. $s = 8.9$ m
 $A =$ _____

11. $s = 3.25$
 $A =$ _____

12. $s = 6.82$
 $A =$ _____

Solve.

13. The 1-inch square tiles for a trivet that is a square 9 inches on a side cost $0.17 each. What is the cost of the tiles?
 _____

RETEACH   Areas of Triangles and Trapezoids

Linda's mother is covering a table top with vinyl material. The table top is in the shape of a trapezoid. The lengths of the bases are 30 in. and 60 in. The height is 25.5 in. How many square in. of vinyl does she need?

Remember

Add the bases before multiplying.

$$A = \tfrac{1}{2}(b_1 + b_2)h$$
$$A = \tfrac{1}{2} \cdot \underline{(30 + 60)} \cdot 25.5$$
$$A = \tfrac{1}{2} \cdot 90 \cdot 25.5$$
$$A = 1{,}147.5$$

She needs 1,147.5 square inches of vinyl.

Find the areas of each triangle or trapezoid.

1.

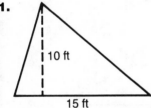

10 ft
15 ft

A = _____

2.

15 ft
9 ft
12 ft

A = _____

3.

10 ft
8 ft
12 ft

A = _____

4.

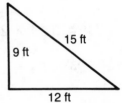

45 in.
35.5 in.
80 in.

A = _____

5. base$_1$ = 40 cm
base$_2$ = 25 cm
height = 17 cm   A = _____

6. base$_1$ = 16.1 cm
base$_2$ = 16.5 cm
height = 3.7 cm   A = _____

Find the areas of the trapezoid and the three triangles.

7. Trapezoid area: _____

8. Triangle A: _____

9. Triangle B: _____

10. Triangle C: _____

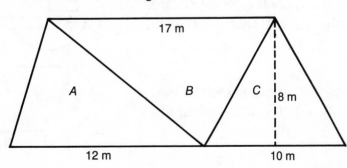

17 m
A
B
C
8 m
12 m
10 m

RETEACH   Area of Circles

Rick's dog is kept in a circular pen. A rope from the outer
edge to a stake in the center would be 15 feet long. How
large is the area in which the dog can move?

> **Remember**
>
> The area of a circle is π times the radius squared.
>
> $$A = \pi r^2 = \pi \cdot r \cdot r$$
> $$A \approx 3.14 \cdot 15^2 \approx 3.14 \cdot 15 \cdot 15$$
> $$A \approx 706.5$$

Rick's dog has approximately 706.5 square feet of running
area.

Find the area of each circle. Use 3.14 for π. Fill in the
blanks.

1. $r = 12$ ft $A = \pi \times r^2 = 3.14 \times 12 \times 12 =$ _____ ft^2

2. $r = 20$ ft $A = \pi \times 20^2 = 3.14 \times 20 \times 20 =$ _____ ft^2

3. $r = 24$ in. $A = 3.14 \times 24 \times 24 =$ _____ in.^{2}

4. $r = 18.5$ in. $A =$ _____ $\times$ _____ $\times$ _____ $=$ _____ in.^{2}

5. $r = 1.3$ cm $A =$ _____ cm^2 **6.** $d = 18$ in. $A =$ _____ in.^{2}

7. $r = 3.7$ m $A =$ _____ m^2 **8.** $r = 6.8$ m $A =$ _____ m^2

9. $d = 18.4$ in. $A =$ _____ in.^{2} **10.** $d = 19.6$ m $A =$ _____ m^2

11. $r = 3.75$ ft $A =$ _____ ft^2 **12.** $r = 8.82$ ft $A =$ _____ ft^2

Solve.

13. A circular rabbit pen is attached to a
corner of a shed. Over how much area
can the rabbit roam? $\left(\text{Use } \frac{3}{4} \text{ of the circle.}\right)$ _____ ft^2

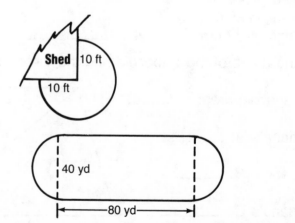

14. A region has the shape shown in the
figure at right. What is the area of the
region? _____ yd^2

Name _____ Date _____

While on vacation, the Schwartz family stopped at a display stand which was built like the one at the right. What is the name of the solid that makes up the top of the stand?

| Remember |
The base of the top has five sides. Be sure to name the base correctly.

The top of the display stand is a pentagonal pyramid.

Write a name for each figure.

Number of sides on base	Name of base	Name of pyramid
1. 3	triangle	
2. 4	rectangle	
3. 5	pentagon	
4. 6	hexagon	

5.

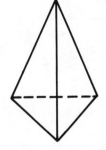

_____ pyramid

6.

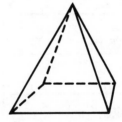

_____ pyramid

7.

_____ pyramid

8.

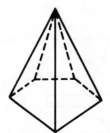

_____ pyramid

RETEACH Surface Area

The third pyramid of Giza in Egypt has the shape of a
square pyramid. The base of the pyramid is 105 m on a side.
Each triangular side has a height of 83.9 m. What is the
surface area of the pyramid?

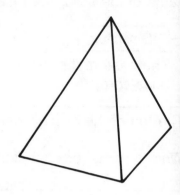

Remember

A square pyramid has 4 sides.

$$S = \text{area of base} + 4(\text{area of face})$$
$$S = \text{side} \times \text{side} + 4\left(\tfrac{1}{2} \text{ base} \times \text{height}\right)$$
$$S = 105 \cdot 105 + 4\left(\tfrac{1}{2} \cdot 105 \cdot 83.9\right)$$

$S = 28{,}644$

The surface area is about 28,644 m^2.

Several of the Egyptian pyramids are square pyramids.
Complete the table.

Pyramid	1. Second Pyramid of Giza	2. Merenre	3. Userkaf
Side of base	214.5 m	78.5 m	73.5 m
Height of triangles	179 m	65.6 m	59.7 m
Area of base	$(214.5)^2 =$ _____	_____	_____
Area of each triangle	$\tfrac{1}{2} \cdot 214.5 \cdot 179 =$ _____	_____	_____
Total surface area	_____	_____	_____

Use with pages 370–371.

RETEACH   Volume

Larry's father has a grain-storage bin on his farm. If the
radius of the base of the bin is 10.5 ft and the height is 21 ft,
what is the volume of the bin to the nearest cubic foot?

Remember

$V = Bh$ $B = \pi r^2$
$V = \pi r^2 h$
$V = 3.14 \cdot 10.5 \cdot 10.5 \cdot 21$
$V = 7{,}269.885$

The volume of the bin is about 7,270 ft³.

Find the volume of each cylinder, and fill in the blanks.

1. $r = 5$ ft, $h = 12$ ft $V = 3.14 \cdot$ _____ $\cdot$ _____ $\cdot$ 12 = _____ ft³

2. $r = 6.2$ ft, $h = 14$ ft $V = 3.14 \cdot$ _____ $\cdot$ _____ $\cdot$ 14 = _____ ft³

3. $r = 10$ ft, $h = 12$ ft $V = 3.14 \cdot$ _____ $\cdot$ _____ $\cdot$ _____ = _____ ft³

4. $r = 6$, $h = 4$ $V = 3.14 \cdot$ _____ $\cdot$ _____ $\cdot$ _____ = _____

Solve for volumes of cylinders with these dimensions.

5. $r = 16$ cm, $h = 5.6$ cm

  $V =$ _____ cm³

6. $r = 16$ m, $h = 22$ m

  $V =$ _____ m³

7. $r = 8$ in., $h = 25$ in.

  $V =$ _____ in.³

8. $r = 23$ in., $h = 72$ in.

  $V =$ _____ in.³

9. $r = 10.1$ m, $h = 14$ m

  $V =$ _____ m³

10. $r = 12.3$ ft, $h = 14.1$ ft

  $V =$ _____ ft³

Find the volumes of these figures.

11.

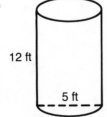

12 ft

5 ft

$V =$ _____

12.

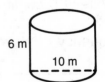

6 m

10 m

$V =$ _____

Name _____ Date _____

The height of each of the 10 girls on the seventh-grade
basketball team was measured. The heights in inches were
62, 63, 60, 59, 58, 61, 57, 65, 62, and 63.
Here is the data organized in a frequency distribution table.

HEIGHTS OF GIRLS (IN INCHES)

Interval	Tally	Frequency	Relative frequency
64–65	/	1	$\frac{1}{10}$, or 10%
62–63	////	4	$\frac{4}{10}$, or 40%
60–61	//	2	$\frac{2}{10}$, or 20%
58–59	//	2	$\frac{2}{10}$, or 20%
56–57	/	1	$\frac{1}{10}$, or 10%
TOTAL	10	10	100%

What percent of the girls are listed in the 62–63 interval?

Remember

Relative frequency is the ratio of the frequency for the
interval to the total.
The frequency of girls in the 62–63 interval is 4.
The total is 10.

$$4 \div 10 = \frac{4}{10} = 40\%$$

The 62–63 interval consists of 40% of the girls.

The height of each of the 10 boys on the seventh-grade
basketball team is measured. The heights in centimeters
are 164, 152, 157, 145, 163, 158, 150, 155, 161, and 165.

1. Draw a frequency distribution table on another page. Start
   with 145 and use intervals of 5 centimeters.

2. What is the relative frequency of players in the
   155–159 class? _____

Name _____ Date _____

RETEACH | Range, Median, and Mode

During the first 10 weeks of school, George had English test scores of 90, 92, 93, 88, 88, 95, 97, 87, 98, and 85. Find the median of these scores.

Remember

The median is the middle number in a set of ordered data. When there are two middle numbers, add the two middle numbers and divide by 2 to find the median.

$$\frac{90 + 92}{2} = \frac{182}{2} = 91$$

The median is 91.

For each set of data, find the range, median, and mode.

Item	Set of data	Range	Median	Mode(s)
1. Points scored in football	7, 13, 18, 24, 9, 3, 18			
2. Stolen bases in a season	60, 35, 47, 85, 85, 75, 70			
3. Push-ups done per day	7, 10, 13, 8, 15, 21, 13			
4. Problems per day	19, 25, 20, 37, 21, 36, 21			
5. Newspapers delivered	125, 120, 118, 130, 125, 133, 127			

Solve.

6. A marathon runner ran these distances during a week of practice: 10 km, 15 km, 12 km, 14 km, 8 km, 16 km, 16 km. Find the range, median, and mode for this data.

RETEACH Mean

Members of the seventh-grade class were asked to vote for their favorite sport. The results of the voting are summarized in the table. Find the mean of this data. Round the answer to the nearest tenth.

FAVORITE SPORT	
Football	5
Basketball	3
Baseball	6
Soccer	7
Gymnastics	1
Track	2
Tennis	5

Remember

The mean, also called the *average,* is the sum of the numbers divided by the number of numbers.

$$\frac{5 + 3 + 6 + 7 + 1 + 2 + 5}{7} = 4.2857$$

The mean is about 4.3 votes.

Find the mean for each set of data.

1. 63, 42, 94, 25, 66 _____

2. 28, 210, 95, 100, 171, 110 _____

3. 317, 473, 257, 397 _____

4. 245, 510, 365, 250, 585 _____

5. $2.50, $3.75, $1.25, $6.10 _____

6. 2.6, 3.5, 5.7, 8.3, 4.9 _____

Find the mean for each set of data. Round to the nearest tenth.

7. 85, 36, 27, 56, 17, 98 _____

8. 12, 14, 17, 21, 19, 15, 18 _____

Members of the seventh-grade class were asked to vote for which of 7 beverages they would like to have at their party. The results of the voting are summarized in this table.

9. Find the range of this data. _____

10. Find the median of this data. _____

11. Find the mode of this data. _____

12. Find the mean of this data to the nearest tenth. _____

FAVORITE BEVERAGE	
Orange juice	6
Grape juice	6
Lemonade	5
Chocolate milk	7
Water	2
Milk	3
Grapefruit juice	1

Use with pages 390–391.

RETEACH   Pictographs and Bar Graphs

The most home runs hit by a Major-League baseball player for the years 1981 to 1984 are listed in the table. Draw a pictograph using the data from this table.

MAJOR-LEAGUE HOME RUNS HIT BY A SINGLE PLAYER	
Year	Home runs
1981	31
1982	39
1983	40
1984	43

Remember

Choose a reasonable scale unit for the pictograph.

Use units of 5 as the scale unit. Use a baseball as the symbol to represent 5 home runs.

Round the results from the table to the nearest 5 home runs. Write the years in order and draw the correct number of symbols next to each year. Indicate the value of the symbol and choose the title.

MAJOR LEAGUE HOME RUNS HIT BY A SINGLE PLAYER	
Year	Home runs
1981	⚾ ⚾ ⚾ ⚾ ⚾ ⚾
1982	⚾ ⚾ ⚾ ⚾ ⚾ ⚾ ⚾ ⚾
1983	⚾ ⚾ ⚾ ⚾ ⚾ ⚾ ⚾ ⚾
1984	⚾ ⚾ ⚾ ⚾ ⚾ ⚾ ⚾ ⚾ ⚾

⚾ = 5 home runs

1. Use the table of runs batted in (RBI) to draw a pictograph on another page.

2. To which place would you round these numbers? _____

3. Which number would represent the scale unit? _____

4. How many symbols would be used for 1980? _____

MAJOR-LEAGUE RUNS BATTED IN BY A SINGLE PLAYER	
Year	RBI's
1976	109
1977	119
1978	139
1979	139
1980	122

RETEACH Broken-Line Graphs

The chart shows the number of patents issued for inventions in the United States every tenth year between the years 1800 and 1850. Draw a broken-line graph using this data.

NUMBER OF U.S. PATENTS (SELECTED YEARS)	
1800	41
1810	223
1820	155
1830	544
1840	458
1850	883

Remember

Be sure to choose appropriate scales for each axis.

For the vertical axis, start at 0 and increase the scale by increments of 100 up to 1,000.

Draw and label the vertical and the horizontal axes. Place a dot on the graph to represent each number from the data, and connect the dots with line segments. Write a title on the graph.

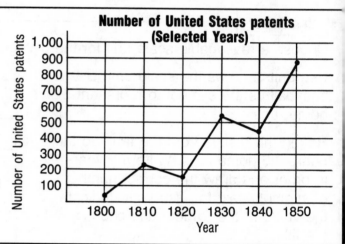

1. Use the data in the table to draw a broken-line graph.

2. Tommy and the Wildfires' hit record "I Love Love" sold 7,000 copies in May, 23,000 copies in June, 37,000 copies in July, 49,000 copies in August, and 28,000 copies in September. Use the information to draw a broken-line graph.

U.S. POPULATION PER SQUARE MILE 1790–1850	
1790	4.5
1800	6.1
1810	4.3
1820	5.5
1830	7.4
1840	9.8
1850	7.9

Use with pages 396–397.

RETEACH   Circle Graphs

A survey taken at Jefferson High School determines which of 5 animals the students like best. The results of the survey are shown in the table. Use this information to draw a circle graph.

FAVORITE ANIMALS		
Type of animal	Number of votes	Percent of total
Cat	55	24%
Dog	59	26%
Deer	40	17%
Raccoon	40	17%
Horse	36	16%

Remember

In order to find the measures of the central angles, multiply each percent by 360°.

24% of 360° ≈ 86°
26% of 360° ≈ 94°
17% of 360° ≈ 61°
16% of 360° ≈ 58°

Use each set of data to draw a circle graph.

1.

VOTING RESULTS FOR CLASS PRESIDENT		
Candidates	Percent of total	Central angle
Regina	17%	$0.17 \cdot 360° = 61.2° \approx 61°$
Larry	22%	$0.22 \cdot 360° = 79.2° \approx 79°$
Betty	13%	$0.13 \cdot 360° = 46.8° \approx 47°$
Reggie	20%	$0.20 \cdot 360° = 72°$
Veronica	28%	$0.28 \cdot 360° = 100.8° \approx 101°$

2.

COMPOSITION OF JEFFERSON JESPER'S JAZZ BAND		
Instrument	Fraction of total	Percent of total
Horn	$\frac{1}{2}$	50%
Guitar	$\frac{5}{28}$	18%
Percussion	$\frac{9}{28}$	32%

Name _____ Date _____

At the Bloomville county fair, there is an apple-bobbing contest. In a barrel of 29 apples, 24 are red and 5 are green. What is the probability of picking a green apple?

Remember

Be sure to use the number of favorable outcomes as the numerator.

$$\text{probability} = \frac{\text{number of green apples}}{\text{number of apples in barrel}}$$

$$P(\text{green}) = \frac{5}{29}$$

There are 5 chances out of 29 that a green apple will be picked.

You are going to spin the spinner once. Find each probability.

1. P(black) ____

2. P(green) ____

3. P(orange or red) ____

4. P(red or black or blue) ____

5. P(not green) ____

6. P(not blue or red) ____

One card is selected at random from a standard deck of 52 cards. Find each probability.

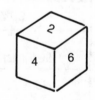

7. P(king) ____

8. P(queen or jack) ____

9. P(not a jack) ____

10. P(a club) ____

11. P(a black card) ____

12. P(not a spade) ____

Determine the number of possible outcomes and the number of favorable outcomes for

13. spinning a spinner.

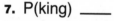

14. tossing a number cube.

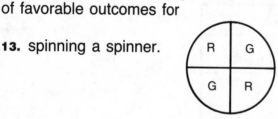

RETEACH **Tree Diagrams and Sample Space**

Mary has 3 blouses and 4 skirts that she can mix and match.
Draw a tree diagram to show how many different outfits Mary
can put together.

Remember

Be sure to list all of the possible outcomes.

Choice Blouse	Choice Skirt	Possible Outcomes

a —1—————— a1
—2—————— a2
—3—————— a3
—4—————— a4

b —1—————— b1
—2—————— b2
—3—————— b3
—4—————— b4

c —1—————— c1
—2—————— c2
—3—————— c3
—4—————— c4

Mary can put together 12 different outfits.

Draw a tree diagram for each event on another page. Write
the number of possible outcomes.

1. Tossing the coin and spinning the
spinner.

_____

2. Rolling the number cube and tossing the
coin.

_____

3. Spinning each spinner.

_____

4. Tossing two coins.

_____

Use with pages 404–405.

RETEACH Probability and Sample Spaces

If you spin the spinner twice, what is the
probability that the spinner will stop on
an even number both times?

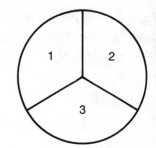

Remember

A probability is found by dividing the number of favorable
outcomes by the number of possible outcomes.

$$\text{probability} = \frac{\text{number of favorable outcomes}}{\text{number of possible outcomes}}$$

$$P(\text{even}) = \frac{1}{6}$$

The probability that the spinner will stop on an even number
both times is $\frac{1}{6}$.

You are going to spin the spinner once. Find each
probability.

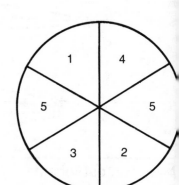

1. P(3) ____

2. P(2 or 4) ____

3. P(5) ____

4. P(odd number) ____

5. P(even number) ____

6. P(7) ____

7. P(5 or 1) ____

8. P(not 7) ____

A six-sided number cube is tossed twice. Prepare a sample
space to help find each probability.

9. P(both tosses a 2) _____

10. P(both tosses an even number) _____

11. P(sum of both tosses greater than 6) _____

12. P(sum of tosses less than 7) _____

13. P(sum of tosses are primes) _____

14. P(sum of tosses less than 5 or greater than 9) _____

Use with pages 406–407.

Name _____ Date _____

A coin is tossed and a six-sided number cube is rolled. What is the probability of tossing heads and a 4?

Remember

Because tossing a coin and rolling the number are independent events, you must multiply.

$$P(\text{heads, then } 4) = P(\text{heads}) \cdot P(4)$$
$$P = \frac{1}{2} \cdot \frac{1}{6} = \frac{1}{12}$$

The probability of tossing heads and a 4 is $\frac{1}{12}$.

Find the probability of each event. Toss a coin and roll a six-sided number cube.

1. P(heads, 3) _____

2. P(tails, 6) _____

3. P(heads, 1 or 2) _____

4. P(heads or tails, 4) _____

5. P(heads, odd number) _____

6. P(tails, not 5) _____

Find the probability of each event. Spin the spinner and toss a six-sided number cube.

7. P(A, 5) _____

8. P(B, 2 or 3) _____

9. P(A or B, odd number) _____

10. P(C, not 6) _____

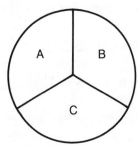

Solve.

11. One bag of marbles contains 3 red marbles and 2 black marbles. Another bag of marbles contains 4 blue marbles and 5 white marbles. Pick one marble from each bag. What is the probability of picking a black marble and a white marble?

_____

Name _____ Date _____

RETEACH Dependent Events

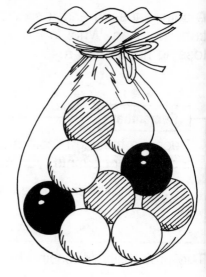

A bag contains 3 red marbles, 4 green marbles, and 2 blue marbles. Pick a marble, but do not replace it. Then, pick a second marble. What is the probability of picking a red marble and then a blue marble?

Remember

In a dependent event, be sure to show the effect of the outcome of the first event on the probability of the second event.

Because the first marble is not replaced, there are only 8 marbles remaining after the red one has been picked. So, the probability of picking a blue marble *after* removing a red marble is $\frac{2}{8}$, not $\frac{2}{9}$.

$$P(\text{red, then blue}) = \frac{3}{9} \cdot \frac{2}{8} = \frac{1}{12}$$

The probability of picking a red marble and then picking a blue marble is $\frac{1}{12}$.

A bag contains 3 blue marbles, 3 red marbles, and 2 green marbles. Pick a marble. Do not replace it. Then, pick another marble. Find the probability of each event.

1. P(blue, then green) _____

2. P(red, then red) _____

3. P(red, then blue or green) _____

4. P(non-red, then red) _____

5. P(non-green, then non-green) _____

6. P(green, then red or blue) _____

Solve.

7. Phillip has 6 red socks, 4 green socks, and 2 blue socks in a drawer. If he picks a blue sock, what is the probability that the second sock will be blue?

_____

Use with pages 412–413.

Name _____ Date _____

Daytona Beach, Florida, is 7 feet above sea level. The lowest point in New Orleans, Louisiana, is 5 feet below sea level. Which city has the higher elevation?

Remember

Use a number line to compare integers. The integer to the right is always greater than the integer to the left.

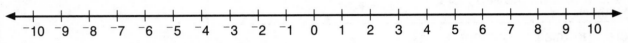

The number 7 is to the right of ⁻5.

Daytona Beach has the higher elevation.

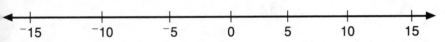

Using the number line as a guide, write >, <, or = for ◯.

1. ⁻7 ◯ 5   **2.** 0 ◯ 3   **3.** 0 ◯ ⁻3   **4.** ⁻2 ◯ ⁻3

5. ⁻6 ◯ ⁻1   **6.** 7 ◯ 4   **7.** ⁻15 ◯ 15   **8.** ⁻2 ◯ ⁻12

9. ⁻3 ◯ ⁻1   **10.** ⁻8 ◯ 2   **11.** 1 ◯ ⁻1   **12.** ⁻13 ◯ ⁻15

Order each set of integers from the least to the greatest.

13. 0, 1, ⁻1, 2, ⁻2   **14.** ⁻5, 6, ⁻6, ⁻4   **15.** 0, ⁻14, ⁻15, 13, 12

_____   _____   _____

Solve.

16. The lowest depth in Asia is the Dead Sea, which is 1,312 feet below sea level. The lowest depth in South America is located in Argentina, and is 131 feet below sea level. Which site has the lower depth? _____

Name _____ Date _____

RETEACH Properties of Integers

Find the missing number in the expression.
$^-3(^-4 + ^-5) = (^-3 \cdot$ _____ $+ ^-3 \cdot ^-5)$

Remember

The Distributive Property also applies to integers. The Distributive Property says that to multiply a sum by a number, you can multiply each addend by the number and then add the products.

Here, the missing number is $^-4$.

Use the properties of addition and multiplication of integers to find the missing integer.

1. _____ $+ ^-3 = ^-3 + ^-4$

2. $^-14 + 7 = 7 +$ _____

3. $^-3 + (^-5 + 6) = ^-3 ($ _____ $+ ^-5)$

4. $(^-11 +$ _____ $) + 6 = (^-3 + ^-11) + 6$

5. $(2 + 5) + ^-3 =$ _____ $+ (5 + ^-3)$

6. $^-14 + (^-7 + ^-6) = (^-7 + ^-6) +$ _____

7. $^-3 \cdot ^-5 =$ _____ $\cdot ^-3$

8. $^-11 \cdot$ _____ $= ^-14 \cdot ^-11$

9. $(^-7 \cdot ^-5) \cdot 4 = (^-5 \cdot$ _____ $) \cdot 4$

10. $35 \cdot (^-7 \cdot ^-11) = 35 (^-11 \cdot$ _____ $)$

11. $(^-4 \cdot ^-3) \cdot ^-14 = ^-4 \cdot ($ _____ $\cdot ^-14)$

12. $(^-14 \cdot$ _____ $) \cdot ^-7 = ^-14 \cdot (^-6 \cdot ^-7)$

13. $^-3 \cdot$ _____ $= 0$

14. $^-3 +$ _____ $= 0$

15. $^-35 \cdot$ _____ $= ^-35$

16. $^-80 =$ _____ $\cdot ^-80$

17. $^-3(5 + ^-4) = ^-3(^-4 +$ _____ $)$

18. $^-18(6 + ^-3) = ^-18(^-3 +$ _____ $)$

19. $^-3(5 + ^-4) =$ _____ $\cdot 5 + ^-3 \cdot ^-4$

20. $^-18($ _____ $+ ^-3) = ^-18 \cdot 5 + ^-18 \cdot ^-$

21. $(7 + ^-2)6 = 6 \cdot 7 + 6 \cdot$ _____

22. $9 + (8 + ^-1) = (9 + 8) +$ _____

23. $(8 + ^-3) + 5 = 8 + (^-3 +$ _____ $)$

24. $^-4(^-6 + ^-1) = (^-4 \cdot$ _____ $+ ^-4 \cdot ^-1$

120

Use with pages 426–427.

Name _____ Date _____

The temperature on a cold night in January reached ⁻12°F.
The temperature rose 42°F the next day. What was the
temperature reading after the increase?

```
━ 110
━ 100
━ 90
━ 80
━ 70
━ 60
━ 50
━ 40
━ 30
━ 20
━ 10
━ 0
━ 10
━ 20
```

Remember

When two integers have different signs, subtract the
numbers without the signs. Use the sign of the integer
farther from zero.

$$^-12 + {}^+42$$
$$= {}^+(42 - 12) = {}^+30°$$

The temperature after the increase was ⁺30°F.

Add. Use a number line if necessary.

1. ⁻3 + 5 = _____

2. 3 + ⁻5 = _____

3. 15 + ⁻7 = _____

4. ⁻15 + 7 = _____

5. ⁻8 + 8 = _____

6. ⁻11 + 5 = _____

7. 3 + ⁻14 = _____

8. ⁻7 + ⁻7 = _____

9. ⁻6 + ⁻3 = _____

10. ⁻14 + 6 = _____

11. ⁻11 + ⁻11 = _____

12. ⁻11 + 11 = _____

13. ⁻41 + 20 = _____

14. ⁻163 + 14 = _____

15. 65 + ⁻50 = _____

Solve.

16. The record low temperature for Indiana is ⁻35°F. The
    record high temperature is 151°F higher. What is the
    record high temperature? _____

17. The lowest temperature ever recorded in the United
    States is ⁻80°F. The highest temperature is 214°F higher.
    What is the record high temperature? _____

RETEACH Subtracting Integers

The highest elevation in California is the top of Mount Whitney, which is 14,494 feet above sea level. The lowest depth is in Death Valley, which is 282 feet below sea level ($^-$282 feet). What is the difference between these locations?

Remember

To subtract an integer, simply add its opposite.

$$\left.\begin{array}{l} 14{,}494 - {}^-282 \\ = 14{,}494 + 282 \\ = 14{,}776 \end{array}\right\} \text{opposites}$$

The difference in altitudes is 14,776 feet.

Subtract.

1. $18 - 6 =$ _____

2. $^-15 - 3 =$ _____

3. $^-10 - 7 =$ _____

4. $14 - {}^-5 =$ _____

5. $16 - {}^-3 =$ _____

6. $4 - {}^-4 =$ _____

7. $^-5 - {}^-3 =$ _____

8. $0 - 14 =$ _____

9. $^-14 - 0 =$ _____

10. $16 - {}^-20 =$ _____

11. $41 - {}^-16 =$ _____

12. $^-11 - 4 =$ _____

13. $^-11 - {}^-4 =$ _____

14. $^-8 - {}^-3 =$ _____

15. $^-8 - 7 =$ _____

Solve.

16. The highest elevation in Louisiana is 535 feet above sea level. The lowest depth in Louisiana is 5 feet below sea level. What is the difference between the depth and the height?

_____

17. The highest elevation in Asia is on top of Mount Everest ($^+$29,028 ft). The lowest depth is in the Dead Sea ($^-$1,312 ft). Find the difference between the locations.

_____

Use with pages 430–431.

Name _____ Date _____

An airplane is descending at the rate of 500 ft/min. How much higher was the plane 5 min ago ($^-5$ min)?

Remember

The product of two integers that have like signs is positive.

$$^-500 \cdot {}^-5 = 2{,}500$$

The plane was 2,500 ft higher 5 min ago.

Find the product.

1. $^-5 \times {}^-3 =$ _____

2. $^-6 \times {}^-5 =$ _____

3. $^-8 \times {}^-6 =$ _____

4. $^-12 \times {}^-13 =$ _____

5. $6 \times 7 =$ _____

6. $11 \times 14 =$ _____

7. $13 \times 6 =$ _____

8. $80 \times 17 =$ _____

9. $^-6 \times {}^-8 =$ _____

10. $^-6 \times {}^+8 =$ _____

11. $14 \times {}^-10 =$ _____

12. $80 \times {}^-11 =$ _____

13. $^-6({}^-10 + 5) =$ _____

14. $^-10({}^-5 + {}^-6) =$ _____

15. $^-11(6 - {}^-3) =$ _____

Solve.

16. A submarine is descending from the surface at the rate of 65 ft/min (ascending at $^-65$ ft/min). What is the depth of the submarine after 3 min? _____

17. A plane is descending at the rate of 300 ft/min (climbing at $^-300$ ft/min). How much higher was the plane 4 min ago (time $= {}^-4$)? _____

18. A meteor falls at the rate of 25 mi/min (climbing at $^-25$ mi/min). How much higher was the meteor 1 minute ago (time $= {}^-1$)? _____

RETEACH Dividing Integers

Divide ⁻2,400 ÷ 12.

Remember

The quotient is negative if the two integers have unlike signs.

⁻2,400 ÷ 12 = ⁻200

Divide.

1. ⁻64 ÷ 4 = _____

2. ⁻8 ÷ 2 = _____

3. 25 ÷ ⁻5 = _____

4. 72 ÷ ⁻4 = _____

5. ⁻100 ÷ ⁻20 = _____

6. ⁻65 ÷ ⁻5 = _____

7. ⁻112 ÷ ⁻4 = _____

8. 64 ÷ 4 = _____

9. 0 ÷ ⁻31 = _____

10. ⁻18 ÷ 6 = _____

11. ⁻22 ÷ ⁻1 = _____

12. ⁻114 ÷ ⁻2 = _____

13. ⁻225 ÷ 15 = _____

14. ⁻225 ÷ ⁻15 = _____

15. ⁻46 ÷ ⁻2 = _____

16. ⁻400 ÷ ⁻4 = _____

17. ⁻115 ÷ 5 = _____

18. 84 ÷ ⁻2 = _____

Solve.

19. A submarine descended from the surface of the water to 600 feet below the surface in 5 minutes. What was the average rate of change in position? Give this depth as a negative number. _____

Use with pages 436–437.

RETEACH · Solving Equations with Integers

The EZ Company manufactures widgets. Overhead is $1,200 a day. They sell each widget for $4. If they produce x widgets per day, the profit for the company is $^-1,200 + 4x$ dollars. How much must the company produce per day to produce a profit of $2,000?

The equation is $^-1,200 + 4x = 2,000$.

Remember

Perform the same operation on both sides of the equation.

$$^-1,200 + 4x = 2,000$$
$$1,200 + {}^-1,200 + 4x = 1,200 + 2,000$$
$$4x = 3,200$$
$$\frac{4x}{4} = \frac{3,200}{4}$$
$$x = 800$$

The company must produce 800 widgets per day.

Solve the equation.

1. $x + {}^-10 = 15$ _____

2. $r + {}^-10 = {}^-15$ _____

3. $e - {}^-10 = 14$ _____

4. $\frac{a}{^-5} = {}^-30$ _____

5. $^-5x = 45$ _____

6. $^-3s = {}^-48$ _____

7. $^-2b = {}^-10$ _____

8. $^-7y = {}^-98$ _____

9. $^-15z = {}^-225$ _____

10. $^-5t + 10 = 25$ _____

11. $^-11p - 15 = 51$ _____

12. $^-12x + 13 = {}^-59$ _____

Solve.

13. The profit function for EZ company is $^-3000 + 12x$, where x is the number of items produced per day. How many items must they produce per day for a profit of $1,800? _____

14. The cost of operating a plant is represented by the expression $8,000 - 2x$. Find a value of x for which the cost is $5,000. _____

Name_____ Date_____

Yoshika's father travels extensively in his job. The company allows a maximum of $95 per day for expenses. If his motel bill for the day is $52.80, how much can he spend for other expenses? This is equivalent to solving the inequality:
$x + \$52.80 \le \$95$.

Remember

Write the answer as an inequality.

$$x + 52.80 = 95$$
$$x + 52.80 - 52.80 = 95 - 52.80$$
$$x = 42.20$$

The solution to the inequality is $x \le 42.20$.

Yoshika's father can spend $42.20 *or less* for other expenses.

Write the solution for the inequality.

1. $m + 15 < 35$ _____

2. $n - 15 > 40$ _____

3. $n + 14 < {}^-8$ _____

4. $p - 31 > {}^-56$ _____

5. $m - 3 \le 17$ _____

6. $r + 16 \ge 46$ _____

7. $2r \le 56$ _____

8. $3r \ge 27$ _____

9. $5r \le {}^-80$ _____

10. $7r \ge {}^-98$ _____

11. $\frac{r}{16} < 1$ _____

12. $\frac{r}{14} > {}^-3$ _____

Solve.

13. A company allows a <u>maximum</u> of $120 per day for expenses. A salesperson spends $24.50 for gasoline and $43.75 for a motel on a particular day. How much can be spent for other expenses? _____

14. Yoshika's father receives a <u>maximum</u> of $36 for gasoline. If gasoline costs $1.20 per gallon, how many gallons can he buy? _____

RETEACH | Graphing Sentences

Eldon's mother has $250 in her checking account. The bank does not charge her for writing checks if she keeps a minimum balance of $200 in the account. What amount can she write her check for and avoid a charge?

Solve the inequality and graph the solution on a number line.

$x + 200 \leq 250$ Use the related equation. $x + 200 = 250$
$x + 200 - 200 = 250 - 200$
$x = 50$

Remember

Write the solution as an inequality. $x \leq 50$

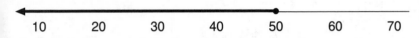

$x \leq 50$ means $x = 50$ or less. It means x includes 50 and all numbers to the left of 50 on a number line.

Eldon's mother's check can be for $50 or less.

Solve and graph each inequality.

1. $x + 8 < 10$ _____   **2.** $x - 8 < 10$ _____

3. $x + 4 \geq 11$ _____   **4.** $x - 4 > 14$ _____

5. $x + 6 < {}^-1$ _____   **6.** $x - 4 < {}^-7$ _____

7. $x + 3 \leq {}^-3$ _____   **8.** $x - 3 \leq {}^-9$ _____

Solve.

9. The 4-H club treasurer has a checking account. The bank does not charge for checks if a $50 balance is maintained. The checking account has an $83 balance. Draw a graph showing the amounts of the checks which can be written without paying a bank charge.

10. Eldon's father delivers appliances for a department store. He receives $25 for each appliance delivered. How many must he deliver in a week to earn <u>at least</u> $550? _____

Name _____ Date _____

Ross has drawn a coordinate system with the location of his family's house at the origin. He then plotted the places that he frequently visits on the coordinate system. What are the coordinates of the grocery store?

Remember

Write the x-coordinate first.

The grocery store is located at (2, ⁻2)

Write the coordinates of the locations.

1. Bill's house _____

2. Mark's house _____

3. Jennifer's house _____

4. the park _____

5. the theater _____

6. the bowling alley _____

7. the school _____

8. the record shop _____

9. the pizza parlor _____

Solve.

10. Draw a coordinate system and locate the points on the graph.

    A(5, 4), B(5, ⁻2), C(2, ⁻4), D(⁻4, ⁻4), E(⁻4, 2), F(⁻1, 4), G(2, 2). Then draw the line segments $\overline{AB}$, $\overline{AG}$, $\overline{AF}$, $\overline{BC}$, $\overline{CD}$, $\overline{CG}$, $\overline{DE}$, $\overline{EF}$, $\overline{EG}$.

11. Draw a coordinate system and locate these points on a coordinate system.

    A(0, 0), B(2, ⁻3), C(6, ⁻3), D(8, 0), E(4, 6), F(4, 1). Then draw solid-line segments $\overline{EA}$, $\overline{EB}$, $\overline{EC}$, $\overline{ED}$, $\overline{AB}$, $\overline{BC}$, $\overline{CD}$. Then draw dashed segments $\overline{FA}$, $\overline{FE}$, $\overline{FD}$.

Use with pages 448–449.

Name _____ Date _____

A junior-achievement company is renting a booth at a craft fair from which to sell cutting boards. They will make $2 profit from each board. The rent for the weekend is $5. The profit, y, for the weekend is represented by the equation

$y = 2x + {}^-5$, where x represents the number of cutting boards sold.

What is the profit if they sell 3, 5, or 7 items?

Remember

Set up a table and substitute values for x in the equation.

If x =	3	5	7
Then y =	1	5	9

If x = 3, y = 2(3) + ⁻5
y = 1

The profit is $1, $5, or $9.

Substitute the given values for x in the equation
$y = {}^-3x + 15$

1. x = 5 $y = {}^-3 \cdot 5 + 15 =$ _____

2. x = ⁻4 $y = {}^-3 \cdot {}^-4 + 15 =$ _____

3. x = ⁻3 _____   4. x = ⁻7 _____   5. x = 0 _____

Complete the table by substituting the given values for x.

6. $y = x - 7$

x	⁻2	⁻1	0	1	2
y	⁻9				

7. $y = {}^-4x - 10$

x	⁻3	0	1	4	7
y	2				

8. $y = \frac{x}{2} - 3$

x	⁻4	0	2	4	8
y	⁻5				

9. $y = 10 - \frac{x}{3}$

x	⁻3	0	3	6	9
y	11				

Name _____ Date _____

An airplane is flying past a flight station (the origin on the graph). The path of flight is described by the equation $y = {}^-2x + 4$. Use $x = {}^-1$, $x = 0$, and $x = 5$ to graph the path of flight.

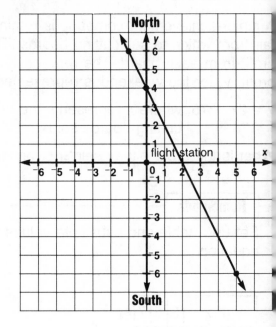

Remember

Plot the points in the correct order.

$$y = {}^-2x + 4$$

If $x =$	$^-1$	0	5
Then $y =$	6	4	$^-6$

The points are $(^-1, 6)$, $(0, 4)$, and $(5, {}^-6)$.

Set up a table and graph each equation. Use the given values of x.

1. $y = x - 5$; $x = {}^-2$, $x = 0$, $x = 6$

2. $y = x + 4$; $x = {}^-6$, $x = 0$, $x = 2$

3. $y = 3x$; $x = {}^-2$, $x = 0$, $x = 2$

4. $y = \frac{x}{4}$; $x = {}^-8$, $x = 0$, $x = 8$

5. $y = 2x - 4$; $x = {}^-1$, $x = 0$, $x = 4$

6. $y = {}^-3x + 2$; $x = {}^-1$, $x = 0$, $x = 2$

7. $y = \frac{x}{2} + 1$; $x = {}^-8$, $x = 0$, $x = 6$

8. $y = \frac{{}^-x}{2} + 1$; $x = {}^-6$, $x = 0$, $x = 8$

9. $y = \frac{x + 4}{3}$; $x = {}^-10$, $x = {}^-1$, $x = 5$

10. $y = \frac{2x - 4}{3}$; $x = {}^-4$, $x = {}^-1$, $x = 5$

Solve.

11. A car is passing a police radar unit (located at the origin) on a path described by the equation $y = 10x - 6$. Graph the equation.

12. A company produces x items at a cost of $y = 2x + 10$. Graph the equation for nonnegative values of x.

RETEACH ANSWER KEY

Page 1

1. ten thousands
2. hundred thousands
3. hundred thousands
4. millions
5. hundred thousands
6. ten millions
7. tens
8. ten thousands
9. ten millions

Page 2

1. >   2. >   3. <   4. <   5. =
6. <   7. >   8. >
9. 896; 8,836; 8,846; 37,733
10. 28,837; 29,375; 263, 398; 283, 389
11. 582, 298; 54,475, 279; 476, 743, 648; 498, 498, 374; 832, 382, 221

Page 3

1. 15, 35   2. 17, 52   3. 56, 33
4. 53, 127
5. 120, 872
6. 52, 53
7. 533; 1,359
8. 108; 1,024
9. 101, 724
10. 66, 810
11. 121 miles
12. $1,545

Page 4

1.–8. *Answers will vary. Accept any reasonable estimate.*
1. 23,000–25,000
2. 16,000–18,000
3. 12–14 million
4. 50,000–60,000
5. 23,000–25,000
6. 16,000–18,000
7. 12–14 million
8. 50,000–60,000
9. <   10. >   11. <

Page 5

1. a   2. a.   3. b.   4. a.   5. b.
6. b.   7. a.   8. a.
Answers will vary. Accept any reasonable estimate.
9. 4,000⁻
10. 8,000⁺
11. 50,000⁻

Page 5 (cont'd.)

12. 4,000,000⁻
13. 7,000,000⁺
14. 20,000⁺

Page 6

1. 5,152   2. 6,691   3. 5,960
4. 4,545   5. 490   6. 446   7. 2,265
8. 10,841   9. 9,482   10. 31,988
11. 21,916   12. 270,059
13. 216,704   14. 9,022,806

Page 7

1. 2,136   2. 813   3. 3,426
4. 6,375   5. 12   6. 158   7. 574
8. 59,039   9. 38,890
10. 49,685   11. 598,720
12. 523,201

Page 8

1. d   2. b   3. c   4. b   5. c
6. five hundredths
7. four thousandths
8. six ten-thousandths
9. nine hundred-thousandths
10. forty-five hundredths
11. forty-five thousandths

Page 9

1. T   2. F   3. F   4. T   5. F
6. <   7. <   8. >   9. >   10. >
11. >   12. >   13. <   14. >
15. 0.0005, 0.005, 0.5
16. 1.349, 1.3492, 1.35

Page 10

1. 0.06
2. 0.060
3. 0.1
4. 0.0025
5. 0.023
6. 0.02
7. 0.019
8. 0.0110

Page 11

1. <
2. >
3. >
4. >
5. <
6. <
Answers will vary. Accept any reasonable estimate.
7. 18–20   8. 40–50   9. 80–90

Page 11 (cont'd.)

10. $300–$400   11. 80–85
12. 90–105   13. 200–300
14. 390–410

Page 12

1. 42.53   2. 42.19   3. 42.48

Page 13

1. 2.55   2. 0.98   3. $5.25
4. $8.06   5. 0.15   6. 1.85
7. 5.068   8. 5.255   9. 86.997
10. 946.623   11. 0.139877
12. 0.003702
13. 0.002 miles per hour
14. 0.104 miles per hour

Page 14

1. Commutativity of multiplication
2. Associativity of multiplication
3. Commutativity of multiplication
4. Distributive principle
5. 8   6. 8   7. 9   8. 31   9. 9
10. 20

Page 15

1. 50; 500; 5,000; 50,000
2. 80; 800; 8,000; 80,000
3. 100; 1,000; 10,000; 100,000
4. 280; 2,800; 28,000; 280,000
5. 1,500; 15,000; 150,000; 1,500,000
6. about $2,000,000
7. about $120,000,000

Page 16

1. b.   2. d.   3. a.   4. 1,200
5. 1,400   6. 2,400   7. 10,000
8. 40,000   9. 1,800,000
10. 2,500,000   11. 16,000,000
Answers will vary. Accept any reasonable estimate.
12. 150⁻   13. 3,200⁺
14. 2,400⁻   15. 6,000
16. 25,000⁺
17. 180,000⁺

Page 17

1. 2,880   2. 1,278   3. 196
4. 414   5. 858   6. 2,520
7. 1,190   8. 3,234   9. 8,032
10. 11,763   11. 19,590
12. 51,444   13. $440.94

RETEACH ANSWER KEY

Page 17 (cont'd.)

14. $11,743.04 15. $546
16. $338.10

Page 18

1. 5,670; 6,048 2. 115,800;
   $1,331.70 3. 4,032 4. 1,116
5. 2,314 6. 1,272 7. 4,997
8. 34,992 9. 23,161 10. 73,640
11. 521,976 12. 1,512 six-packs
13. $88.90

Page 19

1. 2485
    7100
    73,485
2. 4 068
    20 340
    207,468
3. 3,990 4. 11,021 5. 48,972
6. 140,606 7. 597,429
8. 951,405 9. 482,924
10. 11,068,767

Page 20*

1. b. 2. c. 3. d. 4. 6.084
5. 4.1535 6. 0.45898
7. 0.12852
8. 0.7^- 9. 3^+ 10. 0.2^+
11. 1^+ 12. 3^- 13. 8^+

Page 21

1. 25.500 2. 49.634 3. 106.2
4. 193.2 5. 122.98 6. 22.572
7. 10.236 8. 5.075 9. 5.67
10. 17.974 11. $27.68 12. $9.38
13. 40.112 14. 10,954.766
15. 6.5625 g 16. 11.115 g

Page 22

1. 50
2. 3,600
3. 19; 190; 1,900; 19,000
4. 0.4; 4; 40; 400
5. 8.72; 87.2; 872; 8,720
6. 196; 1,960; 19,600; 196,000
7. 0.032; 0.32; 3.2; 32
8. 6,500 lb

Page 23

1. 0.0903 2. 0.00884 3. 0.945
4. 0.0240 5. 0.0255 6. 0.0801

Answers will vary. Accept any reasonable estimate.

Page 23 (cont'd.)

7. 0.5032 8. 0.0504
9. 0.17716 10. 0.3978
11. 0.2548 12. 0.017112
13. 10.8477 14. 0.145 kg
15. 0.10125 kg

Page 24

1. 9, 2, 18 2. 17, 2, 34
3. 0, 32, 0 4. 73, 5, 365
5. 1, 32, 32
6. 25, 4, 100
7. 0, 16, 0
8. 27, 3, 81
9. 19, 2, 38
10. 4, 47, 188
11. 6, 15, 90
12. 18, 1, 18
13. 6, 1, 6
14. 3, 2, 6
15. 3, 9, 27
16. 3, 15, 45
17. 1, 87, 87
18. 6, 6, 36
19. True
20. False
21. $144 \div 16 = 9$
22. $9 \times 16 = 144$

Page 25

1. 30 2. 20 3. 20 4. 300
5. 200 6. 20 7. 25 8. 2
9. 35 10. 20 11. 60 12. 800
13. 80 14. 8
15. 2.5 gallons per hour
16. 500 miles per hour

Page 26*

1. 4 2. 3 3. 3 4. 4 5. 3
6. 3 7. c 8. b 9. c
10. $1,000^+$
11. 500^+
12. 200^+
13. 800^+
14. 500^+
15. $3,000^+$
16. $5,000^+$
17. $10,000^+$
18. $5,000^+$

Page 27

1. 214 2. 128 3. 319 R6 4. 139
5. 36 6. 15 7. 449 8. 449 R5
9. 449 10. 1,002 11. 71,238

Page 27 (cont'd.)

12. 4,013 13. 1,106 R2 14. 1,02
15. $6.59 16. $2.12

Page 28

1. 105 2. 204 R10 3. 207
4. 101 5. 105 R4 6. 809 7.
8. 306 9. 601 10. 1,005 11.
12. 4,005 13. 2,003 R12 14. 10,
15. 107 acres
16. 105 acres

Page 29

1. 105 2. 109 3. 304 4. 207
5. 306 R7 6. 302 7. $18.04
8. $10.45 9. $10.08 10. 2,080
11. 104 12. 1,032 13. 2,008 R30
14. 1,003 15. $1.09

Page 30

1. $0.07 2. $0.06 3. $0.19
4. $0.64 5. $0.11 6. $0.24
7. $0.48 8. $0.04 9. $0.12

Page 31

1. C 2. B 3. A 4. D 5. D
6. B
7. 0.0027 in.
8. 0.00192 in.
9. 0.00215 lb

Page 32

1. 3.2 2. 5.3 3. 8.2 4. 0.05
5. 6.36 6. 0.03 7. 3.7 8. 0.3
9. 9.6 10. 0.78 11. 0.37
12. 0.78
13. 27.5 miles per gallon
14. 86 posts

Page 33

1. 5.3 2. 3.7 3. 5.2 4. 7.4
5. 10.8 6. 20.5 7. 1.68
8. 18.17 9. 0.58 10. 1.07
11. 4.914 12. 299.917 13. 0.433
14. 14.408 15. 1.0909
16. 16.8519 17. 0.4163
18. 1.5744

Page 34

1. no
2. yes
3. yes
4. yes

Page 34 (cont'd.)

5. no
6. no
7. no
8. yes
9. yes
10. no
11. yes
12. no
13. yes
14. no
15. yes
16. yes
17. no
18. yes
19. no
20. yes

Page 35

1. 36
2. 2.8561
3. 7×7; 49
4. $4 \times 4 \times 4$; 64
5. 64 6. 512 7. 255 8. 2.25
9. 29.791 10. 1,024 11. 2^3
12. 4^5 13. 9^2 14. 7^3 15. 3^4
16. 5^4 17. 12^2 18. 11^3 19. 10^5

Page 36

1. 6.25×10^4
2. 8.42×10^3
3. 1.62×10^3
4. 1.5×10^3
5. 1×10^4
6. 1.5×10^4
7. 1.5×10^2
8. 2×10
9. 8.56×10^4
10. 6.537×10^2
11. 5.6212×10^3
12. 8.907×10^6
13. 6.964×10^8
14. 1.55×10^7
15. 18,500
16. 2,000
17. 374.1
18. 189, 320

Page 37

1. 1, 2, 3, 4, 6, 9, 12, 18, 36
2. 1, 2, 3, 5, 6, 10, 15, 30
3. 1, 2, 3, 6
4. 1, 7
5. 1, 2, 7, 14
6. 1, 3, 7, 21
7. 1, 31

Page 37 (cont'd.)

8. 1, 2, 4, 7, 8, 14, 28, 56
9. 1, 5, 25
10. 1, 7, 49
11. 1, 2, 7, 14, 49, 98
12. 1, 2, 4, 5, 10, 20, 25, 50, 100
13. 1, 2, 4, 8, 16, 32
14. No
15. 1×40, 2×20, 4×10, 5×8

Page 38

1. 2, 5
2. 3.3
3. 2, 5, 7, 5
4. $2 \times 3 \times 5$
5. 2×11
6. $2^3 \times 7$
7. $2 \times 5 \times 19$
8. $2 \times 5^2 \times 7$
9. $2^4 \times 5^2$
10. 2^9
11. $2^2 \times 5^4$
12. $2 \times 3^2 \times 5$
13. 126 14. 60 15. 24 16. 270
17. 80 18. 150 19. 4 20. 3

Page 39

1. 5 2. 30 3. 4 4. 11 5. 6
6. 7 7. 10 8. 15 9. 50
10. 12 11. 60 12. 3 13. 1
14. 15 15. 8 ft 16. 8 in.

Page 40

1. 240
2. 120
3. 2×3^2, $2^3 \times 3$, 72
4. $2 \times 3 \times 5$, $3^2 \times 5$, 90
5. 5×19, $2 \times 5 \times 19$, 190
6. 1×13, 2^4, 208
7. 5^2, $2^2 \times 3 \times 5$, 300
8. $2^2 \times 3^2$, $2^4 \times 3$, 144

Page 41

1. 25 2. 35 3. 18 4. 39
5. 12 6. 60 7. 62 8. 72
9. 28 10. 8 11. 41 12. 0
13. 35 14. 95 15. $35

Page 42

1. no
2. yes
3. yes
4. no
5. $x = 6$

Page 42 (cont'd.)

6. $x = 12$
7. no solution
8. no solution
9. $x = 20$
10. $x = 20$
11. $x = 18$
12. $x = 10$
13. $x = 16$
14. $x = 4$
15. $x = 18$
16. no solution

Page 43

1. 25
2. 15
3. $x = 9$
4. $x = 18$
5. $x = 21$
6. $x = 16$
7. $x = 16$
8. $x = 92$
9. $x = 9$
10. $x = 37$
11. $x = 110$
12. $x = 1.7$
13. $x = 11$
14. $x = 37$
15. $57.95
16. $449.95

Page 44

1. 70 2. 112 3. 1 4. 2 5. 84
6. 7 7. 196 8. 98
9. false
10. false
11. true
12. false
13. true
14. false
15. 24
16. 15
17. no solution
18. 9
19. no solution
20. 6
21. no solution
22. 18
23. no solution
24. no solution
25. 18
26. 15

Page 45

1. 0.25 2. 21.6 3. 12 4. 12
5. 9 6. 4 7. 15 8. 72

RETEACH ANSWER KEY

Page 45 (cont'd.)

9. 3.2   10. 3.2   11. 1.2   12. 1.9
13. 28   14. 11.25   15. 8¢   16. 4

Page 46

1. 12   2. 15   3. 7.5, 30   4. 7
5. 5   6. 3   7. 18   8. 36   9. 35
10. 7   11. 5   12. 5   13. 56
14. 180   15. 160   16. 17   17. 5
18. 7   19. 70   20. 45   21. 84
22. 4   23. 13   24. 6   25. 171
26. 40   27. 80

Page 47

1. $\frac{5}{8}$ 2. $\frac{11}{12}$ 3. $\frac{7}{10}$ 4. $\frac{8}{13}$ 5. $\frac{7}{12}$

Page 48

1. $\frac{4}{15}$ 2. $\frac{1}{3}$ 3. $\frac{7}{17}$ 4. $\frac{6}{13}$ 5. $\frac{3}{4}$

6. $\frac{1}{3}$ 7. $\frac{2}{9}$ 8. $\frac{3}{4}$ 9. $\frac{2}{5}$

10. $\frac{2}{3}$ 11. $\frac{2}{5}$

Page 49

1. $\frac{21}{4}$ 2. $\frac{31}{8}$ 3. $\frac{18}{5}$ 4. $\frac{67}{10}$ 5. $\frac{55}{12}$

6. $\frac{17}{16}$ 7. $\frac{63}{20}$ 8. $\frac{75}{8}$ 9. $\frac{77}{10}$

10. c   11. c   12. d   13. a

Page 50

1. <   2. >   3. <   4. >   5. <
6. <   7. <   8. =   9. <
10. $\frac{5}{6}$, $\frac{7}{8}$, $\frac{8}{9}$

11. $\frac{3}{2}$, $\frac{9}{4}$, $\frac{8}{3}$

12. $\frac{13}{4}$, $\frac{10}{3}$, $\frac{7}{2}$

13. 7 half-cup containers
14. $2\frac{5}{8}$, $2\frac{2}{3}$, $2\frac{3}{4}$

Page 51*

1. >   2. <   3. <   4. <   5. >
6. >   7. >   8. <   9. >   10. <
11. 6–7   12. 13–14   13. 9–10
14. 7–8   15. 16–17   16. 1^+
17. $1\frac{1}{2}^-$ 18. $2\frac{1}{2}^-$ 19. 12^-
20. 40–41

Page 52

1. $1\frac{7}{10}$ 2. $\frac{7}{12}$ 3. $\frac{17}{24}$ 4. $\frac{7}{10}$ 5. $\frac{13}{18}$

6. $1\frac{13}{30}$ 7. $1\frac{7}{20}$ 8. $1\frac{7}{16}$ 9. $1\frac{7}{10}$

Page 53

1. $\frac{3}{8}$ 2. $\frac{3}{4}$ 3. $\frac{5}{16}$ 4. $\frac{2}{5}$ 5. $\frac{1}{10}$

6. $\frac{1}{16}$ 7. $\frac{7}{40}$ 8. $\frac{1}{18}$ 9. $\frac{7}{8}$ 10. $1\frac{1}{40}$

Page 54

1. $4\frac{1}{8}$ 2. $2\frac{1}{16}$ 3. $4\frac{17}{20}$ 4. $4\frac{1}{10}$

5. $3\frac{3}{10}$ 6. $4\frac{1}{7}$ 7. $4\frac{4}{9}$ 8. $6\frac{7}{15}$

9. $4\frac{3}{16}$ 10. $8\frac{3}{40}$

11. $5\frac{3}{20}$ yd

12. $4\frac{1}{4}$ yd

13. $4\frac{1}{2}$ yd

Page 55

1. $3\frac{1}{2}$ 2. $1\frac{3}{16}$ 3. $\frac{3}{8}$ 4. $2\frac{1}{6}$ 5. $4\frac{5}{12}$

6. $4\frac{13}{16}$ 7. $2\frac{9}{16}$ 8. $2\frac{3}{16}$ 9. $2\frac{1}{64}$

10. $2\frac{31}{64}$

11. $4\frac{1}{12}$ pages

Page 56

1. $12\frac{3}{4}$

2. $15\frac{1}{2}$

3. $17\frac{5}{8}$

4. $18\frac{11}{16}$

5. $2\frac{7}{8}$

6. $4\frac{15}{16}$

7. $2\frac{21}{40}$

8. $1\frac{33}{40}$

9. $5\frac{11}{20}$

10. $22\frac{23}{24}$

11. $6\frac{87}{100}$

12. $\frac{7}{24}$

13. $6\frac{15}{16}$

14. $8\frac{5}{8}$

Page 57

1. $7\frac{8}{15}$, $7\frac{8}{15}$

2. +, +

3. +, $8\frac{1}{4}$, $8\frac{1}{4}$

4. $4\frac{2}{3}$ 5. $4\frac{7}{20}$ 6. 10

7. $4\frac{37}{64}$ 8. $1\frac{27}{32}$ 9. $10\frac{27}{35}$

10. $F - \frac{2}{3} = 5\frac{3}{4}$;
    $F = 5\frac{3}{4} + \frac{2}{3} = 6\frac{5}{12}$

Page 58

1. 6 mile

2. $7\frac{7}{8}$ mile

3. $8\frac{1}{2}$ mile

4. $11\frac{1}{4}$ mile

5. $6\frac{1}{4}$ mile

6. 9 mile

7. $9\frac{7}{20}$ mile

8. $7\frac{1}{2}$ mile

9. $11\frac{7}{8}$

Page 59

1. $\frac{1 \times 3}{1 \times 20}$, $\frac{3}{20}$ 2. $\frac{1}{6}$ 3. $\frac{7}{30}$

4. $\frac{3}{14}$ 5. $\frac{44}{247}$

Page 60*

1. 30^- 2. 18   3. 8^- 4. 20^+ 5.
6. 66   7. >   8. <   9. <   10. <
11. >   12. >   13. <   14. >
15. <   16. <   17. >   18. <
19. 40   20. 80^+
21. 80   22. 100^-
23. 48^+ 24. 100^-

Page 61

1. $12\frac{4}{5}$ 2. 5   3. $\frac{1}{2}$ 4. $1\frac{2}{3}$

5. $10\frac{15}{16}$ 6. $4\frac{7}{8}$ 7. $17\frac{1}{4}$

8. $11\frac{1}{12}$ 9. 5   10. 20

11. $2\frac{1}{2}$ 12. $9\frac{1}{6}$ 13. $5\frac{1}{12}$

14. $16\frac{8}{49}$ 15. 20   16. $14\frac{1}{4}$

17. $20\frac{5}{8}$ 18. $29\frac{3}{8}$ 19. 10

20. $12\frac{2}{3}$

Page 62

1. 6   2. $4\frac{1}{2}$ 3. $6\frac{2}{3}$ 4. 8   5. $5\frac{1}{3}$

*Answers may vary. Accept any reasonable estimate.

age 62 (cont'd)

$15\frac{5}{9}$ **7.** $\frac{8}{9}$ **8.** $1\frac{1}{15}$ **9.** $1\frac{7}{8}$ **10.** $\frac{7}{10}$

age 63

$\frac{1}{2}$ **2.** $\frac{1}{4}$ **3.** $\frac{11}{24}$ **4.** $\frac{9}{32}$

$\frac{15}{56}$ **6.** $\frac{5}{12}$ **7.** 3 **8.** 12

2 **10.** 6 **11.** $\frac{11}{14}$ pound

age 64

1. 0.1 **2.** 0.05 **3.** 0.025
4. 0.02 **5.** 0.09375 **6.** 0.0125
7. 0.06 **8.** 0.12 **9.** 0.04
0. 2.5 **11.** 0.8125 **12.** 0.078125

age 65

1. $0.2\overline{8}$ **2.** $0.\overline{6}$ **3.** $0.\overline{8}$ **4.** $0.0\overline{8}$
5. $0.91\overline{6}$ **6.** $0.9\overline{3}$ **7.** $0.58\overline{3}$
8. $0.\overline{7}$ **9.** $0.\overline{93}$ **10.** $0.\overline{4}$
1. $0.8\overline{6}$ **12.** $0.7\overline{3}$

age 66

45 **2.** 20 **3.** 12 **4.** 20 **5.** 45
48 **7.** 7 **8.** $3\frac{21}{22}$

$4\frac{1}{2}$ hours, or 4 hours 30 minutes

age 67

1. m or cm **2.** cm **3.** cm
4. cm **5.** cm **6.** km **7.** cm
8. mm **9.** A **10.** B **11.** A
2. B **13.** m **14.** mm

age 68

1. 0.053 **2.** 0.15 **3.** 5 **4.** 315
5. 5.3 **6.** 39,000 **7.** 3 **8.** 2.74
9. 96,740 **10.** 190 **11.** 9,500
2. 315 **13.** 0.0009042
4. 361.06 **15.** 15.2 **16.** 32 km
7. 0.800 km

age 69

1. kg **2.** g **3.** kg **4.** g **5.** kg
6. mg **7.** kg **8.** g **9.** mg
0. 0.035
1. 2,500,000
2. 0.4
3. 0.0025
4. 45,000,000
5. 99,000 mg
6. 5,000
7. 0.045

Page 70

1. 48 **2.** 2 **3.** 2 **4.** 9 **5.** 6
6. 9 **7.** 12 **8.** 3,520 **9.** 72
10. 30 yards
11. 900 feet
12. 20 yards
13. 18 inches
14. 30 feet
15. 360, 120

Page 71

1. 24 **2.** 20 **3.** 23 **4.** 6 **5.** 24
6. 3 **7.** 92 **8.** 432 **9.** 11
10. 3 **11.** 3 **12.** 18 **13.** 18 tons

Page 72

1. 900 **2.** 180 **3.** 600 **4.** 144
5. 480 **6.** 48 **7.** $1\frac{1}{2}$ **8.** 3,600

9. $6\frac{2}{3}$

10. 9 min 44 s
11. 12 h 37 min
12. 9 h 2 min
13. 23 h 14 min
14. 12 h 15 min
15. 5 h 31 min
16. 3,120 hours

Page 73

1. 3 A.M.
2. 8 A.M.
3. 6 A.M.
4. 7 A.M.
5. 7 A.M.
6. 6 A.M.
7. 8 A.M.
8. 6 A.M.

Page 74

1. B **2.** A **3.** C **4.** B **5.** A
6. B **7.** A **8.** 1.2°F

Page 75

1. 8 qt
2. 2,000 mm
3. 730 mm
4. 17.0 oz
5. 300 cm
6. 360 d
7. 48.0°C
8. 6c
9. 7,920 ft
10. 9,000 mg
11. 51 ft
12. 6.09 m

13. 50 cm
14. 1,200 mg
15. 168.50°C
16. 205 mL

Page 76

1. 34:4, $\frac{17}{2}$

2. 290:3, $\frac{290}{3}$

3. 8:2, $\frac{4}{1}$

4. 92:6, $\frac{46}{3}$

5. 500:4, $\frac{125}{1}$

6. 125:10, $\frac{25}{2}$

7. 150:6, $\frac{25}{1}$

8. 162:2, $\frac{81}{1}$

9. 250:5, $\frac{50}{1}$

10. 5:40, $\frac{1}{8}$

Page 77

1. $480x = 3,360, 7h$
2. 480 x; 1,920; 4h
3. $\frac{8}{x} = \frac{4.5}{1,125}$; 4.5 $x = 9,000$;
$x = 2,000$ mi

Page 78

1. $\frac{5}{x} = \frac{1}{22}$; 110

2. $\frac{5.5}{x} = \frac{1}{22}$; 121

3. $\frac{3.2}{x} = \frac{1}{22}$; 70.4

4. $\frac{4.3}{x} = \frac{1}{22}$; 94.6

Page 79

1. 70% **2.** 75% **3.** 95%
4. 64% **5.** 30% **6.** 60%
7. 100% **8.** 50% **9.** 38%
10. 94% **11.** 91% **12.** 90%
13. 80% **14.** 100% **15.** 88%
16. 72% **17.** 80% **18.** 85%
19. 95% **20.** 90%

Page 80

1. 0.5 **2.** 0.125 **3.** 0.075
4. 0.04 **5.** 0.025 **6.** 0.015
7. 0.012 **8.** 0.0175 **9.** 0.43
10. 0.16 **11.** 0.005 **12.** 0.0005
13. 5% **14.** 7.5% **15.** 11.2%

16. 0.3% **17.** 14.2% **18.** 105%
19. 0.018 **20.** 0.125

Page 81

1. 62.5% **2.** 25% **3.** 31.25%

4. 6.25% **5.** 50% **6.** $33\frac{1}{3}$%

7. $16\frac{2}{8}$% **8.** 37.5% **9.** $1\frac{2}{3}$%

10. $20\frac{5}{6}$% **11.** 43.75%

12. 29.6875% **13.** $66\frac{2}{3}$%

14. 20% **15.** $13\frac{1}{3}$%

Page 82

1. 1.1825 **2.** 0.01875
3. 0.0925, $1.20 **4.** 0.1, 0.062
5. 0.0425 **6.** 0.6095 **7.** $0.39
8. $1.99 **9.** 0.735 **10.** 0.5814
11. 0.221375 **12.** 0.12285
13. $4.34 **14.** $5.99

Page 83

1. 50% **2.** $33\frac{1}{3}$% **3.** 26% **4.** 0%

5. $16\frac{2}{3}$% **6.** $50\frac{2}{3}$% **7.** 80%

8. 410, 163, $39\frac{31}{41}$% **9.** $81\frac{3}{7}$%

Page 84

1. 580 **2.** 0.65, 440 **3.** 250
4. 485 **5.** 175 **6.** 400 **7.** 160
8. 360
9. 220 bicycles
10. 375 bicycles

Page 85

1. 250 **2.** 14.4 **3.** 40% **4.** 200
5. 400 **6.** 520 **7.** 4,500 **8.** 170
9. 1 **10.** 82.14 **11.** 5%
12. 4.4% **13.** 15.5%

Page 86

1. 20% decrease
2. 10% decrease
3. 12.5% increase
4. 20% increase
5. 12%

Page 87

1. false
2. true
3. false
4. true

Page 87 (cont'd.)

5. true
6. true
7. true
8. false
9. false
10. true
11. $\overrightarrow{AD}$
12. $\overrightarrow{AB}$
13. Answers will vary.
14. $\angle GAC$
15. $\angle FAD$
16. $\angle EAC$
17. $\angle EAF$ or $\angle FAE$

Page 88

1. true
2. true
3. false
4. false
5. false
6. false
7. Answers will vary. Possible answers include: $\angle ADB$ and $\angle CDB$; $\angle ABD$ and $\angle CBD$; $\angle FBG$ and $\angle GBH$; $\angle MDL$ and $\angle KDL$
8. $\angle PQT$ and $\angle RQS$; $\angle PQT$ and $\angle PQU$; $\angle RQS$ and $\angle RQV$; $\angle PQU$ and $\angle RQV$

Page 89

1.–6. Check students' drawings.
7.–8. Answers will vary.

Page 90

1.–12. *Check students' drawings.*

Page 91

1. vertical
2. vertical
3. supplementary
4. supplementary
5. corresponding
6. vertical
7. corresponding
8. supplementary
9. vertical
10. corresponding
11. corresponding
12. supplementary
13. Answers may vary. Possible answers include: $\angle DGH$ and $\angle EGJ$; $\angle AJB$ and $\angle GJH$; $\angle BJH$ and $\angle AJG$; $\angle JHF$ and $\angle GHC$.

14. Answers will vary. Possible answers include: $\angle BDC$ and $\angle BGF$; $\angle ACD$ and $\angle AHE$.

Page 92

1.–4. *Check students' drawings.*

Page 93

1. $\triangle DAE$; $\triangle CBE$; $\triangle CED$
2. $\triangle DAE$; $\triangle CBE$; $\triangle CED$
3. $\triangle IFG$; $\triangle HGF$; $\triangle FIH$; $\triangle GHI$
4. $\triangle FJI$; $\triangle GHJ$
5. $\triangle IJH$; $\triangle FJG$
6. $\triangle FJI$; $\triangle GJH$; $\triangle IJH$; $\triangle FJG$

Page 94

1. *Answers will vary for 1–10.*

Page 95

1. $\overline{BC} \cong \overline{ZX}$; $\overline{BA} \cong \overline{XY}$; $\overline{CA} \cong \overline{YZ}$; $\angle B \cong \angle X$; $\angle X$; $\angle A \cong \angle Y$; $\angle C \cong \angle Z$
2. $\overline{DA} \cong \overline{MQ}$; $\overline{AB} \cong \overline{QP}$; $\overline{NP} \cong \overline{CB}$; $\overline{MN} \cong \overline{CD}$; $\angle D \cong \angle M$; $\angle A \cong \angle Q$; $\angle B \cong \angle P$; $\angle C \cong \angle N$
3. $\overline{HJ}$; $\angle H$
  $\overline{JL}$; $\angle J$
  $\overline{LM}$; $\angle L$
  $\overline{MH}$; $\angle M$

Page 96

1. $216\frac{2}{3}$; $162\frac{1}{2}$
2. 32; 30
3. 26; 24
4. 13.56; 14.58
5. $x = 22\frac{1}{2}$; $y = 28\frac{1}{2}$
6. $a = 3$; $b = 9$

Page 97

1. $\overline{BD}$; $\overline{AC}$
2. $\overline{OA}$; $\overline{OB}$; $\overline{OC}$; $\overline{OD}$
3. $\overline{AB}$; $\overline{BD}$; $\overline{CD}$; $\overline{AC}$
4. $\angle DOC$; $\angle AOB$; $\angle BOC$; $\angle AOD$
5. radius
6. chord
7. central angle
8. chord; diameter
9. chord
10. chord
11. radius
12. none of these

RETEACH ANSWER KEY

Page 98

1. yes
2. yes
3. no
4. no
5. no
6. no
7. Check students' drawings.
   The name Debbie is symmetrical; answers will vary.

Page 99

1. 3 units up
2. 4 units right
3. 3 units up and 4 units right, or 4 units right and 3 units up
4. 3 units down
5. 4 units left
6. 3 units down and 4 units right, or 4 units right and 3 units down
7.–10. Check students' graphs.
11. *B* 12. A

Page 100

1. $152\frac{1}{2}$ ft 2. $145\frac{1}{2}$ in. 3. 176 cm
4. 137 ft
5. $35\frac{1}{2}$ in.
6. $38\frac{1}{2}$ in.
7. 48.4 cm
8. 41.6 cm
9. 37.6 m
10. 190 ft
11. 320 ft
12. 520 ft

Page 101

1. 84.78
2. 62.8
3. 3.14; 8; 50.24
4. 3.14; 6.5; 40.82
5. 31.4
6. 75.36
7. 84.78
8. 96.084
9. $618\frac{2}{21}$
10. $102\frac{1}{7}$
11. $99\frac{11}{35}$
12. $57\frac{23}{49}$
13. 22 inches

Page 102

1. 400
2. 38; 38; 1,444
3. 7.5^2; 7.5; 75; 56.25
4. 14.5; 14.5; 210.25
5. $12\frac{1}{4}$ in.^{2}
6. $52\frac{9}{16}$ in.^{2}
7. $284\frac{49}{64}$ in.^{2}
8. 18.49 cm^2
9. 46.24 cm^2
10. 79.21 m^2
11. 10.5625
12. 46.5124
13. $13.77

Page 103

1. 75 ft^2
2. 54 ft^2
3. 88 ft^2
4. 2,218.75 in.
5. 552.5
6. 60.31
7. 156
8. 48
9. 68
10. 40

Page 104

1. 452.16
2. 1,256
3. 1,808.64
4. 3.14; 18.5; 18.5; 1,074.665
5. 5.3066
6. 254.34
7. 42.9866
8. 145.1936
9. 265.7696
10. 301.5656
11. 44.15625
12. 244.26813
13. 235.5
14. 4,456

Page 105

1. triangular pyramid
2. rectangular pyramid
3. pentagonal pyramid
4. hexagonal pyramid
5. triangular
6. rectangular
7. hexagonal
8. pentagonal

Page 106

1. 46,010.25 m^2; 19,197.75 m^2; 122,801.25 m^2
2. 6,162.25 m^2; 2,574.8 m^2; 16,461.45 m^2
3. 5,402.25 m^2; 2,193.975 m^2; 14,178.15 m^2

Page 107

1. 5; 5; 942
2. 6.2; 6.2; 1,689, 8,224
3. 10; 10; 12; 3,768
4. 6; 6; 4; 452.16
5. 4,501.504
6. 17,684.48
7. 5,024
8. 119, 596.32
9. 4, 484.3596
10. 6,698.21346
11. 235.5 ft^3
12. 471 m^3

Page 108

1. *Check students' drawings.*
2. 30%

Page 109

1. 21; 13; 18
2. 50; 70; 85
3. 14; 13; 13
4. 18; 21; 21
5. 15; 125; 125
6. range = 8; median = 14; mode = 16

Page 110

1. 58 2. 119 3. 361 4. 391
5. $3.40 6. 5.0 7. 53.2 8. 16.6
9. 6 10. 5 11. 6 12. 4.3

Page 111

1. Check students' drawings.
2. nearest 10
3. 10
4. 12

Page 112

1. Check students' graphs.
2. Check students' graphs.

Page 113

1.–2. Check students' graphs.

RETEACH ANSWER KEY

Page 114

1. $\frac{1}{5}$ 2. $\frac{1}{5}$ 3. $\frac{2}{5}$ 4. $\frac{3}{5}$ 5. $\frac{4}{5}$ 6. $\frac{3}{5}$

7. $\frac{1}{13}$ 8. $\frac{2}{13}$ 9. $\frac{12}{13}$ 10. $\frac{1}{4}$ 11. $\frac{1}{2}$

12. $\frac{3}{4}$

13. 4 possible; 2 favorable
14. 6 possible; 1 favorable

Page 115

Check students' drawings.
1. 6 possible outcomes
2. 12 possible outcomes
3. 8 possible outcomes
4. 4 possible outcomes

Page 116

1. $\frac{1}{6}$ 2. $\frac{1}{3}$ 3. $\frac{1}{3}$ 4. $\frac{2}{3}$ 5. $\frac{1}{3}$

6. 0 7. $\frac{1}{2}$ 8. 1 9. $\frac{1}{36}$ 10. $\frac{1}{4}$

11. $\frac{7}{12}$ 12. $\frac{5}{12}$ 13. $\frac{5}{12}$ 14. $\frac{1}{3}$

Page 117

1. $\frac{1}{12}$ 2. $\frac{1}{12}$ 3. $\frac{1}{6}$ 4. $\frac{1}{6}$ 5. $\frac{1}{4}$ 6. $\frac{5}{12}$

7. $\frac{1}{18}$ 8. $\frac{1}{9}$ 9. $\frac{1}{3}$ 10. $\frac{5}{18}$ 11. $\frac{2}{9}$

Page 118

1. $\frac{3}{28}$ 2. $\frac{3}{28}$ 3. $\frac{15}{56}$ 4. $\frac{15}{56}$ 5. $\frac{15}{28}$

6. $\frac{3}{14}$ 7. $\frac{1}{11}$

Page 119

1. < 2. < 3. > 4. > 5. <
6. > 7. < 8. > 9. < 10. <
11. > 12. >
13. ⁻2, ⁻1, 0, 1, 2
14. ⁻6, ⁻5, ⁻4, 6
15. ⁻15, ⁻14, 0, 12, 13
16. Dead Sea

Page 120

1. ⁻4 2. ⁻14 3. 6 4. ⁻3
5. 2 6. ⁻14 7. ⁻5 8. ⁻14
9. ⁻7 10. ⁻7 11. ⁻3 12. ⁻6
13. 0 14. 3 15. 1 16. 1
17. 5 18. 6 19. ⁻3 20. 5
21. ⁻2 22. ⁻1 23. 5 24. ⁻6

Page 121

1. 2 2. ⁻2 3. 8 4. ⁻8
5. 0 6. ⁻6 7. ⁻11 8. ⁻14

Page 121 (cont'd.)

9. ⁻9 10. ⁻8 11. ⁻22 12. 0
13. ⁻21 14. ⁻149 15. 15
16. 116°F 17. 134°F

Page 122

1. 12 2. ⁻18 3. ⁻17 4. 19
5. 19 6. 8 7. ⁻2 8. ⁻14
9. ⁻14 10. 36 11. 57 12. ⁻15
13. ⁻7 14. ⁻5 15. ⁻15
16. 540 feet
17. 30,340 ft

Page 123

1. 15 2. 30 3. 48 4. 156
5. 42 6. 154 7. 78 8. 1,360
9. 48 10. ⁻48 11. ⁻140
12. ⁻880 13. 30 14. 110
15. ⁻99
16. ⁻195 ft
17. 1,200 ft
18. 25 miles

Page 124

1. ⁻16 2. ⁻4 3. ⁻5 4. ⁻18
5. 5 6. 13 7. 28 8. 16 9. 0
10. ⁻3 11. 22 12. 57 13. ⁻15
14. 15 15. 23 16. 100
17. ⁻23 18. ⁻42
19. ⁻120 feet per minute

Page 125

1. 25 2. ⁻5 3. 4 4. 150
5. ⁻9 6. 16 7. 5 8. 14
9. 15 10. ⁻3
11. ⁻6 12. 6
13. 400 items
14. 1,500

Page 126

1. $m < 20$ 2. $n > 55$
3. $n < ⁻22$ 4. $p > ⁻25$
5. $m \le 20$ 6. $r \ge 30$
7. $r \le 28$ 8. $r \ge 9$ 9. $r \le ⁻16$
10. $r \ge ⁻14$ 11. $r < 16$
12. $r > ⁻42$ 13. $\le \$51.75$
14. ≤30 gallons

Page 127

Check students' graphs.
1. $x < 2$ 2. $x < 18$ 3. $x \ge 7$
4. $x > 18$ 5. $x < ⁻7$
6. $x < ⁻3$ 7. $x \le ⁻6$
8. $x \le ⁻6$

Page 127 (cont'd.)

9. Check students' graphs.
   $x \le 33$
10. $x \ge 22$

Page 128

1. (⁻4,3) 2. (0,4) 3. (⁻2,⁻4)
4. (5,⁻4) 5. (⁻3,2) 6. (⁻5,⁻3)
7. (3,3) 8. (3,0) 9. (6,⁻2)
10.–11. Check students' graphs.

Page 129

1. 0 2. 27 3. 24 4. 36 5. 15
6. ⁻8, ⁻7, ⁻6, ⁻5
7. ⁻10, ⁻14, ⁻26, ⁻38
8. ⁻3, ⁻2, ⁻1, 1
9. 10, 9, 8, 7

Page 130

1. (⁻2,⁻7) (0,⁻5) (6,1)
2. (⁻6,⁻2) (0,4) (2,6)
3. (⁻2,⁻6) (0,0) (2,6)
4. (⁻8,⁻2) (0,0) (8,2)
5. (⁻1,⁻6) (0,⁻4) (4,4)
6. (⁻1,5) (0,2) (2,⁻4)
7. (⁻8,⁻3) (0,1) (6,4)
8. (⁻6,4) (0,1) (8,⁻3)
9. (⁻10,⁻2) (⁻1,1) (5,3)
10. (⁻4,⁻4) (⁻1,⁻2) (5,2)
11. (0,⁻6) (1,4) (⁻1,⁻16)
12. (1,12) (2,14) (3,16)

ENRICHMENT

These masters provide a course of enrichment that
extends the scope and sequence of the pupil's
edition. Most masters enrich the text pages they are
keyed to, but a number of them provide experiences
with mathematics topics not taught at the grade
level or not generally covered in textbooks.

Name _____ Date _____

Number systems can be developed using any number as a base. The system that we use is base ten. It uses the digits 0 to 9. Base five uses five digits.

1. Write the five digits of base five.

_____

Each place value in a number represents a power of 5.

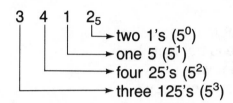

3 4 1 2₅
→ two 1's (5^0)
→ one 5 (5^1)
→ four 25's (5^2)
→ three 125's (5^3)

To write a base-ten number as a base-five number, divide by the place values. For example, to write $2,871_{10}$ in base five:

a. Divide by $625(5^4)$.

$2,871 \div 625 = \boxed{4}$ R371

b. Divide the remainder by 125.

$371 \div 125 = \boxed{2}$ R121

c. Divide the remainder by 25.

$121 \div 25 = \boxed{4}$ R21

d. Divide the remainder by 5.

$21 \div 5 = \boxed{4}$ R$\boxed{1}$

e. Write the base-five numbers from left to right.

$2,871_{10} = \boxed{42441_5}$

Write the number in base five.

2. $1,034_{10}$

_____

3. 679_{10}

_____

4. $3,200_{10}$

_____

5. 809_{10}

_____

6. $2,982_{10}$

_____

7. 345_{10}

_____

8. $6,111_{10}$

_____

9. 247_{10}

_____

10. Choose a number in base ten. Use the guidelines for base five to write the number in base seven and base three.

_____

Name _____ Date _____

ENRICH   **Measurement**

Increased **precision** in measurement does not indicate an increase in **accuracy.**

The precision of a measurement is the positive value of the greatest possible error, the amount which the measurement could be "off" in either direction. The more digits to which a measurement was performed accurately, the smaller the precision. Think of a small precision as precise to a small measure. For example, a measurement with a precision of 0.0005 m is "precise to the nearest $\frac{5}{10,000}$ m."

The accuracy of a measurement is the size of the greatest possible error in relation to the size of the measurement itself. The more digits to which a measurement was performed accurately, the smaller the accuracy. Accuracy, unlike precision, depends upon the value of the number.

Complete the table.

	Number	Possible error (precision)	Accuracy (percent)
	1.25	0.005	$\frac{0.005}{1.25} = 0.004 = 4\%$
	3.841	0.0005	$\frac{0.0005}{3.841} = 0.00013 = 0.13\%$
1.	6.41		
2.	17.857		
3.	10.1		
4.	1.7857		

5. Which two numbers differ in precision but have the same accuracy? _____

You can always see to which place value a decimal measurement has been rounded. With whole numbers, it is more difficult. A measurement of 4,500 yd may only be accurate to the nearest 100 yd.

6. Think of a way to express whole-number measurements to make it clear to what place value they have been rounded. _____

2   **Use with pages 4–5**

ENRICH   Logic

To solve a logic puzzle, you need to use creative thinking and systematic elimination of incorrect possibilities. Solve the puzzle.

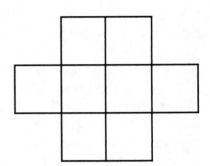

1. Fill in the eight squares with the numbers 1 to 8. Two consecutive numbers cannot be in adjacent squares or in diagonally touching squares.

2. Explain the solution.

_____

3. Use the following clues to figure out how the six people are arranged around the table.
   a. Barbara does not sit next to Ryan or Fernando.
   b. Eileen sits opposite Celia.
   c. Louise sits opposite Ryan.
   d. Eileen sits between Louise and Ryan.

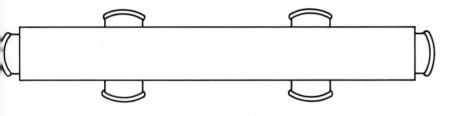

4. If a 3-pound weight is on the left side of a scale and a 1-pound weight is on the right side, the scale will read "2 pounds." Add weights to either or both sides of the scale. Use 1-, 3-, 9-, and 27-pound weights.

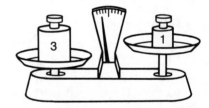

Scale reading	Left	Right
1	1	0
2	3	1
3		
4		
5		
6		
7		

Scale reading	Left	Right
11		
12		
13		
14		
15		
16		
17		

Scale reading	Left	Right
21		
22		
23		
24		
25		
26		
27		

Scale reading	Left	Right
31		
32		
33		
34		
35		
36		
37		

ENRICH   Problem Solving

Irene, Olivia, and Marsha want to go on a shopping trip next Saturday. They plan to leave home at 11:00 A.M. and drive to a shopping mall 20 miles away. Irene wants to buy a pair of shoes. She knows the color that she wants, but has not decided on the style. Olivia wants to buy the newest album of her favorite recording star. Marsha wants to look for a birthday gift for her mother. She has no idea what to buy. In addition to shopping, the sisters plan to eat lunch and to see a movie at the mall. They have to be home by 3:30 P.M.

1. What would be a reasonable estimate for the amount of time each activity will take?

   driving to and from the mall _____

   buying shoes _____

   buying a record _____

   looking for a gift _____

   seeing a movie _____

   eating lunch _____

2. Will they have enough time to do all the things they plan to do at the mall and still get home on time? _____

3. Olivia plans to bring $20.00. Will she have enough money for lunch, the movie, and the album? _____

4. At the movie theater, Irene wants to go to a double feature that starts at 2:00. Would she be able to see the double feature and still be home by 3:30? _____

5. If the sisters leave the mall at 2:30, will they have time to drive by a scenic route home? Driving by a scenic route takes 15 minutes longer than does the direct route home.

   _____

Use with page 8–9.

Name _____ Date _____

You plan to travel from Gloucester, Massachusetts, to
Sarasota, Florida, switching planes in Newark, New Jersey.
After calling airline and train companies, you have the
following information:

	Gloucester to Boston North Station Subway	Logan Airport in Boston to Newark Airport	Newark Airport to Sarasota
First trip	6:30 A.M.	7:45 A.M.	9:05 A.M.
Last trip	9:30 P.M.	8:35 P.M.	9:10 P.M.
Time of trip	1 h 13 min	1 h	3 h
Frequency	2 h 30 min	1 h 50 min	2 h 25 min

The subway from North Station to Logan Airport in Boston
takes 30 minutes and runs every 10 minutes.

1. Complete the schedule.

Lv. Gloucester	6:30							
Ar. Subway	7:43							
Lv. Logan	7:45							
Ar. Newark	8:45							
Lv. Newark	9:05							
Ar. Sarasota	12:05							

Use your schedule to answer the questions.

2. How much time should you allow to
catch the subway and ride it to the
airport? Why? _____

_____

3. What is the latest train you could take
from Gloucester to make it to Sarasota
the same day? What will be your final
arrival time in Sarasota?

_____

4. Your friend Niurca is leaving on an earlier flight so that
she can purchase concert tickets for the evening. Her
plane is delayed in Boston for over 2 hours due to frozen
rain on the plane's wings, and she ends up on your flight.
At what time did she leave Gloucester? _____

ENRICH | Statistics and Probability

The table lists the populations of some counties in South Carolina. The information is the result of the 1980 census. Also, the area of each county is listed in square miles.

1. Estimate the total population for the counties in the table.

_____

2. Estimate the total land area listed in the table.

_____

3. Estimate the population of South Carolina not listed in the table.

_____

4. Estimate the land area of South Carolina not listed in the table.

_____

County	Population	Area (mi²)
Aiken	105,630	1,092
Beaufort	65,364	579
Cherokee	40,983	396
Kershaw	39,015	723
Lee	18,929	411
Oconee	48,611	629
Sumter	88,243	665
Union	30,764	515

Total population in South Carolina = 3,122,717.
Total land area in South Carolina = 30,203 mi².

5. In 1970, Sumter County had a population of 24,555. Estimate the growth in population from 1970 to 1980.

_____

6. Estimate how much larger the land area of Aiken County is than Sumter County.

_____

7. Estimate to find the counties listed in the table with a combined population equal to $\frac{1}{10}$ South Carolina's total population.

_____

8. Estimate to find the county listed in the table with an area equal to $\frac{1}{5}$ the area listed in the table.

_____

ENRICH   Patterns

If the pattern between a group of numbers is due to the addition or subtraction of a constant term, the group of numbers is called an **arithmetic sequence.** Find the pattern, and write the next two numbers.

1. 2, 5, 8, 11, 14, 17, . . . _____

2. 23, 21, 19, 17, 15, . . . _____

3. 98, 96, 97, 95, 96, 94, . . . _____

4. 103, 96, 89, 82, 75, . . . _____

5. 0, 1, 3, 6, 10, 15, . . . _____

To find the nth term of a sequence, first determine the pattern. For example, in the sequence 3, 8, 13, 18, 23, 28, . . . , the common difference between terms is 5.

First term (nth term = 1): $3 + (5 \times 0) = 3$
Second term (nth term = 2): $3 + (5 \times 1) = 8$
Third term (nth term = 3): $3 + (5 \times 2) = 13$

The general formula for this sequence is:
nth term $= 3 + 5(n - 1)$, or nth term $= 5n - 2$

Write a formula to find the nth term.

6. 9, 13, 17, 21, 25, . . . _____

7. 2, 5, 8, 11, 14, 17, . . . _____

8. 23, 21, 19, 17, 15, . . . _____

9. 98, 86, 74, 62, 50, 38, . . . _____

10. 75, 82, 89, 96, 103, . . . _____

11. 0, 1, 3, 6, 10, 15, . . .

_____

12. Find the sum of the terms in Exercises 6 through 11. Does the sum of the first and last number equal the sum of the second and next-to-last number? Which sequence does not follow this rule? Why? _____

_____

ENRICH **Number**

Arithmetic operations often result in patterns of numbers that repeat endlessly. More complex mathematical processes often yield more complex repetitive patterns of numbers. Here is an example of a repetitive pattern, or *loop*.

a. Think of a 2-digit number made up of two different digits.
b. Arrange the digits to make the largest possible number; then arrange the digits to make the smallest possible number (putting zeros in front if needed).
c. Subtract the smaller number from the larger to give a new number with the same number of digits (including zeros). Repeat operations **b** and **c**.

91

91 − 19 = 72
72 − 27 = 45
54 − 45 = 09
90 − 09 = 81
81 − 18 = 63
63 − 36 = 27
72 − 27 = 45
54 − 45 = 09

loop

Complete.

1.   62

62 − 26 =

2.   84

3. Make a loop with some 2-digit numbers of your own. What do you find?

_____

_____

4. Repeat the same operation with these 3-digit numbers.

          364

          802

5. What distinguishes loops from the use of 3-digit numbers?

_____

6. Use 4-digit numbers. What pattern do you find?

_____

Use with pages 16–17.

Name _____ Date _____

ENRICH   Problem Solving

Read the paragraph and problems below. For questions 1–6, find an idea in the Help File that would help each student solve his or her problem.

Darnelle plans to make two beaded necklaces; one for her friend Annie, the other for Kim. Both necklaces will contain a mixture of orange, yellow, and red beads. To make the two necklaces, she will need 505 orange beads and 664 red beads. Annie's necklace will contain 220 orange beads and 345 yellow beads. Kim's necklace will contain 222 yellow beads and 338 red beads.

Problems
a. How many yellow beads will Darnelle need?
b. How many red beads will Annie's necklace contain?
c. How many orange beads will Kim's necklace contain?
d. How many beads in all will Darnelle need to make the two necklaces?

1. Kate is working on Problem **b.** She knows that 664 and 338 are the numbers to use to solve the problem, but she's not sure how to do the necessary math.

_____

2. Pat has found an answer to Problem **a.** Now he wants to make sure his answer is correct. _____

3. Spencer wants to solve Problem **d,** but he doesn't understand the question. _____

4. Mike is working on Problem **c,** but he's not sure what method to use to solve it. _____

5. Yolanda thinks that the answer to Problem **c** is 285, but she isn't certain. _____

6. Roberto understands what Problem **d** is asking, but he doesn't know how to go about answering the question.

_____

Use with pages 18–19.   9

ENRICH   Measurement

The number of **significant digits** is the number of digits to which something has been precisely measured. The numbers 502 in. and 502.0000 in. do not express the same thing. The first would be 502 inches to the nearest inch, and the second would be 502 inches to the nearest ten-thousandths of an inch. The first number has 3 significant digits, and the second has 7.

1. What is the difference between these two statements? "India takes up 2% of Earth's land area" and "India takes up 2.0% of Earth's land area"?

    _____

    _____

2. Which is more precise: 284,655 mm or 284.65 m?   _____

3. A virus molecule can measure as large as 0.0004 mm. How many significant digits are there in this number? Explain why.

    _____

    _____

A number such as 2,700 may have been rounded to the nearest hundred or to the nearest one. Generally, zeros at the end of whole numbers are not considered significant digits. The most precise way to express significant digits is by using exponents. This way, 2,700 m to the nearest 100 m = 2.7×10^3 m (2 significant digits), and 2,700 m to the nearest m = 2.700×10^3 m (4 significant digits).

Write the number of significant digits.

4. 33 ft   _____

5. 4.12 h   _____

6. 9.001×10^3 _____

7. 2.300×10^4 kg _____

8. 0.025 yd _____

9. 20 in.   _____

10. The People's Republic of China has about one thousand twenty-two million inhabitants.   _____

11. Explain why the use of exponents shows more clearly than standard notation whether zeros at the end of a number are significant or not.

    _____

    _____

Name _____ Date _____

In the solar system, there are nine planets orbiting the sun. An *orbit* is one complete revolution. Another scale has been invented for distance in space: **Astronomical Units (AU).** In this scale, Earth's distance from the sun is one unit. A *planet's orbit speed* is the number of miles it travels per second.

Complete the table.

Planet	Distance from sun (Miles)	Distance from sun (AU)	Orbit speed (Miles/Second)
Mercury	36,000,000		29.8
Venus	67,200,000	0.72	21.8
Earth	92,900,000	1	18.5
Mars	141,500,000	1.52	15.0
Jupiter	483,300,000		8.1
Saturn	886,000,000		6.0
Uranus	1,783,000,000		4.2
Neptune	2,791,000,000		3.4
Pluto	3,671,000,000		2.9

1. What is Earth's orbit speed in astronomical units?

_____

2. How many astronomical units does Mercury travel in 1 minute?

_____

3. The planets spin, or *rotate,* causing one side to face the sun and the other to be in darkness. Earth spins once every 24 hours, creating a day. Neptune completes 1 orbit in 165 Earth years and rotates once every 16 hours. Approximately how many Neptune days are there in a Neptune year?

_____

4. Japan is planning to launch a radio-wave satellite to help document information about galaxies beyond our galaxy, the Milky Way. The satellite will orbit beyond Pluto. What must they plan for while building the satellite? (HINT: Analyze the relationship between the distance to the sun and orbit speed.)

_____

5. Is it better to measure distance within our solar system with astronomical units? why or why not?

_____

_____

ENRICH   Measurement

Measurements are always limited by the accuracy of the measuring instrument. With an ordinary ruler, you can measure an object to the nearest millimeter. But you could not accurately give a measurement of 1.253524 cm with the same ruler. When you are given a measurement such as 1.25 cm, you cannot assume that it is 1.25000000 cm. You must assume that the last digit given (0.05) was rounded.

1. What is the range of measures that would round 1.5 cm?

_____

The difference between a rounded measure and the highest and lowest numbers that round to it is the **greatest possible error.** This is the largest amount which the measurement could be "off." The **precision** is the positive value of the greatest possible error. The precision of a measurement cannot be more than the precision of the instrument used.

2. A mechanic rebuilds a car engine. For the engine to work smoothly, two of the pieces must overlap 1.25 cm. What is the greatest possible error and precision? _____

An electrical engineer has to place a microchip into the back of a computer. Precision is extremely important for the data to be stored properly and the computer to be efficient. It is measured to the nearest millimeter.

1.3 cm

2.5 cm

3. Find the area of the microchip to the correct precision.

_____

4. Write the largest and the smallest areas that the chip could have, assuming the measurement was rounded to the proper precision. Write the difference. _____

5. Since the precision of each measurement in Problem 3 is 0.05 cm, what must be the precision of the engineer's measurement of the difference? _____

6. If a key has a length of 2.54371 cm and a width of 1.3 cm, what would be the precision of the measurements of the lock? Why? _____

Use with pages 24–25.

ENRICH   Problem Solving

Read the questions for Topics *A* and *B* below. Under each topic, write three sources of information you could use to find answers to the questions. Then choose *one* of the topics and answer the questions.

Topic *A*: American Space Travel

_____

_____

1. What was the duration of the *Skylab 3* mission?

_____

2. What was the date of the first moon walk? _____

3. About how far is the moon from Earth?

_____

4. Who was the first American in space?

_____

5. What was the launch date of the first United States-Soviet Union joint space flight? _____

6. What is the height of the Apollo Lunar Module?

_____

Topic *B:* Animal Statistics

_____

_____

1. How fast can a cheetah run? _____

2. How many legs does an arachnid have? _____

3. What is the average weight of a hippo?

_____

4. How long is an average rainbow trout?

_____

5. How many pounds of food does an African elephant in the wild eat per day? _____

6. What is the average life span of a gorilla? _____

ENRICH Number

People grow at different rates. Last year, Stanley grew 4.21 cm, and his older brother, David, grew 8.73 cm. This year, Stanley grew 7.06 cm, and David grew 3.9 cm.

Use the table.

It is interesting to look at the average height for various age levels. You can estimate what your height will be next year, and in a few years.

Boys

Age (year)	Height (cm)	Weight (kg)
4	99.0	15.4
5	106.6	17.7
6	114.2	20.9
7	119.3	23.1
8	127.0	25.9
9	132.0	28.6
10	137.1	31.3

Girls

Age (year)	Height (cm)	Weight (kg)
4	99.0	15.0
5	104.1	17.2
6	111.7	20.4
7	119.3	22.2
8	127.0	25.4
9	132.0	28.1
10	137.1	31.3

1. Paul grew 8.32 cm last year. Estimate how old he was.

_____

2. Keiji is 7 years old and 117.01 cm tall. Estimate how tall he will be next year.

_____

3. Cynthia hasn't seen her niece in two years. Laurinda, her niece, was four years old, and her height was 98.7 cm. How tall does Cynthia estimate Laurinda to be now?

_____

4. Laurinda weighed 13.0 kg when she was four years old. Cynthia uses the table to estimate Laurinda's weight at six years. How much does Cynthia think Laurinda weighs?

_____

5. At various times in their growth, boys and girls have the same average weight and height. Write these ages by using estimation.

_____

ENRICH Statistics and Probability

Here is a copy of the ledger page for the bank account of the Hitching Post Restaurant, owned by Jane Tenderleaf. The accountant spilled ink on the ledger. When the ink was removed, so were the numbers underneath it. Complete the ledger page using the information.

1. Twice every calendar month, Mrs. Tenderleaf writes a check for $750.00 to pay rent.
2. Once a week, the bank automatically withdraws $342.15 for payroll checks to employees.
3. Once every calendar month, Mrs. Tenderleaf deposits a check for $101.25 from the Starlight Hotel, which buys three loaves of Mrs. Tenderleaf's homemade bread every day.
4. Every calendar month, Mrs. Tenderleaf withdraws a total of $3,500.00 to pay United Foods, her main food supplier.
5. Every calendar month, Mrs. Tenderleaf deposits a total of $28,000.00 in cash taken in at the restaurant.

Date	Cash/check to/from	Deposit	Withdrawal	Balance
July 1	cash	$10,000.00		$20,000.05
July 2				$19,657.90
July 2	United Foods		$1,200.00	
July 3	Johnson Fruit Co.		$ 450.00	$18,007.65
July 8	cash	$ 8,250.00		$26,257.65
July 8				$25,507.65
July 9	payroll account		$ 342.15	$25,165.50
July 10	Starlight Hotel			
July 15	United Foods		$ 950.00	$24,316.75
July 16	payroll account			
July 19	Midway Dairy		$2,108.40	$21,868.20
July 23				$21,526.05
July 24		$ 4,750.00		
July 29				$25,526.05
July 30	cash	$ 5,000.00		$30,526.05
July 30	payroll account			
July 31				$28,833.90

ENRICH   Statistics and Probability

When you write a check, you authorize the company or person named in the check to withdraw the amount of money written on the check. This is how you write a check.

- Fill in the date.
- Fill in the name of the person or company the check is for.
- Write the amount of money in numbers.
- Write the dollar amount of money in words (cents are written as fractions of 100).
- Sign your name.
- Add a memo about what the check is for.

```
                          Mowata Butler                    712
                          227 Orange Street
                          Typicalville, N.Y.    9/26  , 1992
         Pay to the
         order of    Elm St. Garage           $ 65.36
         Sixty-five and 36/100 _____ DOLLARS
         MEMO  oil change            Mowata Butler
                002-212-5531212
```

1. Complete the check. On October 12, 1992, you spend $73.42 on circuits at the Solar Light Store.

```
                          Mowata Butler                    718
                          227 Orange Street
                          Typicalville, N.Y.    _____ ,19

         Pay to the
         order of    _____    $ [        ]

         _____ DOLLARS

         MEMO  _____    _____
                002-212-5531212
```

A **check register** keeps track of the **balance,** the money left in the checking account after checks are written and deposits are made. This is done by adding the amounts of any deposits to the existing balance and subtracting the amounts of withdrawals.

2. Complete the check register. Enter the check for the Solar Light Store.

					Starting balance $645.20
Check no.	Date	To or for	Deposits	Withdrawals	Balance
713	9/27	Metro. Power Co.		102.86	542.34
714	9/29	Dave's Dry Cleaner	732.46	28.00	
715	9/29	Silver Supermarket		73.45	
716	10/1	Main St. Realty Co.			611.87
717	10/11	Telephone Co.	732.46	24.75	

3. What do you think is the major advantage to paying by check rather than in cash?

_____

_____

Use with pages 32–33.

ENRICH   Problem Solving

You work for Teamspro Sporting Goods. Your main competitor is Playwell Sports Equipment. You are representing the marketing department at the annual board meeting. Use the graph below to help you answer board members' questions.

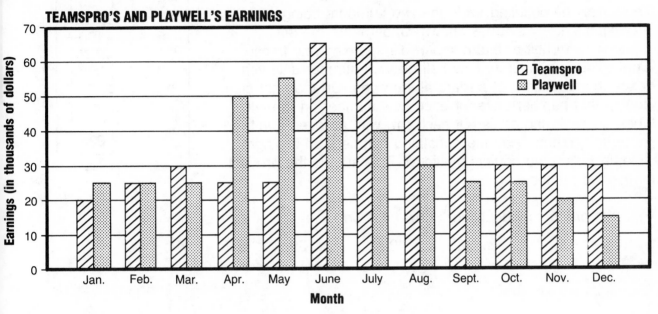

TEAMSPRO'S AND PLAYWELL'S EARNINGS

1. Which company earned more in the first half of the year?

   _____

2. Playwell launched a major advertising campaign at the end of March. Do you think that this campaign helped their sales?

   _____

3. Do you think the Playwell ad campaign had an effect on Teamspro's sales for April and May?

   _____

4. Teamspro launched their summer ad campaign in late May. Do you think that this campaign was successful?

   _____

5. Teamspro and Playwell specialize in summer sporting goods. Did Teamspro earn more than Playwell during the summer months?

   _____

6. How did Teamspro's yearly earnings compare with Playwell's?

   _____

ENRICH   Number

The ancient Egyptians and other peoples did not multiply numbers the way we do. They used a method called **doubling.** This method requires only the ability to halve a number, double a number, and add a column of figures.

To multiply by doubling, write the two numbers being multiplied side by side, as shown. Underneath the left number, write half of that number, disregarding any fraction. Continuing in a column, take half of each number until you reach the number 1. Disregard all fractions. On the right side, double that number once for each new number on the left. Then go back and cross out each row with an even number in the left column. Add the remaining numbers on the right side, including the original multiplier. This sum is the product of the two numbers.

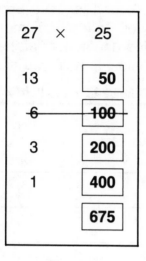

27	×	25
13		50
~~6~~		~~100~~
3		200
1		400
		675

Find the product by doubling. Show your work.

1. 31 × 29

2. 32 × 42

3. 39 × 385

4. 62 × 49

5. 65 × 590

6. 51 × 211

7. Why has conventional multiplication replaced multiplication by doubling?

_____

_____

_____

Use with pages 44–45.

Name _____ Date _____

Angela conducts population research for Clear Springs State University. Much of her work involves estimating future events based on current trends.

1. Angela finds that Florida's population in 1960 was 4,951,560. In 1970, it was 6,789,433. The population of Pennsylvania changed from 11,319,366 in 1960 to 11,793,909 in 1970. Angela uses these figures to estimate which state will have a larger population in the year 2000. Which state does she estimate will be larger?

_____

2. The tiny island of Tranzi had a population of 2,914 in 1960. Its population increased two-fold every 15 years. Estimate its population in 1990.

_____

The Botony Department at Clear Springs State University needs Angela's help in estimating the plant growth in the university's experimental garden.

3. Angela learns that the microscopic Popplenock fern produces a new stalk every hour. The Botony Department has only one specimen. After one hour, there will be two ferns. After two hours, there will be four ferns. After three hours, there will be eight ferns, and so on. How many ferns does she estimate there will be in twelve hours?

_____

4. Write the formula Angela would use to find the exact number of Popplenock ferns after n hours. _____

5. Estimation is helpful in performing mathematical operations. Describe two such situations.

_____

_____

ENRICH   Statistics and Probability

Each arrangement of a group of things in a particular order is called a **permutation**. For example, if you've forgotten the combination of your gym locker but remember that the numbers are 15, 25, and 30, then there are six possible permutations of the numbers for you to try: 15–25–30, 15–30–25, 25–15–30, 25–30–15, 30–15–25, and 30–25–15.

To find the number of possible permutations for a group of things, multiply together the possibilities for each position in the order. An example is the permutations of the five letters in the word *float:* the first position could be any of the five letters; the second could be any of the remaining four letters, and so on, until there is only one letter left for the last position in the order. The number of possible permutations is $5 \times 4 \times 3 \times 2 \times 1 = 120$.

1. The Chinatown Community Association is planning its annual fund-raising carnival. In how many different orders can they arrange the 8 food and game booths? _____

2. In how many different orders can 6 people sit in 5 chairs?

_____

3. By what factor is the set of possible permutations of a series *a, b, c, d* increased if *e* and *f* are added?

_____

4. Explain Abdul's mistake: "There are three letters in the word *dog.* There are three positions and three letters for each position; so, the number of possible permutations for these letters is $3 \times 3 \times 3 = 9$." _____

_____

5. Would $10 \times 9 \times 8 \times 7 \times 6 \times 5 \times 4 \times 3 \times 2 \times 1 = 3,628,800$ be the correct way to determine the number of possible permutations of the word *Madagascar?* why or why not? _____

_____

_____

                                          Use with pages 48–49.

ENRICH **Algebra**

The graph below is used to find $(a \times b) + c$.

- Start at a point, a, on the lower left half of the graph. Draw a vertical line to intersect a line with a b value.
- Draw a horizontal line from the point of intersection to find the value of $(a \times b)$.
- Continue the horizontal line to intersect a line with a c value.
- Draw a vertical line from the point of intersection to find the value of $(a \times b) + c$.

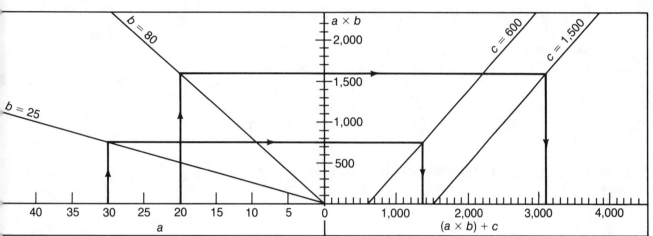

Two examples are shown:
$$(30 \times 25) + 600 = 1{,}350; \qquad (20 \times 80) + 1{,}500 = 3{,}100$$

Draw lines to complete.

1. $(15 \times 80) + 1{,}500 = $ _____   **2.** $(40 \times 25) + 600 = $ _____

Solve.

3. Create the line $b = 60$ by finding two points on the line. Use the equations $60 \times 0 = 0$ and $60 \times 25 = 1{,}500$ to find the points.

4. Create the line $c = 2{,}200$ by finding two points on the line.

5. $(35 \times 60) + 1{,}500 = $ _____   **6.** $(25 \times 60) + 2{,}200 = $ _____

Reverse the order of operations. Start with $(a \times b) + c$ on the table and work backwards.

7. Create the line which shows $(1{,}600 - 600) \div 25 = 40$.

8. Draw a line to find $(4{,}000 - 2{,}200)$ $\div 60 = $ _____

9. On another sheet of paper, create a graph that finds $(a \div b) + c$.

Use with pages 50–51.

ENRICH   Problem Solving

Read the paragraphs below and answer the questions that follow. Consult the chart for additional information. If you don't have all the facts you need, write *not enough information.*

There are two ways to measure a waterfall. One way is to measure its height. But note that some waterfalls fall in one drop, and others fall in a series of drops, or *cascades.* For example, Yosemite Falls, the highest waterfall in North America, is 2,425 feet high. Yosemite Falls is made up of three drops. The upper fall is 1,430 feet high. The lower fall is 320 feet high.

The second way to measure a waterfall is in terms of the volume of water the fall carries. This volume is measured in cubic feet per second *(cusecs).* A low fall may carry a larger volume of water than a higher fall. For example, Victoria Falls has an average flow of 38,000 cusecs, even though it is only 343 feet high.

Waterfall	Average flow (thousands of cusecs)	Height (feet)
Khone	410	70
Guaira	292	213
Niagara	212	186
Grande	106	75
Urubupunga	97	27

1. How much higher is Yosemite's upper fall than its lower fall?

   _____

2. How much greater is the average flow of Urubupunga Falls than the average flow of Yosemite Falls?

   _____

3. Angel Falls in Venezuela is an amazing 3,212 feet high. How much higher is Angel Falls than the highest waterfall in North America?

   _____

4. The height of Guaira Falls is equal to the combined height of which two waterfalls?

   _____

5. It takes about 5 seconds for water to travel from the top to the bottom of Victoria Falls. About how many cubic feet of water pass over the falls in the same amount of time?

   _____

ENRICH — Statistics and Probability

Our **genes** are part of our biological makeup. They carry information about characteristics or traits that we inherit from our parents. For example, eye color is determined from two genes, one gene from each parent. Possible gene combinations are often shown in the form of a diagram similar to a multiplication table.

		Parent	
		B	b
Parent	B	BB	Bb
	b	Bb	bb

In this example, each parent has one gene for brown eye color, indicated by "B," and one gene for blue eye color, indicated by "b." The pairs of letters within the diagram are the possible combinations, or *genotypes,* that the children could inherit.

A genotype of BB or Bb produces brown eyes. This is because the gene for brown eyes is *dominant.* A person can have one or two brown-eye genes and her eyes will always be brown. The gene for blue eyes is *recessive.* The only genotype that gives a person blue eyes is bb.

You can find the likelihood of two parents with genotype Bb having a child with brown eyes. Divide the number of genotypes producing brown eyes by the total number of possible combinations of the parents' genes. This is $\frac{3}{4}$, or 0.75, and can be stated as "3 of 4 children are likely to have brown eyes."

Color	Possible genotypes	Number of possibilities
Brown	Bb, Bb, BB	
Blue	bb	
	Total	

There are five other eye-color genotypes. Complete the diagram. Write 4 of the possibilities of the offspring's eye color.

1.

	b	b
B		
b		

blue _____ : brown _____

_____ : _____

2.

	B	B
b		
b		

blue _____ : brown _____

_____ : _____

3.

	b	b
b		
b		

blue _____ : brown _____

_____ : _____

4.

	B	B
B		
b		

blue _____ : brown _____

_____ : _____

5. If both parents are BB, what is the first generation of offspring that could have blue eyes? Explain why. (HINT: If their child combines with a Bb or bb, could its offspring have blue eyes?)

_____

_____

Name _____ Date _____

| ENRICH | **Patterns** |

Multiplication can result in surprising and curious patterns. Try multiplying any 5-digit number by 100,001.

$$100,001 \times 47,562 = 4,756,247,562$$

Multiply.

1. 100,001
× 67,401

2. 100,001
× 99,999

3. 100,001
× 42,177

4. 100,001
× 21,798

5. Is there a pattern in Questions 1–4? Explain why. (HINT: Look at the number of zeros in 100,001.) _____

_____

_____

6. Write the product of 100,001 times the whole number *xy,zab*. _____

7. What would you do with the number 1,001 to produce a similar pattern? _____

The number 15,873 has interesting properties when multiplied by 7 and multiples of 7.

$$15,873 \times 7 = 111,111$$
$$15,873 \times 21 = 333,333$$

Multiply.

8. 15,873
× 14

9. 15,873
× 49

10. 15,873
× 56

11. 15,873
× 77

12. Write a formula for 15,873 times *n*, when *n* is a multiple of 7. _____

The number 37,037 produces another curious number pattern. Multiply.

13. 37,037
× 3

14. 37,037
× 5

15. 37,037
× 11

16. 37,037
× 13

17. Based on the examples, can you make up a number that will produce an interesting multiplication pattern?

_____

_____

Use with pages 56–57.

ENRICH   Problem Solving

The Drama Club at Basington Junior High School is planning
a budget for the spring play. Consider the facts below and
then use estimation to plan a reasonable budget for the
show. Fill in the budget form on this page.

The last show sold 497 adult tickets at $4.00 each
and 670 student tickets at $3.00 each.
The Drama Club has $1,100 left in its treasury.
The club plans to hold a bake sale and a car wash to earn
extra money. Last year's bake sale earned $167. Last year's
car wash earned $146.
The last show had 12 characters, and the costumes cost
$277.
The spring show has 24 characters.
Sets for the last 3 productions cost $266, $489, and $354.
Posters cost $47 per 100. The club usually prints between
200 and 400 posters.
It will cost $127 to print the programs for the show.

BASINGTON JUNIOR HIGH SCHOOL DRAMA CLUB
ESTIMATED BUDGET FOR SPRING PLAY

Available funds	**Costs**
Drama Club treasury _____	Sets _____
Bake sale profits _____	Costumes _____
Car wash profits _____	Programs _____
Total available funds _____	Posters _____
	Total costs _____
Sales income	**Net results**
Estimated adult ticket sales _____	Total available funds _____
Estimated student ticket sales _____	Minus total costs _____
Estimated total sales _____	Subtotal _____
	Plus sales income _____
	Total funds after show _____

Name_____ Date_____

You can check the sum of an addition operation with an easy technique called **casting out nines.** This technique uses the digit sum. To find the digit sum, add the digits of a number. If the sum is less than 9, that number is the digit sum. If the sum is 9, the digit sum is 0. If the sum is more than 9, add the digits until you have a single-digit number. Here are some examples.

314	3 + 1 + 4 = 8		Digit sum = 8
4,788	4 + 7 + 8 + 8 = 27	2 + 7 = 9	Digit sum = 0
624	6 + 2 + 4 = 12	1 + 2 = 3	Digit sum = 3

To check an addition problem by casting out nines

• find the digit sums of each addend.
• add the digit sums of each addend.
• find the digit sum of this number.
• find the digit sum of the answer.
• compare the two digit sums.

		Step 1	Step 2	Step 3
	6.17 + 3.39 9.56	6 + 1 + 7 = 14; 1 + 4 = 5 3 + 3 + 9 = 15; 1 + 5 = 6 9 + 5 + 6 = 20; 2 + 0 = 2	5 + 6 = 11	1 + 1 = 2
Step 4:				

The number in step 3 equals the digit sum of the correct answer in step 4.

Ring the incorrect sums. Use casting out nines, and show all digit sums.

1.   6.245
    44.400
+ 9.682
  60.027

2.   92.079
    0.495
+ 3.621
  96.195

3.   791.204
    104.679
+ 1,238.166
  2,135.049

4.   94.821
  685.563
+ 227.911
1,008.295

5.   75.102
  347.694
+ 121.710
  546.506

6.   65.421
  279.854
+ 95.718
  440.993

7. Casting out nines is a convenient way to check addition problems, but it will not catch every wrong answer. Can you explain why this is true? _____

_____

ENRICH   Statistics and Probability

The **mean** of a set of numbers equals the sum of the numbers divided by the number of elements in the set. The mean is often referred to as the *average*.

A variation of the mean is the **weighted mean**, a measure that takes into account the **frequency**. The frequency of a value in a set is the number of times it occurs. Suppose 1, 2, 3, and 4 are values in a set {1,1,2,2,2,2,3,4,4,4}. Their frequencies are different. The frequency of the number 1 is 2.

1. What are the frequencies of the numbers 2, 3, and 4? _____

The weighted mean for the set would equal:

$$\frac{(1 \times 2) + (2 \times 5) + (3 \times 1) + (4 \times 3)}{2 + 5 + 1 + 3} = \frac{27}{11} = 2\frac{5}{11}$$

Let a, b, c, and d, represent values in a set, and their frequencies f_a, f_b, f_c, and f_d. Here is the general formula for the weighted mean.

$$\frac{(a \times f_a) + (b \times f_b) + (c \times f_c) + (d \times f_d)}{f_a + f_b + f_c + f_d}$$

2. What is the weighted mean for the set {6,6,4,2,2,4,8,2,6,6,6,4,0,6,6}?

_____

You are in charge of buying fruit for a large community picnic. You have to buy apples, casabas, peaches, papayas, and grapes. Two stores sell fruit, but you can shop at only one. You call each for their prices per pound.

Store	Apples	Casabas	Peaches	Papayas	Grapes
Fruit-Mart	$0.45	$0.35	$0.99	$0.80	$0.25
Lasting Happiness	$0.60	$0.35	$0.75	$0.58	$0.40

3. What is the mean price per pound for each store to the nearest cent? By this measure, which store is cheaper?

_____

4. You need 100 lb of apples, 50 lb of casabas, 25 lb of peaches, 20 lb of papayas, and 200 lb of grapes. What is the weighted mean price per pound (round to the nearest cent) at each store? Which store offers the better price?

_____

5. What would be another way to determine the better price?

_____

ENRICH   Problem Solving

Read each problem carefully and solve. Fill in the blanks in the right-hand column and write the sign of the correct operation.

1. Sally had 27 marbles. Yesterday, she bought 17 more. This morning, she gave away 12 marbles to Sarah. This afternoon, she bought 8 red marbles and sold twice as many marbles. How many marbles does Sally have now?

_____

a. 27 ? 17 = ____

b. ____ ? 12 = ____

c. ____ ? 8 = ____

d. ____ ? ____ = ____

2. Basil is flying a kite. The kite is flying at 540 feet. It rises 47 feet. Then, Basil reels in 23 feet of string. A while later, the kite drops 38 feet. How high is the kite?

_____

a. 540 ? 47 = ____

b. ____ ? 23 = ____

c. ____ ? 38 = ____

3. On Monday, Saul hiked 12 miles south of Green Rock. On Tuesday, he continued south and hiked 3.5 miles less than he had on Monday. On Wednesday, he hiked 10.7 miles north. On Thursday, he hiked 13.6 miles in the same direction that he hiked on Monday. How far south of Green Rock is Saul now?

_____

Monday:

Tuesday:

Wednesday:

Thursday:

4. Trudy works in a luncheonette. She received a 55-cent tip from her first customer. Her second customer left her 75 cents. She used 3 dimes to make a phone call. How much of Trudy's tip money remains? _____

ENRICH | Number

Currency is the form of money a country uses. Dollars are the currency of the United States. When you travel in another country, you must use money in the currency of that country. You can turn your U.S. dollars into foreign currency based on the **rate of exchange** for that country. The rate of exchange changes daily with the changes in the economy.

You are taking a trip to Brazil, so you need

Brazilian currency. The rate of exchange for Brazilian cruzeiros is set at 6,850 for each dollar.

From Brazil, you go to Uruguay. The exchange rate for Uruguayan pesos is 104.2 pesos to the dollar. You still have 1,314,800 cruzeiros, and want to exchange them for pesos. To exchange cruzeiros for pesos, you write an equation.

6,850 cruzeiros
× $300 (U.S.)
2,055,000 cruzeiros

6,850 cruzeiros = 104.2 pesos

$\frac{6,850}{104.2}$ cruzeiros = 1 peso = 65.74 cruzeiros

1. How do you know that 6,850 cruzeiros = 104.2 pesos?

_____

2. Use this equation to write the number of pesos you can get for 1,314,800 cruzeiros.

$$\frac{65.74 \text{ cruzeiros}}{1 \text{ peso}} = \frac{1,314,800 \text{ cruzeiros}}{x \text{ number of pesos}}$$

_____

The table shows how to convert Japanese yen and Hong Kong dollars into U.S. dollars.

3. How many yen can you get for $500 in Hong Kong currency? _____

	Currency	Per U.S. $1
Japan	yen	236.75
Hong Kong	dollar	7.78

4. After spending two-fifths of your yen, you go to Hong Kong and exchange your leftover yen for Hong Kong dollars. How many Hong Kong dollars do you get? (Round to the nearest dollar.)

_____

5. How can you check your answer to Question 4?

_____

_____

_____

ENRICH   Patterns

If the pattern between numbers in a series is one of multiplication or division, the series is a **geometric sequence.**

Write the missing numbers in each sequence.

1. _____, 30, _____, 7.5

2. 100, _____, 1, 0.1, _____

3. 0.11, 1.21, _____, _____

4. 20, 70, 245, _____, _____

5. 100, 20, _____, _____

6. _____, _____, 3.2, 12.8

7. Ring the letter of each geometric sequence.

a. 1, 2, 4, 8, 16
c. 125, 112, 99, 86

b. 102, 103, 104, 105, 106
d. 27, 9, 3, 1

To find the nth term of sequence, figure out the pattern.
For example, in the sequence 3, 6, 12, 24, 48, 96, . . .

First term (nth term = 1):	3	=	3×2^0
Second term (nth term = 2):	3×2	=	3×2^1
Third term (nth term = 3):	$3 \times 2 \times 2$	=	3×2^2
Fourth term (nth term = 4):	$3 \times 2 \times 2 \times 2$	=	3×2^3

8. What is the formula for the sequence in the example?
nth term = _____

Write the formula for each sequence.

9. 7, 21, 63, 189, 567, . . . _____

10. 1,024, 256, 64, 16, . . .   _____

11. 59,049, 6,561, 729, 81, . . .   _____

12. 72, 432, 2,592, 15,552, 93,312, . . . _____

13. 200 100, 50, 25, . . . _____

14. A family tree is a geometric progression. Is there a formula for family trees? why or why not? _____

_____

ENRICH   Problem Solving

Read the paragraph. Then solve each problem that follows.

Mrs. Müller raises cats. May was a very busy month for her business. She began the month with 15 Siamese, 12 Persian, 18 tiger-striped, and 14 calico cats. On May 4, she sold 12 cats. One of her calico cats had kittens on May 6. In the litter, there were 3 calico, 2 gray, and 3 white kittens. On May 12, Mrs. Müller bought 3 Burmese cats and sold 2 Siamese cats. She sold a tiger-striped cat two days later. A week after she sold the tiger-striped cat, one of her Persian cats had a litter of 4 kittens. On May 26, Mrs. Müller sold twice as many cats as she sold on May 4. At the end of the month, she bought 2 black-and-white kittens.

1. What was the total number of cats Mrs. Müller had on each of the following days?

   May 5 _____   May 22 _____   May 31 _____
   May 13 _____   May 28 _____

2. Four of the cats that Mrs. Müller sold on May 4 were calicos. How many calicos did she have on May 8?

   _____

3. Mrs. Müller sold 2 Siamese cats on May 4. She had 5 Siamese cats on May 28. How many Siamese cats did she sell on May 26? _____

4. On which day of the month did Mrs. Müller's Persian cat have kittens? _____

5. At the end of June, Mrs. Müller had 16 more cats than she had at the beginning of May. She sold 11. How many remained? _____

6. In January, one of Mrs. Müller's cats had a litter of 6 kittens. If she sells each kitten for $55, how much more than $300 would she earn? _____

ENRICH Statistics and Probability

Jean got 28 hits in 80 times at bat during last year's softball season. She hit in $\frac{28}{80}$, or 0.35 of her times at bat. A baseball player's **batting average** is his or her batting average expressed as a 3-digit decimal number with a zero place-holder.

Divide the number of hits by the number of times at bat. Jean's batting average last year was 0.350. She has hit 8 times this year out of 24 times at bat. Her batting average now is $\frac{8}{24}$, or 0.333.

1. The table contains batting records for two major-league baseball players. Find their batting averages.

1969	At bats	Hits	Batting average
Pete Rose	627	218	
Reggie Jackson	549	151	

2. Rogers Hornsby's batting average in 1924 was 0.424, the highest season average ever in the major leagues. He had 536 at bats that year. How many hits did he have? _____

Slugging average is the average (as a 3-digit decimal) of total bases a player accumulates divided by the number of times at bat. For example, if a player is at bat 50 times and has 10 singles, 4 doubles, 1 triple, and 3 home runs, his total bases = $(10 \times 1) + (4 \times 2) + (1 \times 3) + (3 \times 4) = 33$. His slugging average = $\frac{33}{50} = 0.660$.

3. Complete the table.

	At bats	Singles	Doubles	Triples	Home runs	Slugging average
Hank Greenberg (1934)	593	105	63	7	26	
Babe Ruth (1920)	458	73	36	9	54	
Pete Rose (1969)	627	158	33	11	16	
Reggie Jackson (1969)	549	65	36	3	47	

4. Would you rather have had the player with the highest batting average at the end of the 1968 season, or the player with the highest batting average two weeks into the 1969 season on your team? why?

_____

_____

Use with pages 82–83.

ENRICH   Number

California is called the Golden State. It lies n the southwestern corner of the United States. It's total population, as of the 1980 census, is 23,688,562. The total area of California is 158,693 mi².

The table lists the population and area of some of the counties in California.

County	Population	Area (mi²)
Alameda	1,105,379	733
Calaveras	20,710	1,024
Marin	222,952	520
Riverside	663,923	7,176
Sacramento	783,381	975
San Francisco	678,974	45
Santa Clara	1,295,071	1,300
Sutter	52,246	603
Tuolumne	33,920	2,252
Yuba	49,733	639

Use the table to estimate your answer.

1. By 2070, Tuolumne County expects to grow by half of its current population. How many more people will live in Tuolumne in 2070 than in 1980?

_____

2. What two counties make up $\frac{1}{100}$ of the total area of California?

_____

3. What part of the area of California is not shown on the table?

_____

4. Estimate how many times larger the land area in Riverside County is than the land area in Alameda County.

_____

5. Estimate how much larger the population in Alameda County is than the population in Riverside County.

_____

6. Look at Problems 4 and 5. What can you determine about Alameda County?

_____

_____

_____

ENRICH **Algebra**

Symbols are used to represent arithmetic functions. Two numbers joined by the symbol $+$, $-$, $\times$, or $\div$ indicate add, subtract, multiply, or divide, respectively. Letters or other symbols are often used to represent more complex arithmetic functions.

Let * represent the operation $x \div 2$, where x is any whole number.

For example:

*(4)	$= 4 \div 2$	$= 2$
*(9) $- 3$	$= 4\frac{1}{2} - 3$	$= 1\frac{1}{2}$
*(16) $+$ *(8)	$= 8 + 4$	$= 12$

Solve.

1. *(84) = _____

2. $10 +$ *(28) = _____

3. $1{,}013 -$ *($2{,}006$) = _____

4. *($64{,}391$) $+$ *($64{,}391$) = _____

5. *($\$456.00$) $-$ *($\$329.00$) = _____

6. $47 +$ *($746{,}009$) $-$ *($746{,}102$) = _____

The symbol α represents the operation $x^2 + 3$. Solve.

7. $\alpha(6)$ = _____

8. $\alpha(3)$ = _____

9. $18 + \alpha(2)$ = _____

10. $2 + \alpha(4) -$ *(16) = _____

11. $12 + \alpha(7)$ = _____

12. *(24) $\times \alpha(3)$ = _____

The symbol § represents the operation $\left(\frac{4x - 2}{3}\right) - (x + 2)$. Solve.

13. §(13) = _____

14. §(16) = _____

15. §(27) = _____

16. §(28) = _____

17. §(29) = _____

18. §(30) = _____

19. Look at Exercises 15–18. Can you solve for §(31) without using the operation? why or why not?

_____

_____

20. $Y(4) = 16$, $Y(24) = 96$, and $Y(28) = 112$. What arithmetic operation(s) does Y represent?

_____

_____

21. Create three different possible arithmetic operations, and assign a symbol to each. Give several examples of performing each operation. _____

ENRICH   Number

Miha, Yoko, and Lynn buy season tickets to see the Sereno Heights soccer team. They each pay $43.20 for a book of 12 tickets. A book of tickets has a 20% discount off the price of 12 single admission tickets.

1. Miha's dog ate 3 of her tickets; so, she has to pay the price of single admission for those games. Did she save any money by buying the discounted book of tickets? ____

2. Yoko misses 2 games of the season. How much did she save by buying season tickets instead of single admission tickets? _____

3. If Yoko had sold the 2 tickets at 60% of their single-admission value, how much would she have saved by buying the book of tickets? What percent would she have saved? Round to the nearest percent. _____

Lynn goes to the first 9 games but then signs up for wind-surfing classes that take place at the same time as the soccer games. Her friend Ashura agrees to buy the 3 tickets she has left.

4. If Lynn sells the tickets for single admission prices, how much will it have cost her to see each of the 9 games she saw? _____

5. If Lynn decides to give Ashura the tickets, how much over single admission price has she paid for each game she has attended? _____

6. Lynn decides to pay single admission prices for each game that she has seen. Ashura pays her the difference between that amount and what Lynn spent on tickets. What percent does Ashura save from paying the single admission ticket price for the 3 games? _____

7. What should you consider when buying season tickets?

_____

_____

_____

_____

Name _____ Date _____

Make a reasonable estimate for each question below. For some of the questions you will need to do some computation. Think carefully before answering.

1. How many hours do you sleep per year?

_____

2. How many hours do you spend eating per month?

_____

3. How long would it take you to walk 10 miles?

_____

4. How long would it take you to bicycle 20 miles?

_____

5. How long would it take you to drive 100 miles?

_____

6. How many days are there in a decade?

_____

7. How many seconds are there in a month?

_____

8. How many students are there in your school?

_____

9. How tall is a 7-story building?

_____

10. How many days old are you?

_____

11. How many words do you know how to spell?

_____

Name _____ Date _____

Venn diagrams can be used to represent true or false
statements and their relationships. Look at some simple sets
and their diagrams. Diagonal lines show the part of the set
that does not exist.

The set defined: Let P = set of all people
                   A = set of all artists
                   C = set of all cooks

Artists are people.	There are no cooks.	No artists are cooks.
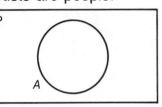	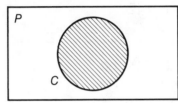	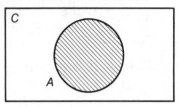

1. Use the defined sets to diagram.   Let M = set of all monsters
                                       H = set of all three-headed monsters
                                       F = set of all fuzzy-footed monsters

All three-headed monsters are monsters.	There are no fuzzy-footed monsters.	The set of all monsters.

2. Write the propositions.   Let P = set of all people
                                  F = set of all field-hockey players
                                  S = set of all soccer players

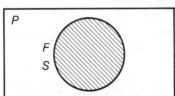	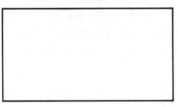	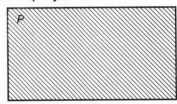
_____	_____	_____
_____	_____	_____

3. Define three sets of your own. Write and diagram four
new propositions.

ENRICH | Number

Here are some curiosities about numbers and their factors. Two numbers are said to be **amicable,** or **friendly,** if the sum of one number's factors, other than the number itself, equals the other number, and vice versa. The Greeks were able to identify only one pair of amicable numbers: 220 and 284.

Factors of 220: 1, 2, 4, 5, 10, 11, 20, 22, 44, 55, 110
      Sum: $1 + 2 + 4 + 5 + 10 + 11 + 20 + 22 + 44 + 55 + 110 = 284$

Factors of 284: 1, 2, 4, 71, 142
      Sum: $1 + 2 + 4 + 71 + 142 = 220$

Amicable pairs are rare and include 5,020 and 5,564; and 1,184 and 1,210.

1. One part of an amicable pair is 2,924. What is the other number? _____

2. Is 3,284 part of an amicable pair? _____

Abundant numbers are those whose factors, other than the number itself, add to sums greater than the number itself. Nearly all abundant numbers have a subset (or several subsets) of their factors that add up to the parent number. **Weird numbers** are abundant numbers that do not have such a subset. For example:

Factors of 12: 1, 2, 3, 4, 6
      Sum: $1 + 2 + 3 + 4 + 6 = 16$
            $2 + 4 + 6 = 12$

12 is therefore abundant, but not weird.

3. There are only two weird numbers under 1,000. A weird number is 836. Is the other 96, 521, 70, or 342? _____

Perfect numbers are numbers that equal the sum of their factors other than the number itself. The Greeks thought them magical.

Factors of 6: 1, 2, 3
      Sum: $1 + 2 + 3 = 6$

4. What is the one perfect number between 20 and 30? _____

5. Are any negative numbers also perfect numbers? Why or why not? _____

Use with pages 94–95.

ENRICH   Problem Solving

Read each problem. Without figuring the exact answer, write the letter of the most reasonable answer.

1. Frieda's family owns an apple orchard. There are 154 rows of trees. Each row has 22 trees. How many trees are there in the orchard? _____

2. Frieda and her family can pick 20 bushels of apples per hour. There are about 120 apples in one bushel. How many apples can Frieda and her family pick in 3 hours? _

3. Oren sells apple pies made from the orchard's apples. Each pie uses 7 apples. He makes 9 pies each day. How many apples does he use in a week? _____

4. Each apple tree yields 8 bushels of apples. Ryan and his friends can pick 18 bushels per day. How many days will it take them to pick 60 trees' worth? _____

5. Claude is making apple butter. He needs 32 apples to make 1 pound of apple butter. Claude wants to make 4.5 pounds of apple butter. How many apples will he need? _

6. Frieda's farm covers 433.6 acres. Her family bought the farm in 4 equal-sized parcels of land. About how many acres were there in each parcel? _____

7. Frieda's family purchased the first parcel of land in 1921. They bought the second parcel 12 years later. They bought the third parcel in 1946 and the last one in 1984. How many years passed between the buying of the second and last parcels? _____

a. 5
b. 8
c. 13
d. 20
e. 26
f. 35
g. 42
h. 51
i. 63
j. 108
k. 144
l. 165
m. 240
n. 306
o. 400
p. 441
q. 480
r. 520
s. 610
t. 720
u. 864
v. 1,864
w. 3,388
x. 6,530
y. 7,200
z. 13,214

ENRICH | Patterns

20–8–9–19   9–19   1   3–15–4–5–4   13–5–19–19–1–7–5

These numbers represent a sentence written in code. There are many types of codes you can use to disguise messages. One kind of code uses different numbers to stand for each letter of the alphabet. In the code used, A = 1, B = 2, C = 3 . . . Z = 26, and the statement can be deciphered.

20–8–9–19   9–19   1   3–15–4–5–4   13–5–19–19–1–7–5.
T H I S   I S   A   C O D E D   M E S S A G E.

Translating a message from a code is called **deciphering** or **decoding**. Writing a message in code is called **enciphering** or **encoding**.

1. Use the same code to decipher the message.

9   12–9–11–5   23–1–12–11–9–14–7   20–15   19–3–8–15–15–12.

_____

2. Encipher the message, MEET ME ON THE CORNER AFTER SCHOOL, using the code A = 2, B = 4, C = 6, D = 8 . . . Z = 52.

_____

_____

3. You can also use letters to stand for other letters. This message uses the code A = Z, B = Y, C = X . . . Z = A. Decode the message.

GSRH ZOKSZYVG RH YZXPDZIW.

_____

4. A famous code uses the sentence "The quick brown fox jumps over the lazy dog." This sentence is used because it contains all twenty-six letters. Write a code, numbering the letters in the sentence in the order in which they occur: T = 1, H = 2, E = 3 . . . G = 26. Decipher the message.
6   22–17   19–11   26–11–11–25   22–1 7–11–25–3–19
6   19–2–11–5–21–25   9–3   22   1–3–22–7–2–3–10.

_____

5. Make up your own code using numbers to represent letters, and encode a message. Trade your coded message with a classmate, and see if you can decipher each other's codes.

ENRICH   Problem Solving

Rachel owns and operates the Mousetrap Cheese Shop. The list at the right shows the prices of some cheeses and other items that Rachel sells. Read the problems below, and decide which operation or operations you will use to solve each one. Then solve.

CHEESE PRICES PER POUND	
Brie	$3.72
Cheddar	$2.80
Edam	$3.44
Gouda	$3.56
Swiss	$3.84
Stay-Krisp crackers	$1.88
Wheatrite crackers	$2.21

1. Mr. Carver wants to buy 3 pounds of Brie. How much change will he receive from $15?

   _____

2. Rachel is weighing cheddar for Mr. Douglas. He asked for 4 pounds. The scale shows 2.2 pounds. How much cheese should Rachel add? How much will Mr. Douglas have to pay?

   _____

3. Belle wants to buy 2 pounds of Edam and a box of Stay-Krisp crackers. Will she have enough left from $20 to buy 3 pounds of Gouda?

   _____

4. Rachel buys a 12-pound wheel of Swiss cheese to sell in her store. She divides it into 16 equal pieces. How much does each piece weigh?

   _____

5. Rachel orders a 24-pound wheel of Gruyere cheese for the store. She pays $47.52. How much should she charge per pound in order to earn a profit of $36.00 from selling the wheel?

   _____

6. Mrs. Kennison wants to buy 0.75 pounds of Brie and twice that much Edam. How much will she have to pay?

   _____

7. The Mousetrap Cheese Shop offers a cheese sampler tray that contains 0.3 pound of each cheese on the list and a box of Wheatrite crackers. The tray and wrapping added $1.15 to the cost. How much does the sampler tray sell for?

   _____

ENRICH   Measurement

Many ancient cultures, such as the Celts, had calendars based on thirteen lunar months each having four 7-day weeks. The first day of the year was the first day of spring. The Celtic calendar, with its months of exactly the same length, uses a finite number system, or **modular system.** In a modular system, things are counted or ordered in a pattern, at the end of which the pattern is repeated. For example, a clock is based upon a repeating pattern of twelve hours.

1. Describe two other modular systems.

_____

The calendar we use is not modular since there are different amounts of days in different months.

2. Examine the relationship between the date of a month and the day of the week it falls on (for example, Thursday). What is the difference between the Celtic calendar and our calendar with regard to this relationship?

_____

_____

_____

3. If today is Tuesday, what day of the week will it be in $2\frac{1}{2}$ months using the Celtic calendar? What if our calendar were used?

_____

4. How would you find the Celtic counterpart of a date on our calendar?

_____

_____

5. Our calendar year is almost exactly one revolution of the Earth around the Sun. Is the Celtic calendar longer or shorter than our year? What happens to fixed events in the solar year (such as equinoxes) in the Celtic calendar?

_____

_____

   Use with pages 102–103.

Name _____ Date _____

Meteorology is the science of studying and forecasting the weather. Meteorologists use specific symbols to represent wind speed, wind direction, and cloud conditions. Meteorologists combine these symbols with the temperature to indicate the weather picture for an area. Complete the table below. Put the symbol in the appropriate place on the map.

Wind speed	Wind direction	Sky cover
5 mph	Northerly	◯ Clear
10 mph	Northeasterly	◐ Scattered clouds
15 mph	Southeasterly	◑ Partly cloudy
25 mph	Easterly	● Cloudy
50 mph	Westerly	⊕ Sky obscured

JUNE 4, 2002

City	Sky cover	Wind speed	Wind direction	°C	Symbol
Boston	Partly cloudy	5 mph	Northerly	20°C	20°C ⊘
New York City	Cloudy	15 mph	Westerly	18°C	
Chicago	Clear	55 mph	Northeasterly	22°C	
Miami	Partly cloudy	Calm	———	27°C	
Houston	Sky obscured	10 mph	Easterly	25°C	
Los Angeles	Scattered clouds	15 mph	Southeasterly	19°C	

Complete your own table like the one above. Use the same six cities for June 4, 2003. Find the sky cover, wind speed, wind direction, and temperature. Use another sheet of paper. Draw a map. Put the appropriate weather-symbol in its place on the map.

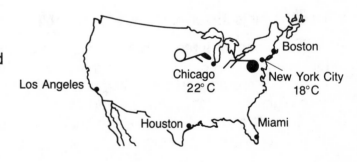

JUNE 4, 2003

City	Sky cover	Wind speed	Wind direction	°C	Symbol
Boston					
New York City					
Chicago					
Miami					
Houston					
Los Angeles					

ENRICH   Patterns

A **cryptarithm** is a puzzle in which alphabet letters are substituted for digits in an arithmetic problem. Each letter represents a unique digit. For example, if the letter M is discovered to represent the digit 7, then no other letter can stand for a 7. In order to solve a cryptarithm, you need to use logical thinking and the process of elimination. Also keep in mind arithmetic rules you have learned. For example, we can solve for A. The only digit that when multiplied by another digit results in itself is 0. A = 0.

$$\begin{array}{r} FE \\ \times\ A \\ \hline AA \end{array}$$

Here is another cryptarithm. To find the digits that are represented by the letters B, Y, C, and A, use these hints.

- Since the product has only three digits, B must be 3 or less. If B were greater than 3, the product B × B would have two digits. 3 × 3 = 9: one digit; 4 × 4 = 16: two digits.
- Y × Y = B, so Y × Y must have 3, 2, or 1 in the ones place.
- Test with Y = 9; then Y = 1.

The other digits follow: Y = 9, C = 3, A = 6.

$$\begin{array}{r} BY \\ \times\ BY \\ \hline CAB \end{array}$$

B = 3, 2, or 1
Y = 9 or 1
B = 1

1. Solve the cryptarithms. Complete the table.

$$\begin{array}{r} IS \\ \times\ IS \\ \hline HISS \end{array} \qquad \begin{array}{r} LU \\ \times\ LU \\ \hline BLU \end{array}$$

I =	H =	U =
S =	L =	B =

2. Use the hints to solve. Complete the table.

- Since the sum of three different digits cannot exceed 24 (for example, 9 + 8 + 7 = 24), U must be 1 or 2. Even if S + U + D regroups in the thousands place, the sum of three digits (24) + 2 cannot exceed 26.
- S + U must equal 10 because the sum of S + U + D has the digit D in the ones place.

$$\begin{array}{r} S,SSS \\ U,UUU \\ +\ D,DDD \\ \hline US,SSD \end{array}$$

S	U	D

3. Complete the table to discover the hidden message.

SE + FE = YE   SE + FE + FE = TE

$$\begin{array}{r} YEE,EEE \\ \times\ \quad FE \\ \hline Y,EEE,EEE \end{array} \qquad \begin{array}{r} AEE \\ \times\ SEE \\ \hline UE,EEE \end{array} \qquad \begin{array}{r} S,EEE \\ \times\ FEE \\ \hline SEE,EEE \end{array} \qquad \begin{array}{r} AE,EEE \\ \times\ A,EEE \\ \hline SE,EEE,EEE \end{array}$$

A = 2	
E =	S =
T =	U =
F =	Y =

This is ___ ___ ___ ___   ___ ___ ___ ___ ___.
        0   2   4   5   4   6   8   1   1

Name _____ Date _____

You are planning the first annual Spring Parade in Akron, Ohio. All the floats and participants will be mounted on bicycles. The parade, moving at a rate of about 2.5 miles per hour, should take between 2 and 3 hours. The parade should pass the University of Akron, Perkins Park, and Summit Lake Park. It should not travel along highways. On the map below, plan the route the parade will take. Then answer the questions.

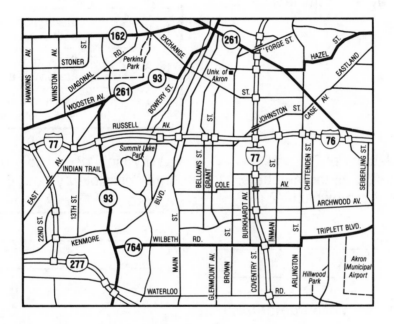

1. Where does the parade begin? Where does it end? About how many miles long is it? _____

2. About how many hours will it take to travel the distance between the University and Perkins Park? _____

3. If the parade begins at noon, at what time will it reach Summit Lake Park? _____

4. Put an *X* on the map to mark the halfway point of the parade route.

5. If the parade route also had to include part of Brown Street, about how many miles would be added to your route? how many hours? _____

ENRICH Number

Here are the rules for divisibility by 3, 4, 5, 6, 8, and 9.

You can use these rules to determine divisibility by larger numbers. For example, a number is divisible by 15 if it is divisible by both 5 and 3. Think of divisibility as factorization: a number's divisibility by 5 means that 5 is a factor of that number. A number is divisible by any combination of its prime factors.

A number is divisible	if
by 3	the sum of the number's digits is divisible by 3.
by 4	the number's last two digits are divisible by 4.
by 5	the number's last digit is 5 or 0.
by 6	the number is divisible by both 3 and 2.
by 8	the number's last three digits are divisible by 8.
by 9	the sum of the number's digits is divisible by 9.

1. Write the prime factors of 72, and combine them to find all the numbers, other than 1 and 72, by which 72 is divisible.

   _____

   _____

2. Why isn't 18 divisible by 12 even though it is divisible by both 6 and 2?

   _____

   _____

   _____

Read each division rule. Write *true* or *false*. Explain your answer.

3. A number is divisible by 30 if it is divisible by 3 and 2, and it ends in 0.

   _____

4. A number is divisible by 18 if it is even, and the sum of its digits is a multiple of 9.

   _____

5. A number is divisible by 48 if its last three digits are divisible by 8, the sum of its digits is divisible by 3, and it is even.

   _____

6. Write a divisibility rule of your own. Check it by prime factorization of the divisors and dividends.

   _____

Use with pages 118–119.

ENRICH   **Algebra**

In the lattices, replace *x* inside each rectangle with the number in the diamond above it. Write the value of each expression in the next diamond below. Follow the arrows until you have completed the lattice.

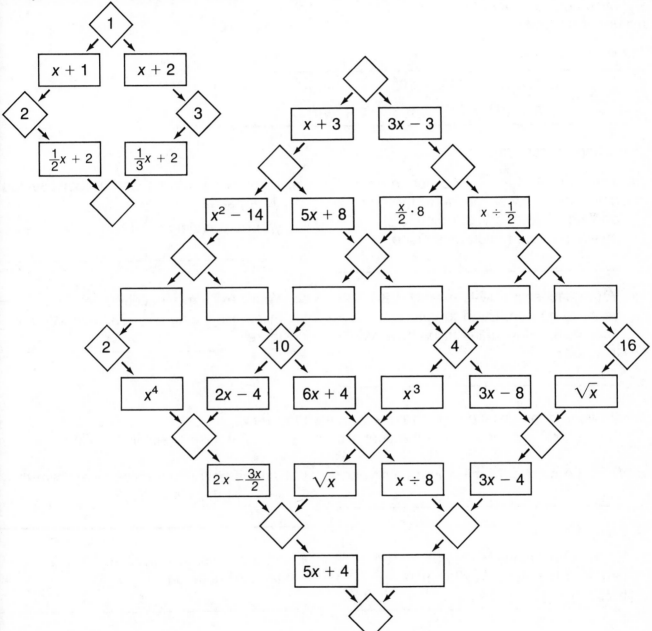

Could answers vary in the second lattice's rectangles? Explain.

_____

_____

_____

ENRICH   Algebra

Scientific notation can be used to express any number, but it is most useful with very large or very small numbers. The speed of light is a number commonly written in scientific notation. Light travels 1.86×10^5 miles per second.

Numbers written in scientific notation can be multiplied and divided without converting them to standard notation. Sometimes, the exponent on the 10 will have to be adjusted

For example:

$$(2.1 \times 10^5) \times (3.2 \times 10^4) = 6.72 \times 10^9$$
$$(9.36 \times 10^3) \div (3.6 \times 10^4) = 2.6 \times 10^{-1}$$

Use scientific notation.

1. There are 8.64×10^4 seconds in one day. How many seconds are there in one week? in one year? Round answers to the hundredths place.

   _____

2. If you were in a spaceship that traveled $\frac{1}{2}$ the speed of light, how fast would you be traveling?

   _____

3. Your spaceship travels exactly 4.2 years to go from Earth to your first destination. How many miles have you traveled?

   _____

4. Your next trip is exactly 7.32×10^{11} miles. How long will it take you to get there? _____

A light year is the distance light travels in one year. The Earth is 32,000 light years from the center of the Milky Way. Use scientific notation.

5. Write the number of miles in a light year.

   _____

6. Earth is how many miles away from the center of the Milky Way?

   _____

7. Earth is how many feet away from the center of the Milky Way? (1 mile = 5,280 ft)

   _____

8. Write the distance in Question 7 in standard notation.

   _____

9. Why is scientific notation useful in measuring astronomical distances, such as the distance from Earth to the center of the Milky Way?

   _____

   _____

Use with pages 122–123.

ENRICH   Patterns

Arithmetic operations often result in **loops,** or patterns, of numbers that repeat endlessly. More complex mathematical operations often yield more complex repetitive patterns of numbers.

Consider the number sequence generated in the following way. Pick a number to serve as an initial term. If it is even, divide it by 2. If it is odd, multiply it by 3 and add 1. Continue the operation using the new result. For example, the initial term 16 gives

16:   8, 4, 2, 1, 4, 2, 1, . . .

Perform this operation on each number until the pattern repeats.

1. 9: _____

_____

2. 3: _____

3. 12: _____

4. 4: _____

5. What pattern results from the number 9 and its factor 3, and from 12 and its factor 4? What is the fastest way to determine a loop?

_____

_____

_____

6. This sequence uses different operations. Continue the sequence. Is there a loop? 37:   110, 55, 164, 82, 41, 122, 61, 182, . . .

_____

_____

7. What operation(s) has generated this sequence?

_____

_____

_____

_____

8. Choose three prime numbers less than 100 and see the loops that are generated by this operation.

_____

_____

_____

_____

ENRICH   **Algebra**

There is a total of 41 ducks and geese on the pond. The number of ducks is 4 less than twice the number of geese. How many geese and how many ducks are there on the pond?

You can solve this riddle by setting up an equation with the information given. Let g = number of geese and d = number of ducks. Since you know that $d = 2g - 4$, you can substitute for d to solve.

$g + d = 41$	Then use the value of g to solve for d.
$g + (2g - 4) = 41$	$d = 2g - 4$
$(g + 2g) - 4 = 41$	$d = 30 - 4$
$3g = 45$	$d = 26$
$g = 15$	

There are 15 geese and 26 ducks on the pond.

Rebecca is twice as old as her cousin. Her cousin is 2 years younger than Rebecca's older brother. The sum of their ages is 26. How old is each child?

You know each person's age in relation to the cousin; so, express each age in terms of the cousin's age: x = cousin's age; $2x$ = Rebecca's age; $(x + 2)$ = brother's age.

1. How old are the three children? Write an equation and solve for x.

   _____

   _____

2. There is a total of 19 mice and hamsters in Mr. Thompson's cages. The number of mice is 5 less than 3 times the number of hamsters. How many mice and how many hamsters are there?

   _____

3. Jeff's younger sister's age is 3 times the difference between Jeff's age and his older sister's age. Jeff's age is 4 times the difference between his age and his older sister's age. The sum of all the children's ages is 36. How old is each child?

   _____

   _____

4. There is another way to do each of the two examples at the top of the page. Write a different equation for each.

   _____

ENRICH   Problem Solving

You are an adviser to the President's Economic Planning Committee. Members of the committee have made statements about the dollar's declining value between 1967 and 1980. The graph below shows the purchasing power of the dollar relative to what $1 could buy in 1967. Use the graph below to help you decide whether each statement is *true* or *false.*

1. JOHN WILTON: "The actual value of the dollar decreased by about 40 cents between 1970 and 1979." _____

2. J. D. SANCHEZ: "The value of the dollar decreased more between 1967 and 1972 than it did between 1972 and 1980." _____

3. HELEN AKAI: "I disagree with J. D. I do think, however, that the dollar decreased more between 1967 and 1974 than it did between 1974 and 1980." _____

4. BRIAN PERSKI: "The greatest one-year drop in the dollar's value occurred between 1969 and 1970." _____

5. JOHN WILTON: "In 1975, the average purchasing value of the dollar was less than 60 cents." _____

6. HELEN AKAI: "The purchasing power of the dollar first fell below 50 cents between 1977 and 1978." _____

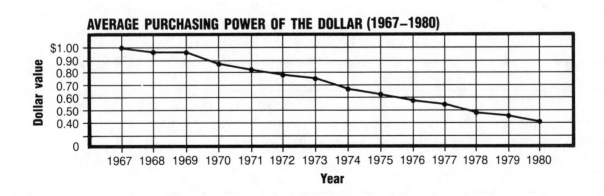

AVERAGE PURCHASING POWER OF THE DOLLAR (1967–1980)

Name _____ Date _____

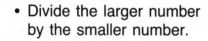 **Number**

Division can be used to quickly find the **greatest common factor (GCF)** of two numbers. For example, to find the GCF of 180 and 384

- Divide the larger number by the smaller number.

- Then take the divisor and divide it by the remainder.

- Repeat this step until a remainder of 0 is reached.

- The divisor that yields a remainder of 0 is the GCF of the two numbers.

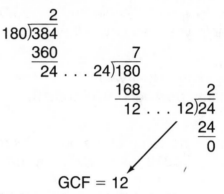

The same process can be used to find the greatest common factor of three numbers. For example, to find the GCF of 72, 198, and 495

- Use division to find the GCF of any two of the numbers.
- Take the GCF and the third number, and find their GCF.
- That number is the GCF of all 3 numbers.

GCF of 72 and 198 = 18
GCF of 18 and 495 = 9
GCF of 72, 198, and 495 = 9

Use this technique, and write the GCF.

1. 432 and 288 _____   **2.** 144 and 300 _____   **3.** 16, 64, and 192 _____

4. 15, 225, and 360 _____   **5.** 8 and 162 _____   **6.** 270, 35, and 60 _____

7. How would you use the same technique to find the GCF of four numbers?

_____

_____

_____

8. Reducing numbers to factors by division could be helpful in other arithmetic operations. Explain how in two other operations.

_____

_____

52   **Use with pages 130–131.**

Name _____ Date _____

To find the **least common multiple (LCM)** of two or more numbers, we can use exponents of prime numbers. Write any repeating prime factors as exponents.

$$252 = 2^2 \times 3^2 \times 7 \qquad 270 = 2 \times 3^3 \times 5$$

Write the common prime factors (in this case, 2 and 3). Multiply these common factors, each raised to the highest power and found in either factorization.

$$2^2 \times 3^3 = 108$$

Multiply this product by any factors which are not in both numbers. This is the LCM.

The LCM of 252 and 270 is
$2^2 \times 3^3 \times 7 \times 5 = 4 \times 27 \times 5 = 3,780.$

Write the LCM.

1. 90 and 42

2. 75 and 165

3. 12, 15, and 18

4. 28, 42, and 45

Five cars compete in an all-day race. The table shows the time it takes for each car to complete one lap. The race starts at 6:00 A.M. Each car does not change speed.

What is the earliest time that each event occurs? (HINT: Use exponents of prime factors to find the LCM of each car's lap time.)

Car	Lap time
Blue	15 minutes
Green	9 minutes
Yellow	18 minutes
Red	14 minutes
Orange	21 minutes

5. The yellow and the orange car pass the starting point at the same time. _____

6. The blue, green, and yellow cars pass the starting point at the same time. _____

7. The red and the orange car pass the starting point at the same time. _____

8. All of the cars pass the starting point at the same time.

_____

9. When is the LCM of a given group of numbers always one of the numbers in the group?

_____

ENRICH   Number

Tien and Chian, survivors of Earth's lost continent of Hisa, are moving to the planet Bulgar-2. On the way, they stop in the United States to investigate its base-ten number system. The Hisan system is rooted in base six.

1. Write the six digits in base six. _____

Convert to Hisan.

2. $6_{10} =$ _____   **3.** $8_{10} =$ _____   **4.** $23_{10} =$ _____   **5.** $36_{10} =$ _____

Tien and Chian reach their final destination, Bulgar-2. There, the Ecto-Qaidam civilization has a different number system and symbols. A thin slash equals 5, and a bold slash equals 25. Thus, the number 56 is written as ▬▬.

Ecto-Qaidam						
1	•	5	—	9	••••
2	••	6	•̶	10	=
3	•••	7	••̶	11	•=
4	••••	8	•••̶	12	••=

Convert from Ecto-Qaidam to Hisan.

6. •••• = _____   **7.** ••≡ = _____   **8.** ▬▬ = _____   **9.** •▬▬ = _____

Convert from Hisan to Ecto-Qaidam.

10. $11_6 =$ _____   **11.** $43_6 =$ _____   **12.** $55_6 =$ _____   **13.** $35_6 =$ _____

Solve. Write the answer in base ten.

14. $134_6 +$ •▬ = _____   **15.** ▬▬ $- 31_6 =$ _____   **16.** $324_6 - 82_{10} =$ _____

17. ••≡ $+ 102_6 =$ _____   **18.** $42_6 - 12_6 =$ _____   **19.** $1_6 + 15_6 =$ _____

Multiply. Write the answer in Hisan.

20. •▬▬ $\times 4_{10} =$ _____   **21.** • $\times$ •••▬▬ = _____   **22.** $56_{10} \times$ ••• = _____

Solve.

23. The highly intelligent insectlike creatures on the planet Bulgar-1 have no number system. See if you can create one for them. Keep in mind that each of these creatures has three fingers on each of its three hands. Convert your telephone number into the new system so that the creatures will be able to contact you.

_____

_____

Use with pages 136–137.

Name _____ Date _____

Fadzai, the bricklayer, uses math to estimate how many bricks she needs for each job. She is asked to build a garden wall 3 yards high and 4 inches thick for a length of 50 yards. If it takes 6 bricks per square yard to build a wall 4 inches thick, how many bricks will she need? The total surface area of the wall will be 3 yards × 50 yards = 150 square yards. Multiply this amount by the number of bricks per square yard to find the number of bricks needed for the wall. 6 × 150 = 900. So, a total of 900 bricks is needed for the wall.

Fadzai is asked to leave space in the wall for a gate 4 yards wide. To find the total number of bricks needed, she subtracts the area of the gate space from the total area of the wall, and then multiplies the answer by the number of bricks per square yard. Area: 150 − (4 × 3) = 138; 138 × 6 = 828. Fadzai will need 828 bricks.

1. Fadzai uses 12 bricks per square foot to build an 8-inch-thick wall. Approximately how many bricks will she need to build this section of the house? The wall will be 8 inches thick. _____

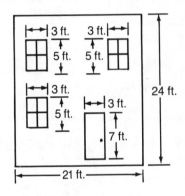

2. If the bricks cost $20 per thousand, how much will Fadzai have to pay for the bricks to build the section shown? _____

3. Fadzai then plans to build a rectangular open-air pottery kiln $2\frac{1}{3}$ yards wide and $3\frac{2}{3}$ yards long. It takes 12 adobe tiles per square foot to build each 8-inch-thick wall. How many tiles would Fadzai need to build the 8-inch-thick and 6-foot-high kiln? _____

4. How many tiles will be needed in Problem 3 if the kiln is to contain two entrances, one 2 feet wide and the other 3 feet wide? _____

5. What would you need to know to find the number of bricks needed to build an entire house?

_____

_____

ENRICH   Logic

Complete each logic table. Eliminate a box by drawing an *X*,
and place a circle in each box that is correct.

1. Louis, Patricia, Emanuel, and Jacqueline
like to swim, fly kites, read, and play
chess. Among these hobbies, each
person favors a different one. Use the
table to find each person's favorite.
  a. No person's name has the same
  number of letters as his or her favorite
  hobby.

b. The person who likes chess the most is
a girl and is friends with both Louis and
Patricia.

c. The person who likes reading the most
is a boy.

	Jacqueline	Patricia	Louis	Emanuel
Chess				
Reading				
Swimming				
Kite flying				

2. Mr. Ncube, Mr. Forest, Mr. Perrotti, Mr.
Lee, and Mr. Clark are bakers. At a
recent cake sale
  a. each baker had a cake for sale.
  b. no one bought cake baked by her
  husband.
  c. Mr. Ncube's cake was bought
  by Mrs. Forest.

d. Mr. Lee's cake was bought by the
woman whose husband's cake was
bought by Mrs. Perrotti.

e. Mrs. Ncube bought the cake baked by
the husband of the woman who bought
Mr. Clark's cake.

Complete the table to indicate who bought
each baker's cake.

	Mr. Ncube	Mr. Forest	Mr. Perrotti	Mr. Lee	Mr. Clark
Mrs. Ncube					
Mrs. Forest					
Mrs. Perrotti					
Mrs. Lee					
Mrs. Clark					

HINT: Think of clues in terms of unknowns.
For example, Clue *d*:

• Mrs. X bought Mr. Lee's cake.

• Mrs. Perrotti bought Mr. X's cake.

ENRICH Problem Solving

You are a librarian at the Seaburg Public Library. The
pictograph below shows the number of books that your
library owns in ten categories. It also shows the approximate
number of times that books in each category were borrowed
last year. Use the pictograph below to answer the questions.

	Category	Number of Books	Books Borrowed
Fiction	Plays	🕮🕮🕮🕮	🕮🕮🕮🕮
	Science fiction	🕮🕮🕮	🕮🕮🕮🕮
	Mysteries	🕮🕮	🕮🕮
	Suspense novels	🕮🕮🕮	🕮🕮🕮🕮🕮🕮
	Other novels	🕮🕮🕮🕮🕮🕮	🕮🕮🕮🕮🕮🕮🕮
Nonfiction	Science	🕮🕮🕮🕮	🕮🕮🕮🕮
	Cookbooks	🕮	🕮🕮🕮🕮
	Arts and crafts	🕮🕮🕮🕮	🕮🕮🕮🕮
	How-to books	🕮🕮🕮	🕮🕮🕮🕮🕮🕮
	Histories	🕮🕮🕮	🕮🕮🕮

Each 🕮 stands for 300 books.

1. How many books does your library own in all the
   categories shown? How many books were borrowed last
   year? _____

2. In nearly all categories, the number of books borrowed
   exceeds the number of books that the library owns. How
   is this possible? In which category was this *not* the case?

   _____

3. How many more fiction books than nonfiction books does
   the library own? Which of the two groups is more
   popular? _____

4. How many more suspense novels than mysteries does the
   library own? _____

5. On the average, about how many how-to books were
   borrowed per week? _____

Name _____ Date _____

ENRICH   Patterns

The numbers in a **magic square** form vertical, horizontal, and diagonal rows that add up to a single magic number. The magic number for the first square is 15. The magic number for the second square is 34.

4	3	8
9	5	1
2	7	6

1	12	7	14
8	13	2	11
10	3	16	5
15	6	9	4

Complete the magic squares. The magic number is 65. Use numbers from 1 to 25.

1.

1				18
7	20			24
		9	17	5
19	2	15	23	
	8	16	4	12

2.

	13	3		23
21	18		6	
22	19		10	2
	8	15	20	17
7				

3.

17	24	1	8	
	5	7	14	
4	6	13		
10			21	
	18	25	2	9

Solve.

4. In this magic square, the rows do not have a magic number through addition. What mathematical operation does the magic square use? What is the magic number?

2,187	1	243
9	81	729
27	6,561	3

_____

5. What mathematical property is used in creating magic squares?

_____

6. This is not a magic square even though it has a magic number. Adding or multiplying in consecutive row order is not important. What mathematic operation(s) does the square use? Explain your answer. What is the magic number?

6	9	2
3	5	7
8	1	4

_____

7. On another sheet of paper, complete your own magic square. Combine three arithmetic operations to create the magic number.

Use with pages 144–145.

Name _____ Date _____

Venn diagrams can be used to show a relationship between two sets. Diagonal lines show the part of the set that does not exist. Areas with diagonal lines are void areas and are no longer part of the set.

First, the sets are defined: P = the set of all people; S = the set of all swimmers; D = the set of all dancers.

Then the diagrams are filled in to illustrate the propositions.

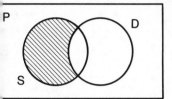

All swimmers are dancers.

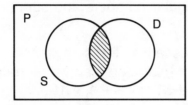

No one is both a dancer and a swimmer.

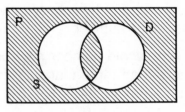

All people are either dancers or swimmers, but no one is both.

1. Use the defined sets to fill in the diagram for each proposition. P = the set of all people; L = the set of all lumberjacks; B = the set of all backpackers.

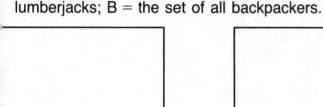

No one is both a lumberjack and a backpacker.

All lumberjacks are backpackers.

All people are either lumberjacks or backpackers, but no one is both.

2. Write the propositions. B = the set of all bicycles in Durango; R = the set of all red bicycles in Durango; T = the set of all 3-speed bicycles in Durango.

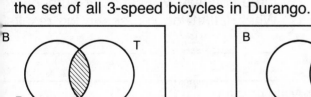

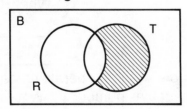

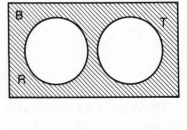

_____

_____

_____

_____

ENRICH | Patterns

A **square number** is the product of a whole number that is multiplied by itself. It can be shown as a square pattern of dots.

The numbers in the series $1 + 2 + 3 + 4 + . . .$ are called **triangular numbers.** They can be shown as equilateral triangles of dots.

Square and triangular numbers are related in many ways. If you add any two consecutive triangular numbers, the sum is a square number.

Every whole number may be expressed as the sum of no more than three triangular numbers. Numbers can be repeated. For example, $14 = 1 + 3 + 10$, and $51 = 49 + 1 + 1$.

$1 = \bullet \qquad 4 = \begin{smallmatrix}\bullet\ \bullet\\\bullet\ \bullet\end{smallmatrix} \qquad 9 = \begin{smallmatrix}\bullet\ \bullet\ \bullet\\\bullet\ \bullet\ \bullet\\\bullet\ \bullet\ \bullet\end{smallmatrix}$

$(1 \times 1) \quad (2 \times 2) \quad (3 \times 3)$

$\bullet = 1 \qquad \begin{smallmatrix}\bullet\\\bullet\ \bullet\end{smallmatrix} = 3 \qquad \begin{smallmatrix}\bullet\\\bullet\ \bullet\\\bullet\ \bullet\ \bullet\end{smallmatrix} = 6$

$(1) \quad (1 + 2) \quad (1 + 2 + 3)$

$\begin{smallmatrix}\bullet\\\bullet\ \bullet\end{smallmatrix} + \begin{smallmatrix}\bullet\\\bullet\ \bullet\\\bullet\ \bullet\ \bullet\end{smallmatrix} = \begin{smallmatrix}\bullet\ \bullet\ \bullet\\\bullet\ \bullet\ \bullet\\\bullet\ \bullet\ \bullet\end{smallmatrix}$

$(3 + 6 = 9 = 3 \times 3)$

Write the number as the sum of three or fewer triangular numbers.

1. 21 _____

2. 43 _____

3. 17 _____

4. 119 _____

5. 140 _____

6. 199 _____

Every whole number may also be expressed as the sum of no more than four square numbers. Numbers can be repeated. For example, $23 = 1 + 4 + 9 + 9$, and $47 = 1 + 1 + 9 + 36$.

Write the number as the sum of four or fewer square numbers.

7. 38 _____

8. 65 _____

9. 128 _____

10. 99 _____

11. 140 _____

12. 199 _____

Solve.

13. Multiply any triangular number by 8 and add 1 to the product. What property does the answer have?

_____

14. Perform the operation in Problem 13 on three consecutive triangular numbers. What pattern do you see in the results?

_____

_____

15. If you are given a square number x, what operations can you perform on it to yield a triangular number y? Write a formula, and test it with some square and triangular numbers that you know. Find one square number which does not yield a triangular number.

_____

ENRICH Problem Solving

Each problem can be solved by completing and then using one of the equations shown. Draw a line from each problem to the correct equation. Complete the equation and solve.

1. The area of the walls that Sam is painting is 800 square feet. He will need 2.5 gallons of paint to do the job. How many square feet does 1 gallon of paint cover?

2. Helene bought 4 gallons of paint for $46.36. She plans to paint a 450-square-foot area. How much did she pay for each gallon of paint?

3. Marco is carpeting a staircase. Twice the amount of carpet he uses minus 15 feet equals 45 feet. How many feet of carpet does he use?

4. Melinda put up 10 feet more than 3 times as much wallpaper as did her sister, Melissa. Melissa put up 21 feet of wallpaper. How many feet of wallpaper did Melinda put up?

5. The number of hours Conrad and Jules needed to paint a house divided by 4 equals 7.25. How many hours did they need?

6. Darla is painting the trim in her room navy blue. The trim takes up 0.1 of the 875 square foot wall space. How many square feet does the trim cover?

$n =$ _____ $\times\ 21\ +$ _____

$n =$ _____

$2n$ _____ $= 45$

$n =$ _____

$4n =$ _____

$n =$ _____

_____ $\div$ _____ $= 7.25$

$n =$ _____

$n = 0.1 \times$ _____

$n =$ _____

$800 =$ _____

$n =$ _____

Name _____ Date _____

ENRICH　**Algebra**

Your family is opening a new pizza restaurant. You have created terrific pizza recipes, and your sister planned the finances on a computer. The large pizza will sell for $6.00, and the small pizza will sell for $4.50. Half of the selling price will be spent on ingredients, and the other half will be kept for living expenses and profit.

Item	Cost per ounce
Dough	$0.05
Sauce	$0.06
Cheese	$0.10

Garlic, Spices, and Oil	
Large pizza	$0.40
Small pizza	$0.39

1. Your recipe for a large pizza calls for $\frac{3}{4}$ as much cheese as dough, and $\frac{5}{6}$ as much sauce as cheese. How many ounces of each does your budget allow you to use? [HINT: (amount of dough × price of dough) + (amount of cheese × price of cheese) + (amount of sauce × price of sauce) + cost of oil and spices = price of all ingredients]

_____

_____

2. Your recipe for a small pizza calls for $\frac{3}{4}$ as much cheese as dough, and $\frac{2}{3}$ as much sauce as cheese. How many ounces of each ingredient can you use on this pizza?

_____

3. Pepperoni and sausage cost 15¢ per ounce. Onions and peppers cost $\frac{2}{3}$ as much. On your deluxe large pizza, you want to put 9 ounces of these extra ingredients, $\frac{1}{3}$ meat and $\frac{2}{3}$ vegetables. How much should you charge for the deluxe large pizza if you must still only spend $\frac{1}{2}$ of the price on ingredients? _____

4. Your sister knows that $\frac{1}{5}$ of the profit made on each pizza will be spent on rent. She expects to sell 400 large pizzas and 700 small pizzas each month. How much is your rent per month? _____

5. Your mother thinks that another location might increase sales, although the rent is $\frac{2}{15}$ higher. Your sister estimates that the better location will help you sell $\frac{1}{8}$ more pizzas of each size. Should you move? why or why not?

_____

62　　　　　　　　　　　　　　　　　　　　　　　**Use with pages 162–16**

ENRICH   Measurement

For a threaded bolt to fit properly into a threaded nut, the space between the threads on both must be precisely matched. Yet the threads of bolts, like the specifications of most manufactured goods, vary in size. It is important that they vary only by amounts that will not affect their performance. The nut must fit its bolt. The amount of variation acceptable in the manufacturing of an item is called the **tolerance.** The tolerance for the distance between threads on a bolt would be very small, about ±0.05 mm. This means that if the threads are ideally 1.00 mm apart, any threads spaced between 0.95 and 1.05 mm apart are acceptable.

Dunn Droll, Inc., manufactures clock gears. The radius of the cog is $2\frac{1}{4}$ inches. In order for it to fit the next cog, the tolerance is $\pm\frac{1}{16}$ inches. Is each measurement acceptable? Write *yes* or *no*.

1. $2\frac{1}{8}$ in. _____   2. $2\frac{3}{16}$ in. _____   3. $2\frac{1}{2}$ in. _____

Solve.

4. Maximilian's Packster Company is testing the tolerance of their fruit packsters and twist-on lids. The space between the threads should be 5 mm. If the tolerance is 0.5 mm, what is the measurement range for the fruit packsters and lids?

    _____

The figure shows the dimensions and tolerance for each part of a metal bolt manufactured by Maxamilian's Packster Company. Write the acceptable range of length for each part.

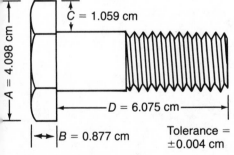

$C = 1.059$ cm

$A = 4.098$ cm

$D = 6.075$ cm

$B = 0.877$ cm

Tolerance = ±0.004 cm

5. A _____

6. B _____

7. C _____

8. D _____

9. What is the reason for having a tolerance? Why would a manufacturer make a tolerance larger or smaller?

_____

_____

ENRICH   Algebra

Flowcharts help you visualize how an algebraic equation works. Each flowchart starts with one or more *input* values. The inputs are modified in the flowchart, and emerge as a different *output.*

1. The algebraic equivalent of each step in the flowchart is shown in Figure 1. Write the output that results from input values of $x = 2$ and $y = 1$. _____

2. Complete the table based on the flowchart in Figure 1.

input x	7	9	$\frac{3}{4}$	$2\frac{2}{3}$
input y	2	11	8	$5\frac{1}{4}$
output z				

3. In Figure 2, write the algebraic equivalents of each step for the flowchart in the spaces provided.

4. Complete the table based on the flowchart in Figure 2.

input x	4	8	2	$5\frac{1}{3}$
input y	3	20	$\frac{9}{14}$	$3\frac{5}{7}$
output z				

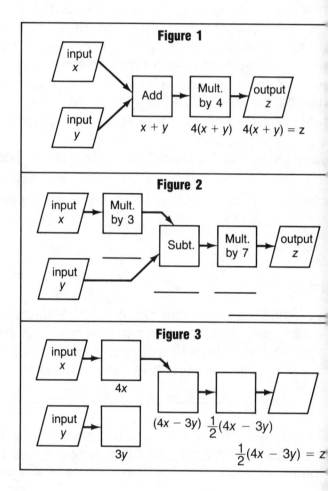

Figure 1

input x → Add → Mult. by 4 → output z
input y →

$x + y$ $4(x + y)$ $4(x + y) = z$

Figure 2

input x → Mult. by 3 → Subt. → Mult. by 7 → output z
input y →

Figure 3

input x →
input y →

$4x$ $3y$ $(4x - 3y)$ $\frac{1}{2}(4x - 3y)$

$\frac{1}{2}(4x - 3y) = z$

5. Use the algebraic equivalents to complete the flowcharts in Figure 3. If input y is $1\frac{1}{3}$, and output z is 8, what must input x be? (HINT: Plug input y into the flowchart to obtain an equation with only one unknown variable.)

_____

6. A *palindrome* is a word, such as *madam,* that reads the same backward and forward. Using only one input, at least two middle steps, and an output, see if you can design a palindrome flowchart.

_____

Use with pages 166–167.

ENRICH   Algebra

Figure A

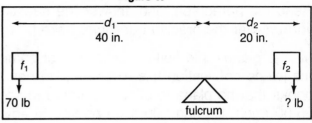

A teeter-totter is a large **lever.** Weights on either end of a lever are balanced on a **fulcrum** (see Figure A). When they are balanced, the following relationship is true

$$f_1 \times d_1 = f_2 \times d_2,$$

where f_1 is the weight, or **force,** pressing down on the left side of the fulcrum, f_2 is the force on the right side, and d_1 and d_2 are the distances of the two weights from the fulcrum. Substitute the values in Figure A to solve for the weight needed to balance the lever.

$$f_1 \times d_1 = f_2 \times d_2$$
$$70 \times 40 = f_2 \times 20$$
$$f_2 = 140$$

To balance the lever, 140 lb is needed.

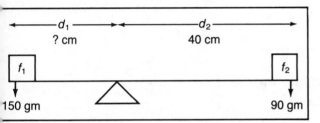

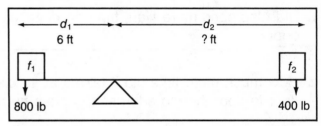

1. What is d_1? _____

2. What is d_2? _____

3. A 900-lb gorilla sits on the right side of the lever in Figure B. The weights of 5 children are shown. To balance the lever, who should sit on the left side?

_____

Figure B

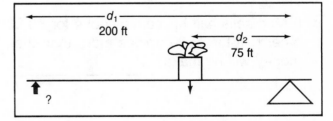

70	95	100	65	55	10
Zulu	Seth	Abdul	Marlena	Tovah	Rocio

When both forces are on the same side of the fulcrum, you can find the upward force needed to balance the lever. Use $f_1 \times d_1 = f_2 \times d_2$.

Figure C

4. A 3,500-lb chest filled with gold trinkets and a 4,500-lb ship's propeller rest on a lever in Figure C. What upward force is needed to lift the chest and the propeller to a level position? _____

5. What do you know if two items of equal weight do not balance on a lever?

_____

ENRICH — Problem Solving

Read the paragraph, and answer the questions. Be sure that you answer the precise questions asked.

Mac is planning to sell his collection of comic books at a magazine convention this weekend. He has 1,100 comic books that he plans to offer at prices ranging from $0.50 to $5.00 each. He had 500 fliers printed to advertise his sale. Each leaflet cost $0.03 to print and $0.22 to mail. He mailed 100 of them to comic-book collectors. It took Mac about an hour to address them. He took half of the remaining fliers and distributed them door-to-door. It took him about a half hour to distribute 50 fliers. He took the rest of the leaflets to school, posted 150 of them, and gave all but 1 of those remaining to friends. That he kept as a souvenir.

1. Did Mac send more fliers than he distributed door-to-door? _____

2. How much more time did it take Mac to distribute the fliers door-to-door than to address the ones he mailed?

   _____

3. Mac is willing to spend up to $50.00 advertising his sale. Can he afford to take out an ad in a local magazine for $12.50 and also mail the 100 fliers? _____

4. How much money will Mac earn if he sells all his comic books at the lowest price? _____

5. Mac estimates that he will sell all but 200 of his comic books at an average price of $0.75 each. How much money does Mac estimate he will earn? _____

6. If Mac sells half his comic books for $0.50 apiece and the other half for $3.00 apiece more than that, how much money will he make? _____

ENRICH   Number

Our number system is called base ten and has ten symbols:
0, 1, 2, 3, 4, 5, 6, 7, 8, and 9. The *base-twelve* number
system has twelve symbols: 0, 1, 2, 3, 4, 5, 6, 7, 8, 9, α, β.

1. Complete the table.

base ten:	1	2	3	4	5	6	7	8	9	10	11	12
base twelve:	1	2	3	4	5	6	7	8	9	α	β	10
base ten:	13	14	15	16	17	18	19	20	21	22	23	24
base twelve:	11											

For numbers greater than 11 in base twelve, another
place is used to show the value of the digits. Each
place is 12 times greater than the place to the right.
For example, number $\beta 7\alpha 5_{12}$ is shown.

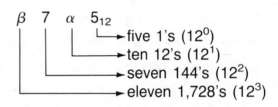

β 7 α 5_{12}
- → five 1's (12^0)
- → ten 12's (12^1)
- → seven 144's (12^2)
- → eleven 1,728's (12^3)

To write a base-ten number as a base-twelve number, divide
the base-ten number by the base-twelve place values. Begin
with the largest place value that can be divided into the
base-ten number.

$412_{10} = x_{12}$

$412 \div 144 =$ ② R124

Divide the remainder by the next greatest base-twelve place
value. Continue to the ones place.

$124 \div 12 =$ ⑩ R④

② ⑩ ④ $= 2\alpha 4_{12}$

Write the number in base twelve.

2. $92_{10} =$ _____

3. $54_{10} =$ _____

4. $59_{10} =$ _____

5. $158_{10} =$ _____

6. $126_{10} =$ _____

7. $443_{10} =$ _____

8. $144_{10} =$ _____

9. $707_{10} =$ _____

10. $154_{10} =$ _____

Solve.

11. In base ten, 1 foot = 12 inches. In base twelve, 1 foot
would equal 10 inches. Use this fact to create a system
in base twelve that uses inches and feet as its basic
units of measure. (HINT: 12_{10} inches = 10_{12} inches)

_____

Name _____ Date _____

The total value of all the goods and services produced by a country during a period of time (usually a year) is called the **Gross National Product (GNP).** In general, a higher GNP indicates more economic activity. The GNP of a country divided by its population gives the GNP per person.

There are four main parts of the GNP.

a. purchases of goods and services by individuals within the country
b. government expenditures within the country
c. business investment within the country
d. import income: the value of goods and services exported less the value of those imported

The table lists the economic figures for Matique, a small island country with a population of 5,000 people.

1. Complete the table. Expenditures are given in thousands.

	Year 1	Year 2	Year 3	Year 4
Individual expenditures	40,000	48,000		48,000
Government expenditures	10,000	14,500	21,000	18,500
Business investment	12,000	15,000	20,500	11,500
Import expenditures	12,000	13,000	14,500	15,500
Export receipts	27,500		13,000	
GNP			90,000	
GNP per person		16		17

2. Which economic trends in Matique reversed in Year 4?

_____

3. Which measure increased by the largest percentage from Year 1 to Year 4?

_____

4. Sometimes one country with a higher GNP than another will have a lower GNP per person. What does this indicate?

_____

_____

5. GNP figures include all money transactions. In what countries are GNP figures likely to reflect less than the total value of all economic activity?

_____

_____

ENRICH | Patterns

An **arithmetic sequence** is a sequence of numbers in which the difference between consecutive terms is a constant. For example, the set of odd numbers has a **common difference** of 2 between each consecutive term. An **arithmetic series** is the sum of the numbers in an arithmetic sequence.

There is a quick way to add large sequences. Write the numbers of a sequence in a row, and then write the numbers in reverse under them. Notice what happens when you add the two sequences as vertical pairs.

$$1 + \ \ 4 + \ \ 7 + 10 + 13 + 16 + 19$$
$$\underline{19 + 16 + 13 + 10 + \ \ 7 + \ \ 4 + \ \ 1}$$
$$20 \quad 20 \quad 20 \quad 20 \quad 20 \quad 20 \quad 20$$

An arithmetic series is the number of terms divided by 2 and multiplied by this common amount (20 in this case). In the example, the series is equal to $70 = \frac{7}{2}(20)$.

1. Why is it necessary to divide by 2?

_____

If n is the number of terms in the sequence, a is the first term, and l is the last term, the arithmetic series $S = \frac{n}{2}(a + l)$.

2. What is the arithmetic series with the first term ⁻5, last term 73, and 40 terms in the series? _____

3. If the sequence in Problem 2 had 30 terms, what would the series be? _____

4. When an arithmetic series is 0, what must be true about the formula? Is n significant? why or why not?

_____

_____

_____

ENRICH   Algebra

If you had a secret message, you might want to send it in code. In one standard code, the numbers 1–26 represent the letters *A–Z* in order. A space is 27, a period is 28, a question mark is 29, and commas separate all numbers.

1. Decode the following message written in this code.

3, 15, 4, 5, 19, 27, 1, 18, 5, 27, 6, 21, 14, 28

_____

Many people know this code, and so, you might need a more complex code. One code uses ordered pairs of numbers in the above code and multiplies these pairs by a **matrix.** Write the above coded message in ordered pairs.

(3,15) (**4, 5**) (_____, _____) (_____, _____) (_____, _____) (_____, _____) (_____, _____)

In matrix coding, each pair will be multiplied by an encoding matrix, $E = \begin{bmatrix} 2 & 4 \\ 1 & 3 \end{bmatrix}$.

The rule for multiplication of an ordered pair and the matrix is:

$$\begin{bmatrix} 2 & 4 \\ 1 & 3 \end{bmatrix} \times (a, b) = \begin{bmatrix} a \times 2 & 4 \times a \\ b \times 1 & 3 \times b \end{bmatrix}$$

$$= (a \times 2 + b \times 1, a \times 4 + b \times 3)$$

For example, using the first ordered pair:

$$\begin{bmatrix} 2 & 4 \\ 1 & 3 \end{bmatrix} \times (3, 15) = \begin{bmatrix} 3 \times 2 & 4 \times 3 \\ 15 \times 1 & 3 \times 15 \end{bmatrix}$$

$$= (3 \times 2 + 15 \times 1, 3 \times 4 + 15 \times 3)$$
$$= (21, 57)$$

2. Complete the matrix multiplication for the second ordered pair.

(4, 5) × E = (4 × _____ + 5 × _____, 4 × _____ + 5 × _____) = (_____, _____)

3. Complete the code for the message at the top of the page.

(21, 57) (13, 31) (_____, _____) (_____, _____) (_____, _____) (_____, _____) (_____, _____)

4. Write the following message in a matrix code using the matrix $A = \begin{bmatrix} 4 & 5 \\ 3 & 2 \end{bmatrix}$: A VERY SNEAKY CODE

(85, 59) (_____, _____) (_____, _____) (_____, _____) (_____, _____)
(_____, _____) (_____, _____) (_____, _____) (_____, _____)

5. Make up your own message, and encode it using your own matrix.

_____

Name _____ Date _____

Jodie wants to save money to take a pottery class at her local arts center. She decides to make a weekly budget to help her plan her spending. She will save all income above her expenses.

Weekly income
$150.00 (after taxes have been taken out of her paycheck)

Expenses	
Rent	$35.00
Food	30.00
Gas	5.00
Transportation	10.00
Entertainment	15.00
Miscellaneous	25.00
Total:	$120.00

1. The cost of the pottery class is $70.00, and the full amount must be paid at the first meeting which will take place in four weeks. In addition to the money she saves for the pottery class, how much will Jodie be saving each week? _____

2. After two weeks on her budget, Jodie's weekly transportation costs increase 50%. If she wants her weekly savings to remain the same, what fraction of her miscellaneous money should she put toward transportation? _____

3. Juliet comes to stay with Jodie for one week, during which time Juliet pays for all of their food. However, at the end of the week, Jodie discovers she spent twice as much on entertainment as she should have with her guest. Was Jodie over her budget or under her budget that week? by how much? _____

4. Juliet wants to stay for two more weeks and will pay half the rent and half the gas. If Jodie stays on budget in all other categories, how much more than usual, per week, can she put in her savings? _____

_____

5. Imagine that you want to save money for something special. You are earning $15.00 per week raking leaves and mowing lawns for your neighbors, but you have to pay for your own entertainment, transportation, and other miscellaneous expenses. Write a budget that allows you to save enough money, and also accounts for all your expenses. _____

ENRICH   **Measurement**

On any globe or world map, the world is divided by lines of
latitude and **longitude.** Latitudes run east to west, parallel to
the equator. As seen in the figure, they range from 0° at the
equator to 90° at the North and South poles. Longitudes are
the North Pole to South Pole lines. The longitudinal line at 0°
is called the **prime meridian,** and goes through Greenwich,
England (see the figure).

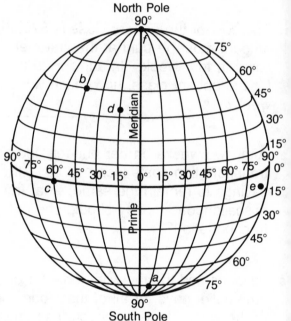

1. The coordinates of point *x* in the figure
   are (45°N, 60°W). Write the coordinates
   of points *a* through *f* in the figure.
   Approximate when necessary.

   a _____   *b* _____

   c _____   *d* _____

   e _____   *f* _____

2. Place the points on the figure, and label
   them *g* through *l*. Ring the letter on the figure.

   g (15°S, 15°W)   *h* (60°S, 45°E)
   i (0°, 90°E)   *j* (54°N, 60°E)
   k (67°N, 0°)   *l* (45°N, 75°W)

3. Earth is not perfectly round. It is 24,900 miles around at
   the equator (latitudes), but only 24,818 miles around the
   poles (longitudes). How many miles is 1° longitude? How
   many miles at the equator is 1° latitude?

   _____

4. Time zones are determined by longitude. If you were
   given the job of determining time zones, how many
   longitudinal degrees would you make each zone? How
   many miles wide at the prime meridian would each zone be?

   _____

5. Is one degree longitude or one degree latitude the same
   distance everywhere? Explain your answer.

   _____

   _____

   _____

ENRICH   Number

Two sets are **equal** if they contain exactly the same elements. The order of the elements is not important. For example:

A = (1, 2, 3, 4)   B = (2, 3, 4, 1)   C = (2, 3, 1, 4)
A = B = C

Two sets are **equivalent** if they have a one-to-one correspondence. Equivalent sets always have the same number of elements. Equivalent sets do not necessarily have identical elements.

A = (2, 4, 6, 8)
B = (1, 3, 5, 7)   A is equivalent to B.

For each set, write one set that is equal, and one that is equivalent but not equal.

1. (3, 5, 7, 9, 11)

_____

2. (A, B, C, D)

_____

3. (12, 24, 48, 96, 182, 364)

_____

4. Are the sets of players on opposing baseball teams equal or equivalent? why?

_____

5. Describe two pairs of sets that are equivalent but not equal.

_____

An **empty set,** shown by the symbol ∅, or by leaving a blank space between a pair of parentheses ( ), is a set containing no elements, such as "the set of all purple giraffes."

6. Use your imagination to describe two empty sets.

_____

7. Examine various objects in your classroom. Use some of the objects to create equal, equivalent, and empty sets. On another sheet of paper, write three of each.

ENRICH Problem Solving

Read the paragraph and answer the questions that follow. If you need help, try solving a simpler problem first.

Laura and Arnold each have a garden plot. Laura's plot is 96 square feet. Arnold's is 72 square feet. Laura plants her plot with vegetables. She divides the plot into 24 equal rows, and plants 7 rows of corn, 6 rows of tomatoes, 5 rows of lettuce, and 2 rows each of green beans, carrots, and celery. Arnold plants his plot with flowers. He divides the plot into 10 equal rows. So far he plants 2 rows of gladiolas, and one row each of asters, daisies, and zinnias. On the average, it takes Laura 48 minutes per week to tend each 20 square feet of her plot. It takes Arnold 32 minutes per week to tend each 19 square feet of his plot.

1. How many square feet does the corn in Laura's garden cover? _____

2. How many square feet do the daisies in Arnold's garden cover? _____

3. Do Arnold's gladiolas take up more room than Laura's carrots? If so, how much more?

_____

4. About how many hours per week does it take Laura to tend her entire garden? _____

5. About how much less time does it take Arnold to tend his garden than Laura to tend hers? _____

6. Laura decides to replace a row of tomatoes with a row of peppers. She plants 3 pepper plants in the row. How many square feet does each plant cover? _____

7. Green beans yield 2 quarts of beans for every 3 square feet planted. How many quarts of beans will Laura's garden yield?

_____

Name _____ Date _____

You can often predict numbers based on other numbers. For example, 20 bushels of apples were picked on Thursday, and 10 on that Sunday. The next Sunday 100 were picked. How many bushels of apples do you think were picked on that Thursday? You would find that $\frac{20}{10} = \frac{n}{100}$, yielding an answer of $n = 200$ bushels.

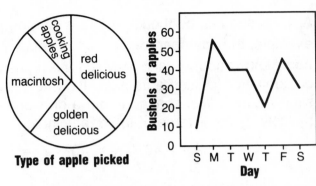

Type of apple picked

Use and compare the graphs to solve.

Average daily number of apples picked
Each figure represents 1 bushel.

1. If 520 bushels were picked on Wednesdays during an entire season, how many would you expect on Tuesdays? _____

2. Cindy is estimating the number of new apple trees to plant. If she plants 200 trees, approximately how many will be macintosh? Why must the answer be approximate?

_____

_____

3. During an entire season, Cindy picked 600 bushels of apples. How many bushels would you expect Jorge and Ashley to accumulate during an entire season?

_____

4. Farmer Perez is selling his apples for a week at the county fair. If he has to pay $5.00 a day for rent on his stall, which graph would be the best to use to see his personal profits and losses? _____

5. Give an example of information that can be stored on a graph. Choose one of the three different types of graphs, and explain why that one is the best choice for your particular information. _____

Use with pages 200–201.

75

ENRICH Number

Any fraction can be thought of as a division problem. For example, the improper fraction $\frac{40}{5}$ is equal to $40 \div 5$. A **complex fraction** is one in which the numerator and/or the denominator, is itself a fraction. To write a complex fraction in simplest form, first change it into a division problem; then multiply by the inverse of the denominator.

$$\frac{40}{\frac{5}{4}} = 40 \div \frac{5}{4} = 40 \times \frac{4}{5} = 32$$

Write each complex fraction in simplest form.

1. $\dfrac{16}{\frac{8}{9}} = $ _____

2. $\dfrac{\frac{3}{4}}{12} = $ _____

3. $\dfrac{\frac{5}{8}}{\frac{15}{16}} = $ _____

4. $\dfrac{\frac{7}{18}}{\frac{28}{45}} = $ _____

If a complex fraction has more than one number in the numerator, the denominator, or both, you must simplify the numerator and the denominator into single fractions, and then divide.

$$\frac{\frac{2}{5} + \frac{4}{5}}{\frac{6}{7} \times \frac{4}{5}} = \frac{\frac{6}{5}}{\frac{24}{35}} = \frac{6}{5} \div \frac{24}{35} = \frac{6}{5} \times \frac{35}{24} = \frac{7}{4} = 1\frac{3}{4}$$

Write each complex fraction in simplest form.

5. $\dfrac{6\frac{6}{7} \div 4\frac{4}{5}}{5\frac{1}{3} - 2\frac{5}{14}} = $ _____

6. $\dfrac{\frac{12}{17} \times \frac{85}{48}}{5\frac{1}{3} - \frac{28}{6}} = $ _____

When the numerator, the denominator, or both contain complex fractions, write the complex fraction in each numerator and denominator in simplest form. Then divide.

Write each complex fraction in simplest form.

7. $\dfrac{\dfrac{\frac{5}{6}}{\frac{12}{11}}}{\frac{18}{4} \div \frac{6}{16}} = $ _____

8. $\dfrac{\dfrac{\frac{9}{10}}{\frac{3}{20}}}{\dfrac{4 - \frac{4}{15}}{3\frac{3}{7} \times 1\frac{19}{30}}} = $ _____

Use with pages 202–203.

ENRICH   Problem Solving

You are the president of the newly formed Student Motion-Picture Association. You are preparing to produce your first movie. Three of the decisions you need to make are

a. what kind of movie to make.
b. how large the budget for the film should be.
c. how to advertise the film.

Each question below relates to one of these decisions. Write the letter of the related decision in the space to the left of each question.

_____ **1.** How much does it cost to rent a movie camera?

_____ **2.** In which local newspaper should you place an ad?

_____ **3.** How much will you pay the actors?

_____ **4.** Where will you put up the posters?

_____ **5.** What kind of movie do most people enjoy?

_____ **6.** How many people will you hire to work on the production?

_____ **7.** Which kinds of movies have been most successful in recent years?

_____ **8.** Which organizations might be willing to contribute money for the film?

_____ **9.** Which aspects of a film might attract moviegoers?

_____ **10.** How much money will you spend on costumes and sets?

_____ **11.** Should the movie have a happy ending?

For each of the three decisions, write one other question that you would need to answer.

a. _____

b. _____

c. _____

ENRICH | Statistics and Probability

Dr. Eleanor Wong brings a box to class containing 1,000 insects. There are four kinds of insects in the box: icky, ugly, cute, and slimy. Several brave students volunteer to take **random samples** from the jar. Each takes out a handful of insects. They use this sample to estimate the number of each kind of insect in the box.

1. Renee reaches into the top of the box and pulls out 3 icky insects, 2 ugly ones, 2 cute ones, and 1 slimy one. What fraction of the insects she pulled out were

   icky? _____ ugly? _____ cute? _____ slimy? _____

2. Use the 8 insects that Renee took as a sample of the box's contents. Approximately how many of the insects in the entire box would you predict to be

   icky? _____ ugly? _____ cute? _____ slimy? _____

3. Josh shook up the box before taking out a sample of 20 insects. Of the 20 insects Josh took, 3 were icky, 6 were ugly, 3 were cute, and 8 were slimy. From this sample, predict how many bugs of each type the box contained.

   _____

   _____

4. After shaking the box, Kit took out a sample of 100 insects. Her sample contained the following: 5 icky, 25 ugly, 15 cute, and 50 slimy. From this sample, predict how many of each type of insect the box contained.

   _____

   _____

Dr. Wong explained that slimy bugs like dark places; so, they tend to stay near the bottom of the box.

5. How might this have affected the samples taken by the students?

   _____

   _____

6. How might shaking up the box have affected the students' sample results?

   _____

   _____

7. From Renee's sample, can you guess which type of insect likes to stay near the top of the box?

   _____

8. An estimate made from a random sample is accurate for only certain populations? Why? _____

   _____

   _____

Use with pages 206–207.

ENRICH   Measurement

A **contour map** is a map divided into regions by lines called **contours.** Each region falls within a certain range of a measured characteristic, such as rainfall or elevation. The elevation map in Figure 1 is a contour map. The *contours* define areas within the same altitude range. The lines give the exact altitude of points on a line. Points between lines have altitudes between the readings of the two lines surrounding their regions.

Use Figure 1 to solve.

1. What three points have the same altitude?

_____

2. What is the difference in altitude from *m* to *e*, and from *l* to *g*?

_____

3. What would the terrain look like in the area where the contour lines are close together? What would the ground look like where the lines are further apart?

_____

4. There may be many points not on a contour line with the same altitude as a contour line. Explain why.

_____

5. Construct a contour map in Figure 2. Each point on the map is designated by its number and letter coordinates. For example, the point A7 is shown.

50 ft: A7, A4, C1, J1, M3, O6, N11, L11, J9, D11
100 ft: B7, C3, K2, M5, L10, J8, D10
150 ft: C7, E5, I4, K5, K8, J7, E9
200 ft: E8, E7, H6, I6, I7

6. Draw a picture of what the map you constructed in Figure 2 would look like if it were viewed at eye level.

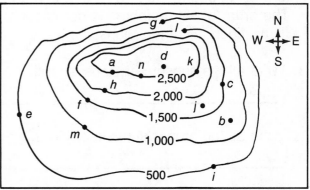

Figure 1: Elevation (in meters) on Mount Flapjack

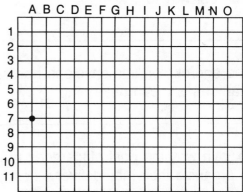

Figure 2: Contour Elevation Map (in feet)

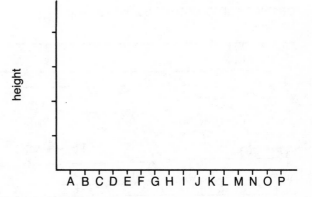

ENRICH   **Number**

Sets can be organized in different ways. Here are two examples:

- *X* is a **subset** of *Y* if each member of *X* is also a member of *Y*. The empty or null set, ∅, is a subset of every set, and every set is a subset of itself.
- *X* is a **proper subset** of *Y* if *X* is a subset of *Y*, and there is at least one member of *Y* that is not a member of *X*. The order of set members is not important. For example, {lions, tigers} = {tigers, lions}.

1. Write all the subsets of {lions, tigers}.

_____

2. Write all the proper subsets of {lions, tigers}.

_____

3. Your baseball team is at the daily workout. The coach divides the team into subsets. Why would she feel this is the best way to practice? _____

_____

4. The address on this envelope has several subsets. List as many as you can determine.

_____

Greg Jung
265 Elm Street
Xenia, MA 02117

5. Explain why the post office does not use proper subsets to organize their mail delivery.

_____

6. Think of a few situations where it would be important to organize into proper subsets.

_____

_____

ENRICH   Number

The ancient Egyptians used a different number system from the Hindu-Arabic system we use. They used symbols to represent numbers as shown in the table.

1	2	3	4	5	6	7	8	9	10	11	12	13	14	15
I	II	III	IIII	IIIII	III III	IIII III	IIII IIII	IIIII IIII	∩	II ∩∪	II ∩∪	III∪	III∪	I∪

16	17	18	19	20	21	22	30	40	50	60	70	100	200	1,000
∩III IIII	∩I IIIIII	∩IIII IIIII	∩II IIIIIII	∩∩	∩∩ I	∩∩ II	∩∩∩	∩∩ ∩∩	∩∩∩ ∩∩	∩∩∩ ∩∩∩	∩∩∩∩ ∩∩∩	𐦥	𐦥𐦥	⚱

They also discovered many ways to perform arithmetic operations. They multiplied two numbers by a process called **simple doubling.**

As an example, multiply 13 × 35.

a. Write the number 1 in the left column and one of the factors in the right column.
b. Double the numbers in both columns.
c. Stop when the number in column 1 exceeds 13, the other factor.
d. Starting at the bottom of the left column, ring the numbers whose sum is 13, the other factor. Ring and add the corresponding numbers in the right column. The sum will equal 13 × 35.

13 × 35

(1)	**35**
2	70
(4)	**140**
(8)	**280**
STOP	16 > 13

280 + 140 + 35 = 455
13 × 35 = 455

Use Egyptian numbers to multiply with the doubling method. On another sheet of paper, make a table to use the simple-doubling method. Put the first factor on the left side and the second factor on the right side. Write the answers using the Egyptian numbering system.

1. 65 × 11 = _____

2. 32 × 12 = _____

3. 91 × 19 = _____

4. 19 × 91 = _____

5. When you multiply two numbers by the simple-doubling method, which number would you double to do as little work as possible? (HINT: Look at Exercises 3 and 4.) _____

6. Explain how the simple-doubling method works in the example 13 × 35. (HINT: Rewrite 13 as the sum of powers of 2.)

_____

_____

_____

_____

Use with pages 212–213.

ENRICH | Measurement

The amount of electricity used by electric appliances is measured in **voltage** and **amperage.** *Voltage,* the measure of electrical force in the circuit, has different standards in different countries. For example, in the United States, the voltage is set at 120 volts. *Amperage* measures the amount of current needed to operate a given appliance.

The product of voltage and amperage is *wattage:* $W = A \times V$. Watts measure the electrical power used by an appliance.

1. These are some household appliances and their power requirements. Complete the table.

Appliance	Volts	Amperes	Watts
Air conditioner	120		1,500
Desk lamp	120	0.5	
Fan	120		72
Typewriter	120		54

Watt hours are the appliance's wattage requirement multiplied by the number of hours the appliance is used. One *kilowatt-hour* is equal to 1,000 watt hours.

2. Complete the table to determine the number of kilowatt-hours of electricity used to run the appliances listed for the month of July.

Appliance	Hours Per Day	Watt Hours Per Day	Kilowatt Hours Per Day	Kilowatt Hours in July
Air conditioner	12	18,000	18	558
Desk lamp	10			
Fan	12			
Typewriter	5			

3. If the charge for electricity is $15.00 per month for the first 250 kilowatt-hours and $0.08 for each additional kilowatt-hour, what is the July bill?

_____

4. Write a formula that determines the number of kilowatt-hours an appliance uses in a month.

_____

_____

Use with pages 216–217.

ENRICH   Problem Solving

You are planning a simple lunch menu for the summer meeting of the Drama Club. You're not sure yet exactly how many people are coming, but you know you'll be making either 24 or 36 servings.

Use the menu below to fill in the boxes of the chart.

MENU FOR DRAMA CLUB SUMMER MEETING

Tuna-salad sandwich	Fruit cocktail	8-oz glass of milk
4 oz tuna	$\frac{2}{3}$ cup chopped apples	
$\frac{1}{2}$ cup celery	$\frac{3}{4}$ cup oranges	
$\frac{1}{4}$ cup mayonnaise	$1\frac{1}{4}$ cups bananas	
$\frac{1}{3}$ cup cucumbers	$\frac{3}{8}$ tablespoon lemon juice	
8 slices bread	1 teaspoon honey	
Makes 4 servings	Makes 6 servings	

Item	Amount needed for 24 servings	Amount needed for 36 servings
tuna (1 pound per can)		
celery		
mayonnaise		
cucumbers		
bread (24 slices per loaf)		
apples		
oranges		
bananas		
lemon juice		
honey		
milk (32 ounces = 1 quart)		

ENRICH   Measurement

There are many different forms of energy, and many different ways to measure it. Heat is one of the most basic kinds of energy, and it is measured in units called *calories.* One calorie is the amount of energy (in the form of heat) that it takes to raise the temperature of one gram of water by 1°C. The energy contained in food is chemical energy, but since chemical energy (along with all other types of energy) is easily changed into heat energy, the energy in food is expressed in Calories also. A food Calorie is actually a *kilocalorie,* 1,000 calories of energy. It is spelled with a capital *C* to distinguish it from the calorie.

1. An apple contains 75 Calories. If the energy it contains were converted to heat, how many degrees Celsius would the heat rise for one gram of water? How much would it raise the temperature of 1 kilogram of water?

_____

A second common unit used to measure heat is the British Thermal Unit (BTU). This is the amount of heat needed to raise one pound of water one degree Fahrenheit. One BTU is equal to approximately 252 calories. The power of air conditioners is commonly measured in BTU's. An air conditioner rated at 20,000 uses 20,000 BTU per hour.

2. If a 10 × 15 × 8 room needs a 5,000 BTU air conditioner to cool it, what size air conditioner will a 20 × 35 × 12 room need? _____

3. Michael's new apartment has two rooms that he would like to keep cool in the summer. One room is 15 × 10 × 10, and the second room is 25 × 12 × 10. If a 10 × 15 × 8 room needs a 5,000 BTU air conditioner, Michael will need how many BTU's?

_____

4. Make up a new unit to measure larger amounts of heat energy, such as the amount used by construction machinery. Write your standard unit, and measure the heat energy of a few things in your town.

_____

_____

   Use with pages 220–221.

Name _____ Date _____

ENRICH **Measurement**

The **Beaufort Scale,** which was devised by Admiral Francis Beaufort in 1807, measures wind force. His scale assigned wind-speed values to different weather conditions. For instance, the number 12 originally indicated a wind "that which no canvas could withstand" and going approximately 74 mph.

Beaufort number	Name	Miles per hour (mph)	Effect on land
0	Calm	less than 1	Calm; smoke rises vertically.
1	Light Air	1–3	Weather vanes inactive; smoke drifts with air.
2	Light Breeze	4–7	Weather vanes active; wind felt on face; leaves rustle.
3	Gentle Breeze	8–12	Leaves and small twigs move; light flags extend.
4	Moderate Breeze	13–18	Small branches sway; dust and loose paper blow about.
5	Fresh Breeze	19–24	Small trees sway; waves break on inland waters.
6	Strong Breeze	25–31	Large branches sway; umbrellas difficult to use.
7	Moderate Gale	32–38	Whole trees sway; difficult to walk against the wind.
8	Fresh Gale	39–46	Twigs break off trees; walking against wind very difficult.
9	Strong Gale	47–54	Slight damage to buildings; shingles blow off roof.
10	Whole Gale	55–63	Trees uproot; considerable damage to buildings.
11	Storm	64–73	Widespread damage; very rare occurrence.
12–17	Hurricane	74 and above	Violent destruction.

1. Is the approximate ratio between a Beaufort unit and miles per hour a consistent ratio throughout the scale?

2. As Beaufort units increase, does the increase in average wind speed get larger or smaller?

3. You are walking near a shore and suddenly a strong wind starts. You hear waves breaking. When you try to open your umbrella, the wind hurls it out of your hands. Soon you see twigs breaking off trees. What is the Beaufort number?

4. If the wind has a Beaufort number of 6, do you know exactly how fast it is traveling? why or why not?

5. Create another wind scale based on different weather conditions. Use situations from your part of the country.

Use with pages 222–223.   85

ENRICH | Problem Solving

You work in the shipping department of the Crystalmite Glassware Company. The company sells drinking glasses and ceramic mugs to stores around the world. To protect the goods, the company uses 3 different packages to ship its glasses and mugs: boxes, cartons, and crates. Each box contains a maximum of 8 glasses or 6 mugs. Each carton can contain 1 to 6 boxes. Each crate can contain 1 to 12 cartons. Fill in the chart below to show what packages will be needed to ship each order.

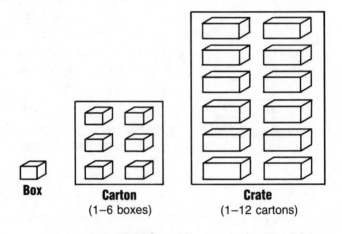

Box

Carton
(1–6 boxes)

Crate
(1–12 cartons)

Items Ordered	Number of Boxes Needed	Number of Cartons Needed	Number of Crates Needed
217 glasses			
434 mugs			
576 glasses			
144 mugs			
1,746 glasses			
4,640 mugs			
1,633 glasses			
2,704 mugs			
200 glasses			
5,778 glasses			

Use with pages 224–225.

ENRICH   Measurement

When we measure something, we put a unit value on it. There are many different types and uses of measurement; so, there are many different **measurement scales.** Here are four.

Nominal—This type of scale numbers things for identification or counting. For example: The 11 players on the Southside soccer team bought new uniforms with their car-wash profits.	*Ordinal*—This type of scale tells us the location of something in a sequence or order. For example: Celia took fourth place in the New York Marathon.
Interval—In interval scales, things are measured in quantitative increments, but the zero point is arbitrary. For example: In the winter, the temperature in Minneapolis averages ⁻10°F.	*Ratio*—These scales are most often used for physical measurement. Zero is absolute and means the empty set, such as zero feet or zero grams. For example: A racketball is $2\frac{1}{2}$ inches in diameter and costs $0.50.

Write the correct measurement scale in the space below.

It was 90 degrees (1) in the shade on July 4 (2). Pat and Tim went to a 3-ring (3) circus. They went to the 25 African Big-Game Animals (4) exhibit and saw the biggest (5) lion in captivity. Then they walked towards the main tent. On the way, they each bought a cup (6) of regular chili for 90¢ (7) each. The vendor wanted them to try Texas four-alarm chili (8), but Pat and Tim knew it would be too hot for them.

In the main tent, a team of 20 (9) acrobats performed on the tight-rope 50 feet (10) overhead for 30 minutes (11). When the clowns came out, they divided into two volleyball teams (12). One team was called First Town, and the other was called Second Town (13). You can imagine what the game was like. After that, they rode the 20-seat Ferris wheel (14) that took them 100 feet (15) above the circus grounds. It was a day they would never forget.

1. _____   2. _____   3. _____

4. _____   5. _____   6. _____

7. _____   8. _____   9. _____

10. _____   11. _____   12. _____

13. _____   14. _____   15. _____

Use with pages 236–237.

ENRICH   Measurement

Many measurement systems were invented by using standard distances between two points. For instance, the French developed a system of measurement based on a fraction of the distance from the North Pole to the equator. It runs along the line known as the prime meridian. This length, the *meter* (from the Greek word *metron,* meaning "measure"), became the basic unit of a new measurement system. As a unit, the meter is used with powers of 10 to create larger or smaller units of measure within the system we call the *metric system.*

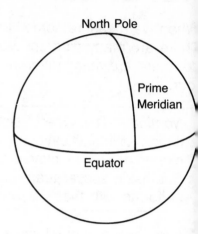

Create your own measurement system based on length. Use something you have with you, besides a ruler or other measuring device, as the standard for your system.

1. Name and define the basic unit of your measurement system.

   _____

2. Use this unit to name and define corresponding units of measure, both larger and smaller. _____

3. Construct a ruler that contains the units of your measurement system. Measure your desk, your height, your book, and your pen. Use both your own system of measurement and the metric system.

   _____

4. Complete the table to illustrate the conversion from your system of measurement to the metric system.

Object	Your System	Metric System
Door		cm
Height		cm
Book		cm
Pen		cm

5. Write a formula that converts measurements from your system of measurement to the metric system, and vice versa.

   _____

Use with pages 238–239

ENRICH **Measurement**

An *inclinometer* is used to find the height of an object which cannot be measured directly.

Use a piece of cardboard, a length of string, and a small weight, such as an eraser, to construct an inclinometer. Mark the degrees on the scale from 0° to 80° as shown.

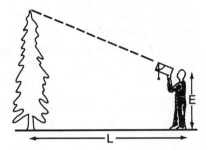

Attach the string at the corner.

Cardboard

To use the inclinometer:

- Measure the distance (L) from the base of the object to the point where you are standing.
- Measure the height of your eye (E) from the ground.
- Sight the inclinometer so that the top of the object is in line with the top of the instrument. Hold the string where it settles, and read the angle.
- Use the table for the value T.
- The height of the object is (L × T) + E.

Angle	0°	5°	10°	15°	20°	25°	30°	35°	40°
T	0	0.088	0.176	0.268	0.364	0.466	0.577	0.7	0.839

Angle	45°	50°	55°	60°	65°	70°	75°	80°	85°
T	1.0	1.192	1.428	1.732	2.145	2.747	3.732	5.671	11.43

1. Assume that you are standing 25 feet from a tree, and the height of your eye from the ground is $4\frac{1}{2}$ feet. You sight the top of the tree, and the angle on the inclinometer reads 45°. What is the height of the tree?

2. The height of the post office is 35 feet. The height of your eye from the ground is $4\frac{1}{2}$ feet, and after sighting the top of the post office, the angle on the inclinometer reads 35°. What is your distance (L) from the post office?

3. Your ship is sailing in shallow waters. A lighthouse, known to sailors to be 150 feet tall, stands on a treacherous reef 750 feet in diameter. Write an equation that will help you chart a safe course around the reef.

4. Use the inclinometer to measure the height of several tall buildings near your school.

ENRICH   Problem Solving

Read the paragraph. Then solve the problems that follow.

Mr. Lee is in charge of solid-waste disposal for Ridgeville, a town of 35,000 people. He is working to reduce the amount of solid waste that must be transported by truck to a regional landfill. His research indicates that the average amount of waste generated in Ridgeville per person per day is 3.74 lb. Of this amount, 0.91 lb is newspaper, 0.45 lb is glass, and 0.31 lb is aluminum. By having each family set aside their newspaper, glass, and aluminum for recycling, Mr. Lee hopes to significantly reduce the amount of solid waste that must be transported to the landfill.

1. How many pounds of solid waste does the average family of 4 people in Ridgeville generate per year?

   _____

2. If Mr. Lee succeeds in having all newspaper, glass, and aluminum separated and recycled, will he reduce by more than one-half the amount of solid waste that must be transported to the landfill? _____

3. How many tons of solid waste are generated by Ridgeville's residents each day? _____

4. Ridgeville pays $17 per ton to the regional landfill to dispose of its waste. If the town can reduce its weekly tonnage from 458 to 253, how much money will Ridgeville save per week? _____

5. Ridgeville receives $0.02 per pound for the newspaper it sends to the recycling center. If the town recycled all its newspaper, how much money would Ridgeville receive each day? _____

6. How many pounds of nonrecyclable material do the residents of Ridgeville generate each year?

   _____

Use with pages 244–245.

ENRICH   Measurement

The shortest distance between two points on a piece of paper is a straight line between them. However, since Earth s round, the shortest distance between two points on Earth s not a straight line. It is the distance between them on a **great circle.** A great circle is a line of symmetry for Earth, a circumference line that divides Earth (or a globe) into two equal halves.

A straight line drawn between two distant points on a map or globe looks like it represents the shortest distance between them. For example, a line can be drawn almost directly east rom New York to Rome. However, the shortest distance etween the two cities entails going far north of the east-west ne. Look at the two maps.

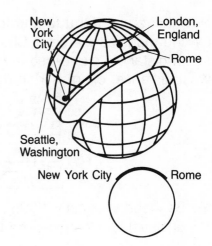

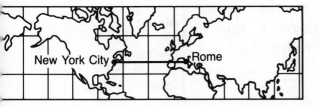 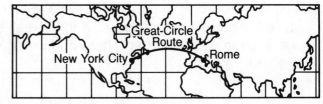

1. A plane from Seattle, Washington, to London, England, will fly close to the North Pole. Why is this?

_____

_____

2. If two cities are close, a map can give a nearly exact measure of their distance apart. Why is this?

_____

3. What line between two cities that are far apart would be shorter than a great circle arc?

_____

4. Are lines of latitude (E–W) and longitude (N–S) great circles? Explain your answers.

_____

_____

_____

_____

ENRICH   **Measurement**

Navigators use **latitude** and **longitude** to measure location. On the modified Mercater Chart below, longitude is north–south distance, expressed in degrees; and latitude is east–west distance, expressed in degrees.

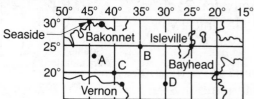

1. Bayhead is exactly 1,725 miles east and 690 miles south of Seaside. Complete the legend and the table.

    Legend: 5° = _____ miles

2. You are treasure hunting in the Salty Sea. Your first trip is from Seaside to location A, and then to Bakonnet. How many degrees latitude and how many degrees longitude will you travel? _____

3. For your second trip, you leave Bakonnet, explore location B, and then go to Bayhead. How many degrees latitude and how many degrees longitude is this trip?

    _____

4. Then you explore location D, where you notice you are leaking fuel. You decide to leave for the nearest port immediately. To what port do you travel? _____

5. After your boat is repaired, you decide to explore two locations on a single trip. What is the shortest trip you can make on which you explore two locations? What is the final destination? _____

6. You have enough gas for 2,587.5 miles. Leaving from Bayhead, you want to explore location B and location A, and then dock in Bakonnet. You find that this involves 12° and 26° travel, so you estimate that you don't have enough gas. Your captain then tells you that you're mistaken. What does the captain realize that you forgot?

    _____

    _____

	Latitude	Longitude
Seaside	30°	45°
Isleville		
Bayhead		
Vernon		
Bakonnet		
A		
B		
C		
D		

Use with pages 248–249

Name _____ Date _____

Kamau's Seaweed Farm must have the correct mixture of liquid plant food and water for the seaweed to grow properly. The mixture varies depending on the type of seaweed. One tank contains 20 gallons of pure water. How many gallons of liquid plant food must Kamau add to make the water in the tank contain 10% liquid plant food?

Let x = the number of gallons of plant food to be added. The final number of gallons in the tank will be $(20 + x)$. Since 10% of $(20 + x)$ is liquid plant food, $0.10(20 + x) = x$. Look at the equation. Kamau must add approximately 2.2 gallons of liquid plant food to make a 10% mixture.

Round to the nearest tenth.
$$0.10(20 + x) = x$$
$$2 + 0.1x = x$$
$$2 = 0.9x$$
$$x = 2.2$$

1. Kamau has another tank with 20 gallons of pure water. To this he adds plant food containing 25% liquid plant food and 75% water. How much should he add to make the water in the tank contain 5% liquid plant food?

_____

Pablo is mixing poster paint with specific pigment contents. One jar of paint contains 85% base and 15% yellow pigment. Another contains 70% base and 30% blue pigment. How much of each must he combine to get 10 oz of green paint containing 25% pigment?

	Number of oz	Amount of pigment
Blue	x	$0.30x$
Yellow	$(10 - x)$	$0.15(10 - x)$
Green	10	$0.25 (10)$

$$0.30x + 0.15(10 - x) = 2.5$$
$$0.30x + 1.5 - 0.15x = 2.5$$
$$0.15x = 1.0$$
$$x = \frac{1}{0.15} = 6\frac{2}{3}$$

Pablo must mix $6\frac{2}{3}$ oz of blue paint, and $10 - 6\frac{2}{3} = 3\frac{1}{3}$ oz of yellow paint.

Write the equation and solve.

2. Pablo is making a different shade of green paint. He needs 80% yellow and 20% blue in his final mixture. How much yellow does he need to add to 5 pints of blue to make the proper mixture? Show the initial equation and solve.

_____

3. How must Pablo combine two paints, one containing 20% and the other 10% pigment, to get 10 oz of paint containing 15% pigment? Write the equation and solve.

_____

_____

ENRICH Problem Solving

You are in charge of the racing team for an Indianapolis 500 racing car. Your crew and driver are preparing for the 500-mile race around the Indianapolis $2\frac{1}{2}$-mile track. Answer the following questions.

1. Your car has done several practice laps around the track at an average speed of 160 mph. At that rate, about how long will it take for your car to complete the race? _____

2. During a time trial, your car completes 2 practice laps in 2 minutes. What is the car's average speed for the 2 laps? $\left(\text{HINT:} 2 \text{ minutes} = \frac{2}{60} \text{ or } \frac{1}{30} \text{ of an hour}\right)$ _____

3. How many laps around the Indianapolis track will each car have to make in order to finish the race? _____

4. If a car races for 30 minutes at an average speed of 144 mph, how many miles will the car travel? _____

5. Your car completes 120 laps at an average speed of 150 mph. How much time has elapsed since the start of the race? _____

6. Your car is neck and neck with another car. Because of poor weather conditions, both cars are traveling at 120 mph. If your car stops for a 30-second pit stop, how far will it fall behind the other car? _____

7. The yellow flag warns the cars to slow down because of an accident. All the cars slow to 80 mph for 8 laps. How long will it take to drive those 8 laps? _____

8. Your car wins the race in $3\frac{1}{2}$ hours. What was the car's average speed for the race? _____

ENRICH   Patterns

Music is divided into sections called **measures**. For example, Figure 1 is divided into three measures.

Figure 1

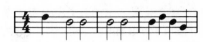

1. How many measures is Figure 2 divided into? _____

Here are some commonly used musical notes.

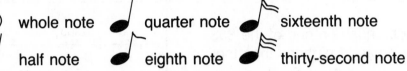

whole note   quarter note   sixteenth note

half note   eighth note   thirty-second note

Half notes have a duration half that of whole notes. Four quarter notes last as long as one whole note, and so on.

Figure 2

2. How many thirty-second notes would it take to equal 2 quarter notes? _____

The numbers on the left side of each figure are called the *time signature.* The top number in Figure 2 indicates that there are 3 beats to a *measure.* The bottom number designates which type of note will count as a beat.

In this example, the 4 indicates that quarter notes will count as a beat (8 would stand for eighth notes, and so on). Each measure in Figure 2 must consist of 3 quarter notes, or their equivalents in time.

Figure 3

3. What number of beats are there in each measure of Figure 2? _____

4. Each beat in Figure 3 is equivalent to what kind of note?

_____

5. How many beats are there in the second measure of Figure 3? _____

6. Complete the time signatures in Figure 4.

Figure 4

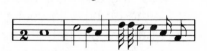

7. Create music on the empty *staff.* Make sure each measure adds up to the correct number of beats. Find a musician to play the music (or play it yourself). How does it sound?

_____

_____

ENRICH   Statistics and Probability

In a museum with 30 strangers, there is a 71% chance that at least 2 people have the same birthday. To come up with this probability, ask the question: What are the odds that every person in the museum has a different birthday?

Unique birthdays to choose from
Total days in the year
$\dfrac{365}{365}$
$\dfrac{364}{365}$
$\dfrac{363}{365}$
$\dfrac{365}{365} \times \dfrac{364}{365} \times \cdots \times \dfrac{336}{365}$

- The first person can have any birthday.
- The second person must have a birthday on one of the 364 other days in the year.
- The third person must have a birthday on one of the 363 other days, since it must be a different birthday than the first 2 people's.

Multiply the probabilities of each person having a unique birthday. This expression is equal to approximately 0.29. There is a 29% probability that everyone has a different birthday, and a 71% probability that at least 2 people in the museum have the same birthday.

1. What are the chances that 2 people in a group of 20 have the same birthday?
_____

2. What is the largest group possible with less than a 50% chance of 2 people having the same birthday? _____

3. What are the chances that 2 people in a group of 20 will have birthdays in the same week? _____

4. What are the chances that 2 people in a group of 20, all born in a leap year, have the same birthday? _____

5. What are the chances that 2 people in a group of 10 will have birthdays in the same week? _____

6. What is the largest group possible that has less than a 50% chance of 2 people having a birthday in the same week? _____

7. Test the accuracy of more than one person having the same birthday in your class. Ask each of your classmates what her or his birthday is. How many do you have to ask before you find two people with the same birthday?

_____

8. Think of another situation where the probability seems logically low, but is statistically high.

_____

_____

ENRICH | Measurement

Changes take place at uneven rates. For example, you may grow 2 feet between the ages of ten and twenty, but you will grow a different amount in each individual year. You can find the **average rate of change** (the average amount of change per each equal time interval) by dividing the total amount of change by the number of equal time intervals.

1. If you grow 2 feet in 10 years, what is your average rate of growth? _____

The table shows the average monthly temperature in New York, New York, in a recent year. The temperatures are in degrees Fahrenheit (°F).

January	February	March	April	May	June
34°F	34°F	39°F	50°F	61°F	70°F

July	August	September	October	November	December
77°F	73°F	66°F	55°F	45°F	36°F

2. What was the monthly average rate of change in temperature from January to June? _____

3. What was the monthly average rate of change in temperature from July to December? Is this expressed as a positive or negative number? Why?

_____

4. What was the monthly average rate of change in temperature for the year (from January to December)?

_____

5. If the temperature was 5°F higher in each of the months between May and November, would this alter the average rate of change? Explain your answer.

_____

_____

_____

ENRICH Problem Solving

You work for the Rapid Transit Bus Company and are helping to design a new bus route from Brownville to Gleason. This week you are making trial runs along the proposed new route in order to complete the time schedule below.

BROWNVILLE TO GLEASON Weekdays Except Major Holidays

Eastbound from Brownville	AM	AM	AM	AM	AM	AM	AM	AM	PM	PM	PM
Brownville .... Lv.	5.40	6.12	...	6.43	...	7.06	...	7.42	...	...	...
Hopatcong .... ″	5.47	6.19	...	6.50	...	7.13	...	7.49	...	...	...
Dover .... ″	5.59		6.45	7.00	7.14	7.23	7.33	7.59	...	...	...
Denville .... ″	6.06	?	...	7.09	...	7.29	...	...	...	...	...
Mountain Road .... ″	6.11	6.40	6.54	...	7.23	...	7.42	8.08	...	...	...
Boonton St. .... ″	6.14	6.43	6.57	...	7.26	...	7.45	?	...	...	...
Towaco .... ″	6.20	6.49	...	7.21	...	7.40	7.51	8.17	...	...	...
Lincoln Ave. .... ″	6.25	6.54	...	?	...	7.45	7.56	8.22	4.35	...	9.25
Mountain View .... ″	6.30	6.59	7.11	7.31	7.40	7.50	8.01	8.27	...	...	...
Great Falls .... ″	6.34	...	7.15	...	7.44	...	8.05	8.31	...	...	...
Little Notch .... ″	...	7.06	...	7.38	...	7.57	...	8.34	4.45	6.23	...
Montclair Heights ...... ″	...	7.08	7.21	...	7.50	...	8.11	8.36	4.47	6.26	9.38
Mountain Ave. .... ″	6.42	...	...	7.41	...	8.00	?	8.38	...	...	...
Harris St. .... ″	6.44	7.11	7.24	...	7.53	...	?	8.40	4.50	...	...
Watchung Ave. .... ″	6.46	7.13	...	7.44	...	8.03	?	8.42	...	...	...
Walnut St. .... ″	6.48	7.15	7.27	...	7.56	...	8.19	8.44	4.54	...	...
Benson St. .... ″	6.51	7.18	...	...	...	8.07	8.22	8.47	...	...	...
Rowe St. .... ″	6.54	7.21	...	7.50	...	...	8.25	8.50	...	...	...
North Ave. .... ″	6.58	7.25	...	...	8.04	...	8.29	8.54	...	...	...
Arlington St. .... ″	7.01	...	...	?	...	...	8.32	...	...	...	...
Gleason .... Ar	7.16	?	7.54	8.11	8.22	8.31	8.45	9.10	5.17	6.50	10.02

Use the schedule to answer the questions.

1. You leave Brownville at 6:12 A.M. You leave Dover 18 minutes later and 6 minutes after that Denville. At what time did you leave Denville? _____

2. The trip from Brownville to Gleason takes 4 minutes less if you leave at 6:12 A.M. rather than at 5:40 A.M. When will you arrive in Gleason if you leave Brownville at 6:12 A.M.? _____

3. If you leave Brownville at 7:42 A.M., it takes twice as long to get from Boonton Street to Towaco as it does from Mountain Road to Boonton Street. When does the bus leave Boonton Street? _____

4. The bus that leaves Brownville at 6:43 A.M. completes exactly one-half of its trip at Lincoln Avenue. At what time does the bus leave Lincoln Avenue? _____

Use with pages 260–261

ENRICH   Number

A **ratio** is a relation between two quantities. For example, from the chart the ratio of the number of days in one Earth year to the distance of Earth from the sun is *365 days:93 million miles.* When two equal ratios are written as equivalent fractions, they form a **proportion.**

In the chart, a *year* is defined as "the number of Earth days it takes each planet to complete an orbit around the sun."

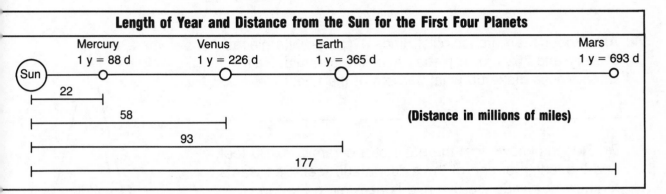

Length of Year and Distance from the Sun for the First Four Planets

Mercury	Venus	Earth	Mars
1 y = 88 d	1 y = 226 d	1 y = 365 d	1 y = 693 d

Sun

22
58
93
177

(Distance in millions of miles)

1. For each planet, write the ratio between its distance from the sun and the number of days in its year (round to express in millions of miles per day).

   _____

2. What would you expect the ratio between distance from the sun and number of days in a year to be for the planet Jupiter? The distance between Jupiter and the sun is 1,082 million miles. What is the approximate length of a year on Jupiter?

   _____

3. A day on Jupiter is only 10 Earth-hours long. What is the ratio between each planet's year in Jupiter days, and its distance from the sun (in millions of miles)? (HINT: How many Jupiter days are there in 1 Earth day?)

   _____

4. Compare the answers in Problems 1 and 2. What similarities do you see? What can you conclude?

   _____

   _____

Name _____ Date _____

ENRICH   **Measurement**

Ratios and proportions are useful when measuring something that is too large or too distant to be measured directly.

1. An Egyptian pharaoh wanted to build a pyramid twice as large as a pyramid built by a previous pharaoh. The existing pyramid was 200 feet high and had a base of 400 feet. How high will the new pyramid be? Use the proportion of height over base: $\frac{200}{400} = \frac{x}{800}$. Solve for x.

_____

2. Ana Roberts, an archeologist, finds 47 pale-white pieces of ivory and 752 brown pieces near the pyramid. Pale-white pieces make up what percent of the total?

_____

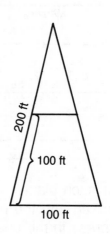

3. Dr. Roberts knows that the base of a pyramid is 100 feet, and the length of one of the sides is 200 feet. She wants to know how wide the pyramid is halfway to the top. Write the proportion she uses and solve.

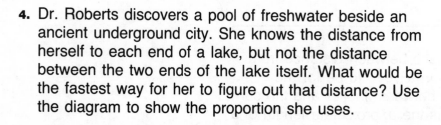

4. Dr. Roberts discovers a pool of freshwater beside an ancient underground city. She knows the distance from herself to each end of a lake, but not the distance between the two ends of the lake itself. What would be the fastest way for her to figure out that distance? Use the diagram to show the proportion she uses.

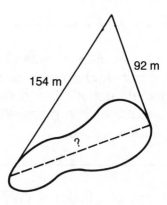

5. The weight of the 250 ivory pieces she finds in a ceramic bowl must be measured before recording them in her daily log. Each piece is too light to weigh on her pound-weight scale. What is the proportion she uses to weigh each piece?

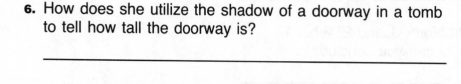

6. How does she utilize the shadow of a doorway in a tomb to tell how tall the doorway is?

_____

_____

_____

Use with pages 272–273

```
ENRICH
```
Problem Solving

You are the great Henri Fournier, a master chef from Europe who is touring restaurants in the United States. In Europe, you do all your measuring using metric units. Measurement in the United States is usually done in customary units. When preparing various dishes in the United States restaurants that you visit, you use the chart below to convert units of measure.

CONVERSION CHART		
3 teaspoons = 1 tablespoon	= 15 mL
4 tablespoons = $\frac{1}{4}$ cup	= 60 mL
$5\frac{1}{3}$ tablespoons = $\frac{1}{3}$ cup	= 79 mL
8 tablespoons = $\frac{1}{2}$ cup	= 118 mL
16 tablespoons = 1 cup	= 237 mL
1 fluid ounce = 2 tablespoons	= 30 mL
8 fluid ounces = 1 cup	= 237 mL
16 fluid ounces = 2 cups or 1 pint	= 473 mL
32 fluid ounces = 4 cups or 1 quart	= 946 mL

Answer the questions below. Use a proportion when appropriate.

1. Your recipe for Fournier's Inside-Out Soufflé calls for 5 teaspoons of salt. How many milliliters of salt is that?

_____

2. While making your famous Eggnog Supreme, you add 1,900 mL heavy cream. About how many pints of heavy cream did you use? _____

3. Your recipe for Henri's Apricot Surprise calls for $1\frac{1}{3}$ cups of sugar. How many milliliters of sugar is this? _____

4. You add $1\frac{1}{4}$ mL of black pepper to a recipe for Shrimp Olé. How much pepper is this in customary units?

_____

5. Your recipe for Potato Soup Parisian calls for 3 quarts water. To the nearest hundred milliliters, how much water is this? _____

ENRICH   Measurement

The **scale** on a map gives the relationship between distance on the map and actual distance. It is usually given as a proportion of map units to actual units. Often the scale is given as a fraction, such as $\frac{1}{63,000}$. Using inches as the unit of measure, this scale means 1 inch on the map represents 1 mile of actual ground (1 mile = 5,280 ft $\times$ 12 in. = 63,000 in.).

1. If two roads were $6\frac{1}{2}$ in. apart on a map with this scale, how far apart are they actually?

_____

Often a map will use different units in its scale. 1 inch on a map might equal a number of miles of actual distance.

2. A map has a scale of $\frac{1\ in.}{35\ mi}$. If two cities are 1.6 in. apart on the map, how far apart are they actually?

_____

3. If one city is 161 miles from another, what is their distance from each other on the map?

_____

The proportion between two actual distances is the same as their proportion on a map.

4. A rectangular parking lot is 37,500,000 square feet on the ground. One side is 7,500 feet long. If a map shows the long side of the parking lot as 20 inches, how long is the short side on the map?

_____

5. What is the scale of the map in Question 4?

_____

6. The United States is about 1,000 miles by 3,000 miles. If you wanted to draw a map of the United States on an $8\frac{1}{2}$-inch by 11-inch sheet of paper, what scale would you use?

_____

Use with pages 276–277

ENRICH   Statistics and Probability

A **percent** expresses a ratio between a number and 100. Tendai correctly answers 17 of 20 questions on her math quiz. Her grade is expressed as a percent.

Percentile is the way to express the position of a number (or score) within a set of numbers (or scores). Of the 100 students who took a quiz, 82 received grades lower or equal to Tendai's. The percentile is 82 (number of students with grades lower than or equal to Tendai's), or Tendai's position in relation to all the students taking the test. Thus, Tendai's percentile is 82, whereas her percent correct is 85%.

$$\frac{\text{(number correct)}}{\text{(number on the test)}} =$$
$$\frac{17}{20} = \frac{85}{100} =$$
85 percent (85%)

Tendai received a grade of 85%.

1. 100 students took a test with 60 questions on it. Complete the table to give the results.

Number of correct answers	60	58	56	55		52	50					
Number of students with that score	1	4	8	3	8	10	16	18	16	8	6	2
Percentage correct	100	97			90			80	70	65	60	55
Percentile rank	100	99										

2. What is the highest percentile in which you can place? What is the lowest? _____

3. Billy's score on the geometry test is the highest in his class. He answers 38 of 50 questions correct for a score of 76%. In what percentile did Billy score?

_____

4. Tendai took a standardized test that many seventh graders take. There were 200 questions, and she answered 44 correctly, or 22%. She placed in the eighty-eighth percentile. Did Tendai do well on the test? Explain your answer. What do you know about the test?

_____

_____

_____

_____

ENRICH | **Measurement**

A measurement can often be expressed in two or more ways, using different units. Sometimes these units might be multiples of each other, such as units of length in the metric system, or they can be wholly unrelated. When different systems of measurement are used to measure the same thing, we often need to convert from one unit to another. A familiar example is degrees Celsius and degrees Fahrenheit. The Celsius scale has the freezing point of water at 0° and the boiling point of water at 100°. The Fahrenheit scale sets the freezing point at 32° and the boiling point a 212°.

1. Using the number of degrees between water's boiling and freezing points, write the ratio of °C to °F. Round to the nearest single-digit ratio.

_____

There is an additional factor in converting from one scale to another: the scales do not have a common starting point.

2. You know the ratio between °C units and °F units. Write a proportion to find the number of °F units in 0°C units. What must you then add to find the °F in 0°C?

_____

3. Write the conversion formula to convert 0°C to °F.

_____

4. Write a proportion again using 0°C. This time, write the equivalent °F in the proportion. What must you do to the °F measure for the proportion to be correct?

_____

5. Write the conversion formula to convert 0°F to °C.

_____

One conversion is 50°F = 10°C. Test your formulas, and ring the correct conversion(s).

6. 25°C = 77°F   **7.** 113°F = 45°C   **8.** 14°F = 5°C   **9.** 99°C = 131°F

Use with pages 280–281.

ENRICH   **Logic**

Venn diagrams are used to show a relationship between two or more sets. Diagonal lines show the part of the set that does not exist. Areas with diagonal lines are void areas and are no longer part of the set. An *asterisk* (*) indicates that some of the set exists.

First, the sets are defined:

P = the set of all people   D = the set of all drivers   B = the set of all bicyclers

Then the diagrams are filled in to illustrate the propositions.

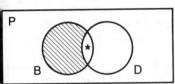

Some drivers are bicyclers; no bicyclers only ride bikes.

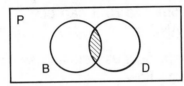

No bicyclers are drivers.

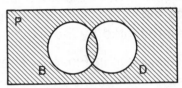

All people are either bicyclers or drivers, but no one is both.

1. Use the defined sets to fill in the diagram for the proposition(s).

M = the set of all musicians   P = the set of all pianists   D = the set of all drummers

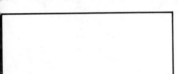

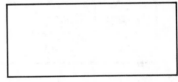

All people are either pianists or drummers; some are both.

All pianists are drummers.

No one is both a pianist and a drummer.

Write the proposition(s) for each diagram.

2. G = the set of all gravy   S = the set of sweet gravy   B = the set of brown gravy

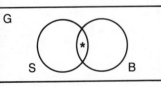

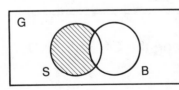

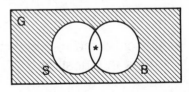

_____

_____

_____

_____

_____

_____

_____

_____

_____

_____

_____

_____

ENRICH   Logic

Computer information is represented by electronic switches that are either "on" or "off." The switch, or *gate,* in Figure 1 is on, or "closed," since it allows electricity to flow from point *a* to point *b.* The gate in Figure 2 is off, or "open," since it prevents the flow, or current, of electricity from point *a* to point *b.*

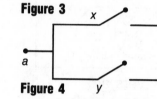

Figure 1

Figure 2

Computers can form more complex circuits, or *statements,* using more than one switch (Figure 3). This circuit is called a *logical AND gate* because the switches at both *x* and *y* must be closed for the current to flow from *a* to *b.* It can be represented by the expression "*x* AND *y.*"

The circuit in Figure 4 is an *OR gate* because closing switch *x, y,* or both will permit the current to flow.

Figure 3

Figure 4   *y*

1. Complete the table for Figure 4.

x	y	Circuit
Open	Open	OFF
Open	Closed	
Closed	Open	
Closed	Closed	

2. Write the expression for the circuit in Figure 4.

_____

3. How would you express the circuit in Figure 5? Use another sheet of paper to determine the possibilities of an on or off circuit.

_____

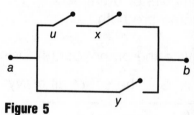

Figure 5   *y*

4. Describe the relationship between the OR and AND gates in Question 3.

_____

_____

_____

Use with pages 284–285.

ENRICH **Number**

Stores buy goods in quantity at **wholesale prices** and sell goods individually to the public at **retail prices.** The difference between the price a store pays and the price it sells the item for is the **profit.** A store's profit on an item is normally expressed as a percent of the wholesale price.

1. Jody's Bait and Tackle Shop makes a 20% profit on fish eggs. He obtains them for $3.00 per 100 eggs. What price does he charge for 100 eggs?

_____

2. Jody's Secret Fish Radar Lures cost him $0.80 to make and he sells them for $2.00 each. What percent profit does he make?

_____

3. Jody sells night crawlers at a low price, hoping that people will buy other items once they come into the store. Jody obtains the night crawlers for $1.80 per box and sells each box for $1.98. What is his profit on each box? Express the profit as a percent.

_____

4. Jody averages $2,000 profit per month. If approximately 30% of the profit comes from night crawler sales, 45% comes from fish egg sales, and 25% comes from Radar lure sales, what quantity of each item does he sell per month on the average?

_____

5. Jody estimates that if he lowered the price of the Radar lures to $1.80 each, he would be able to sell 100 extra lures. If he lowered the price to $1.50, he would be able to sell 200 extra lures. Will he make the most profit by selling the lures at $1.80, $1.50, or $2.00?

_____

6. If Jody's Bait & Tackle Shop raises the price of the night crawlers to $2.16, he will lose an estimated 1% of his sales for all three items he sells. How much profit will he gain or lose each month if he raises the price of the night crawlers to $2.16 per box?

_____

7. Unlike Jody's Bait & Tackle Shop, some supermarkets average only 2% or 3% profit on each item they sell. How do you suppose these stores stay in business?

_____

Name _____ Date _____

1. King Maudi IV of Bean Island decided one day to raise the salary of all workers from 11,000 to 12,000 bean dollars (B$). What percent increase is this? _____

2. People on the island were pleased with their extra money, but soon prices increased. A can of bean soup last year cost 30B¢. This year it cost 36B¢. A Beanmobile car last year cost 5,000B$. This year it costs 6,000B$. What was the percent increase in price?

_____

3. When the price of everything in an economy increases, *inflation* is said to exist. If the rate of inflation on Bean Island was 20% over last year, write the price of the items in the table.

	Bean pie	Computer	Sneakers	3-bean salad
Last year	2.00B$	850B$	24B$	0.75B$
This year				

4. The table shows a breakdown of Edwina Bean's expenses for last year. Inflation is 20% this year. Complete the table.

	Salary	Rent	Fun	Beans	Other
Last year	11,000B$	4,200B$	1,500B$	1,000B$	3,000B$
This year	12,000B$				

5. How much money will Edwina spend this year?

_____

6. Economists often say that the price of an item increases when demand for it increases, and decreases when demand for it decreases. In view of this, see if you can explain how the increase in salary that King Maudi IV gave to his workers might have caused the inflation experienced on Bean Island.

_____

108

Name _____ Date _____

You work at the Highland Savings Bank. You are preparing a report about bank loan policies. The people listed in the chart below have each borrowed money from the bank. Complete the chart by using the simple interest formula $i = prt$. Round the interest to the nearest cent.

	BORROWER	PRINCIPAL	RATE	TERM OF LOAN	INTEREST
1.	A. Zelles	$2,000	12%	1 year	
2.	F. Unger		11%	2 years	$770
3.	E. Zapata	$4,750		1 year	$617.50
4.	R. Clarke	$5,300	10%		$1,060
5.	A. DeLuca	$8,800	12.5%	3 years	
6.	T. Nuñez	$6,100		1 year	$686.25
7.	C. Nasarenko		13.5%	6 months	$175.50
8.	S. Seigal	$9,425	12.75%		$1,802.53

Use the chart to answer the questions below.

9. What was the total amount Mrs. A. Zelles repaid the bank? _____

10. Mr. R. Clarke repaid the bank in 24 equal monthly installments. What was the amount of each payment?

_____

11. Mrs. Seigal repaid her loan 6 months early. She received a reduction of $438 for early payment. What was the total amount she repaid the bank? _____

12. Miss C. Nasarenko repaid her loan in 6 equal monthly payments. Because one payment was late, she had to pay a penalty of $37.50. What was her total payment that month? _____

ENRICH | Statistics and Probability

Here are examples of different types of charts and graphs. Each shows the monthly profits of the Barbizon Automobile Company.

circle graph

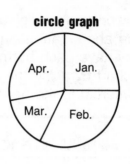

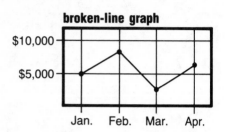

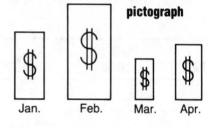

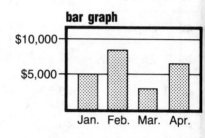

1. Of these charts, which two are most useful in showing the actual amounts of change each month?

_____

2. What is the circle graph most useful in showing?

_____

3. Barbizon Automobile Company wants to compare its output with its competitor. Which type of chart would show the comparison most dramatically at a quick glance?

_____

4. The table shows the Barbizon Automobile Company sales and profits. Use broken lines to complete one graph to show the number of cars sold; then make a bar graph to show profit per car.

	Jan.	Feb.	Mar.	Apr.	May	June	July	Aug.	Sept.
cars sold	500	450	600	550	700	750	900	850	900
profit per car	$425	$400	$350	$400	$325	$300	$275	$275	$250

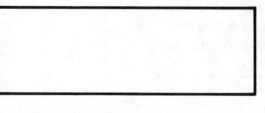

Cars sold

$ profit per car

Use with pages 294–295.

ENRICH   Statistics and Probability

When you have a savings account at a bank, you earn **interest.** *Interest* is the percent of your money per year that the bank pays you for keeping your money there. Interest can be paid in two different ways. With **compound interest,** the interest is totaled at specified intervals and added to your original money, called the **principle.** With compound interest, you begin to earn interest on the money that the bank has already paid you as interest. **Simple interest** is not added to your principle; so, you only continue to earn interest on the principle.

If you had $100.00 in a bank at 8% simple interest, after one year you would have $108.00. If you had $100.00 earning 8% compounded quarterly, $\left(\frac{8\%}{4}\right)$, you would end up with more.

Jan. 1	Apr. 1	July 1	Oct. 1	Jan. 1

$100.00 $\times \frac{8\%}{4}$ = $102.00 $\times \frac{8\%}{4}$ = $104.04 $\times \frac{8\%}{4}$ = $106.12 $\times \frac{8\%}{4}$ = $108.24

Compounded quarterly, an 8% interest rate yields you 8.24% of the money you deposited. This is called the **effective rate of interest.**

1. What is the effective rate of interest on a savings account that paid 12% interest and compounded monthly? _____

2. Which is greater, the difference between 10% simple and 10% compound interest, or the difference between 20% simple and 20% compound interest? Explain why.

_____

_____

3. If you had $10,000 to invest, would you put it in an account that paid 18% compounded monthly, or one that paid 19% simple interest? why?

_____

_____

Use with pages 296–297.   111

ENRICH Problem Solving

You are the state treasurer. You are appearing before the
state legislature to answer questions about your state's
income from taxation. Your assistant has prepared a circle
graph for you that breaks down the sources of the state's tax
income. Use the graph below to help you answer questions
asked by members of the legislature.

STATE INCOME FROM TAXES FOR THE YEAR: $5,320,600,000

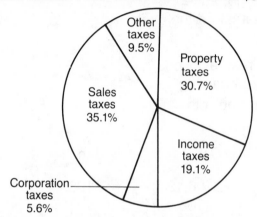

1. Which tax revenue source provides the state with the most
   income? _____

2. Which two tax revenue sources combined provide the
   state with more than 60 percent of its total tax revenue?

   _____

3. Did the tax on corporations bring in more than 1 billion
   dollars in revenue for the year? _____

4. The taxes included in the "other" category were taxes on
   gasoline, public utilities, alcoholic beverages, tobacco
   products, and gifts. Which of these accounted for the
   greatest amount of income?

   _____

5. About 0.7% of total tax revenue came from the tax on
   tobacco products. How much money was this? _____

6. How much money did the state take in during the year
   from income taxes? _____

Use with pages 298–299.

Name_____   Date_____

Ordered pairs (*x,y*) are normally used to plot and identify points on a graph. An alternative system uses **polar coordinates.** These coordinates are:

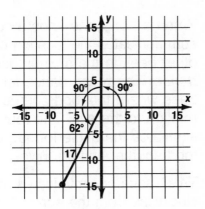

a. The length of a line (the *radian*) drawn from the origin (0 on both axes) to the point.

b. The angle the radian makes with the *x*-axis. The angle is measured counterclockwise from the positive *x*-axis.

Polar coordinates (17,242°)

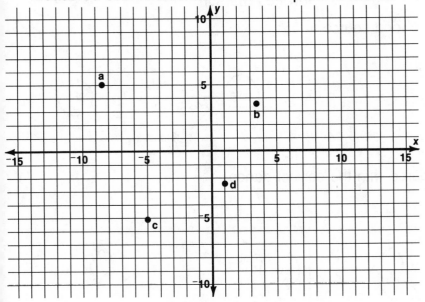

1. Use a protractor and ruler to find the polar coordinates of each point on the graph.

a. _____   **b.** _____   **c.** _____   **d.** _____

2. Draw the points e–h on the graph, and write the ordered pair (*x,y*) for each.

e. (15,29°) _____   **f.** (10,220°) _____

g. (9,300°) _____   **h.** (6,90°) _____

3. The polar coordinates (5,0°–360°) represent the graph of all points that are 5 from the origin, between 0° and 360° from the positive *x*-axis. What does this graph look like? Can you express this using ordered pairs? Explain why or why not. _____

_____

ENRICH   Geometry

When a honeybee finds a source of food, it communicates the location of the food to other bees in the hive by using the *round dance.* The round dance tells the other bees where the food source is located in relation to the sun. The round dance simulates the angle formed by the sun, the food source, and the hive.

A honeybee performs the round dance on one of the vertical walls, called *combs,* inside the hive. The ground directly below the hive indicates the direction of the sun. Therefore, if a bee travels straight down the comb during its dance, other bees know they can locate the food source by flying towards the sun.

This dance communicates that the food source is 45° clockwise from the sun.

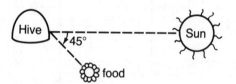

Match the location of the food source with the correct dance. You may use a protractor.

1.

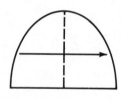

_____

2.

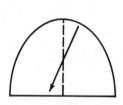

_____

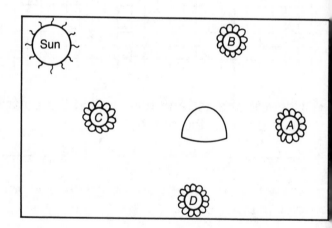

3.

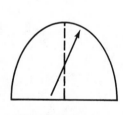

_____

4.

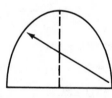

_____

5. In the diagram, draw a flower where you might find food as indicated by a honeybee that dances straight up.

6. If the hive were turned on its side, would this affect the bee's round dance? why? _____

_____

_____

Name _____ Date _____

Given an angle, you can construct an angle congruent to it using only a compass and a straightedge. Put your compass on the vertex of the angle, and draw a circle. It will intersect the two rays of the angle at A and B. Label A and B. Draw a line segment between the two points. Draw a congruent circle, and label the center point C. Use your compass to make two points on this circle that are the same distance from each other as from A to B. Label the points D and E. Draw the two rays from C to D and C to E. The two angles are congruent.

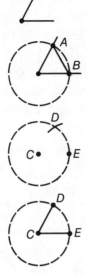

1. Use this method to draw △MNO similar to △JKL. (HINT: Construct two angles equal to two of the angles of △JKL.)

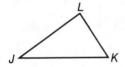

2. Diagram two ways to construct a square using only a compass and a straightedge.

3. Construct a regular hexagon using only a compass and a straightedge, given this 120° angle.

ENRICH   Algebra

An **ordered pair** is a set of two elements in which order is important. A **Cartesian product** is a set of ordered pairs that is formed by taking each element of one set or group and pairing it with each element of a second set. If one set contains as its elements two cars, and a second set contains two drivers, the Cartesian product of the two sets represents the possible pairings of each car with each driver.

$(a,b) \neq (b,a)$

Ordered pairs are enclosed by parentheses.

$\{a,b\} = \{b,a\}$

Cartesian products are enclosed by brackets.

Cars	Drivers	Cartesian product
baby blue	Ms. Ponti	{baby blue, Ms. Ponti}, {baby blue, Mr. Zenith}, {royal blue, Ms. Ponti}, {royal blue, Mr. Zenith}
royal blue	Mr. Zenith	

If set $A = \{x,y,z\}$ and set $B = \{1,2\}$, the Cartesian product of A and B is written as $A \times B$ and is read "A cross B."

1. Write the Cartesian product of $A \times B$.

_____

2. Steve, Chu Yat, and Yukio visit Babe's Pet Store and find a parrot, gopher, and kitten. Each bought one. Use Cartesian products to give the possibilities of who bought which pet.

_____

_____

_____

A subset of a Cartesian product $N \times M$ in which every first element is paired with a different or unique second element is called a *mapping* or a *function* from N to M. For example:

$$P = \{(a,7), (b,9)\}$$

is a subset of $N \times M$. This can be written

as $P \subset (N \times M)$ which reads "P is a subset of N cross M."

Since the first element among the ordered pairs of set P is paired with a unique second element, set P is a mapping or function of N to M.

3. If set $R = \{(a,1), (a, 2), (b,2)\}$, is it a function? Explain.

_____

4. Explain two situations where Cartesian products would be useful to you.

_____

Use with pages 316–317.

ENRICH   Geometry

Swimmers at the ninth Annual Sea Race carry tiny radio transmitters and are tracked from two radar stations located on boats 10 miles apart. Station A gets a 225° reading for Porky Porpoise. Station B's reading for Porky is 315°. The intersection of lines drawn from the stations marks Porky's exact location. Porky's position is shown below.

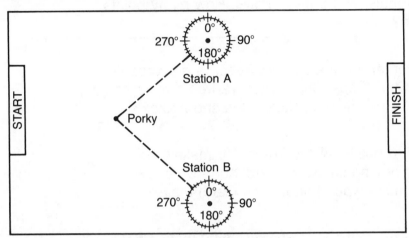

1. Locate the racers listed in the table. Use a protractor to draw lines on the map. Mark each racer's position on the map. In the third column of the table, write the order, from first to fifth place, in which the racers are currently swimming.

Racer	Station A	Station B	Place
Porky Porpoise	230°	310°	
Goldie Goldfish	230°	300°	
Sean Shark	120°	50°	
Fred Flounder	140°	40°	
Tommy Trout	250°	295°	

2. With only a half hour to go in the race, things have changed drastically. Sean Shark and Tommy Trout are battling it out for first place. Sean's radar readings are A: 135°, B: 45°. Tommy's readings are A: 120°, B: 60°. Use the map. Who is closest to the finish line?

_____

_____

3. The radar tracking in next year's race will come from a single boat. Signals will be sent to the swimmers and reflected back. What will the radar trackers measure? What figure will they need to know?

_____

_____

ENRICH   Statistics and Probability

In professional basketball, there are three ways to score points: long shots count for 3 points, field-goal baskets count for 2 points, and free throws count for 1 point.

1. In a game against the Franklin Frogs, Ben makes 3 long shots, 7 field goals, and 5 free throws. How many points does he score?

   _____

2. Abbie plays center for the Oregon Trees. She scores 40 points against the Frogs. She makes 12 free throws and no long shots. How many baskets does she make?

   _____

3. Garth scores 36 points for the Trees. He makes the same number of long shots, baskets, and free throws. How many of each type of shot does Garth make?

   _____

4. Toni, star forward of the Bay Shore Clams, makes none of her long shots against the Trees. She makes 3 times as many field-goal baskets as free throws for a total of 70 points. How many baskets does Toni make?

   _____

5. Jeff scores a total of 23 points for the Rochelle Rebounds. He makes twice as many field-goal baskets as free throws, and 4 times as many free throws as long shots. How many baskets does Jeff make?

   _____

6. Use all three types of shots to create a similar problem. Give it to a classmate to solve.

   _____

Use with pages 322–323.

Name _____ Date _____

Pythagoras, a Greek mathematician and philosopher who lived in the sixth century B.C., discovered a basic property about right triangles. Look at the figures.

In Figure A, Y is a right triangle, and $a = b$. W, X, and Z are squares. In Figure B, C and D have one diagonal drawn, and E has both diagonals drawn. Now there are nine congruent triangles.

Figure A

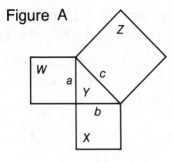

1. If $a = 2$ and $b = 2$, what is the area of W? What is the area of X? Which formula is used to find the area of a square? _____

2. What is the area of Z? _____

3. What is the length of c? (HINT: Use your answer from Problem 2.) What is formula is used to find the length of a side of a square, given its area?

_____

Figure B

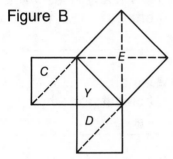

The Pythagorean Theory, one of the building blocks of geometry, is stated as follows: For a right triangle ABC with hypotenuse c, $c^2 = a^2 + b^2$.

Fill in the missing side.

4.

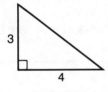

3
4

5.

5
6

6.

5   7

7.

8
6

8.

10
4

9.

6
7

10.

2
1

11. 8   12

12. Can you explain why all the triangles in Figure B are congruent? Use Figures A and B.

_____

_____

_____

_____

Name _____ Date _____

You can construct regular polygons using only a compass, protractor, and straight edge.

To create a hexagon, draw a circle with a compass. The circle can be of any radius. The vertices of the hexagon will be on this circle.

1. Label the center of the circle *A*. Put a point on the circle.

2. How many sides will a hexagon have? How many vertices? What will be the common central angle at *A*?

_____

3. Use a protractor to put another point on the circle. Where should it go? why?

_____

_____

4. How will you complete the hexagon? why?

_____

_____

_____

Construct a regular pentagon.

5. What will the central angle be? why?

_____

6. What will the five pentagon angles be?

_____

7. What do you notice about the answers to Problems 5 and 6? Is there a relation to another geometric figure?

_____

_____

8. Can you conclude anything about the triangles formed by the sides of the pentagon and the radii of the circle at each vertex? _____

_____

_____

9. What can you conclude about the relationship between the angles of the pentagon and the radii of the circle at each vertex? _____

120

Name _____ Date _____

The number system we use in the United States is base ten. Base ten uses ten digits: 0 to 9. Base twelve uses twelve digits: 0, 1, 2, 3, 4, 5, 6, 7, 8, 9, *, ☆. Each place is 12 times greater than the place to the right.

You can add base-twelve numbers. Regroup in base twelve the same way you do in base ten.

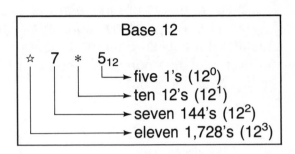

Base 12

☆ 7 * 5_{12}
- five 1's (12^0)
- ten 12's (12^1)
- seven 144's (12^2)
- eleven 1,728's (12^3)

Add.

$$\begin{array}{r} \overset{1}{2}7_{12} \\ + \ 87_{12} \\ \hline 2_{12} \end{array} \qquad \begin{array}{r} \overset{1}{2}7_{12} \\ + 87_{12} \\ \hline ☆2_{12} \end{array}$$

(REMEMBER: $11_{10} = ☆_{12}$)

1. $\begin{array}{r} 67610_{12} \\ + \ 4*204_{12} \\ \hline ☆5814_{12} \end{array}$

2. $\begin{array}{r} 3274☆6_{12} \\ + \ \ **1_{12} \\ \hline \end{array}$

3. $\begin{array}{r} ☆0*_{12} \\ + 147_{12} \\ \hline \end{array}$

4. $\begin{array}{r} 28135_{12} \\ + 92999_{12} \\ \hline \end{array}$

5. Complete the base-twelve multiplication table.

×	1	2	3	4	5	6	7	8	9	*	☆
1											
2											
3											
4											
5											
6											
7											
8											
9											
*											
☆											

Use the table to multiply the following base-twelve numbers.

6. $\begin{array}{r} 75_{12} \\ \times \ \ 3_{12} \\ \hline \end{array}$

7. $\begin{array}{r} 58_{12} \\ \times \ \ *_{12} \\ \hline \end{array}$

8. $\begin{array}{r} 673_{12} \\ \times \ \ 9_{12} \\ \hline \end{array}$

9. $\begin{array}{r} 71*_{12} \\ \times \ \ 4_{12} \\ \hline \end{array}$

10. $\begin{array}{r} ☆3_{12} \\ \times \ \ *_{12} \\ \hline \end{array}$

ENRICH   Patterns

Triangular numbers are those in the sequence $1 + 2 + 3 + \cdots + n$. They can be represented as patterns of dots in equilateral triangles. Square numbers are the numbers you get from squaring numbers. They can be represented as square patterns of dots.

triangular numbers   square numbers

Pentagonal numbers are those numbers that can be arranged to form regular pentagons. The first three pentagonal numbers are shown: 1, 5, 12.

1. Draw the next four pentagonal numbers. Follow the examples, keeping the lower left-hand vertex the same for each pentagon. Write the pentagonal number within each successive pentagon. Note that the nth pentagon has sides of length n.

A formula for pentagonal numbers is $[n^2 + (1 + 2 + 3 + \cdots + [n - 1])]$. You can see from this formula that the nth pentagonal number is the sum of the nth square number and the $(n - 1)^{th}$ triangular number.

2. The third pentagonal number has been arranged in dots to show its square and triangular components. Draw the fourth, fifth, and sixth pentagonal numbers in the same way.

3. Use the formula to write the eighth through the tenth pentagonal numbers.

_____

4. Why do we say that pentagonal numbers can be shown as patterns of dots in *regular* pentagons? Why not any 5-sided figure?

_____

_____

ENRICH   Geometry

Take a strip of paper about 2 inches wide and 15 inches long. Join the ends together with tape to make a band, but first give the band a half-twist. Join A with D and B with C. This is a Möbius strip.

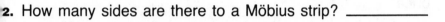

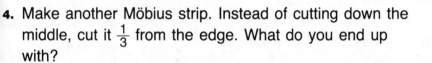

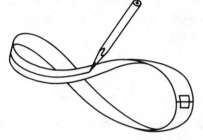

1. Draw a line in the middle of the band completely around the outside. What do you notice? _____

2. How many sides are there to a Möbius strip? _____

3. Cut along the line you have drawn. What do you notice?

_____

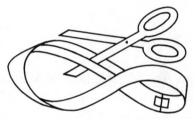

4. Make another Möbius strip. Instead of cutting down the middle, cut it $\frac{1}{3}$ from the edge. What do you end up with? _____

5. How many edges does a Möbius strip have? _____

6. How many edges does a band with two half-twists have? _____

7. Make another band with three half-twists. How many edges are there?

_____

8. What do you predict for bands with four half-twists? _____

9. What generalization can you make about half-twists? _____

10. Make a band with two half-twists in it. Cut it down the middle. What do you end up with?

_____

11. Make a band with three half-twists in it. Cut it down the middle. What do you end up with?

_____

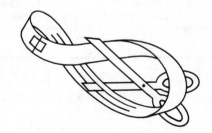

12. Möbius strips have been considered for use in machinery as fan belts. why?

_____

ENRICH   Geometry

A **network** is a figure composed of points, called *vertices,* connected by lines, called *arcs.* The degree of a vertex is the number of arcs that meet at it. If an odd number of arcs meet at a vertex, it is called an *odd-degree vertex.* If an even number of arcs meet, it is called an *even-degree vertex.*

Vertex *A* is of even degree 2.
Vertex *C* is of odd degree 3.
Vertex *D* is of even degree 4.

A network is *traversable* if you can trace it with a continuous path that crosses each arc only once.

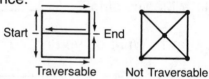

Traversable   Not Traversable

1. Are all of these networks traversable? _____

2. What do the vertices of these networks have in common?

_____

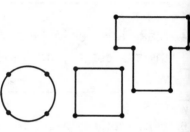

3. Are all the networks in the second set of figures traversable? _____

4. How many vertices of odd degree do each of these networks have? _____

5. What do these networks have in common?

_____

6. Construct some networks of your own on another sheet of paper. Keep them simple. Then complete a table like this one.

Number of even vertices	Number of odd vertices	Traversable

Analyze the findings in your table; then write how to determine the traversability of a network.

_____

_____

Use with pages 338–339

Name _____ Date _____

elations between elements of a set (x,y) may be
iagrammed with arrows and loops. Relations are written with
R. For example:

x is related to y   y is related to x   x is related to x

xRy   yRx   xRx

x ———————→ y   y ———————→ x   x

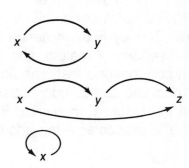

When x is related to y and y is related to x, then the
relation between x and y is **symmetric.**

When x is related to y, y is related to z, and x is related to
z, then the relation between x, y, and z is **transitive.**

If every element in a set is related to itself, the set is
reflexive.

1. Ring the words that describe the relation shown.

L ——→ M ——→ N	symmetric	reflexive	transitive
↻ 3	symmetric	reflexive	transitive
W ⇄ Y ⇄ Z X	symmetric	reflexive	transitive

Diagram the relation.

2. transitive using
elements W, X, Y, and
Z

3. symmetric and
reflexive using
elements R, S, and T

4. transitive and
symmetric using
elements △, ○, and ☆

The following diagram describes a few operations of addition
using the set (0,1,2).

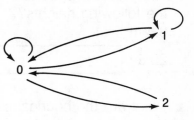

0R0 and 1R1 because 0 + 0 and 1 + 1 are members of the set.
0R1 and 1R0 because 1 + 1 and 0 + 1 are members of the set.
0R2 and 2R0 because 2 + 0 and 0 + 2 are members of the set.

5. On another sheet of paper, make up three addition
problems. Diagram the relation of each.

ENRICH   Problem Solving

Read the paragraph and answer the questions that follow.
Use the picture to find the unstated information.

Dr. Bentley is a scientist studying four exotic species of
insects that live at various heights in the South American rain
forest pictured below. She finds Species 1 living on the forest
floor. Then she climbs 11.4 meters and comes upon Species
2. She continues to climb, and throughout the next 6 meters,
Dr. Bentley finds evidence of both Species 1 and 2. In the
subsequent 7 meters, she finds only Species 2. In the 3.2
meters beyond that, she finds no Species 1 or 2 insects.
Then she comes upon Species 3 and 4. Species 3 lives only
in the Upper Canopy. Dr. Bentley finds no insects of any of
the four species living above 48 meters.

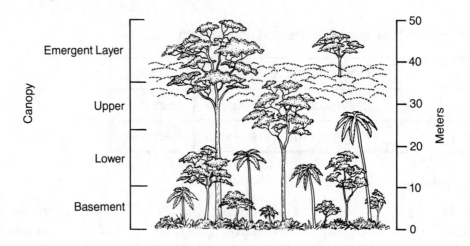

1. Which species of insects did Dr. Bentley find living at each
   level of the rain forest?
   Basement _____   Lower canopy _____

   Upper canopy _____   Emergent layer _____

2. Which insect species would you expect to find at each of
   the following heights?
   8.4 m _____   32.4 m _____

   25.5 m _____   41.0 m _____

3. What are the boundaries of the areas in which Dr. Bentley
   found no insects of the species she was studying?

   _____

ENRICH   Geometry

1. Can you trace a continuous path that passes over each line only once without lifting your pencil?

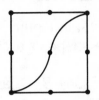

_____

The figure is called a **network.** It is composed of points, called *vertices,* connected to each other by either curved or straight lines, called *arcs.* It is *traversable* because it can be traced with a continuous path that crosses each arc only once. Such a path is known as an **Eüler (oy′ · ler) path.**

You can predict whether a network will have an Eüler path by analyzing its vertices. If an odd number of arcs meet at a vertex, it is called an *odd-degree vertex.* If an even number of arcs meet at a vertex, it is known as an *even-degree vertex.* A network is traversable if all vertices are even or if it contains exactly two odd vertices.

2. Write *traversable* or *not traversable* for each figure. Trace the Eüler path if the figure is traversable.

  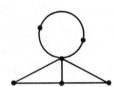

_____   _____   _____

3. The city of Königsberg is composed of four separate areas of land connected by seven bridges. Can the inhabitants of Königsberg take a trip that will allow them to visit all four areas of land while crossing each bridge exactly once? Write *traversable* or *not traversable.*

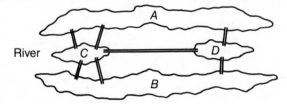

_____

4. If the figure is traversable, trace the path. If not, add or subtract bridges to make it traversable.

_____

ENRICH   Geometry

If section *A* in Figure 1 was cut out, a top view of it would have the shape of a circle.

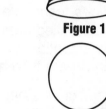

final section

Figure 1

1. If sections *B*, *C*, and *D* were also cut out, what generalization could you make about these sections as they appear closer and closer to the tip of the cone?

_____

2. Suppose sections *E*, *F*, *G*, etc., were cut in Figure 1, each one in succession closer to the top of the cone until the final infinitesimally thin section were cut. What geometric term would you use to label this final section?

_____

top view of *A*

3. What shape would section *K* and section *L* have if they were cut from Figure 2 and seen from a top view?

_____

Figure 2

4. Assume the width of the cone's base in Figure 3 and the sphere's diameter in Figure 2 are equal. Sections *I* and *J* are cut from the cone, and sections *K* and *L* are cut from the sphere. Compare the sum of the area of sections *I* and *J* to that of sections *K* and *L*.

_____

_____

Figure 3

5. What shape would section *N*, cut from the rectangular pyramid in Figure 4, have if it were cut out?

_____

Figure 4

6. What is unique about all the sections you could take in Figure 5?

_____

7. Are there any three-dimensional objects whose sections, no matter how they are cut, will always have the same shape?

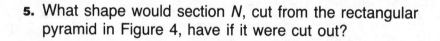

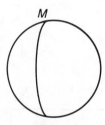

Figure 5

Use with pages 354–355

ENRICH Measurement

The Spokes Bike Club is planning to paint their new bicycle shed. 1 gallon of paint covers 500 ft² for the first coat, and 700 ft² for the second and third coats. To determine how many gallons it takes to paint the back wall of the shed, find its area and set up a proportion. Figure 1 shows that the wall is 20 ft × 30 ft, or 600 ft². For the first coat, use this proportion: $\frac{1 \text{ gal}}{500 \text{ ft}^2} = \frac{x}{600 \text{ ft}^2}$; $x = 1.2$ gal.

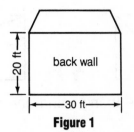

Figure 1

1. How many gallons are needed to paint all three coats of paint on the back wall? Round to the nearest tenth.

_____

2. If the dimensions of the shed's back wall (Figure 1) were doubled to 40 × 60 ft, would twice as much paint be needed? What if the dimensions were tripled? why or why not ?

_____

_____

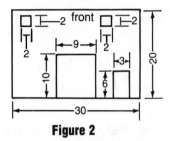

Figure 2

NOTE: All dimensions in Figures 2 and 3 are in feet.

3. Approximately how much paint is used to paint three coats on the front wall of the shed in Figure 2. The doors and windows are not painted. Round to the nearest hundredth.

_____

The club designs a billboard to recruit new members. They paint their logo in purple with a red background. Look at Figure 3.

4. How much of each color will be needed to give the billboard two coats? Remember that the area of a circle is πr^2, and round to the nearest hundredth.

_____

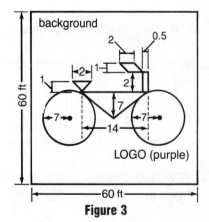

Figure 3

5. Write a general formula for the amount of paint needed if the dimensions of the wall increased n times. (HINT: Use x = the original dimensions of the wall.)

_____

ENRICH   **Geometry**

These are squares that contain two triangles and two quadrilaterals.

Draw one triangle and one pentagon within each regular polygon.

 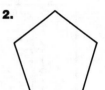 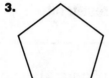 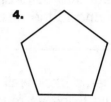

1.   **2.**   **3.**   **4.**

Draw one triangle, one quadrilateral, and one pentagon within each square.

5.   **6.**   **7.**   **8.**

The **axis of symmetry** is the line that divides a figure into identical parts. For example, the axis of symmetry is shown in Problem 13 with arrows.

Draw two symmetrical figures within each square.

  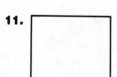

9.   **10.**   **11.**   **12.**

Draw two triangles and two quadrilaterals within each square. Show any axis of symmetry.

13.   **14.**   **15.**   **16.**

ENRICH   Problem Solving

Lila is making an inlaid tabletop using the scale drawing below as her pattern. The center of her tabletop will be a square of ebony wood, each side measuring 8 inches. Use the drawing to answer the questions. Make a plan when needed.

1. When Lila's table is completed, how much more area will the ebony trapezoids cover than the ebony square?

_____

2. How much more rosewood than pine will Lila use?

_____

3. What is the total area of the inlaid pattern?

_____

4. Lila plans to outline every trapezoid with a thin line of gold leaf. About how many inches of gold leaf will she use?

_____

5. It takes Lila $26\frac{1}{2}$ minutes to make each piece of wood that is less than 60 in.^{2} in area. It takes her 44 minutes to make each of the other pieces. How long does it take Lila to make all the pieces? _____

6. Can Lila cut all of the maple she needs from a piece of wood 22 inches by 25 inches? _____

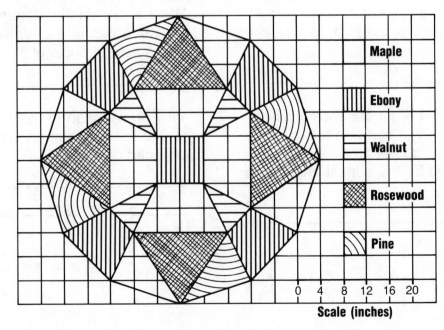

Scale (inches)

Name _____ Date _____

The area of a circle is found with the formula $A = \pi r^2$. The circumference of a circle is given by the formula $C = 2\pi r$. Using these two formulas, we can find the area of different parts of a circle.

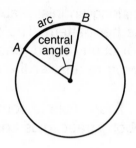

An **arc** is a portion of the circle's circumference. An arc is **encompassed** by a central angle through its two endpoints, A and B. You can determine the length of an arc by using the measurement of its central angle. A central angle of 360° encompasses the entire circumference of the circle.

1. What part of the circumference of a circle is encompassed by a central angle of 180°? by an angle of 90°?

_____

2. If the circumference of a circle is 30 cm, what is the length of an arc encompassed by a 60° angle?

_____

3. Write a formula that determines the length of an arc encompassed by a central angle of $Y°$ in a circle with radius r. (HINT: Use the circumference formula.)

_____

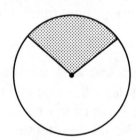

To determine the area of a section of a circle, take the central angle $Y°$. It encompasses an area of $\frac{Y}{360}$ of the circle's area.

4. If the area of a circle is 100 cm², what is the area encompassed by a central angle of 36°?

_____

5. Write a formula that determines the area of a part of a circle with radius r and a central angle of $Y°$.

_____

6. Find the length of an arc encompassed by a central angle of 40° in a circle of radius 7 cm. Find the area encompassed by this central angle. Use 3.14 for π.

_____

7. Why do we need to use central angles to find the length of an arc or the area of a part of a circle?

_____

_____

ENRICH   **Geometry**

You can construct various three-dimensional figures.

1. Draw Figure 1 on a separate sheet of heavy construction paper. Use scissors to cut out the drawing. Then construct the equilateral, triangular-based prism. Fold along all internal lines. Paste the tabs to the corresponding plane (for example, *A* is pasted to *A*).

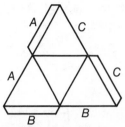

Figure 1: an equilateral, triangular-based pyramid

2. Draw models of Figures 2 and 3 on heavy construction paper. Then construct the regular icosahedron and dodecahedron using the same method.

Figure 2: a regular icosahedron

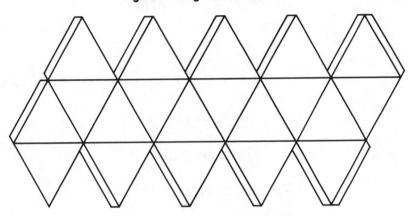

Figure 3: a regular dodecahedron

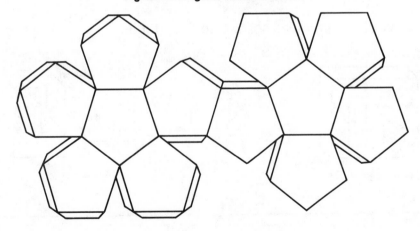

3. Try to design your own polyhedron. Draw the plans on a piece of heavy construction paper. Arrange interlocking regular triangles, quadrilaterals, pentagons, or hexagons into a structure that will become three-dimensional when folded and pasted together.

Name _____ Date _____

To find the surface area of irregular solids, determine the
area of each surface. Then add them to find the total surface
area of the solid. For example, look at the picture of the stick
through the wheel. The solid can be divided into seven
surface areas:

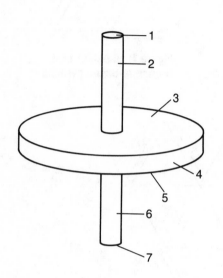

Part	Type of surface	Area (Use 3.14 for π.)
1	circle, $r = 1$	1. _____
2	cylinder wall, $r = 1$, $h = 5$	2. _____
3	circle, $r = 5$, minus circle, $r = 1$	3. _____
4	cylinder wall, $r = 5$, $h = 1$	4. _____
5	Same as part 3	5. _____
6	Same as part 2	6. _____
7	Same as part 1	7. _____

8. What is the total surface area of the solid? _____

Write the surface area of the irregular solid. Use 3.14 for π.

9.

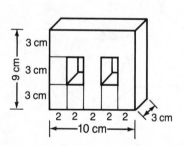

_____

10.

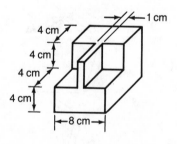

_____

11. A hollow cylinder is 1 cm thick, 10 cm
in length, and 5 cm in diameter. Write
the total surface area.

_____

12. Write a formula for the surface area of
the front and the top of n steps. The
steps are length l, width $\frac{1}{2}l$, and
height $\frac{1}{2}l$.

_____

Name _____ Date _____

Not all solids have volumes that can be found by using one specific formula. The volumes of **composite solids** are found by using two or more formulas. For example, a solid may be a regular cone attached to the top of a regular cylinder. The volume of that solid is the sum of the volumes of the cone and the cylinder. Here is another composite solid: a cube with a smaller cube cut out of one corner. The volume of this composite solid equals the volume of the larger cube minus the volume of the smaller cube.

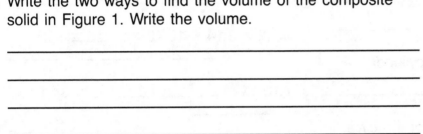

Volume of regular solids
Sphere $= \frac{4}{3}\pi r^2$
Rectangular $= 1 \times w \times h$
Cone $= \frac{1}{3}\pi r^2 \times h$
Cube $= s^3$
Pyramid $= \frac{1}{3}$base $\times h$
Cylinder $= \pi r^2 \times h$
$\pi = 3.14$

1. Write the two ways to find the volume of the composite solid in Figure 1. Write the volume.

_____

_____

_____

_____

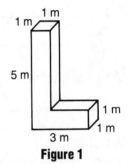

1 m

1 m

5 m

1 m

1 m

3 m

Figure 1

2. A pipe is 2 inches thick, 5 feet long, and has a diameter of 10 inches. How much clay can it hold? How much metal was used to make it? Show all work.

_____

_____

_____

3. Why are the formulas you know inadequate to find the volume of a cylinder with a hole drilled through its curved surface?

_____

_____

4. What is the volume of the composite solid in Figure 2? The lower portion is $\frac{1}{2}$ of a sphere with radius $= 10$ in., $a = 4$ in., and $b = 20$ in. Show all work.

_____

5. Write the dimensions for two pyramids that have volumes of 108 cubic meters.

_____

_____

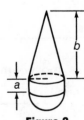

b

a

Figure 2

ENRICH | Problem Solving

Draw a line from each problem to the equation you would use to solve it. Fill in the missing information in each equation and solve.

In the city of Memoria, there is a monument that consists of 14 round pillars supporting a cylinder. The pillars are 34.1 feet tall, and each has a radius of 1.7 feet. They are arranged in a circle whose diameter is 30.3 feet. Inside this circle of pillars is a pool of water that has a radius of 10.42 feet. The pool is 3.6 feet deep. There are 3 solid crystal cubes in the pool. The cubes have sides of 2.1 feet, 2.8 feet, and 3.2 feet. The radius of the cylinder is 18.3 feet. The cylinder is 7.4 feet tall.

1. What is the volume of the largest crystal cube? _____

2. What is the volume of the cylinder?

_____

3. What is the circumference of the circle in which the pillars are arranged? _____

4. The inside of the pool is mirrored. How much area is covered by mirrors?

_____

5. How far are the pillars from the pool?

_____

6. What is the combined volume of the pillars?

_____

7. What is the volume of water contained in the pool? _____

a. $2 \times$ _____ $\times$ _____ $=$ _____

b. $(2 \times 3.14 \times 10.42 \times$ _____$)+$
$(3.14 \times$ _____ $\times$ _____$) =$ _____

c. $3.14 \times$ _____ $\times$ _____ $\times 34.1 \times 14 =$
_____

d. $(30.3 \div 2) -$ _____ $=$ _____

e. $3.2 \times$ _____ $\times 3.2 =$ _____

f. (_____ $\times 10.42 \times$ _____ $\times 3.6) -$
$(2.1^3 +$ _____ $+ 3.2^3) =$ _____

g. $3.14 \times$ _____ $\times$ _____ $\times 7.4 =$
_____

Use with pages 374–375.

Name _____   Date _____

Statistics are used to collect large amounts of information and to present this data in an understandable way. Statistical analysis consists of three steps: defining the problem, collecting data relevant to the problem, and analyzing the data.

Companies use this procedure to predict public interest in their products. They often must take into account various factors, such as age groups, geographic location, and so on.

The Sell and Sell Movie Company is deciding whether to produce the movie, *Hopping Monsters.* They decide to poll the city of Monda.

Age Group	Population	Percent of the Population
0–12	11,400	
13–18	9,300	
19–25	14,600	
26–34	17,100	
35–50	20,100	
50–64	18,900	
65 or more	8,600	

1. Complete the table.

Advertisements are mailed out, and the Sell and Sell Movie Company sets up a polling table at Mahogony Junior High. Of the 100 seventh graders polled, 80 of them thought *Hopping Monsters* was a terrific idea for a movie. The Sell and Sell Movie Company concludes that 4 of every 5 people in Monda would like to see *Hopping Monsters* produced.

2. Assume that the sample group's preferences actually reflect the preferences of the city of Monda. Predict how many people in Monda want *Hopping Monsters* produced.

_____

3. Why is it important that the collection and analysis of data be supervised by people who are not connected with the sample groups? _____

_____

4. Why would age group be a determining factor in whether the sample group accurately reflected Monda's opinion?

_____

5. The rule for sampling is: The larger the sample group, the more accurate the results. How large was the sample group? Did the sample group accurately reflect the opinions of the people of Monda? why or why not?

_____

_____

ENRICH   Statistics and Probability

A **poll** is often taken of a *sample,* or small subset, of the population in order to predict the opinion of the population as a whole. This technique of sampling is used if it is too cumbersome or costly to test everyone in the population. Political polls and television surveys are examples. To accurately represent a larger group, a sample population should be as typical of the larger group as possible.

The Megakola Company has developed a new all-natural soft drink called Melonade. To test whether people will like it enough to buy it, the company performs some market research tests in Weesippem, an average city of 50,000 people. Different sample populations are given Melonade to drink and then asked if they would purchase it if it were sold on the market.

1. On the first day, Jimmie, a novice pollster, polled 500 people. Of these, 100 said they like Melonade enough to buy it. Jimmie told Megakola Company that in a city the size of Weesippem, 100 people would buy Melonade. Explain the mistake in Jimmie's reasoning.

_____

_____

2. Sarah, an expert pollster, polled a representative sample of 500 people. Of these, 50 said they would buy Melonade. How many people did Sarah predict would buy the soft drink in a city like Weesippem? _____

3. Peter, another expert pollster, also polled 500 people, and 150 said they would buy Melonade. How many people in Weesippem would buy Melonade according to Peter's estimate? _____

4. How would you decide if Peter's poll or Sarah's poll is more accurate? _____

5. Based on his poll of 500 people in the city park one day, Dwight told Megakola Company that the new drink would not sell well. The day of Dwight's poll, the Nystraw Soft Drink Company held its annual picnic in the park. Would you accept Dwight's prediction? why or why not?

_____

_____

_____

Use with pages 388–389.

ENRICH   Number

The **mean** of a set is its average. For example, the mean of {3,7,2} is 4. The **mean deviation** tells you how widely a set of numbers varies from its average. It is the average difference between each number of a set and the set's mean.

Prices	Deviation from the mean	Mean deviation
$9.75	$1.25	$\dfrac{\$1.25 + \$0.75 + \$3.00 + \$3.00}{4} = \$2.00$
$7.75 mean = $8.50	$0.75	
$5.50	$3.00	
$11.00	$3.00	

1. It costs 75¢ for a quart of truji on five different planets. A sixth planet charges 66¢. Write the mean deviation.

_____

2. If five planets charge 66¢ and one charges 75¢ for truji, what would the mean deviation be?

_____

The Neptune Lunarwarp fleet has a mission to explore planets in the Alpha-78 galaxy. So far, there have been six missions: one ship explored 5 planets, one explored 4, two ships explored 3 each, and two ships didn't reach any planets.

3. What is the mean deviation?

_____

4. Lunarwarp command expects a mean of 3 planets explored per mission. How many planets would the next mission have to explore to meet this goal? What would the mean deviation then be?

_____

5. If each mission had explored 4 planets, what would have been the mean deviation? _____

6. The same test is given to two Lunarwarp pilot classes. The mean scores in each class are identical. The first class's scores have a small mean deviation, the other a high one. What does this indicate?

_____

_____

ENRICH   Statistics and Probability

In the experimental sciences, an **independent variable (IV)** is a physical quantity that an investigator varies in order to measure its effect on a **dependent variable (DV).** For example, Dr. Dan DeLuca is experimenting with the relationship between temperature and the length of copper rods. The copper rod expands as its temperature rises. He varies the temperature (IV) in order to find its effect on the length of the copper rods (DV). He takes measurements and examines the results by plotting the corresponding variables as points on a graph.

Temperature in °C (IV)	Length of Rod in cm (DV)
10	76.0
80	77.2
150	77.8

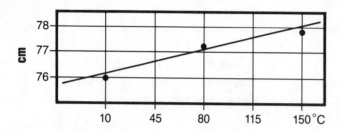

The line drawn is the best-fitting straight line through all three points. Dr. DeLuca can use the graph to predict the length of the copper rod at temperatures not measured.

1. At 115°C, what is the approximate length of the rod? _____

Dr. Robert Kaufman studies the relationship between pressure and the depth of water. He measures pressure at three depths.

2. Which variable is independent, and which is dependent? Plot the points from Dr. Kaufman's results on the graph.

_____

Depth in water	Pressure in atm (atmosphere)
10	1.0
20	1.8
30	2.8

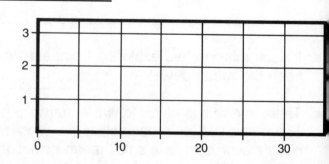

3. Draw the best-fitting straight line on the graph. Make several predictions of pressure at depths not measured by Dr. Kaufman.

_____

Use with pages 392–393.

Name _____ Date _____

A group of 10 athletes competed in 3 different sports: bowling, golf, and archery. After playing the sports, the athletes made statements about their scores. Use the scattergrams on this page to decide if each statement is true or false. Write *true* or *false*.

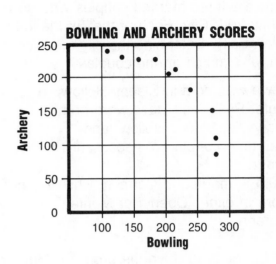

BOWLING AND ARCHERY SCORES

Kyle: In general, the athletes that had the highest bowling scores had the lowest archery scores.

_____

Melanie: Most of the athletes scored more than 80 in golf and more than 200 in archery.

_____

Rick: Most of the athletes who did well at golf did not do so well at bowling. (NOTE: in golf, *low* score wins.)

_____

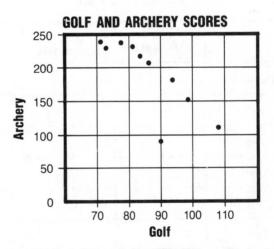

GOLF AND ARCHERY SCORES

Hans: The average archery score was more than twice as high as the average golf score.

_____

Marcella: More than 50% of the bowling scores were lower than 200.

_____

Simone: The athletes who excelled at golf also excelled at archery.

_____

Lars: The widest range of points scored was in archery.

_____

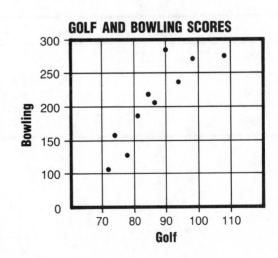

GOLF AND BOWLING SCORES

Svea: The athlete who scored 90 in golf, scored 86 in archery, and 280 in bowling.

_____

Jacob: The same athletes scored in the upper 10% of each sport.

_____

Use with pages 394–395.   **141**

ENRICH | Logic

There are three married couples who go to concerts together in New York City. Each of the six friends was born in a different city. Determine the city in which each person was born, and match up the couples.

- Dave was born in Sleepy Hollow.
- Rufo, Ryan, and Dave were born in Maryville, Sleepy Hollow, and Sacramento, but not necessarily in that order.
- Rufo is married to Carmen, who was not born in either Oberlin or Monte Sereno.

- Dawn was not born in Oberlin.
- Dawn, Carmen, and Joyce were born in Oberlin, New Haven, and Monte Sereno, but not necessarily in that order.
- Ryan, who was born in Maryville, is married to Dawn.

Use the grids to solve the problem. Mark incorrect boxes with an X and correct boxes with an O.

	Maryville	Sacramento	Sleepy Hollow	Oberlin	New Haven	Monte Sereno
Rufo						
Ryan						
Dave						
Dawn						
Carmen						
Joyce						

	Dawn	Carmen	Joyce
Rufo			
Ryan			
Dave			

Name _____ Date _____

ENRICH   **Measurement**

Optical microscopes generally have two sets of lenses. The **eyepiece** lens can magnify objects to appear 10, 30, or 50 times their actual size. This is written as 10x, 30x, and 50x.

The second type of lens on a microscope, the **objective** lens, has three powers of magnification. The three powers of magnification usually fall into groupings of either 20x, 60x, and 100x, or 30x, 50x, and 120x. Normally, objects are viewed simultaneously through both the eyepiece and one power of the objective lens.

1. Suppose you are looking at a salmon egg measuring 0.3 mm in diameter through an eyepiece lens adjusted to 30x. How large in diameter would it appear in the microscope's visual field? _____

2. If the salmon egg in Problem 1 is viewed through a 30x eyepiece and a 20x objective lens, how large would it appear to be? _____

3. Complete the table.

Object viewed	Actual size	Eyepiece power	Objective power	Magnified size
Tick	0.0052 cm		20x	1.04 cm
Fat cell		30x	60x	4.86 mm
Crystal	0.00000546 m	50x	100x	
Microchip	0.78 mm	10x		15.6 m

4. Dr. Brye claims that she can see a smile on the face of an amoeba when it is magnified to 6,000 times its actual size. At what eyepiece and objective-lens settings would the smile be visible? _____

5. Imagine that you are studying to be a detective. You have three human hairs as clues. You use a microscope to match Hair A with either Hair B or Hair C. Which hair is the same size as Hair A? Complete the chart, and ring the matching hair.

	Eyepiece power	Objective power	Size of hair in microscope	Actual size of hair
Hair A	20x	60x	9 cm	
Hair B	30x	20x	1.5 cm	
Hair C	20x	50x	7.5 cm	

Use with pages 398–399.   143

ENRICH | Problem Solving

Read the paragraph. Then estimate or find the exact answer to each question.

You are vice-president in charge of operations for a large football stadium. During the fall, 5 football games were held at the stadium. Attendance was as follows:

Game 1: 48,317
Game 2: 61,081
Game 3: 52,615
Game 4: 58,022
Game 5: 47,796

For each game you hired 232 ushers, 81 security police, and 39 parking attendants. At the conclusion of each game, a maintenance staff of 85 cleaned the stadium and grounds. Food services for the fans were provided by an independent concessionaire.

1. Was total attendance for the 5 football games greater or less than 270,000 people? _____

2. Did you have to hire more or fewer maintenance people per game than security police? How many? _____

3. If the average ticket price is $9.00, about how much money was taken in from the sale of tickets for Game 3?

_____

4. In general, you try to hire one security police officer for every 500 patrons. Did you have as many security police as you wanted at Game 2? _____

5. To the nearest thousand, determine between which 2 games the greatest change in attendance occurred.

_____

6. The breakdown of ticket sales for Game 1 was as follows: 17,547 tickets sold at $7.50 each; 19,149 tickets sold at $9.25; 11,621 tickets sold at $10.25. How much money was taken in altogether? _____

Use with pages 400–401.

ENRICH   Probability and Statistics

The Pals are in second place with three games left to play in the hockey season. The coach plans the different possible outcomes for these final 3 games of the season. The collection of all possible outcomes is called the **sample space.**

1. List the sample space for this situation.

First game — Second game — Third game			First game — Second game — Third game		
WIN —	WIN —	WIN	—		—
WIN —	WIN —	LOSE	—		—
—		—	—		—
—		—	—		—
—		—	—		—
—		—	—		—

2. María has three lizards, Lizzie, Dizzy, and Fizzy. María decides to feed them in a different order each day. List all the possible orders in the sample space for her feeding pattern.

_____

_____

3. Harold, Troy, Lance, and Darrell are quadruplets. Since they are identical, no one can remember the exact order of their birth. Use their initials, and list all the possible orders.

_____ _____ _____ _____ _____ _____

_____ _____ _____ _____ _____ _____

_____ _____ _____ _____ _____ _____

_____ _____ _____ _____ _____ _____

4. An equation for determining the number of outcomes in the sample space for Problem 1 is $2 \times 2 \times 2$. Can you explain what these numbers represent?

_____

Use with pages 402–403.   **145**

ENRICH Algebra

If two people sit in two chairs in a row, they can sit in 2 different orders, AB or BA. If they sit at a round table, there is only one order because each always sits to the left and to the right of the other. This **circular permutation** is an ordered arrangement where the sequential order of set members is important, but the member you begin with is not. Three people at a round table can sit in only 2 orders, ABC or ACB; so, there are 2 circular permutations of the three set members.

1. Write the number of the figure in which each clockwise ordering of the three people occurs.

Figure 1

Figure 2

ABC _____ ACB _____ BAC _____ BCA _____ CAB _____ CBA _____

2. Draw diagrams like the example to show all the circular permutations of four people A, B, C, and D.

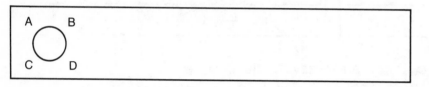

The formula for the number of permutations of a set uses the operation called factorial: n factorial, $n!$, is equal to $1 \times 2 \times 3 \ldots \times n$. The number of permutations with n items is $n!$. For example, if 4 people were to sit in a row of 5 chairs, 1 of the 4 could sit in the first chair, 1 of the 3 remaining in the next, 1 of the 2 remaining in the next, and the last person would have to sit in the last chair. The number of permutations of four people then is $1 \times 2 \times 3 \times 4 = 4! = 24$. However, with circular permutations, the last factor is eliminated. This is so because person A can always stay in the same seat. Only B, C, and D change positions. The circular permutations of a set of n items is $(n - 1)!$.

3. If 5 people sit at a round table, how many circular permutations are there? What if a sixth person joins them?

_____

4. How many times as many circular permutations are there of a group of 37 people than of a group of 36 people? than a group of 35?

_____

5. Can you find another way to write the formula for circular permutations using factorial notation? (HINT: Write out $n!$. What do you need to do to it to get the number of circular permutations of a set of n items?)

_____

Use with pages 404–405.

ENRICH | Statistics and Probability

Your team is at bat. What is the probability of the batter getting a hit? You figure that there are two possibilities: he gets a hit, or he doesn't. This puts the probability of a hit at $\frac{1}{2}$. But this doesn't sound right because you know that the likelihood of someone's getting a hit depends on such factors as how good a hitter he or she is, who is pitching, and so on.

In situations like this, where the occurrence of events is not random, we make **empirical predictions. Empirical probability** is based on the knowledge of past experience. For example, if Suzie has had a hit 32 of the last 100 times at bat, the probability of her hitting safely next time at bat is this.

Probability (hit) $= \frac{32}{100} = 0.32 = 32\%$

We often make empirical predictions. Every time you estimate how much time it will take you to travel home from school on the school bus, you are using empirical probability based on the knowledge of past experience.

1. Waking up for school one morning, you wonder if your sister will beat you to the breakfast table. She has beaten you 85 of the last 100 school days. What is the probability that she will beat you today?

   _____

2. The teacher in your first class has been waiting by the door to catch people coming in late for 12 of the last 15 days. What is the probability he will be there today?

   _____

3. Your favorite lunch has been served in the school cafeteria only twice in the last 24 days. What is the probability of your favorite lunch being served at school today?

   _____

4. For the past three years, every day when you have come home from school, your dog has run to the door to meet you. What is the probability of his doing so today?

   _____

5. Which of the above predictions is most likely to be accurate?

   _____

   _____

Name_____ Date_____

You are trying to organize a livestock-investment partnership. The partnership's area of specialization will be cattle and sheep. Several prospective partners have asked you questions about trends in livestock production since 1950. The two graphs below will help you answer their questions.

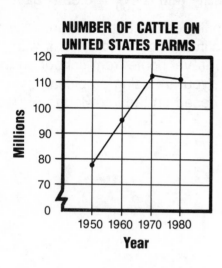

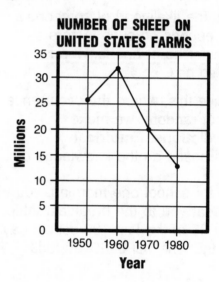

1. Between 1970 and 1980, has the production of cattle or the production of sheep shown the greater decrease in number? How much greater? _____

2. In 1960, were there more cattle or sheep on United States farms? how many more? _____

3. Approximately how many cattle were on United States farms in 1965? _____

4. How many more cattle than sheep were on United States farms in 1950? _____

5. The value of each head of sheep in 1960 was $16.50. What was the total value of all the sheep that year?

_____

6. The total value of all the cattle in 1980 was $5,583,300,000. What was the value of each head?

_____

ENRICH   Number

A **ratio** shows a relationship between two quantities. For example, in the following table, the ratio of computer sales to food sales in Beech County is 18:3. In simplest terms, this ratio becomes 6:1. When two equal ratios are written as equivalent fractions, they form a **proportion.** This means that Beech has $6 million of computer sales for every $1 million of food sales $\left(\text{Example: } \frac{18}{3} = \frac{6}{1}\right)$. Ratios and proportions can be used to make predictions. Where the ratio is constant, if the value of one term changes, the value of the other term will change proportionately so that the new ratio will equal the old. Thus, if food sales increase to $6 million, computer sales will increase to $36 million.

1986 SALES BY COUNTY (IN MILLIONS OF DOLLARS)

County	Food	Computers	Clothing	Other goods
Beech	3	18	24	13
Johnson	40	0	5	5
Clark	30	45	0	10

Use the table to answer the questions. Write all ratios in simplest form.

1. In Johnson County, what is the ratio of clothing sales to the total amount of goods sold in 1986? _____

2. If Johnson County sells a total of $60 million worth of goods in 1987, what will the figure be for clothing? _____

3. If computer sales in Clark County increase to $60 million in 1987, and sales of other goods don't increase, find the ratio of computer sales to total sales. _____

4. Is the ratio in 1987 larger or smaller? _____

5. Suppose Beech County has total sales of $51 million. The ratio of *food:clothing* is 2:5, *food:computers* is 1:3, and *food:other goods* is 1:2. Draw a table like the one above. The sales of computers is $18 million. Find the sales of food, clothing, and other goods. _____

ENRICH   Geometry

To predict how many cylinders will fit into a box, you cannot merely compare the total volume of the cylinders with the box's volume. If the volume of a box is 20 cubic feet, the total volume of cylinders that could fit into it must be less. We must take into account the extra space between the cylinders.

Bright Blossom, Inc., manufactures giant kaleidoscopes. The shipping-and-receiving department delivers them in crates that are 4.5 feet wide, 3 feet high, and 5 feet long. The kaleidoscopes are 5 feet long and have diameters of 1.5 feet.

1. What is the maximum number of giant kaleidoscopes that can be packaged into a single crate?

_____

2. How many cubic feet of space in the crate are wasted if the maximum number of kaleidoscopes is placed inside? (Round to the nearest hundredth.)

_____

Bright Blossoms, Inc., decides to protect the kaleidoscopes by putting each into a plastic-foam tube. These tubes add 2 inches to the diameter of each kaleidoscope.

3. What are the dimensions of the crate that is needed to ship the same number of kaleidoscopes in each crate?

_____

4. How much space will be wasted in the new crates?

_____

Bright Blossoms, Inc., is planning to use the kaleidoscope mold to make glass cylinders. The cylinders will be used to encase cables that have a uniform diameter of 3 inches.

5. What is the total volume (in cubic inches) of a 5-foot-long cable?

_____

6. What is the total volume (in cubic inches) of a 5-foot-long cylinder?

_____

Bright Blossoms, Inc., has planned that 36 cables will be encased in each cylinder.

7. What is this plan based on? Will the plan work? why or why not?

_____

_____

_____

Use with pages 412–413.

Name_____ Date_____

Problem Solving

You are one of a group of engineers and architects planning
a series of structures that will be among the most amazing in
the world. Use an outside source, such as an almanac or
encyclopedia, to help you answer the questions below.

1. Dr. Steger, one of the engineers, plans
to build a suspension bridge 18% longer
than the longest bridge in North America.
How long will Dr. Steger's bridge be?

_____

_____

_____

_____

2. Ms. Murphy is designing a building that
will have twice as many stories as the
John Hancock Tower in Boston. How
many stories will the Murphy Building
have?

_____

_____

_____

_____

3. Mr. Azmed intends to construct a tunnel
as long as the combined length of the
Lincoln Tunnel and Holland Tunnel. How
long will the Azmed Tunnel be?

_____

_____

_____

_____

4. Ms. Diaz is working on a miniature
replica of the Statue of Liberty. The
scale is 1 inches equals 12 feet. How
tall will the replica be, including the
base?

_____

_____

_____

_____

5. You and two other engineers are
designing the Everglades Dome, which
will have a base area $\frac{3}{4}$ the size of the
Everglades National Park. What will the
base area of the dome be?

_____

_____

_____

_____

6. On January 1, 1999, work begins on the
Pluto Observatory. If all goes well,
construction will be completed in the
time it takes Pluto to circle the sun twice.
In what year will the observatory be
finished?

_____

_____

_____

_____

151

ENRICH   Number

The table gives the prices of four companies's stocks during five different weeks. The stock market deletes the dollar sign in order to simplify figures. For example, 38 = $38.

Stock	Week 1	Week 2	Week 3	Week 4	Week 5
J. Foundries	$38\frac{1}{8}$	41	$37\frac{1}{2}$	38	$40\frac{1}{8}$
Tek Oil	$59\frac{5}{8}$	$65\frac{3}{8}$	$69\frac{3}{8}$	$62\frac{1}{2}$	60
Dirks Works	16	$19\frac{7}{8}$	$23\frac{1}{8}$	$18\frac{1}{8}$	16
Telematic	79	$71\frac{1}{8}$	$75\frac{1}{4}$	$74\frac{7}{8}$	$77\frac{1}{4}$

Write the average change in price per week for each of the stocks. (Remember to count decreases in price as negative change.) Use fractions.

1. J. Foundries _____   2. Tek Oil _____   3. Dirks Works _____   4. Telematic _____

5. Do these averages accurately reflect the price movement each week? why or why not?

_____

A way to accurately track the amount of movement is to use **absolute value.** The absolute value of a number x, shown by the symbol $|x|$, gives the amount that the number represents without regard to its sign. For example, $|3| = |^-3| = 3$. A way to picture a number's absolute value is its distance from 0 on a number line in either direction.

Use the absolute value of the price movements each week to find the average movement per week of each stock. Use fractions.

6. J. Foundries _____   7. Tek Oil _____   8. Dirks Works _____   9. Telematic _____

Let x = the movement of the price of a stock. Use absolute value to write a formula for the statement.

10. "Sell if the stock moves 6 points in either direction." _____

11. "Don't sell if the stock's price moves less than 4 points up or down." Use > or <. _____

12. "The stock's price fluctuates by more than 5 points each week." Use > or <.

_____

13. In what other situations would you use absolute value?

_____

_____

_____

ENRICH — Number

Magic squares originated in China thousands of years ago. They were brought to India and Africa and later to Europe and America. In 1732, an African scholar, Muhammad ibn Muhammad, wrote a book in the Arabic language about many types of magic squares.

On the right are two 3 × 3 (3 rows and 3 columns) magic squares. Each digit from 1 to 9 appears exactly once, and the sum of every row, every column, and each of the two diagonals is 15, the **magic sum.** The top magic square is in Hindu-Arabic numbers, the system we use in the United States; the bottom one is in East Arabic. The numbers in each position in the two squares have the same value; only the symbols used are different.

6	1	8
7	5	3
2	9	4

٧	١	٨
٧	٥	٣
٢	٩	٤

1. Under each number, write the corresponding East Arabic number.

Hindu-Arabic	1	2	3	4	5	6	7	8	9	10	11	12	13	20	30
East Arabic										١٠	١١		١٣		٣٠

Use East Arabic numbers for all the magic squares.

2. Complete the magic squares taken from Muhammad's book. The magic sum is 15, written ١٥ .

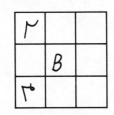
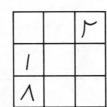
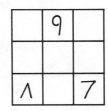

3. Muhammad wrote that exactly eight different 3 × 3 magic squares can be made with the numbers 1 to 9. Construct the three remaining squares.

ENRICH   Patterns

On planet Algaenon, Sasasa deep-sea kelp starts as a single branch. After a month, it starts to send out new branches at a rate of one per month. Each new branch matures in one month and also starts to send out one new branch per month.

1. Complete the table.

Month	1	2	3	4	5	6	7	8	9	10	11	12
Number of branches	1	1	2	3	5		13	21		55		144

This result is a very famous and complex number sequence called the **Fibonacci sequence,** named after a famous Italian mathematician of the 1200's. The value of each term is the sum of the two previous terms.

2. The total number of branches in month n = the number of branches in $(n - 1)$ plus the number of branches in $(n - 2)$. Each month, what part of the plant at $(n - 1)$ does $(n - 2)$ represent?

_____

Oscandra kelp has branches that produce two new branches each month after maturing for one month. The monthly totals for the first six months of this plant's life are 1, 1, 3, 5, 11, 21.

3. What are the next three terms in this sequence?

_____

4. What is the pattern of this sequence?

_____

_____

5. Iaenko kelp also begins with one branch. Its branches have to mature two months before they begin to send out new branches at the rate of one per month. Write the sequence that gives the number of branches each month for a year. What is the nth term for the sequence?

_____

_____

ENRICH   Number

When you have a job and earn money, you must pay income tax on the amount you have earned. This is how the government pays for the many things it does. The table is a tax table. It tells how much income tax must be paid to the government, given different incomes.

FEDERAL INCOME TAX

Taxable income	Single person	Married, filing jointly	Married, filing separately
$ 9,000–10,000	$ 999	$ 753	$1,145
10,001–11,000	1,159	893	1,342
11,001–12,000	1,334	1,003	1,562
12,001–13,000	1,514	1,185	1,789

A married couple can file *jointly,* combining both incomes into a single total, or each person can pay separately. To find the amount of tax owed, look at the row in which the income falls, and the column of the type of tax return being filed.

Exemptions are conditions that make part of a taxpayer's income exempt from taxation. A person may deduct $1,000 from his or her income for each exemption. A person earning $12,000 with 3 exemptions pays the amount of tax owed on $9,000. Exemptions include one for yourself, one for each child, and one for being more than 65 years of age.

1. Mrs. Feinbaum, 34 years old, earned $15,712 and claims exemptions for herself and her two children. How much taxable income does she have? How much tax does she pay if she is married and filing separately?

_____

2. How much tax must Mrs. Edwards pay on $17,052 income if she is 37 years old, has three children, claims the personal exemption, and is married filing jointly? Her husband does not work.

_____

3. If you donate money to charity, you may deduct 15% of your donation from your taxable income. Mr. Weindling earned $14,003 and is single. How much tax must he pay if he exempts himself and his two children, and claims a deduction from a $200 donation to an animal shelter?

_____

4. Last year, Ms. Perez earned $12,000 constructing brick fireplaces. This year, her income went up 15%. How much will she pay in taxes? She is single and is 67 years old.

_____

ENRICH | Algebra

In the code in which $A = 1$, $B = 2$, . . . $Z = 26$, space $= 27$, a period $= 28$, the message CODES CAN BE FUN. is written 3, 15, 4, 5, 19, 27, 3, 1, 14, 27, 2, 5, 27, 6, 21, 14, 28.

1. Write the coded message as ordered pairs (3,15), (4,5),

. . . (28,—). Multiply by the matrix $\begin{bmatrix} 3 & 5 \\ 1 & 2 \end{bmatrix}$, using the

matrix multiplication rule $(a,b) \times \begin{bmatrix} 3 & 5 \\ 1 & 2 \end{bmatrix} = (3a + 1b, 5a + 2b)$.

(24,45), _____

_____

To decode a message written in a matrix code, you multiply the ordered pairs by a decoding matrix. The decoding matrix

D for an encoding matrix $E = \begin{bmatrix} a & c \\ b & d \end{bmatrix}$ (if $ad - bc \neq 0$) is

$D = \begin{bmatrix} \dfrac{d}{ad - bc} & \dfrac{-c}{ad - bc} \\ \dfrac{-b}{ad - bc} & \dfrac{a}{ad - bc} \end{bmatrix}$.

From the encoding matrix in Problem 1, you get the

decoding matrix $D = \begin{bmatrix} \dfrac{2}{3 \cdot 2 - 5 \cdot 1} & \dfrac{-5}{3 \cdot 2 - 5 \cdot 1} \\ \dfrac{-1}{3 \cdot 2 - 5 \cdot 1} & \dfrac{3}{3 \cdot 2 - 5 \cdot 1} \end{bmatrix} = \begin{bmatrix} 2 & -5 \\ -1 & 3 \end{bmatrix}$.

Multiplying the first ordered pair from Problem 1 by this decoding matrix gives you

$(24,45) \begin{bmatrix} 2 & -5 \\ -1 & 3 \end{bmatrix} = (24 \cdot 2 + 45 \cdot (-1), \ ^-5 \cdot 24 + 3 \cdot 45)$

$= (3,15)$.

2. You receive a coded message. It was encoded by using

the matrix $\begin{bmatrix} 2 & 1 \\ 5 & 3 \end{bmatrix}$. Write the decoding matrix, and decode

this message: 125, 70, 177, 102, 94, 56, 85, 48, 145, 86, 137, 82, 21, 11, 56, 30, 69, 36, 50, 27, 10, 5.

$$D = \begin{bmatrix} \quad & \quad \\ \quad & \quad \end{bmatrix}$$

_____

_____

_____

 Use with pages 434–43!

Name _____ Date _____

Figure 1 shows a picture of a bird, drawn on a 1-in. × 1-in. grid. Notice the difference between the picture of the bird in Figure 1 and the picture of the same bird in Figure 2. The bird in Figure 2 is distorted because it is drawn on a 2-in. ×1-in. grid. On a 2-in. × 1-in. grid, the ratio of horizontal to vertical dimension in each box is 2 in.:1 in. This means that all the measurements in the horizontal direction are doubled, while the vertical measurements remain unchanged.

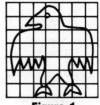

Figure 1

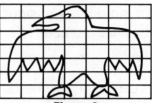

Figure 2

1. Use the grid in Figure 3 to draw the bird with a horizontal to vertical distortion ratio of 1 in.:2 in.

2. Use a horizontal-to-vertical distortion ratio of 3 in.:0.5 in. to draw the bird in Figure 4.

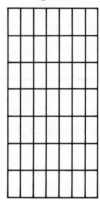

Figure 3

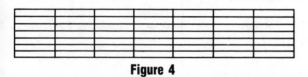

Figure 4

3. Make your own 3-in. × 5-in. grid on a separate sheet of paper. Draw the bird inside it by using a horizontal-to-vertical distortion ratio of 3 in.:5 in.

4. What kind of distortion ratios would you need to convert Figures 2, 3, and 4 back into pictures that are identical to the original bird in Figure 1?

_____

_____

5. Name several professions in which the use of these distortion grids is valuable.

_____

_____

_____

Name _____ Date _____

Index numbers make it easy to compare information. Car racing uses index numbers to compare specific lap times to the average. For example, a driver named Caballo has done the practice lap in an average time of 1 min 10 s over the past year. He wants to compare his lap times on Tuesday, Wednesday, Thursday, and Friday to that average. The average time is assigned the **base index number** of 100. A specific day's lap time is assigned a corresponding index number. This index number is a percent of the base number. Look at the table.

1. What percent of 1:10, the base time, does Caballo's time on Tuesday represent? _____

2. What percent of the base time do Caballo's times for Wednesday, Thursday, and Friday represent?

_____

3. On Saturday, Caballo records a time of 1 minute. What index number does this time represent? _____

4. The index number for Caballo's lap on Sunday is 150. How long does it take Caballo to complete the lap?

_____

Day	Time (min:s)	Index number
Base	1:10	100
Tuesday	1:03	90
Wednesday	1:24	120
Thursday	1:13.5	105
Friday	0:52.5	75

5. On Monday, four drivers did practice laps. Use Caballo's time as the base, and determine the index numbers for each driver. Complete the table.

Driver	Kate	Keiji	Allan	Caballo
Time (min:s)	0:54	1:30	2:20	1:06
Index number				

6. Why do you think that the base index number is always chosen to be the number 100?

_____

_____

_____

Use with pages 440–441

ENRICH | Number

n interesting way to find the product of two numbers is
alled **galley multiplication.** Figure 1 is a **galley.** One
umber is written across the top, in this case 613, and the
econd number is written on the right side, 245. The product
f each pair of digits is written in the appropriate box with a
iagonal separating the tens and the ones places. For
xample, 6 (in 613) × 4 (in 245) = 24. The product of
13 × 245 is found by adding the numbers in each diagonal
olumn, starting at the bottom right, and regrouping if
ecessary to the next diagonal column. Follow the arrows to
nd the product. In the example, 613 × 245 = 150,185.

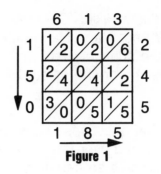

Figure 1

1. Complete the galley in Figure 2. What is 278 × 436?

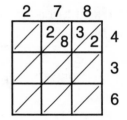

Figure 2

alley multiplication was used by John Napier (born in 1550)
n his primitive calculator, which are known as *Napier's rods.*
hese rods are the columns of a large galley in which the
umbers 1 through 9 are written in order both across the top
nd down the left side. Figure 3 shows the nine Napier's
ods. To multiply 243 and 7, line up the 2, 4, and 3 rods, and
ook at the 7 column (Figure 4). Add like any other galley
Figure 5). Thus, 243 × 7 = 1,701.

ndex	0	1	2	3	4	5	6	7	8	9
1	0/0	0/1	0/2	0/3	0/4	0/5	0/6	0/7	0/8	0/9
2	0/0	0/2	0/4	0/6	0/8	1/0	1/2	1/4	1/6	1/8
3	0/0	0/3	0/6	0/9	1/2	1/5	1/8	2/1	2/4	2/7
4	0/0	0/4	0/8	1/2	1/6	2/0	2/4	2/8	3/2	3/6
5	0/0	0/5	1/0	1/5	2/0	2/5	3/0	3/5	4/0	4/5
6	0/0	0/6	1/2	1/8	2/4	3/0	3/6	4/2	4/8	5/4
7	0/0	0/7	1/4	2/1	2/8	3/5	4/2	4/9	5/6	6/3
8	0/0	0/8	1/6	2/4	3/2	4/0	4/8	5/6	6/4	7/2
9	0/0	0/9	1/8	2/7	3/6	4/5	5/4	6/3	7/2	8/1

Figure 3

Figure 4

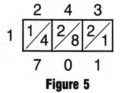

Figure 5

ENRICH Problem Solving

The Hillsdale Hiking Club has nine members: Herb, Esther, Kevin, Bruno, Mary, Hanna, Jennifer, Barbara, and Leo. During the summer, each member recorded the number of miles that he or she hiked. Herb, for instance, hiked 33.5 miles.

Answer the questions below to find out how far each club member hiked over the summer. For questions 1–8, write and then solve an equation.

1. Esther hiked twice as far as Herb did. How many miles did she hike? _____

2. Kevin hiked 25 miles fewer than Esther. How many miles did he hike? _____

3. Bruno hiked a distance equal to the sum of the distances hiked by Esther and Kevin. How far did he hike?

_____

4. Mary hiked 149 fewer miles than 3 times the distance Bruno hiked. How far did Mary hike?

_____

5. Hanna hiked 9.5 miles fewer than half the distance Mary hiked. How far did she hike? _____

6. Jennifer hiked a distance approximately equal to the sum of the distances hiked by Esther and Kevin divided by 4.2. About how many miles did Jennifer hike?

_____

7. Barbara hiked 83.6 miles fewer than 7 times the distance Jennifer hiked. How far did Barbara hike?

_____

8. Leo hiked a distance that was the average of the sum of the distances hiked by Esther, Bruno, Mary, and Barbara. How many miles did Leo hike? _____

Use with pages 444–445

ENRICH | Statistics and Probability

We use **empirical probability** to give the probability of nonrandom events that are influenced by many factors. Empirical predictions are based on knowledge of past experience. If under certain conditions in the past an event has occurred a times in n possibilities, the chance that it will occur under the same conditions in the future is $\frac{a}{n}$. The larger n is, the more accurate the prediction.

An event can be assigned different empirical predictions, depending upon the conditions taken into account. For instance, a baseball player has a batting average that gives the likelihood of his getting a hit each time at bat; yet against left-handed pitchers, he may hit better or worse. The probability of the batter's getting a hit against a left-handed pitcher can be expressed as his overall batting average, or his average against left-handers. The conditions of n should always be understood. The more precise these conditions are, the more accurate the prediction will be, assuming a large enough n.

Solve.

1. How would you determine the probability of a baseball player's getting a hit against a left-handed pitcher?

_____

_____

2. Write the formula for the probability of a player's getting a hit against a left-hander at 8:44 P.M. on a Sunday with a south westerly wind?

_____

_____

3. Even though problem 2 is more specific, problem 1 might be more accurate. Explain why.

_____

_____

4. Weather conditions are one of the most common empirical predictions. They are also one of the most difficult. Why do you think this is so?

_____

_____

_____

ENRICH   Patterns

You can create **codes** based on a rotary telephone and a push-button telephone by using geometric angles and coordinates. For example, the numbers on a rotary telephone are 30° apart.

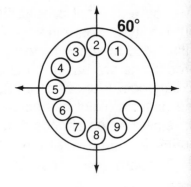

You can use the angles to make a code by substituting angle measures for each digit in a telephone number. For example, the telephone number 101–2568 can be written in code as 60 330 60 90 180 210 270. To simplify the code, drop the final zero: 6, 33, 6, 9, 18, 21, 27.

Write the telephone number in the rotary angle code.

1. 775–0824:

_____

2. 263–8419:

_____

Each digit on a push-button telephone corresponds to coordinates (*x,y*) located on the left side and the bottom of the panel. For example, the coordinates of the number 2 are (2,4). The coordinates of 7 are (3,2).

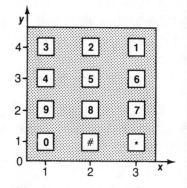

3. Write the coordinates of the other digits.

_____

_____

To simplify the digital code, drop the commas. Thus, the digit 2 = 24. The digit 7 = 31.

4. Write the numbers 555–1212 and 943–6105 in digital code.

_____

_____

Each number represents rotary code numbers. Write the digital code number and the actual telephone number.

5. 18, 27, 21, 9, 30, 15, 15:

_____

6. On another sheet of paper, create your own code by using a combination of the rotary and digital codes. Give your code and an example to one of your classmates.

Use with pages 448–449

Name _____ Date _____

ENRICH   Problem Solving

You are president of Century Airlines. This morning you are
meeting with the board of trustees to answer questions about
the airline's profitability during the 12 months of last year. To
assist you, your staff has prepared a broken-line bar graph
representing the year's earnings. Use the graph to answer
the board's questions.

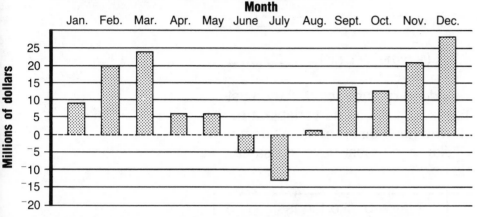

CENTURY AIRLINES: JANUARY–DECEMBER EARNINGS

1. How much more money did Century Airlines earn in May
   than in August? _____

2. Based on the airline's performance during the year, would
   you predict a profit or a loss in January? _____

3. During the holiday season of November and December,
   air travel increased significantly. How much did Century
   Airlines earn during those months? _____

4. During which quarter did Century Airlines earn the most
   money: January through March, April through June, July
   through September, or October through December? how
   much? _____

5. There was a sharp increase in fuel costs during the
   summer. This increase had a negative impact on earnings
   for June, July, and August. What were the airline's total
   profits or losses for those 3 months? _____

6. How much did earnings recover from July to August?

   _____

Use with pages 450–451.   **163**

ENRICH   Algebra

Look at each statement. Write *true* or *false*.

1. $(3 \times 1) + (4 \times 1) = 7 \times 1$ _____

2. $(3 \times 2) + (4 \times 2) = 7 \times 2$ _____

3. $(3 \times 1) + (4 \times 2) = 7 \times (1 + 2)$ _____

4. 4 dimes + 3 dimes = 7 dimes _____

5. 3 dimes + 4 nickels = $7 \times (1$ dime + 1 nickel$)$ _____

In order for two terms to be added or subtracted, they must have the same variable. Terms with the same variable are called **like terms**. **Unlike terms** have different variables and cannot be added together. Like terms must have the same exponents on each variable.

Like terms	Unlike terms
$5a + 3a = 8a$	$5a + 3b = 5a + 3b$
$5ab + 3ab = 8ab$	$5a + 3b = 5a + 3b$
$5xy^2 + 2y^2x = 7xy^2$	$3x^2y - xy^2 = 3x^2y - xy^2$

Add or subtract where possible. Write *unlike* next to problems that contain unlike terms.

6. $3a^3 + 4a^3 =$ _____

7. $5n - 4m =$ _____

8. $8x - 4xy =$ _____

9. $8s^7r^5 - 2s^5r^7 =$ _____

10. $3x + 9x =$ _____

11. $4xy^3 - 2xy^3 =$ _____

12. $\frac{1}{2}x^5 + 5x^2 =$ _____

13. $p + p =$ _____

14. $x^2 + x^2 =$ _____

15. $5a - 5a =$ _____

16. Are like terms necessary for multiplication? Write a rule for multiplying terms with variables and exponents.

_____

_____

ENRICH Geometry

When you graph an equation with two variables, the line made is the set of all values (x,y) for which the equation is true. When you graph two equations, each with two variables, they often intersect. The point of intersection gives the values (x,y) for which both equations are true.

1. Graph $6x + 2y = 14$.

y = _____

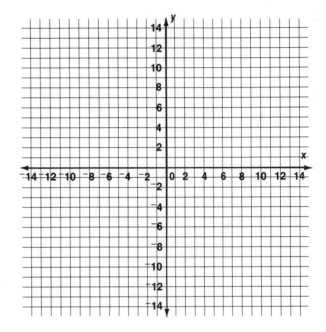

x	−2	−1	0	1	2	3
y						

2. On the same graph, plot $6x - 3y = 9$. Solve for y:

_____

x	−2	−1	0	1	2	3
y						

3. Where do the two lines intersect? _____

You can also graph inequalities with two variables. To do this, you shade the area for which all values (x,y) are true for the inequality. When graphing y, you shade above the line for ≥, and >, and below the line for ≤ and <. When graphing > or <, use a dashed line.

4. The inequality $5x - y > 19$ is graphed. On the same coordinate plane, graph the inequality $x + 3y > 6$. Shade the intersection of the two graphs heavily. Solve for y: _____

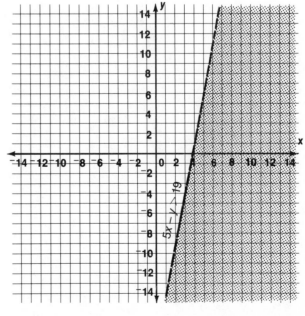

5. If the equation $y > -1$ were added to the last graph, what would be common to all three inequalities? What if $y < -1$ were added?

_____

_____

_____

Page 1

1. 0, 1, 2, 3, 4
2. $3\ 114_5$
3. $10\ 204_5$
4. $100\ 300_5$
5. $11\ 214_5$
6. $43\ 412_5$
7. $2\ 340_5$
8. $143\ 421_5$
9. $1\ 442_5$
10. Answers will vary.

Page 2

1. 0.005; 0.00078; 0.078%
2. 0.0005; 0.000028; 0.0028%
3. 0.05; 0.0049504; 0.49504%
4. 0.00005; 0.000028; 0.0028%
5. 17.857; 1.7857
6. Answers will vary. Use of exponents is deal.

Page 3

1. 4, 6, 7, 1, 8, 2, 3, 5
2. The first and last number must be in the middle.
3. Louise, Barbara, Eileen, Ryan, Fernando, Cella
4. 3, 0, 3 + 1, 0, 9, 3 + 1, 9, 3, 9 + 1, 3, 9 + 3, 1, 9 + 3, 0, 9 + 3 + 1, 0, 27, 9 + 3 + 1, 27, 9 + 3, 27 + 1, 9 + 3, 27 9 + 1, 27 + 3, 9, 27 + 3 + 1, 9, 27, 3 + 1, 27, 3, 27 + 1, 3, 27, 1, 27, 0, 27 + 3 + 1, 0, 27 + 9, 3 + 1, 27 + 9, 3, 27 + 9 + 1, 3, 27 + 9, 1, 27 + 9, 0, 27 + 9 + 1, 0

Page 4

1. Answers will vary. Possible answers are listed below.
   1 hour
   $\frac{1}{2}$–1 hour
   $\frac{1}{4}$–$\frac{1}{2}$ hour
   $\frac{1}{2}$–$1\frac{1}{2}$ hours
   2 hours
   $\frac{1}{2}$–1 hour
2. probably   3. yes   4. no
5. yes

Page 5

1. Students will complete schedule.

Page 5 (cont'd.)

2. 40 minutes; because you must add time between
3. 2:00 P.M.; 9:45 P.M.
4. 11:30 A.M.

Page 6

1. 400,000–440,000 people
2. 4,900–5,100 mi^2
3. 2.6–2.7 million
4. 25,000 mi^2–25,300
5. 63,000–65,000 people
6. 300–400 mi^2
7. all but Aiken; answers will vary.
8. Aiken county
Answers may vary. Accept any reasonable estimate.

Page 7

1. 20 23
2. 13, 11
3. 95, 93
4. 68, 61
5. 21, 28
6. 1 + 4 $(n + 1)$, or $4n + 5$
7. 2 + 3 $(n - 1)$, or $3n - 1$
8. 23 − 2 $(n - 1)$, or 25 − $2n$
9. 98 − 12 $(n - 1)$, or 110 − $12n$
10. 75 + 7 $(n - 1)$, or 68 + $7n$
11. 0 + $\frac{1}{2}n$ $(n - 1)$
12. Yes, except for 11; the number added to each in this sequence increases instead of being constant.

Page 8

1. 62 − 26 = 36
   63 − 36 = 27
   72 − 27 = 45
   54 − 45 = 09
   90 − 09 = 81
   81 − 18 = 63
   63 − 36 = 27
2. 84 − 48 = 36
   63 − 36 = 27
   72 − 27 = 45
   54 − 45 = 09
   90 − 09 = 81
   81 − 18 = 27
   72 − 27 = 45
3. All 2-digit numbers give you exactly the same loop.

Page 8 (cont'd.)

4. 643 − 346 = 297
   972 − 279 = 693
   963 − 369 = 594
   954 − 459 = 495
   954 − 459 = 495
   820 − 028 = 792
   972 − 279 = 693
   963 − 369 = 594
   954 − 459 = 495
   954 − 459 = 495
5. All 3-digit numbers end in 495 repeating over and over.
6. All 4-digit numbers end in a repeating 6,174.

Page 9

1. Ideas should come from Solutions section of Help File.
2. Ideas should come from Checks section.
3. Ideas should come from Questions section.
4. Ideas should come from Tools section.
5. Ideas should come from Checks section.
6. Ideas should come from Tools section.

Page 10

1. The first is accurate to the nearest percent, and the second is accurate to the nearest tenth of one percent.
2. 284,655 mm
3. One; the zero does not contribute to the number's accuracy.
4. 2 5. 3 6. 4 7. 4 8. 2
9. 1 10. 4
11. In standard notation, nonsignificant zeros are needed as place holders; using exponents, they can be dropped.

Page 11

Check students' tables.
1. 0.0000002 AU/s
2. 0.000019 AU/min
3. Approximately 90,000
4. Speed < 2.9 in order to stay in orbit

Page 11 (cont'd.)

5. Yes; distances in space are so large; answers will vary.

Page 12

1. All numbers $\geq 1.45 < 1.55$
2. $\pm$ 0.005 cm; 0.005 cm
3. 3.3 cm^2
4. 3.25 cm^2; 3.0625 cm^2; 0.1875
5. 0.05 cm
6. 0.05 cm; explanations will vary.

Page 13

Topic A:
Sources of information include: almanac, encyclopedia, book about space travel, science magazine, or similar sources.
1. 1,472 hours 9 minutes 4 seconds
2. July 20, 1969
3. 240,000 miles
4. Alan Shephard, Jr.
5. July 15, 1975
6. 7 m ($22\frac{7}{8}$ feet)

Topic B:
Sources of information include: almanac, encyclopedia, dictionary, book about animals, nature magazine, or similar sources.
1. 70 mph
2. 8 legs
3. 2,500 lb
4. 14 inches
5. 650 lb
6. 20 years

Page 14

1. 4 or 7; answers will vary.
2. 125 cm; answers will vary.
3. approximately 112 cm
4. approximately 18 kg
5. Height: 4; 7; 8; 9; 10; weight: 4; 5; 6; 8; 9; 10; answers will vary.

Page 15

Cash:
payroll account
rent
payroll account
cash
rent
united foods
Deposit: $101.25

Page 15 (cont'd.)

Withdrawal:
$342.15
$750.00
$342.15
$342.15
$750.00
$342.15
$1,350.00
Balance:
$18,457.90
$25,266.75
$23,974.60
$26,276.05
$30,183.90

Page 16

1. Students will complete the check.
2. 718, 10/12, Solar Light Store, 561.48, 73.42; 1,246.80; 1,173.35; 1,319.58; 1,246.16
3. You have a record of your transactions; answers will vary.

Page 17

1. Playwell
2. Yes; Playwell's sales increased sharply in April and May.
3. Yes; Teamspro's sales decreased in April and May.
4. Yes; very; sales increased in the following months.
5. yes
6. Teamspro earned more, especially in the second half of the year.

Page 18

1. 15	58
7	116
3	232
1	464
	899
2. 16	84
8	168
4	336
2	672
1	1,344
	1,344
3. 19	770
9	1,540
4	3,080
2	6,160
1	12,320
	15,015

Page 18 (cont'd.)

4. 31	98
15	196
7	392
3	784
1	1,568
	3,038
5. 32	1,180
16	2,360
8	4,720
4	9,440
2	18,880
1	37,760
	38,350
6. 25	422
3	3,376
1	6,752
	10,761

7. Multiplying large numbers by doubling takes too many steps; answers will vary.

Page 19

1. Florida
2. approximately 12,000 people
3. approximately 4,000
4. 2^n
5. Solving problems quickly; predictions are approximate; answers will vary.

Page 20

1. 40,320
2. $6 \times 5 \times 4 \times 3 \times 2 = 720$
3. a factor of 30
4. Once a letter is used, it can't be reused; $3 \times 2 \times 1 = 6$.
5. No; there aren't ten different letters; *a* occurs four times; so, $4 \times 3 \times 2 \times 1$ combinations are just switching around that *a* leaving the arrangement the same.

Page 21

1. 2,700
2. 1,600
3. $b = 60$
4. $c = 2,200$
5. 3,600
6. 3,700
7. Check students' drawings.
8. 30
9. Answers will vary.

ENRICH ANSWER KEY

Page 22

1. 1,110 feet
2. not enough information to answer the question
3. 787 feet
4. Niagara and Urubupunga
5. about 190,000 cubic feet

Page 23

1. 2:2
2. 0:4
3. 4:0
4. 0:4
5. Great-grandchild; child (BB) combines with Bb or bb to produce Bb, who combines with Bb or bb to produce bb.

Page 24

1. 6,740,167,401
2. 9,999,999,999
3. 4,217,742,177
4. 2,179,821,798
5. Yes; any 5-digit number multiplied by 100,001 will produce a product which is the 5-digit number listed twice.
6. x, yza, bxy, zab
7. Multiply it by any 3-digit number.
8. 222, 222
9. 777, 777
10. 888, 888
11. 1,222,221
12. $15,873 \times n = \frac{n}{7} \times 111,111$
13. 111,111
14. 185, 185
15. 407, 407
16. 481, 481
17. Answers will vary; any 5-digit number with pattern xy, 0xy will produce a similar effect.

Page 25

Available Funds
$1,100
$170
$150
$1,420
Costs
$400
$600
$130
$150
$1,280

Page 25 (cont'd.)

Sales income
$2,000
$2,100
$4,100
Net results
$1,420
$1,280
$140
$4,100
$4,240

Page 26

1. Ring 60.027.
   17; 8
   12; 3
   25; 7
   15; 6
2. 27; 0
   18; 0
   12; 3
   30; 3
3. Ring 2,135.049.
   23; 5
   27; 0
   27; 0
   24; 6
4. 24; 6
   33; 6
   22; 4
   25; 7
5. Ring 546.506.
   15; 6
   33; 6
   12; 3
   26; 8
6. 18; 0
   35; 8
   30; 3
   29; 11; 2
7. An incorrect sum could have the same digit as a correct answer.

Page 27

1. 5; 1; 3
2. $4\frac{8}{15}$
3. Fruit-Mart $0.57; Lasting Happiness $0.54; Lasting Happiness
4. Fruit-Mart $0.39; Lasting Happiness $0.48; Fruit-Mart
5. Multiply all the prices by the different amounts, total.

Page 28

1. 24 marbles
   a. +, 44
   b. 44, −, 32
   c. 32, +, 40
   d. 40, −, 16, 24
2. 526 feet
   a. +, 587
   b. 587, −, 564
   c. 564, −, 526
3. 23.4 miles
   12
   $12 + (12 − 3.5) = 20.5$
   $20.5 − 10.7 = 9.8$
   $9.8 + 13.6 = 23.4$
4. $1.00

Page 29

1. Each amount equals one dollar; so, they equal each other.
2. 20,000
3. 15,215
4. 300 Hong Kong dollars
5. Multiply $300 by Hong Kong dollar exchange rate; or find Hong Kong dollar-to-yen rate, and multiply it by $\frac{3}{5}$ of answer to Question 3.

Page 30

1. 60; 15
2. 10; 0.01
3. 13.31; 146.41
4. 857.5; 3,001.25
5. 4; 0.8
6. 0.2; 0.8
7. a.; d.
8. $3 \times 2^{n-1}$
9. $7 \times 3^{n-1}$
10. $1,024 \div 4^{n-1}$
11. $59,049 \div 9^{n-1}$
12. $72 \times 6^{n-1}$
13. $200 \div 2^{n-1}$
14. No; the varying number of children per parents in each generation.

Page 31

1. 47; 59; 37; 56; 35
2. 13 calico cats
3. 6 Siamese cats
4. May 21
5. 64 cats
6. $30

Page 32

1. 0.348
   0.275
2. 227 hits
3. 0.600
   0.847
   0.512
   0.608
4. 1968's leader—average from longer period is more accurate indication of talent; answers will vary.

Page 33

1. 15,000–17,000
2. Marin County and Sacramento County; answers will vary.
3. 143,000–145,000 mi^2
4. about 10 times
5. 400,000–500,000 people
6. It has more large cities; it has a denser population; answers will vary.

Answers may vary. Accept any reasonable answer.

Page 34

1. 42 2. $24 3. 10 4. 64,391
5. $63.50 6. 0.5 7. 39 8. 12
9. 25 10. 13 11. 64 12. 144
13. $1\frac{2}{3}$ 14. $2\frac{2}{3}$ 15. $6\frac{1}{3}$ 16. $6\frac{2}{3}$
17. 7 18. $7\frac{1}{3}$
19. Yes; § (31) will be $\frac{1}{3}$ more than § (30): That is the pattern in this operation.
20. Division by 2; then multiplication by 8; multiplication by 4; answers will vary.
21. Symbols and operations will vary.

Page 35

1. no
2. $1.80
3. $7.20; 13%
4. $3.30
5. $0.30
6. 80%
7. How often you would go; if this rate would be cheaper than buying single admission tickets; answers will vary.

Page 36

Answers will vary. Possible answers are shown.
1. 2,200–3,200 hours
2. 45–60 hours
3. 3–6 hours
4. 1–4 hours
5. 2–4 hours
6. about 3,650 days
7. about 2,500,000 seconds
8. Answers will vary.
9. 70–140 feet
10. Answers will vary.
11. Answers will vary.

Page 37

1. Check students' diagrams.
2. There are no soccer players. There are no soccer or fieldhockey players. There are no people.
3. Answers will vary.

Page 38

1. 2,620
2. no
3. 70
4. 28
5. No; their factors always sum to 0.

Page 39

1. w 2. y 3. p 4. e 5. k 6. j
7. h

Page 40

1. I like walking to school.
2. 26-10-10-40   26-10   30-28
   40-16-10   6-30   36-28-10-36
   2-12-40-10-36   38-6-16-30-30-24
3. This alphabet is backward.
4. I am so good at codes I should be a teacher.
5. Answers will vary.

Page 41

1. $3.84 (subtraction, multiplication)
2. 1.8 pounds; $11.20 (subtraction, multiplication)
3. yes (multiplication, addition, subtraction)
4. 0.75 pound (divide)
5. $3.48 (division, addition)
6. $7.95 (multiplication, addition)
7. $8.57 (multiplication, addition)

Page 42

1. Minutes in hour, days in week, odometer; answers will vary.
2. Every month's dates fall on the same day of the week in the Celtic calendar; with our calendar, a particular date may fall on any day of the week.
3. Tuesday; with our calendar, it depends on what month it is.
4. Find what day of the year it is and divide by 28; whole number answer is month, and remainder is day.
5. Shorter: Fixed celestial events will come earlier each year. For example, summer equinox on 4/21 one year comes on 4/20 the next.

Page 43

June 4, 2002
18°C; symbols for Westerly, 15 mph, and Cloudy
22°C; symbols for Northeasterly, 55 mph, and Clear
27°C; symbol for Partly Cloudy
25°C; symbols for Easterly, 10 mph, and Sky Obscured
19°C; symbols for Southeasterly, 15 mph, and Scattered Clouds
June 4, 2003
All answers will vary.
Check students' maps and use of weather symbols.

Page 44

1. 6 or 5, 3 or 2, 5, 0, 2, 6
2. 9, 1, 8
3. 0, 4, 6, 8, 1, 5
   Code: EASY STUFF

Page 45

1. Answers to the following questions will vary.
2. generally about 1 hour
3. Answers will depend on the starting point.
4. Students will place an X on the map to mark the halfway point of the parade route.
5. generally about 4 miles and 1.5 hours

Page 46

1. $2 \times 2 \times 2 \times 3 \times 3$; 2, 3, 4, 8, 24, 9, 18, 36, 12, 6
2. Because it doesn't have enough 2's in its prime factorization to make a factor of 12; answers will vary.
3. true; divisibility by 6 and 5
4. true; divisibility by 9 and 2
5. false; combines divisibility by 3 and 8 erroneously
6. Answers will vary.

Page 47

3.

Row 1: 5
Row 2: 8; 12
Row 3: 50; 48; 24
Row 4: $x \div 25$; $x \div 5$; $\frac{x}{4} - 2$;
$x \div 6$; $x \div 6$; $\frac{5}{8}x + 1$
Row 5: 16; 64; 4
Row 6: 8; 8
Row 7: 44
Yes: many different operations can take you from one number to another; so, there can't be a single correct answer.

Page 48

1. 6.05×10^5; 3.15×10^7
2. 9.3×10^4 miles per second
3. 1.23×10^{13} miles
4. 0.25 years
5. 5.86×10^{12} miles
6. 1.88×10^{17} miles
7. 9.87×10^{20} ft
8. 987,000,000,000,000,000,000
   The distances are so great; scientific notation is easier to manipulate; answers will vary.

Page 49

1. 28, 14, 7, 22, 11, 34, 17, 52, 26, 13, 40, 20, 10, 5, 16, 8, 4, 2, 1, 4, 2, 1, . . .
2. 10, 5, 16, 8, 4, 2, 1, 4, 2, 1, . . .
3. 6, 3, 10, 5, 16, 8, 4, 2, 1, 4, 2, 1, . . .
4. 2, 1, 4, 2, 1, . . .
5. This operation will always yield an endless 4, 2, 1, loop; test a factor of the number.

Page 49 (cont'd.)

6. 91, 272, 136, 68, 34, 17, 50, 25, 74, 37, 110, 55, 164 . . .; yes
7. If a number is even, divide it by 2. If a number is odd, multiply it by 3 and subtract 1.
8. The numbers 1, 3, 11, 29, 43, 53, 59, 71, and 97 generate a 2, 1, 2, 1, . . . loop. The numbers 5, 7, 13, 19, and 47 generate a 5, 14, 7, 20, 10, 5, . . . loop; answers will vary.

Page 50

1. $x + 2x + (x + 2) = 26$; Rebecca's cousin is 6, her younger brother is 8, and Rebecca is 12; $x = 6$.
2. 13 mice; 6 hamsters
3. older sister = 15, Jeff = 12, younger sister = 9
4. $d + (\frac{1}{2}d + 2) = 41$; $x + \frac{1}{2}x + (\frac{1}{2}x + 2) = 26$

Page 51

1. true 2. false 3. true 4. true
5. false 6. true

Page 52

1. 144 2. 12 3. 16 4. 15 5. 2
6. 5
7. Find the GCF of three pairs of numbers, using all four numbers. Then take the GCF of the GCF's of the three pairs; answers will vary.
8. It saves time when reducing fractions; it helps when reducing equations like $24x + 36y = 48$; answers will vary.

Page 53

1. 630
2. 825
3. 180
4. 1,260
5. 8:06 A.M.
6. 7:30 A.M.
7. 6:42 A.M.
8. 4:30 P.M.
9. when the numbers are all factors of one of the numbers

Page 54

1. 0, 1, 2, 3, 4, 5
2. 10_6
3. 12_6
4. 35_6
5. 100_6
6. 13_6
7. 25_6
8. 104_5
9. 150_6
10. ⋯
11. ⋯
12. ≡
13. ≣
14. 89
15. 31
16. 42
17. 55
18. 18
19. 12
20. 400_6
21. 530_6
22. 440_6
23. A number system in base three; symbols and answers will vary.

Page 55

1. 5,256 bricks
2. $105.12
3. 2,592 tiles
4. 2,232 tiles
5. Numbers of windows, doors; height, width, length; answers will vary.

Page 56

1. Students will fill in the charts with an O for *true,* and an X for *false.*
   Jacqueline: O, X, X, X
   Patricia: X, X, X, O
   Louis: X, O, X, X
   Emanuel: X, X, O, X
2. Students will fill in the charts with an O for *true* and an X for *false.* Read columns down:
   Ncube = X, O, X, X, X
   Forest: X, X, X, O, X
   Perrotti: O, X, X, X, X
   Lee: X, X, X, X, O
   Clark: X, X, O, X, X

ENRICH ANSWER KEY

Page 57

1. 8,550; 10,800 books
2. Books are taken out more than once; other novels.
3. 1,050; Fiction books
4. 150 more suspense novels
5. about 26 how-to books

Page 58

1. 14, 22, 10
   3, 11
   13, 21
   6
   25
2. 1, 25
   11
   12
   5
   16, 24, 4, 14
3. 15
   23, 16
   20, 22
   12, 19, 3
   11
4. multiplication; 531,441
5. the Associative Property
6. adding two of the numbers and subtracting the third; 5
7. Check students' drawings.

Page 59

1. Check students' diagrams.
2. There are no red three-speed bicycles in Durango. All three-speed bicycles in Durango are red. All bicycles in Durango are either red or three-speed.

Page 60

1. $15 + 6$
2. $36 + 6 + 1$
3. $1 + 6 + 10$
4. $91 + 28$
5. $136 + 3 + 1$
6. $190 + 6 + 3$
7. $16 + 9 + 9 + 4$
8. $64 + 1$
9. $64 + 64$
10. $81 + 9 + 9$
11. $100 + 36 + 4$
12. $196 + 1 + 1 + 1$
13. It is a square number.
14. The pattern yields the square of consecutive odd numbers.
15. $(x - 1) \div 8 = y$; answers will vary.

Page 61

1. $2.5n$
   320
   320 square feet
2. $46.36
   $11.59
   $11.59
3. 15
   30
   30 feet
4. 3, 10
   73
   73 feet
5. n; 4
   29
   29 hours
6. 875
   87.5
   87.5 square feet

Page 62

1. 16 ounces dough; 12 ounces cheese; 10 ounces sauce
2. 12 ounces dough; 9 ounces cheese; 6 ounces sauce
3. $8.10
4. $555.00
5. No; $69.38 extra earned will not pay $74.00 extra rent.

Page 63

1. no
2. yes
3. no
4. 4.5 to 5.5 mm
5. 4.094 cm–4.102 cm
6. 0.873 cm–0.881 cm
7. 1.055 cm–1.063 cm
8. 6.071 cm–6.079 cm
9. Tolerance distinguishes between significant and insignificant variations in manufacturing; if the use changed for an item; answers will vary.

Page 64

1. 12
2. 36, 80, 35, $31\frac{2}{3}$
3. $3x$
   $3x - y$; $7 (3x - y)$
   $7 (3x - y) = z$
4. 63, 28, $37\frac{1}{2}$, 86

Page 64 (cont'd.)

5. Mult.
   by 4   Subt.   Mult.   Outpu
                    by $\frac{1}{2}$ z
   mult.
   by 3
   Input $x = 5$
6. Answers will vary.

Page 65

1. 24 cm
2. 12 ft
3. Zulu, Marlena, Tovah, and Rocio
4. 3,000 lb
5. They are not at equal distances from the fulcrum.

Page 66

1. no
2. about 1 hour
3. yes
4. $550
5. $675
6. $2,220

Page 67

1. 12, 13, 14, 15, 16, 17, 18, 19, 1α, 1β, 20
2. 78_{12}
3. 46_{12}
4. $4\beta_{12}$
5. 112_{12}
6. $\alpha6_{12}$
7. $30\beta_{12}$
8. 100_{12}
9. $4\alpha\beta_{12}$
10. $10\alpha_{12}$
11. Answers will vary.

Page 68

1. 50,000, 15,500, 22,500
   77,500, 80,000, 85,000
   15.5, 18
2. The trend of every measure reversed.
3. government expenditures
4. The country with the larger GNP also has a larger population.
5. In countries where people barter, or trade without money; answers will vary.

Page 69

1. because each term of the sequence is used twice
2. 1,360
   1,020
3. $a + 1 = 0$: no; n will never equal 0 unless the series has 0 terms. Answers will vary.

Page 70

1. Codes are fun
   (19,27) (1,18) (5,27) (6,21) (14,28)
2. 2, 1, 4, 3 (13,31)
3. (65,157), (20,58), (37,101), (33,87), (56,140)
4. (103,120) (147,140) (165,173) (71,80) (37,27) (181,179) (57,45) (31,30)
5. Answers will vary.

Page 71

1. $12.50
2. $\frac{1}{5}$
3. under her budget; $15.00
4. Juliet pays $20.00 per week: Jodie saves $20.00 per week more.
5. Answers will vary.

Page 72

1. a (75°S, 15°E)
   b (60°N, 45°W)
   c (0°, 60°W)
   d (50°N, 15°W)
   e (10°S, 85°E)
   f 90°N
2. Check students' placement of the points on the figure and the labels they have written next to the points.
3. 69.2 miles per degree latitude; 68.9 miles per degree longitude
4. 15°; 1,034 miles; answers may vary.
5. Degrees latitude are all the same, since latitudes are parallel; longitude degrees are shorter as you approach the poles, since the lines converge at the poles.

Page 73

1. (7, 3, 11, 9, 5); (1, 2, 4, 6, 8)
2. (D, B, C, A); (1, 3, 7, 9)
3. Answers will vary; (364, 24, 182, 96, 12, 48); (1, 3, 7, 9, 11, 17)
4. Equivalent; they do not contain identical people.
5. Answers will vary; husbands and wives; questions and answers.
6. Answers will vary; unicorns; male hens.
7. Check students' answers.

Page 74

1. 28 square feet
2. $7\frac{1}{5}$ square feet
3. yes; 28 square feet more
4. about 4 hours
5. about 2 hours
6. $1\frac{1}{3}$ square feet
7. $5\frac{1}{3}$ quarts

Page 75

1. 520
2. 50: the exact proportion is not given; answers may vary.
3. 1,800 bushels; 2,400 bushels
4. the line graph
5. Answers will vary.

Page 76

1. 18
2. $\frac{1}{16}$
3. $\frac{2}{3}$
4. $\frac{5}{8}$
5. $\frac{12}{25}$
6. $\frac{15}{8}$
7. $\frac{55}{864}$
8. 9

Page 77

1. b 2. c 3. b 4. c 5. a
6. b 7. a 8. b 9. c 10. b
11. a
Answers will vary.

Page 78

1. $\frac{3}{8}$ $\frac{1}{4}$ $\frac{1}{4}$ $\frac{1}{8}$
2. 375 250 250 125
3. 150 icky; 300 ugly; 150 cute; 400 slimy
4. 50 icky; 250 ugly; 150 cute; 500 slimy
5. Sample taken from the top would have disproportionately few slimy insects.
6. It would have distributed the insects in a more representative way.
7. icky insects
8. It is representative and accurate only for evenly distributed populations; answers will vary.

Page 79

1. f; c, l; a, n, k
2. the same
3. rising steadily; rising gradually
4. There may be broad flat areas; answers will vary.
5. Check students' maps.
6. Answers will vary.

Page 80

1. lions, tigers; lions; tigers; {0}
2. lions; tigers; {0}
3. All pitchers would concentrate on their particular skill needs; answers will vary.
4. ZIP codes, state; answers will vary.
5. A letter or package would not be delivered.
6. A football team, because players are assigned different positions; answers will vary.

Page 81

1	35
4	140
8	280

1. 9999999ⁿ‖‖‖
2. 999ₙₙₙₙₙₙₙ‖‖‖
3. ⅃9999999ₙₙ‖‖‖‖‖‖
4. ⅃9999999ₙₙ‖‖‖‖‖‖‖
5. the larger number
6. $13 = 2^3 + 2^2 + 2^0$; these numbers were checked off; $35 (2^3 + 2^2 + 2^0) = 455$; take powers of 2 that add to

Page 81 (cont'd.)

smaller factor; multiply each by the larger factor; add.

Page 82

1. 12.5
   60
   0.6
   0.45
2. 600, 0.6, 18.6, 864, 0.864, 26.784, 270, 0.27, 8.37
3. $43.94
4. $\dfrac{\text{days in a month} \times \text{hours per day} \times \text{watts}}{1{,}000}$

Page 83

$1\frac{1}{2}$ cans	$2\frac{1}{4}$ cans
3 cups	$4\frac{1}{2}$ cups
$1\frac{1}{2}$ cups	$2\frac{1}{4}$ cups
2 cups	3 cups
2 loaves	3 loaves
$2\frac{2}{3}$ cups	4 cups
3 cups	$4\frac{1}{2}$ cups
5 cups	$7\frac{1}{2}$ cups
$1\frac{1}{2}$ cups	$2\frac{1}{4}$ cups
4 teaspoons	6 teaspoons
6 quarts	9 quarts

Page 84

1. 75,000°; 75°
2. 35,000 BTU
3. 18,750
4. Heat energy needed to propel a truck; answers will vary.

Page 85

1. no
2. larger
3. 8 or higher
4. No; the Beaufort number represents a range.
5. Answers will vary.

Page 86

28, 5, 1
73, 13, 2
72, 12, 1

Page 86 (cont'd.)

24, 4, 1
219, 37, 4
774, 129, 11
205, 35, 3
451, 76, 7
25, 5, 1
723, 121, 11

Page 87

1. interval
2. ordinal
3. nominal
4. nominal
5. ordinal
6. ratio
7. ratio
8. nominal
9. nominal
10. ratio
11. ratio
12. nominal
13. ordinal
14. nominal
15. ratio

Page 88

1–5. Answers will vary.

Page 89

1. $(25 \times 1.0) + 4\frac{1}{2} = 29\frac{1}{2}$ feet
2. 43.57 feet or $L = \dfrac{H\text{-}E}{T} = \dfrac{35 - 4.5}{0.7} = \dfrac{30.5}{0.7} = 43\frac{4}{7}$ feet
3. $L = \dfrac{150 - E}{T} = 750$, $E =$ your height above lighthouse base
4. Answers will vary.

Page 90

1. 5,460.4 pounds
2. no
3. 65.45 tons
4. $3,485
5. $637
6. 26,444,250 pounds

Page 91

1. That is where the great circle route between two cities is, and that is the shortest distance between them.
2. Over short distances, Earth is very nearly flat.
3. a straight line drilled through Earth
4. Lines of longitude are one-half of a great circle—since each connects the two poles, they are one line of symmetry; The only great circle line (of latitude) is the equator; answers will vary.

Page 92

1. 345
2. 13°; 3°
3. 9°; 22°
4. Vernon
5. Vernon to C to A; Bakonnet
6. Straight line travel is a shorter distance than point to point travel involving east to west and north to south directional changes.

Page 93

1. $0.005(20 + x) = 0.25x$; 5 gallons
2. $0.80(x + 5) = x$; 20 pints of yellow
3. $0.20x + 0.10(10 - x) = 0.15(10)$; 5 oz of each paint

Page 94

1. 3 hours
2. 150 mph
3. 200 laps
4. 72 miles
5. 2 hours
6. 1 mile
7. 15 minutes
8. 142.9 mph

Page 95

1. 4
2. 16
3. 3
4. an eighth note
5. 4
6. 2

Page 95 (cont'd.)

7. Answers will vary, but the equivalent of 6 eighth notes should be in each measure.

Page 96

1. 41%
2. 22
3. 98.5%
4. 41%
5. 60%
6. 8 people
7.–8. Answers will vary.

Page 97

1. 0.2 ft/y, or 2.4 in./y
2. 6°F
3. 6.8$\overline{3}$°F; positive; the change is important, not the fact that it goes down.
4. 7.6°F
5. No: since the total amount of change and the number of months remain constant, the average is not affected.

Page 98

1. 6:36 A.M.
2. 7:44 A.M.
3. 8:11 A.M.
4. 7:27 A.M.

Page 99

1. Mercury 4:1; Venus 4:1; Earth 4:1, Mars 4:1
2. 4:1; 4,328 days
3. 9.6:1; 2.4
4. The ratio between each planet's number of days and distance from the sun is 4:1; answers may vary.

Page 100

1. 400 feet
2. $\frac{47}{799} = \frac{x}{100}$; $x = \frac{6}{100}$, or 6%
3. $\frac{100}{200} = \frac{x}{100}$; $x = 50$ feet
4. $\frac{?}{92\,m} = \frac{x}{9.2\,cm}$
5. $\frac{\text{total weight of ivory pieces}}{\text{total number of pieces}} = \frac{\text{weight of 1 ivory piece}}{\text{1 piece of ivory}}$
6. Measure the shadow of known length and form a proportion with the length of the doorway's shadow.

Page 101

1. 25 mL
2. 4 pints
3. 316 mL
4. $\frac{1}{4}$ teaspoon
5. 2,800 mL

Page 102

1. $6\frac{1}{2}$ miles
2. 56 miles
3. 4.6 inches
4. 13.$\overline{3}$ inches
5. 1 inch/375 feet
6. Answers will vary.

Page 103

1. 54, 48, 42, 39, 36, 33
   93, 92, 87, 83
   95, 87, 84, 76, 66, 50, 32, 16, 8, 2
2. 100; 1
3. Billy scored in the hundredth percentile.
4. Tendai did well because she scored better than or equal to 88% of her peers; the test must have been very difficult, since 88% scored 22% or below.

Page 104

1. 100; 180; 5:9
2. 9:5; 32
3. $\left(\frac{9}{5} \times °C\right) + 32$
4. 5:9 subtract 32.
5. $\frac{5}{9}$ (°F − 32)
6–9. 6 and 7 are correct

Page 105

1. Check students' diagrams.
2. First diagram: Some brown gravy is sweet gravy.
   Second diagram: All sweet gravy is brown gravy.
   Third diagram: There is no gravy except sweet gravy and brown gravy; some gravy is sweet and brown.

Page 106

1. Students will fill in the chart. Circuit: on, on, on.
2. x or y
3. y or (u and x)
4. Either y, or both u and x (the AND gate); must be closed for the current to go from point a to point b; Answers will vary.

Page 107

1. $3.60
2. 150%
3. 10%
4. 3,333 boxes crawlers, 150,000 eggs; 417 lures
5. lower the price to $1.80
6. $574.60 more profit per month
7. High volume; low overhead; answers will vary.

Page 108

1. 9.1%
2. 20%
3. 2.40 B $; 1,020 B $; 28.80 B $; 0.90 B $
4. 5,040 B $; 1,800 B $; 1,200 B $; 3,600 B $
5. 11,640 B $
6. Extra money increased demand for goods; answers may vary.

Page 109

1. $240   2. $3,500   3. 13%
4. 2 years   5. $3,300
6. 11.25%   7. $2,600   8. 18 months   9. $2,240   10. $265
11. $10,789.53   12. $500.08

Page 110

1. broken-line and bar graphs
2. The proportion each month is out of the total.
3. pictograph
4. Students will complete the graph.

Page 111

1. 12.68%
2. 20%; a larger amount of interest compounds, and it compounds at a higher rate.
3. 18% compounded monthly; yields effective rate of 19.56%

Page 112

1. sales taxes
2. property and sales taxes
3. no
4. There is not enough information.
5. $37,244,200
6. $1,016,234,600

Page 113

1. A = (10, 150°)
   B = (5, 45°)
   C = (7, 225°)
   D = (3, 290°)
2. E = (13, 7)
   F = ($^-$6.5, $^-$6)
   G = (300°, $^-$8)
   H = (0, 6)
3. Circle; no, a circle contains an infinite number of ordered pairs.

Page 114

1. B 2. C 3. A 4. D
5. Complete the diagram.
6. No; the angle between the sun, the food source, and the hive, as indicated by round dance, would not change.

Page 115

1. Students will draw similar angles.
2. Answers will vary.
3. Answers will vary.

Page 116

1. {X, 1}, {X, 2}, {Y, 1}, {Y, 2}, {Z, 1}, {Z, 2}
2. {Steve, parrot}
   {Steve, gopher}
   {Steve, kitten}
   {Chu Yat, parrot}
   {Chu Yat, gopher}
   {Chu Yat, kitten}
   {Yukio, parrot}
   {Yukio, gopher}
   {Yukio, kitten}
3. No; because a is not paired with one unique value.
4. Picking doubles teams in a tennis match; answers will vary.

Page 117

Check students' drawings.
1. 3, 4, 1, 2, 5
2. Tommy Trout
3. amount of time the radar travels to reach the swimmers; speed of radar in water

Page 118

1. 28 2. 14 3. 6 4. 40 5. 13
6. Answers will vary.

Page 119

1. w = 4; x = 4; A = bh
2. 8
3. $\sqrt{8}$; $l = \sqrt{A}$
4. 5
5. $\sqrt{61}$
6. $\sqrt{24}$
7. 10
8. $\sqrt{116}$
9. $\sqrt{85}$
10. $\sqrt{5}$
11. $\sqrt{80}$
12. All are right triangles; triangles in C and D are congruent to y, since a = b; the triangle in E adjacent to y equals y, forming a square; all triangles of E are also equal to y.

Page 120

1. Label the center of the circle.
2. six; six; 60°
3. $\frac{1}{6}$ of the way around the circle; it should have six central angles of 60° each.
4. With six equal angles of 60°, mark the circle every 60°, with the vertices; joined together, they make the hexagon.
5. 72°, divide 360° by five angles
6. 108°
7. They add up to 180°, the same number of degrees as a triangle.
8. The pentagon gives five congruent isoceles triangles, with angles of 72°, 54°, and 54.
9. The radii bisect angles of the pentagon; answers will vary.

Page 121

1. * 5814$_{12}$
2. 328397$_{12}$
3. 1055$_{12}$
4. ★ ★ ★12$_{12}$
5. Students will complete the chart.
6. 1 * 3$_{12}$
7. 488$_{12}$
8. 4 ★ *3$_{12}$
9. 2474$_{12}$
10. 946$_{12}$

Page 122

1. Students will draw the next four pentagonal numbers.
2. Students will draw the fourth, fifth, and sixth pentagonal numbers in the same way as the first.
3. 92; 117; 145
4. Nearly any number of dots can be arranged in a pattern with five sides.

Page 123

1. There is no outside.
2. one
3. There is only one piece twice the size.
4. a Möbius strip interlock with a band with two half-strips
5. one
6. two
7. one
8. two edges
9. even number; two edges; odd number; one edge
10. two double-twisted bands interlocked
11. one band twisted around itself
12. only one edge, so it would take more time to wear out

Page 124

1. yes
2. They all have even degree 2.
3. yes
4. 2
5. All have 2 odd-degree vertices.
6. Networks are traversable if all vertices are of even degree— or if there are two vertices of an odd degree.

ENRICH ANSWER KEY

Page 125

1. transitive
   reflexive
   symmetric
2.–4. Answers will vary.
5. Answers will vary.

Page 126

1. Species 1; Species 1 and 2;
   Species 3 and 4; Species 4
2. Species 1; Species 3 and 4;
   None; Species 4
3. 24.4 m − 27.6 m and above
   48m

Page 127

1. yes
2. traversable; not traversable;
   traversable
3. no; not traversable
4. corrected picture will vary

Page 128

1. The circles become progres-
   sively smaller.
2. a point
3. a circle
4. Sections I and J will be smaller
   than sections K and L.
5. a rectangle
6. They are always a circle; answers may vary.
7. only a sphere

Page 129

1. 2.9 gal   2. No; no; if the dimensions were tripled, more than
3 times the amount of paint would
be needed.   3. 2.35 gal   4. red:
4.25 gal; purple: 1.24 gal   5. x^n
gal

Page 130

1.–16. Check students' drawings.

Page 131

Answers will vary for problems 1–
4. Approximate answers given.
1. about 224 in.²
2. about 150 in.²
3. about 1,696 in.²
4. about 320 inches
5. 14 hours 52 minutes
6. no

Page 132

1. $\frac{1}{2}$ circumference;

   $\frac{1}{4}$ circumference
2. 5 cm
3. length of arc $= 2\pi Ry \div 360$
4. 10 cm²
5. area $= \pi R^2 y \div 360$
6. 4.9 cm; 17.1 cm²
7. Because you cannot measure a
   curve with a ruler; answers will
   vary.

Page 133

1.–3. Check students'
      constructions.

Page 134

1. $\pi = 3.14$
2. $10\pi = 31.4$
3. $24\pi = 75.36$
4. $10\pi = 31.4$
5. $24\pi = 75.36$
6. $10\pi = 31.4$
7. $\pi = 3.14$
8. $80\pi = 251.2$
9. 330 cm²
10. 384 cm²
11. $(20 + 42\pi)$ cm² $= 162.8$ cm²
12. $n\,(L^2)$

Page 135

1. Separate the figure into rectangular solids, find the volume of
   each, and add; find the volume
   of a $3 \times 5 \times 1$ rectangular
   solid, and subtract the volume
   of the rectangular solid missing
   from the larger one; 7 cubic
   meters.
2. $\left(\frac{10 - 4 \text{ in.}}{2}\right) \times \pi \times 60$ in. $=$
   1,695.6 in.³; $(\pi 5^2 \times 60) -$
   $(\pi 3^2 \times 60) = 3,014.4$
3. The hole is not an exact cylinder; its top and bottom are
   rounded.
4. $\frac{1}{2} \cdot \frac{4}{3} \cdot \pi \cdot 10^2 + \pi \cdot 10^2 \cdot 4 +$
   $\frac{1}{3} \cdot \pi \cdot 10^2 \cdot 20 = 2{,}442\frac{2}{3}$ in.³
   rectangular base: 6 m × 4 m,
   height: 9 m; triangular base:
   9 m × 6 m, height: 12 m; answers will vary.

Page 136

1. 32.77 ft³; e. 3.2, 32.77
2. 7,781.5 ft³; g. 18.3, 18.3,
   7,781.5
3. 95.142 ft; a. 3.14, 15.15,
   95.142
4. 576.5 ft²; b. 3.6, 10.42, 10.42,
   576.5
5. 4.73 ft; d.; 10.42, 4.73
6. 4,332.21 ft³; c. 1.7, 4,332.21
7. 1,163.37 ft³ f. 3.14, 10.42, 2.8^3
8. 1,163.37

Page 137

1. Students will complete the
   table.
2. 80,000 people
3. People connected could influ-
   ence people's opinion.
4. Subject matter appeals to different age groups.
5. 100; no; 100 seventh graders
   is too small and specific a
   group to reflect the opinion of
   the city.

Page 138

1. He treats the sample as the
   whole population; $\frac{1}{5}$ of the sample
   said they would buy it, $\frac{1}{5}$ of the
   population should also.   2. 5,000
   people   3. 15,000   4. Which was
   more representative   5. No, because the sample was not representative; employees of a competing soft-drink company would not
   support a new competing product.

Page 139

1. $2\frac{1}{2}$¢
2. $2\frac{1}{2}$¢
3. $1\frac{2}{3}$ planets
4. 6 planets; $1\frac{5}{7}$ planets
5. o
6. The first class's scores were
   similar; the second's varied
   greatly.

Page 140

1. 77.5 cm
2. Depth = independent; pressure = dependent
3. Answers will vary; 1.4 atm at 15 m; 2.3 atm at 25 m

Page 141

1. true 2. true 3. true 4. true
5. false 6. true 7. false 8. true
9. false

Page 142

Students will mark incorrect boxes X and correct boxes O.

Page 143

1. 9 mm
2. 180 mm
3. 10x, 0.0027 mm, 0.0273 m, 20x
4. eyepiece: 50x; objective lens: 120x
5. 0.0075 cm
   0.0025 cm
   0.0075 cm
   Hair C matches

Page 144

1. less
2. 4 more
3. $477,000 or $473,000
4. no
5. between Game 1 and Game 2: 13,000
6. $427,846

Page 145

1. *First chart:*
   Win—Lose—Win
   Win—Lose—Lose
   Second chart:
   Lose—Win—Win
   Lose—Win—Lose
   Lose—Lose—Win
   Lose—Lose—Lose
2. Lizzie—Dizzy—Fizzy
   Dizzy—Lizzie—Fizzy
   Fizzy—Lizzie—Dizzy
   Lizzie—Fizzy—Dizzy
   Dizzy—Fizzy—Lizzie
   Fizzy—Dizzy—Lizzie

Page 145 (cont'd).

3. Order of listings may vary.
   H–T–L–D   H–T–D–L
   T–H–L–D   T–H–D–L
   L–H–T–D   L–H–D–T
   D–H–T–L   D–H–L–T
   H–L–T–D   H–D–T–L
   T–L–H–D   T–L–D–H
   L–T–H–D   L–D–H–T
   D–T–H–L   D–T–L–H
   H–D–L–T   T–D–L–H
   L–D–T–H   D–L–T–H
   H–L–D–T
   T–D–H–L
   L–T–D–H
   D–L–H–T
4. the number of possible outcomes for each game multiplied together

Page 146

1. 1, 2, 2, 1, 1, 2
2. A—B—D—C
   A—C—D—B
   A—C—B—D
   A—D—C—B
   A—D—B—C
3. 24; 120
4. 36; 1,260
5. $n! \div n$

Page 147

1. $\frac{85}{100}$, or 0.85, or 85%
2. $\frac{12}{15}$, or $\frac{4}{5}$ or 0.8 or 80%
3. $\frac{2}{24}$, or $\frac{1}{12}$ or 0.083$\overline{3}$, or 8.$\overline{3}$%
4. 1, or 100%
5. Dog meeting you at the door; it is based on the largest number of past experience; so, it should be the most accurate.

Page 148

1. sheep; 6 million
2. cattle; 63 million
3. approximately 105 million
4. 52 million
5. 528,000,000
6. $50.30 per head

Page 149

1. 1:10
2. $6 million
3. 3:5
4. larger
5. $6 million; $15 million; $12 million

Page 150

1. 6 giant Kaleidoscopes
2. 14.51 cubic feet
3. 5 ft × 5 ft × 31$\frac{1}{3}$ ft
4. 17.9 ft^3
5. 423.9 in.^{3}
6. 15,260.4 in.^{3}
7. The plan is based on volume because 25,620.4 ÷ 423.9 = 3.6. It won't work because the figures don't account for wasted space in the fit of the cable in the cylinder.

Page 151

1. Verranzano-Narrows Bridge is 4,260 feet long; 5,026.8 feet.
2. The John Hancock Tower has 60 stories; 120.
3. Holland Tunnel is 8,557 feet long, Lincoln Tunnel is 8,216 feet long; 16,773 feet.
4. Statue of Liberty is 305 feet 1 inch tall; 25.42 inches.
5. The Everglades National Park is 1,398,000 acres; 1,048,500 acres.
6. Pluto circles the sun once in 248 years; A.D. 2495.

Page 152

1. $\frac{1}{2}$
2. $\frac{3}{32}$
3. 0
4. $\frac{^-7}{16}$
5. No; because negative and positive changes cancel each other out.

ENRICH ANSWER KEY

Page 152 (cont'd.)

6. $2\frac{1}{4}$

7. $4\frac{25}{32}$

8. $3\frac{1}{2}$

9. $3\frac{11}{16}$

10. Sell if $|X| = 6$.

11. Don't sell if $|X| < 4$.

12. $|X| > 5$ each week

13. Plotting temperature changes; or any movement up and down; answers will vary.

Page 153

1.–3. Students will answer in code.

Page 154

1. 8, 34, 89

2. that part which is one month old and growing new branches

3. 43, 85, 171

4. Each term equals the previous term plus twice the term before it.

5. 1, 1, 1, 2, 3, 4, 6, 9, 13, 19, 28, 41; n^{th} term = sum of first and third terms before it

Page 155

1. $12,712; $1,789

2. $1,185

3. $1,159

4. $1,334

Page 156

1. (17,30), (84,149), (10,17), (69,124), (11,20), (87,147), (77,133); (84,140)

2. 25, 15, 21, 27, 2, 18, 15, 11, 5, 27, 1, 27, 8, 1, 18, 4, 27, 15, 4, 5, 0.
   YOU BROKE A HARD CODE.

Page 157

1. Check students' drawings.

2. Check students' drawings.

3. Check students' drawings.

4. Reciprocal ratios

Page 157 (cont'd.)

5. Answers will vary. Possible answers: art and graphic design; cartography (mapmaking).

Page 158

1. 90%

2. Wednesday: 120%; Thursday: 105%; Friday: 75%

3. 85.7

4. 1:45

5. 81.8, 136, 212, 100

6. The number 100 is the basis for percents. Since index numbers are based on percents, it is logical that the number 100 be used as the base.

Page 159

1. 121,208

Page 160

1. $2 \times 33.5 = n; n = 67$ miles

2. $67 - 25 = n; n = 42$ miles

3. $67 + 42 = n; n = 109$ miles

4. $3 \times 109 - 149 = n$; $n = 178$ miles

5. $\frac{1}{2} \times 178 - 9.5 = n$; $n = 79.5$ miles

6. $(67 + 42) \div 4.2 = n$; $n = 26$ miles

7. $(7 \times 26) - 83.6 = n$; $n = 98.4$ miles

8. $(67 + 109 + 178 + 98.4) \div 4 = n; n = 113.1$ miles

Page 161

1. number of hits against left-handers ÷ number of at-bats against left-handers

2. number of hits against left-handers at 8:44 P.M. Sunday with S.W. wind ÷ number of at-bats against left-handers at 8:44 P.M.

3. Because in 2; N is probably very small, or even O.

4. Weather conditions include so many factors that identical conditions on which to base predictions are rare; answers will vary.

Page 162

1. 24, 24, 18, 33, 27, 9, 15

2. 9, 21, 12, 27, 15, 6, 30

3. 1 = (3,4); 3 = (1,4); 4 = (1,3); 5 = (2,3); 6 = (3,3); 8 = (2,2); 9 = (1,2); 0 = (1,1)

4. 23, 23, 23, 34; 24, 34, 24; 12, 13, 14, 33, 34, 11, 23

5. 23, 22, 33, 24, 12, 13, 13; 586–2944

6. Codes will vary.

Page 163

1. $5,000,000

2. profit

3. $49,000,000

4. October through December; $62,000,000

5. The airline lost $17,000,000.

6. $14,000,000

Page 164

1. true 2. true 3. false

4. true 5. false 6. $7a^3$

7. $5n - 4m$; unlike

8. $8x - 4\,xy$; unlike

9. $8s^7\,r^5 - 2s^5r^7$; unlike

10. $12x$

11. $2xy^3$

12. $\frac{1}{2}x^5 + 5x^2$; unlike

13. $2p$

14. $2x^2$

15. 0

16. No; multiply all numbers and add exponents for similar variables; answers will vary.

Page 165

1. $7 - 3x$; 13, 10, 7, 4, 1, ⁻2

2. $y = 2x - 3$; ⁻7, ⁻5, ⁻3, ⁻1, 1, 3

3. (2,1)

4. $y > 2 - \frac{1}{3}x$

5. The same point of intersection as before; no point of intersection for all three equations. Check students' graphs.

SKILLS INVENTORY

These tests are designed to assess students' readiness for the concepts to be covered in each chapter. A variety of questioning techniques help pinpoint areas of weakness before work in the chapter begins.

An alternate to the Pretests, these tests could also be used as review before the Pretest is given.

Name_____   Date_____

1. What is the standard form for five thousand, six hundred four?

    _____

2. 17 hundred – 10 hundred =

    _____

3.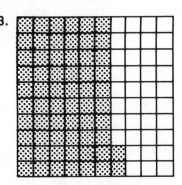

    Write a decimal for the part that is shaded.

    _____

4. $325 \bigcirc 300 + 20 + 5$

    Write $<, >,$ or $=$ in the circle to make a true statement.

5. $(6 + 3) - 4 =$

    _____

6. $300 \bigcirc 400$

    Write $<, >,$ or $=$ in the circle to make a true statement.

7. What is the value of the underlined digit in 6,2̲08?

    _____

8. Circle the least number below.

    one tenth   one hundredth
    one ten   one hundred

    _____

Questions 9 to 11 are based on information in the graph.

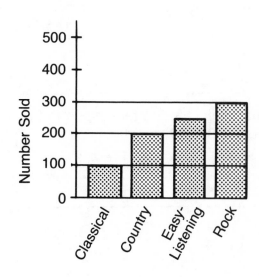

9. For what type of music were the least number of tapes sold in a week?

    _____

10. For what type of music were about 250 tapes sold in a week?

    _____

11. About how many tapes of country music were sold in a week?

    _____

1

Name _____   Date _____

12. Some digits are covered in the numbers below. Which sum is greater, A or B?

_____

A
3,■■■
+ 6,■■■

B
5,■■■
+ 9,■■■

_____

13.   70
     − 23

_____

14. What digit is in the tens place in the number 3,751?

_____

_____

15. (32 − 10) + 7 =

_____

_____

16. Rounded to the nearest ten, 1,265 is

_____

_____

17. Round each number to the nearest hundred and subtract.

812 − 489

_____

_____

18. Roberta had between 8 and 9 dollars. She paid $3.79 for a belt. About how many dollars did she have left?

_____

19. Write seven and four tenths as a decimal.

_____

_____

20.

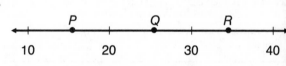

P   Q   R

10   20   30   40

Which point on the number line stands for the largest number, P, Q, or R?

_____

_____

21. Circle all the numbers below that are between 5 and 6.

5.2   4.56   5.7   6.5

_____

22. Rounded to the nearest hundred dollars, $4,762.61 is

_____

_____

23.   19   64   87   32

Write the numbers above from the greatest to the least.

_____

_____

24.   4.29
     + 7.83

SKILLS INVENTORY **Chapter 1 Page 3**

25. Is $7,000 + 600 + 3$ greater than, equal to, or less than 7,063?

_____

26. Some digits are covered in the number 38,■ ■ ■. The number is rounded to the nearest thousand. Circle all numbers below that could be the rounded number.

37,000   38,000   39,000   40,000

27. $12 - (6 + 2) =$

_____

28. Earl found jeans on sale for $8.77 and a sweater on sale for $6.27. How much will both cost?

_____

29.   199   210   189   201

Write the numbers above from the least to the greatest.

_____

30. Jane had $6.79. About how many dollars did she have?

_____

SKILLS INVENTORY Chapter 2 Page 1

1.   8
   ×3

_____

2. Some digits are covered in the numbers below. Which product is greater, A or B?

_____

    A   B
  3■■   4■■
 ×   5   ×   5

_____

3. Round 676 to the nearest hundred.

_____

_____

4.   8,103
   27,900
 + 4,576,000

_____

5. Circle all the numbers that are equal to 0.3.

0.310   0.30   1.3   0.03   0.300

_____

6. Double M Campground has 52 trailer sites and 70 tent sites. Sherwood Campground has 35 tent sites.

Circle all the sentences that give a fact stated above.

1. Pets are allowed at Double M Campground.
2. Double M Campground has 70 tent sites.
3. Sherwood Campground has 52 trailer sites.
4. Double M Campground is 35 miles from Sherwood Campground.

7. $6 \times (2 + 4) =$

_____

_____

8. $2.912 \bigcirc 3$

Write $<, >,$ or $=$ in the circle to make a true statement.

_____

9. $6 \times 8 =$

_____

_____

10. Circle all the multiples of 10.

40   55   106   90   13   70

_____

11. Circle each factor in the following.

$8 \times 4 = 32$ $9 + 7 = 16$ $55 = 5 \times 11$

_____

12. Multiply $9 by 5.

_____

_____

13. $0 \times 8 =$

_____

_____

14. If $7 + 7 + 7 + 7 = \blacksquare \times 7$, then $\blacksquare =$

_____

_____

15.   3,275
 + 51,060

16. Circle the numbers below that are equal to 0.760.

0.76   0.0760   0.76000   0.00760

_____

17. $(7 \times 9) + (1 \times 9) =$

_____

18. Find the product of 6 and 9.

_____

19. Round 4,322 to the nearest thousand.

_____

20. Follow the steps to find the answer.

1. Find the sum of 17, 6, and 12.
2. Divide the sum by 5.

_____

21. $1.8 + 1.8 =$

_____

22. Circle the number below that is closest to $\frac{1}{2}$.

0.12   0.6   0.2   0.8   1.2

_____

23. $19 \times 10 =$

_____

24. $3 \times (5 \times 4) =$

_____

25. 7×4 thousand $=$

_____

26. $0.5 + 0.5 + 0.5 =$

_____

27. Circle the number that is closest to 1.

0.1   1.4   0.8   0.5

_____

28. If $2.4 + 2.4 + 2.4 = \blacksquare \times 2.4$, what number is $\blacksquare$?

_____

29. Doug did 19 push-ups and 5 bench presses.

Circle the questions that can be answered using the above facts.

1. How many bench presses did Doug do?
2. How many sit-ups did Doug do?
3. Did Doug do more push-ups or bench presses?

_____

30. $9 \times 2 \times 4 =$

_____

1.
$$\begin{array}{r} 83 \\ 9)\overline{747} \\ \underline{72} \\ 27 \\ \underline{27} \\ 0 \end{array}$$

In the problem above, the quotient is

_____

2. $35.487 \times 100 =$

_____

3. Write $7 \div 10$ as a fraction.

_____

4. $3 \times 48 \bigcirc 146$

Write $<$, $>$, or $=$ in the circle to make a true statement.

_____

5. $20,000 \times 8 =$

_____

6. Circle each quotient that is greater than $10,000 \div 75$.

   $10,000 \div 175$ $10,000 \div 70$ $10,000 \div 45$

_____

7.
$$\begin{array}{r} 13.7 \\ \times6 \\ \hline \end{array}$$

_____

8. Write 4 divided by 20 using $)\overline{}$.

_____

9.
$$\begin{array}{r} 5R\blacksquare \\ 25)\overline{135} \\ \underline{125} \\ 10 \end{array}$$

In the problem above, $\blacksquare =$

_____

10. $0.0718 \times 10 =$

_____

11.
$$\begin{array}{r} 417 \\ -368 \\ \hline \end{array}$$

_____

12. If $\blacksquare \times 4 = 20$, then $\blacksquare =$

_____

13. Rounded to the nearest hundredth, 392.716 is

_____

14. $5\blacksquare\blacksquare \times 8 =$

_____

Some digits are hidden above. Circle each number that could be the product.

   3   40   1,300   4,200   8,500

15. A long distance swimmer went 21 miles in 7 hours. How many miles did she average per hour?

_____

6. Circle each quotient that is greater than $6,000 \div 4$.

   $600 \div 4$ $60,000 \div 4$ $600 \div 400$

---

7. Some digits are hidden in the numbers below. Which product is larger, A or B?

   _____

   $$
   \begin{array}{cc}
   \text{A} & \text{B} \\
   3\blacksquare\blacksquare & 4\blacksquare\blacksquare \\
   \times \quad 27 & \times \quad 27
   \end{array}
   $$

---

8. $3,000 \times 90 =$

   _____

Use the map below for <u>questions 19 to 21.</u>

MAP OF ALABAMA SPACE AND ROCKET CENTER

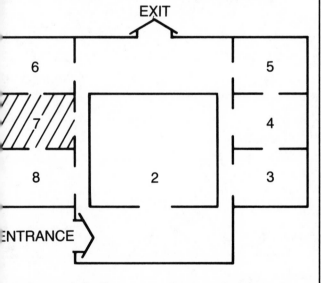

1. Information Center   5. Energy Information
2. Theater   6. Military Projects
3. Space Dimensions   7. Space Projects
4. Rocket Engine   8. Future

19. Circle the place on the map that shows the entrance to the Alabama Space and Rocket Center.

   _____

20. Write a T on the map where the theater is.

   _____

21. What is in the room that is shaded?

   _____

   _____

22. Circle the numbers below that are equal to 0.0169.

   0.169   0.016900   0.01609
   0.01690   0.00169

23. Round the first number to the nearest hundred and multiply.

   623×4

   _____

24. $4.917 \times 1,000 =$

   _____

25. Rounded to the nearest dollar, $87.38 is

   _____

26. Billy correctly answered a question 48 times during 4 days of school. What was the average number of times Billy correctly answered a question each of the 4 days?

   _____

SKILLS INVENTORY   **Chapter 3 Page 3**

27.   825
        − 728

_____

28. $4.3 \times 6.35 =$

_____

29. $0.09130 \times 1,000 =$

_____

                    214
30. $4\overline{)856}$
                    8
                    ■
                    4
                    16
                    16
                    0

In the problem above, ■ =

_____

SKILLS INVENTORY   Chapter 4 Page 1

1. What is the remainder when 54 is divided by 4?

   _____

2. What is the result if you multiply 8 by 10 and then divide by 5?

   _____

3. $4.2 \times 10,000 =$

   _____

4. List all the 1-digit numbers that divide 24 with a remainder of 0.

   _____

5. $10 \times 10 \times 10 =$

   _____

6. Circle the numbers that are factors of 36.

   1   2   3   4   6   9   12   30   36

7. $7\overline{)895}$

8. $2.7156 \times 1,000 =$

   _____

9. $4 + (3 \times 7) =$

   _____

10. Start with 15. Subtract 3. Divide by 4. What is the result?

    _____

11. Is the statement $3 + 4 = 9$ true or false?

    _____

12. $2 \times 2 \times 2 \times 2 =$

    _____

13. $(13 + 5) - 5 =$

    _____

14. $2 \times 10 \times 10 =$

    _____

15. What is the number represented by the last three digits of 53,876?

    _____

16. Is the statement $2 \times 3 = 6$ true or false?

    _____

17. Circle each of the whole numbers below.

    3   2.7   15 $\frac{1}{2}$

18. $2.5 \times 10 \times 10 =$

    _____

SKILLS INVENTORY   **Chapter 4 Page 2**

19. If ■ + 3 = 10, then ■ =

_____

20. List all the 1-digit numbers that divide 32 and leave a remainder of 0.

_____

21. $4.5622 \times 10{,}000 =$

_____

22. What is the remainder when 5,217 is divided by 3?

_____

23. If $3 \times$ ■ = 24, then ■ =

_____

24. What number do you get when you multiply 3 by itself?

_____

25. Circle the numbers that are factors of 26.

1   2   3   6   13   20   26

_____

26. $3 \times 3 \times 3 \times 3 \times 3 =$

_____

27. $6.23 \times 1{,}000 =$

_____

28. $(2 \times 6) - 4 =$

_____

29. What is the sum of the digits of 342?

_____

30. What is the result if you multiply 4 by 6 and then subtract 13?

_____

Name _____ Date _____

1.

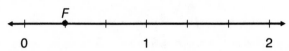

Write a fraction for the point labeled *F* on the number line.

_____

2. $\frac{6}{10} + \frac{1}{10} =$

_____

3. For each of the following, write the whole number that is closest to the given number.

a. $2\frac{7}{8}$ _____   **b.** $2\frac{1}{4}$ _____

c. $\frac{1}{100}$ _____   **d.** $\frac{10}{9}$ _____

4. Place the correct symbol, $>$, $<$, or $=$, in each of the ☐s below.

a. $4 \times 6 \,\square\, 3 \times 8$ **b.** $9 \times 6 \,\square\, 8 \times 7$

c. $10 \times 4 \,\square\, 13 \times 3$ **d.** $4 \times 8 \,\square\, 7 \times 5$

5. What fraction of the shapes are squares?

_____

6. What is the numerator of $\frac{5}{7}$?

_____

7. What is the greatest common factor (GCF) of 12 and 8?

_____

8. If *n* is a number between 5 and 6, and *m* is a number between 2 and 3, then *n* + *m* must be a number between

_____ and _____.

_____

9. What fraction of the circle is shaded?

_____

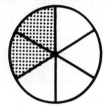

_____

10.

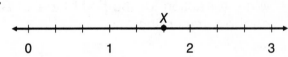

Write a fraction for the point labeled *x* on the number line.

_____

_____

11.

What fraction of the shapes are triangles?

_____

_____

12. If $21 - y = 6$, what is *y*?

_____

_____

13. What is the denominator of $\frac{3}{8}$?

_____

11

Name _____ Date _____

14. $\frac{4}{8} - \frac{1}{8} =$

_____

_____

15. What is the least common multiple (LCM) of 9 and 12?

_____

_____

16. List all the fractions having 2, 4, or 6 as numerator, and 3 or 5 as denominator.

_____

_____

17.

$\overset{\displaystyle\longleftarrow}{\underset{0}{\rule{0pt}{0pt}}\;|\;\;|\;\;|\;\;|\;\;|\;\;\underset{1}{\bullet}^{B}}$

Write a fraction for the point labeled B on the number line.

_____

_____

18. $5\frac{7}{10} - 3\frac{3}{10} =$

_____

_____

19. Shade $\frac{3}{4}$ of the square.

_____

20. If $3 = \frac{\blacksquare}{4}$, then $\blacksquare =$

_____

_____

21. If $x + 14 = 27$, what is x?

_____

22. Write $\frac{18}{24}$ in simplest form.

_____

_____

23. If $4 = \frac{\blacksquare}{1}$, then $\blacksquare =$

_____

_____

24. What is the greatest common factor (GCF) of 15 and 18?

_____

_____

25. Suppose x is a number that is less than 10, and y is a number that is less than 6. How does $x + y$ compare with 16?

_____

_____

26. $1\frac{1}{3} + 2\frac{1}{3} =$

_____

_____

27.

$$\overset{\displaystyle\downarrow}{\overset{\displaystyle\longleftarrow}{\underset{4}{\rule{0pt}{0pt}}\;|\;\;|\;\;|\;\;|\;\;|\;\;|\;\;\underset{5}{\rule{0pt}{0pt}}}}$$

On the number line, the arrow points to

_____.

_____

28. What is the least common multiple (LCM) of 6 and 2?

_____

_____

29. If $x - 12 = 7$, what is x?

_____

_____

30. If $8\frac{1}{5} = 7\frac{\blacksquare}{5}$, then $\blacksquare =$

_____

SKILLS INVENTORY   Chapter 6 Page 1

1. Write $\frac{12}{7}$ as a mixed number. Simplify if necessary.

   _____

2. Write the answer as a decimal.

   $6.6 \div 5 =$

   _____

3. What is the simplest form of $\frac{18}{27}$?

   _____

4. How many tenths are there in 1?

   _____

5. $8\overline{)3,000}$

6. $\frac{1}{2} + \frac{1}{2} + \frac{1}{2} =$

   _____

Use this information for questions 7 and 8.

Recipe for Mixed Nuts

peanuts	6 oz
pecans	3 oz
cashews	3 oz
almonds	4 oz

7. How many oz of pecans are used in this recipe?

   _____

8. How many oz of mixed nuts will this recipe make?

   _____

9. If $1\frac{1}{4} + 1\frac{1}{4} = \blacksquare \times 1\frac{1}{4}$, then $\blacksquare =$

   _____

10. Write $\frac{15}{6}$ as a mixed number. Simplify if necessary.

    _____

11. Circle the number closest to $2\frac{3}{8}$.

    $2 \qquad 2\frac{1}{2} \qquad 3 \qquad 8$

    _____

12. 27 students are going on a field trip. If 8 students can ride in a van, how many vans are needed for the trip?

    _____

13. What whole number is closest to $5\frac{8}{9}$?

    _____

14. Write the answer as a decimal.

    $13 \div 4 =$

    _____

15. If $2x + 2 = 12$, what is x?

    _____

16. Circle the number closest to $\frac{5}{12}$.

    $0 \qquad \frac{1}{2} \qquad 1 \qquad 5 \qquad 12$

    _____

17.

If each of the pies above is cut into sixths, how many pieces will there be?

_____

18. Write $5\frac{2}{3}$ as a fraction.

_____

19. What is the value of the 4 in 2.0457?

_____

20. If $3x - 6 = 12$, what is x?

_____

21. Is $\frac{2}{5}$ in simplest form?

_____

22. Write $\frac{15}{9}$ as a mixed number.
Simplify if necessary.

_____

23.

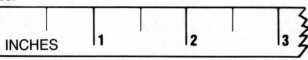

The figure above shows that $3 \div \frac{1}{2} =$

_____

24. Write $1\frac{7}{8}$ as a fraction.

_____

25. If $y - \frac{1}{2} = 7\frac{1}{2}$, what is y?

_____

26. $50 is to be shared equally by 6 clubs.

a. How much money will each club get?

_____

b. How much money will be left over?

_____

27. What is the simplest form of $\frac{12}{16}$?

_____

28. What whole number is $\frac{1}{4}$ closest to?

_____

29. Circle all the numbers below that would round to 5 if rounded to the nearest whole number.

$4\frac{1}{5}$ $5\frac{1}{5}$ $4\frac{9}{10}$ $5\frac{9}{10}$

_____

30. Write $2\frac{4}{10}$ as a fraction.

_____

SKILLS INVENTORY   **Chapter 7 Page 1**

1. $13 \times 60 =$

_____

2. $35.6 \times 100 =$

_____

3. What is the time 2 hours after noon?

_____

4. $276 \div 12 =$

_____

5. $14.3 - 8.9 =$

_____

6. $3 \text{ ft} = 2 \text{ ft} \blacksquare \text{ in}$

_____

7. $108 \div 4 =$

_____

8. $5\frac{1}{4} \times 16 =$

_____

9. $88.4 \div 10 =$

_____

10. What is the time 4 hours before midnight?

_____

11. $3.7 + 12.8 =$

_____

12. $4 \text{ h} = 3 \text{ h} \blacksquare \text{ min}$

_____

13. If $n = 8$, then what is the value of $98 - 7n$?

_____

14. $128 \div 16 =$

_____

15. What is the time 12 hours after midnight?

_____

16. $0.02 \times 1,000 =$

_____

17. $2\frac{1}{2} \times 12 =$

_____

18. $660 \div 60 =$

_____

19. If $x = 5$, then what is the value of $3x + 2$?

_____

SKILLS INVENTORY   **Chapter 7 Page 2**

20.   6 ft   7 in.
     + 2 ft   2 in.

_____

Use this information for <u>questions 21 and 22.</u>

Item	Cost
briefcase	$49.95
pencil set	$26.75
file cabinet	$99.99

21. How much does a pencil set cost?

_____

_____

22. How much more does a file cabinet cost than a briefcase?

_____

_____

23. $1.03 \div 1,000 =$

_____

_____

24. Write the answer as a mixed number.

   $40 \div 16 =$

_____

25. What is the time 3 hours before noon?

_____

_____

26.   4 ft   9 in.
     − 1 ft   3 in.

_____

27. If you add 36 and 48, and divide that sum by 12, what is the result?

_____

28. $0.07 \times 10 =$

_____

29. $3\frac{1}{2} \times 2,000 =$

_____

_____

30. $20 \div 100 =$

_____

Name _____   Date _____

1. Write each of the following as a fraction in simplest form:

   a. $\frac{6}{12}$ _____   **b.** $\frac{150}{100}$ _____

2.

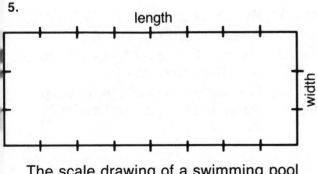

What is the ratio of circles to triangles in the figure?

_____

---

3. What percent of the circle is shaded?

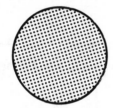

_____

---

4. $0.12 \times \$700 =$

_____

5.

length

width

The scale drawing of a swimming pool has centimeters marked. How long is the scale drawing in centimeters?

_____

---

6. Write whether each change in cost was an <u>increase</u> or a <u>decrease</u>.

   a. Cost was \$50.00   Cost now \$56.00

   _____

   b. Cost was \$1.00   Cost now \$0.85

   _____

   c. Cost was \$71.21   Cost now \$69.95

   _____

---

7. Write the answer as a decimal.

$63 \div 5 =$

_____

---

8. Circle each expression that is equivalent to $1\frac{4}{5}$.

   $\frac{14}{5}$ $1 + \frac{4}{5}$ 1.45 $1 \times \frac{4}{5}$ $\frac{9}{5}$

_____

---

9. $\$2,000 \times 0.14 \times 2 =$

_____

---

10. $500 \div 10 =$

_____

---

11. What is the simplest form of $\frac{48}{100}$?

_____

---

12. One pie will serve 8 people.
Let $n =$ the number of people that 2 pies will serve.

$n =$ _____

Name _____ Date _____

13. What is the ratio of shaded balls to all the balls in the figure?

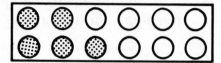

_____

14. $4 \cdot 24 = 8 \cdot x$

$x =$ _____

Questions 15 to 17 are based on the circle graph.

One hundred people were asked what their favorite fruit is.

People's Choice of Favorite Fruit

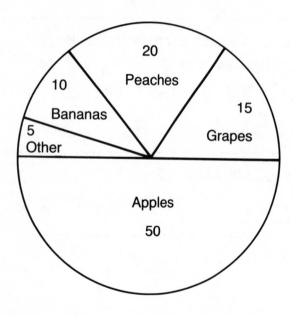

15. Which fruit is the favorite of the greatest number of people questioned?

_____

16. How many of the people questioned have bananas as their favorite fruit?

_____

17. Which two fruits together are the favorite of exactly 35 of the people questioned?

_____

_____

18. Write the answer as a decimal.

$18 \div 100 =$

_____

19. At the track, 1 mile takes 4 laps, 2 miles take 8 laps, and 3 miles take

_____ laps.

20. 20 is $\frac{1}{4}$ of what number?

_____

21. Scale drawing of Gail's room.

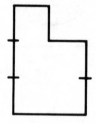

Circle each statement that is true.

1. The scale drawing and Gail's room have the same shape.
2. The scale drawing and Gail's room have the same size.
3. The longest side of the drawing shows the longest wall of Gail's room.

22. Write $\frac{15}{100}$ in simplest form.

_____

SKILLS INVENTORY   **Chapter 8 Page 3**

23. Write the answer as a decimal.

$87.5 \div 7 =$

_____

24. $0.4 \cdot x = 120$

$x =$ _____

25. If $5 \cdot n = 200$, then n is

_____

26. If $\frac{1}{100} \cdot n = 2$, then $n =$

_____

27. $\$700 \times 0.2 \times 3 =$

_____

28. Solve for n.

$3n = 6 \cdot 15$

_____

29. $V = l \cdot w \cdot h$

In the formula above, if $l = 4$, $w = 3$, and $h = 2$, then $V =$

_____

30. Circle each number that is less than 0.15.

0.015   0.150   0.0015   1.5

SKILLS INVENTORY   Chapter 9 Page 1

1. How many times does this curve cross itself?

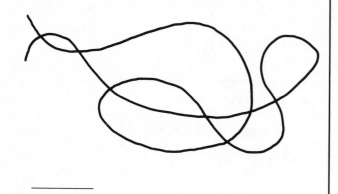

_____

2.

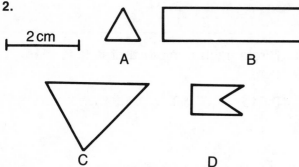

Circle the figures which have a side longer than 2 cm.

3.

Mark the lower right corner of the rectangle with the letter *E*.

4. Write the next two numbers in this pattern.

8, 16, 24, 32, 40, _____, _____

5. $32 \times \frac{5}{8} =$

_____

6. If $\frac{12}{3} = \frac{x}{2}$, then $x =$

_____

7.

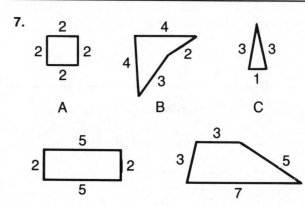

If a klop is a four-sided figure with exactly two equal sides, circle all the figures that are klops.

8.

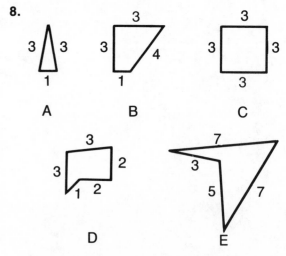

If a klop is a four-sided figure with exactly two equal sides, circle all the figures that are <u>not</u> klops.

Name _____ Date _____

9. 200 − 34 =

_____

10.

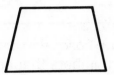

Mark the middle of the top of the figure with the letter *B*.

11. $\frac{1}{3} \times \$234 =$

_____

Use this information for <u>questions 12 to 15.</u>

John ran 3 miles. Then he swam 2 miles. Then he biked 25 miles. Then he ate lunch. Then he took a nap. Then he went to a movie.

12. What did John do last?

_____

13. What was his third activity?

_____

14. What did he do first?

_____

15. $12 \div \frac{3}{4} =$

_____

16.

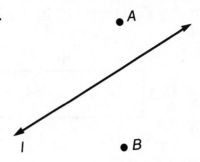

a. Draw a line parallel to line *l*. Make your line go through point *A*.

b. Draw a line perpendicular to line *l*. Make your line go through point *B*.

17. What number corresponds to point *A* on the number line below?

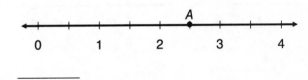

_____

18. The sum of two numbers is 70. If one of the numbers is 12, what is the other?

_____

19. $\frac{3}{4} \times 64 =$

_____

20. $\$275 + \$37.50 =$

_____

21. If $\frac{3}{9} = \frac{5}{x}$, then $x =$

_____

SKILLS INVENTORY   **Chapter 9 Page 3**

22. The length of the rectangle is 10. What is the width?

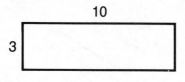

_____

23. $18 \div \frac{2}{3} =$

_____

24. $180 - 57 =$

_____

25. If $\frac{4}{5} = \frac{3}{n}$, then $n =$

_____

26. Write the next two numbers in this pattern.

1, 4, 9, 16, 25, _____, _____

27. If a trobit is a number whose tens digit is even, which of these are trobits? (Circle all the trobits.)

423, 873, 32, 23, 168, 55

28. If a trobit is a number whose tens digit is even, circle all the numbers that are <u>not</u> trobits.

98, 345, 112, 56, 65, 984

29. Write the next two numbers in this pattern.

32, 16, 24, 12, 20, 10, 18, _____, _____

30. If you folded the right side of the rectangle on top of the left side, which point would lie underneath point C?

_____

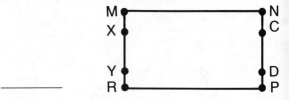

Name _____ Date _____

1. $14.3 + 2.55 =$

_____

2. If $a = 3$ and $b = 4$, what is $2a + b$?

_____

3. How many sides does a rectangle have?

_____

4.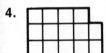

a. In the figure above, if a side of one of the little squares represents 1 inch, what is the distance around the figure?

_____

b. How many of the little squares (□) are there inside the boundary of the figure?

_____

5.
```
    8
 ┌──────┐
4│      │4
 └──────┘
    8
```

What are two names for the figure above?

_____ and

_____

Use this picture for questions 6 to 7.

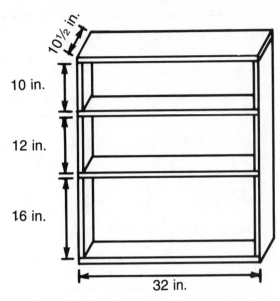

All boards are $\frac{1}{4}$ in. thick.

6. How tall is the tallest shelf of the bookcase?

_____

7. How far from the floor is the top of the bookcase?

_____

8. $8^2 =$

_____

9.
```
      37 in.
 ┌──────────────┐
 │              │9 in.
 └──────────────┘
```

Identify the length and the width of the figure above.

length = _____   width = _____

SKILLS INVENTORY   **Chapter 10 Page 2**

10. $0.7 + 1.4 + 0.9 =$

_____

_____

11. If $k = 5$ and $m = 2$, then $2km =$

_____

_____

12.

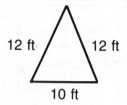

12 ft   12 ft

10 ft

What is the figure called?

_____

13. $2 \times \frac{1}{4} + 2 \times \frac{1}{2} =$

_____

_____

14. How many sides does a pentagon have?

_____

_____

15. $20 \times 3.14 =$

_____

_____

16. How many cubes make up the figure shown?

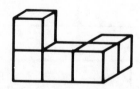

_____

_____

17. $1.8^2 =$

_____

18. If $a = 6$ and $b = 10$, then $\frac{1}{2}(a + b) =$

_____

_____

19.

5

5   5

5

What are two names for the figure?

_____ and

_____

_____

20. What is 20 squared?

_____

_____

21. If $x = 2$ and $y = 7$, what is $y - 3x$?

_____

_____

22. What is the radius of the circle?

_____

_____

23. What is the sum and product of 3 and 8?

sum _____

product _____

_____

24. If $x = 10$, then $x^2 =$

_____

Name _____ Date _____

25. $3 \times \frac{2}{5} =$

_____

26.

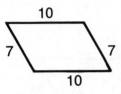

What are two names for the figure above?

_____ and

_____

27. How many of the little blocks (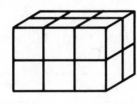) are there in the stack shown?

_____

28. $8 \times 2\frac{1}{3} =$

_____

29.

What is the diameter of the circle?

_____

30. If $d = 15$ and $w = 25$, what is $8w - 2d$?

_____

1. Write $\frac{4}{10}$ as a percent.

   _____

2.   2, 4, 5, 8, 9, 9, 9

   The middle number in the list above is

   _____

3.

   | A | A | A | B | B | B | C |

   How many squares above do <u>not</u> have a B in them?

   _____

4. $\frac{10+7+7+0+6}{6} =$

   _____

5. Circle the numbers below that equal $\frac{6}{18}$.

   $\frac{18}{6}$ $\frac{2}{6}$ 6.18 $\frac{1}{3}$ $\frac{8}{20}$

6. Which pictures are marked off into equal parts?

   A

   B

   C

   D

   _____

7. Round 76,082 to the nearest 5,000.

   _____

8.   11, 7, 8, 20

   The difference between the greatest number and least number above is

   _____.

9. (P) (P) (Q) (Q) (M) (M) (N)

   How many circles above have M or N in them?

   _____

10. Write $\frac{3}{24}$ in simplest form.

   _____

11.   4, 3, 3, 5, 4, 4, 5

   How many numbers above are <u>not</u> 6?

   _____

12. The total number of degrees in a circle is

   _____.

13.   2, 8, 10, 6, 6, 2, 12

   How many numbers above are <u>not</u> even?

   _____

14.   11, 5, 21, 5, 21, 10, 5, 8

   Which number above appears the most often?

   _____

Name _____ Date _____

15.

a. Shade each part that has a 6 on it.

b. What fraction of the parts have a 6 on them?

_____

16. $\frac{5}{6} \times \frac{3}{4} =$

_____

17.   0.2 3.7 2.6 5.2 4.9

1.0 2.3 0.4 2.7 1.3

How many numbers above are between 2.0 and 2.9?

_____

18.   0, 9, 4, 0, 6, 5, 8, 9, 1, 3

How many numbers are listed above?

_____

19. Complete the pattern.

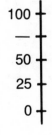

20. Write $\frac{18}{30}$ as a decimal and as a percent.

_____ _____

21.   1, 4, 5, 3, 2, 1, 9, 2

How many numbers above are less than 3?

_____

22. $\frac{238}{7} =$

_____

23. If 🌳 represents 1,000 trees, then

🌳 🌳 🌳 🌳 represents _____ trees.

24.   89, 94, 79, 80, 101, 99

Circle the greatest and the least numbers above.

25. ☐ ◯ △ △ ☐

How many figures above are squares or triangles?

_____

Name _____   Date _____

Use the graph below for <u>questions 26 to 27.</u>

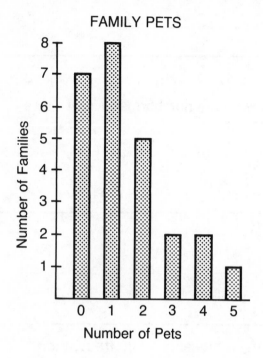

FAMILY PETS

26. How many families have 2 pets?

_____

27. How many more families have 2 pets than have 4 pets?

_____

28. $\frac{1}{4} \times \frac{3}{4} =$

_____

29. Round 681,495 to the nearest 50,000.

_____

30. $\frac{1}{2} \times \frac{1}{2} \times \frac{1}{2} =$

_____

SKILLS INVENTORY Chapter 12 Page 1

1. $90 - 38 =$

_____

2. Circle each correct statement.

$5 < 3$ $5 > 3$ $3 < 3$ $5 < 8$

3.

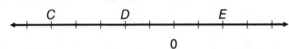

0

Which of the points with a letter name is farthest from 0?

_____

4. Fill in the blanks and complete the pattern.

$1 \times 11 = 11$
$2 \times 11 = 22$
$3 \times \underline{\quad} = 33$
$\underline{\quad} \times 11 = 44$
$5 \times 11 = \underline{\quad}$

Use this figure for questions 5 and 6.

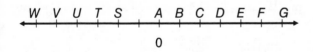

0

5. Which letter is at the point 5 units to the right of 0?

_____

6. Which letter is at the point 4 units to the left of 0?

_____

7. $3 \cdot 10 \cdot 5 =$

_____

8. Write in order from the least to the greatest: 11, 9, 0, 109, 110

_____

9. Fill in the blanks and complete the pattern.

30, 25, 20, _____, 10, _____, _____

10. Circle the number that would be farthest from 0 on the number line.

$\frac{9}{2}$ 3   7   4.8

11. $8 \cdot (4 + 8) = \blacksquare$

$\blacksquare = \underline{\quad}$

12. If $x + 6 = 11$, then $x =$

_____

13.

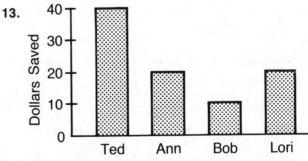

According to the graph Ted has saved how much more than Ann and Bob combined?

_____

29

SKILLS INVENTORY   **Chapter 12 Page 2**

14. How much greater is 11 than 8?

_____

15.

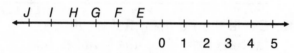

4 is how many units to the left of 10 on the number line?

_____

Use this figure <u>for questions 16 and 17.</u>

$$\begin{array}{ccccccc} J & I & H & G & F & E \\ \end{array}$$
$$\quad\quad\quad\quad 0\ 1\ 2\ 3\ 4\ 5$$

16. Which number shown is as far from 0 as point H is?

_____

17. Which letter shown is as far from 0 as the number 2 is?

_____

18. Solve the equation $4x = 28$.

$x =$ _____

19. $x > 13$

Circle the numbers below that can replace x to make the inequality true.

0   7   13   18   102

20. $\dfrac{6 \cdot 4}{2} =$

_____

21. If $x = 10$, then $\dfrac{x}{2} - 4 =$

_____

22. The greatest integer for which $x + 2 < 9$ is

_____

23.

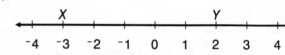

How many units apart are points X and Y above?

_____

24. Solve the equation $\dfrac{y}{3} = 16$.

$y =$ _____

25. $\dfrac{10 + 25}{5} =$

_____

26. If $x = 4$, then $3x + 1 =$

_____

KILLS INVENTORY   **Chapter 12 Page 3**

27.

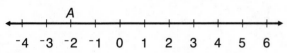

What number is 4 units to the right of point A?

_____

28. On the number line below, place a dot (•) on each mark that represents a number that is less than 3.

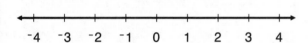

29. Wayne's age is three years less than Cathy's age. Cathy is 21 years old. Circle each equation that could be used to find Wayne's age.

$x - 3 = 21$
$21 \div 3 = x$
$21 - 3 = x$
$21 \cdot 3 = x$

30. Circle the numbers below that can replace n and make the statement $n < 7$ true.

0   4   7   18   106

Skills Inventory Answers

Chapter 1

1. 5,604   2. 7 hundred or 700   3. 0.62   4. =
5. 5   6. <   7. 200, or 2 hundreds   8. one
hundredth   9. Classical   10. Easy Listening
11. 200, or about 200   12. B   13. 47   14. 5
15. 29   16. 1,270   17. 300   18. $4 or $5   19. 7.4
20. R   21. 5.2 and 5.7   22. $4,800.00   23. 87, 64,
32, 19   24. 12.12   25. greater than, or >
26. 38,000 and 39,000   27. 4   28. $15.04   29. 189,
199, 201, 210   30. $7

Chapter 2

1. 24   2. B   3. 700   4. 4,612,003   5. 0.30 and
0.300   6. 2. Double M Campground has 70 tent
sites   7. 36   8. <   9. 48   10. 40, 90, and 70
11. 8, 4, 5, and 11   12. $45   13. 0   14. 4
15. 54,335   16. 0.76 and 0.76000   17. 72   18. 54
19. 4,000   20. 7   21. 3.6   22. 0.6   23. 190
24. 60   25. 28 thousand   26. 1.5   27. 0.8   28. 3
29. 1. How many bench-presses did Doug do? and
3. Did Doug do more push-ups or bench-presses?
30. 72

Chapter 3

1. 83   2. 3,548.7   3. $\frac{7}{10}$ 4. <   5. 160,000
6. $10,000 \div 70$ and $10,000 \div 45$ 7. 82.2   8. $20\overline{)4}$
9. 10   10. 0.718   11. 49   12. 5   13. 392.72
14. 4,200   15. 3 mph   16. $60,000 \div 4$ 17. A
18. 270,000   19.

20.
$$\boxed{\begin{matrix} T \\ 2 \end{matrix}}$$

$\text{(ENTRANCE} \Rightarrow) \ 1$

21. Space Projects   22. 0.016900 and 0.01690
23. 2,400   24. 4,917   25. $87.00, or $87   26. 12
times   27. 97   28. 27.305   29) 91.3, or 91.30
30. 5

Chapter 4

1. 2   2. 16   3. 42,000   4. 1, 2, 3, 4, 6, and 8
5. 1,000   6. 1, 2, 3, 4, 6, 9, 12, and 36   7. 127 R6,
or $127\frac{6}{7}$ 8. 2,715.6   9. 25   10. 3   11. false
12. 16   13. 13   14. 200   15. 876   16. true   17. 3
and 15   18. 250   19. 7   20. 1, 2, 4, and 8
21. 45,622   22. 0   23. 8   24. 9   25. 1, 2, 13, and
26   26. 243   27. 6,230   28. 8   29. 9   30. 11

Chapter 5

1. $\frac{1}{3}$ 2. $\frac{7}{10}$ 3. a. 3   b. 2   c 0   d 1   4. a. =   b. <
c. >   d. <   5. $\frac{2}{5}$ 6. 5   7. 4   8. 7 and 9   9. $\frac{2}{6}$, or $\frac{1}{3}$
10. $1\frac{2}{3}$, or $\frac{5}{3}$ 11. $\frac{4}{9}$ 12. 15   13. 8   14. $\frac{3}{8}$ 15. 36   16. $\frac{2}{3}$,
$\frac{6}{3}$, and $\frac{2}{5}, \frac{4}{5}, \frac{6}{5}$ 17. $1\frac{1}{2}$, or $1\frac{2}{4}$, or $\frac{6}{4}$, or $\frac{3}{2}$ 18. $2\frac{4}{10}$, or $2\frac{2}{5}$
19. any 3 of the 4 rectangles shaded   20. 12
21. 13   22. $\frac{3}{4}$ 23. 4   24. 3   25. $x + y < 16$ 26. $3\frac{2}{3}$
27. $4\frac{2}{5}$ 28. 6   29. 19   30. 6

Chapter 6

1. $1\frac{5}{7}$ 2. 1.32   3. $\frac{2}{3}$ 4. 10   5. 375   6. $1\frac{1}{2}$ 7. 3 oz
8. 16 oz   9. 2   10. $2\frac{1}{2}$ 11. $2\frac{1}{2}$ 12. 4   13. 6
14. 3.25   15. 5   16. $\frac{1}{2}$ 17. 12 pieces   18. $\frac{17}{3}$
19. 0.04   20. 6   21. yes   22. $1\frac{2}{3}$ 23. 6   24. $\frac{15}{8}$
25. 8   26. a. $8.33   b. $0.02   c. $8, or 8 dollars
d. $2, or 2 dollars   27. $\frac{3}{4}$ 28. 0   29. $5\frac{1}{5}$, or $4\frac{9}{10}$ 30. $\frac{24}{10}$,
or $\frac{12}{5}$

Chapter 7

1. 780   2. 3,560   3. 2:00 PM   4. 23   5. 5.4   6. 12
7. 27   8. 84   9. 8.84   10. 8:00 PM   11. 16.5
12. 60   13. 42   14. 8   15. 12:00 noon or 12:00
P.M.   16. 20   17. 30   18. 11   19. 17   20. 8 ft 9 in.
21. $26.75   22. $50.04   23. 0.00103   24. $2\frac{1}{2}$
25. 9:00 A.M.   26. 3 ft 6 in.   27. 7   28. 0.7
29. 7,000   30. 0.2

Chapter 8

1. a. $\frac{1}{2}$ b. $\frac{3}{2}$ 2. 4 to 3, or 4:3, or $\frac{4}{3}$ 3. 100%
4. $84.00   5. 8 cm   6. a. increase   b. decrease
c. decrease   7. 12.6   8. $1 + \frac{4}{5}$ and $\frac{9}{5}$ 9. $560
10. 50   11. $\frac{12}{25}$ 12. 16   13. 5 to 12, or 5:12, or $\frac{5}{12}$
14. 12   15. apples   16. 10   17. peaches and
grapes   18. 0.18   19. 12   20. 80   21. 1 and 3   22. $\frac{3}{20}$
23. 12.5   24. 300   25. 40   26. 200   27. $420.00
28. $n = 30$ 29. 24   30. 0.015 and 0.0015

Chapter 9

1. 7   2. B and C   3. $\boxed{}$ 4. 48, 56   5. 20   6. 8

7. B and E   8. C and E   9. 166   10.

11. $78   12. went to a movie   13. biked   14. ran
15. 16   16.   17. $2\frac{1}{2}$ 18. 58   19. 48

20. $312.50   21. 15   22. 3   23. 27   24. 123
25. 3.75   26. 36, 49   27. 423, 23, and 168   28. 98,
112, and 56   29. 9, 17   30. X

Chapter 10

1. 16.85   2. 10   3. 4   4. (a) 1.6 inches   b. 14
5. Any two of these: rectangle, parallelogram,
polygon, quadrilateral   6. 16 inches   7. 39 inches
8. 64   9. length = 37 in., width = 9 in.   10. 3
11. 20   12. triangle, isosceles triangle   13. $1\frac{1}{2}$
14. 5   15. 62.8   16. 5   17. 3.24   18. 8   19. Any two
of these: square, rectangle, parallelogram, polygon,
quadrilateral   20. 400   21. 1   22. 6.7   23. 11, 24
24. 100   25. $1\frac{1}{5}$ 26. Any two of these:
parallelogram, polygon, quadrilateral   27. 12
28. $18\frac{2}{3}$ 29. 8 m   30. 170

Chapter 11

1. 40% **2.** 8 **3.** 4 **4.** 6 **5.** $\frac{2}{6}$ and $\frac{1}{3}$ **6.** B and C
7. 75,000 **8.** 13 **9.** 3 **10.** $\frac{1}{8}$ **11.** 7, or all
12. 360° **13.** 0, or none **14.** 5
15. a. **b.** $\frac{2}{5}$ **16.** $\frac{5}{8}$ **17.** 3 **18.** 10 **19.** 75

20. 0.6 and 60% **21.** 4 **22.** 34 **23.** 4,000
24. 79,101 **25.** 4 **26.** 5 **27.** 3 **28.** $\frac{3}{16}$
29. 700,000 **30.** $\frac{1}{8}$

Chapter 12

1. 52 **2.** $5>3$ and $5<8$ **3.** *C* **4.** 11, 4, 55 **5.** *E*
6. *V* **7.** 150 **8.** 0, 9, 11, 109, 110 **9.** 15, 5, 0
10. 7 **11.** 96 **12.** 5 **13.** $10 **14.** 3 **15.** 6 **16.** 4
17. *F* **18.** 7 **19.** 18 and 102 **20.** 12 **21.** 1
22. 6 **23.** 5 **24.** 48 **25.** 7 **26.** 13 **27.** 2
28.

29. $21-3=x$ **30.** 0 and 4

PRETESTS

Pretests provide a means to assess student's knowledge of the concepts and skills to be covered in each chapter. Because these tests are parallel to the chapter Posttests, they provide an excellent tool against which to measure students' accomplishments in a given chapter. Information gained from these tests can also help in planning the amount of coverage needed for each lesson.

If the Skills Inventory tests are used exclusively before each chapter, the Pretests could be used as an alternate Posttest or for review.

- Test items are not grouped by objective but are mixed to provide students with more thought-provoking, less predictable tests.

It is assumed that students will have the appropriate measuring devices available for chapter tests on measurement, geometry, and so on.

These tests are in free-response format with some multiple choice items included where that format provides a better testing tool. For multiple choice, students are expected to give the letter of the answer choice.

Turn to the *Other Tests* section for a scoring chart for tests.

PRETEST   Chapter 1 Page 1

1. What is the standard form for the number thirty trillion, one hundred seven thousand?

_____

2. Round 384,497 to the nearest thousand.

_____

3. $205,761 + 884,109 + 307$

_____

4. What is the standard form for the number $60,000 + 8,000 + 30$?

_____

5. What is the value of the 1 in the number 9.2001034?

6. Melissa saved $78.00 from yard work, $36.95 from gifts, and $8.07 from her allowance. How much money did she save in all?

_____

7. What is the short word name for 497,000,006,300?

_____

8. What is the best estimate for $34,085 + 15,998 + 7,307 + 902$?

_____

9. What is the value of the digit in the hundred billions place in the number 5,241,607,038,900?

_____

Name _____ Date _____

Questions 10 to 13 are based on the graph.

STEREO PRICES

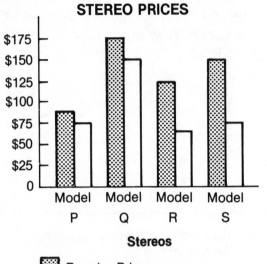

Stereos

▨ Regular Price

☐ End-of-Year Sale Price

10. About how much is the end-of-the year sale price of Model R?

_____

11. Which model has a regular price of $150?

_____

12. What model has the lowest end-of-year sale price?

_____

13. For which model was the difference between the regular price and the end-of-year sale price the greatest?

_____

14. What is the decimal for 6 + 0.07 + 0.0004?

_____

15.   391,085
       − 153,472

_____

16. Rick Mears drove 162.962 miles per hour in an Indianapolis 500 race. Round this rate of speed to the nearest tenth of a mile per hour.

_____

17. Write three ten-thousandths in standard form.

_____

18. If 17,4■9 is less than 17,418, then ■ must be

_____

19. Estimate.
$856.07 − $707.54

_____

20. Write 1.090508 in expanded form.

_____

21. The Frostburg Little League collected $1,283.51 for their season. Round the amount collected to the nearest dollar.

_____

Name _____ Date _____

2. What is the value of the 5 in 4,005,200,830,069?

_____

3. If $456 + 312 = 312 + n$, what is n?

_____

4. What is the value of the digit in the hundred-thousandths place in 107,240.038596?

_____

5. $3,876 + 12,025 - 790 + 88$

_____

6. What is 20.8539 rounded to the nearest hundredth?

_____

7. Write 103,704 in expanded form.

_____

8. A trip for a school band will cost $725.00. The students have $589.64 now. How much do they still need?

_____

29. 5,001; 5,020; 5,099; 5,010

What is the correct order of the above numbers from the greatest to the least?

_____

30.
```
    3 2 7 , 3 9 6
  + ■ ■ ■ , ■ ■ ■
    5 0 2 , 0 9 8
```

What is the missing addend?

_____

31.

Library	Books Checked Out
Annapolis	3.77 million
Honolulu	3.6 million
Louisville	2.89 million
Tucson	3.7 million

The table above shows the number of books checked out from the libraries in four cities. Which library had the greatest number of books checked out?

_____

32. 3.0258
   $- 0.16642$

_____

33. What is the best estimate for $1.35 + 2.716 + 0.849$?

_____

PRETEST   Chapter 1 Page 4

Questions 34 to 37 are based on the graph.

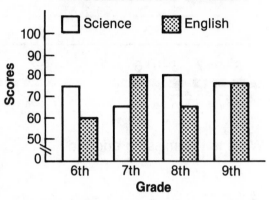

**AVERAGE TEST SCORES
IN SCIENCE AND ENGLISH**

☐ Science   ▨ English

Scores

Grade
6th   7th   8th   9th

34. Which grade has the highest average test score in English?

_____

35. What was the average test score in Science of the sixth grade students?

_____

36. For which grade was the difference between Science and English average test scores the least?

_____

37. About how much was the difference in the Science and English average test scores of the seventh grade students?

_____

38. What is the word name for 42.007?

_____

39. Estimate.
$921.07 − $218.23

_____

40. 27.003, 27.03, 27.33, 27.3
What is the correct order of the numbers above from the least to the greatest?

_____

PRETEST   Chapter 2 Page 1

1. $1,720.69
   ×   8

   _____

2. Compare. Write <, >, or =.
   701 × 51 ● 35,000

   _____

3. 10 × 0.076

   _____

4. If you buy Outdoor Magazine at a
   newsstand, it costs $2.50 for each
   issue. There are 10 issues per year.
   How much would it cost to buy each
   issue at a newsstand for 2 years?

   _____

5.   8,065
   ×   94

6. 2.69 × 37

   _____

7. Emily swims the same number of laps
   each day. If you want to find how many
   laps she swims in 5 days, what
   information do you need to know?

   _____
   _____

8. 76,285 × 400

   _____

9.   0.514
   ×   62

10. A rocket can travel 26,100 miles per
    hour. A supersonic transport can travel
    1,450 miles per hour. What operation
    should you use with 26,100 and 1,450
    to find how much faster the rocket
    travels than the supersonic transport?

    _____

11. Rope to be used on a boat costs $0.33 a foot. At that price, how much would 100 feet of rope cost?

_____

12.   62.004
    ×   508

13. A grocery store manager ordered 20 cases of canned tomato soup. Each case contains 48 cans. To find how many cans of tomato soup he ordered, what operation should you use with 20 and 48?

_____

14. 0.06×0.8

_____

15. $27.■■ × 12

Some digits are hidden in the number above. What is a reasonable estimate of the product?

_____

16. Hamburgers cost $0.99 each at a snack shop. Mrs. Snow had coupons for $0.25 off each hamburger bought. She bought 4 hamburgers. What did she pay for the hamburgers she bought?

_____

17. $0.02 \times 0.4 \times 0.03$

_____

18. Regina received 7 letters and wrote 5 during vacation. It cost $0.22 to buy a stamp to send a letter. How much did Regina spend on stamps to send her letters during vacation?

_____

19.   4.00173
    ×   1,000

20. Jeremiah rode his bike 28.6 kilometers one day and 21.5 kilometers the next day. What operation should you use with 28.6 and 21.5 to find out how many kilometers Jeremiah rode those two days?

_____

1. $12 \times (4 + \blacksquare) = (12 \times 4) + (12 \times 7)$

   What is $\blacksquare$?

   _____

2. Gabe's camera is 9.5 cm wide and weighs 17 oz. Dawn's camera is 8.5 cm wide and weighs 13 oz. How much wider is Gabe's camera than Dawn's camera?

   _____

3.   9,040
     $\times$ 270

4. Nick counted 15 packages of pencils and 9 loose pencils in a drawer. Each package contained 12 pencils. How many pencils were in the drawer?

   _____

25. Gracie had a dream in which she could spend $35 each week in her favorite store for 8 weeks. To find how much she could spend in all, what operation should she use with 35 and 8?

   _____

26. $39.\blacksquare \times 0.4\blacksquare 5$

   Some digits are hidden in the numbers above. What is a reasonable estimate of the product?

   _____

27. $0.03 \times 80 \times 9$

   _____

28. A band uniform costs $41.50. How much must the school pay to buy 28 uniforms?

   _____

29.
```
   0.47
 × 0.19
   423
    47
   893
```

The problem above has not been finished. What is the correct answer?

_____

30. Sliced turkey costs $2.35 a lb. The scale showed 3.4 lb of turkey. How much does the turkey cost in all?

_____

31. A large lion weighs 500 pounds. A large whale is 33 yards long and weighs 150 tons. If you want to find how much longer the whale is than the lion, what information do you need to know?

_____
_____

32. 100 × 23.15

_____

33. The regular price for one can of soup is $0.43. The sale price is $1.05 for 3 cans of soup. How much will be saved by buying 3 cans of soup on sale?

_____

34. Which of the following products is beween 6,000 and 7,000?

91 × 70   90 × 94

66 × 67   91 × 60

_____

PRETEST   Chapter 3 Page 1

1. Tim drove 75 miles per day for 5 days. What operation should you use to find the total number of miles he traveled?

   a. addition   b. subtraction
   c. multiplication   d. division

   _____

2. $73\overline{)66,138}$

   _____

3. Estimate.

   $4\overline{)824}$

   _____

4. Estimate.

   $142 \div 7$

   _____

5. $\dfrac{18.12}{6} =$

   _____

6. Three identical cameras cost $147. What operation should you use to find the price of one camera?

   a. addition   b. subtraction
   c. multiplication   d. division

   _____

7. $2,807 \div 7$

   _____

8. $8\overline{)\$560,016}$

   _____

9. Estimate.

   $\$149.57 \div 3$

   _____

10. $1,000\overline{)205.5}$

   _____

11. The Highland cheerleaders bought 14 uniforms for $840. What is the price of one uniform?

   Choose the most reasonable answer.

   a. $9,000   b. $600
   c. $60   d. $6

   _____

12. $3\overline{)\$121.41}$

   _____

13. $0.17504 \div 3.2$

   _____

14. What is the remainder when 800 is divided by 147?

_____

15. $0.6\overline{)54.36}$

_____

16. $54.62 \div 10$

_____

17. $22\overline{)6,548}$

What is the best estimate of the quotient?

_____

18. A carton containing a microwave oven weighs 43.5 pounds. If the carton itself weighs 1.5 pounds, what is the weight of the microwave oven?

_____

19. $0.09\overline{)7,083}$

_____

20. $62\overline{)\$3,946.85}$

What is the best estimate of the quotient?

_____

Questions 21 to 24 are based on the following map. The heavy lines show the way a class walked to see the sights of New Orleans.

Map of Part of New Orleans

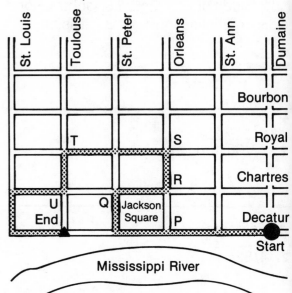

21. The circle (●) shows the spot where a class started walking. Where did they start?

_____

22. The class walked to a video history museum at Chartres and Orleans Streets. What letter on the map shows that place?

_____

23. When the class got to the corner marked U on the map, they had walked how many blocks?

_____

24. The triangle (▲) shows where the class stopped. What location was the halfway point of their walk?

_____

25. 25)42,3▇▇

Some digits are hidden above. How many digits will an estimate of the quotient have?

_____

_____

26. $782.4 \div 1,000$

_____

_____

27. | Shelley drove 750 miles in 15 hours. What was her average speed? |

Choose the most reasonable answer.

a. 5 mph   b. 30 mph
c. 50 mph   d. 80 mph

_____

_____

28. $0.0816 \div 34$

_____

_____

29. Estimate.

$82,490 \div 15$

_____

30. Mr. Preston worked 9 months and earned $28,650. What is a reasonable estimate of $28,650 \div 9$, his monthly pay?

_____

_____

31. $40.05 \div 0.15$

_____

_____

32. It took Scott 71.1 seconds to walk 100 meters. What is $71.1 \div 100$?

_____

_____

33. Julie has $3.59 and buys a few cans of oil for $0.72 each. What amount of money does she have left? Choose the most reasonable answer.

a. $10   b. $5
c. $4   d. $0.71

_____

_____

34. 48)131.04

35. Joel's little brother is 4 feet 2 inches tall but claims he is going to grow another 2 feet. How tall would his brother be then?

_____

36. The Fly-By-Night Mail Service flew 213 night packages into Newark. Each package weighed between 12 lb and 19 lb. Which might be the total maximum weight of all the night packages?

Choose the most reasonable answer.

a. 2,130 lb   b. 2,520 lb
c. 4,000 lb   d. 4,400 lb

_____

PRETEST **Chapter 4 Page 1**

1. Which of the following numbers is divisible by 4?

   8,314   5,524   5,058   4,174

   _____

2. What is 689 in scientific notation?

   _____

3. What is $\sqrt{64}$?

   _____

4. What is the greatest common factor (GCF) of 40 and 90?

   _____

5. Simplify $9 + 5 \cdot 6 - 2$.

   _____

6. Barbara wants 9 baby geese to raise. Assuming that $\frac{1}{4}$ of those that she orders will not arrive alive, she will order more than she wants. Write an equation that shows how many geese she should order.

   _____

7. Which numbers are equal?

   $\sqrt{100}$ $\sqrt{1,000}$ 10

   _____

8. If $x + 17 = 31$, what is x?

   _____

9. Which numbers are divisible by 3?

   216   702   156

   _____

10. If $s = 3$, what is the value of $s + 9$?

   _____

11. What is the least common multiple (LCM) of 48 and 64?

_____

Use the following information for <u>questions 12 to 14.</u>

Every year a school has a plant sale. The graph shows how many plants were sold from 1980–1986.

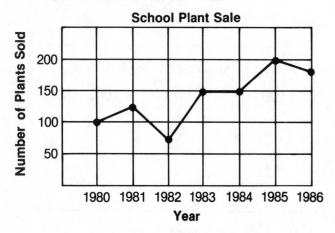

12. In 1983 each plant sold for $8. What were the total sales for that year?

_____

13. One-fifth of the plants sold in 1981 were herbs. About how many were not herbs?

_____

14. The goal in 1986 was to sell three times the number sold in 1982. What was the goal?

_____

15. What is the greatest common factor (GCF) of 18, 20, and 32?

_____

16. What is 6.5×10^2 in standard form?

_____

17. What is $\sqrt{16}$?

_____

18. Which numbers are divisible by 8?

364   5,000   27,640

_____

19. What is the least common multiple (LCM) of 25 and 125?

_____

20. If $x = 6$, what is $2x - 1$?

_____

21. If $30 - 3y = 12$, what is y?

_____

22. Which equations have the same solution?

$3a - 5 = 7$ $3a = 2$ $3a = 12$

_____

PRETEST   **Chapter 4 Page 3**

23. If $n^2 = 144$, what is n?

_____

24. | Sam is 2 in. taller than 3 times the height of his dog. Sam is 65 in. tall. How tall is his dog? |

Which equation would you use to solve the problem?

a. $3d + 2 = 65$ b. $2d - 3 = 65$
c. $65 = d - 2$ d. $d = 65 + 6$

_____

25. Simplify $8 - 4 - 1 + 2$.

_____

26. What is the least common multiple (LCM) of 3, 5, and 10?

_____

27. Which of the following numbers is <u>not</u> divisible by 3?

9,119   8,415   8,118   6,918

_____

Use the following information for <u>questions 28 and 29</u>.

A school organized a scrap paper drive. The graph shows the number of pounds of paper collected.

Pounds of Scrap Paper Collected

Thursday	☐ ☐ ☐
Friday	☐ ☐ ☐ ☐ ☐
Saturday	☐ ☐ ☐ ☐ ☐ ☐ ☐ ☐ ☐ ☐
Sunday	☐ ☐ ☐ ☐ ☐ ☐ ☐ ☐

Each ☐ stands for 100 pounds

28. How many pounds were collected on Saturday?

_____

29. About how many more pounds were collected on Sunday than on Thursday?

_____

30. Two more than one-half the number of coats Carlos took to be dry-cleaned was 6. How many coats did Carlos have dry-cleaned?

_____

_____

31. If $y = 4$, what is $\frac{y}{2} + 8$?

_____

_____

32. If $2q + 7 = 13$, what is q?

_____

_____

33. What is 70,000 in scientific notation?

_____

_____

34. Simplify $6 \cdot 8 \div 4 - 3 \cdot 2$.

_____

_____

35. If $y = 15$, what is $3y - 2$?

_____

_____

36. What is 1.599×10^6 in standard form?

_____

_____

37. Which of the following numbers is divisible by 6?

2,312   2,806   3,018   5,733

_____

_____

38. Simplify $35 \div (5 + 2) \cdot 4 + 5$.

_____

Name_____ Date_____

Write a fraction equivalent to $\frac{9}{12}$.

_____

_____

Which fraction is <u>not</u> equivalent to $\frac{30}{50}$?

a. $\frac{3}{5}$ b. $\frac{10}{30}$

c. $\frac{15}{25}$ d. $\frac{60}{100}$

_____

If $n < \frac{2}{3}$, then n could be

a. $\frac{3}{6}$ b. $\frac{4}{6}$

c. $\frac{3}{4}$ d. $\frac{12}{13}$

_____

$\frac{3}{4} + \frac{2}{5}$

What is the sum written in simplest form?

_____

What is the mixed number for the fraction $\frac{15}{8}$?

_____

Which fraction is greater than $\frac{8}{7}$?

a. $\frac{9}{10}$ b. $\frac{9}{8}$

c. $\frac{7}{6}$ d. $\frac{7}{8}$

_____

$\frac{11}{12} - \frac{3}{4}$

What is the difference written in simplest form?

_____

8.

  8

Suppose you have 3 cards, as shown, and you arrange the cards to form all the different 3-digit numbers possible. Which is a complete list of those numbers that would be greater than 500?

a. None
b. 618, 816
c. 618, 681, 816, 861
d. 681, 816, 861

_____

9. Suppose you are at a craft supply store and want to purchase as many of a certain item as you can. Each of these items costs $2.89. To estimate the number of items you can buy with the money you have, which of the following plans would most likely be simplest? (There is no sales tax.)

a. Round down to $2.50.
b. Round down to $2.75.
c. Round up to $2.90.
d. Round up to $3.00.

_____

10. $x + \frac{5}{6} = \frac{9}{6}$

Solve the equation.

_____

11. $\frac{3}{12} + \frac{1}{6}$

What is the sum written in simplest form?

_____

PRETEST   Chapter 5 Page 2

12. What is the best estimate for
$8\frac{7}{8} - 3\frac{1}{10}$?

_____

13. $\frac{3}{4} = \frac{6}{n}$
Find n.

_____

14. Order the fractions $\frac{5}{6}$, $\frac{3}{4}$, and $\frac{1}{2}$, from the least to the greatest.

_____

15. What is the fraction equal to the mixed number $10\frac{1}{5}$?

_____

Use the following information for questions 16 to 18.

Types of Soil

	Soil 1	Soil 2
Peat moss	$6\frac{3}{4}$ lb	$5\frac{3}{8}$ lb
Sand	$2\frac{1}{4}$ lb	$1\frac{7}{8}$ lb
Fertilizer	$\frac{3}{4}$ lb	$1\frac{1}{8}$ lb

16. If you have 5 lb sand, do you have enough to make 1 batch of each kind of soil?

_____

17. About what part of Soil 1 is fertilizer?

_____

18. About how much peat moss is used altogether in one batch of each soil?

Choose the best plan to simplify the problem.

a. Subtract 5 from 7.
b. Multiply 5 and 7.
c. Add 7 and 5.
d. Double the $6\frac{3}{4}$.

_____

19. Marie has 2 favorite tops that she can wear with any of 3 skirts. How many different outfits can she make with these tops and skirts?

_____

20. $x - \frac{4}{9} = \frac{7}{9}$
Solve the equation.

_____

21. What is the best estimate for
$\frac{2}{3} + \frac{1}{8}$?

_____

22. $6\frac{5}{9} - \frac{2}{3}$
What is the difference written in simplest form?

_____

Name _____ Date _____

23. Which fraction is less than $\frac{8}{18}$?

   a. $\frac{4}{14}$ b. $\frac{4}{9}$

   c. $\frac{8}{10}$ d. $\frac{9}{4}$

   _____

24. What is the best estimate for

$4\frac{11}{12} + \frac{1}{5}$?

   _____

25. Sam's snake grew $\frac{1}{2}$ in. in January and $\frac{2}{3}$ in. in February. How long is the snake now?

   a. $\frac{3}{5}$ in.

   b. $\frac{3}{4}$ in.

   c. $1\frac{1}{6}$ in.

   d. You need more information.

   _____

26. Every night Jay has to take out the trash, walk the dog, and do the dishes. To keep from being bored, he tries to do these things in a different order each night. How many different ways are there to order these three tasks?

   _____

27. $3\frac{2}{3}$
   $+7\frac{3}{4}$

What is the sum written in simplest form?

   _____

28. What whole number or mixed number is equivalent to $\frac{138}{6}$?

   _____

29. $1\frac{3}{10} + x = 2\frac{4}{5}$

Solve the equation.

   _____

30. $3\frac{1}{5} + 4\frac{3}{10}$

What is the sum written in simplest form?

   _____

31. What is the fraction equal to the whole number 7?

   a. $\frac{1}{7}$ b. $\frac{2}{7}$

   c. $\frac{7}{1}$ d. 14

   _____

32. What is the best estimate for

$\frac{5}{6} - \frac{1}{8}$?

   _____

33. Write a fraction equivalent to $\frac{9}{5}$.

   _____

34. $\frac{6}{4} - \frac{1}{3}$

What is the difference written in simplest form?

_____

35. | Sylvia worked $4\frac{7}{10}$ hours to build a stool. Tim worked $8\frac{2}{5}$ hours to build a chair. How much longer did Tim work? |

A student said that the answer to the problem was about 4 h. Was the student right?

a. Yes.

b. No, the problem says Tim worked more than 8 h.

c. No, Sylvia worked almost 5 h and Tim about 8, so the answer is about 13 h.

d. No, it's a little more than 4 h because $\frac{7}{10} > \frac{2}{5}$.

_____

36. Before New Year's Eve, there was $5\frac{7}{8}$ in. of snow on the ground. On New Year's Eve, it snowed $\frac{11}{15}$ in. On New Year's Day, $\frac{2}{5}$ in. melted. How much snow was left on the ground?

_____

37. **SCHEDULE OF SATURDAY ACTIVITIES**

1:00 PM	Swimming, Volley Ball
2:00 PM	Pottery, Weaving
3:30 PM	Candle Making, Macrame, Making Model Cars

If a student wants to sign up for an activity at each of the times scheduled, how many different combinations of activity are possible?

_____

38. How much change should you receive from a $20 bill if you bought two items at $1.69 each and two items at $5.98 each?

_____

39. $3\frac{4}{5} - 1\frac{4}{10}$

What is the difference written in simplest form?

_____

40. $x - 2\frac{1}{3} = 4\frac{1}{2}$

Solve the equation.

_____

PRETEST   Chapter 6 Page 1

1. $\frac{2}{3} \times \frac{3}{5}$

_____

2. Write $\frac{3}{100}$ as a decimal.

_____

3. What is the best estimate for

$\frac{9}{10} \times 2\frac{2}{5}$?

_____

4. $\frac{3}{4} \div 3$

_____

5. Write 1.5 as a mixed number.

_____

6. Jenny paints signs. Each sign takes $2\frac{1}{2}$ gal. of paint. She has 7 gal. of paint to use. How many complete signs can she paint?

_____

7. In a band, $\frac{2}{3}$ of the members are boys and $\frac{1}{4}$ of these have blue eyes. What fraction of the band members are boys with blue eyes?

_____

8. What is the best estimate for

$3\frac{7}{8} \times 5\frac{1}{6}$?

_____

9. $1\frac{7}{8} \times \frac{4}{5}$

_____

10. If $\frac{1}{4}x = \frac{1}{3}$, what is x?

_____

11. Write $\frac{1}{5}$ as a decimal.

_____

12. Write $\frac{1}{3}$ as a decimal.

_____

13. $1\frac{1}{10} \div 1\frac{4}{5}$

_____

14. $2\frac{1}{2} \times 3\frac{1}{4}$

_____

PRETEST   **Chapter 6 Page 2**

Use this information for <u>questions 15 and 16.</u>

A high school is planning a paper drive in the community to recycle scrap newspapers and magazines. A scout troop will furnish pick-up trucks to collect the paper.

15. Which question is <u>not</u> important for the planners to answer?

   a. How much will they get paid for the recycled paper?
   b. How many people will be needed to ride in the trucks?
   c. How much does it cost to subscribe to a news magazine?
   d. How many trucks are needed?

_____

16. Which question is important for the planners to answer?

   a. How much will it cost to advertise the paper drive?
   b. How many people subscribe to magazines?
   c. How many pages are there in the average newspaper?
   d. What color are the trucks?

_____

17. What is the best estimate for $1\frac{1}{7} \times 9\frac{6}{7}$?

_____

18. Write $\frac{1}{4}$ as a decimal.

_____

Use this information for <u>questions 19 to 22.</u>

One batch of gold alloy can be made from the following three metals.

     gold — $5\frac{1}{2}$ pounds
  copper — $2\frac{3}{4}$ pounds
   silver — $1\frac{1}{8}$ pounds

19. How much copper is needed for $2\frac{1}{2}$ batches of alloy?

_____

20. How much silver is needed for $\frac{1}{3}$ batch of alloy?

_____

21. How many batches of alloy could be made with $8\frac{1}{4}$ pounds of gold?

_____

22. If three people each gave an equal amount of gold for one batch of alloy, how much would each person give?

_____

23. Write a fraction in simplest form that is equivalent to 0.8.

_____

24. What is the best estimate for $3\frac{1}{4} \times 8\frac{1}{3}$?

_____

25. $15 \times \frac{3}{5}$

_____

26. There are 140 children going on a field trip. Each bus can hold 40 children. How many buses are needed?

_____

27. Which product is closest to 42?

   a. $7\frac{1}{12} \times 5\frac{9}{10}$ b. $7\frac{1}{4} \times 5\frac{1}{8}$

   c. $7\frac{3}{4} \times 5\frac{5}{6}$ d. $7\frac{5}{6} \times 5\frac{3}{4}$

_____

28. If $\frac{3}{4}w = \frac{6}{8}$, what is w?

_____

29. Write 0.35 as a fraction in simplest form.

_____

30. $\frac{2}{5} \div \frac{3}{5}$

_____

Use this information for questions 31 and 32.

   Jim and Joan are doing the advertising for a school's band concert.

31. Which question is not important for them to answer?

   a. How much will it cost to light the concert?

   b. How much will it cost to print posters?

   c. How much radio advertising time will be donated?

   d. How soon should advertising begin?

_____

32. Which question is important for them to answer?

    a. Will the local newspaper review the concert?

    b. How much does advertising cost on radio and TV?

    c. How much does the music cost for the band to use?

    d. Will the concert be taped for future broadcast?

    _____

33. If $\frac{2}{5}x + 2 = 3\frac{9}{10}$, what is x?

    _____

34. Write 0.89 as a fraction.

    _____

35. A skydivers club has $18\frac{1}{2}$ m of silk to make parachutes. Each parachute requires $3\frac{1}{2}$ m of silk. How many parachutes can they make?

    _____

36. Write $\frac{7}{6}$ as a decimal.

    _____

37. Sue has $5\frac{1}{2}$ hours to conduct job interviews for a restaurant. Each interview takes $\frac{3}{4}$ hour. How many interviews can she conduct?

    _____

38. Write a decimal that is equivalent to $1\frac{3}{5}$.

    _____

39. Marie is working with tiles that are $\frac{2}{3}$ of a foot long. If they are laid end to end, how many of the tiles will fit in $9\frac{1}{3}$ feet?

    _____

40. If $\frac{3}{4}x + \frac{2}{3} = 1\frac{1}{3}$, what is x?

    _____

PRETEST **Chapter 7 Page 1**

1. Which of the following is the best estimate for the weight of a bookbag with 3 school books in it?

   a. 8 oz   **b.** 8 lb
   c. 80 lb   **d.** 8 T

   _____

2.   13 lb   9 oz
   + 7 lb   12 oz

   _____

3. What is $2\frac{1}{2}$ pounds expressed as ounces?

   _____

Questions 4 to 7 are based on the following diagram.

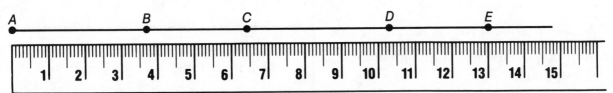

4. What is the distance from *A* to *C* to the nearest millimeter?

   _____

5. What are the two line segments that are closest to 4.0 cm in length?

   _____

6. What is the distance from *C* to *E* to the nearest centimeter?

   _____

7. What are the two points that are 93 mm apart?

   _____

8.   13 h   20 min
   − 11 h   22 min

   _____

9. Which of the measurements are equal?

   0.0025 kL   2.5 L   2,500 mL

        I   II   III

   _____

Name _____ Date _____

Questions 10 and 11 are based on the following information.

**AVERAGE TEMPERATURE ON
THE LAST DAY OF EACH MONTH**

Month	Jul	Aug	Sept	Oct	Nov	Dec
Temperature (°C):	25.1	31.5	21.6	15.8	5.6	8.6

10. How much warmer was it on August 31 than on September 30?

_____

11. How much colder was it on November 30 than on July 31?

_____

Questions 12 and 13 are based on the following information.

**AVERAGE TEMPERATURE ON
THE FIRST DAY OF EACH MONTH**

Month	Jan	Feb	Mar	Apr	May	Jun
Temperature (°F):	22	12	25	42	55	68

12. How much colder was it on March 1 than on April 1?

_____

13. How much colder was it on February 1 than on May 1?

_____

14. How many hours are there in $2\frac{1}{2}$ days?

_____

15.   6 h   47 min
    + 3 h   15 min

_____

16. What is 3.25 cm expressed as millimeters?

_____

17. Sue drove 25 miles in 30 minutes. At that speed, how long would it take her to drive 60 miles?

_____

RETEST   Chapter 7 Page 3

Use the following map for <u>questions 18</u> <u>to 21.</u>

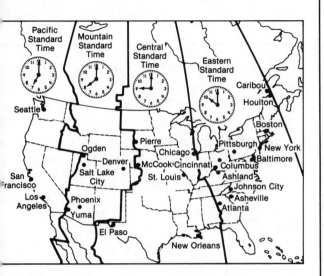

18. If it is 8:00 PM in Atlanta, in which two of the following cities is it 5:00 PM?

a. Denver and Yuma
b. Boston and New York
c. San Francisco and Seattle
d. Chicago and El Paso

_____

19. A plane departs from Chicago at 10:15 AM and arrives in Los Angeles at 12:30 PM. How long was the flight?

_____

20. What time is it in Denver when it is 6:30 PM in New York?

_____

21. A bus leaves San Francisco at 7:50 AM and arrives in Los Angeles at 4:15 PM. How long was the trip?

_____

22.   2 ft   7 in.
    +5 ft   6 in.

_____

23. A plane can fly 1,500 miles in 3 hours. How long would it take to fly 400 miles?

_____

24. What is the appropriate customary unit for measuring the width of a television screen?

_____

25. A cassette tape can record $1\frac{1}{2}$ h of music. A 20-minute song and a 15-minute song have been recorded. How much time is left on the tape?

_____

26. Brendan takes the bus from New York City at 8:42 AM on a trip to Buffalo, N.Y. The bus arrives in Buffalo at 3:51 PM. How long is the trip?

_____

27.   8 yd   1 ft
    − 5 yd   2 ft

_____

28. Hurricane Ann is traveling 12 miles in 45 min. If it maintains its average speed, how long will it take to travel 80 miles?

_____

29.   15 lb   3 oz
    − 14 lb   12 oz
    _____

_____

30. What is the appropriate metric unit for measuring the mass of a stereo radio headset?

_____

_____

Questions 31 to 34 are based on the information in the table.

BUS SCHEDULE (CENTRAL TIME ZONE)

City	Departure	City	Arrival
Mem City	6:45 AM	Hurkle	11:30 AM
Port Game	10:15 AM	Mount Disky	3:30 PM
Hurkle	11:45 AM	Chipville	12:35 PM
Port Game	7:05 AM	Lovesville	11:55 PM

31. How long does it take to travel from Mem City to Hurkle?

_____

32. How long does it take to travel from Port Game to Lovesville?

_____

33. How long does it take to travel from Port Game to Mount Disky?

_____

34. How long does it take to travel from Hurkle to Chipville?

_____

35. Jake jogs $4\frac{1}{5}$ miles per hour. How long would it take him to jog 21 miles?

_____ ____

36. What is 18 in. expressed in yards?

_____

_____

37. Which of the following is the best estimate for the width of a school's stage?

   a. 30 mm   **b.** 30 dm
   c. 30 m   **d.** 30 km

_____

_____

38. Sue walked 2 miles in $\frac{1}{3}$ hour. What was her average speed?

_____

_____

39. Jim drove from Sacramento, California, to San Francisco, California, in $1\frac{1}{2}$ h. His average speed was 52 mph. How far is it from Sacramento to San Francisco?

_____

_____

40. Jerry took the bus on a trip from Richmond, Virginia, to Knoxville, Tennessee, a distance of 457 mi. The trip took $8\frac{1}{2}$ h. What was the average speed of the bus?

Which part of the formula $d = rt$ should you solve for?

   a. rate
   b. time
   c. distance
   d. none of the above

_____

PRETEST   **Chapter 8 Page 1**

1. Solve the proportion. $\frac{6}{8}=\frac{x}{4}$

   _____

2. Write $\frac{80}{100}$ as a percent.

   _____

3. What percent of 100 is 4?

   _____

4. Two rolls of wallpaper cover 56 square feet. Paul's room has 280 square feet of wall to be covered. How many rolls of wallpaper does he need?

   _____

5. Solve the proportion. $\frac{6}{x}=\frac{3}{5}$

   _____

6. Write 0.25 as a percent.

   _____

7. In a scale drawing an object has a width of 7 cm. What is the actual width of the object if the scale is 1 cm = 4 m?

   _____

8. In the proportion $\frac{n}{100}=\frac{16}{20}$, what is the value of n?

   _____

9. If 70% of a number is 140, what is the number?

   _____

10. During a "$5.00 off" sale, what is the percent of decrease on a $20.00 item?

   _____

11. What is 40% of 200?

   _____

12. Jason wants to buy a camera that costs $140. If he borrows the money at a yearly interest rate of 18%, how much interest will he owe for a 2-year period?

   _____

13. 63 is 63% of what number?

   _____

PRETEST   **Chapter 8 Page 2**

14. A scale drawing of a bookshelf is 2.8 cm long. Using the scale 1 cm = 0.5 m, what is the actual length of the bookshelf?

_____

15. What percent of 80 is 40?

_____

16. Write 13.4% as a decimal.

_____

17. The price of an item decreased from $300 to $240. What is the percent of decrease?

_____

18. If 10% of *n* is 6.4, what is *n*?

_____

19. Troy borrowed money to buy a videocassette recorder. The loan was for 4 years at a yearly rate of 20%. If the interest on the loan was $350, how much did the recorder cost?

_____

20. Write 4% as a fraction.

_____

Use the circle graph for <u>questions 21 to 24.</u>

21. The least amount of money was spent on which category?

_____

22. Which pair of items accounts for more than half the cost of the party?

    a. invitations and food
    b. prizes and favors
    c. invitations and favors
    d. invitations and prizes

_____

23. How much money was spent on prizes if the party cost $120?

_____

24. If the party cost $120, which items cost more than $50?

    I. Food   II. Prizes   III. Favors

    a. I only   b. III only
    c. I and II   d. None

_____

25. In the proportion $\frac{3}{7} = \frac{7}{n}$, what is the value of n?

_____

26. A recipe calling for 3 eggs will serve 8 people. In order to serve 24 people, how many eggs will be needed?

_____

27. If the price of a ticket increased from $4.00 to $5.00, what is the percent of the increase?

_____

28. A student is making a larger copy of a chart. The original chart is 2.5 inches wide and 6 inches long. If the copy is to be 25 inches long, which proportion would be used to find the new width in inches?

a. $\frac{2.5}{6} = \frac{25}{x}$

b. $\frac{6}{25} = \frac{x}{2.5}$

c. $\frac{2.5}{6} = \frac{x}{25}$

d. $\frac{2.5}{25} = \frac{6}{x}$

_____

29. A wrestling team sold $224 worth of hoagies. The team receives 30% of the hoagie sales. How much does the team receive?

_____

30. What is 2.1% of 294?

_____

31. If 8 of every 20 students are girls, what percent are girls?

_____

32. In a fish tank, 55 ft³ of water are needed for every 3 fish. To find how many fish can be kept in a tank holding 2,145 ft³ of water, we could use the proportion

a. $\frac{3}{55} = \frac{x}{2,145}$ b. $\frac{3}{55} = \frac{2,145}{x}$

c. $\frac{3}{x} = \frac{2,145}{55}$ d. $\frac{3}{2,145} = \frac{x}{55}$

_____

33. A library ordered 40 magazines. If 15% are news magazines, how many news magazines did the library order?

_____

34. Given the scale 3 cm = 2 m, how long is the scale drawing of an object with an actual length of 15 m?

_____

PRETEST   Chapter 8 Page 4

35. 15 new students enter a school which already has 300 students. What is the percent of increase of students?

_____

36. What percent of 24 is 60?

_____

37. What is 116% of 200?

_____

38. On a town map two buildings are drawn 5 cm apart. If the actual buildings are 20 m apart, what does 1 cm on the map represent?

_____

39. Alice is buying a boat that costs $9,000. She is borrowing the money from a bank and will have to pay $3,000 in interest over a two-year period. What is the annual interest rate?

_____

40. If 110% of a number is 99, what is the number?

_____

Name _____ Date _____

1.

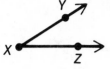

What is a name for the angle shown?

_____

2.

I   II   III

Which line segments are congruent?

_____

3. If the measure of two angles of a triangle are 45° and 55°, what is the measure of the third angle?

_____

Use the following figures for questions 4 and 5.

Figure A   Figure B

Figure C   Figure D

4. Which figure shows perpendicular lines?

_____

5. Which figure shows parallel lines?

_____

6.

Which of the following labels would apply to this triangle?

I	II	III
acute	right	isosceles

_____

7.

The center of this circle is *B*. Which line segment is a diameter?

_____

8.

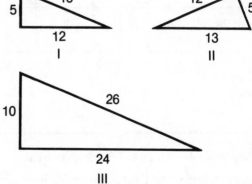

I   II

III

Which figures are congruent?

_____

9.

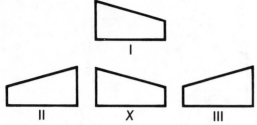

Which of the above are reflections of figure *X*?

_____

10.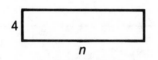

The polygons are similar. What is *n*?

_____

11. How many diagonals can be drawn from one vertex in an octagon?

Complete the table to help you.

Sides	4	5	6			
Diagonals from one vertex	1	2	3			

_____

12. This year there are 75 people in a band. Last year there were 15 less than $\frac{2}{3}$ this number. How many were in the band last year?

_____

Use this figure to answer questions 13 and 14.

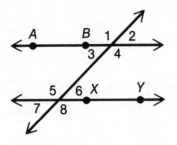

$\overleftrightarrow{AB}$ is parallel to $\overleftrightarrow{XY}$.

13. Name an angle to which $\angle 1$ is congruent.

_____

14. Name an angle to which $\angle 2$ is supplementary.

_____

15.

I   A   II

III

Which of the above could be a result of a translation of figure *A*?

_____

16.

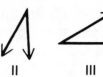

I   II   III

Which angles are congruent?

_____

17.

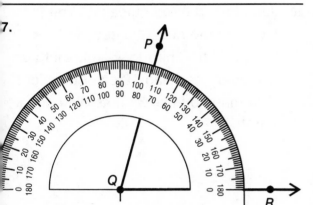

What is the measurement of ∠PQR?

_____

Use the figures below for questions 18 and 19.

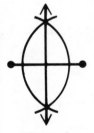

Figure A

Figure B

Figure C   Figure D

18. Which figure shows a construction of the bisector of an angle?

_____

19. Which figure shows a construction of a bisector of a line segment?

_____

Use this figure to answer questions 20 and 21.

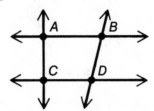

20. Name a pair of parallel lines in the figure.

_____

21. Name a pair of perpendicular lines in the figure.

_____

22.

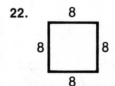

How many lines of symmetry does this figure have?

_____

23. A living room is 12 ft wide and 20 ft long. If its width in a scale drawing is 3 cm, what is its length in the drawing?

_____

24. Which figure shows a construction of a line segment congruent to •————• ?

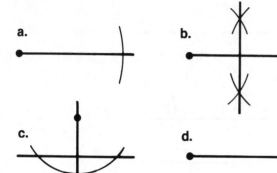

a.

b.

c.

d.

_____

Use this information for <u>questions 25 to 27.</u>

If an even number of equilateral triangles are drawn in a row, the result is a parallelogram.

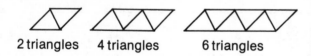

2 triangles   4 triangles   6 triangles

25. If the side of each triangle is 1 cm, how long is the top of the parallelogram if 12 triangles are drawn in a row?

_____

26. If the side of each triangle is 1 cm, how long is the top of the parallelogram if 20 triangles are drawn in a row?

_____

27. If the side of each triangle is 4 cm, how long is the top of the parallelogram if 20 triangles are drawn in a row?

_____

28. Juan baked three nutcakes. The first took $\frac{1}{4}$ of the nuts, the second took 3 oz, and the third took $\frac{2}{3}$ of what was left. Juan then had 12 oz of nuts left. How many ounces of nuts did he start with?

_____

29. If the measurements of two angles of a triangle are 110° and 30°, what is the measurement of the third angle?

_____

30.

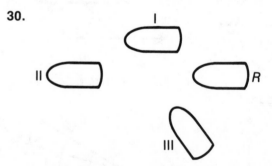

Which of the above are rotations of figure *R*?

_____

31. Which of the following shows the construction of an angle congruent to a given angle?

a.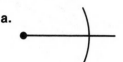

b.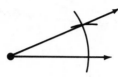

c.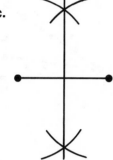

d.

_____

32.

Name this figure.

_____

33.

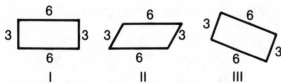

I   II   III

Which figures are congruent?

_____

34. Which figure shows a ray?

a.    b.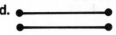

c.   d.

_____

_____

35. In which figure does $\overleftrightarrow{CD}$ bisect $\overline{AB}$?

a. 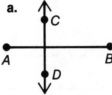   b.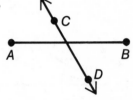

c. 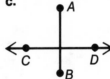   d.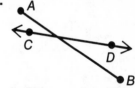

_____

36.

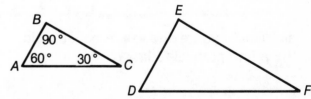

The triangles are similar. What is the measure of ∠F?

_____

37

37.

Which names describes this figure?

square	rectangle	parallelogram
I	II	III

_____

Use the following figures for <u>questions 38 and 39.</u>

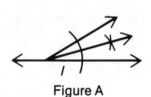

Figure A   Figure B

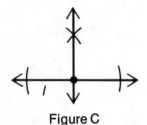

Figure C   Figure D

38. Which figure shows the construction of a line perpendicular to line *l*?

_____

39. Which figure shows the construction of a line parallel to line *l*?

_____

40. This year 60 people graduated. Last year there were 5 less than $\frac{4}{5}$ this number. How many graduated last year?

_____

41. In which figure does $\overrightarrow{SU}$ bisect $\angle RST$?

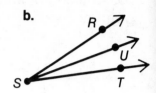

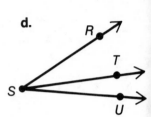

_____

42.

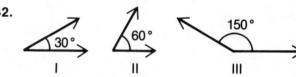

Which pair of angles is complementary?

_____

43.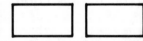

In the row of houses shown, the front of each house is 45 feet wide and the distance between the houses is 5 feet. What is the length of the row?

_____

44.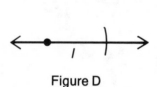

What is the name of this figure?

_____

45.

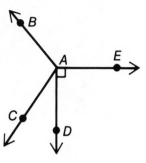

Which angle is acute?

_____

46.

Which of the following labels would apply to this triangle?

I	II	III
equilateral	obtuse	isosceles

_____

47.

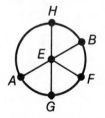

Which segments are chords?

_____

48. Which figure has exactly 2 lines of symmetry?

a.

b.

c.

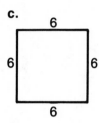

d.

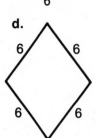

_____

49. A computer desk is 3 m long by 1.5 m wide. If a scale drawing of the desk is 150 mm long, how wide is the desk in the drawing?

_____

50. Which of the following figures are reflections of figure A?

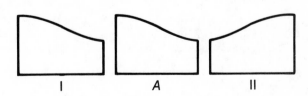

_____

PRETEST   **Chapter 9 Page 8**

51. Mrs. Schwartz bought three gifts. The first cost $\frac{1}{4}$ of her money, the second cost $12, and the third cost half of what was left. She has $60 after buying all three gifts. How much money did she start with?

_____

52.

The two triangles are similar. What is the measure of $\angle B$?

_____

PRETEST Chapter 10 Page 1

1.

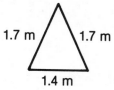

What is the perimeter of the triangle?

_____

2. A world's fair was built in the shape of a square with a measure of 5 km on each side. Joe entered the fair at the center of the south side and walked 1 km due north. Then he walked 1.5 km due east and then 2 km due north. How far is he from the eastern border at that point?

_____

3.

What is the name of this figure?

_____

4. What is the perimeter of a square whose side is 3.1 cm?

_____

5. What is the area of a parallelogram whose base is 3 cm and height is 9 cm?

_____

6.

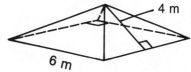

What is the total surface area of this square pyramid?

_____

7. Eva has 37 m of fence to put around a rectangular garden that is 12 m long and 5 m wide. How much fence will be left?

_____

8. The product of the page numbers of the last two pages in a recipe booklet is 420. How many pages are in the booklet?

_____

9. What is the circumference of a circle whose radius is 20 cm? (Use 3.14 for π.)

_____

10. What is the area of a square with a side of 3 ft?

_____

11. What is the volume of a rectangular prism that is 10 cm long, 2.5 cm wide, and 4 cm high?

_____

12.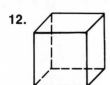

What is the name of this figure?

_____

13.

What is the perimeter of this polygon?

_____

14. A band rehearses 5 days each week for $1\frac{1}{2}$ hours each day. A drama club rehearses 1 day each week for $3\frac{1}{2}$ hours. The band rehearses about how many times as long each week as the drama club?

_____

15.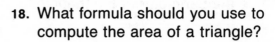

What is the name of this figure?

_____

16. Which represents the area of a circle with a radius of 13 m? (Use 3.14 for π.)

     a. 3.14×13 **b.** $2 \times 3.14 \times 13$
     c. $3.14 \times 3.14 \times 13$ **d.** $3.14 \times 13 \times 13$

_____

17. The area of a rectangular stamp is 432 mm². It is three times as long as it is wide. How wide is it?

_____

18. What formula should you use to compute the area of a triangle?

_____

19.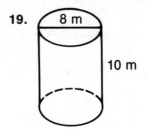

What is the surface area of this cylinder? Use 3.14 for π.

_____

20. What is the volume of a cube with an edge of 3 ft?

_____

21. Jack's poster is a square with a side of 2 ft. Roy's poster is a square with a side of 5 ft. The area of Roy's poster is about how many times as large as that of Jack's?

_____

Name _____ Date _____

22. A park has the shape of a square with 52 m on each side. The city wants to construct a walkway around the park 1 m wide. What will be the area of the park and the walkway together?

_____

23. A circular park has a diameter of 10 mi. A rectangular park is 3 mi long and 2 mi wide.

Which of the following plans will determine how many times larger the area of the circular park is than that of the rectangular park? (Use 3.14 for π.)

$C = 3.14 \times 5 \times 5$ $R = 3 \times 2$ Answer is $R \div C$	$C = 3.14 \times 5 \times 5$ $R = 3 \times 2$ Answer is $C - R$	$C = 3.14 \times 5 \times 5$ $R = 3 \times 2$ Answer is $C \div R$
Plan I	**Plan II**	**Plan III**

_____

24. What is the area of a trapezoid which has bases of 6 cm and 8 cm and a height of 4 cm?

_____

25.

6 cm

Which is a way to determine the perimeter of the square in this figure?

a. 4×6 b. 6×6
c. 4×12 d. 12×12

_____

26.

What is the name of this figure?

_____

27. What is the area of a rectangle with length 6 ft and width 4 ft?

_____

28. If a triangle has a base of 7 cm and a height of 9 cm, what is the area?

_____

29. The perimeter of a rectangular painting is 24 in. It is 2 in. longer than it is wide. How long is it?

_____

30. The product of the ages of 2 brothers is 32. One brother is 4 years older than the other. How old is the younger brother?

_____

31. A family bought a 15 ft by 9 ft rug for their living room. The length of the floor is 18 ft and the width is 12 ft. What is the area of the floor not covered by the rug?

_____

32. What formula should you use to compute the volume of a cube?

_____

_____

33. A circle has a diameter of 10 ft. What is the circumference? (Use $\frac{22}{7}$ for π.)

_____

_____

34. If a rectangle has a length of 4 m and a width of 2 m, what is its perimeter?

_____

35.

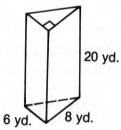

20 yd.

6 yd.   8 yd.

What is the volume of this figure?

_____

36.

14 in.

What is the area of the circle in this figure? (Use $\frac{22}{7}$ for π.)

_____

37.

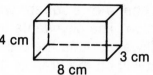

4 cm

8 cm   3 cm

What is the surface area of this prism?

_____

38. A town decided to use rectangular blocks to cover a sidewalk measuring 90 ft by 8 ft. The length of a block is 1 ft and the width is $\frac{1}{2}$ ft. How many blocks are needed to cover the sidewalk?

_____

39.

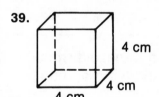

4 cm

4 cm

4 cm

What is the surface area of this prism?

_____

40.

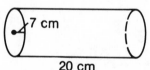

7 cm

20 cm

What is the volume of this cylinder? (Use $\frac{22}{7}$ for π.)

_____

Name _____ Date _____

1. A number cube has the numbers 1, 2, 3, 4, 5, and 6 on the six faces. You are going to toss the cube once. What is the probability of tossing a number greater than 2?

_____

2. What is the mean of 6, 0, 5, 7?

_____

3.

EARLY AMERICAN POPULATION ESTIMATES	
Year	Population
1750	1,200,000
1760	1,600,000
1770	2,100,000
1780	2,800,000

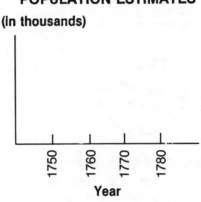

EARLY AMERICAN POPULATION ESTIMATES
(In thousands)

A broken-line graph has been started. Which of the following is a correct way to label the vertical axis?

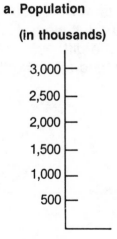
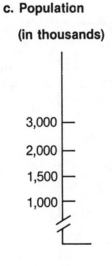
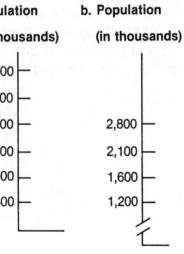

a. Population (in thousands)

3,000 —
2,500 —
2,000 —
1,500 —
1,000 —
500 —

b. Population (in thousands)

2,800 —
2,100 —
1,600 —
1,200 —

c. Population (in thousands)

3,000 —
2,000 —
1,500 —
1,000 —

d. Population (in thousands)

4 —
3 —
2 —
1 —

_____

4.

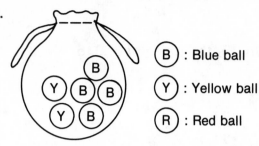

B : Blue ball
Y : Yellow ball
R : Red ball

Jesse will choose a ball from the bag without looking. What is P(red)?

_____

5.

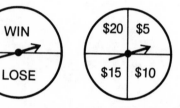

Ramona spins each spinner once. Which of the following is a possible outcome of her spins?

a. WIN, LOSE   b. WIN, $25
c. LOSE, $15   d. $5, $15

_____

6. Three cards with the digits 1 to 3 on them are mixed in a box. Without looking, you are going to pick one card and replace it. Then you are going to pick another card. What is the probability of picking a card with a 2 on it followed by a card with a 3 on it?

_____

7.

| A | B | C | D | E |

The cards above are turned over to their blank side and mixed. Melody picks the card that has C on it. She keeps the card. What is the probability that the next card Melody picks will have B on it?

_____

8.   2, 8, 7, 8, 4, 1

The median of the set of data above is

_____

9. A grab bag has gifts that all look the same. There are 6 gifts worth $0.50, 4 gifts worth $0.75, and 1 gift worth $1.00. If you choose one gift, what is the probability of selecting a gift worth $1.00?

_____

PRETEST   **Chapter 11 Page 3**

Use the following graphs for <u>questions 10 to 13.</u>

TOY DEPARTMENT SALES AT HARVEY'S AND CONNOR'S

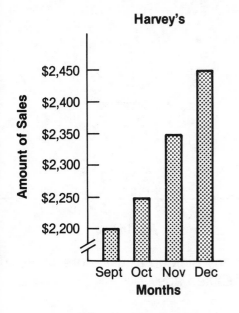

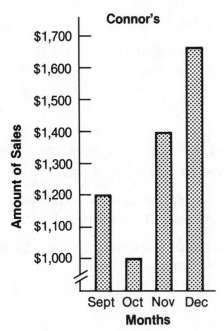

10. What was the total amount of toy sales in both stores in December?

_____

11. The least amount of toy sales was in what month at what store?

_____

12. How much money was spent on toys at Connor's in October?

_____

13. In how many of the months shown were Connor's toy sales higher than Harvey's?

_____

14. The tree diagram below shows the possible outcomes of the first two games of the Rhinos' season

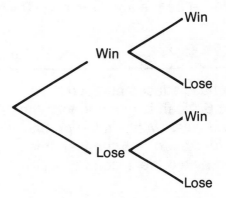

How many possible outcomes are there?

_____

15. There are 7 boys and 3 girls who help in the library. Their names are written on slips of paper and put in a box. Mrs. Williams is going to choose one name, not replace it and then choose another name. What is the probability that the first chosen is a boy and the second chosen is a girl?

_____

Use the following table for questions 16 and 17.

LENGTHS OF CROCODILES (IN FEET)			
Interval	Tally	Frequency	Relative Frequency
0–4	IIII	4	
5–9	III	3	
_____	II	2	
15–19	I	1	
TOTAL		10	

16. What is the missing interval?

_____

17. The relative frequency for interval 0-4 is

_____

18. A cube has its faces numbered 1 through 6. Noah is going to toss the cube two times. What is the probability he will toss a 4 or a 5 the first time followed by a 6 the second time?

_____

19. There are 1 white, 2 black, and 2 yellow balls in a bag. Without looking, you are going to choose a ball. What is P(not white)?

_____

Use the following scattergram for questions 20 to 23.

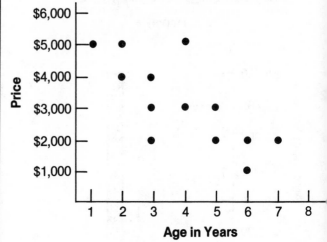

AGES AND SELLING PRICES OF PICK-UP TRUCKS AS FOUND IN CLASSIFIED ADS

20. How many pick-up trucks were found in the classified ads?

_____

21. What is the range of prices of pick-up trucks found in the classified ads?

_____

22. Which of the following can be concluded from the scattergram?

   I. The pick-up trucks less than 3 years old were selling for at least $4,000.

   II. The price of the oldest pick-up truck was the lowest.

_____

23. According to the scattergram, as the age of the trucks increases the price of the trucks

_____

24. Mister Shoes sold 6 pairs of shoes one day. The sizes sold were 12, 8, 9, 6, 9, 7. What was the mode of the sizes?

_____

25.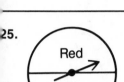

Spinner 1   Spinner 2

The probability of spinning a red on spinner 1 and a Y on spinner 2 can be found using

a. P(red)·P(Y)
b. P(red) + P(Y)
c. P(red) + P(Y after red)
d. P(red)·P(Y after red)

_____

26. A coin is tossed that can land heads or tails. Then a cube with the letters a, b, c, d, e, and f on it is tossed. Which ordered pairs are needed to complete the list of possible outcomes?

(H,a) (H,b) (H,c) (H,d) (H,e) (T,a) (T,b) (T,c) (T,d)

_____

27.

| A | B | C | D | E |

A large prize is behind one of the doors above. Carol picks door C and it is not there. Next she picks door D and it is not there. She is going to pick one more door. What is the probability that she will pick the door with the large prize?

_____

28. $0.65 $1.03 $0.18 $0.35 $0.45 $0.35

Several students counted the money they had in coins. The results are shown above. What is the range of the amounts they had?

_____

29. Barrels of Oil Produced in 1983

Region	Number of Barrels (in trillion)
North & South America	6
Europe	2
Middle East	4
Africa	2
Asia	1
Russia and China	5
	20

In a circle graph showing this information, what is the central angle for the part representing the Middle East?

_____

30.

You are going to spin the spinner two times. What is the probability that the sum of the two spins is 2?

_____

31. For a code, any of 8 different digits can be used in the first position and any of 4 different letters in the second position. How many different codes are possible?

_____

32. A bowl contains 4 red balls and 2 blue balls. Without looking, you are going to pick one ball from the bowl and not replace it. If you then pick a second ball, what is P(red, then red)?

_____

Name _____ Date _____

For questions 1 and 2, use the number line.

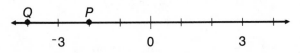

1. Write an integer for the point *P* on the number line.

   _____

2. Write an integer for the point *Q* on the number line.

   _____

3. $^-5 \cdot 3$

   _____

4. It was 18°F below zero in International Falls, Minnesota, on a day when it was 72°F above zero in Tampa, Florida. Write an equation that could he used to find the difference in temperatures.

   _____

5. $^-7 + ^-2$

   _____

Use the graph for questions 6 and 7.

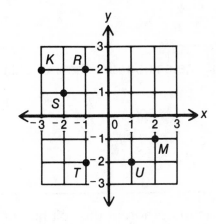

6. Which point is located at $(1, ^-2)$?

   _____

7. What are ordered pairs for points *K* and *M*?

   _____

8. Which number makes the following statement true?

   $x < ^-5$

   a. $^-8$ b. $^-3$
   c. 2   d. 7

   _____

PRETEST   **Chapter 12 Page 2**

9. If $y = 4x - 3$ and $x = {}^-2$, what is y?

_____

10. What is the solution for the inequality $\frac{x}{3} > 12$?

_____

11. Which is the graph of the solution of $x - 2 = {}^-4$?

a.
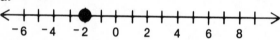

b.
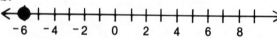

c.
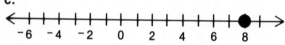

d.
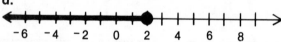

_____

12. A building has 30 floors above ground and 2 floors below ground. Jocelyn got on an elevator in the building on the 21st floor. She got off 7 floors down. What floor did she get off on?

_____

13. $({}^-1,0)$ $(0,1)$ $(1,2)$

The ordered pairs are solutions for $y = x + 1$. Which of the following is the graph for the equation?

a.
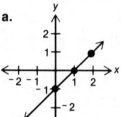

b.
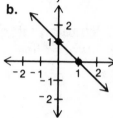

c.
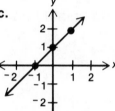

d.
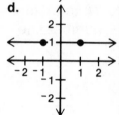

_____

14. An equivalent expression for ${}^-6 - 5$ is

_____

15. $24 \div {}^-4$

_____

16. If $12 + x = {}^-2$, what is x?

_____

Name _____ Date _____

PRETEST   **Chapter 12 Page 3**

17. If $3y = {}^-9$, what is y?

_____

18. Write the letter of the <u>opposite</u> of $^-4$ on the number line.

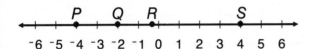

_____

19. Mt. Everest is 29,028 feet above sea level. The Dead Sea is 1,296 feet below sea level. What is the difference in altitude of these two points?

_____

20.

x	4	2	0	$^-2$
y	11	5	$^-1$	$^-7$

The table shown is for the equation $y = 3x - 1$.

What are four solutions for the equation?

_____

_____

21. $^-5 + 23$

_____

22.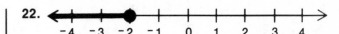

The graph above shows the solution of which inequality?

a. $x > 2$ b. $x < 2$
c. $x \geq {}^-2$ d. $x \leq {}^-2$

_____

23.

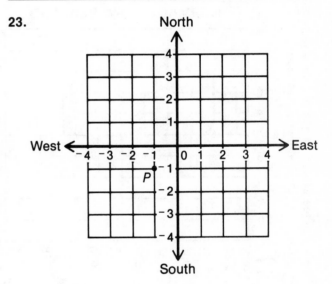

In the graph, what is the ordered pair for the point 3 units north and 4 units east of point P?

_____

24. The graph of $y = {}^-3x - 2$ passes through which of these points?

I. $(0, {}^-5)$ II. $(^-1, {}^-5)$ III. $(1, {}^-5)$

a. I only   b. II only
c. III only   d. I, II, and III

_____

53

25.   4   ⁻3   8   ⁻9

What is the correct order of the numbers from the least to the greatest?

_____

_____

Use the graph below for <u>questions 26 to 29</u>

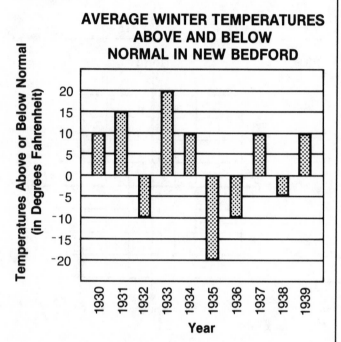

26. How many degrees above or below normal was the average temperature during the winter of 1936?

a. 20° below normal
b. 10° below normal
c. 10° above normal
d. 20° above normal

_____

_____

27. During which winter was the average temperature 20° above normal?

_____

28. Based on the average temperature, which winter was the coldest?

_____

_____

29. During which winter was the average temperature the closest to normal?

_____

_____

30. $x + 1 < {}^{-}4$ is true when x is any number less than what number?

_____

31.

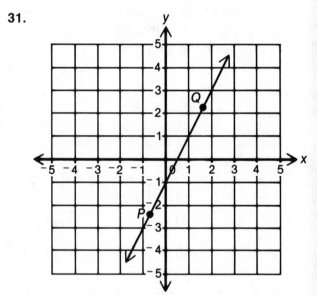

Which of these ordered pairs are on the line connecting points P and Q on the graph above?

I. $({}^{-}1, {}^{-}3)$ II. $(0, {}^{-}1)$ III. $(2, 3)$

a. I and II only   b. I and III only
c. II and III only   d. I, II, and III

_____

32. | Gary awakes to a chilling 5° below zero. During the morning the temperature drops 10° but then rises 15° in the afternoon. What is the temperature then?

Which of the following equations can be used to solve the problem above?

a. $n = {}^-5 + 10 + 15$ b. $n = ({}^-5 - 10) + 15$
c. $n = ({}^-5 + 10) - 15$ d. $n = ({}^-5 - 10) - 15$

_____

33. $^-6 \cdot {}^-3$

_____

34. The graph of the solution of $x \leq 3$ is

a.
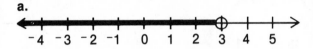

b.
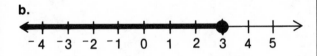

c.
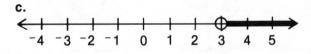

d.
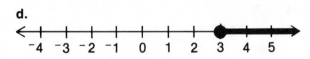

_____

35. What is the ordered pair 3 units above the origin in a coordinate plane?

_____

36. The table shown is for the equation $y = 2x + 3$.

x	2	0	$^-2$	$^-4$
y	7	3	$^-1$	n

What number should replace n in the table?

_____

_____

37. Write $<, >$, or $=$ to make the statement true.

$^-3 \bullet 2$

_____

_____

38.

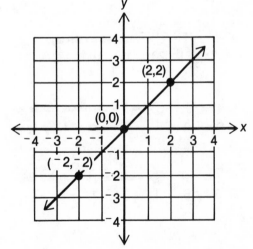

Which of the following equations is shown on the graph?

a. $y = x$ b. $y = {}^-x$
c. $y = x + 2$ d. $y = 2x$

_____

39. The table shown is for the equation $y = {}^-3x$.

x	$^-1$	0	1	2
y	3	0	m	n

What numbers should replace m and n in the table?

_____

40. Which is the graph of the solution of $4x > {}^-16$?

a.

b.

c.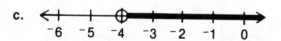

d.

_____

41.

What is the number that is 5 units to the left of $^-2$ on the number line?

_____

42.　　　　　　　　$^-12$　9　$^-10$　11

What is the correct order of the numbers from the greatest to the least?

_____

43. $7 - {}^-13$

_____

44. $\dfrac{^-8}{^-2} =$

_____

Pretest Answers

Chapter 1

Objective	Test Items	Text Pages
1A	1, 7, 17, 38	2–3, 20–21
1B	4, 14, 20, 27	2–3, 20–21
1C	5, 9, 22, 24	2–3, 20–21
1D	18, 29, 31, 40	4–5, 22–23
1E	2, 16, 21, 26	8, 24–25
1F	3, 6, 15, 23, 25, 28, 30, 32	14, 30–33
1G	8, 19, 33, 39	9–13, 28–29
1H	10, 11, 12, 13, 34, 35, 36, 37	34–35

Answers

1. 30,000,000,107,000 **2.** 384,000 **3.** 1,090,177
4. 68,030 **5.** 1 ten-thousandth **6.** $123.02
7. 497 billion, 6 thousand, 3 hundred
8. 50,000–60,000* **9.** 200,000,000,000 **10.** $65*
11. Model S **12.** Model R **13.** Model S
14. 6.0704 **15.** 237,613 **16.** 163.0 mph
17. 0.0003 **18.** 17,410,000 **19.** $150*
20. $1 + 0.09 + 0.0005 + 0.000008$ **21.** $1,284.00
22. 5 billion **23.** 456 **24.** 0.00009 **25.** 15,199
26. 20.85 **27.** $100,000 + 3,000 + 700 + 4$
28. $135.36 **29.** 5,099; 5,020; 5,010; 5,001
30. 174,702 **31.** Annapolis **32.** 2.85938 **33.** 5*
34. 7th Grade **35.** 75* **36.** 9th Grade **37.** 15
points* **38.** Forty-two and seven thousandths
39. $700.00* **40.** 27.003, 27.03, 27.3, 27.33

Chapter 2

Objective	Test Items	Text Pages
2A	1, 5, 8, 21, 23, 28	46–47, 50–51, 54–57
2B	2, 15, 26, 34	48–49, 58–59, 60–61
2C	3, 11, 19, 32	66–67
2D	6, 9, 12, 27	62–63
2E	14, 17, 29, 30	62–63, 68–69
2F	7, 18, 22, 31	52–53
2G	10, 13, 20, 25	64–65
2H	4, 16, 24, 33	70–71

Answers

1. $13,765.52 **2.** > **3.** 0.76 **4.** $50.00
5. 758,110 **6.** 99.53 **7.** The number of laps she
swims in a day **8.** 30,514,000 **9.** 31.868
10. subtraction **11.** $33.00 **12.** 31,498.032
13. multiplication **14.** 0.048 **15.** 200–400*
16. $2.96 **17.** 0.00024 **18.** $1.10 **19.** 4,001.73
20. addition **21.** 7 **22.** 1 cm **23.** 2,440,800
24. 189 pencils **25.** multiplication **26.** 15–20*
27. 21.60 **28.** $1,162.00 **29.** 0.0893 **30.** $7.99
31. the length of the lion **32.** 2,315 **33.** $0.24
34. 91×70

Chapter 3

Objective	Test Items	Text Pages
3A	2, 7, 8, 14	82–83, 88–89, 92–95
3B	3, 4, 9, 17, 20, 25, 29, 30	86–87, 90–91
3C	16, 10, 26, 32	102–103
3D	5, 12, 28, 34	98–99
3E	13, 15, 19, 31	104–105
3F	11, 27, 33, 36	96–97
3G	1, 6, 18, 35	100–101
3H	21, 22, 23, 24	108–109

Answers

1. C **2.** 906 **3.** 200⁺* **4.** 20* **5.** 3.02 **6.** D
7. 401 **8.** $70,002 **9.** $40–$50* **10.** 0.2055
11. C **12.** $40.47 **13.** 0.0547 **14.** 65 **15.** 90.6
16. 5.462 **17.** 300* **18.** 42 lb **19.** 78.7
20. $60⁺* **21.** Decatur and Dumaine **22.** R
23. 9 **24.** Orleans and Royal, or S **25.** 3
26. 0.7824 **27.** C **28.** 0.0024 **29.** $5,000⁺*
30. $3,000⁺* **31.** 267 **32.** 0.711 **33.** D
34. 2.73 **35.** 6 ft 2 in. **36.** C

Chapter 4

Objective	Test Items	Text Pages
4A	1, 9, 18, 27, 37	118–119
4B	3, 7, 17, 23	120–121
4C	2, 16, 33, 36	122–123
4D	4, 11, 15, 19, 26	130–133
4E	5, 25, 34, 38	136–137
4F	10, 20, 31, 35	138–139
4G	8, 21, 22, 32	140–141, 146–149
4H	12, 13, 28, 29	128–129, 142–143
4I	6, 14, 24, 30	150–151

Answers

1. 5,524 **2.** 6.89×10^2 **3.** 8 **4.** 10 **5.** 37
6. $x - \frac{1}{4}x = 9$, $\frac{3}{4}x = 9$, or an equivalent equation
7. $\sqrt{100}$ and 10 **8.** 14 **9.** 216, 702, and 156
10. 12 **11.** 192 or $2^6 \times 3$ **12.** $1,200* **13.** 100*
14. 225* **15.** 2 **16.** 650 **17.** 4 **18.** 5,000 and
27,640 **19.** 125 **20.** 11 **21.** 6 **22.** $3a - 5 = 7$ and
$3a = 12$ **23.** 12 **24.** A **25.** 5 **26.** 30 **27.** 9,119
28. 950 lb **29.** 500 lb **30.** 8 **31.** 10 **32.** 3
33. 7×10^4 **34.** 6 **35.** 43 **36.** 1,599,000
37. 3,018 **38.** 25

*Answers may vary. Accept any reasonable estimate.

*Answers may vary. Accept any reasonable estimate.

Chapter 5

Objective	Test Items	Text Pages
5A	1, 2, 13, 33	164–165
5B	3, 6, 14, 23	168–169
5C	5, 15, 28, 31	166–167
5D	4, 7, 11, 34	174–177
5E	22, 27, 30, 39	182–187
5F	10, 20, 29, 40	188–189
5G	12, 21, 24, 32	172–173
5H	16, 17, 25, 35	170–171
5I	8, 19, 26, 37	180–181
5J	9, 18, 36, 38	190–191

Answers

1. $\frac{3}{4}, \frac{12}{16}, \frac{15}{20}, \ldots$ **2.** B **3.** A **4.** $1\frac{3}{20}$ **5.** $1\frac{7}{8}$ **6.** C **7.** $\frac{1}{6}$
8. C **9.** D **10.** $\frac{2}{3}$ **11.** $\frac{5}{12}$ **12.** 5+* **13.** 8 **14.** $\frac{1}{2}, \frac{3}{4}, \frac{5}{6}$
15. $\frac{51}{5}$ **16.** yes **17.** $\frac{1}{10}$* **18.** C **19.** 6 **20.** $1\frac{2}{9}$
21. 1* **22.** $5\frac{8}{9}$ **23.** A **24.** 5* **25.** D **26.** 6 **27.** $11\frac{5}{12}$
28. 23 **29.** $1\frac{1}{2}$ **30.** $7\frac{1}{2}$ **31.** C **32.** 1* **33.** $\frac{18}{10}, \frac{27}{15}, \frac{36}{20}, \ldots$
34. $1\frac{1}{6}$ **35.** A **36.** $6\frac{5}{24}$ in. **37.** 12 **38.** $4.66 **39.** $2\frac{2}{5}$
40. $6\frac{5}{6}$

Chapter 6

Objective	Test Items	Text Pages
6A	1, 7, 9, 14, 25	200–203, 208–209
6B	4, 13, 30, 39	210–213
6C	5, 23, 29, 34	216–217
6D	2, 11, 12, 18, 36, 38	220–221
6E	10, 28, 33, 40	222–223
6F	3, 8, 17, 24,27	206–207
6G	15, 16, 31, 32	204–205
6H	19, 20, 21, 22	218–219
6I	6, 26, 35, 37	224–225

Answers

1. $\frac{2}{5}$ **2.** 0.03 **3.** 2* **4.** $\frac{1}{4}$ **5.** $1\frac{1}{2}$ **6.** 2 signs **7.** $\frac{1}{6}$
8. 20* **9.** $1\frac{1}{2}$ **10.** $1\frac{1}{3}$ **11.** 0.2 **12.** 0.3 **13.** $\frac{11}{18}$ **14.** $8\frac{1}{8}$
15. C **16.** A **17.** 10* **18.** 0.25 **19.** $6\frac{7}{8}$ pounds
20. $\frac{3}{8}$ pounds **21.** $1\frac{1}{2}$ batches **22.** $1\frac{5}{6}$ pounds **23.** $\frac{4}{5}$
24. 24+* **25.** 9 **26.** 4 buses **27.** A **28.** 1 **29.** $\frac{7}{20}$
30. $\frac{2}{3}$ **31.** A **32.** B **33.** $4\frac{3}{4}$ **34.** $\frac{89}{100}$ **35.** 5
parachutes **36.** 1.16 **37.** 7 interviews **38.** 1.60
39. 14 tiles **40.** $1\frac{1}{3}$

Chapter 7

Objective	Test Items	Text Pages
7A	4, 5, 6, 7	236–237
7B	1, 24, 30, 37	236–237, 240–241, 246–249
7C	3, 9, 16, 36	238–241, 246–249
7D	2, 22, 27, 29	246–249
7E	10, 11, 12, 13	256–257
7F	8, 14, 15, 26	250–251
7G	18, 19, 20, 21	254–255
7H	17, 23, 25, 28	244–245
7I	35, 38, 39, 40	252–253
7J	31, 32, 33, 34	260–261

Answers

1. B **2.** 21 lb 5 oz **3.** 40 oz **4.** 64 mm **5.** AB and CD **6.** 7 cm **7.** B and E **8.** 1 h 58 min **9.** I, II and III **10.** 9.9°C **11.** 19.5°C **12.** 17°F
13. 43°F **14.** 60 h **15.** 10 h 2 min **16.** 32.5 mm
17. 1 h 12 min, or $1\frac{1}{5}$ h **18.** C **19.** 4 h 15 min
20. 4:30 PM
21. 8 h 25 min **22.** 8 ft 1 in. **23.** 48 min
24. inch **25.** 55 minutes **26.** 7 h 9 min **27.** 2 yd 2 ft **28.** 5 h **29.** 7 oz **30.** gram **31.** 4 h 45 min
32. 16 h 50 min **33.** 5 h 15 min **34.** 50 min **35.** 5 h **36.** 0.5 yd **37.** C **38.** 6 mph **39.** 78 mi **40.** A

Chapter 8

Objective	Test Items	Text Pages
8A	1, 5, 8, 25	272–273
8B	7, 14, 34, 38	276–277
8C	2, 6, 16, 20	280–283
8D	11, 30, 33, 37	284–285
8E	3, 15, 31, 36	288–289
8F	9, 13, 18, 40	290–291
8G	10, 17, 27, 35	296–297
8H	4, 26, 28, 32	274–275
8I	12, 19, 29, 39	286–287, 292–293
8J	21, 22, 23, 24	298–299

Answers

1. 3 **2.** 80% **3.** 4% **4.** 10 **5.** 10 **6.** 25% **7.** 28 m **8.** 80 **9.** 200 **10.** 25% **11.** 80 **12.** $50.40
13. 100 **14.** 1.4 m **15.** 50% **16.** 0.134
17. 20% **18.** 64 **19.** $437.50 **20.** $\frac{1}{25}$
21. invitations **22.** invitations and food **23.** $30
24. A **25.** $16\frac{1}{3}$ **26.** 9 **27.** 25% **28.** C
29. $67.20 **30.** 6.174 **31.** 40% **32.** A **33.** 6
34. 22.5 cm **35.** 5% **36.** 250% **37.** 232 **38.** 4 m **39.** $16\frac{2}{3}$% **40.** 90

*Answers may vary. Accept any reasonable estimate.

Chapter 9

Objective	Test Items	Text Pages
9A	4, 5, 34, 44	310–311
9B	1, 17, 42, 45	312–313
9C	2, 16, 24, 31	314–315
9D	18, 19, 35, 41	316–317
9E	20, 21, 38, 39	322–323
9F	3, 6, 29, 46	326–327
9G	7, 32, 37, 47	328–329, 336–337
9H	8, 22, 33, 48	330–331, 338-339
9I	10, 23, 36, 49	332–333
9J	9, 15, 30, 50	338–341
9K	11, 25, 26, 27	318–319
9L	12, 28, 40, 51	334–335
9M	13, 14, 43, 52	342–343

Answers

1. $\angle X$, $\angle YXZ$, or $\angle ZXY$ **2.** I and III only **3.** 80°
4. figure C **5.** figure D **6.** I, II and III **7.** $\overline{AC}$ or
$\overline{CA}$ **8.** I and II only **9.** figures II and III only
10. 16 **11.** 5 **12.** 35 **13.** $\angle 5$, $\angle 4$, or $\angle 8$ **14.** $\angle 8$,
$\angle 5$, $\angle 4$, or $\angle 1$ **15.** III only **16.** I, II, and III
17. 74° **18.** figure D **19.** figure A **20.** $\overleftrightarrow{AB}$ and $\overleftrightarrow{CD}$
21. $\overleftrightarrow{AB}$ and $\overleftrightarrow{AC}$, or $\overleftrightarrow{CD}$ and $\overleftrightarrow{AC}$ **22.** 4 **23.** 5 cm
24. A **25.** 6 cm **26.** 10 cm **27.** 40 cm **28.** 52
oz **29.** 40° **30.** III only **31.** C **32.** octagon **33.** I
and III only **34.** C **35.** B **36.** 30° **37.** I, II, and
III **38.** figure C **39.** figure B **40.** 43 **41.** B **42.** I
and II only **43.** 195 ft **44.** line **45.** $\angle CAD$ **46.** I, II
and III **47.** $\overline{AB}$ and $\overline{HG}$ **48.** D **49.** 75 mm **50.** II
only **51.** $176.00 **52.** 103°

Chapter 10

Objective	Test Items	Text Pages
10A	1, 4, 9, 13, 33, 34	352–355
10B	5, 10, 16, 24, 27, 28	356–359, 362–363
10C	3, 12, 15, 26	366–367
10D	6, 19, 37, 39	370–371
10E	11, 20, 35, 40	372–373
10F	7, 14, 21, 23	360–361
10G	8, 17, 29, 30	364–365
10H	2, 22, 31, 38	368–369
10I	18, 25, 32, 36	374–375

Answers

1. 4.8 m **2.** 1 km **3.** sphere **4.** 12.4 cm **5.** 27
cm² **6.** 84 m² **7.** 3 m **8.** 21 **9.** 125.6 cm **10.** 9
ft² **11.** 100 cm³ **12.** cube, or rectangular prism
13. 11 in. **14.** 2 times **15.** triangular prism
16. D **17.** 12 mm **18.** $A = \frac{1}{2} bh$ **19.** 351.68 m²
20. 27 ft³ **21.** 6 times **22.** 2,809 m² **23.** Plan III
only **24.** 28 cm² **25.** C **26.** triangular pyramid
27. 24 ft² **28.** 31.5 cm² **29.** 7 in. **30.** 4 years old
31. 81 ft² **32.** $V = e^3$ **33.** $31\frac{3}{7}$ ft **34.** 12 m **35.** 480
yd³ **36.** 154 in.² **37.** 136 cm² **38.** 1,440 **39.** 96
cm² **40.** 3,080 cm³

Chapter 11

Objective	Test Items	Text Pages
11A	3, 16, 17, 29	386–387
11B	2, 8, 24, 28	388–391
11C	5, 14, 26, 31	404–407
11D	1, 4, 9, 19	402–403
11E	6, 18, 25, 30	410–411
11F	7, 15, 27, 32	412–413
11G	20, 21, 22, 23	394–395
11H	10, 11, 12, 13	408–409

Answers

1. $\frac{2}{3}$ **2.** 4.5 **3.** A **4.** 0 **5.** C **6.** $\frac{1}{9}$ **7.** $\frac{1}{4}$ **8.** 5.5 **9.** $\frac{1}{11}$
10. $4,100 **11.** October at Connor's **12.** $1,000
13. 0 **14.** 4 **15.** $\frac{7}{30}$ **16.** 10–14 **17.** 40% **18.** $\frac{1}{18}$
19. $\frac{4}{5}$ **20.** 13 **21.** $4,000 **22.** I only
23. decreases **24.** 9 **25.** A **26.** (H, f), (T, e), (T,
f) **27.** $\frac{1}{3}$ **28.** $0.85 **29.** 72° **30.** 0 **31.** 32 **32.** $\frac{2}{5}$

Chapter 12

Objective	Test Items	Text Pages
12A	1, 2, 18, 41	424–425
12B	8, 25, 37, 42	424–425
12C	5, 14, 21, 43	428–431
12D	3, 15, 33, 44	434–437
12E	10, 16, 17, 30	440–441
12F	11, 22, 34, 40	446–447
12G	9, 20, 36, 39	452–453
12H	6, 7, 23, 35	448–449
12I	13, 24, 31, 38	454–455
12J	4, 12, 19, 32	444–445
12K	26, 27, 28, 29	450–451

Answers

1. ⁻2 **2.** ⁻4 **3.** ⁻15 **4.** $n = 72 - (^-18)$ **5.** ⁻9
6. U **7.** $K = (^-3,2)$ and $M = (2, ^-1)$ **8.** ⁻8 **9.** ⁻11
10. $x > 36$ **11.** A **12.** 14th **13.** C **14.** $^-6 + ^-5$
15. ⁻6 **16.** ⁻14 **17.** ⁻3 **18.** S **19.** 30,324 ft
20. (4, 11), (2, 5), (0, ⁻1), (⁻2, ⁻7) **21.** 18 **22.** D
23. (3, 2) **24.** III only **25.** ⁻9, ⁻3, 4, 8 **26.** B
27. 1933 **28.** 1935 **29.** 1938 **30.** ⁻5 **31.** D
32. B **33.** 18 **34.** B **35.** (0, 3) **36.** $n = ^-5$
37. < **38.** A **39.** $n = ^-3$ and $m = ^-6$ **40.** C
41. ⁻7 **42.** 11, 9, ⁻10, ⁻12 **43.** 20 **44.** 4

POSTTESTS

Posttests are designed to assess students' accomplishment of the learning objectives for each chapter. When used in conjunction with the chapter Pretest, these tests will provide a means by which to measure actual learning.

Tests items are not grouped by objective but are mixed to provide students with more thought-provoking, less predictable tests.

It is assumed that students will have the appropriate measuring devices available for chapter tests on measurement, geometry, and so on.

These tests are in free-response format with some multiple choice items included where that format provides a better testing tool. For multiple choice, students are expected to give the letter of the answer choice.

Turn to *Other Tests* section for a scoring chart for tests.

POSTTEST   **Chapter 1 Page 1**

1. What is the standard form for the number 39 billion, 76 thousand?

   _____

2. What is 42,735,800 rounded to the nearest million?

   _____

3. 700,963
   − 426,718

4. What is the standard form for 100,000 + 7,000 + 90?

   _____

5. What is the value of the digit 6 in 9,060,470,325,180?

   _____

6. Dawn wanted to find out how much a new car stereo system would cost. The radio and cassette player cost $89.95, the speakers cost $13 a pair, and an antenna costs $8.30. What would the total cost be?

   _____

7. Write eighteen hundred-thousandths in standard form.

   _____

8. What is the best estimate for 97.365 − 15.823?

   _____

9. What is the value of the 4 in 24,700,900,505,683?

   _____

POSTTEST   **Chapter 1 Page 2**

Questions 10 to 13 are based on information in the graph.

**PUBLIC LIBRARY BOOKS
READ BY SEVENTH GRADE STUDENTS**

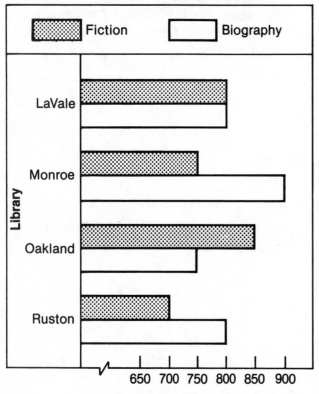

10. How many biographies were read by seventh grade students using the Ruston Library?

    _____

11. Seventh grade students read about 800 books of fiction at which library?

    _____

12. Seventh grade students using which library read the greatest number of books of fiction?

    _____

13. About how many more biographies than books of fiction were read by seventh graders using Monroe Library?

    _____

14. Write 4.060097 in expanded form.

    _____

15. $8.67 - 2.04 + 4.91$

    _____

16. What is 51.03476 rounded to the nearest thousandth?

    _____

17. What is the word name for 0.017?

    _____

18.   2,358; 2,547; 2,538; 2,549

    What is the correct order of the numbers above from the least to the greatest?

    _____

19. What is the best estimate for $3,287,321 + 6,532,719$?

    _____

20. What is the decimal for $8 + 0.02 + 0.0005$?

    _____

1. The price of a bike is $137.53. What is the price rounded to the nearest dollar?

   _____

2. What is the value of the 2 in 81.092705?

   _____

3. 849.007
   − 93.16
   _____

4. What is the value of the 8 in 35,010.92784?

   _____

5. ■ ■ ■ , ■ ■ ■
   + 8 0 7 , 6 1 9
   1 , 4 9 1 , 3 5 0

   What is the missing addend in the problem above?

   _____

6. There were 909,647 copies of a magazine sold. What is the number of copies rounded to the nearest thousand?

   _____

7. If 186,375 = 100,000 + ■ + 6,000 + 300 + 70 + 5, then what is ■ ?

   _____

28. A television that cost $298.50 is now on sale for $239.95. How much would be saved by buying the television on sale?

   _____

29.

Airport	Number of Passengers
Frankfurt	17.030 million
Osaka	16.306 million
Paris	16.060 million
St. Louis	16.000 million

The table above shows the number of passengers during one year at four airports. Which airport had the fewest number of passengers?

   _____

30. 970,326 + 805 + 59,041 + 98

   _____

31. Which of the following is closest in value to 877,775?

   857,775   876,725
   876,775   877,725

   _____

32. If 125 − 17 = 108, then 125 − 108 = n. What is n?

   _____

33. What is the best estimate for $1,247.69 − $381.47?

   _____

POSTTEST   **Chapter 1 Page 4**

Questions 34 to 37 are based on the graph.

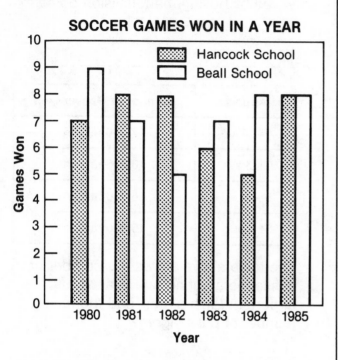

SOCCER GAMES WON IN A YEAR

34. How many soccer games did Beall School win in 1983?

_____

35. In what year did Hancock and Beall win the same number of soccer games?

_____

36. In which year did Hancock School win three more games than Beall School?

_____

37. In which year did Hancock School win the fewest games?

_____

38. What is the word name for the number 702.0085?

_____

39. A PTA is buying a computer and a printer for a school. A computer will cost between $400 and $500. A printer will cost between $300 and $400. Estimate the total cost.

_____

40.   4.66, 4.066, 4.666, 4.11

What is the correct order of the numbers above from the greatest to the least?

_____

POSTTEST   **Chapter 2 Page 1**

1. $1,608.50
   $$\times \qquad 9$$

   _____

2. Compare. Write <, >, or =.

   790×599 ● $48,000$

   _____

3. 10×0.089

   _____

4. The regular price is $0.98 for one skein of yarn. The sale price is $3.00 for 4 skeins of yarn. Pamela is buying 4 skeins of yarn. How much will she save by buying the yarn on sale?

   _____

5.   9,406
   $$\times \qquad 85$$

   _____

6. 28×3.36

7. A grocery store received 12 cases of grapefruit. Each case contained the same number of grapefruit. If you want to know how many grapefruit the store received, what information do you need to know?

   _____

   _____

8. $59,612 \times 300$

   _____

9.   0.407
   $$\times \qquad 83$$

   _____

10. Matt bought some apples. He bought 3.6 pounds of one kind and 2.4 pounds of another kind. What operation should he use with 3.6 and 2.4 to find out how many pounds of apples he bought?

   _____

11. Floor tiles cost $0.57 each. At that price, how much would 100 tiles cost?

   _____

12. 71.058
     $\times \quad 306$

     _____

13. Mr. Minetti bought 6 door knobs. They cost $19 each. To find how much they cost altogether, what operation should you use with 6 and 19?

    _____

14. 0.08×0.6

    _____

15. $17.■■ × 39

    Some digits are hidden in the number above. What is a reasonable estimate of the product?

    _____

16. The regular price is $2.19 for a can of tennis balls. During an end-of-season sale, cans of tennis balls were sold for $0.35 off the regular price. Jeff bought 2 cans of tennis balls on sale.

    What did he pay?

    _____

17. $0.04 \times 1.5 \times 0.01$

    _____

18. Del took 8 pictures of animals. He wanted enlargements made of 2 of them. It cost $0.95 for each enlargement. How much did Del pay for the enlargements he wanted?

    _____

19. 6.00281
     $\times \quad 1,000$

     _____

20. David has 93 newspapers to deliver each day. One morning his mom helped by delivering 31 of his papers. What operation should you use with 93 and 31 to find out how many papers David delivered that day?

    _____

21. $6 \times (9 + 2) = (6 \times 9) + (6 \times ■)$

    What is ■ ?

    _____

22. Dee jumped 1.3 m in the high jump and 1.85 m in the long jump. Linda jumped 1.1 m in the high jump and 1.90 m in the long jump. What was the difference in the long jump distances of Dee and Linda?

_____

23.   7,008
     ×   305

24. Jim bought 4 cartons of paper clips. Each carton contained 12 boxes of paper clips. Each box contained 100 paper clips. How many paper clips did Jim buy?

_____

25. A pep club is making pom-poms. It will take 60 strips of paper ribbon 10 inches long for each pom-pom. What operation should be used with 60 and 10 to find out how many inches of paper ribbon are needed for each pom-pom?

_____

26. 51.■ × 0.6■2

Some digits are hidden in the numbers above. What is a reasonable estimate of the product?

_____

27. 0.09 × 70 × 4

_____

28. It costs $21.80 a month to receive cable TV programs. How much will it cost to receive the programs for 36 months?

_____

29.   0.34
     × 0.28
        272
         68
        952

The problem above has not been finished. What is the correct answer?

_____

30. Sherry and Cindy saved 7.5 pounds of empty aluminum cans. They took the cans to be recycled and received $0.12 a pound. How much did they receive?

_____

31. A large shark was 15 yards long. A large crocodile was 16 feet long and weighed 1,150 pounds. If you want to find how much more the crocodile weighed than the shark, what information do you need to know?

_____

32. 100×46.57

_____

33. A store received a box of eggs. The box had 20 cartons of eggs and each carton had 12 eggs. A store clerk found 8 eggs broken. How many eggs were <u>not</u> broken?

_____

34. The product of two numbers is between 0.05 and 0.1. The two numbers could be

   a. 7.4 and 1   **b.** 7.4 and 0.1

   c. 7.4 and 0.01   **d.** 7.4 and 0.001

_____

POSTTEST   **Chapter 3 Page 1**

1. Malted Milk Nail Enamel costs $2.49 each. What operation should you use to find out how much it will cost to buy 5 nail enamels?

   a. addition   **b.** subtraction
   c. multiplication   **d.** division

   _____

2. $42\overline{)34,398}$

   _____

3. $820\overline{)13,694}$

   What is the best estimate of the quotient?

   _____

4. $5,495 \div 25$

   What is the best estimate of the quotient?

   _____

5. $\dfrac{72.36}{9} =$

   _____

6. Five identical bicycles cost $625. What operation should you use to find the price of one bicycle?

   a. addition   **b.** subtraction
   c. multiplication   **d.** division

   _____

7. $2,408 \div 8$

   _____

8. $\$47,000 \div 100$

   _____

9. $\$34,178 \div 62$

   What is the best estimate of the quotient?

   _____

10. $\dfrac{0.096}{100} =$

    _____

11. Ty's T-Shirts bought a box of 240 T-shirts for $480. They want to make a $2 profit on each of the T-shirts they sell. What is the price for a T-shirt?

    Choose the most reasonable answer.

    a. $4.00   **b.** $9.00
    c. $40.00   **d.** $700.00

    _____

12. $8\overline{)\$16.72}$

    _____

13. $4.836 \div 1.2$

    _____

14. What is the remainder for 6)9,050?

_____

15. 0.7)63.49

_____

16. 781.5 ÷ 10

_____

17. 78)9,762

What is the best estimate of the quotient?

_____

18. Vern and Herb's ages together total 42 years. Vern is 14. What is Herb's age?

_____

19. 80.04 ÷ 0.03

_____

20. 74)$6,058.29

What is the best estimate of the quotient?

_____

Questions 21 to 24
are based on the following map. The heavy lines show the way a class walked to see the sights of Philadelphia.

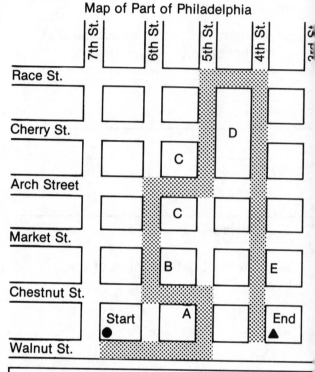

Map of Part of Philadelphia

A Independence Hall   D U.S. Mint
B Liberty Bell   E Franklin Court
C Independence Park

21. The circle (●) shows the spot where a class started walking. Where did it start?

_____

22. What did the class see at the location marked B?

_____

3. How many blocks had the class walked when they got to the corner of Arch St. and 5th St.?

_____

4. Which of the following streets does not go by the U.S. Mint?

a. Arch Street   b. 4th Street
c. 5th Street   d. Market Street

_____

25. 74)‾88,9■■

Some digits are hidden above. How many digits will an estimate of the quotient have?

_____

26. 1,000)‾5.16

27. Mary Christine jogs 3.5 miles each day. She has now jogged 210 miles. What is the number of days she has jogged?

Choose the most reasonable answer.

a. 6   b. 20
c. 60   d. 80

_____

28. $0.1066 \div 41$

_____

29. $735,480 \div 24$

What is the best estimate of the quotient?

_____

30. Alice is carefully cutting strips of ribbon for a banner, and she wants each strip to be 7 cm long. She has a 300-cm roll of ribbon. What is a reasonable estimate of $300 \div 7$, the number of strips she can cut?

_____

31. 0.12)‾20.4

32. $0.0271 \div 100$

33. Jim has $4.79 and buys a few bottles of juice for $0.89 each. What is the amount of money he has left?

Choose the most reasonable answer.

a. $0.34   b. $4
c. $5   d. $10

_____

34. $78\overline{)163.956}$

_____

35. A class has 26 students who walk to
    school or come by car. One day 16
    students came by car. How many
    students walked?

    _____

_____

36. Between 170 and 190 band members
    are going to a concert in vans that can
    carry 20 students each. What is the
    number of vans needed?

    Choose the most reasonable answer.

    a. 40   b. 18
    c. 10   d. 8

    _____

POSTTEST   **Chapter 4 Page 1**

1. Which of the following numbers is divisible by 4?

   1,654   3,276   4,022   5,638

   _____

2. What is 130,000 in scientific notation?

   _____

3. What is $\sqrt{100}$?

   _____

4. What is the greatest common factor (GCF) of 36 and 60?

   _____

5. Simplify $5 + 2 \cdot 7 - 4$.

   _____

6. Cassandra had a balance of $92.78 in her savings account after she deposited $15. Write an equation that shows how much she had before her deposit.

   _____

7. Which numbers are equal?

   5     $\sqrt{125}$ $\sqrt{25}$

   _____

8. If $y - 26 = 45$, what is y?

   _____

9. Which numbers are divisible by 8?

   224   3,000   516

   _____

10. If $a = 21$, what is the value of $a - 7$?

   _____

11. What is the least common multiple (LCM) of 28 and 40?

_____

Use the following information for <u>questions 12 to 14.</u>

A school has an annual T-shirt sale. The graph shows how many shirts were sold from 1980 to 1986.

12. In 1984 each shirt sold for $5. What were the total sales for that year?

_____

13. One-third of the shirts sold in 1985 were size small. About how many were <u>not</u> size small?

_____

14. The goal in 1986 was to sell 25 fewer shirts than twice the number sold in 1982. What was the goal?

_____

15. What is the greatest common factor (GCF) of 9, 15, and 21?

_____

16. What is 8.2×10^3 in standard form?

_____

17. What is $\sqrt{36}$?

_____

18. Which numbers are divisible by 3?

411   405   414

_____

19. What is the least common multiple (LCM) of 40 and 120?

_____

20. If $w = 8$, what is $2w + 3$?

_____

21. If $10 + 2x = 16$, what is x?

_____

Name ______________________ Date ______________

POSTTEST **Chapter 4 Page 3**

22. Which equations have the same solution?

$\frac{x}{4}=7$ $\frac{x}{4}=3$ $\frac{x}{4}+2=5$

______

23. If $n^2=196$, what is n?

______

24. An art contest was held at school. Three more than one-third of the number of blue ribbons awarded was 12. How many blue ribbons were awarded?

Which equation would you use to solve the problem?

a. $3r=12$ b. $3+\frac{1}{3}r=12$

c. $r=12+1$ d. $3-\frac{1}{3}r=12$

______

25. Simplify $9-3-2+4$.

______

26. What is the least common multiple (LCM) of 4, 6, and 9?

______

27. Which of the following numbers is <u>not</u> divisible by 9?

518 603 729 819

______

Use the following information for <u>questions 28 and 29</u>.

The graph below shows the number of students at a school who could do at least 20 pushups.

At Least 20 Pushups

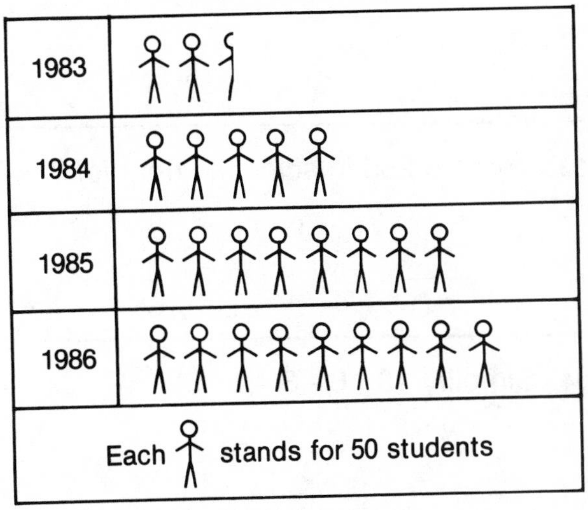
1983
1984
1985
1986
Each
stands for 50 students

28. About how many students could do at least 20 pushups in 1983?

______

29. About how many more students could do at least 20 pushups in 1986 than in 1985?

______

30. The price of a certain type of calculator in 1980 was \$50. The price of the calculator in 1980 was \$10 less than one-sixth of the price in 1972. What was the price in 1972?

______

POSTTEST   **Chapter 4 Page 4**

31. If $y = 12$, what is $\frac{y}{3} + 6$?

    _____

32. If $3x + 5 = 17$, what is x?

    _____

33. What is 255 in scientific notation?

    _____

34. Simplify $10 \cdot 6 \div 3 - 2 \cdot 5$.

    _____

35. If $x = 12$, what is $4x - 3$?

    _____

36. What is 2.821×10^5 in standard form?

    _____

37. Which of the following numbers is divisible by 6?

    6,114   5,948   4,066   3,915

    _____

38. Simplify $100 \div (5 + 5) \cdot (4 - 2)$.

    _____

Name_____ Date_____

1. Write a fraction equivalent to $\frac{5}{6}$.

_____

2. Which is <u>not</u> equivalent to $\frac{6}{8}$?

   a. $\frac{3}{4}$ b. $\frac{4}{6}$

   c. $\frac{9}{12}$ d. $\frac{12}{16}$

_____

3. If $n < \frac{16}{64}$, then n could be

   a. $\frac{1}{4}$ b. $\frac{8}{32}$

   c. $\frac{14}{66}$ d. $\frac{24}{72}$

_____

4. $\frac{5}{16} + \frac{2}{4}$

   What is the sum written in simplest form?

_____

5. What is the mixed number for the fraction $\frac{7}{3}$?

_____

6. Which fraction is greater than $\frac{10}{14}$?

   a. $\frac{0}{4}$ b. $\frac{6}{10}$

   c. $\frac{20}{28}$ d. $\frac{14}{10}$

_____

7. $\frac{4}{6} - \frac{2}{5}$

   What is the difference written in simplest form?

_____

8.

| 4 | 5 | 7 |

Which is a list of all the 3-digit numbers greater than 500 that can be made by arranging the 3 cards shown above?

   a. 547,745   b. 574

   c. 547,574,745,754   d. 574,745,754

_____

9. Suppose you have a sheet of tagboard that is $10\frac{1}{2}$ in. by $13\frac{1}{2}$ in. and want to cut as many 3 in. squares as possible from the sheet. Which of the following plans would enable you to do this most simply.

   a. Consider the sheet to be 9 in. by 12 in.
   b. Round the dimensions down to 10 in. by 13 in.
   c. Round the dimensions up to 11 in. by 14 in.
   d. Divide $10\frac{1}{2}$ by 3 and $13\frac{1}{2}$ by 3 and add your answers.

_____

10. $x + \frac{1}{4} = \frac{3}{4}$

    Solve the equation.

_____

11. $\frac{3}{6} + \frac{1}{4}$

    What is the sum written in simplest form?

_____

12. What is the best estimate for $5\frac{4}{5} - 2\frac{1}{6}$?

_____

---

13. $\frac{n}{12} = \frac{28}{24}$

Find n.

_____

---

14. Order the fractions $\frac{2}{3}$, $\frac{4}{5}$, and $\frac{3}{4}$, from the least to the greatest.

_____

---

15. What is the fraction equal to the mixed number $12\frac{3}{4}$?

_____

---

16. One recipe for soup calls for $3\frac{1}{8}$ lb beef and a second recipe calls for $6\frac{3}{4}$ lb beef. About how many times as much beef is used in the second recipe as in the first?

_____

---

17. Roger's prize pecan tree had grown to a height of $4\frac{7}{12}$ ft. A storm broke off $2\frac{5}{6}$ ft. from the top. How tall was the tree then?

A student estimated that the answer to the problem was about $1\frac{1}{2}$ ft. Was this a good estimate?

a. No, the problem says the tree is $4\frac{7}{12}$ ft., which is closer to $4\frac{1}{2}$ ft.

b. No, because $2 + 4$ is about 6.

c. No, because $2\frac{5}{6}$ is about 3, and $4\frac{7}{12}$ is about $4\frac{1}{2}$, so the answer is about $7\frac{1}{2}$ ft.

d. The student's estimate is about right.

_____

---

18. During one weekend, it rained $5\frac{11}{20}$ in. on Saturday and $3\frac{2}{5}$ in. on Sunday. What was the total rainfall for that weekend?

Choose the best plan to simplify the problem.

a. Subtract 4 from 6.
b. Multiply 4 and 6.
c. Add 6 and 4.
d. Divide 6 by 4.

_____

---

19. Jerry is going to paint his room, but he cannot decide on a color scheme. There are 2 colors he likes for the ceiling, and 4 colors for the walls. How many different choices does he have for a color scheme?

_____

20. $x - \frac{1}{3} = \frac{2}{3}$

Solve the equation.

_____

21. What is the best estimate for

$\frac{1}{5} + \frac{6}{7}$?

_____

22. $3\frac{7}{18} - \frac{5}{6}$

What is the difference written in simplest form?

_____

23. Which fraction is less than $\frac{3}{8}$?

a. $\frac{1}{6}$ b. $\frac{3}{7}$

c. $\frac{5}{8}$ d. $\frac{8}{3}$

_____

24. What is the best estimate for

$6\frac{2}{3} + \frac{1}{7}$?

_____

25. One recipe for bread calls for $5\frac{2}{3}$ cups flour and another calls for $7\frac{1}{8}$ cups flour. If you have 10 lb flour, do you have enough for both recipes?

a. $12\frac{3}{4}$
b. Yes.
c. No.
d. You need more information.

_____

26. Mae has a dog, a cat, and a bird. So that none of the pets feels neglected, she feeds them in a different order each day. In how many different orders can she feed her pets?

_____

27. $4\frac{11}{12}$

      $+ \quad \frac{5}{6}$

What is the sum written in simplest form?

_____

28. What whole number or mixed number is equivalent to $\frac{256}{8}$?

_____

29. $1\frac{2}{3} + x = 2\frac{5}{6}$

Solve the equation.

_____

30. $1\frac{1}{3} + 2\frac{1}{6}$

What is the sum written in simplest form?

_____

31. What is a fraction equal to the whole number 9?

_____

32. What is the best estimate for

$\frac{4}{5} - \frac{1}{10}$?

_____

33. Write a fraction equivalent to $\frac{24}{18}$.

_____

34. $\frac{13}{10} - \frac{1}{5}$

What is the difference written in simplest form?

_____

35. For a cake-baking demonstration, one kind of cake required $\frac{8}{9}$ lb flour and another required $1\frac{2}{3}$ lb flour. Will 2 lb flour be enough for both cakes?

   a. Yes, because one cake needs less than 1 lb and the other needs more.
   b. Yes, because only about 1 lb is needed altogether.
   c. No, about 3 to 4 lb are needed.
   d. No, about $2\frac{1}{2}$ lb are needed.

_____

36. Cindy painted $2\frac{7}{12}$ yd of fence on Friday afternoon, and Gertrude painted $8\frac{5}{6}$ yd on Saturday. If the fence is 20 yd, how many yd are left to be painted?

_____

37.
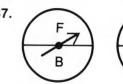

Two spinners are used in a certain board game. The first spinner determines whether you move forward (F) or backward (B). The second spinner tells you how many spaces to move. How many different moves can be determined using the two spinners?

_____

38. How much change would you receive from a $10 bill if you bought 3 items at $1.49 each and 1 item at $4.79?

_____

39. $5\frac{3}{5} - 2\frac{1}{10}$

What is the difference written in simplest form?

_____

40. $x - 3\frac{7}{12} = 4\frac{1}{4}$

Solve the equation.

_____

POSTTEST   Chapter 6 Page 1

1. $\frac{1}{6} \times \frac{6}{7}$

   _____

2. Write a decimal that is equivalent to $\frac{3}{5}$.

   _____

3. What is the best estimate for
   $5\frac{1}{3} \times 3\frac{11}{12}$?

   _____

4. $1\frac{1}{6} \div 7$

   _____

5. Write 0.47 as a fraction.

   _____

6. Charles packs pecans in boxes. Each box holds $2\frac{1}{2}$ lb. How many boxes can be filled with 9 lb of pecans?

   _____

7. In a theater club, $\frac{1}{2}$ of the members are girls, and $\frac{2}{5}$ of these have brown hair. What fraction of the members are girls with brown hair?

   _____

8. What is the best estimate for
   $4\frac{1}{4} \times 7\frac{5}{6}$?

   _____

9. $1\frac{1}{4} \times \frac{8}{9}$

   _____

10. If $\frac{1}{2}w = \frac{1}{4}$, what is w?

    _____

11. Write $\frac{8}{5}$ as a decimal.

    _____

12. Write $\frac{7}{11}$ as a decimal.

    _____

13. $\frac{4}{9} \div \frac{7}{9}$

    _____

POSTTEST   **Chapter 6 Page 2**

14. $8 \times \frac{3}{4}$

_____

_____

Use this information for questions 15 and 16.

A school is planning a 10 kilometer race to raise money for a charity. Prizes will be awarded to the fastest boy and the fastest girl runners in each grade.

15. Which question is important for the planners to answer?

   a. How many hours of daylight are there on race day?
   b. What is the height of the tallest runner?
   c. How much does it cost to repair running shoes?
   d. How many people might run?

_____

16. Which question is <u>not</u> important for the planners to answer?

   a. How much do the prizes cost?
   b. What will the route of the race be?
   c. How much does the heaviest runner weigh?
   d. What is the weather likely to be on race day?

_____

17. What is the best estimate for $\frac{9}{10} \times \frac{9}{7}$?

_____

_____

18. Write $1\frac{1}{5}$ as a decimal.

_____

_____

Use this information for questions 19 to 22

   One batch of bread dough can be made from the following ingredients.

   flour — $2\frac{1}{4}$ cups
   water — $1\frac{1}{3}$ cups
   yeast — $3\frac{1}{2}$ tsp
   salt — $1\frac{1}{2}$ tsp

19. How many batches of dough can be made from 6 tsp of salt?

_____

20. How many cups of flour are needed for $3\frac{1}{2}$ batches of dough?

_____

21. How many cups of water are needed for $\frac{1}{3}$ batch of dough?

_____

22. If 2 kinds of flour are used in equal amounts to make one batch, how much of each kind is needed?

_____

_____

23. Write 2.8 as a mixed number.

_____

_____

24. Which product is closest to 9?

a. $2\frac{1}{8} \times 3\frac{11}{12}$ b. $2\frac{11}{12} \times 3\frac{1}{8}$

c. $2\frac{4}{5} \times 3\frac{11}{12}$ d. $2\frac{11}{12} \times 3\frac{4}{5}$

_____

25. $\frac{4}{9} \div \frac{2}{3}$

_____

_____

26. A recipe for bread calls for $\frac{1}{2}$ cup of soy flour. Each recipe makes one loaf of bread. What is the greatest number of loaves of bread that can be made with $3\frac{3}{4}$ cups of soy flour?

_____

_____

27. What is the best estimate for $2\frac{1}{5} \times 3\frac{4}{5}$?

_____

_____

28. If $\frac{3}{4}x = \frac{15}{8}$, what is x?

_____

29. Write a fraction in simplest form that is equivalent to 0.35.

_____

_____

30. A hockey team has $12\frac{3}{4}$ yd of cloth to use to make banners. Each banner requires $\frac{3}{4}$ yd of cloth. How many banners can they make?

_____

_____

Use this information for questions 31 and 32.

A carnival will be held in a school's gym. The school is donating the space. There will be 15 booths for games and 10 booths for food. Each game booth will have prizes to give away. The food will be donated by parents.

31. Which question is important for the planners to answer?

a. What will the weather be?
b. How much will it cost to rent the gym?
c. How much will the prizes cost?
d. Who will win the most prizes?

_____

32. Which question is <u>not</u> important for the planners to answer?

    a. How much time will it take to set up the booths?
    b. How much will it cost to build the booths?
    c. How much space does each booth need?
    d. How much will the food cost?

    _____

33. If $\frac{2}{3}x + \frac{1}{2} = 1\frac{1}{2}$, what is x?

    _____

34. Write a mixed number that is equivalent to 2.66.

    _____

35. A store manager wants to order 100 gallons of milk. The milk comes in cases with 6 gallons of milk in each case. How many cases does he have to order to get at least 100 gallons of milk?

    _____

36. Write $\frac{3}{4}$ as a decimal.

    _____

37. George has $6\frac{1}{2}$ hours to judge a piano contest. Each contestant takes $\frac{3}{4}$ hour. How many contestants can he judge?

    _____

38. Write $\frac{6}{9}$ as a decimal.

    _____

39. Wanda and Herman wrap gifts in a store. Yesterday Wanda put paper on $\frac{7}{8}$ of the gifts. Herman put tape on $\frac{2}{3}$ of the packages Wanda wrapped. What part of the gifts were completely wrapped?

    _____

40. If $5x - \frac{1}{3} = 3\frac{1}{3}$, what is x?

    _____

Name _____ Date _____

1. Which of the following is the best estimate for the mass of a personal computer?

   a. 5 mg   b. 5 g
   c. 5 kg   d. 50 kg

   _____

2.   27 lb   12 oz
   + 15 lb   13 oz

   _____

3. What is 3 quarts expressed in pints?

   _____

Questions 4 to 7 are based on the following diagram.

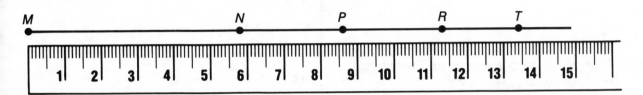

4. What is the distance from *M* to *P* to the nearest millimeter?

   _____

5. What are the two line segments that are closest to 6.0 cm long?

   _____

6. What is the distance from *N* to *T* to the nearest centimeter?

   _____

7. What are the two points which are closest to 75 mm apart?

   _____

8.   5 h   15 min
   − 3 h   23 min

   _____

9. Which of the measurements are equal?

   3,400 mg   0.0034 kg   3.4 g
       I   II   III

   _____

Name _____ Date _____

Questions 10 and 11 are based on the following information.

AVERAGE TEMPERATURE ON THE LAST DAY OF EACH MONTH

Month:	Jul	Aug	Sep	Oct	Nov	Dec
Temperature (°C):	25.1	31.5	21.6	15.8	5.6	8.6

10. How much warmer was it on July 31 than on October 31?

_____

11. How much colder was it on December 31 than on August 31?

_____

Questions 12 and 13 are based on the following information.

AVERAGE TEMPERATURE ON THE FIRST DAY OF EACH MONTH

Month:	Jan	Feb	Mar	Apr	May	Jun
Temperature (°F):	22	12	25	42	55	68

12. How much warmer was it on April 1 than on February 1?

_____

13. How much warmer was it on May 1 than on March 1?

_____

14. How many days are there in 108 hours?

_____

15.   13 h   25 min
     + 18 h   52 min

_____

16. What is 8.05 L expressed as milliliters?

_____

17. Bertha rode 6 miles in 20 minutes on her bicycle. At that speed, how long would it take her to ride 27 miles?

_____

Name _____ Date _____

Use the following map for <u>questions 18 to 21.</u>

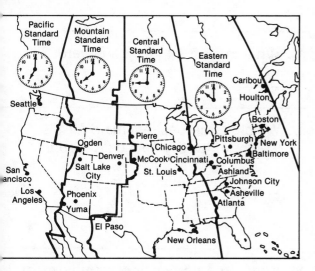

18. If it is 10:00 AM in El Paso, in which two of the following cities is it 8:00 AM?

A. Atlanta and Boston
B. Chicago and St. Louis
C. Salt Lake City and Yuma
D. Los Angeles and Seattle

_____

19. A bus leaves St. Louis at 12:30 PM and arrives in Cincinnati at 7:45 PM. How long was the trip?

_____

20. What time is it in Denver when it is midnight in Johnson City?

_____

21. A plane leaves Pittsburgh for New York at 11:30 AM. If the flight takes 1 h 10 min, at what time should the plane land in New York?

_____

22.   4 yd   2 ft
    +1 yd   2 ft
   _____

23. A plane can fly 2,000 miles in 4 hours. How long would it take to fly 750 miles?

_____

24. What is the appropriate customary unit for measuring the width of a room?

_____

25. A video tape can record 4 h of TV shows. A 90-minute show and an 85-minute show have been recorded. How much time is left on the tape?

_____

26. Marilyn drives from Norfolk, Virginia, to Raleigh, North Carolina. She leaves Norfolk at 10:10 AM and arrives in Raleigh at 2:57 PM. How long is the trip?

_____

27.   8 ft   4 in.
    −3 ft   7 in.
   _____

28. Hurricane Harry has been traveling 11 miles in 10 minutes. If it maintains its average speed, how long will it take to travel 220 miles?

_____

29.   16 lb   5 oz
    − 9 lb 11 oz

_____

30. Which is the best estimate for the length of a city parade route for a Fourth-of-July parade?

    a. 2 cm   b. 2 dam
    c. 2 m   d. 2 km

    _____

Questions 31 to 34 are based on the information in the following table.

BUS SCHEDULE (EASTERN TIME ZONE)			
City	Departure	City	Arrival
Leadtown	8:45 AM	Tin City	11:20 AM
Ironwood	10:35 AM	Slagville	12:25 PM
Port Silver	9:15 AM	Mount Pyrite	4:05 PM
Leadtown	8:10 AM	Port Silver	10:25 PM

31. How long does it take to travel from Leadtown to Tin City?

    _____

32. How long does it take to travel from Port Silver to Mount Pyrite?

    _____

33. How long does it take to travel from Leadtown to Port Silver?

    _____

34. How long does it take to travel from Ironwood to Slagville?

    _____

35. Max's horse ran 4 miles in $\frac{1}{4}$ hour. What was his average speed?

    _____

36. What is 18 ft expressed in yards?

    _____

37. Which is the best estimate for the weight of an Olympic gold medal?

    a. 0.4 oz   b. 4 oz
    c. 4 lb   d. 4 T

    _____

38. Water in a particular stream flows at $3\frac{1}{3}$ miles per hour. How long would it take a leaf to float 20 miles downstream if it maintains the speed of the stream?

    _____

39. Brian drove from St. Louis, Missouri, to Kansas City, Kansas, in $4\frac{1}{2}$ h. His average speed was 55 mph. How far is it from St. Louis to Kansas City?

    _____

40. Carol took the train on a trip from New York to Chicago. The distance between the two cities is 806 miles. The average speed of the train was 50 mph. How long did the trip take?

Which part of the formula $d = rt$ should you solve for?

    a. time
    b. rate
    c. distance
    d. none of the above

    _____

POSTTEST Chapter 8 Page 1

1. Solve the proportion. $\frac{15}{20} = \frac{x}{8}$

   _____

2. Write $\frac{30}{100}$ as a percent.

   _____

3. What percent of 6 is 3?

   _____

4. A seventh-grade class is selling muffins to raise money for a class project. If they make $1.25 for every $2.00 sold, how much will they make if the total sales are $600.00?

   _____

5. Solve the proportion. $\frac{x}{6} = \frac{6}{4}$

   _____

6. Write 0.12 as a percent.

   _____

7. Given the scale 1 cm = 15 m, what is the actual length of an object which is 30 cm long in a scale drawing?

   _____

8. In the proportion $\frac{4}{5} = \frac{3}{n}$, what is the value of n?

   _____

9. If 50% of a number is 78, what is the number?

   _____

10. If an item decreased in cost from $18.00 to $12.00, what is the percent of decrease?

    _____

11. What is 3% of 30?

    _____

12. Edward has $3,300 to invest. How much interest will he earn in 4 years if the interest rate is 12%?

    _____

13. 80 is 8% of what number?

    _____

14. Using the scale 2 cm = 5 m, what is the actual length of a boat if the length of the scale drawing is 24 cm?

_____

15. What percent of 50 is 15?

_____

16. Write 0.14% as a decimal.

_____

17. If an item which originally sold for $20.00 is on sale for $16.00, what is the percent of decrease in price?

_____

18. If 3% of n is 1.5, what is n?

_____

19. Tom and Linda want to buy a new house. The interest rate is 12% per year. The interest over a 20-year period will be $180,000. What is the price of the house?

_____

20. Write 96% as a fraction.

_____

Use the circle graph for <u>questions 21 to 24.</u>

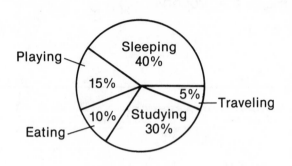

21. The least amount of time in an average day is spent on which category?

_____

22. Which of the following groups of categories accounts for more than half of the time?

    a. eating, sleeping, and traveling
    b. studying and traveling
    c. playing and traveling
    d. eating, playing, and traveling

_____

23. In an average day, how many hours are spent playing?

_____

24. How many hours are spent sleeping in an average day?

_____

25. In the proportion $\frac{27}{n} = \frac{45}{100}$, what is the value of n?

_____

26. Two large rolls of wallpaper cover 72 square feet. Diane's room has 288 square feet of wall to be covered. How many rolls of paper does she need?

_____

27. After a tune-up, a car which was getting 25 miles per gallon gets a 2-mile-per-gallon increase. What is the percent of increase?

_____

28. A scale model of a castle has a banquet table 20 cm long and 7 cm wide. If the actual table is 4 m wide, which proportion can be used to find the length?

I. $\frac{20}{7} = \frac{x}{4}$ II. $\frac{20}{7} = \frac{4}{x}$ III. $\frac{20}{x} = \frac{7}{4}$

a. I only   b. II only
c. I and III only   d. I, II, and III

_____

29. Kristi sells Country-Craft materials at home parties. She receives a commission of 30% on total sales. Her sales at two parties were $120 and $160. How much did she receive in commission for the two parties?

_____

30. What is 7.9% of 100?

_____

31. During the month of June there were 10 rainy days and 20 sunny days. What percent of the days were rainy?

_____

32. The pep club expects 7 out of every 10 students to buy a school button. The school has 450 students. Which proportion shows how many buttons to order?

a. $\frac{7}{10} = \frac{450}{x}$ b. $\frac{7}{10} = \frac{x}{450}$
c. $\frac{7}{450} = \frac{x}{10}$ d. $\frac{10}{450} = \frac{x}{7}$

_____

33. The original cost of an item is $360. How much money will be saved with a discount of 18%?

_____

34. If the scale is 5 cm = 3 m, how wide is the scale drawing of a playground with an actual width of 30 m?

_____

35. Twins were born to a family with 3 other children. What is the percent of increase of the number of children in the family?

    _____

36. What percent of 80 is 200?

    _____

37. What is 375% of 750?

    _____

38. A scale drawing of a room is 6 in. wide. If the actual room is 12 feet wide, what is the scale?

    _____

39. Bill borrowed $600 to buy a color TV. A bank charged $270 interest for a 3-year loan. What is the annual rate of interest on his loan?

    _____

40. 120% of what number is 36?

    _____

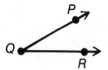 **POSTTEST** | **Chapter 9 Page 1**

1. What is a name for the angle shown?

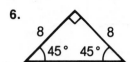

_____

2.

Which line segments are congruent?

_____

---

3. If the measurements of two angles of a triangle are 50° and 65°, what is the measurement of the third angle?

_____

Use the following figures for questions 4 and 5.

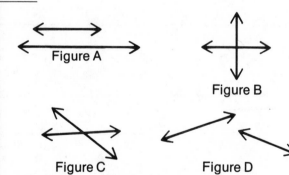

4. Which figure shows parallel lines?

_____

---

5. Which figure shows perpendicular lines?

_____

6.

Which of the following labels would apply to this triangle?

I	II	III
right	isosceles	acute

_____

7.

The center of this circle is *P.*

Which segment is a diameter?

_____

8.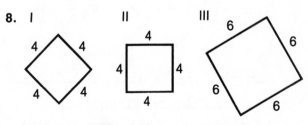

Which figures are congruent?

_____

9.

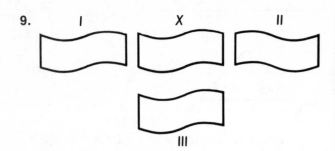

Which of the above are reflections of figure *X*?

_____

10.

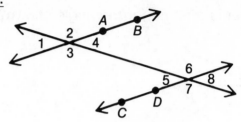

The parallelograms are similar. What is *n*?

_____

11.

Sides	4	5	6			
Triangles	2	3	4			

If you draw all the diagonals from one vertex, how many triangles are formed in a polygon with 11 sides?

Complete the table to help you.

_____

12. This year there are 50 people in a drama club. Last year there were 10 more than $\frac{1}{2}$ this number. How many were in the club last year?

_____

Use this figure to answer questions 13 and 14.

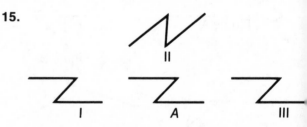

Lines $\overleftrightarrow{AB}$ and $\overleftrightarrow{CD}$ are parallel.

13. Name an angle to which $\angle 8$ is congruent.

_____

14. Name an angle to which $\angle 5$ is supplementary.

_____

15.

Which of the figures could be the result of a translation of figure *A*?

_____

16.

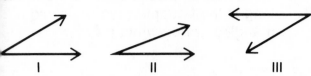

| I | II | III |

Which angles are congruent?

_____

7.

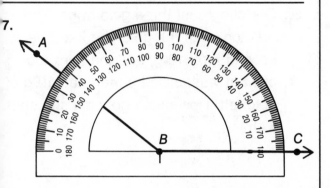

What is the measure of ∠ABC?

_____

Use the figures below for questions 18 and 19.

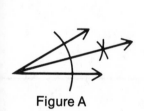

Figure A

Figure B

Figure C   Figure D

18. Which figure shows a construction of a bisector of a line segment?

_____

19. Which figure shows a construction of the bisector of an angle?

_____

Use this figure to answer questions 20 and 21.

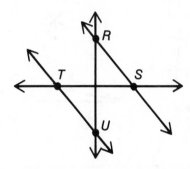

20. Name a pair of parallel lines in the figure.

_____

21. Name a pair of perpendicular lines in this figure.

_____

22.

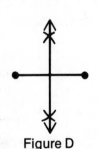

How many lines of symmetry does this figure have?

_____

23. A painting is 6 ft long and 4 ft wide. If a copy with the same shape has a width of 2 ft, what is its length?

_____

24. Which figure shows the construction of a line segment congruent to ●———● ?

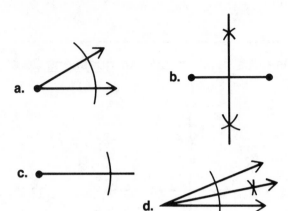

a.

b.

c.

d.

_____

Use this information for <u>questions 25 to 27</u>.

If an odd number of equilateral triangles are drawn in a row, the result is a trapezoid.

  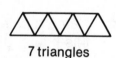

3 triangles   5 triangles   7 triangles

25. If the side of each triangle is 1 cm, how long is the top of the trapezoid if 13 triangles are drawn in a row?

_____

26. If the side of each triangle is 1 cm, how long is the top of the trapezoid if 21 triangles are drawn in a row?

_____

27. If the side of each triangle is 1 cm, how long is the bottom of the trapezoid if 2: triangles are drawn in a row?

_____

28. Gretchen cast three gold rings. The first took $\frac{1}{5}$ of the gold she had, the second took 10 g, and the third took $\frac{3}{4}$ of what was left. She then had 10 g of gold left. How much gold did she start with?

_____

29. The measure of two angles of a triangle are 120° and 40°; what is the measure of the third angle?

_____

30.

Of the above, which are rotations of figure *B*?

_____

1. Which of the following shows the beginning of a construction of an angle congruent to ∠P?

a.

b.

c.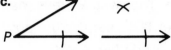

d.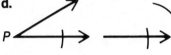

_____

2.

What is the name of this figure?

_____

3.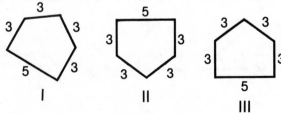

I   II   III

Which figures are congruent?

_____

34. Which figure shows a line?

a.    b. ●———●

c.   d. ●———→

_____

_____

35. In which figure does $\overline{AB}$ bisect $\overline{CD}$?

a. 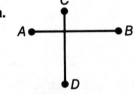   b.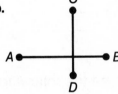

c. 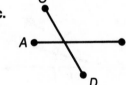   d.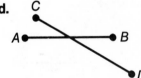

_____

36.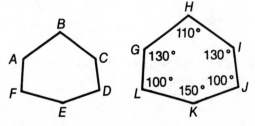

The polygons are similar. What is the measure of ∠E?

_____

37.

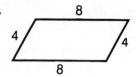

quadrilateral   parallelogram   rectangle

    I   II   III

Which names describe this figure?

_____

Use the following figures for questions 38 and 39.

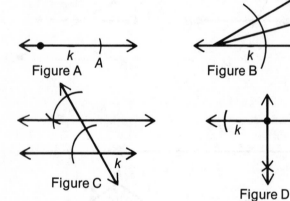

38. Which figure shows the construction of a line parallel to line *k*?

_____

39. Which figure shows a construction of a line perpendicular to line *k*?

_____

40. This year there were 100 people in a class parade. That was 20 less than $\frac{3}{4}$ of the number last year. How many were in the parade last year?

_____

41. In which figure does $\overrightarrow{BD}$ bisect $\angle ABC$?

a.
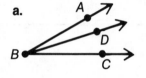

b.
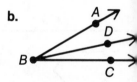

c.
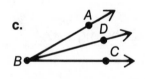

d.
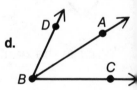

_____

42.
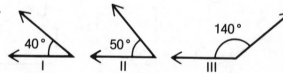

Which pair of angles is supplementary?

_____

3.

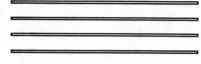

The shelves shown are 1 inch thick and 11 inches apart. How far is the top of the top shelf from the bottom of the bottom shelf?

_____

4.

What is the name of this figure?

_____

5.

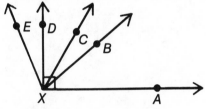

Which angle is obtuse?

_____

6.

9
7
3

Which of the following labels would apply to this triangle?

I	II	III
obtuse	scalene	isosceles

_____

47.

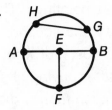

Which segments are chords?

_____

48. Which figure has exactly 3 lines of symmetry?

a.
   5
   5   5

b.
   4 / \ 4
     2

c.
   7
   4   4
   7

d.
   3   3
   3   3

_____

49. A dining table is 2 m wide by 5 m long. If a scale drawing of the table is 10 cm wide, how long is the table in the drawing?

_____

50.

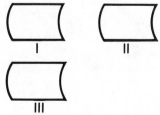
I   II
III

Which figures are reflections of one another?

_____

POSTTEST   **Chapter 9 Page 8**

51. Mr. Garcia bought three paintings. The first cost $\frac{1}{3}$ of his money, the second cost $24, and the third cost $\frac{1}{2}$ of what was left. He had $90 after buying all three paintings. How much money did he start with?

_____

52.

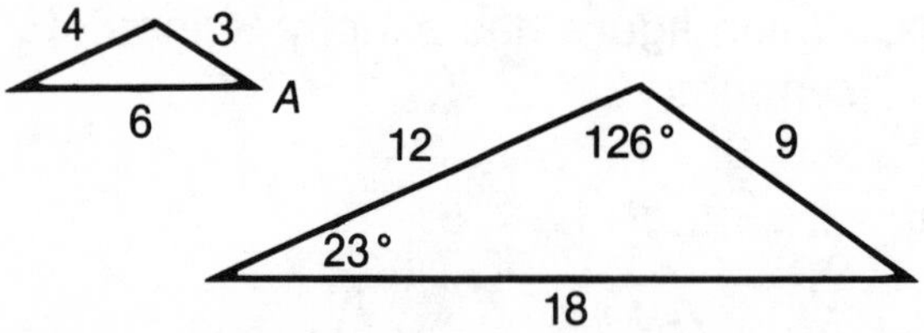

The two figures are similar. What is the measure of $\angle A$?

_____

ame _____   Date _____

.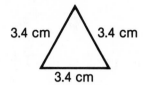

3.4 cm   3.4 cm

3.4 cm

What is the perimeter of the triangle?

_____

_____

. A zoo has a square shape with 6 km on each side. Jim enters the zoo at the center of the east side and walks 1.5 km due west. Then he walks 1 km due north and then 2.5 km due west. How far is he from the northern border at that point?

_____

_____

.

What is the name of this figure?

_____

_____

. What is the perimeter of a square whose side is 2.5 ft?

_____

_____

. What is the area of a parallelogram whose base is 9 m and height is 12 m?

_____

6.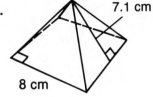

7.1 cm

8 cm

What is the total surface area of this square pyramid?

_____

_____

7. Lynn has 20 in. of gold braid to wrap around the outside of a rectangular picture frame with a length of 6 in. and a width of 2 in. How much braid will be left?

_____

_____

8. The sum of the page numbers of the last two pages in a novel is 501. How many pages are there?

_____

_____

9. What is the circumference of a circle with a radius of 100 ft? (Use $\frac{22}{7}$ for π.)

_____

_____

10. What is the area of a square whose side is 9 m?

_____

POSTTEST   Chapter 10 Page 2

11. What is the volume of a rectangular prism that has a length of 5 in., a width of 4 in., and a height of 3 in.?

_____

12.

What is the name of this figure?

_____

13.

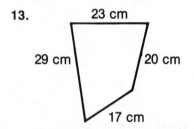

What is the perimeter of this polygon?

_____

14. A health movie is shown in 2 sessions of 55 minutes each, and a science movie is shown in 5 sessions of 40 minutes each. The total time for the science movie is about how many times as long as the total time for the health movie?

_____

15.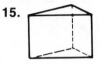

What is the name of this figure?

_____

16. Which represents the area of a circle with a radius of 8 cm? (Use 3.14 for π.)

a. $3.14 \times 8 \times 8$ b. $3.14 \times 3.14 \times 8$
c. 3.14×8 d. $2 \times 3.14 \times 8$

_____

17. The area of a rectangular floor is 72 ft². It is twice as long as it is wide. How long is it?

_____

18.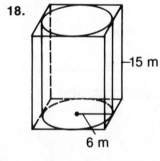

What is the volume of this cylinder? (Use 3.14 for π.)

_____

9.

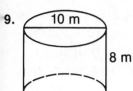

10 m

8 m

What is the surface area of this cylinder? (Use 3.14 for π.)

_____

20. What is the volume of a cube with an edge of 10 m?

_____

21. Sue's banner is a rectangle $1\frac{1}{3}$ ft by 2 ft. Sam's banner is a rectangle 2 ft by 4 ft. Sam's banner is about how many times as large as Sue's?

_____

22. A swimming pool is 10 m long and 8 m wide. A patio 2 m wide is to be built around the swimming pool. What will be the area of the swimming pool and the patio together?

_____

23. Summerville has the shape of a square with a side of 4.5 mi. Autumn City is rectangular, with a length of 2.1 mi and a width of 1.8 mi. Which of the following plans will determine how many times as large the area of Summerville is as the area of Autumn City?

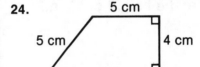

$S = 4.5 \times 4.5$	$S = 4.5 \times 4.5$	$S = 4.5 \times 4.5$
$A = 2.1 \times 1.8$	$A = 2.1 \times 1.8$	$A = 2.1 \times 1.8$
Answer is $S \div A$	Answer is $A - S$	Answer is $S - A$
Plan I	**Plan II**	**Plan III**

_____

24.

5 cm

5 cm   4 cm

8 cm

What is the area of this figure?

_____

25. What formula should you use to compute the perimeter of a rectangle?

_____

26.

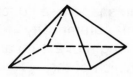

What is the name of this figure?

_____

27. What is the area of a rectangle whose length is 12 ft and width is 7 ft?

_____

28. What is the area of a triangle with a base of 10 in. and a height of 12 in.?

_____

29. The perimeter of a rectangular garden is 140 m. It is 10 m longer than it is wide.

How long is it?

_____

30. The sum of the ages of a parent and a child is 48. The parent is 3 times as old as the child. How old is the child?

_____

31. A square piece of property measures 38 ft to the side. The owner uses a rectangular piece, 15 ft by 12 ft, to plant flowers. What is the area of the property not used?

_____

32. What formula should you use to compute the volume of a rectangular prism?

_____

33. What is the circumference of a circle whose diameter is 7 cm? (Use 3.14 for π.)

_____

34. If a rectangle has a length of 2.4 cm and a width of 1.6 cm, what is its perimeter?

_____

35.

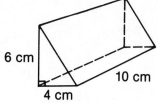

6 cm

10 cm

4 cm

What is the volume of this figure?

_____

36.

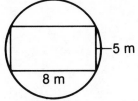

5 m

8 m

What is the area of the rectangle in this figure?

_____

37.

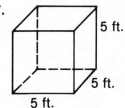

5 ft.

5 ft.

5 ft.

What is the surface area of this prism?

_____

38. Sue decided to change the tile on her rectangular kitchen floor. The floor is 20 ft by 10 ft. If each square tile is $1\frac{1}{4}$ ft long, how many tiles are needed?

_____

39.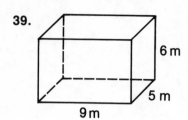

6 m

5 m

9 m

What is the surface area of this prism?

_____

40.

4 m

13 m

What is the volume of this cylinder?
(Use 3.14 for π.)

_____

Name _____ Date _____

1. A number cube has the numbers 1, 2, 3, 4, 5, and 6 on the six faces. You are going to toss the cube once. What is the probability of tossing a 1 or a 6?

_____

2.   3, 11, 13

What is the mean of the scores above?

_____

3.

UNITED STATES POPULATION	
Year	**Population**
1950	152,000,000
1960	181,000,000
1970	205,000,000
1980	223,000,000

UNITED STATES POPULATION

(in millions)

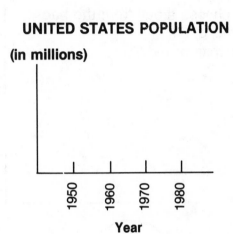

A broken-line graph has been started above. Which of the following is a correct way to label the vertical axis?

a. Population

(in millions)

223
205
181
152

b. Population

(in millions)

220
200
180
150

c. Population

(in millions)

250
225
200
175
150

d. Population

(in millions)

5
4
3
2
1

_____

Name _____   Date _____

POSTTEST   **Chapter 11 Page 2**

4.

R : Red ball
W : White ball

Wynn will choose a ball from the bag without looking.
What is P(white or red)?

_____

5.

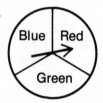 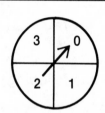

Craig spins each spinner once. Which of the following is a possible outcome of his spins?

a. Red, Blue   b. 1, 2
c. Red, 4   d. Green, 0

_____

6. Five cards with the digits 1 to 5 on them are mixed in a box. Without looking, you are going to pick one card and replace it. Then you are going to pick another card. What is the probability of picking a card with a 3 on it followed by a card with a 5 on it?

_____

7.

P Q R S T U V

The cards above are turned to their blank side and mixed. Clay picks the card that has Q on it. He keeps the card. What is the probability that the next card Clay picks will have S on it?

_____

8.   9, 4, 6, 5, 4, 2

The median of the set of data above is

_____

9. Mystery packages all look the same. There are 8 packages worth $0.50 each, 1 package worth $1.00, and 2 packages worth $2.00. If you choose one package, what is the probability of choosing a package worth $0.50?

_____

Use the following graphs for <u>questions 10 to 13.</u>

**AMOUNT OF SALES
AT BEST'S AND MOORE'S**

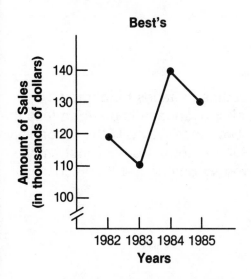

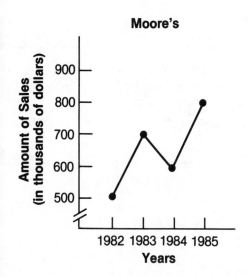

10. What was the total amount of sales at both stores in 1983?

_____

11. The greatest amount of sales in a year was in what year at what store?

_____

12. How much money was spent at Best's in 1984?

_____

13. In how many of the years shown were Best's sales higher than Moore's?

_____

14. The tree diagram below shows the possible ways that Lena can choose one flavor of ice cream and one topping to go on it.

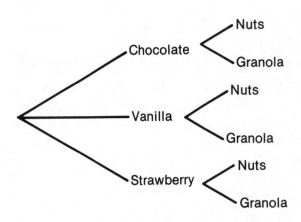

How many different possibilities are there?

_____

Name_____   Date_____

POSTTEST   **Chapter 11 Page 4**

15. Of the eleven members of the math club, 4 are seventh-graders and 7 are eighth-graders. Two of the members will be chosen to plan the club's first program. The names of all of the members will be placed in a hat. The club's adviser will draw one name, not replace it, and then draw a second name. What is the probability that the first name chosen is that of a seventh-grader and the second name chosen is also that of a seventh-grader?

_____

Use the following table for questions 16 and 17.

NUMBER OF STORIES IN BUILDINGS IN GLEN RIDGE

Interval	Tally	Frequency	Relative Frequency
1–19	JHT	5	
20–39	II	2	
_____	II	2	
60–79	I	1	
TOTAL		10	

16. What is the missing interval?

_____

17. The relative frequency for the interval 1–19 is

_____

18. A cube has its faces numbered 1 through 6. Candace is going to toss the cube two times. What is the probability she will not get a 4 on the first time followed by getting a 4 the second time?

_____

19. There are 2 purple, 3 yellow, and 2 green balls in a bag. Without looking, you are going to choose one ball. What is P (not yellow)?

_____

Name _____ Date _____

Use the following information for <u>questions 20 to 23.</u>

Mrs. Westfall gave a quiz in English and a quiz in mathematics. The results of her students' scores are shown in the scattergram.

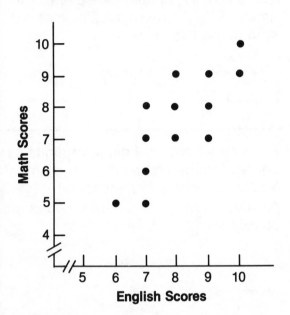

English Scores

20. How many students scored below 8 in the math quiz?

_____

21. What is the range of English quiz scores?

_____

22. Which of the following can be concluded from the scattergram?

I. All of the students who scored more than 7 points on the English quiz scored more than 6 points on the mathematics quiz.

II. All of the students who scored more than 6 points on the mathematics quiz scored more than 7 points on the English quiz.

_____

23. In general, the scattergram shows that as the mathematics scores increased the English scores

_____

24. A hardware store kept a record of the sizes of drill bits sold in a week. The sizes in inches were $\frac{1}{8}$, $\frac{1}{16}$, $\frac{1}{4}$, $\frac{1}{2}$, $\frac{1}{8}$, 1. What was the mode of the sizes sold?

_____

25.

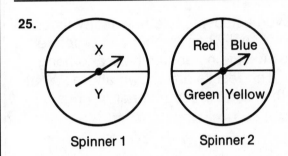

Spinner 1   Spinner 2

The probability of spinning a Y on spinner 1 and a Green on spinner 2 can be found using

a. P(Y) + P(Green after Y)
b. P(Y) · P(Green after Y)
c. P(Y) + P(Green)
d. P(Y) · P(Green)

_____

26. A chip that is blue on one side and white on the other is tossed. Then a cube with the numbers 1, 2, 3, 4, 5, and 6 on it is tossed. Which ordered pairs are needed to complete the list of possible outcomes?

(B,1) (B,2) (B,3) (B,4)
(W,1) (W,2) (W,3) (W,4) (W,5)

_____

27. Felix has a friend's phone number but the last digit is missing. He guesses the last digit and calls but that is the wrong number. He makes another guess, calls, and gets the wrong number. He is going to make one more guess and call the number. What is the probability that he will pick his friend's number?

_____

28.   8, 6, 12, 8, 5, 3

Several students told how many times they usually hear a phone ring before they decide no one is there and hang up. The results are shown above. What is the range of the number of rings?

_____

29. 200 parents were asked what they disagree with their children about most. The results were

Topic	Number of parents
Behavior	60
Homework	30
House chores	60
School grades	40
Other	10
Total	200

In a circle graph showing this information, what is the central angle for the part representing house chores?

_____

30.

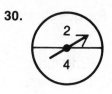

You are going to spin the spinner two times. What is the probability that the sum of the two spins is 2?

_____

31. For a code, any of 9 different digits can be used in the first position and any of 3 different letters in the second position. How many different codes are possible?

_____

32. A bowl contains 2 yellow balls, 2 blue balls, and 3 red balls. Without looking, Winona is going to pick one ball, not replace it, and then pick a second ball from the bowl. P (yellow, then yellow) can be found using

a. $\frac{2}{7} \cdot \frac{2}{6}$ b. $\frac{2}{7} \cdot \frac{1}{7}$

c. $\frac{2}{7} \cdot \frac{1}{6}$ d. $\frac{2}{7} \cdot \frac{2}{7}$

_____

Name _____ Date _____

For <u>questions 1 and 2,</u> use the number line.

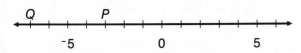

1. Write an integer for the point P on the number line.

   _____

2. Write an integer for the point Q on the number line.

   _____

3. $^-2 \cdot {}^-7$

   _____

4. The highest recorded temperature in the U.S. was 134°F above zero. The lowest temperature was 80°F below zero. Write an equation that could be used to find the difference in temperatures.

   _____

5. $^-6 + {}^-1$

   _____

For <u>questions 6 and 7,</u> use the graph.

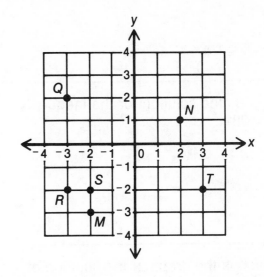

6. Which point is located at $(^-3, {}^-2)$?

   _____

7. What are the ordered pairs for points M and N?

   _____

8. Which number makes the following statement true?

   $x < {}^-7$

   a. 10   **b.** 5
   c. $^-6$ **d.** $^-9$

   _____

9. If $y = {}^-x + 2$ and $x = 6$, what is y?

_____

10. What is the solution for the inequality $7x < 28$?

_____

11. Which is the graph of the solution of $x - 1 = 3$?

a.
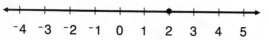

b.
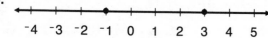

c.
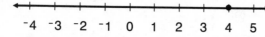

d.
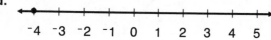

12. The first motorcycle was built in 1869. The first bicycle was built 78 years earlier. When was the first bicycle built?

_____

13. $(^-1, ^-2)$ $(0, ^-1)$ $(1, 0)$

The ordered pairs are solutions for $y = x - 1$. Which of the following is the graph for the equation?

a.
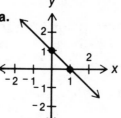

b.
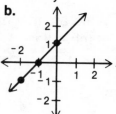

c.
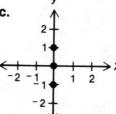

d.
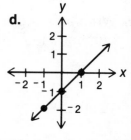

_____

14. An equivalent expression for $^-4 - 7$ is

_____

15. $^-9 \div 3$

_____

16. If $x + 10 = {}^-13$, what is x?

_____

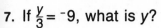

7. If $\frac{y}{3} = {}^-9$, what is y?

_____

_____

8. Which letter represents the <u>opposite</u> of 3 on the number line.

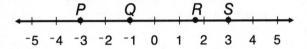

_____

9. Mt. McKinley is 20,320 feet above sea level. Death Valley is 282 feet below sea level. What is the difference in altitude of these two points?

_____

20.

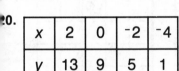

x	2	0	-2	-4
y	13	9	5	1

The table shown is for the equation $y = 2x + 9$. What are four solutions for the equation?

_____

21. $5 + {}^-32$

_____

22.

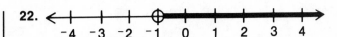

The graph above shows the solution of which inequality?

a. $x = {}^-1$ b. $x \le {}^-1$

c. $x \ge {}^-1$ d. $x > {}^-1$

_____

23.

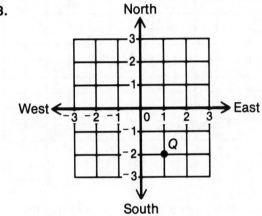

On the graph, what is the ordered pair for the point 3 units north and 2 units west of point Q?

_____

24. The graph of $y = {}^-4x + 5$ passes through which of these points?

I. (0,1)   II. ($^-1$,9)   III. (1,1)

a. III only   b. I and II only

c. II and III only   d. I, II, and III

_____

25.   5 ⁻2 6 ⁻9

What is the correct order of the numbers from the greatest to the least?

_____

Use the graph below for <u>questions 26 to 29.</u>

MOVEMENT OF PEOPLE IN AND OUT OF METROPOLIS

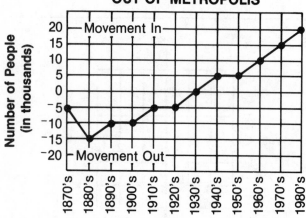

26. During which ten-year period did the most people move out of Metropolis?

_____

27. During which ten-year period did about 15,000 people move to Metropolis?

_____

28. How many people moved in or out in the 1910's?

  a. about 5,000 people moved in
  b. about 5,000 people moved out
  c. about 10,000 people moved in
  d. about 10,000 people moved out

_____

29. During which ten-year period did the fewest people move in or out of Metropolis?

_____

30. $x - 3 > 6$ is true when x is any number greater than what number?

_____

31.

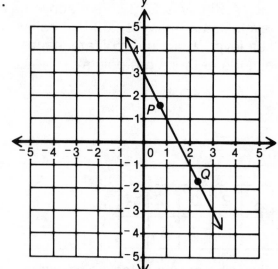

Which of the ordered pairs are on the line connecting points P and Q above?

  I. (0,3)   II. (1,0)   III. (2,⁻1)

  a. I only   **b.** I and II only
  c. I and III only   **d.** I, II, and III

_____

2. | Cheryl owed her dad $10. She earned $13 babysitting and spent $6. She paid her dad the rest of the money she earned. How much does she owe her dad now? |

Which of the following equations can be used to solve this problem?

  a. $n = {}^-10 + (13 + {}^-6)$
  b. $n = {}^-10 + (13 + 6)$
  c. $n = {}^-10 - (13 + 6)$
  d. $n = {}^-10 - (13 + {}^-6)$

_____

3. $6 \cdot {}^-4$

_____

4. The graph of the solution of ${}^-2x = {}^-6$ is

  a.
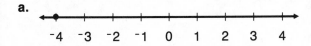

  b.

  c.

  d.
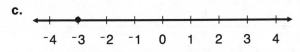

_____

35. What are the coordinates of the point 4 units to the left of the origin?

_____

36.

x	${}^-2$	0	2	4
y	4	${}^-2$	${}^-8$	n

The table shown is for the equation $y = {}^-3x - 2$. What number should replace the n in the table?

_____

37. Write $<, >,$ or $=$ to make the statement true.

  ${}^-5 \bullet {}^-7$

_____

38.

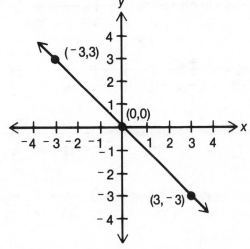

Which of the following equations is shown by the graph above?

  a. $y = x - 1$ **b.** $y = 1 - x$
  c. $y = x$ **d.** $y = {}^-x$

_____

39.

x	-2	-1	0	1
y	-4	-2	m	n

The table shown is for the equation
$y = 2x$. What numbers should replace m
and n in the table?

_____

40. Which is the graph of the solution of
$x \leq -2 \cdot -6$?

a.

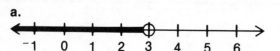

b.

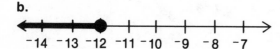

c.

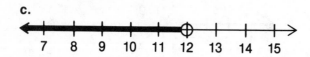

d.

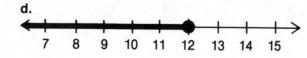

_____

41.

```
  -10      -5       0       5       10
```

What is the number 7 units to the right
of -8 on the number line?

_____

42.   -8   7   3   -5

What is the correct order of the
numbers from the least to the greatest?

_____

43. $5 - {}^{-}16$

_____

44. $\dfrac{-12}{-3} =$

_____

Posttest Answers

Chapter 1

Objective	Test Items	Text Pages
1A	1, 7, 17, 38	2–3, 20–21
1B	4, 14, 20, 27	2–3, 20–21
1C	5, 9, 22, 24	2–3, 20–21
1D	18, 29, 31, 40	4–5, 22–23
1E	2, 16, 21, 26	8, 24–25
1F	3, 6, 15, 23, 25, 28, 30, 32	14, 30–33
1G	8, 19, 33, 39	9–13, 28–29
1H	10, 11, 12, 13, 34, 35, 36, 37	34–35

Answers

1. 39,000,076,000 **2.** 43,000,000 **3.** 274,245
4. 107,090 **5.** 60 billion **6.** $111.25 **7.** 0.00018
8. 80* **9.** 4 trillion **10.** 800* **11.** LaVale
12. Oakland **13.** 150
14. $4 + 0.06 + 0.00009 + 0.000007$ **15.** 11.54
16. 51.035 **17.** seventeen thousandths **18.** 2,358;
2,538; 2,547; 2,549 **19.** 9,500,000–10,000,000*
20. 8.0205 **21.** $138.00 **22.** 2 thousandths
23. 755.847 **24.** 8 ten-thousandths **25.** 683,731
26. 910,000 **27.** 80,000 **28** $58.55 **29.** St. Louis
30. 1,030,270 **31.** 877,725 **32.** 17 **33.** $800.00*
34. 7 **35.** 1985 **36.** 1982 **37.** 1984 **38.** Seven
hundred two and eighty-five ten-thousandths
39. $700–$900* **40.** 4.666, 4.66, 4.11, 4.066

Chapter 2

Objective	Test Items	Text Pages
2A	1, 5, 8, 21, 23, 28	46–47, 50–51, 54–57
2B	2, 15, 26, 34	48–49, 58–59, 60–61
2C	3, 11, 19, 32	66–67
2D	6, 9, 12, 27	62–63
2E	14, 17, 29, 30	62–63, 68–69
2F	7, 18, 22, 31	52–53
2G	10, 13, 20, 25	64–65
2H	4, 16, 24, 33	70–71

Answers

1. $14,476.50 **2.** < **3.** 0.89 **4.** $0.92
5. 799,510 **6.** 94.08 **7.** The number of grapefruit
in each case **8.** 17,883,600 **9.** 33.781
10. addition **11.** $57.00 **12.** 21,743.748
13. multiplication **14.** 0.048 **15.** $600–$800*
16. $3.68 **17.** 0.00060 **18.** $1.90 **19.** 6,002.81
20. subtraction **21.** 2 **22.** 0.05 m **23.** 2,137,440
24. 4,800 paper clips **25.** multiplication
26. 30–40* **27.** 25.20 **28.** $784.80 **29.** 0.0952
30. $0.90 **31.** the weight of the shark **32.** 4,657
33. 232 eggs **34.** C

*Answers may vary. Accept any reasonable estimate.

Chapter 3

Objective	Test Items	Text Pages
3A	2, 7, 8, 14	82–83, 88–89, 92–95
3B	3, 4, 9, 17, 20, 25, 29, 30	86–87, 90–91
3C	16, 10, 32, 26	102–103
3D	5, 12, 28, 34	98–99
3E	13, 15, 19, 31	104–105
3F	11, 27, 33, 36	96–97
3G	1, 6, 18, 35	100–101
3H	21, 22, 23, 24	108–109

Answers

1. C **2.** 819 **3.** 10+* **4.** 200* **5.** 8.04 **6.** D
7. 301 **8.** $470 **9.** $500* **10.** 0.00096 **11.** A
12. $2.09 **13.** 4.03 **14.** 2 **15.** 90.7 **16.** 78.15
17. 100* **18.** 28 yr **19.** 2,668 **20.** $80+*
21. Walnut St. and 7th St. **22.** Liberty Bell **23.** 7
24. D **25.** 4 **26.** 0.00516 **27.** C **28.** 0.0026
29. 30,000* **30.** 40–50* **31.** 170 **32.** 0.000271
33. A **34.** 2.102 **35.** 10 **36.** C

Chapter 4

Objective	Test Items	Text Pages
4A	1, 9, 18, 27, 37	118–119
4B	3, 7, 17, 23	120–121
4C	2, 16, 33, 36	122–123
4D	4, 11, 15, 19, 26	130–133
4E	5, 25, 34, 38	136–137
4F	10, 20, 31, 35	138–139
4G	8, 21, 22, 32	140–141, 146–149
4H	12, 13, 28, 29	128–129, 142–143
4I	6, 14, 24, 30	150–151

Answers

1. 3,276 **2.** 1.3×10^5 **3.** 10 **4.** 12 **5.** 15
6. $b + 15 = 92.78$, or equivalent equation **7.** 5 and
$\sqrt{25}$ **8.** 71 **9.** 224 and 3,000 **10.** 14 **11.** 280, or
$2^3 \times 5 \times 7$ **12.** $1,000* **13.** 100* **14.** 225*
15. 3 **16.** 8,200 **17.** 6 **18.** 411, 405, and 414
19. 120 **20.** 19 **21.** 3 **22.** $\frac{x}{4} = 3$ and $\frac{x}{4} + 2 = 5$
23. 14 **24.** B **25.** 8 **26.** 36 **27.** 518 **28.** 125
29. 50 **30.** $360 **31.** 10 **32.** 4 **33.** 2.55×10^2
34. 10 **35.** 45 **36.** 282,100 **37.** 6,114 **38.** 20

*Answers may vary. Accept any reasonable estimate.

Chapter 5

Objective	Test Items	Text Pages
5A	1, 2, 13, 33	164–165
5B	3, 6, 14, 23	168–169
5C	5, 15, 28, 31	166–167
5D	4, 7, 11, 34	174–177
5E	22, 27, 30, 39	182–187
5F	10, 20, 29, 40	188–189
5G	12, 21, 24, 32	172–173
5H	16, 17, 25, 35	170–171
5I	8, 19, 26, 37	180–181
5J	9, 18, 36, 38	190–191

Answers

1. $\frac{10}{12}, \frac{15}{18}, \frac{20}{24}, \ldots$ **2.** B **3.** C **4.** $\frac{13}{16}$ **5.** $2\frac{1}{3}$ **6.** D **7.** $\frac{4}{15}$
8. C **9.** A **10.** $\frac{1}{2}$ **11.** $\frac{3}{4}$ **12.** 3^{+}* **13.** 14 **14.** $\frac{2}{3}, \frac{3}{4}, \frac{4}{5}$
15. $\frac{51}{4}$ **16.** 2 **17.** D **18.** C **19.** 8 **20.** 1 **21.** 1*
22. $2\frac{5}{9}$ **23.** A **24.** 7* **25.** D **26.** 6 **27.** $5\frac{3}{4}$
28. 32 **29.** $1\frac{1}{6}$ **30.** $3\frac{1}{2}$ **31.** $\frac{9}{1}, \frac{18}{2}, \ldots$ **32.** 1* **33.** $\frac{4}{3}, \frac{8}{6}, \frac{12}{9}$,
$\frac{16}{12}, \frac{20}{15}, \frac{28}{21}, \ldots$ **34.** $1\frac{1}{10}$ **35.** D **36.** $8\frac{7}{12}$ **37.** 8
38. $0.74 **39.** $3\frac{1}{2}$ **40.** $7\frac{5}{6}$

Chapter 6

Objective	Test Items	Text Pages
6A	1, 7, 9, 14, 25	200–203, 208–209
6B	4, 13, 30, 39	210–213
6C	5, 23, 29, 34	216–217
6D	2, 11, 12, 18, 36, 38	220–221
6E	10, 28, 33, 40	222–223
6F	3, 8, 17, 24, 27	206–207
6G	15, 16, 31, 32	204–205
6H	19, 20, 21, 22	218–219
6I	6, 26, 35, 37	224–225

Answers

1. $\frac{1}{7}$ **2.** 0.60 **3.** 20* **4.** $\frac{1}{6}$ **5.** $\frac{47}{100}$ **6.** 3 boxes **7.** $\frac{1}{5}$
8. 32* **9.** $1\frac{1}{9}$ **10.** $\frac{1}{2}$ **11.** 1.6 **12.** 0.63 **13.** $\frac{4}{7}$
14. 6 **15.** D **16.** C **17.** 1* **18.** 1.2 **19.** 4
batches **20.** $7\frac{7}{8}$ cups **21.** $\frac{4}{9}$ cup **22.** $1\frac{1}{8}$ cups **23.** $2\frac{4}{5}$
24. B **25.** $\frac{2}{3}$ **26.** 7 loaves **27.** 8* **28.** $2\frac{1}{2}$ **29.** $\frac{7}{20}$
30. 17 banners **31.** C **32.** D **33.** $1\frac{1}{2}$ **34.** $2\frac{33}{50}$
35. 17 cases **36.** 0.75 **37.** 8 contestants **38.** $0.\overline{6}$
39. $\frac{7}{12}$ **40.** $\frac{11}{15}$

Chapter 7

Objective	Test Items	Text Pages
7A	4, 5, 6, 7	236–237
7B	1, 24, 30, 37	236–237, 240–241, 246–249
7C	3, 9, 16, 36	238–241, 246–249
7D	2, 22, 27, 29	246–249
7E	10, 11, 12, 13	256–257
7F	8, 14, 15, 26	250–251
7G	18, 19, 20, 21	254–255
7H	17, 23, 25, 28	244–245
7I	35, 38, 39, 40	252–253
7J	31, 32, 33, 34	260–261

Answers

1. C **2.** 43 lb 9 oz **3.** 6 pt **4.** 86 mm **5.** MN and
RN **6.** 8 cm **7.** N and T **8.** 1 h 52 min **9.** I, II
and III **10.** 9.3°C **11.** 22.9°C **12.** 30°F
13. 30°F **14.** $4\frac{1}{2}$ d **15.** 32 h 17 min **16.** 8,050
mL **17.** 1 h 30 min **18.** D **19.** 6 h 15 min
20. 10:00 PM **21.** 12:40 PM **22.** 6 yd 1 ft **23.** 1 hr
30 min **24.** foot **25.** 1 h 5 min **26.** 4 h 47 min
27. 4 ft 9 in. **28.** 3 h 20 min **29.** 6 lb 10 oz
30. D **31.** 2 h 35 min **32.** 6 h 50 min **33.** 14 h 15
min **34.** 1 hr 50 min **35.** 16 mph **36.** 6 yd
37. B **38.** 6 h **39.** $247\frac{1}{2}$ mi **40.** A

Chapter 8

Objective	Test Items	Text Pages
8A	1, 5, 8, 25	272–273
8B	7, 14, 34, 38	276–277
8C	2, 6, 16, 20	280–283
8D	11, 30, 33, 37	284–285
8E	3, 15, 31, 36	288–289
8F	9, 13, 18, 40	290–291
8G	10, 17, 27, 35	296–297
8H	4, 26, 28, 32	274–275
8I	12, 19, 29, 39	286–287, 292–293
8J	21, 22, 23, 24	298–299

Answers

1. 6 **2.** 30% **3.** 50% **4.** $375 **5.** 9 **6.** 12%
7. 450 m **8.** $3\frac{3}{4}$ **9.** 156 **10.** $33\frac{1}{3}$% **11.** 0.9
12. $1,584.00 **13.** 1,000 **14.** 60 m **15.** 30%
16. 0.0014 **17.** 20% **18.** 50 **19.** $75,000.00 **20.**
21. traveling **22.** A **23.** 3.6 h **24.** 9.6 h **25.** 60
26. 8 **27.** 8% **28.** C **29.** $84.00 **30.** 7.9 **31.** $33\frac{1}{3}$
32. B **33.** $64.80 **34.** 50 **35.** $66\frac{2}{3}$% **36.** 250%
37. 2,812.5 **38.** 1 in. = 2 ft **39.** 15% **40.** 30

*Answers may vary. Accept any reasonable estimate.

Chapter 9

Objective	Test Items	Text Pages
9A	4, 5, 34, 44	310–311
9B	1, 17, 42, 45	312–313
9C	2, 16, 24, 31	314–315
9D	18, 19, 35, 41	316–317
9E	20, 21, 38, 39	322–323
9F	3, 6, 29, 46	326–327
9G	7, 32, 37, 47	328–329, 336–337
9H	8, 22, 33, 48	330–331, 338-339
9I	10, 23, 36, 49	332–333
9J	9, 15, 30, 50	338–341
9K	11, 25, 26, 27	318–319

Answers

1. $\angle Q$, $\angle PQR$, or $\angle RQP$ **2.** II and III only
3. 65° **4.** figure A **5.** figure B **6.** I and II only
7. $\overline{RS}$ **8.** I and II only **9.** Figure II only **10.** 21
11. 9 **12.** 35 **13.** $\angle 1$, $\angle 4$, or $\angle 5$ **14.** $\angle 2$, $\angle 3$,
$\angle 6$, or $\angle 7$ **15.** figures I and III only **16.** I and III
only **17.** 143° **18.** figure D **19.** figure A **20.** $\overrightarrow{RS}$
and $\overrightarrow{TU}$ **21.** $\overrightarrow{RU}$ and $\overrightarrow{TS}$ **22.** 2 **23.** 3 ft **24.** C
25. 6 cm **26.** 10 cm **27.** 12 cm **28.** 62.5 g
29. 20° **30.** figure III only **31.** A **32.** pentagon
33. I, II, and III **34.** A **35.** C **36.** 150°
37. quadrilateral, parallelogram **38.** figure C
39. figure D **40.** 160 **41.** C **42.** I and III only
43. 49 inches **44.** line segment **45.** $\angle EXA$,
$\angle AXE$ **46.** I and II only **47.** $\overline{HG}$ and $\overline{AB}$ **48.** A
49. 25 cm **50.** I and III only **51.** $306 **52.** 31°

Chapter 10

Objective	Test Items	Text Pages
10A	1, 4, 9, 13, 33, 34	352–355
10B	5, 10, 16, 24, 27, 28	356–359, 362–363
10C	3, 12, 15, 26	366–367
10D	6, 19, 37, 39	370–371
10E	11, 20, 35, 40	372–373
10F	7, 14, 21, 23	360–361
10G	8, 17, 29, 30	364–365
10H	2, 22, 31, 38	368–369
10I	18, 25, 32, 36	374–375

Answers

1. 10.2 cm **2.** 2 km **3.** cylinder **4.** 10 ft **5.** 108
cm² **6.** 177.6 cm² **7.** 4 in. **8.** 251 **9.** $628\frac{4}{7}$ ft
10. 81 m² **11.** 60 in³ **12.** rectangular prism **13.** 89
cm **14.** 2 times **15.** triangular prism **16.** A
17. 12 ft **18.** 1,695.6 m³ **19.** 408.2 m² **20.** 1,000
in³ **21.** 3 times **22.** 168 m² **23.** Plan I only
24. 26 cm² **25.** $P = 2l + 2w$ **26.** rectangular
pyramid **27.** 84 ft² **28.** 60 in.² **29.** 40 m **30.** 12
years old **31.** 1,264 ft² **32.** $V = lwh$ **33.** 21.98
m **34.** 8.0 cm **35.** 120 cm³ **36.** 40 m² **37.** 150
ft² **38.** 128 **39.** 258 m² **40.** 653.12 m³

Chapter 11

Objective	Test Items	Text Pages
11A	3, 16, 17, 29	386–387
11B	2, 8, 24, 28	388–391
11C	5, 14, 26, 31	404–407
11D	1, 4, 9, 19	401–403
11E	6, 18, 25, 30	410–411
11F	7, 15, 27, 32	412–413
11G	20, 21, 22, 23	394–395
11H	10, 11, 12, 13	408–409

Answers

1. $\frac{1}{3}$ **2.** 9 **3.** C **4.** 1 **5.** D **6.** $\frac{1}{25}$ **7.** $\frac{1}{6}$ **8.** 4.5 **9.** $\frac{8}{11}$
10. $810,000 **11.** 1985 at Moore's **12.** $140,000
13. 0 **14.** 6 **15.** $\frac{6}{55}$ **16.** 40–59 **17.** 50% **18.** $\frac{5}{36}$
19. $\frac{4}{7}$ **20.** 6 **21.** 4 **22.** I only **23.** increased **24.** $\frac{1}{8}$
25. D **26.** (B, 5), (B, 6), (W, 6) **27.** $\frac{1}{8}$ **28.** 9
29. 108° **30.** 0 **31.** 27 **32.** $\frac{2}{7} \cdot \frac{1}{6}$

Chapter 12

Objective	Test Items	Text Pages
12A	1, 2, 18, 41	424–425
12B	8, 25, 37, 42	424–425
12C	5, 14, 21, 43	428–431
12D	3, 15, 33, 44	434–437
12E	10, 16, 17, 30	440–441
12F	11, 22, 34, 40	446–447
12G	9, 20, 36, 39	452–453
12H	6, 7, 23, 35	448–449
12I	13, 24, 31, 38	454–455
12J	4, 12, 19, 32	444–445
12K	26, 27, 28, 29	450–451

Answers

1. ⁻3 **2.** ⁻7 **3.** 14 **4.** $n = 134 - (^-80)$ **5.** ⁻7
6. R **7.** $M = (^-2, ^-3)$ and $N = (2,1)$ **8.** D **9.** ⁻4
10. $x < 4$ **11.** C **12.** 1791 **13.** D **14.** $^-4 + ^-7$
15. ⁻3 **16.** ⁻23 **17.** ⁻27 **18.** P **19.** 20,602 feet
20. (2, 13), (0, 9), (⁻2, 5), (⁻4, 1) **21.** ⁻27 **22.** D
23. (⁻1, 1) **24.** C **25.** 6, 5, ⁻2, ⁻9 **26.** 1880's
27. 1970's **28.** B **29.** 1930's **30.** 9 **31.** C
32. A **33.** ⁻24 **34.** B **35.** (⁻4, 0) **36.** $n = ^-14$
37. > **38.** D **39.** $n = 0$ and $m = 2$ **40.** D **41.** ⁻1
42. ⁻8, ⁻5, 3, 7 **43.** 21 **44.** 4

PLACEMENT TEST

The Placement Test is a survey that can be used to test students' retention of material covered in the previous grade. An analysis of class scores can provide the teacher with information about which topics students may have more or less difficulty with during the year.

To test for each student's readiness for Chapter 1, or any chapter, it is recommended that the Skills Inventory test for that chapter be used. These tests are designed to assess students on prerequisite skills for the concepts to be covered in each chapter. A variety of questioning techniques help pinpoint areas of weakness before work in the chapter begins.

CUMULATIVE TESTS

Three tests allow for periodic testing of learning objectives. They are designed to be used after Chapters 3, 6, and 9.

FINAL TEST

The Final Test assesses students' accomplishment of the learning objectives of the grade. It is recommended that this test be used in conjunction with the cumulative tests to insure a thorough evaluation of students' retention of skills and concepts.

A student answer sheet for use with all multiple choice tests can be found in the Management section of this book.

A scoring chart for tests can be found on the reverse side of this page.

NUMBER OF ITEMS ON TEST

No. of Items Missed	15	16	20	22	24	25	28	30	31	32	33	34	36	37	38	40	44	48	50	52
0	100	100	100	100	100	100	100	100	100	100	100	100	100	100	100	100	100	100	100	100
1	93	94	95	95	96	96	96	97	97	97	97	97	97	97	97	98	98	98	98	98
2	87	88	90	91	92	92	93	93	94	94	94	94	94	95	95	95	95	96	96	96
3	80	81	85	86	88	88	89	90	90	91	91	91	92	92	92	93	93	94	94	94
4	73	75	80	82	83	84	86	87	87	88	88	88	89	89	89	90	91	92	92	92
5	67	69	75	77	79	80	82	83	84	84	85	85	86	86	87	88	89	90	90	90
6	60	63	70	73	75	76	79	80	81	81	82	82	83	84	84	85	86	88	88	88
7	53	56	65	68	71	72	75	77	77	78	79	79	81	81	82	83	84	85	86	87
8	47	50	60	64	67	68	71	73	74	75	76	76	78	78	79	80	82	83	84	85
9	40	44	55	59	63	64	68	70	71	72	73	74	75	76	76	78	80	81	82	83
10	33	38	50	55	58	60	64	67	68	69	70	71	72	73	74	75	77	79	80	81
11	27	31	45	50	54	56	61	63	65	66	67	68	69	70	71	73	75	77	78	79
12	20	25	40	45	50	52	57	60	61	63	64	65	67	68	68	70	73	75	76	77
13	13	19	35	41	46	48	54	57	58	59	61	62	64	65	66	68	70	73	74	75
14	7	13	30	36	42	44	50	53	55	56	58	59	61	62	63	65	68	71	72	73
15	0	6	25	32	38	40	46	50	52	53	55	56	58	59	61	63	66	69	70	71
16		0	20	27	33	36	43	47	48	50	52	53	56	57	58	60	64	67	68	69
17			15	23	29	32	39	43	45	47	48	50	53	54	55	58	61	65	66	67
18			10	18	25	28	36	40	42	44	45	47	50	51	53	55	59	63	64	65
19			5	14	21	24	32	37	39	41	42	44	47	49	50	53	57	60	62	63
20			0	9	17	20	29	33	35	38	39	41	44	46	47	50	55	58	60	62
21				5	13	16	25	30	32	34	36	38	42	43	45	48	52	56	58	60
22				0	8	12	21	27	29	31	33	35	39	41	42	45	50	54	56	58
23					4	8	18	23	26	28	30	32	36	38	39	43	48	52	54	56
24					0	4	14	20	23	25	27	29	33	35	37	40	45	50	52	54
25						0	11	17	19	22	24	26	31	32	34	38	43	48	50	52
26							7	13	16	19	21	24	28	30	32	35	41	46	48	50
27							4	10	13	16	18	21	25	27	29	33	39	44	46	48
28							0	7	10	13	15	18	22	24	26	30	36	42	44	46
29								3	6	9	12	15	19	22	24	28	34	40	42	44
30								0	3	6	9	12	17	19	21	25	32	38	40	42
31									0	3	6	9	14	16	18	23	30	35	38	40
32										0	3	6	11	14	16	20	27	33	36	38
33											0	3	8	11	13	18	25	31	34	37
34												0	6	8	11	15	23	29	32	35
35													3	5	8	13	20	27	30	33
36													0	3	5	10	18	25	28	31
37														0	3	8	16	23	26	29
38															0	5	14	21	24	27
39																3	11	19	22	25
40																0	9	17	20	23
41																	7	15	18	21
42																	5	13	16	19
43																	2	10	14	17
44																	0	8	12	15
45																		6	10	13
46																		4	8	12
47																		2	6	10
48																		0	4	8
49																			2	6
50																			0	4
51																				2
52																				0

Name _____ Date _____

1. What is the value of 9.2468 rounded to the nearest tenth?

   a. 9.25   b. 9.3
   c. 9.2   d. 9.0

2. If $32 - n = 21$, then n equals

   a. 11   b. 21
   c. 32   d. 53

3.

   Classify this angle.

   a. acute   b. obtuse
   c. right   d. straight

4. $30)\overline{1,566}$

   a. 52   b. 52.2
   c. 520   d. 522

5. 0.3×0.2

   a. 6.0   b. 60
   c. 0.6   d. 0.06

6. What is the greatest common factor of 24 and 42?

   a. 2   b. 4
   c. 6   d. 8

7. In a room of 27 adults, there are 16 women. What is the ratio of men to women?

   a. $\frac{11}{16}$ b. $\frac{27}{16}$
   c. $\frac{16}{27}$ d. $\frac{11}{27}$

8. The sum of 18.782 and 18.86 is

   a. less than 36
   b. between 36 and 37
   c. between 37 and 38
   d. greater than 38

9. The short word name for 37,483,209 is

   a. 3 million, 748 thousand, 3209
   b. 37 million, 483 thousand, 209
   c. 3 billion, 748 million, 3 thousand, 209
   d. 37 billion, 4 million, 83 thousand, 209

10. What percent of 80 is 40?

   a. 2%   b. 32%
   c. 40%   d. 50%

11.

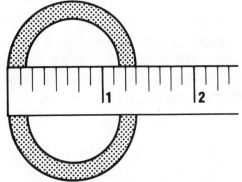

   To the nearest $\frac{1}{8}$ inch, the letter "O" above measures

   a. 1 in.   b. $1\frac{1}{4}$ in.
   c. $1\frac{3}{8}$ in.   d. $1\frac{1}{2}$ in.

1

12.

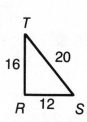 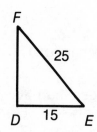

If △RST ~ △DEF in the figure above, what is the length of $\overline{DF}$?

a. 21   b. 20
c. 19   d. 10

---

13. Jack has a $\frac{2}{3}$ chance of carrying his pail of water home without spilling it. Jill's chance is $\frac{3}{5}$. What is the probability that both Jack and Jill will make it home with full pails of water?

a. $\frac{2}{5}$ b. $\frac{5}{8}$
c. $\frac{9}{10}$ d. $\frac{19}{15}$

---

14. My house number is a two-digit odd number. The tens digit is the square of the ones digit. Which of these numbers is on my house?

a. 24   b. 42
c. 39   d. 93

---

15. The number 1,845 is <u>not</u> divisible by

a. 3   b. 5
c. 6   d. 9

---

16. On which number line does *P* mark the opposite of ⁻4?

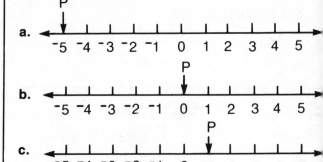

---

17. Which decimal is equal to $\frac{1}{4}$?

a. 0.14   b. 0.25
c. 0.4   d. 0.5

18.

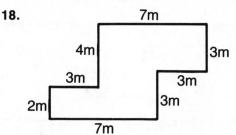

What is the perimeter of the figure?

a. 20 m   b. 26 m
c. 32 m   d. 39 m

---

19. Al Oerter has won 4 Olympic gold medals for the discus throw. The last time he won was in 1968, with a throw that was 27 ft $7\frac{1}{2}$ in. farther than his throw the first time he won in 1956. To find how far he threw the discus in 1956, you would need to know

a. how far he threw the discus in 1968.
b. the weight of the discus.
c. how far he threw the discus in 1960.
d. how many Olympics he entered.

0. In the metric system, the amount of gasoline, milk, or juice in a container is measured in

   a. centimeters   **b.** liters
   c. meters   **d.** kilograms

---

1. Which of the following is equivalent to $\frac{3}{5}$?

   a. $\frac{5}{7}$ **b.** $\frac{9}{25}$ **c.** $\frac{32}{52}$ **d.** $\frac{60}{100}$

---

2. $\frac{3}{5} + \frac{3}{4}$

   a. $\frac{3}{9}$ **b.** $\frac{6}{9}$ **c.** $\frac{27}{20}$ **d.** $\frac{27}{40}$

---

3. Dale had dark slacks and white slacks. Dale also had 3 different shirts. They were plaid, plain, and striped. How many different outfits (slacks and shirt) could Dale wear?

   a. 2   **b.** 3   **c.** 5   **d.** 6

---

4. Liz wrote this addition problem on her paper:

$$
\begin{array}{r}
6.32 \\
4.3 \\
+\,0.113 \\
\hline
0.788
\end{array}
$$

Her teacher marked it wrong. Which one of the following best explains why it was marked wrong?

   a. Liz does not know her basic addition facts.
   b. Liz does not understand decimal places.
   c. Liz does not know the rule for "carrying" in addition.
   d. The teacher made a mistake; Liz's answer is correct.

25.

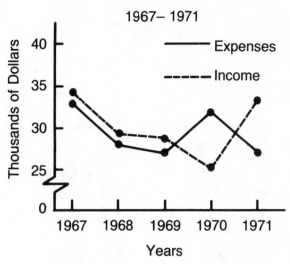

Income and Expenses of Metro, Co.
1967– 1971

According to the graph, in which year did the Metro Company make the largest dollar amount of profit?

   a. 1968   **b.** 1969
   c. 1970   **d.** 1971

26.

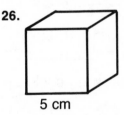

5 cm

What is the surface area of the cube?

   a. 150 cm²   **b.** 125 cm²
   c. 30 cm²   **d.** 25 cm²

---

27. If $\frac{a}{b} = \frac{c}{d}$, then which one of the following statements is true?

   a. $\frac{a}{d} = \frac{b}{c}$ **b.** $\frac{c}{b} = \frac{a}{d}$
   c. $a \times c = b \times d$ **d.** $a \times d = b \times c$

28.

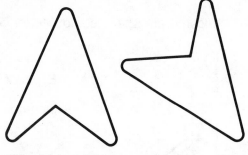

What kind of movement does this pair of figures demonstrate?

a. translation   b. reflection
c. rotation   d. symmetry

29.

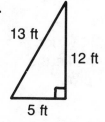

13 ft
12 ft
5 ft

The area of the triangle shown above is

a. 25 ft²   b. 30 ft²   c. 32.5 ft² d. 84 ft²

30. $\frac{1}{5}$ is equivalent to what percent?

a. $\frac{1}{5}$%   b. 5%   c. 15%   d. 20%

31. If $x > ^-2$, which of the following could be the value of x?

a. $^-1$ b. $^-3$ c. $^-4$ d. $^-10$

32.

Time (P.M.)	1:00	1:30	2:00	2:30	. . .
Temperature	80.6°	81.7°	82.8°	83.9°	

A scientist, who was doing an experiment, used the chart above to keep a record of the temperature. According to the chart, what temperature would be expected at 3:00 PM?

a. 84°   b. 84.6°   c. 84.91° d. 85°

33. Of the following numbers, which is the largest prime?

a. 19   b. 29
c. 39   d. 49

34. $62\overline{)25,014}$

Which of the following is the best estimate of the quotient?

a. 4   b. 40
c. 400   d. 4,000

35. What is another way of writing $7\frac{3}{5}$?

a. $7 \times \frac{3}{5}$ b. $7 \div \frac{3}{5}$
c. $7 - \frac{3}{5}$ d. $7 + \frac{3}{5}$

36. At a carnival booth, you can win a prize by guessing the color of a marble drawn from a jar. If you know that there are 25 red, 25 green, 25 yellow, and 25 blue marbles in the jar, what are your chances of winning a prize on your first try?

a. 1 out of 4   b. 1 out of 25
c. 4 out of 25   d. 25 out of 75

37.

What is the dotted line in this circle called?

a. radius   b. diameter
c. chord   d. tangent

8. In numeral form, seven and six hundred forty-five ten-thousandths is

a. 7.645   b. 7.0645
c. 7.00645   d. 0.7645

9. If $6 \times n = 30$, then n equals

a. 90   b. 36
c. 24   d. 5

0.

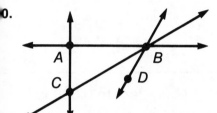

Which of the following is a pair of perpendicular lines?

a. $\overleftrightarrow{AB}$ and $\overrightarrow{BD}$ b. $\overleftrightarrow{AB}$ and $\overleftrightarrow{CB}$
c. $\overleftrightarrow{AB}$ and $\overleftrightarrow{AC}$ d. $\overleftrightarrow{BD}$ and $\overleftrightarrow{CB}$

1. $1\frac{1}{2} \times \frac{1}{4}$

a. $\frac{3}{8}$ b. $\frac{3}{4}$
c. $1\frac{1}{8}$ d. $1\frac{3}{8}$

2. 25, 34, 47, 34, 21, 43

For the set of numbers above, the range is

a. 204   b. 47
c. 34   d. 26

43. The best estimate of $\frac{2}{3}$ of 200 is

a. between 6 and 7
b. between 12 and 14
c. between 60 and 70
d. between 120 and 140

44. $2 - \frac{2}{3}$

a. 0   b. $\frac{1}{3}$ c. $1\frac{1}{3}$ d. $1\frac{2}{3}$

45.

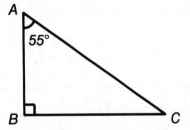

$\triangle ABC$ is a right triangle. What is the measure of $\angle ACB$?

a. 35°   b. 45°   c. 55°   d. 90°

46. $39.00 + ■ = $60.00

■ is closest to which of the following?

a. $10.00   b. $20.00
c. $30.00   d. $50.00

47. What number is 4 more than ⁻1?

a. ⁻3   b. 3   c. ⁻5   d. 5

48. The shop manager is planning a new display of slacks. Each of four racks will hold 3 dozen pair. Which equation could you use to find how many dozen slacks will be on display?

a. $4 \times 3 = n$ b. $n \times 3 = 4$
c. $n \times 4 = 3$ d. $4 \div 3 = n$

49.

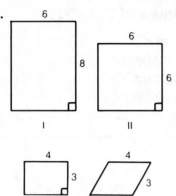

Which pair of figures is similar?

a. I and II
b. I and III
c. II and III
d. I and IV

50. What is the estimated product of 6,025 and 30?

a. 180
b. 1,800
c. 18,000
d. 180,000

51. 3.045×100

a. 0.03045
b. 30.45
c. 304.5
d. 3.04500

52.

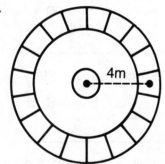

The figure above shows a circular sidewalk around a fountain in a park. About how long is the sidewalk?

a. 16 m
b. 25 m
c. 50 m
d. 64 m

53.

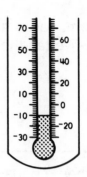

What temperature is shown on this thermometer?

a. ⁻10°   b. ⁻5°   c. 5°   d. 10°

54. $5 - 0.43$

a. 0.07
b. 0.38
c. 4.57
d. 5.43

55. The percent equivalent to 0.625 is

a. 0.00625%
b. 0.625%
c. 6.25%
d. 62.5%

56.

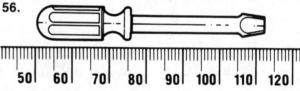

The length of this miniature screwdriver to the nearest centimeter is

a. 6 cm
b. 10 cm
c. 60 cm
d. 110 cm

57. 8,1■4

What value of the missing digit would allow rounding to 8,200?

a. none
b. less than 50
c. greater than or equal to 50
d. all values

58. 7,342
    − 1,018

    a. 6,036   b. 6,324
    c. 6,334   d. 6,336

_____

59. Boris bought 13 shares of Chem, Inc.
    for $13.25 per share. He then sold 6
    shares of this stock for $15.75 per
    share. Later, he sold the rest of the
    stock for $19.50 per share. Excluding
    any fees, how much profit did Boris
    make on Chem, Inc. stock?

    a. $40.63   b. $58.75
    c. $77.75   d. $231

_____

60.

    P   Q   R   S

    You win the game if 3 is spun. Which
    spinner would you choose?

    a. P   b. Q
    c. R   d. S

_____

61. $\frac{0.0867}{100}$

    a. 86.7   b. 8.67
    c. 0.00867   d. 0.000867

_____

62. Which of the following is between 0.4
    and 0.8?

    a. 0.72   b. 0.39
    c. 0.12   d. 0.84

Questions 63 and 64 are based on the
information below.

A survey was taken of 1,000
households in each of three cities.
Each household was asked which TV
station they used to watch the
presidential news conference. This is
the data collected:

City	Station #1	#2	#3
A	302	225	290
B	224	313	204
C	230	206	348

63. The data can be displayed on a
    pictograph with a scale of 1🏠 = 25
    households. How many 🏠 will represent
    listeners to station #2 in City A?

    a. 40   b. 9   c. $4\frac{1}{2}$ d. $2\frac{1}{4}$

---

64. From the data given, which of these
    statements is false?

    a. Station #1 had the most listeners in
       City A.
    b. Station #2 was the least popular in
       City C.
    c. Station #3 was watched by more
       families than either of the other two
       stations.
    d. All 3,000 households watched the
       news conference.

_____

65. The Central Standard Time zone is the
    next zone west of the Eastern Standard
    Time zone.

    A plane left a city at 11:45 AM Eastern
    Standard Time and reached its
    destination at 1:25 PM Central Standard
    Time. How long did the trip take?

    a. 1 h 40 min   b. 2 h 20 min
    c. 2 h 40 min   d. 3 h 40 min

66. $3\frac{1}{8} \div \frac{1}{8}$

  a. $\frac{25}{64}$ **b.** 3   **c.** 4   **d.** 25

67.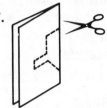

What will the figure above look like when it is cut out and unfolded?

  a.   **b.**

  c.   **d.**

---

68. $4^3 = \blacksquare$

What is $\blacksquare$?

  a. $4 \times 4 \times 4$ **b.** 4×3
  c. $4 + 4 + 4$ **d.** $3 + 3 + 3 + 3$

---

69. The least common multiple of 10 and 36 is

  a. 2   **b.** 36   **c.** 180   **d.** 360

70.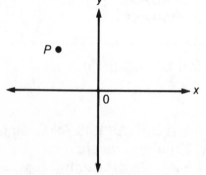

Which of the following could be the coordinates of point P above?

  a. (3,⁻3) **b.** (⁻3,3) **c.** (3,3) **d.** (⁻3,⁻3)

71.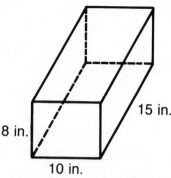

15 in.

8 in.

10 in.

This rectangular carton will hold

  a. 33 in.³   **b.** 132 in.³
  c. 700 in.³   **d.** 1,200 in.³

---

72. Tina has collected 583 pennies and wants to wrap them in rolls of 50 to take to the bank. She does not want any pennies left, so she looks for

  a. no more   **b.** 8 more
  c. 17 more   **d.** 33 more

---

73. A department store received a shipment of 250 glasses. 2% were broken. How many glasses in the shipment were broken?

  a. 125   **b.** 50   **c.** 25   **d.** 5

---

74. The fraction $\frac{6}{4}$ is between

  a. 0 and 1   **b.** 1 and 2
  c. 2 and 4   **d.** 4 and 6

---

75. Shirley's recipe for fruit salad calls for 4 cups of cherries, 2 cups of grapes, and 3 cups of orange sections. This recipe serves 6 people. Shirley is having 10 people over for dinner. How many cups of cherries will she need?

  a. 15 cups   **b.** 7 cups
  c. $6\frac{2}{3}$ cups   **d.** 6 cups

CUMULATIVE TEST Chapters 1–3 Page 1

1. Three hundred nine and fifty-one thousandths can be written

   a. 309.0050
   b. 309.0051
   c. 309.051
   d. 309.51

2. $64,089 \times 7$

   a. 448,603
   b. 448,623
   c. 449,323
   d. 454,023

3. The Atherton Band had $1,027.39 for their trip. Rounded to the nearest dollar this amount is

   a. $1,027.00
   b. $1,027.40
   c. $1,028.00
   d. $1,030.00

4. A store manager ordered 25 skirts at $14.25 each. Which of the following would be reasonable for the total cost of his order?

   a. less than $15
   b. about $40
   c. about $100
   d. over $250

5.

SUNDAY EDITION

State	Number of Newspapers
Colorado	1.010 million
Georgia	1.076 million
Tennessee	1.028 million
Washington	1.091 million

The table above shows the number of newspapers printed on Sunday in four states. Which state prints the greatest number of papers on Sunday?

   a. Colorado
   b. Georgia
   c. Tennessee
   d. Washington

6. $\begin{array}{r} 8,006 \\ \times\ \ 304 \end{array}$

   a. 2,433,824
   b. 2,434,824
   c. 2,436,864
   d. 2,720,204

7. If $68.3 \div \blacksquare = 0.683$, then $\blacksquare =$

   a. 0.01
   b. 0.1
   c. 10
   d. 100

8. Bricks cost $0.52 each. At that price, how much would 1,000 bricks cost?

   a. $5.20
   b. $52.00
   c. $520.00
   d. $5,200.00

9. $62\overline{)5.332}$

   a. 0.086
   b. 0.86
   c. 8.6
   d. 86.0

10. $71.\blacksquare \times 0.4\blacksquare9$

    Some digits are hidden in the numbers above. Which of the following estimates of the product is the most reasonable?

    a. 0
    b. 35
    c. 70
    d. 120

11. $\begin{array}{r} 406,575 \\ -263,189 \end{array}$

    a. 162,386
    b. 143,486
    c. 143,386
    d. 142,386

12. $0.14\overline{)72.8}$

    a. 0.52
    b. 5.2
    c. 52
    d. 520

9

13.
$$
\begin{array}{r}
0.48 \\
\times\,0.15 \\
\hline
240 \\
48 \\
\hline
720
\end{array}
$$

The problem above has not been finished. What is the correct answer?

a. 0.0072   b. 0.072
c. 0.7200   d. 7.20

Use the graph below for <u>questions 14 and 15.</u>

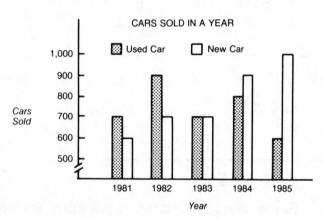

CARS SOLD IN A YEAR

14. The greatest number of used cars was sold in

a. 1982   b. 1983
c. 1984   d. 1985

15. In what year were the same number of new and used cars sold?

a. 1981   b. 1982
c. 1983   d. 1984

16.

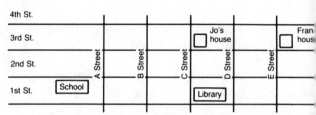

About how many blocks is it from Jo's house to the school?

a. 2   b. 3
c. 5   d. 6

17. There are 41 classes in an elementary school. Which of the following is a reasonable estimate for the number of students in the school?

a. 100   b. 200
c. 1,000   d. 4,000

18. $89\overline{)57{,}2\blacksquare\blacksquare}$

Some digits are hidden above. How many digits will the quotient have?

a. 4   b. 3
c. 2   d. 1

19. $0.06 \times 90 \times 2$

a. 10.8   b. 1.08
c. 0.108   d. 0.0108

20. $101.5 \div 0.5$

a. 20.3   b. 25.1
c. 203   d. 251

UMULATIVE TEST   **Chapters 1–3 Page 3**

1. What is the remainder if 903 is divided by 216?

   a. 39   b. 49
   c. 59   d. 161

2. The product of two numbers is between 0.2 and 0.25. The two numbers could be

   a. 2.1 and 1   b. 2.1 and 0.1
   c. 2.1 and 0.01   d. 2.1 and 0.001

Use the following information for <u>questions 3 to 26.</u>

Memorial Bridge has a toll of $1.20 per vehicle and $2,550 was collected one day. Woodrow Wilson Bridge has a toll of $0.70 per vehicle and 950 vehicles crossed the bridge the same day.

3. What operation would you use with $1.20 and $2,550 to find how many vehicles crossed Memorial Bridge on that day?

   a. addition   b. subtraction
   c. multiplication   d. division

4. What was the total amount of money collected from both bridges that day?

   a. $3,215.00   b. $3,500.00
   c. $3,501.90   d. $3,725.00

5. What was the total number of vehicles that crossed both bridges that day?

   a. 2,125   b. 3,075
   c. 3,500   d. 3,690

26. Which of the following facts is needed to find out about how many people crossed the Woodrow Wilson Bridge in vehicles that day?

   a. The Woodrow Wilson Bridge is about 1 mile long.
   b. About 800 of the vehicles were cars.
   c. About 550 of the drivers were men.
   d. An average of about 2 people were in each vehicle.

27. $6■■.08 – $419.■3

   Some digits are hidden in each of the numbers above. Which of the following estimates of the difference is the most reasonable?

   a. $2.03   b. $20.00
   c. $250.00   d. $1,000.00

28. What is the place-value of the 4 in the number 5,471,020,690,131?

   a. hundred billions   b. billions
   c. hundred millions   d. millions

29. 48)‾5‾7‾0‾

   a. 1 R9   b. 11 R42
   c. 12 R4   d. 12 R14

30. A fire officer's jacket costs $73.50. How much must a city pay to buy 28 jackets?

    a. $205.80   b. $218.80
    c. $2,058.00   d. $2,188.00

31. $280.49 ÷ 7

    a. $4.07   b. $4.70
    c. $40.07   d. $40.70

32. 800 + 7 + 0.06 + 0.0002

    a. 87.62   b. 807.0602
    c. 807.062   d. 8,007.06002

33. What is the best estimate for 36,420 ÷ 41?

    a. 90   b. 600
    c. 900   d. 9,000

CUMULATIVE TEST   Chapters 4–6 Page 1

1. Which number is equivalent to $\frac{9}{4}$?

   a. $9\frac{1}{4}$ b. $2\frac{3}{4}$

   c. $2\frac{1}{4}$ d. $1\frac{2}{4}$

2. $\frac{5}{7} \div 5$

   a. 7   b. $\frac{25}{7}$

   c. $\frac{25}{35}$ d. $\frac{1}{7}$

3. If $\frac{1}{6} + \frac{12}{13} = n$, then n is closest to

   a. 0   b. 1
   c. 2   d. 19

4. If $\frac{4}{5}x = \frac{8}{15}$, then x is

   a. $\frac{4}{15}$ b. $\frac{2}{3}$

   c. $\frac{32}{75}$ d. $1\frac{1}{2}$

5. In which list are the fractions correctly ordered from the greatest to the least?

   a. $\frac{9}{10}, \frac{9}{11}, \frac{9}{12}$ b. $\frac{8}{11}, \frac{9}{11}, \frac{10}{11}$

   c. $\frac{9}{12}, \frac{9}{11}, \frac{9}{10}$ d. $\frac{8}{11}, \frac{9}{10}, \frac{10}{9}$

6. In scientific notation, 12,000 is

   a. 1.2   b. 1.2×10^4

   c. 12×10^3 d. 1.2×10^5

7. If $2\frac{7}{8} \times 6\frac{1}{10} = n$, then n is closest to

   a. 12   b. 14
   c. 18   d. 21

8. Which fraction is not written in simplest form?

   a. $\frac{5}{6}$ b. $\frac{6}{7}$

   c. $\frac{7}{12}$ d. $\frac{8}{12}$

9. A gymnastics team has $6\frac{1}{2}$ yd of cloth to make banners. Each banner requires $1\frac{1}{4}$ yd of cloth. How many complete banners can the team make?

   a. 6   b. $5\frac{1}{5}$

   c. 5   d. 4

10. An ice sculpture weighed $25\frac{1}{3}$ lb. During the day. $6\frac{3}{4}$ lb ice melted. How much ice was left?

   a. $18\frac{5}{12}$ lb   b. $18\frac{7}{12}$ lb

   c. $19\frac{5}{12}$ lb   d. $19\frac{7}{12}$ lb

11.
$2\frac{3}{5}$	2.6	$\frac{13}{5}$
I	II	III

   Which of the above numbers are equivalent?

   a. I and II only   b. I and III only
   c. II and III only   d. I, II, and III

12. Which product is closest to 8?

   a. $2\frac{1}{4} \times 3\frac{8}{9}$ b. $2\frac{8}{9} \times 4\frac{1}{4}$

   c. $2\frac{11}{12} \times 3\frac{19}{20}$ d. $2\frac{19}{20} \times 2\frac{11}{12}$

CUMULATIVE TEST   **Chapters 4–6 Page 2**

13.

If $x = 5$, then $x + 3 = 8$	If $y = 2$, then $13 - y = 15$	If $z = 8$ then $10 = z - 2$
I	II	III

Which of the above is true?

a. I only   b. II only
c. III only   d. I and II only

14. What is the least common multiple (LCM) of 9 and 15?

a. 3   b. 6
c. 45   d. 135

15. Which number is equivalent to 0.45?

a. $\frac{9}{20}$ b. $\frac{4}{5}$
c. $2\frac{2}{9}$ d. $4\frac{1}{2}$

16. In a chess club, $\frac{1}{2}$ of the members are girls, and $\frac{3}{4}$ of these have blond hair. What part of the club members are girls with blond hair?

a. $\frac{1}{4}$ b. $\frac{3}{8}$
c. $\frac{2}{3}$ d. $1\frac{1}{4}$

17. What is $\frac{5}{9}$ written as a decimal?

a. 0.55   b. 0.5
c. $0.\overline{5}$ d. $5.\overline{5}$

18. What is the greatest common factor (GCF) of 6, 8, and 12?

a. 1   b. 2
c. 6   d. 24

19. Simplify $14 - 3 \cdot 4 - 2$.

a. 42   b. 22
c. 8   d. 0

20. What fraction is equivalent to $5\frac{1}{5}$?

a. $\frac{6}{10}$ b. $\frac{6}{5}$
c. $\frac{26}{5}$ d. $\frac{51}{5}$

21. $\frac{1}{8} \times \frac{8}{9}$

a. $\frac{1}{9}$ b. $\frac{9}{64}$
c. $\frac{8}{17}$ d. 9

22. Sam installed $12\frac{2}{3}$ yd of fence one morning and $10\frac{5}{6}$ yd fence that afternoon. How much did he install during that day?

a. $22\frac{1}{2}$ yd   b. $22\frac{7}{9}$ yd
c. 23 yd   d. $23\frac{1}{2}$ yd

23. Sara is 3 in. taller than 2 times her little brother's height. Sara is 63 in. tall. How tall is her little brother?

a. 57 in.   b. 33 in.
c. 30 in.   d. $20\frac{1}{3}$ in.

24.

$\frac{5}{6}$	$\frac{8}{10}$	$\frac{15}{18}$
I	II	III

Which of the above fractions are equivalent to $\frac{10}{12}$?

a. I only   b. II only
c. I and II only   d. I and III only

25.

P E T C A R E	T R E E S	J U L I E

J U L I E	T R E E S	P E T C A R E

Mary has 3 books. Two different ways to arrange the books are shown. How many different ways are there altogether to arrange the books?

a. 4
c. 6

b. 5
d. 9

26.

5	$\sqrt{25}$	$\sqrt{5}$
I	II	III

Which of the above numbers are equal?

a. I and II only
c. II and III only

b. I and III only
d. I, II, and III

27. A recipe for homemade noodles uses the following ingredients:

$1\frac{1}{2}$ cups flour
1 cup water
2 eggs

How many cups of flour are used for 3 recipes of the noodles?

a. $\frac{1}{2}$ cups
c. $2\frac{1}{2}$ cups

b. 2 cups
d. $4\frac{1}{2}$ cups

28. The graph below shows the number of students who joined school clubs.

YEAR	NUMBER OF STUDENTS JOINING CLUBS
1984	✶ ✶ ✶ ✶ ✶ ✶ ✶ ✶ ✶
1985	✶ ✶ ✶ ✶ ✶ ✶ ✶ ✶ ✶ ✶ ✶ ✶
1986	✶ ✶ ✶ ✶ ✶ ✶ ✶ ✶ ✶ ✶

Each ✶ stands for 20 students

How many more students joined clubs in 1985 than in 1984?

a. 3
c. 180

b. 60
d. 240

29. $\frac{3}{4} + \frac{5}{6}$

a. $\frac{7}{11}$
c. $\frac{9}{10}$

b. $\frac{8}{10}$
d. $1\frac{7}{12}$

30.

240	204	405
I	II	III

Which of the above numbers are divisible by both 4 and 5?

a. I only
c. I and II only

b. II only
d. II and III only

CUMULATIVE TEST   **Chapters 4–6 Page 4**

31. In standard form, 7.1×10^5 is

    a. 0.000071   b. 71,000
    c. 710,000   d. 7,100,000

_____

32. If $\frac{3}{2}r + \frac{1}{2} = 2\frac{1}{2}$, then r is

    a. $\frac{1}{2}$ b. $1\frac{1}{3}$
    c. 2   d. 3

33. A school is planning a dance in the gym to raise money for charity. Prizes will be awarded to the best dancers in three different catagories. Which of the following questions is the <u>least</u> important for the planners to answer?

    a. How many people might attend the dance?
    b. How much will the prizes cost?
    c. Who will clean up after the dance is over?
    d. Will there be an even number of people at the dance at 9:00 PM?

CUMULATIVE TEST   Chapters 7–9 Page 1

1.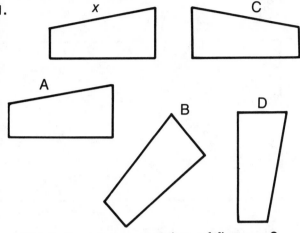

Which figure is a rotation of figure *x*?

a. A
b. B
c. C
d. D

2. Written as a percent, $\frac{15}{20}$ is

a. 0.75
b. 0.75%
c. 15%
d. 75%

3. A tornado moved 72 miles in 3 hours. What was its average speed in miles per hour (mph)?

a. $\frac{1}{24}$
b. 24
c. 69
d. 216

4. Which of the following fractions equals 2%?

a. $\frac{1}{50}$
b. $\frac{2}{50}$
c. $\frac{1}{5}$
d. $\frac{1}{2}$

5. Which of the following is the best estimate for the length of a walking tour of historic Philadelphia?

a. 1 cm
b. 1 dm
c. 1 m
d. 1 km

6. If two angles of a triangle are 33° and 67°, what is the third angle?

a. 34°
b. 80°
c. 100°
d. 147°

7.   14 lb   3 oz
    –   7 lb   8 oz

a. 6 lb 5 oz
b. 6 lb 11 oz
c. 7 lb 5 oz
d. 7 lb 11 oz

8. George bought two gifts. The first cost $\frac{1}{4}$ of the money he had, and the second cost $\frac{1}{2}$ of what was left. If he had $30 after buying the two gifts, how much money did he start with?

a. $60
b. $75
c. $80
d. $120

9. In the proportion, $\frac{5}{8} = \frac{8}{n}$, what is *n*?

a. 3.2
b. 5
c. 11
d. 12.8

10. What percent of 50 is 40?

a. 10%
b. 40%
c. 80%
d. 125%

11. A plane left Chicago at 11:00 AM Central Standard Time and arrived in San Francisco at 5:04 PM Pacific Standard Time. Pacific Standard Time is 2 hours earlier than Central Standard Time. How many hours did the flight take?

a. 4 h 4 min
b. 5 h 56 min
c. 6 h 4 min
d. 8 h 4 min

12.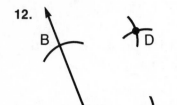

What do you have to do to complete the construction of the angle bisector of ∠BCA?

a. Draw $\overrightarrow{AD}$ b. Draw $\overrightarrow{BD}$
c. Draw $\overrightarrow{CD}$ d. Draw $\overline{AB}$

13.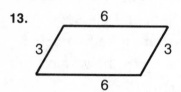

How many lines of symmetry does the figure have?

a. 0   b. 2
c. 3   d. 4

14. What is 55% of $500?

a. $27,500   b. $275
c. $11   d. $2.75

15. Molly used $10.00 of her spending money on movies, $7.50 on food, $8.00 on a video tape, and she had $16.50 left. How much spending money did Molly start with?

a. $16.50   b. $25.50
c. $42.00   d. $45.00

16.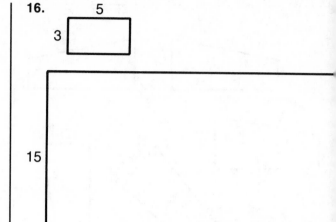

The rectangles are similar.

What is the missing length n?

a. 9   b. 23
c. 25   d. 45

17.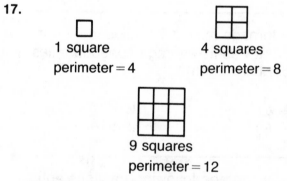

1 square   4 squares
perimeter = 4   perimeter = 8

9 squares
perimeter = 12

Small squares, each with side 1, can be used to make larger squares.

perimeter = 4   perimeter = 8   perimeter = 12

What would the perimeter be if 49 small squares were used to make a larger square?

a. 7   b. 28
c. 49   d. 52

8. The high temperature on April 1 was 25.7°C. The high temperature on April 15 was 7.9°C. How much colder was it on April 15 than on April 1?

a. 17.8°C   b. 18.2°C
c. 18.8°C   d. 33.6°C

9. In a scale drawing of a sailboat, the sail has a height of 4 cm. What is the actual height, in meters, of the sail if the scale is 1 cm = 2 m?

a. 0.08 m   b. 2 m
c. 8 m   d. 800 m

0. 50 is 25% of what number?

a. 2   b. 12.5
c. 20   d. 200

1.

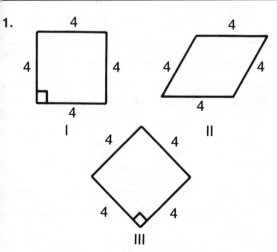

Which figures are congruent?

a. None   b. I and II only
c. I and III only d. I, II, and III

22.

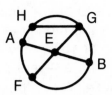

Which line segments are chords?

a. $\overline{EF}$ and $\overline{EB}$ b. $\overline{AB}$ and $\overline{HG}$
c. $\overline{AE}$ and $\overline{BE}$ d. $\overline{HG}$ and $\overline{EB}$

23.

BUS SCHEDULE			
Port City	**Essex**	**Inletville**	**Arthur**
7:30 AM	8:42 AM	10:18 AM	10:58 AM
8:30 AM	9:42 AM	11:18 AM	11:58 AM
9:30 AM	10:41 AM	12:15 PM	12:55 PM
10:30 AM	11:40 AM	1:14 PM	1:54 PM

Ms. McNeal left Port City on the 9:30 AM bus. If the bus arrived in Inletville on time, how long did the trip take?

a. 2 h 45 min   b. 2 h 85 min
c. 3 h 15 min   d. 3 h 25 min

24.   7 ft   5 in.
        − 3 ft   8 in.

a. 3 ft 4 in.   b. 3 ft 7 in.
c. 3 ft 9 in.   d. 4 ft 3 in.

25.

What is the measure of the angle shown above?

a. 25°   b. 35°
c. 155°   d. 165°

CUMULATIVE TEST   Chapters 7–9 Page 4

26. Susan wants to buy a stove for $600. If she borrows the money at an annual interest rate of 15%, how much interest will she owe for a 4-year period? (Use the formula i = prt.)

a. $22.50   b. $60.00
c. $90.00   d. $360.00

27. A recipe calls for 8 lb meat to feed 12 people. Which proportion would be used to find the amount of meat needed for 15 people?

a. $\frac{8}{12} = \frac{15}{x}$ b. $\frac{8}{12} = \frac{x}{15}$
c. $\frac{8}{x} = \frac{15}{12}$ d. $\frac{x}{8} = \frac{12}{15}$

28.

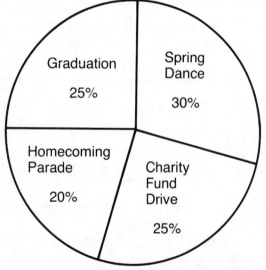

The circle graph shows the ways a school club spends its money. Which of the following pair of items accounts for more than half of the spending?

a. spring dance and homecoming parade
b. charity fund drive and graduation
c. spring dance and graduation
d. homecoming parade and graduation

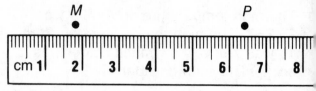

29. In the figure, the distance from M to P is closest to

a. 46 mm   b. 50 mm
c. 46 cm   d. 50 cm

30. During a sale, a shirt was reduced from $10 to $8. What percent is the decrease?

a. 2%   b. 20%
c. 25%   d. 80%

31.

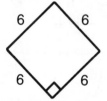

Which are names for the figure above?

square   rectangle   parallelogram
I   II   III

a. I only   b. III only
c. I and II only   d. I, II, and III

32. Dana used 6 boxes of roofing shingles to cover 200 square feet. Dana's roof is 1,500 square feet. At that rate, how many boxes will Dana need?

a. 7.5   b. 45
c. 250   d. 50,000

33. Which of the following measurements are equal?

5100 mg   0.0051 kg   5.1 g
I   II   III

a. I and II only   b. I and III only
c. II and III only   d. I, II, and III

FINAL TEST   Page 1

1. a.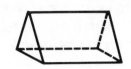
b.

c.
d.

Which figure is a triangular pyramid?

---

2. What is the greatest common factor GCF of 8 and 20?

a. 2   b. 4
c. 8   d. 40

---

3. Mr. Wagner had some money. He spent $\frac{1}{5}$ of it on books. Then he spent $\frac{2}{3}$ of what was left on a microwave oven. That left $60. How much did he have to begin with?

a. $8   b. $225
c. $450   d. $900

---

4. Simplify. $9.37 - 2.18 + 4.05$

a. 3.14   b. 10.24
c. 11.24   d. 15.60

---

5.   2, 2, 8, 9, 10

Which of the following is greatest for the data above?

a. mean only
b. median only
c. mode only
d. mean and median

---

6. $\frac{^-42}{^-6}$

a. $^-48$ b. $^-36$
c. $^-7$ d. 7

---

7. $77\blacksquare,\blacksquare\blacksquare\blacksquare + 43\blacksquare,\blacksquare\blacksquare\blacksquare =$

Some digits are hidden in each of the numbers above. Which of the following is the best estimate of the sum?

a. 110,000   b. 120,000
c. 1,200,000   d. 1,300,000

---

8. Which is equivalent to 3.55?

a. $\frac{3}{55}$ b. $3\frac{1}{2}$
c. $3\frac{5}{11}$ d. $3\frac{11}{20}$

---

9. A scale model of a museum is 4 ft wide and 9 ft long. If the actual museum is 240 ft wide, which proportion can be used to find the length in ft?

$\frac{4}{9} = \frac{240}{x}$ $\frac{4}{9} = \frac{x}{240}$ $\frac{4}{x} = \frac{9}{240}$
  I   II   III

a. I only   b. II only
c. III only   d. I and II only

---

10. A circle has a radius of 20 cm. Which is closest to the circumference of that circle?

a. 31.4 cm   b. 62.8 cm
c. 125.6 cm   d. 1,256 cm

11.

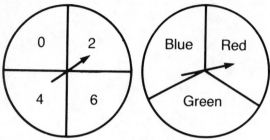

Belinda spins each spinner once. Which of the following is a possible outcome of her spins?

a. 0, Green   b. 2,4
c. Blue, Red   d. 3, Blue

12. 13 − ⁻9

a. 4   b. ⁻4
c. 22   d. ⁻22

13. What is the remainder if 701 is divided by 283?

a. 418   b. 265
c. 235   d. 135

14. $\frac{5}{6} - \frac{3}{4}$

a. $\frac{1}{12}$ b. $\frac{1}{5}$
c. $\frac{5}{8}$ d. 1

15.

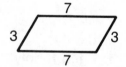

Which names describe this figure?

I. quadrilateral
II. rectangle
III. parallelogram

a. I only   b. I and III only
c. II and III only   d. I, II, and III

16. A roller coaster has 4 cars with 6 seats in each car. A haunted house ride has 5 cars with 8 seats in each car. What is the total number of seats on the roller coaster and haunted house rides?

a. 16   b. 23
c. 48   d. 64

17.

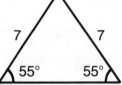

Which of the following labels would apply to the triangle?

I. equilateral
II. right
III. isosceles

a. I only   b. II only
c. III only   d. I and III only

18. $7\frac{8}{9}$
       $+\ \frac{2}{3}$

a. $7\frac{5}{9}$ b. $7\frac{5}{6}$
c. $8\frac{1}{9}$ d. $8\frac{5}{9}$

19. There are 1 white, 3 purple, and 3 green balls in a bag. Without looking, Ahmad is going to choose a ball. P (not purple) =

a. $\frac{1}{3}$ b. $\frac{3}{4}$
c. $\frac{3}{7}$ d. $\frac{4}{7}$

0. 69.1   69.101   69.01   69.11

    Which of the following shows the numbers above in order from the least to the greatest?

    a. 69.01   69.1   69.101   69.11
    b. 69.01   69.1   69.11   69.101
    c. 69.101   69.01   69.11   69.1
    d. 69.101   69.11   69.1   69.01

1.

The distance from *P* to *Q* is closest to

    a. 40 cm   b. 36 cm
    c. 40 mm   d. 36 mm

2. Which of the following is the best estimate for $2\frac{9}{10} + 7\frac{1}{8}$?

    a. 9   b. 10
    c. 11   d. 12

3. Wendy is going to toss a number cube two times. Each face has a different one of the numbers 1, 2, 3, 4, 5, and 6 on it. What is the probability she will not get a 3 the first time, followed by getting a 3 the second time?

    a. 1   b. $\frac{1}{6}$
    c. $\frac{5}{36}$ d. $\frac{1}{36}$

Use this information for questions 24 and 25.

One recipe for biscuits uses the following ingredients.

$2\frac{1}{2}$ cups flour

$\frac{1}{4}$ cup shortening

3 tsp baking powder

$\frac{3}{4}$ cup milk

1 tsp salt

24. How many cups of milk are used for 6 batches of biscuits?

    a. $2\frac{1}{4}$ b. $4\frac{1}{2}$
    c. $6\frac{3}{4}$ d. 8

25. How many batches of biscuits can be made from $3\frac{3}{4}$ cups flours?

    a. $1\frac{1}{4}$ b. $1\frac{1}{2}$
    c. $6\frac{1}{4}$ d. $9\frac{3}{8}$

26.

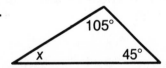

What is the measure of angle *x*?

    a. 30°   b. 40°
    c. 60°   d. 150°

27. Forty billion and seven hundredths can be written

    a. 40,000,000,000.07
    b. 40,000,000,000.007
    c. 40,000,700.00
    d. 40,000,000.07

28. 0.07
       × 0.6

a. 42.0   b. 4.2
c. 0.42   d. 0.042

---

29. ⁻3   11   ⁻14   0

Which of the following shows the
numbers above in order from the
greatest to the least?

a. 11, 0, ⁻3, ⁻14   b. 11, 0, ⁻14, ⁻3
c. ⁻14, 11, ⁻3, 0   d. ⁻14, ⁻3, 0, 11

---

30.   13 lb   5 oz
       − 4 lb   11 oz

a. 9 lb 10 oz   b. 9 lb 6 oz
c. 8 lb 10 oz   d. 8 lb 6 oz

31.

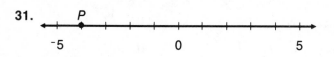

On the number line above, what
number is point *P*?

a. ⁻6   b. ⁻5
c. ⁻4   d. 1

---

32. 1.6)‾0.864‾

a. 0.054   b. 0.54
c. 5.4   d. 54.0

---

33. Which of the following measurements
are equal?

0.0345 kL   34.5 L   3,450 mL
     I   II   III

a. I and II only   b. I and III only
c. II and III only   d. I, II, and III

---

34.   387.006
       −   29.54

a. 356.566   b. 357.466
c. 358.520   d. 362.546

---

35. The product of the page numbers of
the last two pages in a driver's manual
is 992. How many pages are in the
manual?

a. 30   b. 31
c. 32   d. 33

Use the table and pictograph below for
questions 36 and 37.

PEOPLE IN SPORTS

Sport	Number
Aerobics	5,500,000
Camping	6,000,000
Exercising with Equipment	E
Fishing	6,500,000

PEOPLE IN SPORTS

Sport	
Aerobics	🏃🏃🏃🏃🏃🏃
Camping	🏃🏃🏃🏃🏃🏃
Exercising with Equipment	🏃🏃🏃🏃🏃🏃🏃🏃
Fishing	F

🏃 represents 1 million people

🏃 represents ½ million people

36. What number goes at E in the table?

a. 8,000,000   b. 7,500,000
c. 6,250,000   d. 6,000,000

7. Which set of pictures goes at F?

a. ![stick figures]

b. ![stick figures]

c. ![stick figures]

d. ![stick figures]

8. What is 37,000,000 in scientific notation?

a. 3.7×10^6 b. 37×10^6
c. 3.7×10^7 d. 3.7×10^8

9. The soluton for the inequality $x + 4 > 12$ is

a. $x > 3$ b. $x > 8$
c. $x > 16$ d. $x > 48$

0. What is the surface area of a cube if the area of each face is 9 in.²?

a. 729 in.³   b. 81 in.²
c. 54 in.²   d. 36 in.²

1. What is 42.784 rounded to the nearest tenth?

a. 42.7   b. 42.78
c. 42.8   d. 42.884

2. A new radial tire costs $290.50. How much would new tires for a truck with 18 wheels cost?

a. $5,265.00   b. $5,257.00
c. $5,229.00   d. $5,225.00

43. $\frac{4}{7} \times \frac{5}{14}$

a. $\frac{10}{49}$ b. $\frac{10}{7}$
c. $\frac{20}{7}$ d. 10

44.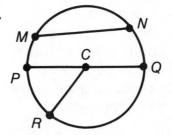

Which segments are chords?

a. $\overline{CQ}$ and $\overline{CR}$ b. $\overline{PC}$ and $\overline{CQ}$
c. $\overline{CR}$ and $\overline{MN}$ d. $\overline{MN}$ and $\overline{PQ}$

45. The Wolodkins have 50 yards of fencing that is 2 feet high. They are going to fence a square garden that is 7 yards on each side. What is the least amount of fence that would be extra?

a. 1 yd   b. 22 yd
c. 59 yd   d. 72 yd

46. These are the number of stories for some buildings.

21 46 51 33 58 44 29 65 81
67 34 38 72 37 66 30 25 25

What is the frequency for the interval 20–35?

a. 18   b. 9
c. 7   d. 6

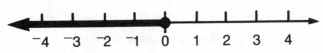

47. The graph above shows the solution of

a. $x = 0$ b. $x \geq 0$
c. $x < 0$ d. $x \leq 0$

48. Choose the best estimate for 30,700 ÷ 61.

a. 50   b. 300

c. 500   d. 700

49. Marlene got on a plane in Atlanta, Georgia, when it was 45°F above zero. When she got off the plane in Buffalo, New York, it was 9°F below zero. Which equation could be used to find the difference d in temperatures?

a. $d = 45 - (^-9)$ b. $d = 45 - 9$

c. $d = 9 - 45$ d. $d = ^-9 + 45$

50.

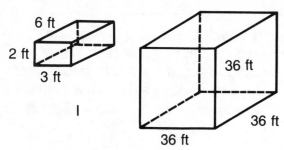

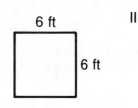

III

Which figure has a volume of 36 ft³?

a. I only   b. II only

c. III only   d. I and III

51. Which fraction is equivalent to $\frac{5}{8}$?

a. $\frac{1}{4}$ b. $\frac{5}{13}$

c. $\frac{8}{5}$ d. $\frac{10}{16}$

52. If $y = x - 4$ and $x = ^-3$, then y is

a. $^-7$ b. $^-1$

c. 1   d. 7

53. Which of the following is a formula for computing the area of a triangle?

a. $A = \pi r^2$ b. $A = lwh$

c. $A = \frac{1}{3}bh$ d. $A = \frac{1}{2}bh$

54. The original cost of a stereo is $264. How much money will be saved with a discount of 33%?

a. $33.00   b. $80.00

c. $87.12   d. $88.00

55.

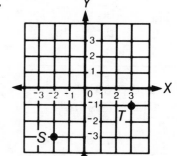

The ordered pairs for points S and T are

a. $S = (^-2,^-3)$ and $T = (3,^-1)$

b. $S = (^-2,3)$ and $T = (3,1)$

c. $S = (^-3,^-2)$ and $T = (^-1,3)$

d. $S = (3,^-2)$ and $T = (1,3)$

56. $\frac{9}{10} \div \frac{6}{5}$

a. $\frac{3}{4}$ b. 1

c. $\frac{27}{25}$ d. $\frac{3}{2}$

57. $^-5 \cdot {}^-9$

a. $^-45$ b. $^-14$
c. 14 d. 45

---

58. Which rectangle has a perimeter of 6?

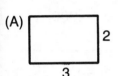
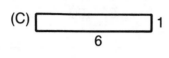
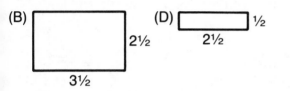

---

59. Written as a fraction, $62\frac{1}{2}\%$ is

a. $\frac{25}{4}$ b. $\frac{5}{8}$
c. $\frac{31}{50}$ d. $\frac{4}{25}$

---

60. It costs $5 to rent a small tractor. In addition, it costs $3 per hour of use. Paul paid $23 in all. How many hours did he use the tractor?

a. 3   b. 4
c. 6   d. 8

---

61. $\frac{3}{5}$ is less than which of the following?

$\frac{2}{3}$ $\frac{4}{7}$ $\frac{3}{4}$

I   II   III

a. I only   b. II only
c. III only   d. I and III

---

62. PAY PER HOUR AND HOURS OF BABYSITTING PER MONTH FOR FIFTEEN STUDENTS

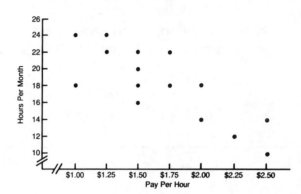

According to the scattergram above, the fewer hours of babysitting, the pay per hour in general

a. decreased
b. increased
c. stayed the same
d. varied

---

63. Choose the best estimate of 0.49×12.01.

a. 3   b. 6^-
c. 12^+ d. 24

---

64. A 38-year old man bought 2 records and a book. The records were $6.98 each. The tax was $1.89. How much should his bill have been?

What information is needed to solve this problem?

a. the man's age
b. the cost of a tape
c. the cost of the book
d. the height of the man

65.

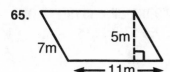

Which of the following gives the area, in square meters, of the parallelogram?

a. 5×11 b. 7×11
c. $5 \times 7 \times 11$ d. $\frac{1}{2}(5 \times 11)$

---

66.   6 h   40 min
        $+$ 7 h   55 min

a. 13 h 35 min   b. 14 h 35 min
c. 14 h 45 min   d. 22 h 5 min

67.

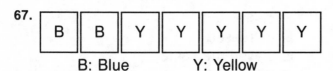

B: Blue   Y: Yellow

The cards above will be turned over and mixed. Kurt is going to pick one card, not replace it, and then pick another. P(Yellow, then Yellow) =

a. $\frac{5}{21}$ b. $\frac{10}{21}$

c. $\frac{20}{49}$ d. $\frac{25}{42}$

---

68. What does the digit 6 stand for in the number 206,425.38?

a. 60   b. 600
c. 6,000   d. 600,000

---

69. What percent of 85 is 17?

a. 2%   b. 5%
c. 20%   d. 68%

---

70. $41.$■■$\times 59$

Some digits are hidden in the numbers above. Which of the following is the most reasonable estimate of the product?

a. $100   b. $2,000
c. $2,500   d. $3,000

---

71. Which of the following is a formula for computing the volume of a cylinder?

a. $V = 2\pi r$ b. $V = \pi r^2$
c. $V = \pi r^2 h$ d. $V = \pi d h$

---

72. If $y = 18$, which expression has a value of 6?

a. $2y + 3$ b. $2y - 3$

c. $\frac{y}{2} + 3$ d. $\frac{y}{2} - 3$

---

73. Mrs. Lee has $8\frac{1}{2}$ yards of fabric. She needs $2\frac{1}{2}$ yards for each skirt she makes. How many complete skirts can she make?

a. 3 skirts   b. 3.4 skirts
c. 4 skirts   d. 21 skirts

---

74. The solution for the equation $3x - 6 = 18$ is

a. $x = 4$ b. $x = 6$
c. $x = 8$ d. $x = 72$

5.

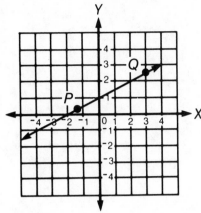

Which of these ordered pairs are on the line connecting points *P* and *Q*?

I (1,0)   II (1,1)   III(⁻2,0)

a. I only   **b.** III only
c. I and III only   **d.** I, II, and III

Test Answers

Placement Test Answers

1. C	16. D	31. A	46. B	61. D
2. A	17. B	32. D	47. B	62. A
3. C	18. C	33. B	48. A	63. B
4. B	19. A	34. C	49. B	64. D
5. D	20. B	35. D	50. D	65. C
6. C	21. D	36. A	51. C	66. D
7. A	22. C	37. C	52. B	67. B
8. C	23. D	38. B	53. A	68. A
9. B	24. B	39. D	54. C	69. C
10. D	25. D	40. C	55. D	70. B
11. C	26. A	41. A	56. A	71. D
12. B	27. D	42. D	57. C	72. C
13. A	28. C	43. D	58. B	73. D
14. D	29. B	44. C	59. B	74. B
15. C	30. D	45. A	60. C	75. C

Cumulative Test   Chapters 1–3

Objective	Test Items	Text Pages
1A	1	2–3, 20–21
1B	32	2–3, 20-21
1C	28	2–3
1D	5	22–23
1E	3	24–25
1F	11	16–17
1G	27	28–29
1H	14, 15	34–35
2A	2, 6, 30	50–51, 54–57
2B	10, 22	60–61
2C	8	66–67
2D	19	62–63
2E	13	62–63, 68–69
2F	26	52–53
2H	24, 25	70–71
3A	21, 29, 31	88–89, 92–95
3B	18, 33	86–87, 90–91
3C	7	102–103
3D	9	98–99
3E	12, 20	104–105
3F	4, 17	96–97
3G	23	100–101
3H	16	108–109

Answers

1. C	10. B	19. A	28. A
2. B	11. C	20. C	29. B
3. A	12. D	21. A	30. C
4. D	13. B	22. B	31. C
5. D	14. A	23. D	32. B
6. A	15. C	24. A	33. C
7. D	16. B	25. B	
8. C	17. C	26. D	
9. A	18. B	27. C	

Cumulative Test   Chapters 4–6

Objective	Test Items	Text Pages
4A	30	118–119
4B	26	120–121
4C	6, 31	122–123
4D	14, 18	130–133
4E	19	136–137
4F	13	138–139
4H	28	142–143
4I	23	150–151
5A	8, 24	164–165
5B	5	168–169
5C	1, 20	166–167
5D	29	174–175
5E	10, 22	186–187
5G	3	172–173
5I	25	180–181
6A	16, 21	200–203
6B	2	210–211
6C	11, 15	216–217
6D	17	220–221
6E	4, 32	222–223
6F	7, 12	206–207
6G	33	204–205
6H	27	218–219
6I	9	224–225

Answers

1. C	10. B	19. D	28. B
2. D	11. D	20. C	29. D
3. B	12. A	21. A	30. A
4. B	13. A	22. D	31. C
5. A	14. C	23. C	32. B
6. B	15. A	24. D	33. D
7. C	16. B	25. C	
8. D	17. C	26. A	
9. C	18. B	27. D	

Cumulative Test Chapters 7–9

Objective	Test Items	Text Pages
7A	29	236–237
7B	5	236–237
7C	33	240–241
7D	7, 24	246–249
7E	18	256–257
7G	11	254–255
7H	15	244–245
7I	3	252–253
7J	23	260–261
8A	9	272–273
8B	19	276–277
8C	2, 4	282–283
8D	14	284–285
8E	10	288–289
8F	20	290–291
8G	30	296–297
8H	27, 32	274–275
8I	26	292–293
8J	28	298–299
9B	25	312–313
9D	12	316–317
9F	6	326–327
9G	22, 31	328–329, 336–337
9H	13, 21	330–331, 338–339
9I	16	332–333
9J	1	340–341
9K	17	318–319
9L	8	334–335

Answers

1. B	10. C	19. C	28. C
2. D	11. D	20. D	29. A
3. B	12. C	21. C	30. B
4. A	13. A	22. B	31. D
5. D	14. B	23. A	32. B
6. B	15. C	24. C	33. D
7. B	16. C	25. A	
8. C	17. B	26. D	
9. D	18. A	27. B	

Final Test Chapters 1–12

Objective	Test Items	Text Pages
1A	27	2–3, 20–21
1C	68	2–3
1D	20	22–23
1E	41	24–25
1F	34	32–33
1G	7	9–11
2A	42	54–55
2B	63, 70	60–61
2E	28	62–63, 68–69
2F	64	52–53
3A	13	94–95
3B	48	86–87
3E	32	104–105
4C	38	122–123
4D	2	130–131
4E	4	136–137
4F	72	138–139
4G	74	148–149
4I	60	150–151
5A	51	164–165
5B	61	168–169
5D	14	176–177
5E	18	182–183
5G	22	172–175
6A	43	200–203
6B	56	210–213
6C	8	216–217
6H	24, 25	218–219
6I	73	224–225
7A	21	236–237
7C	33	240–241
7D	30	248–249
7F	66	250–251
8C	59	282–283
8D	54	284–285
8E	69	288–289
8H	9	274–275
9F	17, 26	326–327
9G	15, 44	328–329, 336–337
9L	3	334–335
10A	10, 45, 58	352–355
10B	65	356–357
10C	1	366–367
10D	40	370–371
10E	50	372–373
10F	16	360–361
10G	35	364–365
10I	53, 71	374–375
11A	36, 37, 46	386–387
11B	5	388–391
11C	11	404–407

Objective	Test Items	Text Pages
11D	19	402–403
11E	23	410–411
11F	67	412–413
11G	62	394–395
12A	31	424–425
12B	29	424–425
12C	12	430–431
12D	6, 57	434–437
12E	39	440–441
12F	47	446–447
12G	52	452–453
12H	55, 75	448–449
12J	49	444–445

Answers

1. B	20. A	39. B	58. D
2. B	21. D	40. C	59. B
3. B	22. B	41. C	60. C
4. C	23. C	42. C	61. D
5. B	24. B	43. A	62. B
6. D	25. B	44. D	63. B
7. C	26. A	45. B	64. C
8. D	27. A	46. C	65. A
9. A	28. D	47. D	66. B
10. C	29. A	48. C	67. B
11. A	30. C	49. A	68. C
12. C	31. C	50. A	69. C
13. D	32. B	51. D	70. C
14. A	33. A	52. A	71. C
15. B	34. B	53. D	72. D
16. D	35. C	54. C	73. A
17. C	36. A	55. A	74. C
18. D	37. B	56. A	75. B
19. D	38. C	57. D	

MANAGEMENT

This section provides a variety of forms to help in the management of the Mathematics Unlimited program.

- *Individual Record* — A listing of all testing objectives in a format suitable for tracking individual students.

- *Class Record Form* — A form on which to record all students' test scores for all tests in the program.

- *Assignment Guide* — A form for recording students' individual assignments on a chapter-by-chapter basis.

- *Progress Reports* — A form that serves as a report card to be sent to students' families at the end of each chapter.

- *Test Answer Sheet* — A form on which students record answers to multiple-choice tests.

INDIVIDUAL RECORD

Mathematics UNLIMITED

GRADE 7

STUDENT _____

TEACHER _____

Placement Test Score: _____

CHAPTER 1

Test Scores:	Skills Inv. _____	Pretest _____	Posttest _____	Needs More Work	Accomplished
A To write short word names for whole numbers and decimals expressed as standard numerals and vice versa, through 15 digits					
B To write expanded numerals for whole numbers and decimals expressed as standard numerals and vice versa, through 10 digits					
C To identify the value of a digit in whole numbers and decimals, through 13 digits					
D To compare and order whole numbers, money amounts, or decimals					
E To round whole numbers, money amounts, or decimals					
F To add or subtract whole numbers, money amounts, or decimals					
G To estimate sums and differences of whole numbers, money amounts, or decimals					
H To use information from a double bar graph to solve problems					

CHAPTER 2

Test Scores:	Skills Inv. _____	Pretest _____	Posttest _____	Needs More Work	Accomplished
A To multiply a whole number or money amount by a whole number					
B To estimate products of whole numbers and decimals					
C To multiply a decimal by powers of 10					
D To multiply a decimal by a whole number					
E To multiply a decimal by a decimal					
F To identify extra or needed information in a problem and solve					
G To choose the operation to solve problems					
H To identify subgoals and solve 2-step problems					

CHAPTER 3

Test Scores:	Skills Inv. _____	Pretest _____	Posttest _____	Needs More Work	Accomplished
A To divide a whole number or money amount by a whole number					
B To estimate quotients of whole numbers and decimals					
C To divide a decimal by powers of 10					
D To divide a decimal by a whole number					
E To divide a decimal by a decimal					
F To check that an answer is reasonable					
G To choose the operation to solve problems					
H To use information from a road map to solve problems					

Cumulative Test Score: _____

CHAPTER 4

Test Scores:	Skills Inv. _____	Pretest _____	Posttest _____	Needs More Work	Accomplished
A To determine if a number is divisible by 2, 3, 5, 6, 8, 9 or 10					
B To find square roots of perfect squares					
C To write standard numerals in scientific notation and vice versa					
D To find the LCM or GCF of up to 3 numbers by prime factorization with exponents					
E To find the value of numerical expressions using the rules for the order of operations					
F To evaluate algebraic expressions					
G To solve 1-step and 2-step equations					
H To use information from a broken-line graph or pictograph to solve problems					
I To write an equation for a 1-step or 2-step problem and solve					

INDIVIDUAL RECORD

CHAPTER 5

Test Scores:	Skills Inv.	Pretest	Posttest	Needs More Work	Accom- plished
A To find a fraction equivalent to a given fraction					
B To compare and order fractions and mixed numbers					
C To write a fraction as a whole or mixed number and vice versa					
D To add or subtract fractions					
E To add or subtract mixed numbers					
F To solve 1-step equations involving addition or subtraction of fractions					
G To estimate sums and differences of fractions and mixed numbers					
H To check that the solution answers the question					
I To make an organized list to solve a problem					
J To write a simpler problem as a strategy for solving problems					

CHAPTER 6

Test Scores:	Skills Inv.	Pretest	Posttest	Needs More Work	Accom- plished
A To multiply with fractions, whole numbers, and mixed numbers					
B To divide with fractions, whole numbers, and mixed numbers					
C To write a decimal as a fraction in simplest form					
D To write a fraction as a terminating or repeating decimal					
E To solve 1-step and 2-step equations involving fractions					
F To estimate products of fractions and mixed numbers					
G To formulate sensible questions to solve problems					
H To use information from a recipe to solve problems					
I To interpret the quotient and the remainder					

Cumulative Test Score: _____

CHAPTER 7

Test Scores:	Skills Inv.	Pretest	Posttest	Needs More Work	Accom- plished
A To measure length to the nearest centimeter and nearest millimeter					
B To choose or estimate the appropriate metric or customary unit of length, mass, or capacity					
C To change between measures of length, mass, volume, or capacity in the metric and customary systems					
D To add or subtract with regrouping in the customary system					
E To find temperature changes (Fahrenheit and Celsius)					
F To add, subtract, or change between units of time					
G To find elapsed time within and across time zones					
H To identify subgoals and solve multistep problems					
I To use the formula $d = rt$ to solve problems					
J To use information from a schedule to solve problems					

CHAPTER 8

Test Scores:	Skills Inv.	Pretest	Posttest	Needs More Work	Accom- plished
A To solve proportions					
B To find actual measure given scale and scale measurement and vice versa					
C To write a decimal or a fraction as a percent and vice versa					
D To find the percent of a number					
E To find what percent a number is of a given number					
F To find the number given the percent of it					
G To find the percent of increase or decrease					
H To write a proportion to solve problems					
I To solve problems involving commission and the interest formula ($i = prt$)					
J To use information from a circle graph to solve problems					

Holt, Rinehart and Winston, Publishers

INDIVIDUAL RECORD

CHAPTER 9

Test Scores:	Skills Inv. _____	Pretest _____	Posttest _____	Needs More Work	Accom-plished
A To name points, lines, line segments, and rays and to identify parallel and perpendicular lines					
B To name, measure, and classify angles and to find the complement or supplement of an angle					
C To construct an angle or segment congruent to a given angle or segment					
D To construct the bisector of a line segment or an angle					
E To construct perpendicular or parallel lines					
F To classify triangles according to the measure of their angles or side and to find the measure of an angle given the measures of the other two angles					
G To identify and name polygons and to identify the parts of a circle					
H To identify congruent figures and lines of symmetry					
I To solve problems involving corresponding parts of similar polygons					
J To identify translations, rotations, or reflections					
K To organize information in a table to find a pattern to solve problems					
L To use working backwards as a strategy to solve problems					
M To use information from a picture or model to solve problems					

Cumulative Test Score: _____

CHAPTER 10

Test Scores:	Skills Inv. _____	Pretest _____	Posttest _____	Needs More Work	Accom-plished
A To find the perimeter of polygons and the circumference of circles					
B To find the area of squares, rectangles, parallelograms, triangles, trapezoids, and circles					
C To recognize solid figures					
D To find the surface area of prisms, pyramids and cylinders					
E To find the volume of prisms and cylinders					
F To identify subgoals and solve multistep problems					
G To use a guess-and-check strategy to solve problems					
H To draw a picture to solve a problem					
I To choose a formula to solve a problem					

INDIVIDUAL RECORD

CHAPTER 11

Test Scores:	Skills Inv. _____	Pretest _____	Posttest _____	Needs More Work	Accomplished
A To collect and record data by making a table, bar graph, broken-line graph, circle graph or pictograph					
B To find the mean, median, mode, and range					
C To list the elements of a sample space for an experiment					
D To find the probability of a simple event					
E To find the probability of independent events					
F To find the probability of dependent events					
G To use information from a scattergram to solve problems					
H To interpret information from graphs and statistics					

CHAPTER 12

Test Scores:	Skills Inv. _____	Pretest _____	Posttest _____	Needs More Work	Accomplished
A To identify integers on a number line					
B To compare and order integers					
C To add or subtract integers					
D To multiply or divide integers					
E To solve 1-step equations or inequalities with integers					
F To graph the solutions of equations or inequalities in one variable					
G To solve equations in two variables					
H To name or locate an ordered pair in a coordinate plane					
I To graph the solutions of equations in two variables					
J To write an equation or inequality for a problem and solve					
K To use information from a broken-line or bar graph with scales above and below zero to solve problems					

Final Test Score: _____
Final Grade: _____

Holt, Rinehart and Winston, Publishers •

CLASS RECORD FORM

Mathematics UNLIMITED

GRADE 7

TEACHER _____

SCHOOL _____

STUDENT NAMES DATE:	PLACEMENT TEST	CHAPTER 1			CHAPTER 2			CHAPTER 3		
		Skills Inventory	Pretest	Posttest	Skills Inventory	Pretest	Posttest	Skills Inventory	Pretest	Posttest
1.										
2.										
3.										
4.										
5.										
6.										
7.										
8.										
9.										
10.										
11.										
12.										
13.										
14.										
15.										
16.										
17.										
18.										
19.										
20.										
21.										
22.										
23.										
24.										
25.										
26.										
27.										
28.										
29.										
30.										
31.										
32.										
33.										
34.										
35.										

	CUM TEST Chapters 1 to 3	CHAPTER 4			CHAPTER 5			CHAPTER 6			CUM TEST Chapters 4 to 6	CHAPTER 7			CHAPTER 8		
		Skills Inventory	Pretest	Posttest	Skills Inventory	Pretest	Posttest	Skills Inventory	Pretest	Posttest		Skills Inventory	Pretest	Posttest	Skills Inventory	Pretest	Posttest
1.																	
2.																	
3.																	
4.																	
5.																	
6.																	
7.																	
8.																	
9.																	
10.																	
11.																	
12.																	
13.																	
14.																	
15.																	
16.																	
17.																	
18.																	
19.																	
20.																	
21.																	
22.																	
23.																	
24.																	
25.																	
26.																	
27.																	
28.																	
29.																	
30.																	
31.																	
32.																	
33.																	
34.																	
35.																	

	CHAPTER 9			CUM TEST Chapters 7 to 9	CHAPTER 10			CHAPTER 11			CHAPTER 12			FINAL TEST Chapters 1 to 12	FINAL GRADE
	Skills Inventory	Pretest	Posttest		Skills Inventory	Pretest	Posttest	Skills Inventory	Pretest	Posttest	Skills Inventory	Pretest	Posttest		
1.															
2.															
3.															
4.															
5.															
6.															
7.															
8.															
9.															
10.															
11.															
12.															
13.															
14.															
15.															
16.															
17.															
18.															
19.															
20.															
21.															
22.															
23.															
24.															
25.															
26.															
27.															
28.															
29.															
30.															
31.															
32.															
33.															
34.															
35.															

ASSIGNMENT GUIDE

LESSON PAGE	LESSON OBJECTIVE	BASIC	AVERAGE	EXTENDED	MORE PRACTICE	FOLLOW UP ACTIVITY	RETEACH	PRACTICE	ENRICH	CLASSROOM ACTIVITY BOOK
1	Chapter Opener (Use MMW 1, 2)	1	1	1						
2, 3	To learn whole number place value	1–19, 25–27	2–26 e, Chlg	1–27 o, Chlg	475	P&G, RM	1	1	1	
4, 5	To compare and order whole numbers	1–26, 27–32, 35–39	1–11 o, 13–19, 27–42	2–12 e, 20–42	475	MM, IND	2	2	2	EST 1
6, 7	To identify and use the properties of addition and subtraction	1–19, Chlg	1–22, Chlg	5–26, Chlg		P&G, MM	3	3	3	
8	To round whole numbers	1–15 o	2–16 e	1–17 o					4	
9	To estimate in problem solving	1–3	1–3	1–3				4		
10, 11	To estimate sums of whole numbers and amounts of money	1–15, 20	2–20	3–21		EST, P&G	4	5	5	
12, 13	To estimate differences of whole numbers and amounts of money	1–16, 23–24	1–8, 23–24, F	3–24, F		P&G, EST	5	6	6	
14, 15	To add whole numbers	1–18, 27–30, F 1–5	1–27 o, 29–30, F 1–5	11–30, F		PS, PS	6	7	7	EST 2, FI 1
16, 17	To subtract whole numbers	1–19, 30–32, MCR	13–27, 30–33, MCR	13–33, MCR		CNS, P&G	7	8	8	CALC 1, LSN T2, 1
18, 19	To use the Help File in problem solving	1–6	1–7	1–8		PS, CALC		9	9	
20, 21	To write a decimal in standard, word-name, and expanded form	1–14, 16–32 e, Chlg	1–29 o, 30–32, Chlg	11–32, Chlg		IND, CALC	8	10	10	
22, 23	To compare and order decimals	1–12, 13–23 o, 25–26	1–12, 14–24 e, 25–27	7–27		PS, IND	9	11	11	
24, 25	To round a decimal	1–8, 9–21 o, 25–28	2–14 e, 17–28, Chlg	1–15 o, 21–28, Chlg		CMP, RFM	10	12	12	

ASSIGNMENT GUIDE

LESSON PAGE	PUPIL EDITION — LESSON OBJECTIVE	BASIC	AVERAGE	EXTENDED	MORE PRACTICE	TE FOLLOW UP ACTIVITY	RETEACH	PRACTICE	ENRICH	CLASSROOM ACTIVITY BOOK
26, 27	To use information from the Infobank in problem solving	1–6	1–7	1–8		PS, CALC		13	13	
28, 29	To estimate sums and differences of decimals	1–15, 26	1–19, 26, 27	3–27		CNS, MM	11	14	14	
30, 31	To add decimals	1–15, 25–28, Chlg	6–22, 25–28, Chlg	11–28, Chlg	475	CNS, P&G	12	15	15	MR 1
32, 33	To subtract decimals	1–15, 25–27, AL	1–23 o, 25–28, AL	2–24 e, 25–28, AL	476		13	16	16	EST 3, 4, CNS 1, CALC 2, CMP 1, 2
34, 35	To use information from a graph in problem solving	1–4	2–8	3–12	RFM, PS			17	17	
36	Calculator									
37	Group Project									
38, 39	Chapter Test									
40	Reteaching									
41	Enrichment									
42	Cumulative Review									

PROBLEM SOLVING WORKBOOKS Pages 1–4 of The Best Problems Ever workbook and pages 1–2 of the Unlimited Challenges for Problem Solvers workbook accompany this chapter.

ASSIGNMENT GUIDE

LESSON PAGE	LESSON OBJECTIVE	BASIC	AVERAGE	EXTENDED	MORE PRACTICE	FOLLOW UP ACTIVITY	RETEACH	PRACTICE	ENRICH	CLASSROOM ACTIVITY BOOK
43	Chapter Opener (Use MMW 3, 4)	43	43	43						
44, 45	To identify and use properties of multiplication	1–33 o	1–34, Chlg	9–34, Chlg		PS, PS	14	18	18	LSN T3, 2
46, 47	To multiply by multiples of 10, 100, 1,000	1–27 o, 31–36, Calc	2–30 e, 31–36, Calc	7–27 o, 28–37, Calc		PS, RFM	15	19	19	
48, 49	To estimate products of whole numbers	1–22, 33–34	1–26, 33–34	5–34		EST, PS	16	20	20	
50, 51	To multiply by a 1-digit number	1–25 o, 26–30, AL	2–28 e, 29–32, AL	10–28 e, 29–32, AL		PS, CNS	17	21	21	
52, 53	To identify extra/needed information in problem solving	1–6	2–7	3–8		PS, CALC		22	22	
54, 55	To multiply by a 2-digit number	1–23 o, 25–26	2–24 e, 25–26, F 1–3	2–24 e, 25–27, F 1–4		PS, EST	18	23	23	EST 5, FI 2
56, 57	To multiply by a 3-digit number	1–19 o, 23–24, MCR	6–22 e, 23–24, MCR	11–22 o, 23–24, MCR	476	CALC, CPR	19	24	24	
58, 59	To estimate in problem solving	1–6	2–8	3–10		PS, CALC		25	25	
60, 61	To estimate products of decimals	1–31, 38–39	5–34, 38–39	5–39		RFM, PS	20	26	26	EST 7
62, 63	To multiply decimals	1–27 o, 32–33, F	2–30 e, 32–33, F	9–31 o, 32–33, F		EST, PS	21	27	27	CNS 2, MM 2
64, 65	To choose the operation in problem solving	1–6	2–7	3–8		PS, CALC		28	28	
66, 67	To multiply decimals by powers of 10	1–23 o, 27–29, Calc	2–24 e, 27–29, Calc	6–26 e, 27–29, Calc		IND, CNS	22	29	29	
68, 69	To multiply decimals with products less than 1	1–23 o, 32, F	2–28 e, 32, F	13–32, F	476	PS, EST	23	30	30	MR 2, CALC 4, CPR 3, 4
70, 71	To solve two-step problems/to make a plan	1–6	2–7	3–8		PS, CALC		31	31	

Column groups: PUPIL EDITION (LESSON PAGE, LESSON OBJECTIVE); BASIC, AVERAGE, EXTENDED, MORE PRACTICE; TE (FOLLOW UP ACTIVITY); TEACHER'S RESOURCE BOOK OR WORKBOOK PAGES (RETEACH, PRACTICE, ENRICH); CLASSROOM ACTIVITY BOOK

Mathematics UNLIMITED

ASSIGNMENT GUIDE

PUPIL EDITION		BASIC	AVERAGE	EXTENDED	MORE PRACTICE	TE FOLLOW UP ACTIVITY	TEACHER'S RESOURCE BOOK OR WORKBOOK PAGES			CLASSROOM ACTIVITY BOOK
LESSON PAGE	LESSON OBJECTIVE						RETEACH	PRACTICE	ENRICH	
72	Reading Math									
73	Group Project									
74, 75	Chapter Test									
76	Reteaching									
77	Enrichment									
78, 79	Technology									
80	Cumulative Review									

PROBLEM SOLVING WORKBOOKS Pages 5–9 of The Best Problems Ever workbook and pages 3–4 of the Unlimited Challenges for Problem Solvers workbook accompany this chapter.

ASSIGNMENT GUIDE

Mathematics UNLIMITED

PUPIL EDITION		BASIC	AVERAGE	EXTENDED	MORE PRACTICE	TE FOLLOW UP ACTIVITY	TEACHER'S RESOURCE BOOK OR WORKBOOK PAGES			CLASSROOM ACTIVITY BOOK
LESSON PAGE	LESSON OBJECTIVE						RETEACH	PRACTICE	ENRICH	
81	Chapter Opener (Use MMW 5, 6)	81	81	81						
82, 83	To relate division to multiplication; to identify the properties of division	1–21	1–21, Chlg	1–22, Chlg		MNP, CALC	24	32	32	MM 3
84, 85	To use basic facts in division examples that involve multiples of 10, 100, or 1,000	1–39 o, 41–43	1–39 o, 41–43, F	2–40 e, 41–44, F		MM, PS	25	33	33	
86, 87	To estimate quotients of whole numbers	1–17, 22–23	1–17, 22–23, Chlg	3–23, Chlg	477	MM, CALC	26	34	34	
88, 89	To divide by a 1-digit number	1–39 o, 49, 50	9–47 o, 49–51	14–48 e, 49–52		EST, CNS	27	35	35	CNS 4, FI 3
90, 91	To estimate in problem solving	1–5	1–6	1–7		PS, P&G		36	36	EST 8
92, 93	To divide by 2-digit numbers in examples requiring long division	1–29 o, 33	2–30 e, 33, 31–34, F	10–32 e, 33–35, F		PS, CPR	28	37	37	FST 9, 10
94, 95	To divide by 3-digit numbers	1–12, 33, 37, MCR	13–20, 21–39 o, MCR	21–39, MCR		RM, PS	29	38	38	MR 3, CALC 5
96, 97	To check for a reasonable answer in problem solving	1–6	1–7	2–9		PS, P&G		39	39	
98, 99	To divide decimals by whole numbers	1–31 o, 41	1–39 o, 41, F	10–40 e, 41–42, F	477	CALC, PS	30	40	40	FST 11, 12
100, 101	To choose the operation in problem solving	1–6	2–7	3–8		PS, CALC		41	41	
102, 103	To divide a decimal by a power of 10	1–24, F	5–33, F	9–34, F		MNP, MM	31	42	42	MR 4
104, 105	To divide a decimal by a decimal	1–35 o, 37–38	2–38 e, 39, Chlg	17–40, Chlg	477	MNP, CALC	32	43	43	
106, 107	To round decimal quotients	1–4, 5–39 o, 41–42	1–39 o, 41–42	6–40 e, 41–42		IND, PS	33	44	44	CALC 6, LSN T4, CPR 5, 6
108, 109	To use information from a map in problem solving	1–5	1–6	1–7		PS, RFM		45	45	

5

Mathematics
UNLIMITED

ASSIGNMENT GUIDE

PUPIL EDITION							TE	TEACHER'S RESOURCE BOOK OR WORKBOOK PAGES			CLASSROOM ACTIVITY BOOK
LESSON PAGE	LESSON OBJECTIVE	BASIC	AVERAGE	EXTENDED	MORE PRACTICE	FOLLOW UP ACTIVITY		RETEACH	PRACTICE	ENRICH	
110	Calculator										
111	Group Project										
112, 113	Chapter Test										
114	Reteaching										
115	Enrichment										
116	Cumulative Review										LSN T1

PROBLEM SOLVING WORKBOOKS Pages 10–14 of The Best Problems Ever workbook and pages 5–7 of the Unlimited Challenges for Problem Solvers workbook accompany this chapter.

ASSIGNMENT GUIDE

LESSON PAGE	PUPIL EDITION LESSON OBJECTIVE	BASIC	AVERAGE	EXTENDED	MORE PRACTICE	TE FOLLOW UP ACTIVITY	RETEACH	PRACTICE	ENRICH	CLASSROOM ACTIVITY BOOK
117	Chapter Opener (Use MMW 7, 8)	117	117	117						
118, 119	To use divisibility tests to determine whether a number is divisible by 2, 3, 4, 5, 6, 8, 9, or 10	1–39 o, 41–42, AL	1–39 o, 41–46, AL	2–40 e, 41–47, AL		MM, PG		46	46	
120, 121	To write and evaluate numbers in exponential notation to find square roots of numbers	1–41 o	1–46 o, Chlg	2–34 e, 36–37, Chlg		EST, PS	34	47	47	LSN T5
122, 123	To write numbers, using scientific notation	1–35	1–35, F	1–36, F	478	IND, RFM	35	48	48	LSN T5, 3
124, 125	To identify prime numbers and composite numbers	1–10, 16–35	2–44 e, 46, Chlg	5–45 o, 46, Chlg		MNP, RFM	36	49	49	FI 4
126, 127	To find the prime factorization of a number, using a factor tree	1–27, F	1–29 o, 31–32, F	2–24 e, 25–32, F		CALC, PG	37	50	50	MR 5, MM 4
128, 129	To use information from a graph in problem solving	1–6	2–14 e	1–13 o		IND, PS	38	51	51	
130, 131	To find the GCF of two or more numbers	1–23, 37–40, MCR	1–28, 37–42, MCR	9–44, MCR	478	MM, RM		52	52	
132, 133	To find the LCM of two or more numbers	1–4, 9–16, 29–32, F	1–39, F	2–32 e, 33–48, F	478	RM, PS	39	53	53	MR 6
134, 135	To practice in problem solving	1–4, 7–16	3–18	3–22		CALC	40	54, 55		CALC 7
136, 137	To use rules for orders of operations to evaluate numerical expressions	1–12, 25–28, 33–34	1–31 o, 33–36-F	14–32, 33–36, F		PG, PS		56	54	
138, 139	To write and evaluate algebraic expressions by inverse operations	2–26, e	2–28 e, Calc	1–27 o, 28–32, Calc		MM, CPR	41	57	55	EST 13
140, 141	To solve addition and subtraction expressions that involve multiplication or division	1–15, 33–34	11–35 o, Chlg	10–32 e, 33–36, Chlg	479	MM, CNS	42	58	56	
142, 143	To use a pictograph in problem solving	1–9	2–11	3–12		PS, CALC	43	59	57	
144, 145	To write and evaluate algebraic expressions that involve multiplication or division	1–25 o, AL	1–15 o, 16–33, AL	2–16 e, 17–34, AL		RM, CPR		60	58	

Note: Columns RETEACH, PRACTICE, ENRICH are under the heading "TEACHER'S RESOURCE BOOK OR WORKBOOK PAGES".

Mathematics UNLIMITED

Mathematics UNLIMITED

ASSIGNMENT GUIDE

PUPIL EDITION						TE	TEACHER'S RESOURCE BOOK OR WORKBOOK PAGES			CLASSROOM ACTIVITY BOOK
LESSON PAGE	LESSON OBJECTIVE	BASIC	AVERAGE	EXTENDED	MORE PRACTICE	FOLLOW UP ACTIVITY	RETEACH	PRACTICE	ENRICH	
146, 147	To solve multiplication and division equations algebraically by using inverse operations	1–9, 19–27, 34–36, AL	1–39 o, AL	2–32 e, 34–39, AL	479	FST, CNS	44	61	59	
148, 149	To solve two-step equations using inverse operations	1–18, Calc	1–37 o, Calc	19–37, Calc	479		45	62	60	CNS 4
150, 151	To write an equation in problem solving	1–6	1–7	1–8		PS, CALC	46	63	61	CALC 8, CPR 7, 8
152	Logical Reasoning									
153	Group Project									
154, 155	Chapter Test									
156	Reteaching									
157	Enrichment									
158, 159	Technology									
160	Cumulative Review									

PROBLEM SOLVING WORKBOOKS Pages 15–20 of The Best Problems Ever workbook and pages 8–10 of the Unlimited Challenges for Problem Solvers workbook accompany this chapter.

ASSIGNMENT GUIDE

PUPIL EDITION						TE FOLLOW UP ACTIVITY	TEACHER'S RESOURCE BOOK OR WORKBOOK PAGES			CLASSROOM ACTIVITY BOOK
LESSON PAGE	LESSON OBJECTIVE	BASIC	AVERAGE	EXTENDED	MORE PRACTICE		RETEACH	PRACTICE	ENRICH	
161	Chapter Opener (Use MMW 9, 10)	161	161	161						
162, 163	To write fractions for parts of an object or parts of a set	1–20, 22–25, 30	1–26, 28–30	3–31		RFM, PG	47	64	62	
164, 165	To write equivalent fractions and to write a fraction in simplest form	1–28, 32–33	1–30, 32–33, Chlg, 1–3	5–33, Chlg 1–4		MNP, CNS	48	65	63	EST 14
166, 167	To write fractions as mixed numbers and mixed numbers as fractions	1–21, 24, F 1–3	1–22, 24–25, F	4–26, F 1–5	480	MM, RFM	49	66	64	
168, 169	To compare and order fractions and mixed numbers	1–27, 31–34, AL	3–28, 31–34, AL	4–34, AL		CALC, MM	50	67	65	
170, 171	To check that the solution answers the question in problem solving	1–6	2–7	3–8		PS, PG		68	66	
172, 173	To estimate sums and differences of mixed numbers and fractions	1–19 o, 21–24, 33–34	2–20 e, 21–28, 33–34	5–19 o, 21–34		MM, PS	51	69	67	
174, 175	To add fractions that have like and unlike denominators	1–25, 29, F 1–3	1–26, 29–30, F	5–30, F		PS	52	70	68	EST 15, FI 5
176, 177	To subtract fractions that have like and unlike denominators	1–24, 27, MCR	1–25, 27–28, MCR	4–24, MCR		IND, PS	53	71	69	CALC 9
178, 179	To practice solving problems	1–8	1–15 o	2–16 e		PS, CALC		72, 73		
180, 181	To make an organized list in problem solving	1–5	1–6	1–6		PS, CALC		74, 75		
182, 183	To add mixed numbers	1–20, 26–27, Calc	1–22, 26–27, Calc	4–27, Calc	180	MNP	54	76	70	
184, 185	To subtract mixed numbers without renaming	1–30, 33–35	1–31, 33–35	5–36		EST, MM	55	77	71	
186, 187	To subtract mixed numbers with renaming	1–25, 28, 32–33, AL	1–26, 28–33, AL	5–33, AL	180	MM, MNP	56	78	72	MR 7, EST 16, MM 5, LSN T6
188, 189	To solve equations that have fractions and mixed numbers	1–24, 27, 29	1–25, 28–29, Chlg	4–29, Chlg	481	PS	57	79	73	MR 8, CNS 5, CALC 10, CPR 9, 10

Mathematics UNLIMITED

ASSIGNMENT GUIDE

PUPIL EDITION						TE	TEACHER'S RESOURCE BOOK OR WORKBOOK PAGES			CLASSROOM ACTIVITY BOOK
LESSON PAGE	LESSON OBJECTIVE	BASIC	AVERAGE	EXTENDED	MORE PRACTICE	FOLLOW UP ACTIVITY	RETEACH	PRACTICE	ENRICH	
190, 191	To write a simpler problem in problem solving	1–5	1–6	1–6		PS, CALC		80	74	
192	Calculator									
193	Group Project									
194, 195	Chapter Test									
196	Reteaching									
197	Enrichment									
198	Cumulative Review									

PROBLEM SOLVING WORKBOOKS Pages 21–24 of The Best Problems Ever workbook and pages 11–13 of the Unlimited Challenges for Problem Solvers workbook accompany this chapter.

ASSIGNMENT GUIDE

LESSON PAGE	PUPIL EDITION — LESSON OBJECTIVE	BASIC	AVERAGE	EXTENDED	MORE PRACTICE	TE FOLLOW UP ACTIVITY	TEACHER'S RESOURCE BOOK OR WORKBOOK PAGES — RETEACH	PRACTICE	ENRICH	CLASSROOM ACTIVITY BOOK
199	Chapter Opener (Use MMW 11, 12)	199	199	199						
200, 201	To multiply by a fraction	1–19, 30–32, Calc	1–29 o, 30–32, Calc	16–32, Calc		MNP, PS	58	81	75	FI 6
202, 203	To use a shortcut for multiplying fractions	1–19, 24–25, F 1–5	1–13 o, 15–25, F	2–14 e, 15–26, F		MM, PS	59	82	76	
204, 205	To choose/write a sensible question in problem solving	1–6	1–6	2–6		PS, PG		83	77	
206, 207	To estimate products of mixed numbers and fractions	1–21 o	2–22 e, 23–26, 29–30	5–21 o, 23–30		RFM, P&G	60	84	78	
208, 209	To multiply by a mixed number	1–19, 26–27, F 1–5	11–22, 26–28, F	11–28, F	481	IND, MM	61	85	79	CNS 6, MM 6, LSN 7
210, 211	To divide by a fraction or by a whole number	1–25, 36–38, AL	2–24 e, 26–38, AL	1–25 e, 26–38, AL		MNP, RFM	62	86	80	
212, 213	To divide with mixed numbers	1–15, 29–31, MCR	1–15 o, 16–25, 29–31, MCR	16–31, MCR	481	EST, PS	63	87	81	MR 9, CALC 11
214, 215	To select notation in problem solving	1–6	1–6	1–6		PS, PG		88, 89		
216, 217	To write a decimal as a fraction or a fraction as a decimal	1–20, 31–33	2–24 e, 26–34	1–25 o, 26–34, Chlg	482	PS, RFM	64	90	82	
218, 219	To use a recipe in problem solving	1–7	2–8	3–9		PS, PG		91	83	
220, 221	To identify and to write terminating and repeating decimals for given fractions	1–17, 24, AL	1–9 o, 11–24, AL	11–26, AL	482	RFM, CALC	65	92	84	LSN T8, 4
222, 223	To solve an equation that involves the multiplication or division of fractions	1–16, 21–25 o, 26–28	1–11 o, 13–28	10–20 e, 21–28	482	RFM, PS	66	93	85	MR 10, CALC 12, CPR 11, 12
224, 225	To interpret the quotient and the remainder	1–6	2–7	3–8		PS, CALC		94	86	

Mathematics
UNLIMITED

ASSIGNMENT GUIDE

PUPIL EDITION						TE	TEACHER'S RESOURCE BOOK OR WORKBOOK PAGES			CLASSROOM ACTIVITY BOOK
LESSON PAGE	LESSON OBJECTIVE	BASIC	AVERAGE	EXTENDED	MORE PRACTICE	FOLLOW UP ACTIVITY	RETEACH	PRACTICE	ENRICH	
226	Reading Math									
227	Group Project									
228, 229	Chapter Test									
230	Reteaching									
231	Enrichment									
232, 233	Technology									
234	Cumulative Review									

PROBLEM SOLVING WORKBOOKS Pages 25–30 of The Best Problems Ever workbook and pages 14–15 of the Unlimited Challenges for Problem Solvers workbook accompany this chapter.

ASSIGNMENT GUIDE

LESSON PAGE	PUPIL EDITION — LESSON OBJECTIVE	PUPIL EDITION — BASIC	PUPIL EDITION — AVERAGE	PUPIL EDITION — EXTENDED	MORE PRACTICE	TE FOLLOW UP ACTIVITY	TEACHER'S RESOURCE BOOK OR WORKBOOK PAGES — RETEACH	TEACHER'S RESOURCE BOOK OR WORKBOOK PAGES — PRACTICE	TEACHER'S RESOURCE BOOK OR WORKBOOK PAGES — ENRICH	CLASSROOM ACTIVITY BOOK
235	Chapter Opener (Use MMW 13, 14)	235	235	235						
236, 237	To estimate and measure lengths in metric units	1–12, 13–17 o, 23, AL	2–22 e, 23, AL	1–23 o, AL		MNP, RM	67	95	87	MM 7
238, 239	To identify and rename metric units of length	1–18, 28–30, 34–36	7–24, 31–36	13–36	483	RM, PS	68	96	88	MR 11
240, 241	To identify and rename metric units of capacity and mass	1–18, 28, MCR	1–27 o, 28, MCR	1–3, 4, 28 e, MCR	483	IND, PS, CPR	69	97	89	
242, 243	To practice solving problems	1–5, 7–12	1–13	1–14		CALC		98, 99		CALC 13
244, 245	To solve multi-step problems/making a plan in problem solving	1–5	1–6	2–8		PS, CALC		100	90	
246, 247	To identify and rename customary units of length	1–15, 23–27, AL	1–20, 23–27, AL	1–3, 7–27, AL	483	MNP, MM	70	101	91	FI 7
248, 249	To identify and rename customary units of capacity and weight	1–18, 32–35, F 1–3	1–29 o, 32–35, F 1–6	2–25 e, 24–35, F	484	MNP, PS	71	102	92	
250, 251	To rename and compute time and to determine elapsed time	1–18, 22–26, Calc	1–15, 19–28, Calc	4–15, 18–28, Calc		PS, MM	72	103	93	EST 17
252, 253	To use a formula in problem solving (d = rt)	1–8	1–9	1–10		PS, CALC		104	94	
254, 255	To identify and determine the time in different time zones	1–11, 13–19, 21–30, 32	1–19, 21–32, Chlg	1–32, Chlg		RFM, PS	73	105	95	ISN T16
256, 257	To recognize, estimate, and compute with temperature measurements	1–16	1–16, Chlg	1–16, Chlg		EST, IND	74	106	96	
258, 259	To determine which measurement is the most precise	1–19	1–19, Chlg 1–2	1–19, Chlg		MNP, PS	75	107	97	
260, 261	To use a schedule in problem solving	1–4	2–6	5–8		MNP, PS		108	98	
262	Calculator									

14

Mathematics
UNLIMITED

ASSIGNMENT GUIDE

PUPIL EDITION						TE		TEACHER'S RESOURCE BOOK OR WORKBOOK PAGES			CLASSROOM ACTIVITY BOOK
LESSON PAGE	LESSON OBJECTIVE	BASIC	AVERAGE	EXTENDED	MORE PRACTICE	FOLLOW UP ACTIVITY		RETEACH	PRACTICE	ENRICH	
263	Group Project										
264, 265	Chapter Test										
266	Reteaching										
267	Enrichment										
268	Cumulative Review										LSN T9

PROBLEM SOLVING WORKBOOKS Pages 31–36 of The Best Problems Ever workbook and pages 16–19 of the Unlimited Challenges for Problem Solvers workbook accompany this chapter.

ASSIGNMENT GUIDE

| PUPIL EDITION | | BASIC | AVERAGE | EXTENDED | MORE PRACTICE | TE FOLLOW UP ACTIVITY | TEACHER'S RESOURCE BOOK OR WORKBOOK PAGES | | | CLASSROOM ACTIVITY BOOK |
LESSON PAGE	LESSON OBJECTIVE						RETEACH	PRACTICE	ENRICH	
269	Chapter Opener (Use MMW 15, 16)	269	269	269						
270, 271	To write ratios, rates and equal ratios	1–28, 33, AL	1–33, AL	5–34, AL		MM, PS	76	109	99	
272, 273	To define a proportion and solve for a missing term	1–28, 31, AL	1–28, 31–32, AL	5–32, AL	484	CNS, PS	77	110	100	MR 12
274, 275	To write a proportion in problem solving	1–6	1–8	1–8		PS, CALC		111	101	
276, 277	To find actual and scale measurements by using scale drawings	1–6, 8–9	1–10, F	1–10, F		MNP, IND	78	112	102	
278, 279	To find a percent	1–22, 25–31	1–32, Calc	5–32, Calc	484	IND, PS	79	113	103	FI 8
280, 281	To write a percent as a decimal and a decimal as a percent	1–24, 29–32	1–32	3–32, Chlg	485	MM, PS	80	114	104	
282, 283	To write a percent as a fraction and a fraction as a decimal	1–29, 37–38, MCR	1–33, 37–38, MCR	3–38, MCR	485	MM, CALC	81	115	105	CALC 15
284, 285	To find the percent of a number	1–16, 21–22, 31–32	1–29 o, 31–32, F 1–4	2–30 e, 31, 34, F		EST, RFM	82	116	106	
286, 287	To solve a problem involving commissions	1–5	1–6	1–7		PS, CALC		117, 118		
288, 289	To find the percent one number is of another number	1–18, 25–26, F 1–4	1–22, 25–27, F 1–4	3–27, F		IND, RFM	83	119	107	EST 18
290, 291	To find the total number when a percent of it is known	1–20, 27–29	1–24, 27–29	7–30		MM, CPR	84	120	108	MR 13
292, 293	To use a formula in problem solving (I = prt)	1–6	2–8	2–8				121	109	
294, 295	To use proportions to solve percent problems	1–16, 24, F	2–21, 24, F	3–24, F	485	MM, PS	85	122	110	
296, 297	To find the percent of increase or decrease	1–8, 13–15, AL	1–10, 13–16, AL	3–16, AL	486	EST, PS	86	123	111	CALC 16, MM 8, CPR 15, 16

Mathematics
UNLIMITED

ASSIGNMENT GUIDE

| LESSON PAGE | PUPIL EDITION | | | | | | | | TE | TEACHER'S RESOURCE BOOK OR WORKBOOK PAGES | | | CLASSROOM ACTIVITY BOOK |
	LESSON OBJECTIVE	BASIC	AVERAGE	EXTENDED	MORE PRACTICE	FOLLOW UP ACTIVITY			RETEACH	PRACTICE	ENRICH	
298, 299	To use a circle graph in problem solving	1–6	2–10	3–14		PS, CALC				124	112	
300	Logical Reasoning											
301	Group Project											
302, 303	Chapter Test											
304	Reteaching											
305	Enrichment											
306, 307	Technology											
308	Cumulative Review											

PROBLEM SOLVING WORKBOOKS Pages 37–42 of The Best Problems Ever workbook and page 20 of the Unlimited Challenges for Problem Solvers workbook accompany this chapter.

ASSIGNMENT GUIDE

PUPIL EDITION		BASIC	AVERAGE	EXTENDED	MORE PRACTICE	TE FOLLOW UP ACTIVITY	TEACHER'S RESOURCE BOOK OR WORKBOOK PAGES			CLASSROOM ACTIVITY BOOK
LESSON PAGE	LESSON OBJECTIVE						RETEACH	PRACTICE	ENRICH	
309	Chapter Opener (Use MMW 17, 18)	309	309	309						
310, 311	To understand basic ideas of geometry	1–16, 19–24	1–26	1–27		MNP, RMF	87	125	113	MM 9
312, 313	To measure angles and classify angles by their measures or their relationships with other angles	1–17 o, 19–23, 29–33, 39, AL	1–41 o, AL	2–40 e, AL		EST, RM	88	126	114	LSN T13, 5, 6
314, 315	To identify and construct congruent segments and angles	1–7, 10, 11	1–12, Chlg	1–13, Chlg		RFM, MNP	89	127	115	EST 19
316, 317	To bisect segments and angles	1–13, 14–20 e, AL	1–13, 14–20 e, 22, 23, AL	3–23, AL		MNP, MM	90	128	116	
318, 319	To solve problems by organizing information and looking for a pattern							129, 130		
320, 321	To identify and use parallel lines, perpendicular lines, vertical lines, and corresponding angles	1–27	3–34	3–38		MNP, PS	91	131	117	
322, 323	To construct perpendicular lines and parallel lines	1–4, MCR	1–6, MCR	1–8, MCR		MNP, RM	92	132	118	CALC 17
324, 325	To practice solving problems	1–3, 5–13	1–13	1–15		CALC		133, 134	119	
326, 327	To classify triangles by their sides or angles, and to compute the measure of the third angle if two angle measures are given	1–27	1–31	4–33		MM, IND	93	135		
328, 329	To classify polygons and to identify properties of quadrilaterals	1–20	1–25	1–28		MNP, PS	94	136	120	FI 9, LSN T13, 7
330, 331	To identify congruent polygons and corresponding parts of congruent polygons	1–17	1–18	1–19		MNP, IND	95	137	121	
332, 333	To identify similar polygons and to solve for corresponding parts in similar polygons	1–10	1–11	1–12		MNP, PS	96	138	122	
334, 335	To work backwards in problem solving	1–4	1–5	1–6		PS, CALC		139, 140		

Mathematics UNLIMITED

ASSIGNMENT GUIDE

LESSON PAGE	PUPIL EDITION LESSON OBJECTIVE	BASIC	AVERAGE	EXTENDED	MORE PRACTICE	TE FOLLOW UP ACTIVITY	TEACHER'S RESOURCE BOOK OR WORKBOOK PAGES RETEACH	PRACTICE	ENRICH	CLASSROOM ACTIVITY BOOK
336, 337	To identify, use, and construct circles and basic geometric figures associated with circles	1–17, 19, 27		1–31		MNP, MR	97	141	123	
338, 339	To identify and use lines of symmetry and reflections	1–16	1–17	1–18		MNP, IND	98	142	124	MR 14, LSN T13, 8, 9
340, 341	To identify, use, and draw translations and rotations	1–7	1–7	1–8		MNP, PS	99	143	125	MR 15, CNS 9, CALC 18, CMP 17, 18
342, 343	To solve problems using a picture or a diagram	p. 342 1–3, p. 343 1–2	p. 342 1–3, p. 343 2–3	p. 342 1–3, p. 343 3–4		PS, CALC		144	126	
344	Calculator									
345	Group Project									
346, 347	Chapter Test									
348	Reteaching									
349	Enrichment									
350	Cumulative Review									LSN T9

PROBLEM SOLVING WORKBOOKS Pages 43–46 of The Best Problems Ever workbook and pages 21–23 of the Unlimited Challenges for Problem Solvers workbook accompany this chapter.

ASSIGNMENT GUIDE

LESSON PAGE	LESSON OBJECTIVE	BASIC	AVERAGE	EXTENDED	MORE PRACTICE	FOLLOW UP ACTIVITY	RETEACH	PRACTICE	ENRICH	CLASSROOM ACTIVITY BOOK
351	Chapter Opener (Use MMW 19, 20)	351	351	351						
352, 353	To find the perimeter of a polygon	1–13, 18–19, F	2–10 e, 12–19, F	1–11 o, 12–19, F	486	EST, PS	100	145	127	MM 10
354, 355	To find the circumference of a circle	1–16, 25–28	1–4, 13–28	17–30, Chlg	486	MM, PS	101	146	128	
356, 357	To find the area of a square, a rectangle, or a parallelogram	1–11, 16–19, 24–26	1–3, 4–22 e, 24–28	1–3, 5–23 o, 24–28	487	CNS, EST	102	147	129	CNS 10
358, 359	To find the area of a triangle or a trapezoid	1–10, 15–18, 23–24	1–6, 7–21 o, 23–24	8–22 e, 23–25	487	MNP, CPR	103	148	130	
360, 361	To solve multi-step problems/make a plan in problem solving	1–2	1–4	1–5		PS, PS		149	131	
362, 363	To find the area of a circle	1–9, 20–26, 31–33, MCR	1–3, 4–26 e, 31–33, MCR	1–3, 5–27 o, 28–33, MCR	487	EST, PS	104	150	132	
364, 365	To guess and check in problem solving	1–4	1–5	1–6				151, 152		
366, 367	To identify types and parts of polyhedrons	1–39	1–39	1–39		MNP, IND	105	153	133	LSN T13, 10
368, 369	To make a picture or diagram model in problem solving	1–11	1–12	1–15		PS, CALC		154, 134		
370, 371	To find the surface area of a prism, a pyramid, and a cylinder	1–11	1–11	1–11, Chlg	488	CPR, RFM	106	156	134	
372, 373	To find the volume of a rectangular prism, a cube, and a cylinder	1–16	1–16	1–16, Chlg	488	CALC, CNS	107	157	135	MR 16, CALC 20, CPR 19, 20
374, 375	To choose a formula, solve problems	1–4	2–6	3–8		IND, PS		158	136	
376	Reading Math									
377	Group Project									

Mathematics UNLIMITED

ASSIGNMENT GUIDE

PUPIL EDITION		BASIC	AVERAGE	EXTENDED	MORE PRACTICE	TE — FOLLOW UP ACTIVITY	TEACHER'S RESOURCE BOOK OR WORKBOOK PAGES			CLASSROOM ACTIVITY BOOK
LESSON PAGE	LESSON OBJECTIVE						RETEACH	PRACTICE	ENRICH	
378, 379	Chapter Test									
380	Reteaching									
381	Enrichment									
382, 383	Technology									
384	Cumulative Review									LSN T9

PROBLEM SOLVING WORKBOOKS Pages 47–52 of The Best Problems Ever workbook and pages 24–26 of the Unlimited Challenges for Problem Solvers workbook accompany this chapter.

ASSIGNMENT GUIDE

LESSON PAGE	LESSON OBJECTIVE	BASIC	AVERAGE	EXTENDED	MORE PRACTICE	FOLLOW UP ACTIVITY	RETEACH	PRACTICE	ENRICH	CLASSROOM ACTIVITY BOOK
	PUPIL EDITION					**TE**	**TEACHER'S RESOURCE BOOK OR WORKBOOK PAGES**			
385	Chapter Opener (Use MMW 21, 22)	385	385	385						
386, 387	To organize data by using a frequency table	1–8, AL	1–9, AL	1–10, AL		MNP, RFM	108	159	137	FI 11, MR 11
388, 389	To determine the range, the median, and the mode of a set of data	1–15, 25, 26	1–18, 25, 26	7–28	488	RFM, PS	109	160	138	
390, 391	To calculate the mean of a set of data	1–23, 26, 27	3–27	5–29	489	MM, PS	110	161	139	
392, 393	To draw, read, and interpret pictographs and bar graphs	1–9	1–9	1–10		MNP, IND	111	162	140	
394, 395	To use information from a scattergram in problem solving	1–7	1–7	1–7		PS, P&G		163	141	
396, 397	To draw, read, and interpret broken-line graphs	1–6	1–7	2–9		PS, RFM	112	169	142	
398, 399	To draw, read, and interpret circle graphs	1, 2, 4, MCR	1–5, MCR	1–5, MCR		FST, PS	113	165	143	CNS 11, CALC 21
400, 401	To estimate in problem solving	1–6	2–7	3–8				166	144	
402, 403	To find the probability of equally likely outcomes and events	1–22, F	1–25, F	1–25, F		MNP, PS	114	167	145	
404, 405	To use tree diagrams to construct sample spaces and to use the fundamental principle of counting	1–7	1–10	1–11	489	PG, PS	115	168	196	
406, 407	To use sample spaces in determining probabilities and to determine whether events are impossible or certain	1–12, AL	1–16, AL	1–16, AL		MM, PS	116	169	147	
408, 409	To correctly interpret information from a graph in problem solving	1–4	2–6	6–10		PS, CNS		170	148	
410, 411	To find the probability of independent events	1–20, 25–26	1–26	1–28		CMP	117	171	149	
412, 413	To find the probability of dependent events	1–14	1–14, Chlg	1–15, Chlg		RFM, PS	118	172	150	MR 18, CALC 22, CPR 21, 22

Mathematics
UNLIMITED

ASSIGNMENT GUIDE

PUPIL EDITION						TE	TEACHER'S RESOURCE BOOK OR WORKBOOK PAGES			CLASSROOM ACTIVITY BOOK
LESSON PAGE	LESSON OBJECTIVE	BASIC	AVERAGE	EXTENDED	MORE PRACTICE	FOLLOW UP ACTIVITY	RETEACH	PRACTICE	ENRICH	
414, 415	To use information from the Infobank in problem solving	1–8	2–9	3–10		PS, IND		173	151	CNS 12
416	Calculator									
417	Group Project									
418, 419	Chapter Test									
420	Reteaching									
421	Enrichment									
422	Cumulative Review									

PROBLEM SOLVING WORKBOOKS Pages 53–58 of The Best Problems Ever workbook and pages 27–29 of the Unlimited Challenges for Problem Solvers workbook accompany this chapter.

ASSIGNMENT GUIDE

| PUPIL EDITION | | BASIC | AVERAGE | EXTENDED | MORE PRACTICE | TE FOLLOW UP ACTIVITY | TEACHER'S RESOURCE BOOK OR WORKBOOK PAGES | | | CLASSROOM ACTIVITY BOOK |
LESSON PAGE	LESSON OBJECTIVE						RETEACH	PRACTICE	ENRICH	
423	Chapter Opener (Use MMW 23, 24)	423	423	423						
424, 425	To identify and order integers	1–23, 25–31 o, 33–36	1–29, 33–36	6–36		MNP, IND	119	174	152	MM 12
426, 427	To identify and use properties of addition and multiplication of integers	1–28, F, 1–6	5–32, F, 1–9	9–32, F, 1–15		RFM, MM	120	175	153	
428, 429	To add integers	1–20, 21–29 o, 30–32, AL	1–23, 30–32, AL	5–32, AL		PG, PS	121	176	154	
430, 431	To subtract integers	1–20, 29–31, AL	5–24, 29–31, AL	5–31, AL		CALC, PS	122	177	155	FI 12
432, 433	To practice solving problems	1–9	2–10	3–11		CALC		178, 179		
434, 435	To multiply integers	1–24, 31–32	1–32, F	1–33, F		MM, PS	123	180	156	
436, 437	To divide integers	2–24 e, 29–30, MCR	1–33 o, MCR	13–34, MCR	489	EST, PS	124	181	157	MR 19, CALC 23
438, 439	To practice solving problems	1–9, 11	1–11	1–12				182, 183		
440, 441	To solve equations involving positive and negative integers	1–20 o, 24–25	5–25, F	5–26, F	490	RFM, PG	125	184	158	MR 20
442, 443	To solve inequalities by using related equations	1–12, 21–24, 29	1–29 o, Chlg	13–30, Chlg	490	MM, CPR	126	185	159	
444, 445	To write equations and inequalities in problem solving	1–3, 5–6	1–7 o	2–8 e		PS, CALC		186	160	
446, 447	To graph an equation or an equality on a number line	1–19 o, 25–32, Calc	2–22 e, 25–32, Calc	5–32, Calc		PG, PS	127	187	161	
448, 449	To graph ordered pairs in a coordinate plane	1–23 o, 25–29	2–24 e, 25–29, Chlg	9–29, Chlg		MNP, IND	128	188	162	
450, 451	To use graphs above and below zero in problem solving	1–8	1–9	2–11		PS, CALC		189	163	

Mathematics UNLIMITED

ASSIGNMENT GUIDE

LESSON PAGE	PUPIL EDITION LESSON OBJECTIVE	BASIC	AVERAGE	EXTENDED	MORE PRACTICE	TE FOLLOW UP ACTIVITY	RETEACH	PRACTICE	ENRICH	CLASSROOM ACTIVITY BOOK
452, 453	To solve equations in two variables	1–13, AL	1–15, AL	4–17, AL	490	MM, PS	129	190	164	
454, 455	To graph equations in two variables	1–15 o	2–20 e, Chlg	13–24, Chlg		MM, MNP	130	191	165	CALC 24, CPR 23, 24
456	Logical Reasoning									
457	Group Project									
458, 459	Chapter Test									
460	Reteaching									
461	Enrichment									
462, 463	Technology									
464	Cumulative Review									

(Column groups: TEACHER'S RESOURCE BOOK OR WORKBOOK PAGES covers RETEACH, PRACTICE, ENRICH)

PROBLEM SOLVING WORKBOOKS Pages 59–64 of The Best Problems Ever workbook and pages 30–32 of the Unlimited Challenges for Problem Solvers workbook accompany this chapter.

STUDENT _____

PROGRESS REPORT

Dear Family:
This is a report of your child's accomplishments in the chapter we have just completed. The chart shows which objectives have been met and those that need more work.

CHAPTER 1	Needs More Work	Accomplished
A To write short word names for whole numbers and decimals expressed as standard numerals and vice versa, through 15 digits		
B To write expanded numerals for whole numbers and decimals expressed as standard numerals and vice versa, through 10 digits		
C To identify the value of a digit in whole numbers and decimals, through 13 digits		
D To compare and order whole numbers, money amounts, or decimals		
E To round whole numbers, money amounts, or decimals		
F To add or subtract whole numbers, money amounts, or decimals		
G To estimate sums and differences of whole numbers, money amounts, or decimals		
H To use information from a double bar graph to solve problems		

POST TEST SCORE: _____

TEACHER

STUDENT _____

 **PROGRESS REPORT**

Dear Family:
This is a report of your child's accomplishments in the chapter we have just completed. The chart shows which objectives have been met and those that need more work.

CHAPTER 2	Needs More Work	Accomplished
A To multiply a whole number or money amount by a whole number		
B To estimate products of whole numbers and decimals		
C To multiply a decimal by powers of 10		
D To multiply a decimal by a whole number		
E To multiply a decimal by a decimal		
F To identify extra or needed information in a problem and solve		
G To choose the operation to solve problems		
H To identify subgoals and solve 2-step problems		

POST TEST SCORE: _____

TEACHER _____

Mathematics UNLIMITED

PROGRESS REPORT

ear Family:
his is a report of your child's accomplishments in the chapter we have just
ompleted. The chart shows which objectives have been met and those that need
ore work.

CHAPTER 3	Needs More Work	Accomplished
A To divide a whole number or money amount by a whole number		
B To estimate quotients of whole numbers and decimals		
C To divide a decimal by powers of 10		
D To divide a decimal by a whole number		
E To divide a decimal by a decimal		
F To check that an answer is reasonable		
G To choose the operation to solve problems		
H To use information from a road map to solve problems		

OST TEST SCORE: _____

UMULATIVE TEST SCORE: _____

TEACHER _____

STUDENT _____

PROGRESS REPORT

Dear Family:
This is a report of your child's accomplishments in the chapter we have just completed. The chart shows which objectives have been met and those that need more work.

CHAPTER 4	Needs More Work	Accomplished
A To determine if a number is divisible by 2, 3, 4, 5, 6, 8, 9, or 10		
B To find square roots of perfect squares		
C To write standard numerals in scientific notation and vice versa		
D To find the LCM or GCF of up to 3 numbers by prime factorization with exponents		
E To find the value of numerical expressions using the rules for the order of operations		
F To evaluate algebraic expressions		
G To solve 1-step and 2-step equations		
H To use information from a broken-line graph or pictograph to solve problems		
I To write an equation for a 1-step or 2-step problem and solve		

POST TEST SCORE: _____

TEACHER _____

STUDENT _____

PROGRESS REPORT

Dear Family:
This is a report of your child's accomplishments in the chapter we have just completed. The chart shows which objectives have been met and those that need more work.

CHAPTER 5	Needs More Work	Accomplished
A To find a fraction equivalent to a given fraction		
B To compare and order fractions and mixed numbers		
C To write a fraction as a whole or mixed number and vice versa		
D To add or subtract fractions		
E To add or subtract mixed numbers		
F To solve 1-step equations involving addition or subtraction of fractions		
G To estimate sums and differences of fractions and mixed numbers		
H To check that the solution answers the question		
I To make an organized list to solve a problem		
J To write a simpler problem as a strategy for solving problems		

POST TEST SCORE: _____

TEACHER _____

STUDENT _____

PROGRESS REPORT

Dear Family:
This is a report of your child's accomplishments in the chapter we have just completed. The chart shows which objectives have been met and those that need more work.

CHAPTER 6	Needs More Work	Accomplished
A To multiply with fractions, whole numbers, and mixed numbers		
B To divide with fractions, whole numbers, and mixed numbers		
C To write a decimal as a fraction in simplest form		
D To write a fraction as a terminating or repeating decimal		
E To solve 1-step and 2-step equations involving fractions		
F To estimate products of fractions and mixed numbers		
G To formulate sensible questions to solve problems		
H To use information from a recipe to solve problems		
I To interpret the quotient and the remainder		

POST TEST SCORE: _____

CUMULATIVE TEST SCORE: _____

_____

TEACHER

PROGRESS REPORT

Dear Family:
This is a report of your child's accomplishments in the chapter we have just completed. The chart shows which objectives have been met and those that need more work.

CHAPTER 7	Needs More Work	Accomplished
A To measure length to the nearest centimeter and nearest millimeter		
B To choose or estimate the appropriate metric or customary unit of length, mass, or capacity		
C To change between measures of length, mass, volume, or capacity in the metric and customary systems		
D To add or subtract with regrouping in the customary system		
E To find temperature changes (Fahrenheit and Celsius)		
F To add, subtract, or change between units of time		
G To find elapsed time within and across time zones		
H To identify subgoals and solve multistep problems		
I To use the formula $d = rt$ to solve problems		
J To use information from a schedule to solve problems		

POST TEST SCORE: _____

_____
TEACHER

Holt, Rinehart and Winston, Publishers • 7

STUDENT _____

PROGRESS REPORT

Dear Family:
This is a report of your child's accomplishments in the chapter we have just completed. The chart shows which objectives have been met and those that need more work.

CHAPTER 8	Needs More Work	Accom-plished
A To solve proportions		
B To find actual measure given scale and scale measurement and vice versa		
C To write a decimal or a fraction as a percent and vice versa		
D To find the percent of a number		
E To find what percent a number is of a given number		
F To find the number given the percent of it		
G To find the percent of increase or decrease		
H To write a proportion to solve problems		
I To solve problems involving commission and the interest formula ($i = prt$)		
J To use information from a circle graph to solve problems		

POST TEST SCORE: _____

TEACHER

PROGRESS REPORT

ear Family:
his is a report of your child's accomplishments in the chapter we have just
ompleted. The chart shows which objectives have been met and those that need
ore work.

CHAPTER 9	Needs More Work	Accomplished
A To name points, lines, line segments, and rays and to identify parallel and perpendicular lines		
B To name, measure, and classify angles and to find the complement or supplement of an angle		
C To construct an angle or segment congruent to a given angle or segment		
D To construct the bisector of a line segment or an angle		
E To construct perpendicular or parallel lines		
F To classify triangles according to the measures of their angles or sides and to find the measure of an angle given the measures of the other two angles		
G To identify and name polygons and to identify the parts of a circle		
H To identify congruent figures and lines of symmetry		
I To solve problems involving corresponding parts of similar polygons		
J To identify translations, rotations, or reflections		
K To organize information in a table to find a pattern to solve problems		
L To use working backwards as a strategy to solve problems		
M To use information from a picture or model to solve problems		

POST TEST SCORE: _____

CUMULATIVE TEST SCORE: _____

TEACHER _____

STUDENT _____

PROGRESS REPORT

Dear Family:
This is a report of your child's accomplishments in the chapter we have just completed. The chart shows which objectives have been met and those that need more work.

CHAPTER 10	Needs More Work	Accomplished
A To find the perimeter of polygons and the circumference of circles		
B To find the area of squares, rectangles, parallelograms, triangles, trapezoids, and circles		
C To recognize solid figures		
D To find the surface area of prisms, pyramids, and cylinders		
E To find the volume of prisms and cylinders		
F To identify subgoals and solve multistep problems		
G To use a guess-and-check strategy to solve problems		
H To draw a picture to solve a problem		
I To choose a formula to solve a problem		

POST TEST SCORE: _____

_____
TEACHER

Mathematics UNLIMITED

PROGRESS REPORT

ear Family:
his is a report of your child's accomplishments in the chapter we have just
ompleted. The chart shows which objectives have been met and those that need
ore work.

CHAPTER 11	Needs More Work	Accom-plished
A To collect and record data by making a table, bar graph, broken-line graph, circle graph, or pictograph		
B To find the mean, median, mode, and range		
C To list the elements of a sample space for an experiment		
D To find the probability of a simple event		
E To find the probability of independent events		
F To find the probability of dependent events		
G To use information from a scattergram to solve problems		
H To interpret information from graphs and statistics		

OST TEST SCORE: _____

TEACHER _____

STUDENT _____

 **PROGRESS REPORT**

Dear Family:
This is a report of your child's accomplishments in the chapter we have just completed. The chart shows which objectives have been met and those that need more work.

CHAPTER 12	Needs More Work	Accom plished
A To identify integers on a number line		
B To compare and order integers		
C To add or subtract integers		
D To multiply or divide integers		
E To solve 1-step equations or inequalities with integers		
F To graph the solutions of equations or inequalities in one variable		
G To solve equations in two variables		
H To name or locate an ordered pair in a coordinate plane		
I To graph the solutions of equations in two variables		
J To write an equation or inequality for a problem and solve		
K To use information from a broken-line or bar graph with scales above and below zero to solve problems		

POST TEST SCORE: _____

FINAL TEST SCORE: _____

_____

TEACHER

NAME _____ DATE _____

TEST ANSWER SHEET

TEST _____

1. ⓐ ⓑ ⓒ ⓓ	26. ⓐ ⓑ ⓒ ⓓ	51. ⓐ ⓑ ⓒ ⓓ
2. ⓐ ⓑ ⓒ ⓓ	27. ⓐ ⓑ ⓒ ⓓ	52. ⓐ ⓑ ⓒ ⓓ
3. ⓐ ⓑ ⓒ ⓓ	28. ⓐ ⓑ ⓒ ⓓ	53. ⓐ ⓑ ⓒ ⓓ
4. ⓐ ⓑ ⓒ ⓓ	29. ⓐ ⓑ ⓒ ⓓ	54. ⓐ ⓑ ⓒ ⓓ
5. ⓐ ⓑ ⓒ ⓓ	30. ⓐ ⓑ ⓒ ⓓ	55. ⓐ ⓑ ⓒ ⓓ
6. ⓐ ⓑ ⓒ ⓓ	31. ⓐ ⓑ ⓒ ⓓ	56. ⓐ ⓑ ⓒ ⓓ
7. ⓐ ⓑ ⓒ ⓓ	32. ⓐ ⓑ ⓒ ⓓ	57. ⓐ ⓑ ⓒ ⓓ
8. ⓐ ⓑ ⓒ ⓓ	33. ⓐ ⓑ ⓒ ⓓ	58. ⓐ ⓑ ⓒ ⓓ
9. ⓐ ⓑ ⓒ ⓓ	34. ⓐ ⓑ ⓒ ⓓ	59. ⓐ ⓑ ⓒ ⓓ
10. ⓐ ⓑ ⓒ ⓓ	35. ⓐ ⓑ ⓒ ⓓ	60. ⓐ ⓑ ⓒ ⓓ
11. ⓐ ⓑ ⓒ ⓓ	36. ⓐ ⓑ ⓒ ⓓ	61. ⓐ ⓑ ⓒ ⓓ
12. ⓐ ⓑ ⓒ ⓓ	37. ⓐ ⓑ ⓒ ⓓ	62. ⓐ ⓑ ⓒ ⓓ
13. ⓐ ⓑ ⓒ ⓓ	38. ⓐ ⓑ ⓒ ⓓ	63. ⓐ ⓑ ⓒ ⓓ
14. ⓐ ⓑ ⓒ ⓓ	39. ⓐ ⓑ ⓒ ⓓ	64. ⓐ ⓑ ⓒ ⓓ
15. ⓐ ⓑ ⓒ ⓓ	40. ⓐ ⓑ ⓒ ⓓ	65. ⓐ ⓑ ⓒ ⓓ
16. ⓐ ⓑ ⓒ ⓓ	41. ⓐ ⓑ ⓒ ⓓ	66. ⓐ ⓑ ⓒ ⓓ
17. ⓐ ⓑ ⓒ ⓓ	42. ⓐ ⓑ ⓒ ⓓ	67. ⓐ ⓑ ⓒ ⓓ
18. ⓐ ⓑ ⓒ ⓓ	43. ⓐ ⓑ ⓒ ⓓ	68. ⓐ ⓑ ⓒ ⓓ
19. ⓐ ⓑ ⓒ ⓓ	44. ⓐ ⓑ ⓒ ⓓ	69. ⓐ ⓑ ⓒ ⓓ
20. ⓐ ⓑ ⓒ ⓓ	45. ⓐ ⓑ ⓒ ⓓ	70. ⓐ ⓑ ⓒ ⓓ
21. ⓐ ⓑ ⓒ ⓓ	46. ⓐ ⓑ ⓒ ⓓ	71. ⓐ ⓑ ⓒ ⓓ
22. ⓐ ⓑ ⓒ ⓓ	47. ⓐ ⓑ ⓒ ⓓ	72. ⓐ ⓑ ⓒ ⓓ
23. ⓐ ⓑ ⓒ ⓓ	48. ⓐ ⓑ ⓒ ⓓ	73. ⓐ ⓑ ⓒ ⓓ
24. ⓐ ⓑ ⓒ ⓓ	49. ⓐ ⓑ ⓒ ⓓ	74. ⓐ ⓑ ⓒ ⓓ
25. ⓐ ⓑ ⓒ ⓓ	50. ⓐ ⓑ ⓒ ⓓ	75. ⓐ ⓑ ⓒ ⓓ